Multimedia Data Engineering Applications and Processing

Shu-Ching Chen
Florida International University, USA

Mei-Ling Shyu
University of Miami, USA

Information Science
REFERENCE

Managing Director:	Lindsay Johnston
Editorial Director:	Joel Gamon
Book Production Manager:	Jennifer Yoder
Publishing Systems Analyst:	Adrienne Freeland
Assistant Acquisitions Editor:	Kayla Wolfe
Typesetter:	Erin O'Dea
Cover Design:	Jason Mull

Published in the United States of America by
Information Science Reference (an imprint of IGI Global)
701 E. Chocolate Avenue
Hershey PA 17033
Tel: 717-533-8845
Fax: 717-533-8661
E-mail: cust@igi-global.com
Web site: http://www.igi-global.com

Library of Congress Cataloging-in-Publication Data

Multimedia data engineering applications and processing / Shu-Ching Chen and Mei-Ling Shyu, editors.
    pages cm
 Includes bibliographical references and index.
 Summary: "This book presents different aspects of multimedia data engineering and management research, including recent theories, technologies and algorithms for providing a detailed understanding of multimedia engineering and its applications"--Provided by publisher.
 ISBN 978-1-4666-2940-0 (hardcover) -- ISBN 978-1-4666-2941-7 (ebook) -- ISBN 978-1-4666-2942-4 (print & perpetual access) 1. Multimedia systems. I. Chen, Shu-Ching, 1963- II. Shyu, Mei-Ling.
 QA76.575.M7926 2013
 006.7--dc23
                                       2012039280

British Cataloguing in Publication Data
A Cataloguing in Publication record for this book is available from the British Library.

The views expressed in this book are those of the authors, but not necessarily of the publisher.

Associate Editors

List of Reviewers

Table of Contents

Section 2
Multimedia Content Management

Sheila M. Pinto-Cáceres, University of Campinas, Brazil

Jurandy Almeida, University of Campinas, Brazil

Vânia P. A. Neris, Federal University of Sao Carlos, Brazil

M. Cecília C. Baranauskas, University of Campinas, Brazil

Neucimar J. Leite, University of Campinas, Brazil

Ricardo da S. Torres, University of Campinas, Brazil

Qiusha Zhu, University of Miami, USA

Lin Lin, University of Miami, USA

Mei-Ling Shyu, University of Miami, USA

Dianting Liu, University of Miami, USA

Kasturi Chatterjee, Florida International University, USA

Shu-Ching Chen, Florida International University, USA

Raluca-Diana Petre, TELECOM SudParis and Alcatel-Lucent Bell Labs, France

Titus Zaharia, TELECOM SudParis and UMR CNRS 8145 MAP5, France

Section 3
Multimodal Content Retrieval

Jyh-Ren Shieh, National Taiwan University, Taiwan

Ching-Yung Lin, IBM T. J. Watson Research Center, USA

Shun-Xuan Wang, National Taiwan University, Taiwan

Ja-Ling Wu, National Taiwan University, Taiwan

Ning Yu, University of Central Florida, USA

Kien A. Hua, University of Central Florida, USA

Danzhou Liu, Symantec Corporation, USA

Detailed Table of Contents

Section 1
Multimedia Content Analysis

Chapter 1

Ehsan Younessian, Nanyang Technological University, Singapore
Deepu Rajan, Nanyang Technological University, Singapore

In this paper, the authors propose an effective content-based clustering method for keyframes of news video stories using the Near Duplicate Keyframe (NDK) identification concept. Initially, the authors investigate the near-duplicate relationship, as a content-based visual similarity across keyframes, through the Near-Duplicate Keyframe (NDK) identification algorithm presented. The authors assign a near-duplicate score to each pair of keyframes within the story. Using an efficient keypoint matching technique followed by matching pattern analysis, this NDK identification algorithm can handle extreme zooming and significant object motion. In the second step, the weighted adjacency matrix is determined for each story based on assigned near duplicate score. The authors then use the spectral clustering scheme to remove outlier keyframes and partition remainders. Two sets of experiments are carried out to evaluate the NDK identification method and assess the proposed keyframe clustering method performance.

Chapter 2

Liping Zhou, The University of Alabama at Birmingham, USA
Wei-Bang Chen, The University of Alabama at Birmingham, USA
Chengcui Zhang, The University of Alabama at Birmingham, USA

This paper describes a framework to detect authorship of eBay images. It contains three modules: editing style summarization, classification and multi-account linking detection. For editing style summarization, three approaches, namely the edge-based approach, the color-based approach, and the color probability approach, are proposed to encode the common patterns inside a group of images with similar editing styles into common edge or color models. Prior to the summarization step, an edge-based clustering algorithm is developed. Corresponding to the three summarization approaches, three classification methods are developed accordingly to predict the authorship of an unlabeled test image. For multi-account linking detection, to detect the hidden owner behind multiple eBay seller accounts, two methods to measure the similarity between seller accounts based on similar models are presented.

Chapter 3

Tao Meng, University of Miami, USA
Mei-Ling Shyu, University of Miami, USA
Lin Lin, University of Miami, USA

Biomedical imaging technology has become an important tool for medical research and clinical practice. A large amount of imaging data is generated and collected every day. Managing and analyzing these data sets require the corresponding development of the computer based algorithms for automatic processing. Histology image classification is one of the important tasks in the bio-image informatics field and has broad applications in phenotype description and disease diagnosis. This study proposes a novel framework of histology image classification. The original images are first divided into several blocks and a set of visual features is extracted for each block. An array of C-RSPM (Collateral Representative Subspace Projection Modeling) models is then built that each model is based on one block from the same location in original images. Finally, the C-Value Enhanced Majority Voting (CEWMV) algorithm is developed to derive the final classification label for each testing image. To evaluate this framework, the authors compare its performance with several well-known classifiers using the benchmark data available from IICBU data repository. The results demonstrate that this framework achieves promising performance and performs significantly better than other classifiers in the comparison.

Chapter 4

Seunghan Han, Technische Universität München, Germany
Walter Stechele, Technische Universität München, Germany

Default reasoning can provide a means of deriving plausible semantic conclusion under imprecise and contradictory information in forensic visual surveillance. In such reasoning under uncertainty, proper uncertainty handling formalism is required. A discrete species of Bilattice for multivalued default logic demonstrated default reasoning in visual surveillance. In this article, the authors present an approach to default reasoning using subjective logic that acts in a continuous space. As an uncertainty representation and handling formalism, subjective logic bridges Dempster Shafer belief theory and second order Bayesian, thereby making it attractive tool for artificial reasoning. For the verification of the proposed approach, the authors extend the inference scheme on the bilattice for multivalued default logic to L-fuzzy set based logics that can be modeled with continuous species of bilattice structures. The authors present some illustrative case studies in visual surveillance scenarios to contrast the proposed approach with L-fuzzy set based approaches.

Sheila M. Pinto-Cáceres, University of Campinas, Brazil
Jurandy Almeida, University of Campinas, Brazil
Vânia P. A. Neris, Federal University of Sao Carlos, Brazil
M. Cecília C. Baranauskas, University of Campinas, Brazil
Neucimar J. Leite, University of Campinas, Brazil
Ricardo da S. Torres, University of Campinas, Brazil

The fast evolution of technology has led to a growing demand for video data, increasing the amount of research into efficient systems to manage those materials. Making efficient use of video information requires that data be accessed in a user-friendly way. Ideally, one would like to perform video search using an intuitive tool. Most of existing browsers for the interactive search of video sequences, however, have employed a too rigid layout to arrange the results, restricting users to explore the results using list- or grid-based layouts. This paper presents a novel approach for the interactive search that displays the result set in a flexible manner. The proposed method is based on a simple and fast algorithm to build video stories and on an effective visual structure to arrange the storyboards, called Clustering Set. It is able to group together videos with similar content and to organize the result set in a well-defined tree. Results from a rigorous empirical comparison with a subjective evaluation show that such a strategy makes the navigation more coherent and engaging to users.

Qiusha Zhu, University of Miami, USA
Lin Lin, University of Miami, USA
Mei-Ling Shyu, University of Miami, USA
Dianting Liu, University of Miami, USA

Traditional image classification relies on text information such as tags, which requires a lot of human effort to annotate them. Therefore, recent work focuses more on training the classifiers directly on visual features extracted from image content. The performance of content-based classification is improving steadily, but it is still far below users' expectation. Moreover, in a web environment, HTML surrounding texts associated with images naturally serve as context information and are complementary to content information. This paper proposes a novel two-stage image classification framework that aims to improve the performance of content-based image classification by utilizing context information of web-based images. A new TF*IDF weighting scheme is proposed to extract discriminant textual features from HTML surrounding texts. Both content-based and context-based classifiers are built by applying multiple correspondence analysis (MCA). Experiments on web-based images from Microsoft Research Asia (MSRA-MM) dataset show that the proposed framework achieves promising results.

Chapter 7

Kasturi Chatterjee, Florida International University, USA
Shu-Ching Chen, Florida International University, USA

This paper proposes a hybrid query refinement model for distance-based index structures supporting content-based image retrievals. The framework refines a query by considering both the low-level feature space as well as the high-level semantic interpretations separately. Thus, it successfully handles queries where the gap between the feature components and the semantics is large. It refines the low-level feature space, indexed by the distance based index structure, in multiple iterations by introducing the concept of multipoint query in a metric space. It refines the high-level semantic space by dynamically adjusting the constructs of a framework, called the Markov Model Mediator (MMM), utilized to introduce the semantic relationships in the index structure. A k-nearest neighbor (k-NN) algorithm is designed to handle similarity searches that refine a query in multiple iterations utilizing the proposed hybrid query refinement model. Extensive experiments are performed demonstrating an increased relevance of query results in subsequent iterations while incurring a low computational overhead. Further, an evaluation metric, called the Model_Score, is proposed to compare the performance of different retrieval frameworks in terms of both computation overhead and query result relevance. This metric enables the users to choose the retrieval framework appropriate for their requirements.

Chapter 8

Raluca-Diana Petre, TELECOM SudParis and Alcatel-Lucent Bell Labs, France
Titus Zaharia, TELECOM SudParis and UMR CNRS 8145 MAP5, France

Automatic classification and interpretation of objects present in 2D images is a key issue for various computer vision applications. In particular, when considering image/video, indexing, and retrieval applications, automatically labeling in a semantically pertinent manner/huge multimedia databases still remains a challenge. This paper examines the issue of still image object categorization. The objective is to associate semantic labels to the 2D objects present in natural images. The principle of the proposed approach consists of exploiting categorized 3D model repositories to identify unknown 2D objects, based on 2D/3D matching techniques. The authors use 2D/3D shape indexing methods, where 3D models are described through a set of 2D views. Experimental results, carried out on both MPEG-7 and Princeton 3D models databases, show recognition rates of up to 89.2%.

Section 3
Multimodal Content Retrieval

Chapter 9

Jyh-Ren Shieh, National Taiwan University, Taiwan
Ching-Yung Lin, IBM T. J. Watson Research Center, USA
Shun-Xuan Wang, National Taiwan University, Taiwan
Ja-Ling Wu, National Taiwan University, Taiwan

The abundance of Web 2.0 social media in various media formats calls for integration that takes into account tags associated with these resources. The authors present a new approach to multi-modal media search, based on novel related-tag graphs, in which a query is a resource in one modality, such as an image, and the results are semantically similar resources in various modalities, for instance text and video. Thus the use of resource tagging enables the use of multi-modal results and multi-modal queries, a marked departure from the traditional text-based search paradigm. Tag relation graphs are built based on multi-partite networks of existing Web 2.0 social media such as Flickr and Wikipedia. These multi-partite linkage networks (contributor-tag, tag-category, and tag-tag) are extracted from Wikipedia to construct relational tag graphs. In fusing these networks, the authors propose incorporating contributor-category networks to model contributor's specialization; it is shown that this step significantly enhances the accuracy of the inferred relatedness of the term-semantic graphs. Experiments based on 200 TREC-5 ad-hoc topics show that the algorithms outperform existing approaches. In addition, user studies demonstrate the superiority of this visualization system and its usefulness in the real world.

Ning Yu, University of Central Florida, USA
Kien A. Hua, University of Central Florida, USA
Danzhou Liu, Symantec Corporation, USA

During the last decade, high quality (i.e. over 1 megapixel) built-in cameras have become standard features of handheld devices. Users can take high-resolution pictures and share with friends via the internet. At the same time, the demand of multimedia information retrieval using those pictures on mobile devices has become an urgent problem to solve, and therefore attracts attention. A relevance feedback information retrieval process includes several rounds of query refinement, which incurs exchange of images between the mobile device and the server. With limited wireless bandwidth, this process can incur substantial delay, making the system unfriendly to use. This issue is addressed by considering a Client-side Relevance Feedback (CRF) technique. In the CRF system, Relevance Feedback (RF) is done on client side along. Mobile devices' battery power is saved from exchanging images between server and client and system response is instantaneous, which significantly enhances system usability. Furthermore, because the server is not involved in RF processing, it is able to support more users simultaneously. The experiment indicates that the system outperforms the traditional server-client relevance feedback systems on the aspects of system response time, mobile battery power saving, and retrieval result.

Ruxandra Tapu, TELECOM SudParis, France
Titus Zaharia, TELECOM SudParis, France

This paper introduces a complete framework for temporal video segmentation. First, a computationally efficient shot extraction method is introduced, which adopts the normalized graph partition approach, enriched with a non-linear, multiresolution filtering of the similarity vectors involved. The shot boundary detection technique proposed yields high precision (90%) and recall (95%) rates, for all types of transitions, both abrupt and gradual. Next, for each detected shot, the authors construct a static storyboard by introducing a leap keyframe extraction method. The video abstraction algorithm is 23% faster than existing techniques for similar performances. Finally, the authors propose a shot grouping strategy that iteratively clusters visually similar shots under a set of temporal constraints. Two different types of visual features are exploited: HSV color histograms and interest points. In both cases, the precision and recall rates present average performances of 86%.

This paper examines video retrieval based on Query-By-Example (QBE) approach, where shots relevant to a query are retrieved from large-scale video data based on their similarity to example shots. This involves two crucial problems: The first is that similarity in features does not necessarily imply similarity in semantic content. The second problem is an expensive computational cost to compute the similarity of a huge number of shots to example shots. The authors have developed a method that can filter a large number of shots irrelevant to a query, based on a video ontology that is knowledge base about concepts displayed in a shot. The method utilizes various concept relationships (e.g., generalization/specialization, sibling, part-of, and co-occurrence) defined in the video ontology. In addition, although the video ontology assumes that shots are accurately annotated with concepts, accurate annotation is difficult due to the diversity of forms and appearances of the concepts. Dempster-Shafer theory is used to account the uncertainty in determining the relevance of a shot based on inaccurate annotation of this shot. Experimental results on TRECVID 2009 video data validate the effectiveness of the method.

Section 4
Multimedia Delivery and Applications

Geographic Information Systems (GISs), which map spatiotemporal event data on geographical maps, have proven to be useful in many applications. Time-based Geographic Information Systems (GISs) allow practitioners to visualize collected data in an intuitive way. However, while current GIS systems have proven to be useful in post hoc analysis and provide simple two-dimensional geographic visualizations, their design typically lacks the features necessary for highly targeted real-time surveillance with the goal of spread prevention. This paper outlines the design, implementation, and usage of a 3D framework for real-time geospatial temporal visualization. In this case study, using livestock movements, the authors show that the framework is capable of tracking and simulating the spread of epidemic diseases. Although the application discussed in this paper relates to livestock disease, the proposed framework can be used to manage and visualize other types of high-dimensional multimedia data as well.

Chapter 14

Video transmission over wireless networks has quality of service (QoS) requirements and the time-varying characteristics of wireless channels make it a challenging task. IEEE 802.11 Wireless LAN has been widely used for the last mile connection for multimedia transmission. In this paper, a cross-layer design is presented for video streaming over IEEE 802.11e HCF Controlled Channel Access (HCCA) WLAN. The goal of the cross-layer design is to improve the quality of the video received in a wireless network under the constraint of network bandwidth. The approach is composed of two algorithms. First, an allocation of optimal TXOP is calculated which aims at maintaining a short queuing delay at the wireless station at the cost of a small TXOP allocation. Second, the transmission of the packets is scheduled according to the importance of the packets in order to maximize the visual quality of video. The approach is compared with the standard HCCA on NS2 simulation tools using H.264 video codec. The proposed cross-layer design outperforms the standard approach in terms of the PSNRs of the received video. This approach reduces the packet loss to allow the graceful video degradation, especially under heavy network traffic.

Chapter 15

Massimiliano Albanese, George Mason University, USA

Antonio d'Acierno, ISA, National Research Council, Italy

Vincenzo Moscato, University of Naples, Italy

Fabio Persia, University of Naples, Italy

Antonio Picariello, University of Naples, Italy

One of the most important challenges in the information access field, especially for multimedia repositories, is information overload. To cope with this problem, in this paper, the authors present a strategy for a recommender system that computes customized recommendations for users' accessing multimedia collections, using semantic contents and low-level features of multimedia objects, past behaviour of individual users, and social behaviour of the users' community as a whole. The authors implement their strategy in a recommender prototype for browsing image digital libraries in the Cultural Heritage domain. They then investigate the effectiveness of the proposed approach, based on the users' satisfaction. The preliminary experimental results show that the approach is promising and encourages further research in this direction.

Preface

The ubiquitous nature of the Internet, and the advances in electronic imaging, video devices, and wireless networking technologies have enabled the users to collect a massive amount of heterogeneous multimedia data with rich semantics, and to interact with each other in the rapidly evolving social networks. In particular, social phenomena are the incontrovertible evidence of users' migration to a new Web overwhelmed by multimedia data. For instance, under the Web 2.0 umbrella, social aspects of software are gaining importance, and a number of trends have created the challenges and opportunities for the development of multimedia technologies.

In social network websites such as Flickr, Twitter, Facebook, and YouTube, some major features of Web 2.0 include the user-created websites, self-publishing platforms, tagging, and social bookmarking. People are becoming more and more active. They share huge amounts of photos and videos in various Web communities via social networks. In fact, studies showed that about 99% of the Web today is constituted by images, videos, music, audios, tweets, tags, animation, and other kinds of multimedia objects. However, the chances of a successful search in such large amounts of multimedia data to meet users' needs are not proportionally supported. The knowledge and management of the spatio-temporal phenomena and the rich semantics in the data are of increasing relevance and importance in a variety of applications such as homeland security, health, education, entertainment, digital libraries, and adaptive games, to name a few.

More and more research efforts have been dedicated to the aforementioned challenges. To better utilize such multimedia data and to fill in the gap between the data and application requirements, advanced representation and analysis techniques need to be developed to address the challenges in multimedia content processing, analysis, retrieval, and management. For example, techniques and tools are needed for content-based and semantic-based multimedia data analysis, reasoning, clustering, detection, indexing, and fusion, with the utilization of multi-modal information such as context and ontology information for multimedia data management and retrieval. Moreover, novel methods for the delivery of extremely large bodies of data at very high rates with real-time constraints and the enabling of spatio-temporal knowledge visualization, even on mobile devices and dissemination through the Web, are to be considered. The successful development of these advanced novel techniques and tools in multimedia research makes it possible to realize and deploy many applications from forensic visual surveillance, eBay authorship detection, biomedical disease surveillance networks, to cultural heritage study.

This book consists of fifteen (15) chapters that are organized into four (04) sections with each section focusing on a distinct content. These four sections are "Multimedia Content Analysis," "Multimedia Content Management," "Multimedia Content Retrieval," and "Multimedia Delivery and Applications." These sections make the focused ideas accessible to the readers who are interested in grasping the basics, as well as to those who would like more technical depth. These chapters are contributed by the researchers, scientists, professionals, software engineers, and graduate students from academia and/or industry, and novel theories, approaches, frameworks, and implementations from different aspects in multimedia data processing, management, and engineering are included in these chapters.

Section 1: Multimedia Content Analysis

The first section includes four (4) chapters that present the techniques and tools in multimedia content analysis. Due to the complex nature of multimedia data, content-based multimedia data analysis that aims at automatically extracting low-level features from audiovisual content to identify high-level semantic features or the effective combination of semantic features derived from different modalities becomes increasingly important. Many challenges exist in multimedia content analysis: for example, how to group video shots/images for video/image content classification, browsing, and retrieval; how to annotate the data and select the fusion strategy of multimodal data for a given application; and how to enable user-friendly interactive search and visualization to display the results to the users. To address these challenges, existing approaches or new solutions suitable for multimedia content analysis need to be adapted or developed.

The first chapter is contributed by Younessian and Rajan in their paper entitled "Content-Based Keyframe Clustering Using Near-Duplicate Keyframe Identification." The authors proposed an effective content-based clustering method for keyframes of news video stories using the Near Duplicate Keyframe (NDK) identification concept. NDKs are referred to as those keyframes in a video data set that are closely similar to each other despite the minor variations caused by the lighting conditions, capturing conditions, and editing operations. In this chapter, a near-duplicate score is first assigned to each pair of keyframes within a story. Next, keypoint matching together with matching pattern analysis are applied to handle the extreme zooming and significant object motion situations in the video data. Then for each story, a weighted adjacency matrix is determined based on the assigned near duplicate score. Finally, the authors utilize the score as the visual similarity function for keyframe clustering through a spectral clustering scheme to remove the outlier keyframes and partition the remainders. In their proposed method, the number of clusters is determined by the within-cluster similarity score and the eigengap score. The authors conducted two sets of experiments to evaluate their proposed NDK identification method, and the performance evaluation shows that their proposed keyframe clustering method performs well in terms of both precision and recall values and is able to estimate the number of clusters accurately. A storyboard presentation of news video data was also generated using the resulting content-based partitioning of the news story and the obtained clusters of keyframes.

In the second chapter, Liping Zhou, Wei-Bang Chen, and Chengcui Zhang proposed an authorship detection and encoding framework in "Authorship Detection and Encoding for eBay Images" to detect authorship from eBay images. The capability of detecting the authorships is critical in many applications and research areas such as forensic evidence, plagiarism detection, email filtering, document categorization, near-duplicate detection, and web information management. Due to the popularity of the Internet, a large number of multimedia data such as images and videos are created and uploaded for various purposes. An example is online shopping where the sellers and buyers worldwide interact through transactions for a variety of goods/products and services online. To better enhance the customer purchase decision-making process, the pictures/images of the goods/products are mostly available on the website so that the customers can see the visual details of the goods/products. Some sellers even add their own touch to produce image design to attract buyers' attention. This calls for automatic image data analysis to detect and encode the editing styles for each seller using the visual features extracted from the product images, and then use the encoded editing styles to automatically predict the ownership for unlabeled images. Such a seller profiling system can be utilized to detect and prevent account taken-over and other related fraudulent behaviors during online shopping activities. In this chapter, the authors focus on the authorship detection and encoding for eBay images. Their proposed framework consists of three modules, namely editing style summarization, classification, and multi-account linking detection. To summarize the editing styles, the authors developed the edge-based, color-based, and color probability approaches to encode the common patterns inside a group of images with similar editing styles into common edge or color models. In the classification module, three classification methods with respect to the three summarization approaches were developed to predict the authorship of an unlabeled test image. To detect the hidden owner behind multiple eBay seller accounts, the authors developed two methods to measure the similarity between seller accounts based on similar models for multi-account linking detection. Two image data sets that consist of product listing images downloaded from 10 sellers and another 47 sellers at eBay are first used to evaluate the summarization and classification modules, and their results indicate that the edge-based classification method is the most promising in identifying the authorship of eBay images. Another experiment using 100 sellers' account data was also conducted to measure the similarity between seller accounts in terms of common image editing styles.

Chapter 3 presents a histology image classification framework by Tao Meng, Mei-Ling Shyu, and Lin Lin in their paper entitled "Multimodal Information Integration and Fusion for Histology Image Classification." The advances in bio-imaging techniques have made it possible to generate and collect a large amount of imaging data to explore the structures and functions of organisms for medical research and clinical practice, resulting in the need for advanced computing technologies in automatic imaging processing and analyses to develop computer-based algorithms for managing, indexing, and analyzing the bio-image data sets. In this chapter, the authors develop a novel framework for histology image classification which has broad applications in phenotype description and disease diagnosis. In their proposed framework, each training image is divided into several blocks and a set of visual features is extracted for each block. The advantages of dividing one image into blocks are (1) to decrease the space and computation complexities for feature extraction, (2) to utilize the local features in each block, and (3) to utilize the distinct location-related information from each block. Next, an array of the Collateral Representative Subspace Projection Modeling (also called C-RSPM) models is built, where each model is trained using the features of one block at the same locations in the original training images. The authors extracted 505 visual features from each block, and applied normalization and feature selection to dynamically keep only those features that can better represent the data characteristics in each block. After that, each testing image was divided into the same number of blocks and each block was input into the corresponding C-RSPM model and got a classification result and a C-value. To integrate and fuse all the classification results for one testing image, a C-value Enhanced Weighted Majority Voting (CEWMV) algorithm was proposed to give the final classification label. There are two modules in the CEWMV algorithm, namely the Weighted Majority Voting Module which outputs the voting score for each class, and the C-Value Enhancement Module which makes the final classification decision. The C-value generated from each C-RSPM model carries the quantitative measurement of the confidence that the block of the testing image belongs to a certain class, and the smaller the C-value is, the more confidence the decision has. This CEWMV algorithm considers both the classification accuracy from the macro view of the model and the C-value information from the micro view of the model in the final classification decision. Evaluations on the IICBU Biological Image Repository data sets are conducted, and the performance (both fusion and classification) is compared among their proposed framework and two other fusion methods (namely early feature fusion and late result decision fusion) using several classifiers available in Weka. The evaluation results demonstrate that their proposed framework achieves promising performance and performs significantly better than those classifiers in the comparison.

In Chapter 4, Han and Stechele presented a default reasoning approach using subjective logic that acts in a continuous space for forensic visual surveillance in their paper "Default Reasoning for Forensic Visual Surveillance based on Subjective Logic and its Comparison with L-Fuzzy Set Based Approaches." The wide proliferation of visual surveillance systems in various application domains motivates the authors to develop a more flexible and powerful approach for higher-level forensic semantic understanding and analysis of visual surveillance scenes, since such forensic analysis requires an appropriate reuse of the observed evidential metadata generated from vision analytics and then mates it with additional high-level contextual knowledge. It is even more challenging that such contextual knowledge and the vision analytic results suffer from uncertainties, incompleteness, and inconsistencies. To address such challenges and to meet the needs, the authors propose an approach to model default reasoning based on subjective logic operators by analyzing the default reasoning mechanism on bilattice and identifying the corresponding and analogous behavior. Default reasoning can express a segment of knowledge as being true by default or generally true, but could be proven false upon arrival of new information (i.e., nonmonotonicity). It can also provide a means of deriving plausible semantic conclusion under imprecise and contradictory information in forensic visual surveillance. In addition, subjective logic can bridge the Dempster Shafer theory and the second order Bayesian to provide better insights on the correlations among different uncertainty formalisms. The authors also applied the L-fuzzy set based logics such as intuitionistic fuzzy logic to contrast the properties and advantage of the subjective logic, and the results show that subjective logic and L-fuzzy set based approaches can be an alternative tool to model default reasoning, but enabling default reasoning to subjective logic can offer a better expressive power for modeling and reflecting real-world situations.

Section 2: Multimedia Content Management

Section 2 discusses the methodologies and tools in content management for multimedia data in four (4) chapters. The rapid progress in information technology has made an enormous amount of multimedia data being easily exchanged through the communication networks and Internet. Excellent examples include Web 2.0 and social networks. There is no doubt that Web 2.0 has marked a new paradigm of generating and distributing Web content itself, characterized by its freedom to share and re-use. We have also witnessed the popularity of social networks. More and more people upload and share images and videos on social networks to demonstrate their seeing and feeling. With such an explosion of multimedia data available on the Internet, desktops, and mobile devices, multimedia data management, search, and retrieval have become more and more important for efficient indexing and intelligent access for audio-video material.

In Chapter 5, Pinto-Caceres *et al.* presented a novel approach in "Navigating through Video Stories Using Clustering Sets" for interactive search that displays the results in a more flexible and intuitive way. The recent technology development has facilitated the generation, storage, and distribution of digital videos for various applications such as search engines and digital libraries. Such phenomena have created the need to efficiently manage video material and effectively access the data in a user-friendly way.

Their proposed approach relies on the storyboard generation and visualization of story strategies. In this chapter, stories are the meaningful and manageable units to be presented to the users. Each story has multiple shots represented by a collection of frames. To build storyboards, an algorithm was developed that produces video stories in a reasonable time and with acceptable quality, enabling online usage. It consists of three steps: feature extraction, content selection, and noise filtering. For each frame, visual features are extracted to describe its visual content. Next, groups of video frames with a similar content are detected, and a representative frame per group is selected. Finally, those potentially redundant or meaningless frames are filtered from the selected frames to build the storyboards. After the storyboards are built, the authors developed an effective technique for the displaying and visualization of the stories. The authors proposed the design concept of Clustering Sets that merge the positive aspects of different visualization strategies into a single structure. Such a visualization design groups video stories into clusters which are displayed in a radial manner. It not only takes advantages of a radial distribution, but also preserves the relationships between similar videos. Therefore, their proposed approach allows the user to view the relationship between several clusters at once with an experience of more comfortable exploration and better navigability. A subjective evaluation with 38 subjects was conducted to evaluate the layout employed by the proposed approach and to compare the proposed approach with several visualization techniques. The results have demonstrated that it outperforms most of the compared methods in most of the evaluated criteria.

Chapter 6 presents a novel two-stage image classification framework by Qiusha Zhu, Lin Lin, Mci-Ling Shyu, and Dianting Liu in their paper entitled "Utilizing Context Information to Enhance Content-Based Image Classification" with the aim to improve the performance of content-based image classification by utilizing the context information of web-based images. The rationale of this study lies in the facts that there are rich HTML surrounding texts associated with images in a web environment, and such texts naturally serve as the context information that can be complementary to the content information. Traditional image classification approaches are text-based such as keywords and tags, which requires a lot of manual efforts to annotate them. When the amount of images increases, manual annotations become infeasible. This leads to the area of content-based image classification, which trains the classifiers directly on visual features extracted from image content. Though the performance of content-based image classification has improved steadily, it is still far below users' expectation. On the other hand, context information for images can be utilized to complement the content information since context information may better capture the semantics of the images assuming that the textual terms are actually related to the images. In their proposed framework, a new TF*IDF weighting scheme was proposed to calculate the term weights for textual feature extraction. In the first stage of the training phase, the content-based MCA classifier is trained using the visual features based on the transaction weights from the MCA (Multiple Correspondence Analysis) model and an initial class label is assigned to each training data instance. In the second stage of the training phase, two context-based MCA classifiers are trained – one from the training data instances with initial positive class label and one from the training data instances with initial negative class label – to eliminate as many false positive data instances and to keep as many false negative data instances as possible. In the first stage of the testing phase, an initial class label will be assigned to each testing data instance. In the second stage of the testing phase, if the testing data instance was classified as positive then it goes to the context-based MCA classifier trained by the positive data instances; while if it was classified as negative, then it goes to the context-based MCA classifier trained by the negative data instances. After that, the final class label will be assigned to this testing data instance. Experiments were conducted to evaluate the proposed new TF*IDF weighting scheme and the whole two-stage classification framework, and the experimental results demonstrate that with the effective utilization of the context-based information, the content-based image classification performance is enhanced.

In Chapter 7, Kasturi Chatterjee and Shu-Ching Chen proposed a hybrid query refinement model for distance-based index structures in their paper, "Hybrid Query Refinement: A Strategy for a Distance Based Index Structure to Refine Multimedia Queries," that supports content-based image retrieval. It is well-acknowledged that an index structure is one of the major components of a database management system since it helps organize the data efficiently to achieve quick and accurate retrieval. However, due to the inherent rich semantic information in multimedia data, traditional index structures are no longer feasible, resulting in the development of the multidimensional index structures. Unfortunately, the semantic interpretation of the multimedia data is subjective and varies from user to user and/or from iteration to iteration for the same user. Hence, it is still very challenging to enable them to efficiently support the content-based image and video retrieval. One of the reasons is that the similarity queries issued for multimedia data are imprecise in nature, and thus a single iteration or a fixed query representation is not enough to capture the user requirements during the retrieval process. To address such a challenge, the query refinement strategy is typically adopted to capture the users' interest pattern. In this chapter, the authors proposed a hybrid query refinement model for distance-based index structures to organize and manage images. Their proposed model refines a query by considering both the low-level feature space and the high-level semantic interpretations separately so that it can handle the queries where the gap between the feature components and the semantics is large. The low-level feature space which is indexed by the distance-based index structure is refined in multiple iterations by introducing the concept of multipoint query in a metric space; whereas the high-level semantic space is refined by dynamically adjusting the Markov Model Mediator (MMM) to introduce the semantic relationships in the index structure. In order to handle the similarity searches that refine a query in multiple iterations utilizing their proposed hybrid query refinement model, the authors designed a k-nearest neighbor (k-NN) algorithm. To compare the retrieval performance in terms of both computation overhead and query result relevance, the authors also developed and proposed the Model_Score evaluation metric which can enable the users to choose the retrieval framework appropriate for their requirements. Experiments were conducted, and the experimental results demonstrate that their proposed hybrid query refinement model achieves an increased relevance of query results in subsequent iterations while incurring a low computational overhead.

In Chapter 8, the paper entitled "3D Model-Based Semantic Categorization of Still Image 2D Objects" by Petre and Zaharia examines the issue of still image object categorization. The authors attempted to propose a solution to determine automatically the semantic meaning of an object present in an image or video, rather than manual annotation. This is particularly needed when a large multimedia database is involved, since user access to specific material of interest from the huge amount of multimedia data is not possible without efficient search engines and tools. Traditional retrieval tools were exclusively based on keywords, but the linguistic barriers represent an important drawback of such approaches. Hence, the need of automatic object categorization tools appears as a crucial challenge, especially when there are a large number of categories and the number of recognition criteria increases. Towards such a demand, the authors presented a new recognition method that is able to handle a large variety of objects by exploiting categorized 3D models from existing 3D repositories in the classification process. The main idea of their proposed 2D/3D indexing approach is to represent a 3D model as a set of 2D views obtained according to different projection angles. This is under the hypothesis that if the models are similar, then they should present similar views; whereas if two 3D models are different, then there is no correspondence between the sets of views. The main advantage of such an indexing methodology is to have different types of comparisons. For instance, a 3D model can be compared with other 3D models based on their respective projections, or a 3D model can be compared with a 2D object extracted from a 2D image. Furthermore, in their proposed approach, the projection represents a binary image (the silhouette of the object) since their goal is to match the 2D objects, which do not have any depth information, with a set of 3D models. Hence, each projection is described by a 2D shape descriptor, and the set of all descriptors yields the 2D/3D representation of the considered 3D object. The experimental results obtained from both MPEG-7 and Princeton 3D models databases show that their proposed approach achieves up to 89.2% recognition rates.

Section 3: Multimodal Content Retrieval

In the third section, several techniques to address the challenges and issues in multimodal analysis and indexing for multimedia retrieval are presented in four (4) chapters. Searching and retrieving information in multimedia databases via keywords is not feasible anymore for large multimedia databases. For example, many existing multimedia data repositories such as YouTube, Google Videos, DailyMotion, etc. include millions of multimedia objects. Take Flickr as an illustration: as of October 2009, it hosted more than four billion images with manual, user-annotated tags. Attempting to manually annotate such huge multimedia databases is simply not possible, not only in terms of money and time, but also with respect to the quality of annotation. More importantly, more and more metadata and user-annotated tags and texts are made available in addition to the multimedia objects, which help describe an item and allow it to be found again by browsing or searching. This calls for the development of multi-modal data analysis and retrieval methods to support different kinds of search by integrating resources across various modalities.

In Chapter 9, Shieh *et al.* presented a new multi-modal media search method that is based on novel related-tag graphs in their paper entitled "Building Multi-Modal Relational Graphs for Multimedia Retrieval." In their proposed method, a query is a resource in one modality such as an image, and the results are semantically similar resources in various modalities such as text and video. The authors attempt to enhance the quality of the search term suggestions by utilizing the "collective intelligence" that is embedded in user-intensive social media such as Wikipedia. The use of resource tagging can enable the use of multi-modal results and multi-modal queries, which is different from the traditional text-based search paradigm. Their proposed framework consists of ten components, namely: tag parsing, disambiguation, multi-partite data sampling, soft clustering, contributor specialization incorporation, context integration, relation fusion, relative importance ranking, multimedia visualization interface, and recommendation and evaluation interface. In their proposed framework, given the search media, its related documents or tags are parsed to find the meaningful (i.e., non-spam) tags. Next, Wikipedia is used as an interpreter to deal with tags that have more than one meaning by adopting the top meaning from the corresponding Wikipedia disambiguation page. Multi-partite data sampling starts from the query keyword tag, and an iterative process is designed to glean a large set of related tags and contributors. Using such information, a multi-partite network composed of layers of contributors and terms is constructed. In their proposed method, a soft clustering technique is applied to fold these networks into a term relationship graph called the related-tag graph. That is, the tag relation graphs are built based on multi-partite networks of existing Web 2.0 social media such as Flickr and Wikipedia. These multi-partite linkage networks (contributor-tag, tag-category, and tag-tag) are extracted from Wikipedia to construct relational tag graphs. In fusing these networks, the authors propose incorporating contributor-category networks to model contributor's specialization. It is shown that this step significantly enhances the accuracy of the inferred relatedness of the term-semantic graphs. The authors conducted experiments on 200 queries tags in TREC-5 *ad hoc* topics and user studies. The experimental results show that the algorithms outperform existing approaches, and the user studies demonstrate the superiority of this visualization system and its usefulness in the real world.

Chapter 10 is contributed by Yu, Hua, and Liu who presented a client-side relevance feedback approach for image retrieval on mobile devices in their paper entitled "Client-Side Relevance Feedback Approach for Image Retrieval in Mobile Environment." The purpose of this study is to enable multimedia information retrieval using the high-resolution pictures taken from the mobile devices. During the last decade, many handheld devices are facilitated with high quality (i.e., over 1 megapixel) built-in cameras, and users often take high-resolution pictures and share with friends via the internet. However, with limited wireless bandwidth and the demand of fast multimedia information retrieval using those pictures on mobile devices, this retrieval process can incur substantial delay, making the system unfriendly to use. To address this issue, the authors proposed a Client-side Relevance Feedback (CRF) technique. A relevance feedback information retrieval process includes several rounds of query refinement, which incurs exchange of images between the mobile device and the server. In the CRF system, Relevance Feedback (RF) is done on the client side. This can be achieved since given a RFS structure stored on the mobile device, this structure can be used to process the user's relevance feedback without any support from the remote server. Though the capacity of flash memory continues to increase, it is preferable to keep this RFS structure small. Under such a design, mobile devices' battery power is saved from exchanging the images between server and client, and system response can be instantaneous, which significantly enhances system usability. Furthermore, because the server is not involved in RF processing, more users can be supported simultaneously. After the CRF process, the final query will be sent to the server who will perform the localized k-NN queries to retrieve the semantically relevant images. These images will then be ranked to form the final result. To better present the information to the users, the authors designed an interface considering the different screen sizes of the smart phones and cell phones. Due to the small screen sizes, thumbnails are used for browsing. To evaluate the performance of their proposed approach, the CRF technique was compared with the existing client-server technique using the image database the authors constructed. This image database has 19,200 images with about 15,000 Corel images and new images. The experimental results indicate that their proposed approach outperforms the traditional server-client relevance feedback approaches on the aspects of system response time, mobile battery power saving, and retrieval result. Moreover, substantial improvement in retrieval precision and recall are also achieved.

In Chapter 11, Ruxandra Tapu and Titus Zaharia tackled the issue of video structuring, examined temporal video segmentation, and proposed a complete and automatic segmentation methodology in "Video Segmentation and Structuring for Indexing Applications." Considering the issues of video indexing and retrieval applications, it is more desirable to structure the video into its constitutive elements: keyframes, shots, scenes, and DVD chapters. These require the development of various techniques in shot boundary detection, keyframe extraction, and scene identification. Correspondingly, the authors proposed a novel methodological framework for temporal structuring and segmentation with the following main contributions: (1) an enhanced shot boundary detection method based on multi-resolution non-linear filtering and with low computational complexity; (2) a leap keyframe extraction strategy that generates adaptively static storyboards; and (3) a novel shot clustering technique that creates semantically relevant scenes by exploiting a set of temporal constraints, a new concept of neutralized/non-neutralized shots, as well as an adaptive thresholding mechanism. For shot boundary detection, the authors adopted the normalized graph partition approach with a non-linear and multiresolution filtering of the similarity vectors involved. The video is segmented using a sliding window that selects a constant number of frames centered on the current frame of interest. They showed that their shot boundary detection technique yields high precision (90%) and recall (95%) rates for all types of transitions, both abrupt and gradual. Next, for each detected shot, the authors constructed a static storyboard by introducing a leap keyframe extraction method that analyzes only the frames spaced by multiple integers of the window size and not the entire set of frames. To select a new keyframe, the current image is compared with all the keyframes already extracted using the chi-square distance of HSV color histograms. In addition, the number of keyframes necessary to describe the informational content of a shot can be automatically adapted to the dynamics of the content. The authors showed that the video abstraction algorithm is 23% faster than existing techniques for similar performances. Finally, the authors proposed a shot grouping strategy that iteratively clusters those visually similar shots under a set of temporal constraints. A neutralization process was developed that can identify the most representative shots for a current scene, which are the remaining non-neutralized shots, so that the influence of outlier shots which might correspond to some punctual digressions from the main action in the considered scene is minimized. Two different types of visual features are exploited: HSV color histograms and interest points. In both cases, the authors demonstrated that the precision and recall rates present an average performance of 86%.

In Chapter 12, Kimiaki Shirahama and Kuniaki Uehara proposed a method that can filter a large number of shots irrelevant to a query based on a video ontology serving as a knowledge base about the concepts displayed in a shot in their paper "Constructing and Utilizing Video Ontology for Accurate and Fast Retrieval." For video retrieval, based on how to represent a query, the existing methods can be classified as Query-By-Keyword (QBK) or Query-By-Example (QBE). QBK approaches take the keywords (representing the query) provided by the user and the system retrieves those shots that are annotated with the same or related keywords. QBE approaches take the example shots (representing the query) provided by the user and the system retrieves those shots that are similar to the example shots in terms of features like color, edge, motion, etc. QBE has two advantages over QBK. Unlike QBK, in QBE, the query is represented with no subjectivity and it requires no shot annotation. Hence, the authors examine video retrieval based on QBE, where the shots relevant to a query are retrieved from a large-scale video data repository based on their similarity to the example shots. Two issues need to be addressed. The first issue is that similarity in features does not necessarily imply similarity in semantic content; whereas the second issue is the expensive computational cost to compute the similarity of a huge number of shots to example shots. The authors developed a method to filter a large number of shots irrelevant to a query and used various concept relationships (e.g., generalization/specialization, sibling, part-of, and co-occurrence) defined in their manually constructed video ontology. In addition, the video ontology assumes that shots are accurately annotated with concepts. However, it is not easy to obtain accurate annotations due to the diversity of forms and appearances of the concepts. Therefore, the authors utilized the Dempster-Shafer theory to account the uncertainty in determining the relevance of a shot based on inaccurate annotation of this shot. The authors conducted the experiment on TRECVID 2009 video data, and the experimental results validated the effectiveness of their proposed method.

Section 4: Multimedia Delivery and Applications

Section 4 includes three (3) chapters that present the research studies in multimedia networking and multimedia applications. There has been growing interests in using multimedia data in real-world applications across the computer networks including wireless networks. Since different multimedia data types (such as text, video, audio, and image) are brought together into one single unit, all controlled by a computer, the development of advanced transmission and delivery techniques to synchronize the various multimedia data types from distributed data sources needs to be sought. Assuming that the main challenges and issues of multimedia delivery and transmission are addressed, various multimedia applications can be then realized using the advances in multimedia technologies. It is well-recognized that multimedia data not only allow fast and effective communication and sharing of information about people – their lives, behaviors, and interests, but also present the digital testimony of facts, objects, and locations.

Chapter 13 presents "A Real-Time 3D Visualization Framework for Multimedia Data Management, Simulation, and Prediction: Case Study in Geospatial-Temporal Biomedical Disease Surveillance Networks" by Nathaniel Rossol, Irene Cheng, Iqbal Jamal, John Berezowski, and Anup Basu. In this study, the authors outlined the design, implementation, and usage of a 3D framework for real-time geospatial temporal visualization and showed that their proposed 3D framework is capable of tracking and simulating the spread of epidemic diseases using livestock movements. Unlike Geographic Information Systems (GISs) which map the spatio-temporal event data on the geographical maps, Time-based Geographic Information Systems (GISs) allow the practitioners to visualize the collected data in an intuitive way. Both GISs and Time-based GISs have proven to be useful in *post hoc* analysis and can provide simple two-dimensional geographic visualizations for many applications. Unfortunately, these designs typically lack the features necessary for highly targeted real-time surveillance with the goal of spread prevention. This motivates the authors to design and develop a visualization framework that can present cross data streams collected from multiple sources in an interactive and intuitive format. Such a design can enable the domain experts to navigate within the visualization space and identify the trends that would not have been discovered using traditional analysis techniques. For example, a biomedical GIS visualization can display a variety of health surveillance data over a geographical overview of the area of interest. The authors applied a network-based modeling approach and used the data livestock disease as their application. This case study used a data set that contains 1418 vertices with 6 dimensions per vertex, and 218,391 transactions with 14 dimensions per transaction, spread over 365 timesteps where each time-step corresponds to a single day of the year. Then the implemented visualization framework was presented to several groups of scientists and middle managers in the government food safety and animal health divisions to get their feedback. Overall, the users described the visualization interface as straightforward and easy to understand. Using the implemented visualization framework, the veterinarian epidemiologist practitioners were already able to make several preliminary discoveries and new knowledge gains, which demonstrated the usefulness and potentials of this study. In addition, the authors also claimed that their proposed framework can be used to manage and visualize other types of high-dimensional multimedia data as well.

Chapter 14 is contributed by Hongli Luo in the paper "A Cross-Layer Design for Video Streaming Over 802.11e HCCA Wireless Network," which attempts to improve the quality of the video received in a wireless network under the constraint of network bandwidth using a cross-layer design for video streaming over IEEE 802.11e HCF Controlled Channel Access (HCCA) WLAN. The explosion of multimedia data and the increasing popularity of wireless devices have made wireless multimedia transmission over the Internet an important and challenging issue. Multimedia data transmission has its quality of service (QoS) requirements, such as bandwidth, packet loss, and delay. The dynamics of the wireless channels as well as the quality of service (QoS) requirements have posed challenges to the design of the wireless networks. Due to its low cost and ease of configurations, IEEE 802.11 Wireless LAN (WLAN) has been widely used for mobile and ubiquitous multimedia networking. It is well-acknowledged that video transmission over the wireless networks has quality of service (QoS) requirements, but the time-varying characteristics of wireless channels make it a challenging task. Recently, the cross-layer design of wireless multimedia transmission provides a promising direction to improve the overall performance of wireless networks since it takes into account the interactions among layers. In this chapter, the cross-layer design is focused on MAC layer scheduling since it can improve the quality of video under heavy traffic load. The author developed two algorithms for the proposed cross-layer video transmission design. The first algorithm is to calculate an allocation of optimal TXOP with the aim to maintain a short queuing delay at the wireless station at the cost of a small TXOP allocation. In the second algorithm, the transmission of the packets is scheduled according to the importance levels of the packets so that the visual quality of video can be maximized. The author conducted serveral performance evaluation simulations, where the proposed approach was compared with the standard HCCA on NS2 simulation tools using H.264 video codec. The simulation results indicated that the proposed cross-layer design outperforms the standard approach in terms of the PSNRs of the received video. That is, the PSNRs of the received video sequence under the proposed cross-layer approach are much higher than the standard HCCA since it reduces the packet loss to allow the graceful video degradation, especially under heavy network traffic.

In the last chapter, Massimiliano Albanese *et al.* presented their proposed strategy to cope with the information overload challenge in "A Novel Strategy for Recommending Multimedia Objects and its Application in the Cultural Heritage Domain" using the cultural heritage domain as a case study. A massive amount of data collections, in the forms of digital video and image libraries, digital documents, news archives, shopping catalogs, virtual museums, and so on, are widely available to the users. However, such a huge amount of multimedia data collections makes it difficult for the users to obtain, retrieve, and/or suggest information of their interests and preferences. In this chapter, the authors addressed the information overload challenge through the development of a recommendation system that can facilitate the browsing of large data repositories to realize the transition from the "era of search" to the "era of discovery." Recommender systems are able to help people retrieve information that matches their preferences by recommending products or services from a large number of candidate products or services, and then support people in making their decisions. Such an idea can be extended to build the multimedia recommendation systems that allow an automatic selection of a small subset of multimedia objects (or items with rich semantics) that appears to fit to the user's need by bridging the semantic gap between the users and the contents using multimedia technologies. Such multimedia recommendation systems are especially useful in the environments with lots of the information where it is difficult to express the semantics of the queries. In such a context, the authors proposed a strategy based on an "importance ranking" algorithm that computes the customized recommendations for accessing multimedia collections, considering the information from semantic contents, intrinsic features of multimedia objects (low-level and semantic similarities), past behavior of individual users, and social behavior of the users' community as a whole. The authors implemented their strategy in a recommender prototype system for browsing the image digital libraries in two scenarios in the Cultural Heritage domain to show how a multimedia recommendation system can desirably work during both a virtual and a real visit of an art gallery. It is hoped that in both scenarios, from the user perspective, it is good to have a guide suggesting paintings which the users might be interested in; whereas from the system perspective, it is also very helpful to use the suggestions for pre-fetching and caching the objects that are more likely to be requested. The authors then investigated the effectiveness of the proposed approach with respect to a user-centric evaluation, based on the users' satisfaction. The preliminary experimental results showed that the approach is promising and encourages further research in this direction.

Shu-Ching Chen
Florida International University, USA

Mei-Ling Shyu
University of Miami, USA

Section 1
Multimedia Content Analysis

Chapter 1
Content–Based Keyframe Clustering Using Near Duplicate Keyframe Identification

Ehsan Younessian
Nanyang Technological University, Singapore

Deepu Rajan
Nanyang Technological University, Singapore

ABSTRACT

In this paper, the authors propose an effective content-based clustering method for keyframes of news video stories using the Near Duplicate Keyframe (NDK) identification concept. Initially, the authors investigate the near-duplicate relationship, as a content-based visual similarity across keyframes, through the Near-Duplicate Keyframe (NDK) identification algorithm presented. The authors assign a near-duplicate score to each pair of keyframes within the story. Using an efficient keypoint matching technique followed by matching pattern analysis, this NDK identification algorithm can handle extreme zooming and significant object motion. In the second step, the weighted adjacency matrix is determined for each story based on assigned near duplicate score. The authors then use the spectral clustering scheme to remove outlier keyframes and partition remainders. Two sets of experiments are carried out to evaluate the NDK identification method and assess the proposed keyframe clustering method performance.

INTRODUCTION

Effective clustering of video shots is an important step in applications involving content-based video analysis and retrieval. For instance Rui and Huang (2000) investigated how a proper grouping of video shots can be useful for video content browsing and retrieval. Clustering of video shots also has been applied to understand associated semantics in video organization which can lead to detecting of scenes in the video (Rasheed & Shah, 2005). Furthermore a wide range of other video-related applications from content-based annotation of video to video summarization can benefit from

DOI: 10.4018/978-1-4666-2940-0.ch001

effective clustering of similar shots (Gao & Dai, 2008). Generally speaking, the different shot clustering approaches utilize either all frames in a video (Chen, Wang, & Wang, 2009; Zhang, Sun, Yang, & Zhong, 2005) or only a particular frame representing the shot, called the keyframe (Odobez, Gatica-Perez, & Guillemot, 2003) as the initial unit of video. In this study, we consider keyframe as the representative of a video shot and tackle the keyframe clustering problem.

One of the most critical issues in keyframe clustering is the similarity measure of visual information. In the video retrieval literature, scholars refer to this problem as Near Duplicate Keyframe identification. Near-Duplicate Keyframe (NDK) refers to the pair of keyframes in a video dataset that are closely similar to each other despite the minor variations due to capturing conditions, lighting, motion and editing operations. The task of NDK detection involves finding NDK pairs while that of NDK retrieval involves ranking all keyframes in the dataset with respect to their probability of being NDK to an input query keyframe. The former is useful for multimedia search (Zhao & Ngo, 2007) and linking news stories and grouping them into threads (Zhang & Chang, 2004), while the latter finds applications in query by example applications and copyright infringement detection (Ke, Suthankar, & Huston, 2004). The real challenge in identifying NDK is the moderate to significant degree of the variations caused by

zooming and object motion (Zhu, Hoi, Lyu, & Yan, 2008). Figure 1 shows four pairs of NDKs varied in term of view point, camera lens and object locations.

In near duplicate analysis, local features invariant to the kind of variations mentioned above are becoming more important compared to global features. Local features are composed of detected keypoints and their associated descriptors extracted from local patches in the image. One of the most popular among them is the scale invariant feature transform (SIFT) descriptor (Lowe, 2004) and their variants such as PCA-SIFT. The former is shown to be scale invariant as well as robust to a certain degree of affine transformation. Similarly, the latter is known to be tolerant to color and photometric changes (Chang et al., 2005).

We use an efficient keypoint matching technique followed by matching pattern analysis in the NDK identification algorithm (Younessian, Rajan, & Chng, 2009) to handle extreme zooming and significant object motion. For each pair of keyframes within the story we calculate a near-duplicate score based on which a weighted adjacency matrix for the graph representation of keyframes is determined. Then we use spectral clustering to remove outlier keyframes and partition the rest of keyframes. The number of clusters is determined automatically so as to obtain well-separated and also balanced clusters.

Figure 1. Examples of NDKs with zooming, object motion and the color change

RELATED WORK

In the literature, various supervised and unsupervised shot-based clustering methods have been reported. Adami, Benini, and Leonardi (2006) overviewed video shot clustering methods comprehensively. In unsupervised clustering category, various approaches used different clustering frameworks like *k-means* (Gatica-Perez, Loui, & Sun, 2003), *Ant_Tree* (Damnjanovic, Piatrik, Djordjevic, & Izquierdo, 2007), and lately spectral clustering (Damnjanovic et al., 2007; Odobez et al., 2003; Zhang et al., 2005). Due to its effectiveness to reflect the perceptual organization in videos, we choose the spectral clustering framework in this paper (Adami et al., 2006). The main challenges in unsupervised spectral clustering approaches are determination of a good similarity measure and the number of clusters. For instance, Odobez et al. (2003) formed a similarity matrix across keyframes according to some global features and temporal information of keyframes. Spectral clustering is adopted to group the keyframes based on the feature distance. Using low-level visual features, this approach has low computational cost and performs well on videos which have long shots in which the similarity (based on the used features) of visual content is high, e.g., slow rhythm videos like documentaries and home videos. Since this study is done on news videos, which generally have a fast rhythm, and also possess large variations in layouts, context (e.g., object displacement and camera angle variations) together with editing effects (e.g. zooming and occlusion), we argue that instead of global fingerprints, visual similarity based on local features can be helpful to handle these variations more effectively. In addition, the temporal order of keyframes is not meaningful in news videos since there might be anchor or reporter shots interspersed in the story stream or there might be repetition of some shots due to lack of raw material. As another spectral approach, Zhang et al. (2005) utilized temporal information along with color-based information

through a frame-based framework to model each shot as a GMM based on which cross-shot similarity is determined and corresponding affinity matrix is computed. Using all frames in the video shot, they could not achieve significant improvement compared to the conventional method proposed by Odobez et al. (2003) (less than 2% improvement in both precision and recall scores). In (Peker & Bashir, 2005), the similarity across keyframes is determined based on the facial features like number, location and size of existing faces in the keyframes. The number of clusters is adaptively determined in this approach based on the cluster validity score. This approach cannot perform well in news videos domain where a large portion of keyframes might include no face. Furthermore, the face detection algorithm is only capable of detecting frontal faces.

The two main approaches for near duplicate keyframe identification can be roughly grouped into appearance-based methods and local feature based methods (Zhu et al., 2008). Global features such as color, texture and edge property play an important role in appearance-based approaches (Qamra, Meng, & Cheng, 2005; Zhang & Chang, 2004). However, they are not tolerant to variations like photometric changes, object dynamics and other geometric transformations. Zhang and Chang (2004) proposed a stochastic Attributed Relational Graph (ARG) matching with part-based representation for NDK identification. This method suffers from the limitations of slow matching process and the requirement of heuristically determined parameters for learning. Generally speaking, local feature based approaches focus on extracting interesting keypoints from the images and matching them to identify Near-Duplicate (Ke et al., 2004; Zhao & Ngo, 2006, 2007). Although these approaches overcome the problems corresponding to appearance-based approaches, but the large number of keypoints generated leads to computationally expensive algorithms.

Utilizing PCA-SIFT, Ke et al. (2004) employed a point set matching method using the locality sensitive hashing (LSH) technique. LSH, nevertheless, requires several user-defined parameters which affect the distortion and granularity of search. Moreover, their study is focused on art images with the high resolution, and its robustness remains unclear when the target database includes keyframes with low-resolution, motion-blur and compression artifacts. Zhao and Ngo (2006) used Pattern Entropy (*PE*) score to measure the similarity of two images containing keypoints extracted by their proposed One-to-One Symmetric (OOS) matching method. However, this method is unsatisfactory when it comes to identifying NDK pairs with large variations, e.g. due to zooming and partial occlusion (Zhu et al., 2008). Zhu et al. (2008) proposed a Non-rigid Image Matching (NIM) approach. The key idea is motivated by computer vision techniques of determining an explicit mapping between two images. The deformation parameters in the mapping along with a ranking scheme to filter out irrelevant matches have ended up with the approach achieving state-of-the-art performance. Although Multi-Level Ranking (MLR) framework improves the efficiency and scalability, some NDKs are incorrectly filtered out through the first ranking stage, since the imposed ranking criterion in this stage is based on global features. Technically, an NDK pair that differs due to extreme zooming or significant object displacement may have distant global features, e.g. in Figure 1(a), features like grid color moment and the edge properties are significantly far away. Similarly, the edge features are different in the NDK pair shown in Figure 1(b). NDK retrieval experiments by Zhu et al. (2008) do not identify the correct result for top-1 retrieval for some query images, e.g. those shown in Figure 1(c) and Figure 1(d). This is due to significant variation in camera lens and/or object dynamics. However our method handles these cases successfully. Chum, Philbin, Isard, and Zisserman (2007) addressed large-scale near identical image detection by utilizing both global features and local SIFT descriptors.

A bag-of-words model is employed to deal with SIFT features. The downside of such methods is that each region is matched independent to others and without considering spatial information. Lazebnik, Schmid, and Ponce (2006) introduced the Spatial Pyramid Matching (SPM) algorithm as a block-to-block matching scheme for scene classification by incorporating the spatial information of location regions. The method implicitly assumes the association between blocks; however, this association is not scale or rotation invariant. Xu, Cham, Yan, and Chang (2008) proposed a multi-level spatial matching framework with two-stage matching to deal with spatial shifts and scale variation for image near duplicate identification task. The block-based distance between image pair is used and multiple alignment hypotheses are explored. Cheng, Hu, and Chia (2008) analyzed the local dependencies in spatial-scale space. To do so, they integrated both appearance, spatial and scale co-occurrence information to handle cases with spatial transformation and scale changes. Wu, Zhao, and Ngo (2007) explored both visual and textual modalities from visual vocabulary and semantic context, respectively for NDK retrieval purpose. The vocabulary, including visual keywords, is constructed by the clustering of keypoints and semantic context is obtained from speech transcripts surrounding a keyframe. Finally a weighted linear fusion is used to integrate visual and textual cues under different similarity measures for NDK retrieval.

The NDK concept also has been investigated in term of different applications. For instance, Das, Farmer, Gallagher, and Loui (2008) proposed an approach to reliably retrieve photos taken at a particular location. Their major contribution is to provide a set of constraints that narrow down probable matched features to retrieve more reliable matching. In this method first, keypoints are spatially clustered. Then paired keypoints are filtered according to the assumption that all keypoint clusters in the scene move in the same general direction which is not always correct particularly in case of several objects displacements like Figure 1(b).

In this paper, we aim to utilize a semantic measure for visual similarity across keyframes. Next, we use this content-based relation between keyframes (i.e. near-duplicate property) for clustering purpose.

NDK IDENTIFICATION

Our NDK identification method is motivated by (Zhao & Ngo, 2007) in which one of the main issues addressed is that of finding reliable matching keypoints across two keyframes. In our approach as shown in Figure 2, first we detect interesting keypoints using Difference of Gaussian detector and determine the SIFT feature as the keypoints descriptor. SIFT descriptors are computed as a 128-dimensional descriptor vector that captures the spatial structure and local orientation in a patch of size 4 × 4 and an 8-bin histogram of orientations. Then each keypoint is matched independently to other keyframe set of keypoints using cosine similarity of their descriptors. Next we remove less reliable keypoint matches using symmetric property of near-duplicate and a ratio of nearest and second-nearest neighbor distances as explained later. Then, a pattern coherency score is assigned to each pair of keyframes. We use the number of matching keypoints across keyframe pairs and the pattern coherency score as two discriminative features. Since these two features hold different degrees of distinguishing power,

we linearly combine them with different weights obtained by Linear Discriminant Analysis (LDA). Finally, the separating boundary is trained using SVM. We will show that our method can handle cross-NDK large variations such as extreme zooming and significant object dynamics, while improving the performance of near duplicate retrieval on the standard databases.

Constraint Symmetric Keypoint Matching Scheme

Given two sets of keypoints, the association across them can be grouped as many-to-many (M2M), many-to-one (M2O), one-to-many (O2M) and one-to-one (O2O) matching (Zhao & Ngo, 2006). The choice of the association type affects the matching effectiveness, efficiency, and reliability. For instance, one of the conventional M2O matching schemes is the well-known nearest neighbor search which has been used for keypoint matching in (Lowe, 2004). Although its effectiveness is shown in (Lowe, 2004), it imposes an expensive computational cost and it does not perform well in noisy dataset. Zhao and Ngo (2007) have shown O2O matching scheme is a suitable choice and noise tolerant at the cost of missing some correct matches for news keyframes, which might suffer from low-resolution.

$$RoD(k_i^A, k_j^B) = \frac{Max_{l=1,..,n_B}(\langle D_i^A, D_l^B \rangle)}{\langle D_i^A, D_j^B \rangle}, l \neq j.$$

$$(1)$$

Figure 2. Our NDK identification framework

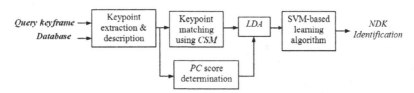

and D_j^B are the SIFT vectors of the ith keypoint of keyframe A and the jth keypoint of keyframe B, respectively, n_B is the number of keypoints in the keyframe B and $\langle,\rangle$ is the cosine similarity between two vectors. Next, we define the association rule between the keypoints across keyframe A and B as

$$k_i^A \Rightarrow k_j^B \text{ if } RoD(k_i^A, k_j^B) < \tau, \qquad (2)$$

where τ is a threshold $(0 < \tau \le 1)$. As stated in the experimental results, τ is specified from corresponding probability density function for correct and incorrect top-1 NDK retrievals. It gives an idea of how much of the true and false keyframe pairs are eliminated for each particular value of τ. As τ is decreased from 1, it enforces more restriction on the association of two keypoints since their similarity must be much farther away from the similarity to other keypoints. It leads to less number of detected matching keypoints but they are more reliable. Based on Equation (2), we define a matrix $R_{A \to B} = [r_{ij}]_{n_A \times n_B}$ whose elements are

$$r_{ij} = \begin{cases} 1 & if \quad k_i^A \Rightarrow k_j^B \\ 0 & if \quad Otherwise \end{cases} \qquad (3)$$

Similarly, we define the matrix $R_{B \to A}$ for the keyframe B. Considering the symmetric property of matching keypoints in NDKs together with the SIFT keypoint matching scheme, we employ a symmetric pairing mechanism for the keypoints through the matrix R_S defined as

$$R_S = R_{A \to B} \circ R_{B \to A} \qquad (4)$$

where $\circ$ indicates element-by-element multiplication. The ith keypoint from keyframe A and the jth keypoint from keyframe B are paired if $R_S(i, j)$

is 1. We call this keypoint matching scheme as constrained symmetric matching (CSM) and evaluate it for different values of τ later in NDK identification evaluation section. It can be shown using Equations (1) and (2) that the association rule results in a O2O matching which is noise-tolerant like other O2O matching schemes as explained earlier.

Forming a simple binary matrix R_S for each keyframe pair, via CSM scheme we can process 7 pairs of keyframes per second, which is comparable to 10 frames per second in (Zhu et al., 2008).

The effectiveness of CSM is also illustrated in NDK identification evaluation section where the numbers of correct retrievals in top-1 are ascertained. Note if the numbers of matching keypoints across two keyframe pairs are the same, we resolve the contention by considering the color-based feature. Specifically, the keyframe is divided into blocks of size 5×5 and the mean and variance of each color channel in each block is computed and collected to form a 150 dimensional vector per keyframe. The cosine similarity, as defined above, between the two color vectors is used to re-rank the retrieval results.

Pattern Coherency Score

Most of the previous NDK identification approaches using keypoint matching techniques have used the number of matching lines (i.e. joining matching keypoints across pair of keyframes) to measure the probability of being NDK (Zhao & Ngo, 2007; Zhu et al., 2008). The more number of matching lines, the higher is the probability of the pair being NDK. In addition to this discriminative feature, we observe that the matching of keypoints across keyframes results in a pattern formed by the lines joining the matching keypoint from one keyframe to the matching keypoint in the other keyframe. This pattern recognition in the context of near duplicate problem was addressed by Zhao and Ngo (2006) earlier. They introduced Pattern Entropy (*PE*) score for each pair of keyframe derived from the angles that the matching lines make with the vertical and horizontal direction. The horizontal and vertical directions are shown by the yellow arrows in Figure 3(b) and Figure 3(c), respectively. Any pair of images with *PE* < 0.5 is considered as near duplicates. Zhu et al. (2008) have shown that the *PE* method fails in cases where there is a change in illumination, object motion or zooming, e.g. in Figure 3 and Figure 4.

In this part we employ a more effective method to recognize the pattern of matching lines for NDK pairs. The key idea is that across NDK pairs, the matching lines joining the keypoint of an identical object in two keyframes are relatively coherent. We utilize a robust score called Pattern Coherency (*PC*) to measure the total coherency of groups of matching lines that join objects in pairs of keyframes. This is explained using an example shown in Figure 3. First, we split the matching lines across Figure 3(a) and Figure 3(b) into two clusters (Q and Q') based on the angles that they make with the horizontal direction. Our choice of two as the number of clusters comes from the observation that, gener-

Figure 3. Pattern coherency score determinations using both vertical and horizontal alignments

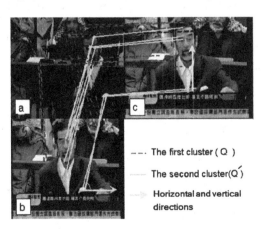

--- The first cluster (Q)

The second cluster(Q´)

Horizontal and vertical directions

Figure 4. An example of extreme zooming. Blue solid lines and red dash lines form the first and the second cluster respectively

ally, objects located in the background or the foreground have roughly the same matching direction in NDK pairs. A simple *k-means* algorithm is used to perform the clustering. The mean distance of the angles in the cluster Q to its centroid, Q_C, is obtained as

$$\Omega_Q = \frac{1}{\left|S_Q\right|} \sum_{i=1}^{\left|S_Q\right|} (\theta_{Qi} - Q_C)^2, \qquad (5)$$

where $\left|S_Q\right|$ is the number of matching lines in cluster Q and θ_{Qi} is the ith matching line angle with the horizontal direction. Similarly we determine $\Omega_{Q'}$ using Equation (5). In Figure 3, Q and Q' are shown as blue solid and red dash lines respectively between (a) and (b). Next, we compute pattern coherency score for the vertical alignment (PC_v) as

$$PC_v = \Omega_Q + \Omega_{Q'} \qquad (6)$$

The advantage of the clustering method lies in this fact that matching lines as a result of significant object displacement and extreme zooming can be divided into two sets and analyzed independently (i.e. clusters of lines between Figure 3(a) and Figure 3(b)) and the PC_v score will be determined by summation of Ω_Q and $\Omega_{Q'}$ as mentioned in Equation (6). Note that considering them as a single set, as in (Zhao & Ngo, 2006) would result in a combined contribution of horizontal and vertical angles in cases of motion/zooming/occlusion which ends up with high values of *PE*. However, in Figure 3(a) and Figure 2(b), due to within coherency of two clusters computed by Equation (5), the determined PC_v based on Equation (6) will be reasonably low.

We determine PC_h similarly using matching lines in horizontal alignment (i.e. matching lines between (a) and (c) in Figure 3). Although the object displacement cannot be observed in this alignment, PC_h computed by Equations (5) and (6) is still low. We conclude that *PC* score works well either in the presence or in the absence of object displacement.

Since we claim that the low value of either PC_v or PC_h is sufficient for being NDK, we impose a weaker constraint by taking the minimum of *PC* scores in vertical and horizontal directions as $PC = \min(PC_h, PC_v)$. Later in NDK identification evaluation section, we will justify the choice of *min* based on experimental results. Figure 3 is a good example of such cases which were misclassified as non-NDK by (Zhao & Ngo, 2006) due to significant object displacement while our method retrieves it correctly as an NDK pair. Figure 4 illustrates an example of extreme zooming whose pattern coherency score is determined relatively low while corresponding *PE* score, determined according to (Zhao & Ngo, 2006), is high based on which it is misclassified. This observation confirms that when compared to *PE*, *PC* can handle extreme zooming cases as well. At the same time, other variations due to illumination and small regional changes are also handled well by *PC*.

Training

In this part, we consider the number of matching keypoints and the *PC* score as two features to train

the SVM learning algorithm. Figure 5 shows the scatter diagram of these features for NDK and non-NDK samples from the Columbia dataset (Zhang & Chang, 2004). It is evident that the non-NDK samples are clustered along the *PC* axis while the NDK clusters are distributed along the horizontal axis. From the obtained SVM boundary separating NDKs from non-NDKs, it is evident that the features have remarkable discriminative power to recognize NDK from non-NDK pairs. We employ linear discriminate analysis (LDA) to determine the linear combination of these two features that best separate the two classes of data. In addition, we also treat the two features independently and train the SVM using a 2-D vector of these features. The outputs of the SVM in either case are the probabilities that the features have been derived from an NDK or a non-NDK pair. An RBF kernel is chosen for the SVM with the penalty parameter *C* set to 10.

CONTENT-BASED CLUSTERING OF KEYFRAMES

The SVM probabilities from the previous section serve as a similarity metric in the proposed keyframe clustering algorithm. For this purpose, the set of keyframes are represented in a graph structure where each keyframe is a vertex and the edge weight between a pair of keyframes is the probability of the pair being an NDK. We call this probability as Near Duplicate Score (*NDS*). Hence, each story is represented as a graph $G = \{V, E\}$, with $V = \{v_i\}$ is the set of vertices and the edge weight between vertices i and j is given by

$$E_{i,j} = NDS(v_i, v_j), \; i, j = 1, 2, ..., n, \;\; i \neq j,$$

(7)

where n is the number of keyframes in the story and $NDS(v_i, v_j)$ refers to the probability that the ith and j^{th} keyframes are NDKs. Hence the problem boils down to finding the representative subgraphs

$G_i, i = 1, 2, .., k$ within G so that the intra-subgraph similarity is maximum and the inter-subgraph similarity is minimum, simultaneously. This problem is also called the *mincut* problem in the graph theory. One of the most common objective functions for this problem is the RatioCut introduced by (Hagen & Kahng, 1992):

$$RatioCut(G_1, G_2, .., G_k) := \frac{1}{2} \sum_{i=1}^{k} \frac{W(G_i, \bar{G}_i)}{|G_i|},$$

(8)

where $W(G_i, \bar{G}_i) := \sum_{i \in G_i, j \in \bar{G}_i} E_{i,j}$, $\bar{G}_i$ denotes the complement of G_i and k is the number of clusters. Although this optimization problem is NP-hard, its relaxed version leads to an unnormalaized spectral clustering problem whose steps are outlined in Figure 6 (Luxburg, 2007). In the spectral clustering scheme, we need to provide a meaningful graph similarity measure and pick a suitable k as the number of clusters as shown as the inputs in Figure 6. We utilize E defined in Equation (7) to construct the weighted adjacency matrix, $W = [w_{i,j}]_{n \times n}$ whose elements are:

$$w_{i,j} = \begin{cases} E_{i,j} & if & E_{i,j} > \tau_S \\ 0 & if & Otherwise \end{cases},$$

(9)

where τ_S is a threshold ($0 < \tau_S < 1$). By thresholding the Near Duplicate Score, we prune outlier keyframes whose visual information is rare in the entire news story. Since *NDS* is determined as a semantically enriched similarity measure, we demonstrate its effectiveness in removing the outlier keyframes in the experiments.

It should be mentioned that *NDS* meets the condition of an appropriate similarity function in the spectral clustering algorithm since local neighborhood induced by this similarity function is meaningful and robust to lighting and camera lens variations, object motion and editing effects. Furthermore, in other clustering schemes like k-means using Euclidean based similarity metric, the triangle inequality is applicable. However, *NDS* as a content-based similarity function does not follow the triangle inequality property necessarily and the spectral clustering framework does not suffer due to this fact. Recall that triangle inequality states that the similarity between keyframes X and Z is at most as large as the sum of the similarity between keyframes X and Y and the similarity between keyframes Y and Z.

To address the second challenge of choosing a suitable number of clusters, we utilize Within-Cluster Similarity (*WCS*) Score for the cluster κ:

$$WCS(\kappa) = \sum_{c=1}^{\kappa} \frac{1}{|G_c|} \sum_{i,j \in G_c} E_{i,j}, \quad \kappa = 1,..,\lfloor \frac{n}{2} \rfloor$$

(10)

where G_c denotes the cluster c, $|G_c|$ is the number of keyframes in G_c and n is the total number of keyframes in the story and also the eigengap heuristic (Luxburg, 2007) which is particularly designed for spectral clustering given by

Figure 5. Scatter diagrams of NDKs and non-NDKs in the Columbia dataset

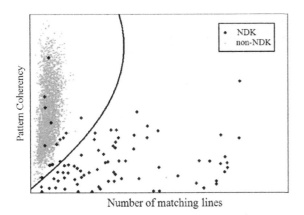

$$\delta(\kappa) = \left| \lambda_\kappa - \lambda_{\kappa+1} \right|, \quad \kappa = 1,..,\lfloor \frac{n}{2} \rfloor,$$

(11)

where λ_κ refers to the κ smallest eigenvalues of graph Laplacian matrix (i.e. L in Figure 6). The number of clusters that maximizes Equation (10), k_{wcs}, and Equation (11), k_δ, are determined. In practice, we iterate the spectral clustering algorithm for $\kappa = 1,..,\left\lfloor \frac{n}{2} \right\rfloor$ and the appropriate number of clusters is then given by

$$k_T = \left\lfloor \frac{k_{wcs} + k_\delta}{2} \right\rfloor . \tag{12}$$

Eigengap statistic has been shown to work well when the clusters in data are well separated (Luxburg, 2007). For instance in Figure 7, we plot the eigengap score for different number of clusters for the news story shown in Figure 8. In this example, it turns out that after pruning the outliers according to Equation (9), we are left with three connected components, i.e., three disjoint subgraphs. This causes the associated graph Laplacian to have three zero eigenvalues. Thus, the eigengap is equal to zero for k from 1 to 3. $k_\delta = 4$ maximizes the eigengap score in this example.

However, since we deal with noisy and overlapping clusters in some news stories, we also use the *WCS* score which indicates normalized within-cluster similarities for a particular partitioning of data for a specific k. It is expected that clusters obtained by maximizing *WCS* will be more balanced. More specifically, it avoids having numerous singleton clusters as can be driven from Equation (10) (e.g. in extreme case of n singleton clusters, *WCS* will be zero). The avoidance of singleton clusters is desirable in our case since we filter out outlier keyframes earlier through Equation (9) and the remaining keyframes are more likely to be part of the reasonably large clusters.

As shown in Figure 7, k_{wcs} equals to 10 maximizes the *WCS* in this example. From Equation (12), we get k_T equals to $\left\lfloor \frac{4+10}{2} \right\rfloor = 7$ as the number of clusters in this example. The clustering result is shown in Figure 8 where the last row indicates keyframes filtered out through Equation (9) and other rows indicate constructed clusters with respect to the k_T. The first, second and fifth clusters refer to anchors and reporter shots and other clusters depict different scenes captured in the *Saddam court* event.

To demonstrate an application of the keyframe clusters, we generate a storyboard for the news story. Storyboard refers to a set of images representing summarized version of video (Chen et al., 2009). To do so, we find the medoid of each

Figure 6. The unnormalized spectral clustering steps

Input: Weighted adjacency matrix $W \in \Re^{n \times n}$ k, number of clusters to construct

1. Construct the unnormalized Laplacian L as $L=D-W$, where D is the diagonal matrix whose (i,i)-element is the sum of W's i^{th} row.

2. Compute matrix $U \in \Re^{n \times k}$, whose columns are the eigenvectors corresponding to the first k smallest eigenvalues of L.

3. Form the normalized eigenvector matrix Y by renormalizing each of U's rows to have unit length, $Y_{i,j} = \dfrac{U_{ij}}{(\sum_j U_{ij}^2)^{\frac{1}{2}}}$.

4. Use *k-means* clustering on the rows of Y to form k clusters of $C_1, C_2,.., C_k$.

Output: Subgraphs $G_1, G_2,.., G_k$ with $G_j = \{v_i \mid Y_{i.} \in C_j\}$.

Figure 7. Variations of eigengap score and within-cluster similarity score with the number of clusters

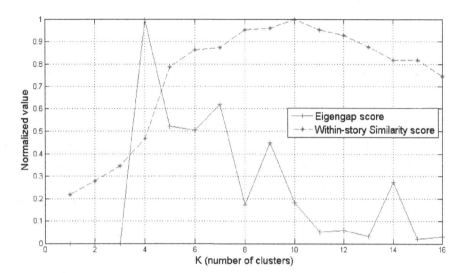

Figure 8. An example of our proposed keyframe clustering algorithm result

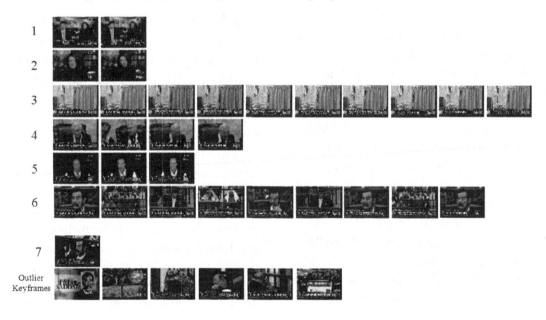

cluster, M_i as the representative member of cluster. The generated storyboard for story mentioned in Figure 8, is shown in Figure 9(a). Note that in addition to filtered out keyframes, the singleton clusters like the 7th cluster in Figure 8, is not considered for storyboard generation. For a smoother representation of the news story, we may select two or even more representative keyframes for the cluster with low within-cluster similarity like the 6th cluster in above example. This smoother version is shown in Figure 9(b).

EXPERIMENTAL RESULTS

In this section, first we evaluate our NDK identification algorithm. Then we assess our proposed keyframe clustering approach compared to another existing method to investigate the effectiveness of the semantic visual similarity measure and our proposed clustering performance.

NDK Identification Evaluation

We separately evaluate our NDK identification algorithm on two NDK datasets the Columbia dataset (Zhang & Chang, 2004) and the NTU dataset which is extracted from keyframes of *TRECVID* 2005 and 2006 corpora (Cheng et al., 2008). Each dataset consists of 150 NDK pairs (i.e., 300 NDKs) and 300 non-NDKs.

Selection of the threshold: In order to arrive at a suitable value of the threshold τ and to evaluate the CSM algorithm, we implement the NDK retrieval task on the NTU dataset using number of matching keypoints feature. Figure 10 indicates the correct and incorrect top-1 NDK retrievals for different τ values. For a threshold of 0.9, about 85% of the incorrect retrievals are rejected; at the same time, about 15% of the correct retrievals are also not detected correctly. As shown in Figure 10, about 97% of the wrong retrievals are rejected for $0.4 < \tau < 0.7$. While less than 6% of correct retrievals are rejected, which indicates the reliability of matching lines for this range of τ. On the other hand we need as many reliable matching lines as possible for computing *PC* score and as mentioned earlier, the higher value of τ, the more number of matching lines can be gained. Therefore, we set τ to 0.7. In doing so, there might be pairs of keyframes that do not contain any matching keypoints. In

such cases, the *PC* score cannot be calculated. Obviously, NDK pairs will be missed if no matching keypoints are detected, as is the case with other methods.

NDK retrieval evaluation: Similar to other approaches addressing NDK retrieval problem, we evaluate our method along the leave-one-out framework. As the name suggests, through leave-one-out cross-validation we use a single keyframe from the original dataset as the test data, and the remaining keyframes as the training data. This procedure is repeated such that each NDK in the dataset is used once as the test data. The probabilities generated by the determined SVM kernel are used to rank the keyframes. The retrieval performance is quantified by the probability of retrieving a correct NDK in the top-k position of the ranked list given by Zhang & Chang (2004) as $p(k) = Z_C / Z$, where Z_c is the number of queries that rank their corresponding NDKs within the top-k position and Z is the total number of queries. Table 1 shows the top-1 retrieval accuracy and the average retrieval accuracy of the top-5 retrievals for the Columbia dataset. It can be seen that in NDK retrieval task, generally keypoint matching techniques like our method, NIM method and OOS-SIFT method outperforms others that used block-to-block matching technique (Lazebnik et al., 2006) and visual keyword method (Wu et al., 2007). Our method using both CSM and *PC* score is comparable to NIM, which is the best result reported in this dataset. Our method outperforms (Zhao & Ngo, 2007) with the large margin, which confirms the effectiveness

Figure 9. (a) Generated storyboard using clusters medoid, (b) extended storyboard including extra images for clusters with low WCS

Figure 10. The correct (solid lines) and incorrect (dashed lines) top-1 NDK retrievals for different τ values

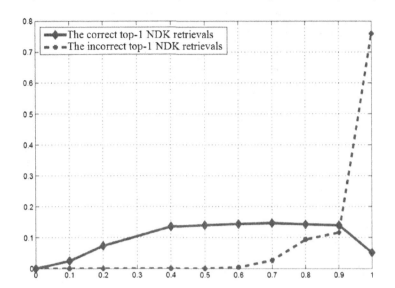

of the CSM scheme compared to its matching algorithm (OOS) and also demonstrates the distinguishing power of *PC* score in the NDK retrieval task. In Figure 11 we show top-30 retrieval results on the Columbia dataset using different features with $\tau = 0.75$. The results show the effectiveness of LDA for feature weighting and justify choice of *min* instead of *max* of $K_{GT}(i)$. CSM performs better than *max* for the top-17 retrievals after which the latter shows slightly improved performance. Training the SVM using the 3-D vector consisting of CSM, PC_v and PC_h gives the worst top-1 and average of top-5 NDK results on the Columbia dataset. Hence, we can conclude that in order to retrieve NDK pairs, it is sufficient to investigate having the

coherent alignment of keypoints in either the vertical or horizontal direction, instead of mixing the quantized alignments as in (Zhao & Ngo, 2006).

Table 2 shows the top-1 retrieval accuracy (%) for the NTU dataset using our method and comparisons with the results reported recently in (Cheng et al., 2008). Moreover, we implemented the NIM method (Zhu et al., 2008) on this dataset. Our method surpasses the LDSS method which is the best result reported for the NTU dataset. There is a slight improvement when using the *PC* score along with the number of matching keypoints (CSM) compared to using only CSM because the number of matching line is the meaningfully more discriminative feature than *PC* score as illustrated in Figure 5 and *PC* score can affect the

Table 1. Comparison of retrieval performance for top-1 and average of top-5 NDK on the Columbia dataset

Method	CSM	CSM+PC	OOS-SIFT (Wu et al., 2007)	LIP-IS+OOS (Zhao & Ngo, 2007)	NIM (Zhu et al., 2008)	LDSS (Cheng et al., 2008)	VK (Wu et al., 2007)	SPM (Lazebnik et al., 2006)
Top-1 (%)	84.33	**85.67**	84.67	79	86.33	84.67	76.67	78.67
Average Top-5 (%)	87.93	**88.62**	88.06	83.06	88.53	87.59	80.73	80.86

Table 2. Comparison of retrieval performance for top-1 NDK on the NTU dataset

Method	CSM	CSM +PC	BOW (Chum et.al, 2006)	LDSS (Cheng et al., 2008)	NIM (Zhu et al., 2008)
Top-1 (%)	94.33	**95.67**	88	92	89.67

Figure 11. Top-k NDK retrieval results on the Columbia dataset

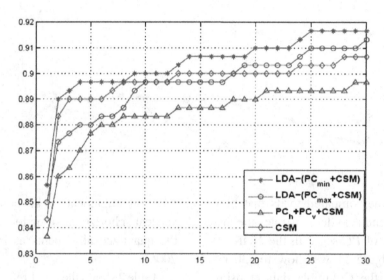

result only for a small portion of samples located in the left side of plot in Figure 5 (i.e. samples with less number of matching lines).

As mentioned earlier, our method is capable of identifying NDK pairs in the presence of extreme zooming and significant object motion. However, there are very few of such instances in the Colombia dataset. This explains why the performance on the NTU dataset, which does include several NDK pairs with large variations, is remarkably higher and NIM method (Zhu et al., 2008) does not perform as well in this dataset. In NTU dataset, there are 18 number of NDK pairs which could not be correctly detected in top-1 via NIM method mostly due to zooming and object motion or combination of them as expected. However, this method handles these cases well.

Content-Based Keyframe Clustering Evaluation

We utilize 20 stories extracted from *TRECVID* 2006 video. Each news story consists of group of keyframes provided by National Institute of Standard and Technology (NIST) (TRECVID, 2006). It includes a master keyframe as the middle I-frame of each shot and some auxiliary keyframes extracted from every two-second period of the video shots to cover more information within shots.

We compare our proposed keyframe clustering approach to another spectral-clustering-based approach (Odobez et al., 2003) where authors utilize Bhattacharayya coefficient of color histogram in RGB space to measure the visual similarity across the keyframes. They adopt the spectral clustering algorithm to group the keyframes with respect to the number of clusters determined. The proposed criteria for the number of clusters are that firstly, all generated clusters must have large enough eigengap and secondly fraction of total weight of edges not covered by clusters must be less than a specific threshold. Although the spirit of our method and that of (Odobez et al., 2003) is similar and based on spectral clustering, our proposed approach benefits from content-based visual similarity function and an effective strategy to choose a suitable number of clusters.

To evaluate the quality of the clustering, we determine Precision Recall measures. For this purpose, we use a set of classes in an evaluation benchmark produced by human judges with a good level of inter-judge agreement. Then according to human-assigned class labels, we index keyframes within all generated clusters. To evaluate how well our clustering method performs we compute the contingency table mentioned in Table 3. To determine each of *TP*, *FN*, *FP*, and *TN* values, we count all number of keyframe pairs belonging to the same\different cluster with the same\different class labels. For more detail about evaluation of clustering we refer to Manning et al. (2008).

Computing contingency matrix for each story, we determine Precision (*P*), Recall (*R*), and F-measures based on following Equations.

$$p = \frac{TP}{TP + FP}, \tag{13}$$

$$R = \frac{TP}{TP + FN}, \tag{14}$$

$$F = 2 \times \frac{P.R}{P + R}. \tag{15}$$

In Figure 12, we illustrate box plot of these three measures for our proposed keyframe clustering approach and the color histogram based approach (Odobez et al., 2003). On each box, the central mark is the median, the edges of the box are the 25th and 75th percentiles, the whiskers extend to the most extreme data points not considered outliers, and outliers are plotted individually. Since the similarity function significantly affect the number of clusters determination, to purely study the similarity function effectiveness, we used ground truth number of clusters to implement spectral clustering in (Odobez et al., 2003). However we use our own strategy to choose the suitable number of clusters in our method. Our proposed keyframe clustering approach outperforms the other with large-margin improvement of 24%, 16%, and 21% in Precision, Recall and F-measure respectively as indicated in Table 4.

The possible explanation for relatively low values of Recall compared to Precision score in our approach is due to semantic gap exists between what our NDK identification algorithm can find as NDK and the ground truth; there might be different clusters containing keyframes from the same class (e.g. cluster 1 and 2 in Figure 8). This fact ends up with high value of FN in Table 3. Furthermore, due to reliable similarity measure we propose, we generally observe high purity

Table 3. Contingency table

	Same Cluster	Different Cluster
Same Class	TP	FN
Different Class	FP	TN

Table 4. Precision, recall and f-measure for our proposed method and the color histogram method

	Precision (%)	Recall (%)	F-measure
Our method	80.7	35.7	48.9
Color Histogram method (Odobez et al., 2003)	56.8	19.6	27.8

Figure 12. Precision, recall and f-measure comparisons for 20 news stories. CH method refers to (Odobez et al., 2003)

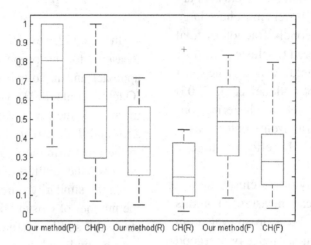

within the cluster (i.e. containing keyframes from the same class rather than different class) which leads to low value of FP and accordingly high value of Precision in our approach. In addition, the shorter varying range of precision, gained by our approach, shows that our proposed similarity appears more robust and less sensitive to data rather than the color-based approach.

In Figure 13, the keyframe clustering result based on (Odobez et al., 2003) is shown. This method performs appropriately for keyframes which are roughly the same like first three clusters.

However, the poor discriminative power is observed when we deal with semantically distant keyframes with the similar color property like fourth clusters which leads to poor precision. Moreover, another by-product of its general incapability to discriminate keyframes appears in filtering out irrelevant keyframes as shown in the last row in Figure 13.

At last, we examine our proposed approach to find the appropriate number of clusters (i.e. K_T) against the ground truth number of clusters (K_{GT}) determined by human. To compare these two sets

Figure 13. Keyframe clustering results based on (Odobez et al., 2003)

of data, we perform a paired *t*-test of the null hypothesis that the data in the difference (i.e. $K_T - K_{GT}$) are random samples from a normal distribution with mean 0 and an unknown variance, against the alternative that the mean is not 0. It is generally agreed that if the sample size is greater than or equal to 20, the null distribution can be approximated by a normal distribution (Rice, 2007). We compute *t* score for our 20 stories dataset based on Equation (16).

$$t = \frac{\bar{K}_D}{\text{var}(K_D)/\sqrt{n}}, \qquad (16)$$

where $K_D(i) = K_T(i) - K_{GT}(i)$ for *i=1,..,n*, and *n* is the total number of samples (i.e. *n=20*). Then we determine associated *p-value* equals to 0.0563 with respect to the degree of freedom of *t* statistic (i.e. *n-1*). The test fails to reject the null hypothesis at the default value of the significance level $\alpha = 0.05$. Under the null hypothesis, the probability of observing a value at least as extreme of the test statistic, as indicated by the *p*-value, is greater than α. In other word, the 95% confidence interval (i.e. [-0.64, 0.14]) on the mean contains 0. This result confirms the satisfying closeness of paired data points (i.e. $K_T(i)$ and $K_{GT}(i)$ for *i=1,..,n*).

CONCLUSION AND FUTURE WORK

In this study, we first tackle NDK identification problem to reach a reliable content-based visual similarity measure across keyframes which can handle large variations in object appearance due to zooming and object movement. Along the leave-one-out framework, two features of the number of matching lines and the *Pattern Coherency* score are learnt based on training NDKs and non-NDKs provided by the Columbia dataset as a ground

truth and trained SVM classifier is used to retrieve NDKs from the Columbia and NTU datasets for the test keyframe. The NDK retrieval evaluation results confirm the effectiveness of our keypoint matching method and usefulness of the *PC* score. Then we utilize the determined SVM score as the visual similarity function to tackle the keyframe clustering problem through the spectral clustering approach. We determine the number of clusters based on two scores of within-cluster similarity and eigengap score. Quantitative assessments show our proposed keyframes clustering algorithm performs well both in terms of precision-recall scores and estimating the number of clusters accurately. Accordingly it results in a content-based partitioning of the news story. We generate a storyboard presentation of news story with respect to obtained clusters of keyframes. In future, we will try to extend our proposed keyframe clustering idea to reach an effective and also compressed content-based signature of news story which can be used for the news video indexing and retrieval.

REFERENCES

Adami, N., Benini, S., & Leonardi, R. (2006). An overview of video shot clustering and summarization techniques for mobile applications. In *Proceedings of the 2nd International Conference on Mobile Multimedia Communications,* Alghero, Italy. New York: ACM.

Chang, S.-F., Hsu, W., Kennedy, L., Xie, L., Yanagawa, A., Zavesky, E., et al. (2005). *Columbia university trecvid-2005 video search and high-level feature extraction.* Paper presented at the NIST TRECVID Workshop, Gaithersburg, MD.

Chen, B. W., Wang, J. C., & Wang, J. F. (2009). A novel video summarization based on mining the story-structure and semantic relations among concept entities. *IEEE Transactions on Multimedia, 11,* 295–312. doi:10.1109/TMM.2008.2009703

Cheng, X., Hu, Y., & Chia, L.-T. (2008). Image near-duplicate retrieval using local dependencies in spatial-scale space. In *Proceedings of the ACM 2008 Conference on Multimedia,* Vancouver, BC, Canada (pp. 627-630).

Chum, O., Philbin, J., Isard, M., & Zisserman, A. (2007). Scalable near identical image and shot detection. In *Proceedings of the ACM Conference on International Video Retrieval,* Amsterdam, The Netherlands (pp. 549-556).

Damnjanovic, U., Piatrik, T., Djordjevic, D., & Izquierdo, E. (2007). Video summarisation for surveillance and news domain. In *Proceedings of the 2nd International Conference on Semantics and Digital Media Technologies,* Genoa, Italy.

Das, M., Farmer, J., Gallagher, A., & Loui, A. (2008). Event-based location matching for consumer image collections. In *Proceedings of the International Conference on Image and Video Retrieval* (pp. 339-348).

Gao, Y., & Dai, Q. H. (2008). Shot-based similarity measure for content-based video summarization. In *Proceedings of the 15th IEEE International Conference on Image Processing,* San Diego, CA (pp. 2512-2515).

Gatica-perez, D., Loui, A., & Sun, M.-T. (2003). Finding structure in home video by probabilistic hierarchical clustering. *Circuits and Systems for Video Technology, 13*(6), 539–548. doi:10.1109/TCSVT.2003.813428

Hagen, L., & Kahng, A. (1992). New spectral methods for ratio cut partitioning and clustering. *Transactions on Computer-Aided Design, 11*(9), 1074–1085. doi:10.1109/43.159993

Ke, Y., Suthankar, R., & Huston, L. (2004). An efficient parts-based near-duplicate and sub-image retrieval system. In *Proceedings of the ACM Multimedia Conference* (pp. 869–876).

Lazebnik, S., Schmid, C., & Ponce, J. (2006). Beyond bags of features: Spatial pyramid matching for recognizing natural scene categories. In *Proceedings of the IEEE Computer Society Conference on Computer Vision and Pattern Recognition* (pp. 2169-2178).

Lowe, D. (2004). Distinctive image features from scale-invariant key points. *International Journal of Computer Vision, 60*(2), 91–110. doi:10.1023/B:VISI.0000029664.99615.94

Luxburg, U. V. (2007). A tutorial on spectral clustering. *Statistics and Computing,* 17.

Manning, C. D., Raghavan, P., & Schütze, H. (2008). Introduction to information retrieval. In *Evaluation of Clustering* (pp. 356–360). Cambridge, UK: Cambridge University Press.

Odobez, J.-M., Gatica-Perez, D., & Guillemot, M. (2003). Spectral structuring of home videos. In *Proceedings of the ACM International Conference on Image and Video Retrieval. Urbana (Caracas, Venezuela), IL,* 310–320.

Peker, K. A., & Bashir, F. I. (2005). *Content-based video summarization using spectral clustering.* Paper presented at the International Workshop on Very Low-Bitrate Video, Sardinia, Italy.

Qamra, A., Meng, Y., & Cheng, E. Y. (2005). Enhanced perceptual distance functions and indexing for image replica recognition. *IEEE Transactions on Pattern Analysis and Machine Intelligence, 27,* 379–391. doi:10.1109/TPAMI.2005.54

Rasheed, Z., & Shah, M. (2005). Detection and Representation of scenes in videos. *IEEE Transactions on Multimedia, 7*(6), 1097–1105. doi:10.1109/TMM.2005.858392

Rice, J. A. (2007). *Mathematical statistic and data analysis* (3rd ed.). Belmont, CA: Duxbury.

Rui, Y., & Huang, T. (2000). A unified framework for video browsing and retrieval. In *Image and Video Processing Handbook* (pp. 705–715). New York: Academic Press.

TRECVID. (2006). *Guidelines.* Retrieved January, 24, 2006, from http://www-nlpir.nist.gov/projects/tv2006/ tv2006.html#3

Wu, X., Zhao, W. L., & Ngo, C. W. (2007). Near-duplicate keyframe retrieval with visual keywords and semantic context. In *Proceedings of the ACM Conference of International Video Retrieval,* Amsterdam, The Netherlands (pp. 162-169).

Xu, D., Cham, T., Yan, S., & Chang, D.-F. (2008). Near duplicate image identification with spatially aligned pyramid matching. In *Proceedings of the IEEE Computer Vision and Pattern Recognition Conference,* Anchorage, AK (pp. 1-7).

Younessian, E., Rajan, D., & Chng, E. S. (2009). *Improved keypoint matching method for near-duplicate keyframe retrieval.* Paper presented at the International Symposium on Multimedia, San Diego, CA.

Zhang, D. Q., & Chang, S. F. (2004). Detecting image near-duplicate by stochastic attributed relational graph matching with learning. In *Proceedings of the ACM Multimedia Conference* (pp. 877-884).

Zhang, J., Sun, L., Yang, S., & Zhong, Y. (2005). Joint inter and intra shot modeling for spectral video shot clustering. In *Proceedings of the International Conference of Multimedia and Expo,* Amsterdam, The Netherlands (pp. 1362-1365).

Zhao, W.-L., & Ngo, C.-W. (2006). Fast tracking of near-duplicate keyframes in broadcast domain with transitivity propagation. In *Proceedings of the ACM Special Interest Group on Multimedia Conference,* Santa Barbara, CA (pp. 845-854).

Zhao, W.-L., & Ngo, C.-W. (2007). Near-duplicate keyframe identification with interest point matching and pattern learning. *IEEE Transactions on Multimedia*, *9*, 1037–1048. doi:10.1109/TMM.2007.898928

Zhu, J., Hoi, S. C. H., Lyu, M. R., & Yan, S. (2008). Near-duplicate keyframe retrieval by nonrigid image matching. In *Proceedings of the ACM Multimedia Conference,* Vancouver, BC, Canada (pp. 41-50).

This work was previously published in the International Journal of Multimedia Data Engineering and Management, Volume 2, Issue 1, edited by Shu-Ching Chen, pp. 1-21, copyright 2011 by IGI Publishing (an imprint of IGI Global).

Chapter 2
Authorship Detection and Encoding for eBay Images

Liping Zhou
The University of Alabama at Birmingham, USA

Wei-Bang Chen
The University of Alabama at Birmingham, USA

Chengcui Zhang
The University of Alabama at Birmingham, USA

ABSTRACT

This paper describes a framework to detect authorship of eBay images. It contains three modules: editing style summarization, classification and multi-account linking detection. For editing style summarization, three approaches, namely the edge-based approach, the color-based approach, and the color probability approach, are proposed to encode the common patterns inside a group of images with similar editing styles into common edge or color models. Prior to the summarization step, an edge-based clustering algorithm is developed. Corresponding to the three summarization approaches, three classification methods are developed accordingly to predict the authorship of an unlabeled test image. For multi-account linking detection, to detect the hidden owner behind multiple eBay seller accounts, two methods to measure the similarity between seller accounts based on similar models are presented.

INTRODUCTION

Authorship detection has a range of applications in a large number of fields such as forensic evidence, plagiarism detection, email filtering, and web information management (Chen, 2010; Love, 2002; Rafailidis, Nanopoulos, & Manolopoulos, 2010). In recent years, an application with grow-ing interests is web information management. The World Wide Web provides a powerful publication platform, where a large number of images are created for different purposes. For instance, online shopping websites such as eBay enable sellers and buyers to transact on the platform for a broad variety of goods and services worldwide. The goods/products are mostly visualized by hav-

DOI: 10.4018/978-1-4666-2940-0.ch002

ing their pictures displayed on the website so that customers can see the visual details of products which often play an important role in customers' purchase decision-making. EBay sellers, especially those power sellers, often add their own touch to product image design in order to attract buyers' attention. For example, some sellers add a frame and/or some promotion texts to their listing images (Figure 1), and some sellers embed the name of their store as watermarks or logos in their images. We assume that many eBay sellers have developed distinctive editing styles over time to embed to their product images (logos, background, and so on.). Such editing styles are highly repetitive within one seller's images, but mostly distinctive among different sellers. We detect and encode such editing styles for each seller using visual features extracted from product images, and in turn use the encoded editing styles to automatically predict the ownership for unlabeled images. Through a collaborative effort between the authors' institution and eBay, the output of this study will be used as added clues in eBay's seller profiling system to detect and prevent account taken-over and other related fraudulent behaviors.

There are several challenges in this study. First, we found that sellers may use more than one image editing style in composing their product images posted on eBay. For example, in Figure 1, the images in the first two rows all belong to the same seller "6ubuy6" but apparently they have visually different editing styles. Therefore, a simple image averaging technique applied to the images within the same seller will not work in the presence of multiple editing styles. Another challenge is that the same product image can be used by multiple sellers who re-edit the image according to their own style, and thus clustering based on global visual features will generate a large amount of false positives due to the common features extracted from the product itself. In this paper, we present a new edge-based clustering method to divide all images within one seller into image groups each of which corresponds to one

editing style of that seller in terms of image edge maps (Abdel-Mottaleb, 2000). The clustering algorithm is based on the similarity of image edge maps. After that, summarization can be done to find the common pattern in each image group.

In order to summarize editing styles, we present three summarization methods: 1) edge-based summarization by applying Hough transform (Fernandes & Oliveira, 2008) on edge map images, which generates an edge template for each image group; 2) color-based summarization in HSV color space (Zhao, Bu, & Chen, 2002) by using a mean image to represent the centroid of an image group, resulting in a HSV color model for each group; 3) color probability based summarization which generates a probability model to represent the spatial color distribution within an image group. The templates or models generated from the summarization step are then used to identify the authorship of unlabeled images using the corresponding classification methods which are edge-based classification with Hough transform, color-based classification, and color probability based classification. Based on our experiments, edge-based classification with Hough transform performs the best in term of accuracy. However, it is more time-consuming than the other two methods. Color-based classification

Figure 1. Examples of product images from online shopping websites such as eBay

by using overlay method in HSV color space is the most efficient among the three methods, but its accuracy is lower than that of the edge-based method. Since the three methods are based on different features, our guess is that they may be able to complement each other, which is actually evidenced by our experimental results. In fact, by combining the edge features and color features in our classification method, the performance has been improved, and the overall accuracy goes up to 94%.

In this framework, we label images with the predicted seller ID based on their image editing styles. However, some sellers may have multiple accounts (IDs), and they tend to use the same or similar editing styles in all of their accounts. Some of these sellers are indeed honest sellers who register for multiple accounts for the purpose of either self-promoting (e.g., giving positive feedbacks to each other to establish a high reputation) or selling different categories of products (rarely seen), but some others are real fraudsters who use multiple accounts to conduct self-promoting and fraudulent transactions. In either case, being able to know the linking between and among seller accounts would be very valuable information for eBay to fight online fraud. In this study, we assume that if the images from two seller accounts have a very similar editing style, then they probably belong to the same seller. By summarizing and encoding the image editing style(s) of each seller with image editing templates, we can discover the linking between sellers through the similarity analysis of their image editing templates. In particular, in this study, we propose two methods to indentify similar editing styles from across sellers, namely the covariance method and the clustering based method.

The arguments for our framework start with a brief discussion on authorship detection and encoding framework. Next, the implementation of proposed framework is followed by the discussion of the edge-based clustering algorithm, the three summarization methods including an edge-

based summarization method and two color-based summarization methods and three classification methods. Thirdly, two multi-account linking detection approaches are described. Finally, the evaluation of system performance with experimental results is presented, followed by the summary and conclusion.

RELATED WORK

Authorship detection has been widely applied in electronic text, which identifies the author of an anonymous text, or the text whose authorship is in doubt. Due to the vast electronic text that have become available on the Internet recently, authorship detection techniques have become to play an increasingly significant role in areas such as document categorization, plagiarism analysis and near-duplicate detection (Zhao & Zobel, 2005). However, the dimension of multimedia analysis is largely missing in these efforts.

Robine, Hanna, Ferraro, and Allali (2007) reported a method to detect near-duplicate music documents and plagiarisms, where the similarity of two music documents is evaluated by the similarity of a pair of musical segments. In recent years, image authorship detection becomes an interesting application domain. Hirose et al. (2008) described a method of identifying authorship of Ukiyoe prints by using Rakkan images found in the prints, which is the seal, or signature included in the paintings. In their approach, the distance between dictionary templates and test data is calculated in order to identify artists and creation dates of Ukiyoe prints.

Watermarking is a commonly used approach for image authentication. However, existing watermark detection cannot be directly applied to eBay images for authorship detection due to the following reasons. First, although human can perceive visible watermarks on an image, the embedded pattern of a visible watermark should be difficult or even impossible to be removed unless intensive and expensive human labors are involved (Huang & Wu, 2004). In Huang and Wu (2004), a visible watermarking attacking scheme is proposed which manually selects watermarked areas and applies image recovery techniques to remove watermarks. However, this approach is impractical for analyzing a large-scale data set such as eBay images, especially given that many sellers do not have watermarks but exhaustive manual check cannot be avoided. There have been several other attempts to automatically extract watermarks by adopting Independent Component Analysis (ICA) (Pei & Zeng, 2006; Yu, Sattar, & Ma, 2002). Performing ICA requires multiple observations of the source signals including observations for at least the original image and the mix of the original image and the watermark. However, the original image is not readily available for eBay images with watermarks. In Pei, et al. (2006), the paper proposes to use manual intervention to generate multiple observations. However, again this is not practical for analyzing a large-scale data set such as eBay images. Further, watermark detection is not applicable to the images of those sellers who do not use watermarks in their editing templates.

In this research, an innovative framework based on image editing style analysis is proposed for online listing image authorship identification. Like the work presented in Hirose, Yoshimura, Hachimura, and Akama (2008), we look for "signatures" of an authorship rather than the global visual features in an image for the reason mentioned in previous section. Specifically, the framework is able to discover all editing styles created by a seller in an automatic manner by clustering the images owned by that seller on the basis of the edge map similarity. Ideally, each cluster produced corresponds to a distinctive editing style created by that seller. Therefore, all images in a cluster can be further encoded into a template (model) that represents an editing style either based on their common edge maps or common HSV color features. When predicting the authorship of an unlabeled image, the proposed framework measures the similarity between the unlabeled image and each template produced. A higher similarity value indicates more likely that the unlabeled image may have the same editing style as the template, and therefore, the image is more likely to belong to the seller who creates the template.

EDGE-BASED CLUSTERING

In this section, we present an edge-based clustering algorithm to divide images of each seller into different image groups based on their editing styles. Edge features are chosen because they are more robust than color features which often vary according to re-editing, re-compression, and change of fill-in colors. For example, in Figure 1, the three images in the second row belong to the same seller and have almost identical editing styles, but their frame colors are quite different.

In most images, the product usually occupies a large area; therefore, clustering based on global edge features will incorrectly cluster those images with common edges on the product area into the same group. To reduce the negative impact of edges on products, we only focus on the edges with strong intensities since image areas with added editing effects usually have strong edges, and also we try to ignore the edges in a fixed area around the center of the image, because products are almost always located in the center of images.

To calculate the similarity between two edge maps E_1 and E_2, we apply Generalized Hough transform (GHT) which is essentially a method originally used for object recognition. The basic process starts by assuming that one of the two edge maps has the predefined object. And the edge points from another edge map are mapped to the parameter space, which represents all the possible instances of edge features in the predefined object. Each matched edge point votes for the location of the predefined object, and the instance with the most votes defines the features present in the edge map, which defines the best matched points of two edge maps. Our proposed similarity measure further decides how likely an edge map has the predefined object. Based on the best matched points, we do the overlay of two edge maps to find the common area of two edge maps. The common pixels are defined as the pixels in the corresponding positions of two edge maps which have the same 1 or 0 value (edge or non-edge) within the common area. Finally, the ratio of the number of common pixels to the common area is used to measure the similarity of edge maps. The similarity of two edge maps is defined in Equation 1 where C denotes their common area after image overlay, area(C) denotes the area of C, and $sum(pix)$ represents the number of common pixels in the two edge maps.

$$Similarity(E_1, E_2) = \frac{sum(pix)}{area(C)} \qquad (1)$$

A threshold is used in the clustering. If the similarity is greater than the threshold value, we consider the two images to be in the same group. The threshold value is experimentally set to 0.8 in this study.

SUMMARIZATION METHODS

After clustering, the images of each seller are clustered into image groups each of which represents one distinctive editing style of that seller's. In this section, based on edge and color features of images, three summarization methods are proposed to encode the editing styles with templates or models.

Edge-Based Summarization

In this method, we summarize each image group with an edge template by finding the common edges of images. After the clustering step, the images of each seller are clustered into image

groups based on the similarity of their edge maps; therefore, the images in each group must have similar edge features. These image groups are used as the training set to generate edge templates. In this process, edge detection is first performed to extract the edge map features for each image in an image group according to the clustering results, and then image overlay is conducted based on the best matched points which are generated in the clustering step. In the new edge template, each pixel value is the average of all pixel values (edge intensities) at that same location in the edge maps of all the training images in that group.

In order to reduce the noise, we choose to use binary values to describe the edge template, that is, the pixel value under 0.5 is set to 0, and the pixel value equal to or greater than 0.5 is set to 1. Further, if one image group has only one or two images, there is not enough training data for summarizing the common edge pattern in that image group. Therefore, we ignore the image groups containing less than 3 images.

The steps to generating an edge template are summarized as follows:

1. Convert color images in a group to grayscale images.
2. Use Sobel filter (Jahne, Scharr, & Korkel, 1999) for edge detection and extract edge maps for the images.
3. Convert each edge map image into intensity image, and keep only those edges with strong intensities.
4. Compute the average value of each pixel, i.e., its average edge intensity, across all the edges maps.
5. Convert the edge intensity value of each pixel into a binary value to generate a new edge template.

Color-Based Summarization

In the edge-based summarization method, we summarize and encode image editing styles of sellers into a set of edge templates by applying Hough transform on edge maps. Though image matching with Hough transform performs well, it is time-consuming. Therefore, based on the same edge-map clustering results, we also design two alternative color-based approaches to summarize common color patterns in HSV color space. HSV color space is chosen because it is more perceptually uniform.

Based on our clustering algorithm, we assume that images in each image group should have the same or similar editing style, so there is less distinction of color between images in the same image group but more distinction between images from different image groups. According to this assumption, we compute a mean image for each image group, and then a template can be represented by a sequence of pixel-level mean values.

An alternative color-based method is based on the assumption that all images associated with a template have perceptually similar color and layout because they have the same or similar editing style, and all color values associated with a pixel at a specific location in all training images may form a normal distribution. This pixel-level color distribution can be further represented as the mean and the standard deviation of all the color values at that pixel location. In this way, a color template can be described by a set of pixel-level color distributions as a probability model.

In both methods, all images are converted from RGB color space to HSV color space. In order to reduce the computational complexity, we have tested various image down-sampling rates in our experiments. The experimental results suggest that the performance has no significant difference between down-sampling to 200×200 pixels and 100×100 pixels. Thus, we down-sampled all images to 100×100 pixels in this study. The model generated from an image group is also a 100×100 image. In addition, to reduce the influence of product areas, we remove a central region with a fixed ratio of area from each image.

CLASSIFICATION METHODS

In order to predict the authorship of an unlabeled image, we implement three classification methods that correspond to the three summarization methods, respectively. The edge templates and color models generated in the summarization step are further used to identify the authorship of unlabeled images. More specifically, each test image is compared against each template/model and the best matched model/template will be used to predict the authorship for that image. In other words, a test image will be associated with the seller one of whose editing styles (models/templates) has the best match with the test image.

Edge-Based Classification

In this method, we match the edge map extracted from a test image with each edge template generated from the summarization step. The edge map of the test image is also generated by using Sobel filter. The proposed algorithm then uses Hough transform to find the best matched point in the edge map of the test image when it is matched with an edge template. The calculation of similarity scores is similar to the method mentioned in the edge-based Summarization Method. Then the edge template which has the maximum similarity with the test image will be considered as its matched template. In our dataset, some images do not have any editing style, so they usually have a low similarity with each edge template. In order to avoid incorrectly associating such images with a template, we define a cutoff value. Therefore, if the maximum similarity score received by a test image is less than the cutoff value, that image cannot be matched with any template.

Color-Based Classification

Using color-based summarization method, we summarize the color patterns in an image group to a mean color model in HSV color space. The similarity between a test image and a mean color model in HSV space is calculated as Equation 3. For each pixel in the test image, we calculate the distance between its pixel value and the corresponding pixel value in a color model, and the sum of the distances of pixel values is used to represent the relative distance between the test image and the model. The distance between a pair of pixels can be computed in Equation 2 where H_{test} is the "Hue" value of the pixel in the test image; H_{model} is the "Hue" value of the pixel in the model. S_{test} denotes the "Saturation" value of the pixel in the test image and V_{test} is the "Value" value of that pixel in the test image.

$$\text{dist}(pix_{test}, pix_{model}) = (H_{test} - H_{model})^2 + (S_{test} - S_{model})^2 + (V_{test} - V_{model})^2 \quad (2)$$

$$\text{DIST}(I_{test}, I_{model}) = \text{sum}(\text{dist}(pix_{test}, pix_{model})) \quad (3)$$

In this method, we also define a cutoff value to identify the images without any editing style. Therefore, if the relative distance between the test image and a model is greater than the cutoff value, the test image cannot be matched with that model.

Probability Model Classification

An alternative color-based approach for the image authorship classification is color probability based classification. For this purpose, we build a color probability model for each image group. Each model describes the pixel-level color distribution of all the images in that group. When performing the authorship identification, we measure the likelihood a test image belongs to each model.

In this method, given a pixel location, after collecting all the corresponding pixel values at that location from all images in the group, we can simply use z-test (Sprinthall, 2002), a statistical hypothesis test, to tell whether a color value comes from the same color distribution at a particular location, and thus, can predict whether a pixel's

value belongs to the same pixel value distribution at the corresponding location in the template. This idea can be extended to test all pixels in a test image against a color probability model. Therefore, we define the overall likelihood between a test image and a color probability model as the mean probability of all pixels.

A cutoff value is used to again identify those images that do not have significant editing styles. More specifically, only those likelihood values exceeding our predefined cutoff values will be collected. A test image will be assigned to the seller who owns the model which yields the maximum likelihood for that image among all models.

EXPERIMENTS

The proposed framework is applied on two datasets in order to evaluate the performance of the proposed system. The first dataset (Dataset-I) consists of 919 images from 10 sellers, and the second dataset (Dataset-II) consists of 3980 images from 47 sellers. In Dataset-I, images procured from 7 sellers have significant editing styles while the rest of the images collected from the other 3 sellers do not have an obvious editing style. In Dataset-II, 7 sellers do not use any editing style in their images while the other 40 sellers create at least one editing style in their images.

In our experiments, a 10-fold cross-validation is performed on Dataset-I and a 3-fold cross-validation is performed on Dataset-II. The reason we did not perform 10-fold cross-validation on Dataset-II is that some sellers have less than 10 images. In an n-fold cross-validation (Kohavi, 1995), we partition the images of seller's into n roughly equal subsets and repeat the training/testing process n times. In each round, one subset is treated as testing data while the other nine subsets are used as training data. In the training phase, we first use our proposed edge-based clustering algorithm to group the images of each seller's into one or more image groups in order to automatically discover a seller's editing styles. By applying the editing style summarization methods on image groups, each group is associated with an edge template, a mean color model, and a color probability model. In the testing phase, the proposed classification methods, i.e., edge-based classification, color-based classification, and color probability based classification, are applied to match a test image with an edge template, a color model, and a color probability model, or none at all (for images without editing styles). The authorship of a test image is then assigned to be the seller who owns the model/template that best matches that image.

Two evaluation scenarios, i.e., within a seller and across different sellers, are defined and used to measure the performance of the proposed framework.

1. **Within a seller:** In this scenario, we mainly focus on finding whether an image belongs to a specific seller within the scope of that seller. This kind of classification can be put into efficient use for account taken over detection when a fraudster tries to upload a product image that does not conform to the editing styles of that seller. In this scenario, if the test image is matched with any of the templates of that seller, that image is said to belong to that seller, and vice versa. Therefore, an image with some editing style is said to be correctly predicted if it is assigned the same seller's ID as indicated by its ground-truth label. Otherwise, the prediction fails. For an image without any significant editing style, a successful prediction is that the image is assigned a "no template" label after classification.

2. **Across different sellers:** In this scenario, we like to know whether the proposed framework can differentiate between editing styles created by different sellers. In this scenario, all the test images from each seller will be tested against all templates from all sellers. Since different seller accounts may have

similar editing styles (e.g., multiple seller accounts associated with the same seller), therefore, if an image with some editing style is assigned to any template that summarizes that editing style, we say it is a correct predication. Otherwise, the prediction fails.

As aforementioned, there is a cutoff value used in each classification method proposed. In our experiments, we experiment with different cutoff values and determine experimentally a threshold value for each approach.

Figure 2 and Figure 3 present the experimental results for Dataset-I and Dataset-II, respectively. In Figures 2 and 3, the first and the second rows show the classification performance in "within seller" and "across sellers" scenarios, respectively.

In Figure 2, the best average accuracy values of the edge-classification method are 0.803 and 0.875 for "within seller" and "across sellers", respectively. The best average accuracy values of the color based classification are 0.843 and 0.799 for "within seller" and "across sellers", respectively. The best average accuracy values of the probability model classification are 0.535 and 0.871 for "within seller" and "across sellers", respectively.

In Figure 3, the highest average accuracy values of the edge-based classification method are 0.868 and 0.717 for "within seller" and "across sellers", respectively. The best average accuracy values of the color-based classification are 0.618 and 0.735 for "within seller" and "across sellers", respectively. And the best average accuracy values of color probability classification are 0.748 and 0.56 for "within seller" and "across sellers", respectively.

From the results, the proposed framework performs well on Dataset-I. However, there are cases where images with similar edge features on their product areas are grouped together during clustering, which may introduce noise into the summarization process. This indicates that removing a fixed percent of central area from

Figure 2. The evaluation results for images of 10 sellers. The three columns from left to right are the results corresponding to the three classification methods, i.e., the color-based classification, the edge-based classification, and the color probability classification.

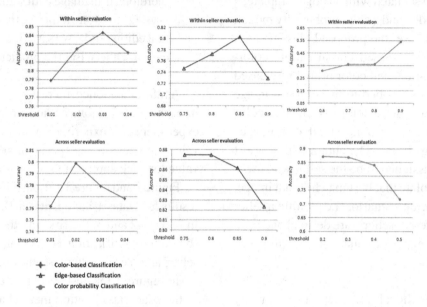

Figure 3.The evaluation results for images of 47 sellers. The three columns from left to right are the results corresponding to the three classification methods, i.e., the color-based classification, the edge-based classification, and the color probability classification.

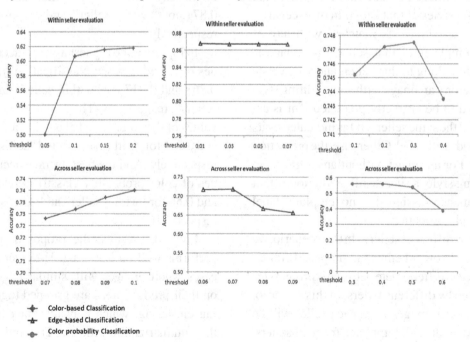

each image cannot eliminate the product features entirely, causing false positives during clustering and classification.

In addition, we observe that the edge-based approach and the color-based approaches can complement each other. Our experimental results show that when we combine edge-based approach with either color-based summarization approach, i.e., the color-based approach or the color probability approach, the accuracy of classification can be drastically improved. For Dataset-I, the overall accuracies are 94% (edge + color-based) and 89% (edge + color probability model) for "within seller" evaluation.

We further analyze the result of each fold for Dataset-I and show the 10-fold accuracy values in Table 1. The results in Table 1 show that the highest accuracy values of edge-classification method, across 10-fold cross validations, are 0.870 and 0.902 for "within seller" and "across sellers", respectively. For color-based classification, the highest accuracy values are 0.891 and 0.846 for "within seller" and "cross seller", respectively.

And the corresponding accuracy values for color probability method are 0.804 and 1, respectively.

From the "across sellers" evaluation results, we can observe that all the accuracies of the edge-based method are close to its maximum accuracy 0.9. However, for the color probability method, a larger range of accuracy values can be observed with the maximum accuracy being 1 and the minimum value being 0.370. For the "within seller" evaluation, the accuracies of the probability method are lower than that of the other two methods in almost all cases. The reason is that the probability method uses mean and standard deviation to represent the color distribution of training images. The standard deviation is largely affected by the size of the training set. In case a training set contains only 2~3 images, the color variance within the same group may still be high. As a consequence, dissimilar image could be incorrectly matched to the model. The performance of the color-based classification method is in between the other two methods and is the most time efficient.

Table 1. The accuracies of 10-fold evaluation for dataset-I

ith fold	Edge-based		Color-based		Color Probability	
	across	within	across	within	across	within
1	0.835	0.835	0.813	0.846	0.703	0.176
2	0.882	0.763	0.839	0.817	1	0.613
3	0.860	0.828	0.774	0.807	1	0.462
4	0.891	0.761	0.750	0.870	1	0.011
5	0.859	0.837	0.837	0.870	0.637	0.294
6	0.902	0.837	0.739	0.804	0.370	0.489
7	0.880	0.870	0.794	0.891	1	0.283
8	0.870	0.739	0.826	0.837	1	0.804
9	0.901	0.769	0.846	0.868	1	0.022
10	0.868	0.791	0.769	0.824	1	0.154
max	0.902	0.870	0.846	0.891	1	0.804
min	0.835	0.739	0.774	0.807	0.370	0.011
mean	0.875	0.803	0.799	0.843	0.871	0.362

MULTI-ACCOUNT LINKING DETECTION

In the previous section, we identify the authorships of images based on their editing styles, and the authorship of each image is described by its assigned sellers' ID. The encoded editing styles (templates/models) can also be used to reveal the same owner behind multiple eBay accounts. We propose two methods to identify the linking of multiple accounts based on their editing styles. The first method, the covariance method, is based on the mean color model and uses covariance as a similarity measure to find similar mean color models. The second method, a clustering based method, uses Hough transform to group similar edge templates into groups. Since the mean color based model outperforms the color probability model in both datasets and is more time efficient than the latter, we only test the performance of the mean color based models in multi-account linking experiments, in addition to testing the edge-based models.

Similarity Measure by Using Covariance

Covariance (Baker, 1973) is a measure of how two variables change together. In this method, we define a similarity measure for mean color based models based on the covariance concept. More specifically, we calculate the similarity between two color models in each color channel separately. Then the sum of the similarities from all three channels is used as the similarity between the two models. To calculate the similarity in each channel, we sequence the pixels of each mean color model into one vector, and then calculate the covariance of the two vectors. The pixel values in each color channel in HSV color space are used as features of models in calculating the similarity.

In each channel in HSV color space, a color model is represented by a feature vector. t_i and t_j represent the feature vectors of two color models,

respectively. We define the similarity between models t_i and t_j using the following correlation as defined in Equation 4.

$$sim(t_i, t_j) = \frac{cov(t_i, t_j)}{\sqrt{cov(t_i, t_i)}\sqrt{cov(t_j, t_j)}} \qquad (4)$$

where $cov(t_i, t_j)$ is given by

$$cov(t_i, t_j) = E[(t_i - E[t_i])(t_j - E[t_j])^T] \qquad (5)$$

We define a similarity matrix for the color models. After sorting the similarities, we start from the best matched model pair, which is a pair of models with the highest similarity value. Then, we find the other models that are matched with the pair of models, that is, if a model is sufficiently similar to either model in the best matched pair, that model will be linked with the model pair.

The steps to find similar color models are presented as follows:

1. Compute a similarity matrix S in which an element s_{ij} is the similarity of models t_i and t_j. Initialize $k = 0$ and choose a threshold value th;
2. Group[k] = [ ];
3. Find the best matched model pair s_{mn} whose similarity is equal to max(s_{ij}), set Group[k] = [t_m, t_n];
4. In the mth and n^{th} rows of matrix S, find all the models whose similarity with m or n is greater than the threshold, then add those models into Group[k] and remove their corresponding columns and rows in S;
5. $k = k + 1$; go to Step 2.

In selecting the threshold value, we normalize the similarity scores between models to a value between 0 and 1. The threshold value is thus experimentally set to 0.95, roughly corresponding to 95% similarity.

Similarity Measure by Using Hough Transform

In this method, we apply Hough transform to cluster similar edge templates into groups. Similar to the proposed edge-based clustering method, this method uses Hough transform to find the best matched point of each pair of edge templates. Then image overlay is performed based on the best matched point to find the common area of the two edge templates. The similarity of two edge template is then computed according to Equation 1.

A threshold value is selected so that if the similarity is greater than the threshold value, the two corresponding edge templates will be linked together. The threshold value is again experimentally set to 0.95 in this study. It means that if two edge templates are 95% similar with each other, they will be linked together. We start from an edge template, find all the templates linked to it based on the similarity measure and the threshold, and remove this group (cluster) from the subsequent clustering process.

Experiments

To evaluate the effectiveness of the proposed multi-account linking detection algorithms, we collected a larger dataset (Dataset-III) consisting of 6053 images from 100 seller accounts. In this dataset, half of the sellers do not use any editing style in their images while the other half of the sellers create at least one editing style in their images. Compared with the classification experiments, here the ground truth is defined in a different way which uses the actual templates/models representing the editing style of an image as the ground truth of that image rather than associating it with a specific seller's account. In this ground truth, images with the same editing style should be in the same group no matter to which seller account they belong. In collecting ground truth, we first visually identify all the distinct image editing styles in the dataset, and then assign the same label to images with the same editing style. We performed a 3-fold cross validation on Dataset-III, and the three sets of clustering results as shown in Tables 2 and 3.

To compare the resultant clusters with the ground truth, we use V-measure (Rosenberg & Hirschberg, 2007), a weighted harmonic mean of homogeneity (*hm*) and completeness (*cm*). V-measure is a conditional entropy-based method to evaluate the clustering results and is independent of the clustering algorithm being used. The definition of V-measure is given in Equation 6, where β is a constant, which if greater than 1 would mean that cm is weighted β times more strongly than *hm*; otherwise *hm* is weighted more in the calculation. In this study, we compare our clustering results with the ground truth using this measure with different β value (ranging from 1 to 3). Tables 2 and 3 show the evaluation results.

$$v_\beta = \frac{(1 + \beta^2) \times hm \times cm}{(\beta^2 \times hm) + cm} \tag{6}$$

We can observe that edge-based templates perform better than color based models, but as aforementioned, the former has a higher complexity than the latter. In Dataset-III, we also observe

Table 2. V-measures of color model based linking

i^{th} fold	hm	cm	v1	v2	v3
1	0.73	0.71	0.72	0.71	0.71
2	0.66	0.70	0.68	0.69	0.69
3	0.65	0.70	0.67	0.69	0.69

Table 3. V-measures of edge template based clustering

i^{th} fold	hm	cm	v1	v2	v3
1	0.81	0.71	0.76	0.73	0.72
2	0.82	0.69	0.75	0.71	0.70
3	0.83	0.68	0.75	0.71	0.70

that there are three pairs of sellers that have almost identical editing styles. The three pairs of sellers are presented in Figure 4. Our proposed two algorithms successfully group each pair into the same group according to the similar editing styles present in each pair.

CONCLUSION

A framework of detecting sellers' authorship of eBay images is proposed in this paper by analyzing and encoding their distinctive image editing styles. Through a collaborative effort between the authors' institution and eBay, the output of this study will be used as added clues in eBay's seller profiling system to detect and prevent account taken-over and other related fraudulent behaviors. This framework includes three modules that target editing style summarization, classification and multi-account linking detection respectively. Three different summarization methods are developed to encode editing styles into templates (models) based on edge or color features, including an edge-based summarization and two color-based summarization methods. Accordingly, in order

to predict the authorship of previously unlabeled images, we implement three classification methods corresponding to the three summarization methods, namely edge-based classification, color based classification, and color probability based classification. We applied these three algorithms to two image data sets that consist of product listing images downloaded from 10 sellers and another 47 sellers at eBay, respectively. *n*-fold cross-validation was performed to evaluate the experimental results. The three summarization and classification methods are compared, and our results indicate that the edge-based classification method is the most promising in identifying authorship of eBay images. The encoded image editing styles can also be used to predict the same owner behind multiple eBay seller accounts. In this study, we collected a larger data set consisting of 100 seller accounts. To measure similarity between seller accounts in terms of common image editing styles, we propose two methods for this purpose, including a covariance based method which uses covariance as a similarity measure for HSV color models, and a clustering based method by using Hough transform for edge template matching.

Figure 4. Examples of multi-account linking results: each row shows the IDs of the sellers linked together and their sample images

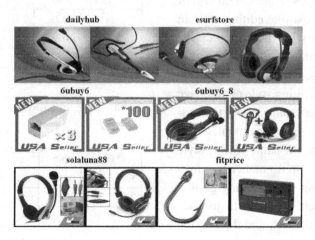

ACKNOWLEDGMENT

This work is supported in part by eBay Inc. and Dr. Chengcui Zhang's NSF grant (DBI-0649894).

REFERENCES

Abdel-Mottaleb, M. (2000). Image retrieval based on edge representation. In *Proceedings of the 2000 International Conference on Image Processing,* Vancouver, BC, Canada (Vol. 3, pp. 734-737).

Al-Asmari, A. K., & Al-Enizi, F. A. (2009). A pyramid-based watermarking technique for digital color images copyright protection. In *Proceedings of the International Conference on Computing, Engineering and Information,* Fullerton, CA (pp. 44-47).

Baker, C. R. (1973). Joint measures and cross-covariance operators. *Transactions of the American Mathematical Society, 2,* 273–289. doi:10.1090/S0002-9947-1973-0336795-3

Chen, S. C. (2010). Multimedia databases and data management: A survey. *International Journal of Multimedia Data Engineering and Management, 1*(1), 1–11. doi:10.4018/jmdem.2010111201

Fernandes, L. A. F., & Oliveira, M. M. (2008). Real-time line detection through an improved hough transform voting scheme. *Pattern Recognition, 41*(1), 299–314. doi:10.1016/j.patcog.2007.04.003

Hirose, S., Yoshimura, M., Hachimura, K., & Akama, R. (2008). Authorship identification of ukiyoe by using rakkan image. In *Proceedings of the Eighth IAPR Workshop on Document Analysis Systems,* Nara, Japan (pp.143-150).

Huang, C. H., & Wu, J. L. (2004). Attacking visible watermarking schemes. *IEEE Transactions on Multimedia, 6*(1), 16–30. doi:10.1109/TMM.2003.819579

Jahne, B., Scharr, H., & Korkel, S. (1999). Principles of filter design. In *Handbook of Computer Vision and Applications* (pp. 125–152). New York, NY: Academic Press.

Kohavi, R. (1995). A study of cross-validation and bootstrap for accuracy estimation and model selection. In *Proceedings of the Fourteenth International Joint Conference on Artificial Intelligence* (Vol. 2, pp. 1137-1143).

Lee, C. F., & Lee, H. E. (2008). A blind associative watermark detection scheme using self-embedding technique. In *Proceedings of the International Conference on Intelligent Information Hiding and Multimedia Signal Processing* (pp.1122-1125).

Love, H. (2002). *Attributing authorship: An introduction.* Cambridge, UK: Cambridge University Press. doi:10.1017/CBO9780511483165

Pei, S. C., & Zeng, Y. C. (2006). A novel image recovery algorithm for visible watermarked images. *IEEE Transactions on Information Forensics and Security, 1*(4), 543–550. doi:10.1109/TIFS.2006.885031

Rafailidis, D., Nanopoulos, A., & Manolopoulos, Y. (2010). Building tag-aware groups for music high-order ranking and topic discovery. *International Journal of Multimedia Data Engineering and Management, 1*(3), 1–18. doi:10.4018/jmdem.2010070101

Robine, M., Hanna, P., Ferraro, P., & Allali, J. (2007). Adaptation of string matching algorithms for identification of near-duplicate music documents. In *Proceedings of the International SIGIR Workshop on Plagiarism Analysis, Authorship Identification, and Near-Duplicate Detection (PAN),* Amsterdam, The Netherlands (pp. 37-43).

Rosenberg, A., & Hirschberg, J. (2007). V-Measure: A conditional entropy-based external cluster evaluation measure. In *Proceedings of the 2007 Joint Conference on Empirical Methods in Natural Language Processing and Computational Natural Language Learning (EMNLP-CoNLL),* Prague, Czech Republic (pp. 410-420).

Sprinthall, R. C. (2002). *Basic Statistical Analysis* (7th ed.). Boston, MA: Allyn and Bacon Publishers.

Yu, D., Sattar, F., & Ma, K. K. (2002). Watermark detection and extraction using independent component analysis method. *Journal on Applied Signal Processing, 1,* 92–104. doi:10.1155/S111086570200046X

Zhao, M., Bu, J. J., & Chen, C. (2002). Robust Background Subtraction in HSV Color Space. In. *Proceedings of SPIE: Multimedia Systems and Applications, 4861,* 325–332.

Zhao, Y., & Zobel, J. (2005). *Effective and scalable authorship attribution using function words.* Melbourne, Australia: RMIT University.

This work was previously published in the International Journal of Multimedia Data Engineering and Management, Volume 2, Issue 1, edited by Shu-Ching Chen, pp. 22-37, copyright 2011 by IGI Publishing (an imprint of IGI Global).

Chapter 3
Multimodal Information Integration and Fusion for Histology Image Classification

Tao Meng
University of Miami, USA

Mei-Ling Shyu
University of Miami, USA

Lin Lin
University of Miami, USA

ABSTRACT

Biomedical imaging technology has become an important tool for medical research and clinical practice. A large amount of imaging data is generated and collected every day. Managing and analyzing these data sets require the corresponding development of the computer based algorithms for automatic processing. Histology image classification is one of the important tasks in the bio-image informatics field and has broad applications in phenotype description and disease diagnosis. This study proposes a novel framework of histology image classification. The original images are first divided into several blocks and a set of visual features is extracted for each block. An array of C-RSPM (Collateral Representative Subspace Projection Modeling) models is then built that each model is based on one block from the same location in original images. Finally, the C-Value Enhanced Majority Voting (CEWMV) algorithm is developed to derive the final classification label for each testing image. To evaluate this framework, the authors compare its performance with several well-known classifiers using the benchmark data available from IICBU data repository. The results demonstrate that this framework achieves promising performance and performs significantly better than other classifiers in the comparison.

DOI: 10.4018/978-1-4666-2940-0.ch003

1. INTRODUCTION

The bio-imaging techniques such as fluorescent microscopy, two-photon-laser canning microscopy, and electron microscopy have become essential tools for exploring the structures and functions of organisms. With the advancement in the automatic imaging technologies, there is a rapid increase of biomedical imaging data sets in recent years, ranging from X-ray, CT for disease diagnosis, to in situ hybridization (ISH) imaging for analyzing gene expression patterns. The number of bio-images is increasing on a scale comparable to that of the genomic revolution (Hamilton et al., 2006).

The huge amounts of biomedical image datasets present significant challenges for traditional analysis methods based on manual annotation and human labeling. Therefore, utilizing computing technologies in automatic image processing and analyses has become popular research topics. With the collaboration of biomedical scientists and computer scientists, the area of "bio-image" informatics (Peng, 2008), which is a new branch of bioinformatics, was developed and a huge amount of computer-based algorithms for managing, indexing, and analyzing bio-image data sets has been introduced. Examples of such applications include automatic cell detection systems (Long, Cleveland, & Yao, 2010; Huang, Sun, & Hu, 2009), bio-image segmentation systems (Bae, Pan, Wu, & Badea, 2009; Madhloom, Kareem, Ariffin, & Zaidan, 2010), cell phenotype classification systems (Minamikawa et al., 2003), etc. A good review of this area was given in (Peng, 2008).

Histology is an essential tool in biomedical research field to examine microscopical anatomy of cells and tissues of plants and animals in order to infer the functional semantics of organisms. In one assay of histology experiment, the tissues or cells are stained so that the structure could be examined by human experts for annotating structural characteristics. With the deluge of the histology data sets, computer-based histology image analysis, which saves human labors and decreases the inter-intra variance, is demanded for automatic management and analyses of histology data and databases.

One of the critical tasks in this area is to classify the raw histology images based on the phenotype. By classifying images into different categories, it not only helps the medical scientists to make comparison within and cross varieties but also facilitates the computer scientists to build efficient indexing and retrieval systems. As a matter of fact, the diagnosis procedure is a binary classification problem itself. However, the task is quite challenging in this scenario for three reasons. First, histology images are non-stationary images. In other words, each region of the raw image could have distinct characteristics. Second, the variance in operating conditions in the laboratory increases the effect of artifacts, which leads to the increase of the intra-class differences. Third, the inter-class difference is relatively small and it is difficult for human to distinguish. In comparison among performances for different benchmark data sets in (Huang, Sun, & Hu, 2009), it showed that the accuracies of three histology data sets, Liver Aging, Liver Gender, and Lymphoma were relatively lower than those of others, which demonstrated the challenge of classifying these data sets.

There are some applications developed for analyzing histology data sets. The current state-of-art technologies can be summarized into three categories. The first category is developed for general biological image classifications. In order to accommodate to heterogeneous characteristics for different data sets, these applications usually encompass a large pool of features and carry the burden of huge computational complexity for feature extraction and feature selection. One example is the Wndchrm (Shamir et al., 2008) developed in the Laboratory of Genetics in National Institute of Aging. It contained 2659 features from raw pixels and transforms of images, such as Gabor Filters and Chebyshev-Fourier features, and utilized the nearest neighbor algorithm to perform the classification. CellProfiler (Carpenter et al., 2006) and EnhancedCellClassifier (Misselwitz et al., 2010) applied the support vector machine with radial basis function (RBF) kernel as the classifier and demonstrated relatively good performance especially on cell images.

The other category of research endeavor lies in developing specific applications for one or few data sets. In order to perform these tasks, many researchers in this domain bring techniques from image processing and pattern recognition fields. In the field of pattern recognition, transforming the images into good feature measurements is crucial for success. Therefore, a lot of approaches have been proposed to extract data-dependent features for a certain histology data set. A typical work of this type was presented in (Qureshi, Raipoot, Nattkemper, & Hans, 2009), in which the authors extracted features using the adaptive discriminant wavelet packet transformation. In that paper, a full wavelet packet transform (FWPT) for each image in the texture sample was first acquired and then the multi-resolution wavelet texture templates was used to calculate the pseudo-probability density estimates of a particular sub-band across all training samples of a particular class. However, the parameters in their process, such as the number of sub-bands, were adapted to the specific data set and the testing data sets contained images for only four patients. Another work in (Sertel, Catalyurek, Shimada, & Guican, 2009), Fractal Geometry based texture features were utilized to grade prostate carcinoma but their work relied on human experts for segmenting the region of interest (ROI). In Caicedo, Cruz, and Gonzalez (2009), the bag of words feature was used to represent the original images but it suffered from the relatively high time complexity for building the codebook. Another approach applies the image segmentation technique before performing classification (Wang, Ozolek, & Rohde, 2010). Their main

idea was that by segmenting the region of interest from the original images, the classification results could be improved. Their proposed approach achieved 100% accuracy by using a simple lazy learning algorithm on the testing data sets after segmenting the nuclei region from the original images and extracting features of chromatin patterns. A recent work showed that segmentation could help for automated Gleason grading of the prostatic carcinoma tissue images (Nguyen, Jain, & Allen, 2010).

However, there are some limitations of those aforementioned methods. First, the general applications do not adapt to the specific properties of histology data sets and rely heavily on human experts to perform further analyses. In addition, they depend on a huge number of extracted features, which increases the computational complexity. On the other hand, the feature extraction oriented classification applications rely heavily on certain data sets and require domain knowledge. For the segmentation-based applications, it suffers from the problem of information loss because no computer-based segmentation algorithms could ensure 100% accuracy under all conditions. In order to address these issues, the research of developing a general light-weight histology classification system, which does not rely on sophisticated segmentation and specific data set, becomes a hot topic. For example, in (Doyle, Feldman, Tomaszewski, & Madabhushi, 2010), the authors built a multi-resolution representation of histology images and used the ensemble learning method by taking a weighted combination of nearest-neighbor, nearest-mean, Bayesian and support vector machine classifiers to make decisions. In their work, the un-relevant region was eliminated by analyzing the images at a lower resolution to save the computation time in the feature extraction step. In (Kwitt et al., 2010), a probabilistic based model, which is commonly used in content-based image retrieval (CBIR), was tested on 269 RGB images taken by endoscope and showed relatively good performance. In their model, they made use of the dual-tree complex wavelet transform as the feature representations and class label was inferred by minimizing the probability of retrieval errors.

Our framework falls into the third category. In our proposed framework, the histology image is first divided into blocks. The division scheme, which is simpler than segmenting the actual objects from the image, decreases the computational complexity tremendously. After feature extraction and a data-dependent feature selection procedure, the subspace-based learning algorithm, Collateral Representative Subspace Projection Modeling (C-RSPM) (Quirino, Xie, Shyu, Chen, & Zhang, 2006) is used to build the models for all the blocks. For each testing image, different models generate classification results and the C-value Enhanced Weighted Majority Voting (CEWMV) algorithm is proposed to give the final classification label. To evaluate the proposed framework, the benchmark histology data sets from IICBU (Shamir et al., 2008) are tested and the classification results of our framework are compared with those of several well-known classifiers as well as the highest classification performance reported so far. The results demonstrate that our proposed framework achieves promising performance and performs constantly better than others in comparison.

The paper is organized as follows. In Section 2, the proposed framework and each component of the framework are discussed. The experiment results and analysis are shown in Section 3. The last section concludes the paper.

2. THE PROPOSED FRAMEWORK

The general architecture of the proposed framework is shown in Figure 1. It is composed of two components. They are *feature preparation component* and *classification & fusion component*.

Figure 1. The general framework

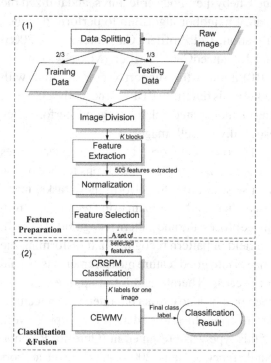

In the feature preparation component, raw images are split to training sets (two thirds of the whole data) and testing sets (one third of the whole data). All images in the training and testing sets are first divided to K equal-sized blocks. The value K could be adjusted according to the applications. In this study, K is set to 25 based on empirical studies. The specific division scheme will be introduced in section 2-A. For data in the training set, the k-th block which has the same location from the original raw images forms the block set B_k, $1 \leq k \leq K$. A set of 505 visual features are extracted from each block. After normalizing the features, the chi-square based feature selection and ranking method is used to select the set of features with high ranking scores, which will be discussed in section 2-B. The processed data are ready to input to the classification and fusion component.

For the data in the testing set, the same set of 505 features is extracted from each block. Those features selected by the feature selection and ranking method in the training process are kept and normalized using the parameters from the normalization step in the training process. Similarly, a testing image is divided to K blocks in the feature preparation component. Each block b_k, $1 \leq k \leq K$ will be classified by the model which is trained using the training blocks in B_k. Since the testing image is composed of K blocks, there will be K labels correspondingly. A CEWMV is proposed to perform the task of late fusion to derive the final class label, which will be discussed in sections 2-C and 2-D.

A. Image Division

The main reasons of performing image division are threefold. First, this method decreases the space complexity for extracting the features (Browning & Tanimoto, 1982). Second, previous studies have shown that when each image captures very many cells, dividing the image into blocks to extract local features of each block can, in some cases, achieve better results than using the global features (Shamir, Eckley, & Goldberg, 2007). Third, different blocks carry distinct information which is dependent on their locations, and thus the factor of relative location can be utilized (Meng, Lin, Shyu, & Chen, 2010).

The division scheme is shown in Figure 2. Each original image, which has the size of 1388x1040, is divided into 16 Type I blocks (shown as the blocks marked by blue solid line, from blocks 1 to 16) and 9 Type II blocks (marked by the black broken lines, from blocks 17 to 25). All the Type I blocks and Type II blocks have the same size. It can be seen that if all 16 Type I blocks are spliced together in sequence, the original image could be reconstructed. Because the division of Type I blocks is arbitrary and may lead to information loss at the border area near the dividing line, Type II blocks are added to recover the information near the border area among neighboring Type I blocks.

Figure 2. The division scheme

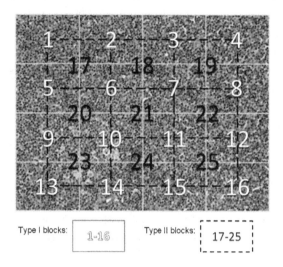

Type I blocks: 1-16   Type II blocks: 17-25

B. Feature Extraction, Normalization and Feature Selection

In our proposed framework, a general classification system for histology images is developed. Therefore, a wide range of visual features are extracted at the beginning. A set of 505 visual features are extracted from each block (Lin & Shyu, 2010; Lin, Chen, Shyu, Fleites, & Chen, 2009), including Color Dominant (16 features), Color Histogram (51 features), Color Moment (108 features), Edge Histogram (47 features), Texture Co-occur (36 features), Texture Wavelet (219 features), Texture Tamura (3 features), Texture Gabor (24 features), and Local Binary Patterns (1 feature).

The Z score normalization is applied to each block set B_k. $1 \leq k \leq K$. For each instance in B_k, the Z score is computed using Equation (1).

$$Z_{i,j} = \frac{W_{i,j} - \mu_j}{\sigma_j}, \tag{1}$$

where $1 \leq i \leq N$, $1 \leq j \leq 505$, $W_{i,j}$ is the raw feature value of the j-th feature for the i-th image in one block set, the total number of images is N, and μ_j & σ_j are the mean and standard deviation values of the j-th feature in one block set. In this work, the normalization is done within each block set. Therefore, the differences among locations are taken into considerations. In addition, this normalization method also helps to improve the feature selection step by keeping the discriminations among the features.

Since feature selection is not the focus of this paper, the chi-square feature selection methodology available in Weka (Witten & Frank, 2005) is applied. The chi-square measure evaluates features by ranking the chi-square statistics of each feature with respect to the class. After computing the ranking scores of all the features, it is necessary to determine the number of features to be kept for our proposed framework. If there are too few features, it could not represent the characteristics of the image thoroughly. On the other hand, if too many features are kept, the computational complexity of the classification steps increases. In addition, the number of features that can represent the data characteristics should be adaptive to the image data. Therefore, the number of features to be kept is determined dynamically given the following two factors in our proposed framework. First, in order to address the issue of the curse of dimensionality, the number of features retained needs to be smaller than or equal to the number of training instances of the class that has the smallest number of instances. Second, based on our empirical study, we retain the features whose scores are greater than or equal to the sum of the mean value and half of the standard deviation value of the ranking scores of all features. Experimental results show that the classification performance is better with an adaptive number of features than using a fixed number of features for various data sets, since it better captures the characteristics of each data set.

C. Collateral Representative Subspace Projection Modeling (C-RSPM)

The characteristics of relatively smaller inter class difference and relatively large noise in a histology data set pose great challenges for the classifiers. In order to address these issues, the Collateral Representative Subspace Projection Modeling (C-RSPM), which is a subspace-based learning algorithm developed in our previous studies (Quirino, Xie, Shyu, Chen, & Zhang, 2006), is utilized in this framework. This classifier has been used in many domains including network intrusion detection (Sainani & Shyu, 2009; Shyu, Quirino, Xie, Chen, & Chang, 2007) and concept detection of multimedia databases (Chen, Shyu, & Chen, 2008; Shyu, Xie, Chen, & Chen, 2008; Xie, Shyu, & Chen, 2007) with good performance. By utilizing the principal component subspace in C-RSPM, the feature values are projected to the new space in which the discrimination characteristics of all the feature values are better represented. In addition, instead of building a single model for classifying all the data sets, C-RSPM builds one binary classification model for each class and utilizes the outputs from the models to make a final decision. As a matter of fact, reducing the complicated problem to a small & manageable task actually increases the robustness of the overall classifier. Given these advantages, C-RSPM is utilized in our proposed framework.

The general idea of this classification method is to build an array of principal component classifiers (PCCs), where the number of classifiers is determined by the number of classes in a specific application. Each PCC is trained to learn the similarities among training instances of a particular class and used to recognize the testing data that are normal to this class. The overall modeling is divided to the training module and testing module. In the training module, the training data of class o ($1 \le o \le H$, H indicates the total number of classes) forms a matrix $X_o = \{x_{ln}\}$, $l = 1, 2, \ldots,$

$M, n = 1, 2,\ldots, P$, which has a dimension of M by P with M training instances which all belong to class o and P selected features from the previous step. First, some training instances which lie too far from the center of the data set are removed to make the remaining data set a good representation for a certain class. Let $\mathbf{x}_l = [x_{l1}, x_{l2}, \ldots, x_{lP}]^T$ be a column vector that represents the features for the l-th instance. The Mahalanobis distance is calculated using Equation (2).

$$d_l^2 = (\mathbf{x}_l - \bar{\mathbf{x}})^T \mathbf{S}^{-1}(\mathbf{x}_l - \bar{\mathbf{x}}), \tag{2}$$

where $\bar{\mathbf{x}} = \dfrac{1}{M}\sum_{l=1}^{M}\mathbf{x}_l$ and

$\mathbf{S} = \dfrac{1}{M-1}\sum_{l=1}^{M}(\mathbf{x}_l - \bar{\mathbf{x}})(\mathbf{x}_l - \bar{\mathbf{x}})^T.$

In order to decide how many instances are trimmed, the parameter trimming percentage ($\gamma\%$) is used so that the number of instances to be trimmed is set to $\gamma\% \bullet M$. After this step, the new feature instance matrix $F_o = \{f_{bn}\}$, $b = 1, 2, \ldots, L, n = 1, 2,\ldots, P$, which has L instances $(L \leq M)$, is formed. The matrix is then normalized to get $Z_o = \{z_{bn}\}$, in which z_{bn} is calculated using Equation (3)

$$z_{bn} = \frac{f_{bn} - \mu_n}{\sigma_n}, \tag{3}$$

where $\mu_n = \dfrac{1}{L}\sum_{a=1}^{L} f_{an}$ and $\sigma_n = \sqrt{\dfrac{\sum_{a=1}^{L}(f_{an} - \mu_n)^2}{L - 1}}.$

The correlation matrix of Z_o is calculated and it is denoted as C_o. The P eigenvalue-eigenvector pairs $(\lambda_1, e_1), (\lambda_2, e_2),\ldots, (\lambda_P, e_P)$ are then calculated for matrix C_o. The matrix Z_o is projected to the P-dimensional eigenspace which is composed of all P principal components from C_o to get $Y_o = \{y_{bn}\}$ in which the row vector $y_i = [y_{b1}, y_{b2},\ldots, y_{bP}]$ is the projection of each normalized training data instance in Z_o onto the eigenspace. Then the principal components whose corresponding eigenvalues are greater than the threshold η are kept as the representative principal components. Let the set G contain the indexes of the features corresponding to representative principal components in Y_o. A distance vector $c=\{c_b\}$, $b=1, 2,\ldots, L$ is computed using Equation (4).

$$c_b = \sum_{g \in G} \frac{(y_{bg})^2}{\lambda_{f(g)}}, \tag{4}$$

where $\lambda_{f(g)}$ is the eigenvalue corresponding to column g. Afterwards, the elements of c are sorted in the ascending order and only the β smallest values are retained. Assuming $\alpha(0 < \alpha < 1)$ is the false alarm rate, β is calculated as the value of the nearest integer to which the value of $(1 - \alpha)L$ is rounded. The threshold value $c_{thres(o)}$ is set to the maximum value of the elements in c for class o. The $c_{thres(o)}$ value is calculated for the training data set for each class o. For a testing instance (i.e., a testing image), in order to check whether it belongs to class o, the following steps are carried out. Let $\mathbf{x} = [x'_1, x'_2 \ldots x'_P]^T$ be the vector representing features for that testing instance. After normalization, the projection vector $\mathbf{y} = [y'_1, y'_2 \ldots y'_P]^T$ is computed by projecting the normalized vector onto the same P-dimensional eigenspace composed of all P principal components from C_o. The c' value is calculated using Equation (5).

$$c' = \sum_{g \in G} \frac{(y'_g)^2}{\lambda_{f(g)}}. \tag{5}$$

The testing instance is classified as statistically negative to the class o if $c' > c_{thres(o)}$ and classified as positive to class o if $c' \leq c_{thres(o)}$. The testing instance is checked for each class. Theoretically, the instance should be positive to one and only one class and negative to all others. However, there are typically two other possible cases. One is that the testing instance is labeled as positive for more than one class; while the other is that the testing instance is negative to all classes. In order to cope with these two situations, the attaching proportion for class o defined as follows is utilized.

$$s_o = \frac{c_o'}{c_{thres(o)}}, \text{where } 1 \leq o \leq H \qquad (6)$$

The testing instance is labeled as the class which has the smallest s_o. The specific details of the classifier could be found in (Quirino, Xie, Shyu, Chen, & Chang, 2006). The parameters such as γ, β and η used in this process are tuned adaptively and automatically by maximizing the classification accuracy on the training set in the model training stage.

D. Weighted Majority Voting Module

After the training setup, there are K C-RSPM models, one for each block set B_k, $1 \leq k \leq K$. In the testing phase, one image is divided to K blocks and each block is classified using its corresponding model. Therefore, one testing image gets K class labels (Table 1) and a final decision needs to be made. The most intuitive way to reach a final conclusion is to use the majority voting. However, some models may have more information than simply the classification results, such as the classification accuracy. Therefore, in order to make use of such information, the C-value Enhanced Weighted Majority Voting (CEWMV) algorithm is proposed in our proposed framework. The CEWMV contains two modules. The first module is the Weighted Majority Voting Module, which outputs the voting score for each class. After getting the scores, the C-Value Enhancement Module will be applied to the make the final decision.

Table 1. Classification results of a testing instance

Testing Instance	Model 1	Model 2	...	Model k	...	Model K
Testing Instance 1	Q_1 =Class 3	Q_2 =Class 1	...	Q_k =Class o	...	Q_k =Class 1

Let $A_1, A_2, ..., A_K$ be the K models, $D_1, D_2, ..., D_K$ be the classification results of the blocks from one testing image, and H classes in the data set (labeled as class 1, class 2, ... class o, ... class H, correspondingly). An example of the classification results of a testing instance is shown in the following table. Here, Q_k is the class label of the testing instance given by the model k. Then an appropriate scheme to calculate the weight of model k for class o is required. The simplest way is to assign 1 to each weight with the majority voting scheme, which may be too coarse. Hence, in our proposed framework, the classification accuracy of each model for a specific class is considered as the weight of each model, which should better capture the overall membership information. Let the total numbers of blocks and classes be K and H, respectively. In this work, $K = 25$ and H depends on the data sets used. The pseudo code for calculating the weight is presented in Table 2.

A weight matrix $R(k,o) = \{r_{ko}\}$, $1 \leq k \leq K$, $1 \leq o \leq H$, in which r_{ko} represents the weight of model k for class o, is calculated based on the training instances. Table 3 shows an example of the weight matrix. The final score for class o is calculated using the Equation (7), where $\Phi = \{k| Q_k = \text{Class } o, 1 \leq k \leq K\}$. The testing image is classified to the label which gets the highest score. As shown in Equation (7), the weight matrix (Table 3) is an important factor for the result of the score.

Table 2. Pseudo-code for calculating the weight from the percentage information

```
1 for model_k ← model_1 to model_K
2 for class_o ← class_1 to class_H
3 NumTP(k,o) = Number of true positive instances in the training data set for class o of model_h
4 NumClass(o) = Number of ground truth instances for class_o in the training data set
5 AccuracyM(k,o) = NumTP(h,o)/ NumClass(o)
6 next
7 next
8 SMax = Maximum(AccuracyM(k,o))
9 SMin = Minimum(AccuracyM(k,o))
10 SDif = SMax - SMin
11 for model_k ← model_1 to model_K
12 for class_o ←class_1 to class_H
13 R(k,o) = (AccuracyM(k,o)-SMin)/SDif
14 next
15 next
```

Table 3. Weight matrix R

Classes	Model 1	Model 2	...	Model k	...	Model K
Class 1	r_{11}	r_{21}	...	r_{k1}	...	r_{K1}
Class 2	r_{12}	r_{22}	...	r_{k2}	...	r_{K2}
...	...	...	...	...	...	...
Class o	r_{1o}	r_{2o}		r_{ko}	...	r_{Ko}
...	...	...	...	...	...	...
Class H	r_{1H}	r_{2H}	...	r_{kH}	...	r_{KH}

$$\text{Score}(\text{Class } o) = \sum_{k \in \Phi} r_{ko} \qquad (7)$$

E. C-Value Enhancement Module

The second module, C-value Enhancement Module is designed to solve the ambiguous voting results from the previous step. If the largest and the second largest voting scores are too close, it indicates that using the weighted majority voting alone is not enough to discriminate the two classes. Therefore, further information is needed to make the final decision. Generally speaking, this module needs to solve two problems: (1) whether the scores are too close so that another round of decision needs to be made; and (2) if the scores are too close, how to make the final decision.

After the weighted majority voting step, a testing instance receives H scores $(e_1, e_2, \ldots, e_H)$ corresponding to the H classes. Let e_{max} and e_{smax} be the largest and the second largest values for all the scores and let σ_e be the standard deviation of $e_1, e_2, \ldots, e_H$. If $e_{max} - e_{smax} < \sigma_e$ holds, a further decision needs to be made. Otherwise, the testing instance is assigned to the class label that corresponds to e_{max}.

In order to make a better decision, the information of the c value from C-RSPM is taken into consideration. The testing data entering this procedure are those ambiguous cases after the accuracies of the models were used. Therefore, more detailed information from the model is needed to clarify such ambiguity. C-RSPM not only outputs the classification result but also provides the output of the c value, which carries the quantitative measurement of the confidence that the testing instance belongs to a certain class. Specifically, if the condition $c \leq c_{thes(o)}$ is met, the testing instance is deem to be positive to the class *o*. In this case, the smaller the *c* value is, the more confidence the decision has. In order to take this factor into consideration, the attaching proportion which is defined in Equation (6) is calculated for each class. Equation (8) is used to calculate the new score, where $\Phi = \{k| Q_k = \text{Class } o, 1 \leq k \leq K\}$.

$$\text{Score}(\text{Class } o) = \sum_{k \in \Phi} r_{ko} \Big/ \left(c'^{k}_{o} \Big/ c^{k}_{thres(o)} \right) \qquad (8)$$

Here, r_{ko} is the weight derived from the Weighted Majority Voting Module in Section 2-D. c'^{k}_{o} is the c' value of this testing instance computed in the C-RSPM classification procedure of model *k* for class *o*. $c^{k}_{thres(o)}$ is the threshold value for *c* of model *k* for class *o*. Therefore, the factor $c'^{k}_{o} / c^{k}_{thres(o)}$ is the attaching proportion of the testing instance corresponding to model *k* and class *o*. In order to maximize the score, the attaching proportion acts as the denominator. In this way, both the classification accuracy from the macro view of the model and the *c* value information from the micro view of the model are considered in the final decision. Experimental results show that such integrated information scheme yields better results.

3. EXPERIMENTS AND RESULTS

Our framework is evaluated on four benchmark histology data sets from the IICBU Biological Image Repository (Shamir, Orlov, Eckley, Macura, & Goldberg, 2008) using the average accuracy from the three-fold cross validation process. The first three data sets are from the cell biology research field and the last one is from the clinical research field.

The Female Mice Liver Aging data set contains 528 microscopy images, each of which has the size of 1388x1040. The class labels are 1 month female mice on ad-libitum diet (99 images), 6 month female mice on ad-libitum diet (115 images), 16 month female mice on ad-libitum diet (162 images) and 24 month female mice on ad-libitum diet (152 images). The liver tissue was extracted from the sacrificed female mice of different ages. The tissue was then sectioned and stained using H&E staining method. The sample images are shown in Figure 3. Due to the fact that these images are taken from the tissues of different mice, the variances among individuals could increase the intra-class difference and confuse the classifier.

The Male Mice Liver Aging data set contains 499 images and each of which has the size of 1388x1040. The class labels are 1 month male mice on ad-libitum diet (100 images), 6 month male mice on ad-libitum diet (150 images), 16 month male mice on ad-libitum diet (100 images), and 24 month male mice on ad-libitum diet (149 images). They were prepared in the same way as that in the previous data set. The sample images are shown in Figure 4.

The Liver Gender data set contains 265 images in this data set. They have the same size of those in the previous data set. The class labels are 6 month male mice on ad-libitum diet (150 images) and 6 month female mice on ad-libitum diet (115 images). They were prepared in the same

Figure 3. The sample image from female mice liver aging data set

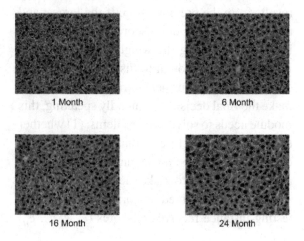

Figure 4. The sample image from male mice liver aging data set

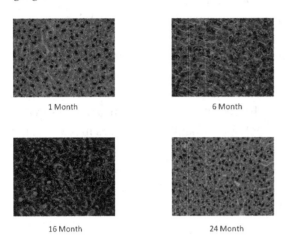

way as those in the previous two data sets. The sample images are shown in Figure 5.

The Malignant Lymphoma data set is from the clinical field. Malignant lymphoma is a cancer affecting lymph node. In this data set, 376 images with the size of (1388x1040) of three types of malignant lymphoma are represented. They are chronic lymphocytic leukemia (CLL) cells (114 images), follicular lymphoma (FL) cells (139 images), and mantle cell lymphoma (MCL) cells (123 images). The sample images are shown in Figure 6. It should be pointed out that since the images are taken in different medical service centers, the variances of operations and imaging quality are larger than those of the previous three data sets, which were taken under laboratory controlled conditions. This factor increases the difficulty for classification.

In our proposed framework, the number of selected features is adaptive to the data sets. After applying the algorithms described in section 2, the number of features selected for the four data sets are: 64 for the Female Mice Liver Aging data set, 68 for the Male Mice Liver Aging data set, 55 for the Liver Gender data sets, and 114 for the Malignant Lymphoma data set.

In order to evaluate the effectiveness of our proposed framework, the performance is compared with that of two other fusion methods using common classifiers in Weka (Witten & Frank, 2005), including Decision Tree C4.5, Rule based JRIP, AdaBoost (with C4.5), k-Nearest Neighbors (k=3), Support Vector Machine (with poly-kernal), Bayes-Net, and Naïve-Bayes applications. Then two fusion frameworks called early feature fusion and late result decision are performed. In early feature fusion framework, one feature vector is computed for each image by averaging the feature values of the K blocks. Supposing the feature values for all the blocks are summarized in the matrix $\mathbf{V} = \{v_{ku}\}$, where $1 \leq k \leq K$, $1 \leq u \leq P$, and P is the number of selected features. $\mathbf{v}_k = [v_{k1}, v_{k2}, \ldots v_{ku}, \ldots, v_{kP}]$ is the row vector of the feature values for block k. The new feature vector $\mathbf{v'} = [v'_u]$ in which v'_u is calculated using Equation (9). The new feature vector $\mathbf{v'}$ is used for classification.

Figure 5. The sample image from liver gender data set

Figure 6. The sample image from malignant lymphoma data set

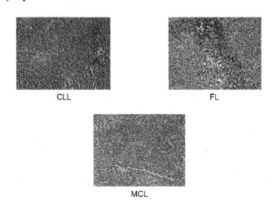

$$v'_u = (\sum_{k=1}^{K} v_{ku}) / K \qquad (9)$$

The late decision framework is to treat all the blocks equally without considering the different locations of the blocks. After getting the class label for each block of a testing image, the majority voting scheme is used to deduce the final label of the image. The evaluation criterion is the classification accuracy which is defined as the percentage of the images in the testing data set whose classification results match the ground truth as determined by the class label. The classification accuracies for four data sets are shown in Table 4, Table 5, Table 6, and Table 7.

From the classification results, it can be seen that the average classification accuracies are higher in the first three data sets than that of the last one. The possible reason for this is that the fourth data set is from the clinical centers in different hospitals and the variances in the imaging conditions among different institutes increase the intra-class variance, which confuses the classifiers. This also can be seen from the fact that after the feature selection step, the largest number

Table 4. Classification accuracy for female mice liver aging data set

TABLE 4 (A)	Published on the website	C-RSPM+ CEWMVA
Accuracy	51.00%	**98.29%**
TABLE 4 (B)	Early Feature Fusion	Late Result Decision
C4.5	90.29%	89.40%
JRIP	88.57%	87.80%
AdaBoost	95.43%	89.10%
3NN	96.00%	90.60%
SVM	95.28%	86.23%
BayesNet	82.86%	78.1%
NaiveBayes	70.22%	64.6%
Average	88.38%	83.69%

Table 5. Classification accuracy for male mice liver aging data set

TABLE 5 (A)	Published on the website	C-RSPM+ CEWMVA
Accuracy	NA	**97.78%**
TABLE 5 (B)	Early Feature Fusion	Late Result Decision
C4.5	87.28%	83.23%
JRIP	88.52%	85.17%
AdaBoost	92.94%	88.95%
3NN	93.98%	90.32%
SVM	90.99%	85.63%
BayesNet	80.30%	75.40%
NaiveBayes	67.79%	63.54%
Average	85.79%	81.75%

of features is kept in the fourth data set because many features are compatible with each other and fewer features take dominate position.

From the experimental results, it can be observed that our proposed framework constantly outperforms other classifiers. For the compared classifiers, k-Nearest Neighbor (k=3 in our study) and Adaboost (with C4.5) classifiers perform better than the other classifiers in general. The possible reason is that the k-Nearest Neighbor classifier sometimes identifies the same animal or patient by finding the most similar instances in the training sets. Therefore, it takes advantages of the data set itself because there are some images taken from the same individual. The Adaboost (with C4.5) has been shown to give good performance in many cases, especially in the binary classification task (Zhu, Zou, Rosset, & Hastie, 2009).

Compared with the other two frameworks, the proposed framework takes the relative locations of the blocks into consideration to build the model for each block. This adapts to the characteristics of the histology image data set because different regions of an image are different internally in

Table 6. Classification accuracy for liver gender data set

TABLE 6(A)	Published on the web site	C-RSPM+ CEWMVA
Accuracy	69.00%	**99.24%**
TABLE 6(B)	**Early Feature Fusion**	**Late Result Decision**
C4.5	86.64%	91.05%
JRIP	83.23%	88.77%
AdaBoost	90.91%	93.32%
3NN	91.18%	93.31%
SVM	89.77%	90.9%
BayesNet	87.53%	83.50%
NaiveBayes	78.09%	76.18%
Average	86.76%	88.15%

Table 7. Classification accuracy for malignant lymphoma

TABLE 7(A)	Published on the website	C-RSPM+ CEWMVA
Accuracy	85.00%	**96.81%**
TABLE 7(B)	**Early Feature Fusion**	**Late Result Decision**
C4.5	80.49%	76.52%
JRIP	79.24%	77.78%
AdaBoost	87.94%	80.05%
3NN	88.93%	82.32%
SVM	72.11%	79.57%
BayesNet	72.29%	73.53%
NaiveBayes	67.29%	64.10%
Average	78.33%	76.27%

terms of the structure and distribution of cells. On the other hand, the early feature fusion and late result decision frameworks both treat the blocks in the same manner, and thus lose the information of the locations. In addition, by comparing the classification results with those reported on the IICBU website (please note that there is no reported classification accuracy for Male Mice Liver Aging set), it can be seen that the proposed framework improves the classification results to a great extent. Since our framework does not depend on features from a certain data set, it could be applied for all histology image classification tasks.

CONCLUSION

In this paper, a novel histology classification framework based on subspace-based classifiers and multimodal information integration is proposed. The histology image is first divided into several blocks and each block is used to train a C-RSPM model. After all the blocks from a testing image are classified, a C-value Enhanced Weighted Majority Voting (CEWMV) algorithm is designed to derive the final label. Experimental results on the IICBU histology benchmark data sets compared with several well-known classifiers in two fusion methods show that our proposed framework gives promising performance on data from different sources, indicating its possible broad applications in both biomedical research and clinical practice.

REFERENCES

Bae, M. H., Pan, R., Wu, T., & Badea, A. (2009). Automated segmentation of mouse brain images using extended MRF. *NeuroImage, 46*(3), 717–725. doi:10.1016/j.neuroimage.2009.02.012

Browning, J. D., & Tanimoto, S. L. (1982). Segmentation of pictures into regions with a tile-by-tile method. *Pattern Recognition, 15*(1), 1–10. doi:10.1016/0031-3203(82)90055-3

Caicedo, J. C., Cruz, A., & Gonzalez, F. A. (2009). Histopathology image classification using bag of features and kernel functions. *Artificial Intelligence in Medicine, 5651*, 126–135. doi:10.1007/978-3-642-02976-9_17

Carpenter, A. E., Jones, T. R., Lamprecht, M. R., Clarke, C., Kang, I. H., & Friman, O. (2006). CellProfier: Image analysis software for identifying and quantifying cell phenotypes. *Genome Biology, 7*(10), 100. doi:10.1186/gb-2006-7-10-r100

Chen, S.-C., Shyu, M.-L., & Chen, M. (2008). An effective multi-concept classifier for video streams. In *Proceedings of the IEEE International Conference on Semantic Computing* (pp. 80-87).

Doyle, S., Feldman, M., Tomaszewski, J., & Madabhushi, A. (2010). A boosted bayesian multi-resolution classifier for prostate cancer detection from digitized needle biopsies. *IEEE Transactions on Bio-Medical Engineering, 99*, 1.

Hamilton, N., Pantelic, R., Hanson, K., Fink, J. L., Karunaratne, S., & Teasdale, R. D. (2006). Automated sub-cellular phenotype classification: An introduction and recent results. In *Proceedings of the Workshop on Intelligent Systems for Bioinformatics* (pp. 67-72).

Huang, Y., Sun, X., & Hu, G. (2009). An automatic integrated approach for stained neuron detection in studying neuron migration. *Microscopy Research and Technique, 73*(2), 109–118.

Kwitt, R., Uhl, A., Hafner, M., Gangl, A., Wrba, F., & Vecsei, A. (2010). Predicting the histology of colorectal lesions in a probabilistic framework. In *Proceedings of the IEEE Computer Society Conference on Computer Vision and Pattern Recognition Workshops* (pp.103-110).

Lin, L., Chen, C., Shyu, M.-L., Fleites, F., & Chen, S.-C. (2009). *Florida International University and University of Miami TRECVID 2009-high level feature extraction.* Retrieved from http://www-nlpir.nist.gov/projects/tvpubs/tv9.papers/fiu-um.pdf

Lin, L., & Shyu, M.-L. (2010). Correlation-based ranking for large-scale video concept retrieval. *International Journal of Multimedia Data Engineering and Management, 1*(4), 60–74. doi:10.4018/jmdem.2010100105

Long, X., Cleveland, W., & Yao, Y. (2010). Multiclass detection of cells in multicontrast composite images. *Computers in Biology and Medicine, 40*(2), 168–178. doi:10.1016/j.compbiomed.2009.11.013

Madhloom, H. T., Kareem, S. A., Ariffin, H., Zaidan, A. A., Alanazi, H. O., & Zaidan, B. B. (2010). An automated white blood cell nucleus localization and segmentation using image arithmetic and automatic threshold. *Journal of Applied Sciences, 10*(11), 959–966. doi:10.3923/jas.2010.959.966

Meng, T., Lin, L., Shyu, M.-L., & Chen, S.-C. (2010). Histology image classification using supervised classification and multimodal fusion. In *Proceedings of the IEEE International Symposium on Multimedia* (pp. 145-152).

Minamikawa, R., Kabuyama, N., Gotoh, T., Kagei, S., Naruse, M., & Kisu, Y. (2003). High-throughput classification of images of cell transfected with cDNA clones. *Molecular Biology and Genetics, 326*, 993–1001.

Misselwitz, B., Strittmatter, G., Periaswamy, B., Schlumberger, M. C., Rout, S., & Horvath, P. (2010). Enhanced cell classifier: A multi-class classification tool for Microscopy images. *BMC Bioinformatics, 11*(30).

Nguyen, K., Jain, A. K., & Allen, R. L. (2010). Automated gland segmentation and classification for Gleason grading of prostate tissue images. In *Proceedings of the 20th International Conference on Pattern Recognition* (pp. 1497-1500).

Peng, H. (2008). Bioimage informatics: A new area of engineering biology. *Bioinformatics (Oxford, England), 24*(17), 1827–1836. doi:10.1093/bioinformatics/btn346

Quirino, T., Xie, Z., Shyu, M.-L., Chen, S.-C., & Chang, L. (2006). Collateral representative subspace projection modeling for supervised classification. In *Proceedings of the IEEE International Conference on Tools with Artificial Intelligence* (pp. 98-105).

Qureshi, H., Raipoot, N., Nattkemper, T., & Hans, V. (2009). A robust adaptive wavelet-based method for classification of Meningioma histology images. In *Proceedings of the MICCAI Workshop on Optical Tissue Image Analysis in Microscopy, Histology and Endoscopy.*

Sainani, V., & Shyu, M.-L. (2009). A hybrid layered multiagent architecture with low cost and low response time communication protocol for network intrusion detection system. In *Proceedings of the IEEE International Conference on Advanced Information Networking and Applications* (pp. 154-161).

Sertel, O. Catalyurek, Shimada, U. V., & Guican, M. N. (2009). Computer-aided prognosis of Neuroblastoma: Detection of Mitosis and Karyorrhexis cells in digitized histological images. In *Proceedings of the IEEE International Conference on Engineering in Medicine and Biology Society* (pp.1433-1436).

Shamir, L. Eckley, D. M., & Goldberg, I. G. (2007). Image tiling vs. cell segmentation – a case study. In *Proceedings of the 47th American Society for Cell Biology Meeting* (p. 35).

Shamir, L., Orlov, N., Eckley, D. M., Macura, T., Johnston, J., & Goldberg, G. (2008). Wndchm - an open source utility for biological image analysis. *Source Code for Biology and Medicine, 3*(13), 943–947.

Shyu, M.-L., Quirino, T., Xie, Z., Chen, S.-C., & Chang, L. (2007). Network intrusion detection through adaptive sub-eigenspace modeling in multiagent systems. *ACM Transactions on Autonomous and Adaptive Systems, 2*(3), 1–37. doi:10.1145/1278460.1278463

Shyu, M.-L., Xie, Z., Chen, M., & Chen, S.-C. (2008). Video semantic event/concept detection using a subspace-based multimedia data mining framework. *IEEE Transactions on Multimedia, 10*(2), 252–259. doi:10.1109/TMM.2007.911830

Wang, W., Ozolek, J. A., & Rohde, G. K. (2010). Detection and classification of Thyroid Follicular lesions based on nuclear structure from histopathology images. *Cytometry. Part A, 77*(5), 485–494.

Witten, I. H., & Frank, E. (2005). *Data mining: Practical machine learning tools and techniques* (2nd ed.). San Francisco, CA: Morgan Kauffman.

Xie, Z., Shyu, M.-L., & Chen, S.-C. (2008). Video event detection with combined distance-based and rule-based data mining techniques. In *Proceedings of the IEEE International Conference on Multimedia & Expo* (pp. 2026-2029).

Zhu, J. Zou, H., Rosset, S., & Hastie, T. (2009). Multi-class AdaBoost. *Statics and its Interface, 2*(3), 349-360.

This work was previously published in the International Journal of Multimedia Data Engineering and Management, Volume 2, Issue 2, edited by Shu-Ching Chen, pp. 54-70, copyright 2011 by IGI Publishing (an imprint of IGI Global).

Chapter 4

Default Reasoning for Forensic Visual Surveillance Based on Subjective Logic and its Comparison with L-Fuzzy Set Based Approaches

Seunghan Han
Technische Universität München, Germany

Walter Stechele
Technische Universität München, Germany

ABSTRACT

Default reasoning can provide a means of deriving plausible semantic conclusion under imprecise and contradictory information in forensic visual surveillance. In such reasoning under uncertainty, proper uncertainty handling formalism is required. A discrete species of Bilattice for multivalued default logic demonstrated default reasoning in visual surveillance. In this article, the authors present an approach to default reasoning using subjective logic that acts in a continuous space. As an uncertainty representation and handling formalism, subjective logic bridges Dempster Shafer belief theory and second order Bayesian, thereby making it attractive tool for artificial reasoning. For the verification of the proposed approach, the authors extend the inference scheme on the bilattice for multivalued default logic to L-fuzzy set based logics that can be modeled with continuous species of bilattice structures. The authors present some illustrative case studies in visual surveillance scenarios to contrast the proposed approach with L-fuzzy set based approaches.

DOI: 10.4018/978-1-4666-2940-0.ch004

INTRODUCTION

Recent advances in computer vision technology have been bestowing increased vision analytic power such as detecting specific patterns of human or object behavior on intelligent visual surveillance systems. However, due to the wide proliferation of visual surveillance systems in various domains, the demand for more flexible and powerful higher-level forensic semantic understanding and analysis of visual surveillance scenes is also growing. One of the important types of higher-level semantic analysis is the forensic sense of semantic analysis after an incident. Such forensic semantic analysis deals with a propositional assumption to be investigated and the answer to the propositional assumption should be an epistemic reasoning result upon observed evidential and contextual cues. Considering the wide variety of semantics possibly implied in visual surveillance scenes, such forensic analysis requires appropriate reuse of observed evidential metadata generated from vision analytics, and mating it with additional high-level contextual knowledge. However, unlike domains that can solely rely on deterministic knowledge model, such contextual knowledge as well as vision analytic results suffered from *uncertainties*, *incompleteness* and *inconsistencies*. Therefore, forensic analysis of visual surveillance data essentially requires a flexible and powerful means of knowledge representation together with a proper uncertainty representation and handling formalism. To cope with this aspect, *extensional approaches* (aka. rule-based systems) are gaining gradually increasing attention. Extensional approaches treat knowledge as conditional rules that are labeled with uncertainty (Pearl, 1988) and logic programming is one that is used for modeling contextual rules. When it comes to uncertainty representation formalisms, there are number of formalisms such as Bilattice (Ginsberg, 1988), fuzzy set based fuzzy logic (Zadeh, 1965, 1973), Dempster Shafer belief theory (Shafer, 1976) and traditional probability based Bayesian approaches, etc. Therefore, for the proper choice

of uncertainty formalism, it is important to know their characteristics and behind philosophy on representing and handling uncertainty. Subjective logic (Jøsang, 2001) is also one such uncertainty representation and handling formalism that can be seen as extended theory derived from both the Dempster Shafer belief theory and second order Bayesian. From Dempster Shafer belief theory, subjective logic inherits the philosophy of explicit representation of ignorance about knowledge in a model called subjective opinion triangle that can be also mapped into beta distribution. The operators of subjective logic are also derived in the sense of Bayesian. Unlike traditional Dempster Shafer evidence fusion method, that is known to yield counter intuitive result when it is operated with highly contradictory evidences and also known to be inconsistent with Bayes' rule, subjective logic comes with similar opinion fusion operators that are robust even with such highly contradictory evidences (Jøsang, 1997). Compared with bilattice that mainly consists of two lattices, one representing degree of truth and the other representing degree of information respectively, the degree of information concept is similar to degree of ignorance in subjective opinion. The main difference between bilattice and subjective logic is the operators. While bilattice comes with four operators that are compositionally defined based on two lattice operators *meet* and *join* from the perspective of set theory, subjective logic comes with 12 operators defined rather in Bayesian sense. Another formidable uncertainty handling formalism, fuzzy logic is based on fuzzy set theory that relies on degree of membership concept for a knowledge segment and again this is similar to the concept of partial ignorance in subjective logic. Interestingly, it is known that some extensions of fuzzy logics can be modeled with (bi-)lattice structures. One thing worth to note concerning fuzzy logic is that, even though there are Zadeh's original logical operators, there are yet another ways of defining logical operators as well. However, due to this aspect, there is inconsistent between fuzzy logic operators and classical probability calculus, thereby often criticized by statisticians who prefer Bayesian (Zadeh, 2008). Thus, we advocate that above aspects make the use of subjective logic attractive as a means of representing and handling uncertainty for artificial reasoning.

In addition to uncertainty representation aspect, what is also important is the uncertainty handling in a way supporting nonmonotonic property. In reality, the truthness of a partial knowledge segment is often easy to be fragile, because there can be potentially possible contradictions or counter examples about the given knowledge segment. Due to this aspect, the property of retracting and updating existing beliefs upon acquisition of new information (aka. belief revision) is essential. Default reasoning introduced by Reiter (1980) is one such nonmonotonic reasoning method especially under contradictory knowledge segments. Default reasoning allows expressing a segment of knowledge as being *true by default* or *generally true,* but could be proven false upon arrival of new information. A discrete species of bilattice structure that represents multivalued default logic is one that is used to model default reasoning and demonstrated the usefulness on performing human identity maintenance and contextual reasoning of event in visual surveillance domain (Shet, Harwood, & Davis, 2006a, 2006b). As noted above, the degree of truth and the degree of information concepts in bilattice are similar to the ones in subjective logic. Focusing on the similarity, we examine subjective logic operators that have corresponding semantic behavior to the operators defined on bilattice framework. As mentioned above, what is also interesting is that some continuous species of bilattice structures are often used to represent two different species of fuzzy logic. Namely, intuitionistic (or interval-valued) fuzzy logic that can be modeled with so-called *triangle* bilattice and fuzzy Belnap logic (aka, fuzzified four-valued logic or fuzzy $\mathcal{FOUR}$) that can be also modeled with so-called square bilattice (Arieli, Cornelis, Deschrijver, & Kerre 2004). The relationship between these two fuzzy species of bilattice structures is studied in

the work of Corneli et al. (2003a, 2003b) and Arieli et al. (2004, 2005). Interestingly, the uncertainty representation in intuitionistic fuzzy logic (*triangle*) is very similar to that of the opinion triangle. Therefore, to verify the proposed subjective logic based default reasoning approach and to study its similarity and dissimilarity with fuzzy logics, we further extend the inference scheme defined on the discrete bilattice structure for the multivalued default logic onto the two continuous species of bilattice structures. To better verify and contrast the characteristics of the proposed approach, we present some illustrative case study examples in typical visual surveillance scenarios. We then compare the default reasoning results yielded from the proposed subjective logic based approach, bialttice for multivalued default logic, the intuitionistic fuzzy logic (*triangle*) and the fuzzy four-valued logic (*square*). We believe this way of comparison better position the subjective logic as a tool for artificial reasoning and also give us better insights on the correlations among different uncertainty formalisms. Namely, by the inherent nature of subjective logic, it gives a bridge between Dempster Shafer belief theory and Bayesian. Then by the comparison in this work on modeling default reasoning, it shows the bridge among subjective logic, fuzzy logics and bilattices as well.

The rest of the article is organized as follows. In the next section, we further review related work. Then we give a brief introduction to preliminaries that covers subjective logic, bilat- tice theory, and *L*-fuzzy logics such as interval-valued fuzzy logic, intuitionistic fuzzy logic and fuzzy Belnap logic. Given the preliminary background, we come up with an overview of default reasoning that covers the inference mechanism of bilattice based multivalued default logic. Next, we introduce our approach to modeling default reasoning using subjective logic, and we also present extensions of discrete multivalued default logic into its possible continuous species of bilattice based extensions of default logic that models *L*-fuzzy logics. For comparison and verification of the proposed inference mechanism, we present illustrative examples from the visual surveillance domain. The next section gives discussions on the two approaches and reviews the differences especially in terms of epistemic semantics and logical soundness and feasibility in terms of characteristics of visual surveillance. Finally, we conclude with summary of the work and future research directions.

RELATED WORK

As higher-level semantic analysis of visual surveillance data is gaining growing attention, the flexibility on knowledge representation and proper uncertainty handling mechanism is becoming more important. To address this aspect, there has been some work on the use of logic programming languages due to the expressive power and on the use of different uncertainty handling formalisms. In general, such approaches can be referred to as *'extensional approach'*. Extensional approaches also known as rule-based systems treat uncertainty as a generalized truth value attached to formulas and compute the uncertainty of any formula as a function of the uncertainties of its sub formulas (Pearl, 1988). Akdemir et al. (2008) used an ontology structure for activity analysis, but with no uncertainty handling mechanism. Shet et al. (2005) introduced a system that adopts Prolog based logic programming for higher-level situation reasoning in visual surveillance. The same authors adopted bilattice based multivalued default reasoning for identity maintenance of human detection results and context reasoning (Shet, Harwood, & Davis, 2006a, 2006b). Jianbing et al. (2009) adopted Dempster Shafer belief theory with the use of rule-based system for bus surveillance scenario. Anderson et al. (2007) adopted fuzzy logic to model and analyze human activity for video based eldercare scenario. Han et al. (2010a, 2010b) proposed the use of logic programming and subjective logic to encode contextual knowledge with uncertainty handling, and demonstrated

bidirectional conditional inference and reputation based uncertain rule modeling for forensic visual surveillance scenarios. While different uncertainty handling formalisms are introduced with logic programming based knowledge modeling, principled handling of default reasoning has been only demonstrated by the bilattice based approach (Shet, Harwood, & Davis, 2006a, 2006b).

When it comes to bilattice framework itself, it is known that some continuous species of bilattice structures that are called *triangle* and *square* correspond to intuitionistic fuzzy logic and fuzzy Belnap logic, respectively (Arieli, Cornelis, Deschrijver, & Kerre 2004). Naturally, there has been comparative study on the characteristics between intuitionistic fuzzy logic and fuzzy Belnap logic (Cornelis, Deschrijver, & Kerre, 2003b). Atanassov (2002) introduced a transformation between these two fuzzy logics and proved that the transformation is bijective. The use of square bilattice is demonstrated to improve human detection results by the use of rule-based reasoning given high false alarm rate and partial occlusion based output of different body parts based detectors (Shet, Neumann, Ramesh, & Davis, 2007) with the similar inference scheme shown in their previous work (Shet, Harwood & Davis, 2006a, 2006b). In this work, we show that the default reasoning behavior on multivalued default and square bilattice can be also modeled using subjective logic. Relying on the study of Atanassov (2002) and Cornelis et al. (2003a, 2003b) we also show the correspondence among subjective logic, intuitionistic fuzzy logic (*triangle*) and fuzzy Belnap logic (*square*).

PRELIMINARIES

This section gives an overview of the fundamental background about uncertainty representation and handling formalisms that will be discussed in this article in the view of default reasoning. The preliminaries will cover subjective logic theory, bilattice theory, and two extensions of fuzzy logics, namely, intuitionistic fuzzy logic and fuzzy Belnap logic.

Subjective Logic Theory

Jøsang (1997, 2001) introduced subjective logic as a framework for artificial reasoning. Unlike traditional binary logic or probabilistic logic (the former can only consider true or false, and the latter can consider degrees of truth or falseness), subjective logic explicitly represents the amount of 'lack of information (ignorance) on the degree of truth about a proposition' in a model called *subjective opinion* (Jøsang, 1997). The idea of explicit representation of ignorance is inherited from the Dempster Shafer belief theory (Jøsang, 1997) and the interpretation of an opinion in bayesian perspective is possible by mapping opinions inftо beta distributions (Jøsang, 2001). Subjective logic also comes with a rich set of operators for the manipulation of opinions. In addition to the standard logical operators, subjective logic provides some operators specific for Dempster Shafer belief theory such as consensus and recommendation. However, unlike Dempster Shafer's evidence fusion rule that is inconsistent with Bayes' rule, it provides an alternative consensus rule with a solid mathematical basis (Jøsang, 1997). It is also different from fuzzy logic: While fuzzy logic maps quantitative measure to non-crisp premises called fuzzy sets (e.g. *fast, slow, cold, hot,* etc.), subjective logic deals with the uncertain belief itself on a crisp premise (e.g. *intrusion happened, accident happened,* etc.). However, in the sense of interpretation, mapping of an opinion into the linguistic certainty fuzzy set (i.e., *very certainly true, less certainly true,* etc) is also possible. In general, subjective logic is suitable for modeling real situations under partial ignorance on a proposition's being true or false. Known application areas are trust network modeling, decision supporting, modeling and analyzing Bayesian network, etc. However, to the best of our knowledge, the ap-

plication of subjective logic in computer vision related domains has been limited to some work of Han et al. (2010a, 2010b), that demonstrated the capability of bidirectional interpretation of conditional rules using abduction and deduction operators and modeling uncertain rules relying on reputation operator in subjective logic. In this section, we will give a brief introduction to subjective logic theory.

Definition 1 (Opinion) (Jøsang, 2001): *Let* $\Theta = \{x, \bar{x}\}$ be a state space containing x and its complement $\bar{x}$. Let b_x, d_x, i_x represent the belief, disbelief and ignorance in the truth of x satisfying the equation: $b_x + d_x + i_x = 1$ and let a_x be the base rate of x in Θ. Then the opinion of an agent ag about x, denoted by ω_x^{ag}, is the tuple $\omega_x^{uy} = (b_x^{ag}, d_x^{ag}, i_x^{ag}, a_x^{ag})$.

Definition 2 (Probability Expectation) (Jøsang, 2001): *Let* $\omega_x^{ag} = (b_x^{ag}, d_x^{ag}, i_x^{ag}, a_x^{ag})$ be an opinion about the truth of x, then the probability expectation of ω_x^{ag} is defined by: $E(\omega_x^{ag}) = b_x^{ag} + a_x^{ag} i_x^{ag}$.

Opinions can be represented on a so called opinion triangle as shown in Figure 1. A point inside the triangle represents a (b_x, d_x, i_x) triple. The corner points marked with Belief, Disbelief and Ignorance represent the extreme cases, i.e., full belief $(1, 0, 0)$, full disbelief $(0, 0, 1)$ and no knowledge $(0, 0, 1)$. The base rate a_x represents the prior knowledge on the tendency of a given proposition $x's$ being true and can be indicated along the base line (the line connecting Belief and Disbelief). For example, in the case we toss a balanced coin with the proposition x as '*get head*', then we put $a_x = 1/2$ however, in the case of biased coin we could set different values. Usually, when we consider balanced binomial cases, the default value is $1/2$. The probability expectation E is then formed by projecting the opinion onto the base line, parallel to the base rate projector line (see the blue line) that is built by connecting the a_x point with the Ignorance corner (see the red line). An interesting property of subjective opinions is their direct mapping to beta distributions. Beta distributions are normally denoted as $Beta(\alpha, \beta)$, where α and β are its two parameters (α represents the number of positive observations and β represents amount of negative observations about a crisp proposition respectively). The Beta distribution of an opinion $\omega_x = (b_x, d_x, i_x, a_x)$ is the function $Beta(\alpha, \beta)$ where $\alpha = 2b_x / i_x + 2a_x$ and $\beta = 2d_x / i_x + 2(1 - a_x)$ (Jøsang, Daniel, & Vannoorenberghe, 2003). Figure 1, Example 1 shows an opinion about a proposition of an agent, that can be linguistically interpreted as '*seems likely and slightly uncertain true*', and Example 2 shows full ignorance (aka. '*vacous*' opinion) at the time of judgment about a proposition. Assuming base rate to be 0.7 in the example we get expectation value also to be 0.7 and the beta distribution appears biased towards '*true*' though the opinion represents full ignorance.

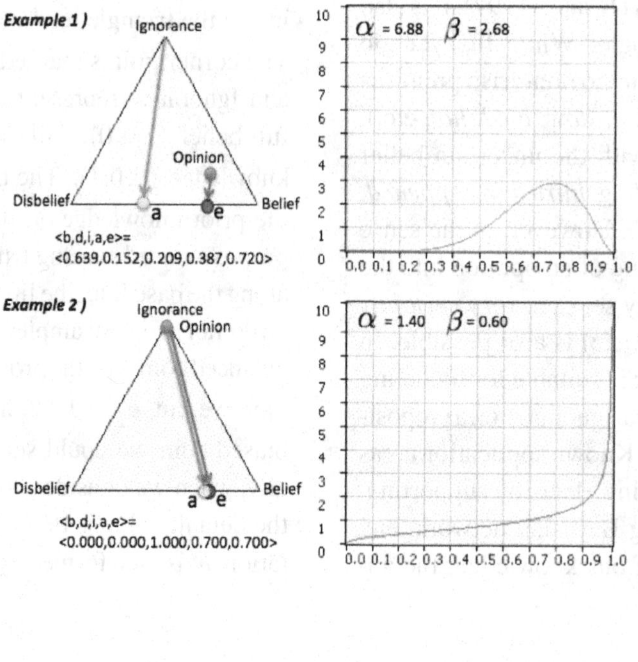

Bilattice Theory

Bilattices (Figure 2) are algebraic structures which are mainly built on top of the concept *poset* introduced by Ginsberg (1988) and elaborated by Fitting (1990). Ginsberg's formal definition of bilattice is as follows (Ginsberg, 1988).

Definition 3 (Partial Order): *A partial order is a binary relation* $\leq$ *over a set* S which is reflexive, antisymmetric and transitive, i.e., for all a, b and c in S, satisfies: a) $a \leq a$ (reflexive) b) if $a \leq b$ and $b \leq a$ then $a = b$ (antisymmetric) c) if $a \leq b$ and $b \leq c$ then $a \leq c$ (transitive).

Definition 4 (Poset): *A set* S *with a partial order* $(S, \leq)$ is called partially ordered set (or poset).

Definition 5 (Lattice): *A poset* L *with a partial order is a lattice* $(L, \leq, \wedge, \vee)$ if it satisfies the following two axioms: *a) for any two elements* a *and* b *of* L, *the set* $\{a, b\}$ *has a least upper bound* $\vee$ (join); *b) for any two elements* a *and* b *of* L, *the set* $\{a, b\}$ *has a greatest lower bound* $\wedge$ (meet).

Figure 1. Opinion triangle and beta distribution

Figure 2. Examples of lattice and bilattices: (a) a lattice, (b) bilattice corresponding to traditional binary logic, (c) bilattice corresponding to three-valued logic, (d) bilattice corresponding to Belnap's four-valued logic, $\mathcal{FOUR}$

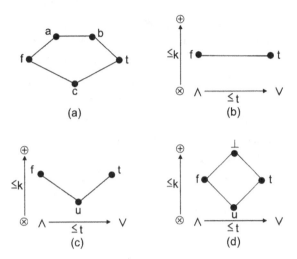

Definition 6 (Prebilattice): *A pre-bilattice is a structure $\mathcal{B} = (B, \leq_t, \leq_k)$, such that B is a nonempty set containing at least two elements, and $(B, \leq_t)$, $(B, \leq_k)$ are complete lattices (for which all subsets are also lattices).*

Definition 7 (Bilattice): *A bilattice is a structure $\mathcal{B} = (B, \leq_t, \leq_k, \neg)$, such that $(B, \leq_t, \leq_k)$ is a pre-bilattice, and $\neg$ is a unary operation on B that has the following properties: for every x, y in B*

a. if $x \leq_t y$ then $\neg x \geq_t \neg y$;

b. if $x \leq_k y$ then
$$U \simeq (0,0,1)_{sl} \simeq (0,0)_{\mathcal{L}} \simeq (0,0)_{\mathcal{L}^2},$$

c. $\neg\neg x = x$.

The name '*bi*' - lattice indicates that it is a structure consists of two lattices. Lattices are any *poset* that are possible to define *meet* $\wedge$ (aka. greatest lower bound) and *join* $\wedge$ (aka. least

upper bound) for any two elements in it. A partial order is a generalization of ordering, i.e., a binary relation $\leq$ over a set S which is *reflexive*, *antisymmetric* and *transitive*. Lattices are often expressed as a graph whose edges represent the binary relation of '*partial order*' between two elements that can be directly compared. There can be elements a and b in the lattice L for which an order between them cannot be determined. However, greatest lower bound *meet* $(a \wedge b)$ and the lowest upper bound *join* $(a \wedge b)$ can always be determined for any of two elements a and b in the lattice L. Namely, by considering two sets that contain elements that are greater than a and greater than b respectively, the lowest element which can be found in both of the sets is the meet (and join can be similarly defined). Figure 2 (a) shows a lattice that some elements in it, for example, a and c are incomparable but still has $a \wedge c = f$ and $a \vee c = t$. Conventionally in lattice theory, '1' represents the greatest elements and '0' is the lowest elements and therefore for any element a in a lattice L, $a \wedge 1 = a$, $a \vee 1 = 1$, $a \wedge 0 = 0$ and $a \vee 0 = a$. Bilattices provide semantics for reasoning by considering one lattice with partial order in terms of degree of truth $\leq_t$ and the other lattice with partial order in terms of degree of information $\leq_k$ (note that, the semantics of degree of information often can be seen as degree of specificity of the information as well). To avoid the confusion that would arise from using the same symbols *meet* $\wedge$ and *join* $\wedge$ for both the lattices, following Fitting (1990), we use the symbols *meet* $\otimes$ and *join* $\oplus$ for the lattice with partial order $\leq_k$. While the meaning of $\wedge$ and $\vee$ corresponds to the standard logical role of conjunction and disjunction, the meaning of $\otimes$ and $\oplus$ are less intuitive. Fitting (1990, 1994) named $\otimes$ as *consensus* operator in the sense that it derives the most degree of information agreed upon two operands. Likewise $\oplus$ is named as *gullibility* operator in the sense that it accepts any degree of information upon two operands. In bilattices, therefore, when the *gullibility* operator $\oplus$ is used, getting more information pushes the overall belief towards true or false with more degree of information except in case of contradiction. Figure 2 shows different bilattice structures that can model different logics.

L-Fuzzy Set Based Logics (Interval-Valued Fuzzy Logic, Intuitionistic Fuzzy Logic, Fuzzy Four-Valued Logic)

Since the introduction of fuzzy set theory and fuzzy logic (Zadeh, 1965, 1973), it became popular as formalism for representing imprecise or vague linguistic concepts (e.g. *hot, cold, fast*, etc.). The basic idea is to introduce a fuzzy membership function (conventionally denoted as μ) as a measure of vagueness to elements in a set and it is called fuzzy set. The membership functions are defined to map an element u in concerned universe to a value within the interval $[0,1]$ (i.e. $\mu(u) \to [0,1]$), thereby assigning exact value makes all elements in the fuzzy set to be ordered and comparable. Due to this aspect, there has been arguing that this makes them in adequate for dealing with incomparable uncertain information (Cornelis, Atanassov, & Kerre, 2003a). There have been some remedies for this aspect. Noting on the footnote comment of Zadeh (1965) saying "in a more general setting, the range of the membership function can be taken to be a suitable partially ordered set P" (p. 359). Goguen (1967) introduced L-fuzzy set that uses a membership function that maps an element u to a value in a lattice L (i.e. $\mu(u) \to L$). Interval based representation of degree of membership is also introduced with the name of interval-valued fuzzy sets (IVFSs) (Gehrke, Walker, & Walker, 1996). In IVFSs, an element x is mapped into a subinterval within $[0,1]$ (i.e. $\mu(u) \to (x_l, x_u) \in [0,1]^2, x_l \leq x_u$). Intuitionistic

fuzzy set theory (IFSs, for short) introduced by Atanassov (1986) additionally adopts a non membership function ν, with a weaker constraint $\nu \leq 1 - \mu$ (note that, in the sense of Zadeh's original fuzzy set the ν is implicitly assumed to be $\nu = 1 - \mu$). Naturally, the so-called amount of indeterminacy or missing information can be defined by the value $\pi = 1 - \nu - \mu$. By dropping the constraint $\mu + \nu \leq 1$ and introducing even weaker constraint $\mu + \nu \leq 2$, we get fuzzy Belnap set. Unlike IVFSs that requires one to address values to be $x_l \leq x_u$ as lower bound and upper bound of imprecision, IFSs allows one to address the positive and the negative side of an imprecise concept separately. Cornelis et al. (2004), however, showed that IVFSs can also be represented in the form of IFSs, in other words the two are isomorphic and the truth values in IFSs can be represented as intervals (e.g. by the mapping $f(x_l, x_u) = (x_l, 1 - x_u)$). As traditional fuzzy set is used for fuzzy logic as a measure of uncertainty on a proposition p, IVFSs, IFSs and fuzzy Belnap set are adopted for interval-valued fuzzy logic (IVFL, for short), intuitionistic fuzzy logic (IFL, for short) and the fuzzy Belnap logic (aka. Fuzzified four-valued logic, $\mathcal{FOUR}$). Following Goguen (1967), IVFL and IFL (Figure 3) can be defined on '*triangle*' species of lattices denoted $\mathcal{L}^I$ and $\mathcal{L}^*$ respectively. Fuzzy Belnap logic can be defined on the '*square*' lattice denoted $\mathcal{L}_\square$. Therefore, IVFSs, IFSs and Fuzzy Belnap logics are kind of L-fuzzy logic. The formal definition of these '*square*' and *triangle*' are as follows (Arieli, Cornelis, Deschrijver, & Kerre, 2005; Cornelis, Deschrijver, & Kerre, 2003b; Fitting, 1990).

Definition 8 ($\mathcal{L}_\square$ Square lattice for fuzzy Belnap logic): $\mathcal{L}_\square = (L_\square, \leq_\square)$, *where* $L_\square = [0,1]^2$ *and* $(x_1, x_2) \leq_\square (y_1, y_2)$ *iff* $x_1 \leq y_1$ *and* $x_2 \geq y_2$.

Figure 3. Lattices: (a) $\mathcal{L}^*$ triangle corresponding to intuitionistic fuzzy logic (and also can be seen as $\mathcal{L}^I$ triangle for interval-valued fuzzy logic), and (b) $\mathcal{L}_\square$ square corresponding to fuzzy Belnap logic

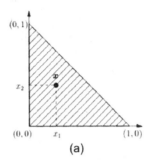 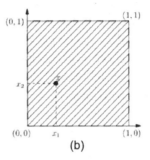

(a)   (b)

Definition 9 ($\mathcal{L}^*$ Triangle lattice for IFSs):

$$\mathcal{L}^* = (L^*, \leq_{L^*}), \text{ where } \begin{array}{l} L^* = \{(x_1, x_2) \in \\ [0,1]^2 \mid x_1 + x_2 \leq 1\} \end{array}$$

and $(x_1, x_2) \leq_{L^*} (y_1, y_2)$ iff $x_1 \leq y_1$ and $x_2 \geq y_2$.

Definition 10 ($\mathcal{L}^I$ Triangle lattice for IVFSs):

$\mathcal{L}^I = (L^I, \leq_{L^I})$, where

$L^I = \{[x_1, x_2] \mid (x_1, x_2) \in [0,1]^2, x_1 \leq x_2\}$

and $[x_1, x_2] \leq_{L^I} [y_1, y_2]$ iff $x_1 \leq y_1$ and $x_2 \leq y_2$.

Figure 3 shows the corresponding graphical interpretation of IFL and fuzzy Belnap logic. As it was shown in Figure 2 (c) and (d), they correspond to continuous extension of three valued logic and Belnap logic (Figure 3 (a) and (b), respectively). In epistemic sense, the values $(0,0)$ corresponds to *unknown*, $(1,0)$ corresponds to *true*, $(0,1)$ corresponds to *false* and $(1,1)$ corresponds to *contradiction*. In IFL and IVFL, however, the explicit *contradiction* state is not allowed.

DEFAULT REASONING

Defaults (default assumptions) are statements that can be interpreted as normally, typically, generally true or false as a rule. Contrary to defaults, statements that express explicit truth or falsity are called definite rules. In practice, the need to make default assumptions often occurs in cases where the information at hand is uncertain, incomplete and potentially contradictory. Default reasoning attempts to draw plausible conclusions based on known defaults and definite rules. Therefore, in default reasoning, conclusions can be changed upon acquisition of new information (i.e., *non-monotonicity*). In logic, Reiter (1980) formalized such reasoning aspects as default logic theory using default rules. In the following we give a brief overview on how rules are expressed in logic programming and a brief introduction to default logic.

Logic Programming

Logic programming mainly consists of two types of logical formulae, rules and facts, Rules are of the form $'A \leftarrow f_1, f_2, ..., f_m'$ where A is rule head and the right hand side is called body. Each f_i is an atom and ',' represents logical conjunction. Each atom is of the form $'p(t_1, t_2, ..., t_n)'$, where t_i is a term and p is a predicate symbol of arity n. Terms could either be variables or constant symbols. Rules of the form $'f \leftarrow'$ (denoted by just $'f'$) is called facts and can serve as an atom when used in a rule body. Negation is represented with the symbol $'\neg'$ such that $'\neg\neg A = A'$. Both positive and negative atoms are referenced to as literals. Given a rule $'head \leftarrow body'$, we interpret the meaning as $'IF\ body\ THEN\ head'$. Traditionally, a resolved set of facts that matches to a rule is called *extension*. In logic programming language based visual surveillance applications as the one mentioned in the related work section, rules have been used to define and reason about various contextual events or activities.

Default Logic

This section describes Reiter's formalization of default logic and an example of default reasoning in visual surveillance.

Definition 11 (Default Theory) (Reiter, 1980):
Let $\Delta = (D, W)$ be a default theory, where W is a set of logical formulae (rules and facts) also known as the definite rules and D is a set of default rules of the form $\dfrac{\alpha : \beta}{\gamma}$, where α is known as the precondition, β is known as the justification and γ is known as the conclusion.

Any default rule $dr \in D$ can be also written as $'\gamma \leftarrow \alpha_1, not(\neg\beta)'$, where not means the negation by failure to prove. The interpretation of such rule is that, if the precondition α is known to be true, and if there were no explicit violations of the justification (facts and rules that entails $\neg\beta$) then it is possible to derive the conclusion γ.

Figure 4. Illustrative scenario setup of example 1

Example 1: Assume a scene as depicted in Figure 4 with two cameras observing the upper and lower parts of an escalator respectively. The scene also shows stairs next to the escalator. Consider the following set of rules:

$\neg escalator\_working(T) \leftarrow people\_take\_stairs(T),$
$not(escalator\_blocked(T))$
$escalator\_working(T) \leftarrow crowd\_at\_stairs(T)$

$where,\quad \neg escalator\_working(T) \in D$
$and\quad\quad escalator\_blocked(T) \in W$

Assume that Cam1 continuously observes that people appear to be using the stairs and generates a set of facts as $\{people\_take\_stairs(T_1)\}_{Cam1}$. Based on the current set of facts and rules, by default, the rule $\neg escalator\_working(T_1)$ is satisfied because we can not explicitly prove $escalator\_blocked(T_1)$. However, at a later time we observe a crowd in front of the escalator and as soon as of Cam2 generates a set of facts $\{crowd\_at\_entrance(T_2)\}_{Cam2}$ from its observations, then, the proposition $\neg escalator\_working(T_2)$ is no longer supported and is withdrawn.

Bilattice Based Multivalued Default Logic

Ginsberg (1988) showed the use of bilattice structure to model default reasoning aspect and

extended the structure to generalized default reasoning framework called multivalued default logic (aka. prioritized default logic) for artificial reasoning. Ginsberg's bilattice structures also inherits the behind philosophy of Belnap logic in the sense that they also adopt the epistemic states *unknown* and *contradictory*. To distinguish definite truth and default truth value, default truth values assumed to have different amount of truth and different amount of information are also introduced. Figure 5 shows Belnap logic that has no default truth values, default logic and multivalued default logic respectively. Based on this truth value setup and the four bilattice operators, each bilattice operator can be seen as a truth functional binary operator on those values. Figure 6 shows (a) the truth table of Belnap logic that has no defaults and (b) default logic that has default true and default false as epistemic states. Based on the truth functional binary operators, inference on the bilattice framework is defined in terms of truth assignment and closure as follows (Ginsberg, 1988).

Definition 12 (Truth Assignment): *Given a declarative language L and a Bilattice $\mathcal{B}$, a truth assignment is a function $\phi : L \to \mathcal{B}$.*

Definition 13 (Truth Assignment): *Given a knowledge base $\mathcal{K}$ in form of declarative language and a truth assignment labeling each sentence $k \in \mathcal{K}$ with a truth value and a Bilattice $\mathcal{B}$, then the closure ϕ of a given*

query sentence q denoted $cl(\phi)(q)$ is the truth assignment function such that:

$$cl(\phi)(q) : \{p, p' \mid \forall S, S' \subseteq \mathcal{K}, S \vDash q, S' \vDash \neg q, p \in S, p' \in S'\} \to \mathcal{B}$$

In other words, the implication of $cl(\phi)(q)$ is a functional mapping from the '*enumeration of all sentences*' that can entail (denoted by the symbol '$\vDash$') q and its contradictory information $\neg q$ to a '*truth value in bilattice $\mathcal{B}$*'. For example, if ϕ labels sentences $\{p, q \leftarrow p\} \in \mathcal{K}$ as true; i.e., $\phi(p) = T$ and $\phi(q \leftarrow p) = T$, then $cl(\phi)$ should also label q as true as it is information entailed by $\mathcal{K}$.

Definition 14 (Default Inference): *Given a query sentence q and given S and S' that are sets of sentences such that $S \vDash q$ and $S' \vDash q$, then the default inference is the truth value assignment closure $cl(\phi)(q)$ given by:*

$$cl_{di}(\phi)(q) = \bigoplus_{S \vDash q} u \vee [\bigwedge_{p \in S} cl(\phi)(p)] \oplus \neg \bigoplus_{S' \vDash \neg q} u \vee [\bigwedge_{p \in S'} cl(\phi)(p)]$$

(1)

Informally, Equation 1 states that for n sets of sentences S that entails q, we first collect the lowest upper bound ('$\wedge$') that every sentence in S_i can agree on, then take it if the result contains more truth than u (unknown) along the partial order $\leq_t$. For each of these truth values of S_i, we evaluate the amount of information and choose

Figure 5. (a) Belnap logic, (b) default logic, (c) multivalued (prioritized) default logic

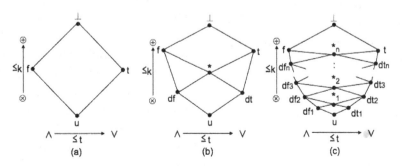

Figure 6. Truth table of Bilattice operators on: (a) Belnap logic, (b) default logic

(a)

∧	⊥	T	F	U
⊥	⊥	⊥	F	F
T	⊥	T	F	U
F	F	F	F	F
U	F	U	F	U

∨	⊥	T	F	U
⊥	⊥	T	⊥	T
T	T	T	T	T
F	⊥	T	F	U
U	T	T	U	U

⊗	⊥	T	F	U
⊥	⊥	T	F	U
T	T	T	U	U
F	F	U	F	U
U	U	U	U	U

⊕	⊥	T	F	U
⊥	⊥	⊥	⊥	⊥
T	⊥	T	⊥	T
F	⊥	⊥	F	F
U	⊥	T	F	U

(b)

∧	⊥	T	F	*	DT	DF	U
⊥	⊥	⊥	F	F	F	F	F
T	⊥	T	F	*	DT	DF	U
F	F	F	F	F	F	F	F
*	F	*	F	*	*	DF	DF
DT	F	DT	F	*	DT	DF	U
DF	F	DF	F	DF	DF	DF	DF
U	F	U	F	DF	U	DF	U

∨	⊥	T	F	*	DT	DF	U
⊥	⊥	T	⊥	T	T	T	T
T	T	T	T	T	T	T	T
F	⊥	T	F	*	DT	DF	U
*	T	T	*	DT	*	DT	* DT
DT	T	T	DT	DT	DT	DT	DT
DF	T	T	DF	*	DT	DF	U
U	T	T	U	DT	DT	U	U

⊗	⊥	T	F	*	DT	DF	U
⊥	⊥	T	F	*	DT	DF	U
T	T	T	*	*	DT	DF	U
F	F	*	F	*	DT	DF	U
*	*	*	*	*	DT	DF	U
DT	DT	DT	DT	DT	DT	U	U
DF	DF	DF	DF	DF	U	DF	U
U	U	U	U	U	U	U	U

⊕	⊥	T	F	*	DT	DF	U
⊥	⊥	⊥	⊥	⊥	⊥	⊥	⊥
T	⊥	T	⊥	T	T	T	T
F	⊥	⊥	F	F	F	F	F
*	⊥	T	F	*	*	*	*
DT	⊥	T	F	*	DT	*	DT
DF	⊥	T	F	*	*	DF	DF
U	⊥	T	F	*	DT	DF	U

the most informative (certain or specific) one among them using greatest lower bound ('⊕') along the partial order $\leq_k$. We do the same process for all S_i' and by understanding the result from S' as contradictory hypothesis, we again collect the most informative one and apply the negation operation. Finally, both resulting intermediate values for S_i and S_i' are joined along the partial order $\leq_k$ again using greatest lower bound ('⊕').

DEFAULT REASONING USING SUBJECTIVE LOGIC

This section describes an inference mechanism for default reasoning using subjective logic. We will discuss how multiple logical values (i.e., default and definite truth values) can be modeled in subjective logic's opinion space. Thereafter, we propose an approach to modeling default reasoning based on subjective logic operators by analyzing the default reasoning mechanism on bilattice and identifying corresponding and analogous behaviour.

Mapping Multi-Logic-Values into Opinion Space

We first note that the implications of $\leq_t$ and $\leq_k$ in bilattice are similar to the concept of truth and ignorance in subjective opinion space when visualized in the opinion triangle. As shown in Figure 5 (b) and (c), d_{tn} and d_{fn} indicate different levels of incomplete truth or falsity. The more certain and specific knowledge is obtained, the higher level of default values result. The degree of certainty or specificity can be considered as degree of information, therefore, the levels of default values can be ordered along the partial order *where*, $DT_1 \simeq (0.5, 0, 0.5)$ *and* $DT_2 \simeq (0.8, 0, 0.2)$ Along the information order $\leq_k$, for each pair of d_{tn} and d_{fn} there exist corresponding undecidible states $*_n$. As shown in Figure 5 (b) and (c), $*_n$ are assumed to have more information than their corresponding d_{tn} and d_{fn}. Unknown state U is one of the undecidible states with zero degree of information. Similarly, the full contradictory state ⊥, that can be reached via definite true (full belief) and definite false (full disbelief), is also one of the undecidible states with maximum degree of information. In the sense of degree of information, however, assigning even higher degree of information than definite true or false to the full contradiction point ⊥ is an interesting aspect to discuss. When considering the result of fusing definite truth and definite false, the definitions in bilattice and subjective logic indicate slightly different views: In bilattice, the interpretation is that there is an overspecification in the system indicated by the full contradiction point $\perp$. In subjective logic, such a contradictory point $\perp$ having even more information than definite true or false is not allowed by its nature. The interpretation is rather that the result should again have full degree of information. To distinguish this slight difference we will denote the maximum undecidible point (namely, full contradictory point) in bilattice as $\perp_{bl}$ and $\perp_{sl}$ for subjective logic (henceforth, the subscripts $_{bl}$ and $_{sl}$ denote bilattice and subjective logic respectively). Except the full contradictory point, the rest of the undecidible states $*_n$ can be defined in the opinion triangle as of bilattice. Additionally, such $*_n$ should be able to reach via an operation as of *join* operator $\oplus_{bl}$ in bilattice on the partial order $\leq_k$. This aspect can be modeled with subjective logic consensus operator $\oplus_{sl}$ (Definition 17). By definition, when d_{tn} and d_{fn} (having the same level of ignorance) are fused with the consensus operator $\oplus_{sl}$, it always yields an opinion in the middle of opinion triangle with less ignorance. The only exception to this is the case of fusing definite true and definite false that yields an opinion in the middle between definite true and definite false again with no ignorance. For example, if we consider a tiny amount of ignorance ε and take $(1-\varepsilon, 0, \varepsilon) = t'$ and $(0, 1-\varepsilon, \varepsilon) = f'$ as any default true or default false, then fusing t' and f' in terms of degree of information in subjective logic $t' \oplus_{sl} f' = *'$ will always draw the values with less ignorance $\varepsilon' < \varepsilon$ (see definition of i in the case of $k \neq 0$ in Definition 17). This behavior is exactly the same as what bilattice based default structures capture, thus, in the sense of ordering along $\leq_k$, $t' \leq_k *'$ and $f' \leq_k *'$.

The only exception to this is when definite true and false are fused namely, $t \oplus_{sl} f = \perp_{sl}$ (Definition 17). This means that only for this single point there is no exact correspondence but rather an approximate correspondence. Consequently this point in the opinion triangle is denoted as $\perp_{sl}$ as depicted in Figure 7 (a). Figure 7 (a) depicts that the correspondence of the bilattice used for Belnap logic, $\mathcal{FOUR}$ and the opinion triangle by mapping $t_{bl} \simeq t_{sl} = (1,0,0)$, $f_{bl} \simeq f_{sl} = (0,1,0)$, $u_{bl} \simeq i_{sl} = (0,0,1)$ and $\perp_{bl} \simeq \perp_{sl} = (0.5, 0.5, 0)$. For the default values, following the discussion above and nontheless values in bilattice are elements of a finite set and the opinion triangle is of continuous domain, we could pick points along the side edges of the opinion triangle. Figure 6 (b) shows this mapping of default true and default false to the opinion triangle. In the same manner, we can extend such mapping to the generalized multivalued default logic in which each of the defaults can be considered with different priority levels as shown in Figure 7 (c).

Default Inference Using Subjective Logic Operators

Now, bearing in mind the default inference mechanism defined on bilattice (Equation 1), we examined subjective logic operators corresponding to $\wedge_{bl}$, $\vee_{bl}$, $\otimes_{bl}$ and $\oplus_{bl}$. Concerning the semantic interpretation of $\wedge_{bl}$ and $\vee_{bl}$ representing the standard logical role of *conjunction* and *disjunction*, subjective logic *conjunction* $(\cdot_{sl})$ and *disjunction* $(\sqcup_{sl})$ operators are examined. For the $\otimes_{bl}$ and $\oplus_{bl}$ operators representing *consensus* and *gullibility*, subjective logic *consensus* $\oplus_{sl}$ and *addition* $+_{sl}$ operators are examined. Figure 8 shows the examination results about the correspondence between each of semantically corresponding operator pairs. Interestingly, the interpretation of *consensus* operator $\otimes_{bl}$ does not

Figure 7. (a)The bilattice and opinion triangle space for Belnap $\mathcal{FOUR}$, (b) the bilattice and opinion triangle space for default logic, (c) the bilattice and opinion triangle space for multivalued default logic

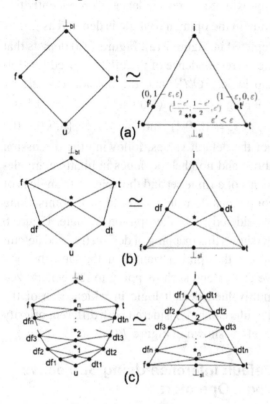

match to the *consensus* $\oplus_{sl}$ in subjective logic. Rather, *consensus* $\oplus_{sl}$ exhibits characteristics corresponding to the *gullibility* operator ($\oplus_{bl}$) in bilattice. The subjective logic *addition* operator $+_{sl}$ showed completely different truth table compared to both the $\oplus_{bl}$ and the $\otimes_{bl}$. This is because the operator

$$cl_{bl_{di}}(\phi)(theft(P,B,T))$$
$$= [U \vee (T \wedge T \wedge T \wedge T \wedge DT_1)]$$
$$\quad \oplus \neg[U \vee (T \wedge T \wedge T \wedge T \wedge T \wedge T \wedge DT_2)]$$
$$= [U \vee DT_1] \oplus \neg[U \vee DT_2]$$
$$= DT_1 \oplus \neg DT_2$$
$$= DT_1 \oplus DF_2$$
$$= DF_2$$

is about adding any beliefs, subtracting any disbelief and averaging ignorance from both the operands. Thereby, it tends to force rapid change of belief towards truth direction. The operator $\otimes_{bl}$ seems not to have any corresponding operator in subjective logic. In Figure 8, the black points represent that those values are identical to the ones in bilattice space. Contrary, the red points indicate that the values are slightly different from the ones in bilattice space. This is due to the difference that the bilattice operators are defined on a discrete set and the operators in subjective logic are defined on continuous space. However, the semantics of the corresponding operators are the same as it is explained below.

Definition 15 (Conjunction $cl^F_{\mathcal{I}^*(\mathcal{L})}$) (Jøsang, 2004): *Let* Θ_X *and* Θ_Y *be two frames and let* x *and* y *be propositions about state in* Θ_X *and* Θ_Y *respectively. Let* $\omega_x = (b_x, d_x, i_x, a_x)$ *and* $\omega_y = (b_y, d_y, i_y, a_y)$ *be an agent's opinions about* x *and* y, *then conjunctive opinion denoted as* $\omega_x \cdot \omega_y$ *is* $\omega_{x \wedge y} = (b_{x \wedge y}, d_{x \wedge y}, i_{x \wedge y}, a_{x \wedge y})$ *such that:*

$$
\begin{cases}
b_{x \wedge y} = b_x b_y + \dfrac{(1-a_x)a_y b_x i_y + a_x(1-a_y)i_x b_y}{1 - a_x a_y} \\
d_{x \wedge y} = d_x + d_y - d_x d_y \\
i_{x \wedge y} = i_x i_y + \dfrac{(1-a_y)b_x i_y + (1-a_x)i_x b_y}{1 - a_x a_y} \\
a_{x \wedge y} = a_x a_y
\end{cases}
$$

Definition 16 (Disjunction

$$cl^F_{\mathcal{I}^*(\mathcal{L})}(cl^{drastic}_{\mathcal{L}^2_{di}}(\phi)(theft(P,B,T)))$$
$$= cl^F_{\mathcal{I}^*(\mathcal{L})}((0.5, 0.8)) = (0.3, 0.49) = DF'_1$$
$$cl^G_{\mathcal{I}^*(\mathcal{L})}(cl^{drastic}_{\mathcal{L}^2_{di}}(\phi)(theft(P,B,T)))$$
$$= cl^G_{\mathcal{I}^*(\mathcal{L})}((0.5, 0.8)) = (0.25, 0.55) = DF'_1)$$

(Jøsang, 2004): *Let* Θ_X *and* Θ_Y *be two frames and let* x *and* y *be propositions about state in and* Θ_Y *respectively. Let* $\omega_x = (b_x, d_x, i_x, a_x)$ *and*

Figure 8. Comparison of operators used in $cl(\phi)$ shown in Equation (1) (black - exact match and red - slight different match)

$\wedge_{bl}$	⊥	T	F	*	DT	DF	U
⊥	⊥	⊥	F	F	F	F	F
T	⊥	T	F	*	DT	DF	U
F	F	F	F	F	F	F	F
*	F	*	F	*	*	DF	DF
DT	F	DT	F	*	DT	DF	U
DF	F	DF	F	DF	DF	DF	DF
U	F	U	F	DF	U	DF	U

$\vee_{bl}$	⊥	T	F	*	DT	DF	U
⊥	⊥	T	⊥	T	T	T	T
T	T	T	T	T	T	T	T
F	⊥	T	F	*	DT	DF	U
*	T	T	*	*	DT	*	DT
DT	T	T	DT	DT	DT	DT	DT
DF	T	T	DF	*	DT	DF	U
U	T	T	U	DT	DT	U	U

$\oplus_{bl}$	⊥	T	F	*	DT	DF	U
⊥	⊥	⊥	⊥	⊥	⊥	⊥	⊥
T	⊥	T	⊥	T	T	T	T
F	⊥	⊥	F	F	F	F	F
*	⊥	T	F	*	*	*	*
DT	⊥	T	F	*	DT	*	DT
DF	⊥	T	F	*	*	DF	DF
U	⊥	T	F	*	DT	DF	U

(Adjacent to each operator table, triangle-diagram illustrations labeled $\bullet_{sl}$, $\sqcup_{sl}$, and $\oplus_{sl}$ are shown.)

$\wedge_{bl}$ ($\vee_{bl}$) should pick the greatest upper bound (lowest upper bound) element of given two operands. This forces, for example, $T \wedge_{bl} DT$ ($F \vee_{bl} DF$) to be DT (DF). However, if we were not restricted by discrete set of values, as is the case in subjective logic, we would expect values in between T and DT (F and DF) in a sense that the conjunction (disjunction) operation are interpreted as intersection (union) of both belief values. This aspect is mainly captured by the definition of $b_{x \wedge y}$ ($b_{x \vee y}$). The amount of ignorance is also captured by $i_{x \wedge y}$ ($i_{x \vee y}$) so that it can consider both ignorance values of given two belief values. This aspect is the main source where the differences of the truth table come from in Figure 8. Thus, considering the semantics of conjunction and disjunction, subjective logic's conjunction and disjunction operators model the meaning of the operators under partial ignorance correctly, but with an additional aspect that is only meaningful in a continuous space.

Definition 17 (Consensus $\oplus_s$) (Jøsang, 2006): *Let* $\omega_x^A = (b_x^A, d_x^A, i_x^A, a_x^A)$ *and* $\omega_x^B = (b_x^B, d_x^B, i_x^B, a_x^B)$ *be opinions respectively held by agents* A *and* B *about the same state* x, *and let* $k = i_x^A + i_x^B - i_x^A i_x^B$. *When* $i_x^A, i_x^B \to 0$, *the relative dogmatism between* ω_x^A *and* ω_x^B *is defined by* γ *so that* $\gamma = i_x^B / i_x^A$. *Let* $\omega_x^{A,B} = (b_x^{A,B}, d_x^{A,B}, i_x^{A,B}, a_x^{A,B})$ *be the opinion such that:*

$$k \neq 0: \begin{cases} b_x^{A,B} = (b_x^A i_x^B + b_x^B i_x^A) / k \\ d_x^{A,B} = (d_x^A i_x^B + d_x^B i_x^A) / k \\ i_x^{A,B} = (i_x^A i_x^B) / k \\ a_x^{A,B} = \dfrac{a_x^A i_x^A + a_x^B i_x^B - (a_x^A + a_x^B) i_x^A i_x^B}{i_x^A + i_x^B - 2 i_x^A i_x^B} \end{cases}$$

$\omega_y = (b_y, d_y, i_y, a_y)$ be an agent's opinions about x and y, then disjunctive opinion denoted as $\omega_x \sqcup \omega_y$ is $\omega_{x \vee y} = (b_{x \vee y}, d_{x \vee y}, i_{x \vee y}, a_{x \vee y})$ such that:

$$\begin{cases} b_{x \vee y} = b_x + b_y - b_x b_y \\ d_{x \vee y} = d_x d_y + \dfrac{a_x (1 - a_y) d_x i_y + (1 - a_x) a_y i_x d_y}{a_x + a_y - a_x a_y} \\ i_{x \vee y} = i_x i_y + \dfrac{a_y d_x i_y + a_x i_x d_y}{a_x + a_y - a_x a_y} \\ a_{x \vee y} = a_x + a_y - a_x a_y \end{cases}$$

The truth functional table of logical conjunction (disjunction) in discrete space should be a function that is closed to its discrete set of truth values. Therefore, considering the interpretation of conjunction (disjunction), the binary operator

$$k = 0 : \begin{cases} b_x^{A,B} = \dfrac{\gamma b_x^A + b_x^B}{\gamma + 1} \\[2mm] d_x^{A,B} = \dfrac{\gamma d_x^A + d_x^B}{\gamma + 1} \\[2mm] i_x^{A,B} = 0 \\[2mm] a_x^{A,B} = \dfrac{\gamma a_x^A + a_x^B}{\gamma + 1} \end{cases}$$

Then $\omega_x^{A,B}$ is called the consensus opinion between ω_x^A and ω_x^B, representing an imaginary agent $[A, B]$'s opinion about x, as if that agent represented both A and B. By using the symbol $\oplus$ to designate this operator, we define $\omega_x^{A,B} = \omega_x^A \oplus \omega_x^B$.

Similarly to conjunction and disjunction, the operator $\oplus_{bl}$ is also defined to pick a value among the given discrete set of values. The selection is done in the sense that it chooses any information that can be accepted upon both the operands. In subjective logic, the consensus operator $\oplus_{sl}$ sees each of operands as one that have observed continuous amount of positive and negative evidence, thereby, summing up both the observations into one opinion. This is similar to interpreting the semantics of consensus from a bayesian perspective and it will increase the amount of information but cannot be restricted to be a discrete value. This aspect is captured by the definition of $i_x^{A,B}$ except in the case of dogmatic opinions having no ignorance. Therefore, the meaning of $\oplus_{bl}$ is modeled also in the sense of partial order $\leq_k$ in bilattice, i.e., that the derived value of given two operands should have more information (less ignorance in subjective logic). Thus, $\oplus_{sl}$ operator in subjective logic models fusing uncertain beliefs in a way that it increases the degree of information.

Based on the consideration about the semantics of operators shown above, we now defined the truth assignment and closure operation for default reasoning using subjective logic.

Definition 18 (Truth Assignment $_{sl}$) : *Given a declarative language* L *and Subjective Opinion Space* O, *a truth assignment is a function* $\phi_{sl} : L \rightarrow O$.

Definition 19 (Closure $_{sl}$) : *Given a knowledge base* $\mathcal{K}$ *in form of declarative language and a truth assignment labeling each sentence* $k \in \mathcal{K}$ *with a truth value and Subjective Opinion Space* O, *then* $cl_{sl}(\phi)(q)$, *the closure* ϕ *of a given query sentence* q, *is the truth assignment function such that:*

$$cl_{sl}(\phi)(q) : \{p, p' \mid \forall S, S' \subseteq \mathcal{K}, S \vDash q,$$
$$S' \vDash \neg q, p \in S, p' \in S'\} \rightarrow O.$$

Definition 20 (Default Inference $_{sl}$) : *Given a query sentence* q *and given* S *and* S' *that are sets of sentences such that* $S \vDash q$ *and* $S' \vDash \neg q$, *then the default inference is the truth value assignment closure* $cl_{sl_{di}}(\phi)(q)$ *given by:*

$$cl_{sl_{di}}(\phi)(q) = \bigoplus_{S \vDash q} u \sqcup [\prod_{p \in S} c\, l_{sl}(\phi)(p)]$$
$$\oplus \neg \bigoplus_{S' \vDash \neg q} u \sqcup [\prod_{p \in S'} c\, l_{sl}(\phi)(p)] \qquad (2)$$

DEFAULT REASONING USING L-FUZZY LOGICS

In this section, as it was done for subjective logic, we extend the discrete bilattice based multivalued default logic to L-fuzzy logics in continuous space. We then describe some properties of L-fuzzy logic representations on bilattice structure and review the possibility of enabling default reasoning. In the preliminaries section, we have considered IVFL, IFL and fuzzy Belnap logic in terms of truth value order ($\leq_t$). However, as we have examined in the previous section, the operators (especially, $\oplus_{bl}$) on degree of information ($\leq_k$) play an important role to model default reasoning aspect as to the case of discrete species bilattice of multivalued default logic. There has been some work on representing IVFSs, IFSs and Fuzzy Belnap using bilattice. Following is the definitions of '*triangle*' and '*square*' in the context of bilattice. Arieli et al. (2005) introduced the following definitions of '*square*' bilattice for fuzzy-belnap logic and '*triangle*' bilattice for IVFL.

Definition 21 ($\mathcal{L}^2$ Square bilattice): *Let* $\mathcal{L} = (L, \leq_L)$ be a complete lattice. A (bilattice-based) square is a structure $\mathcal{L}^2 = (L \times L, \leq_t, \leq_k, \neg)$, where

$$\neg(x_1, x_2) = (x_2, x_1), \quad \text{and} \quad (a)$$
$$(x_1, x_2) \leq_t (y_1, y_2) \Leftrightarrow x_1 \leq_L y_1 \text{ and } x_2 >_L y_2 ; \quad (b)$$
$$(x_1, x_2) \leq_k (y_1, y_2) \Leftrightarrow x_1 \leq_L y_1 \text{ and } x_2 \leq_L y_2 .$$

When we set $L = [0,1]$, this captures the Atanassov's idea on intuitionistic fuzzy sets in the sense that it distinguishes between membership function μ and a non-membership ν, but without imposing the restriction $\mu + \nu \leq 1$. Denoting the join and meet operations of the complete lattice $\mathcal{L}$ by $\wedge_L$ and $\vee_L$, the following four operators are defined for (x_1, x_2), (y_1, y_2) in L^2,

$$(x_1, x_2) \wedge (y_1, y_2) = (x_1 \wedge_L y_1, x_2 \vee_L y_2)$$
$$(x_1, x_2) \vee (y_1, y_2) = (x_1 \vee_L y_1, x_2 \wedge_L y_2)$$
$$(x_1, x_2) \otimes (y_1, y_2) = (x_1 \wedge_L y_1, x_2 \wedge_L y_2) \quad (3)$$
$$(x_1, x_2) \oplus (y_1, y_2) = (x_1 \vee_L y_1, x_2 \vee_L y_2)$$

The $\wedge_L$ and $\vee_L$ can be defined by a *t-norm* and a *t-conorm* in the sense that they generalize intersection and union in lattice space that can be seen as a metric space that satisfies triangle inequity. (note that, a *t-norm* is a function $\mathcal{T} : [0,1] \times [0,1] \rightarrow [0,1]$ that satisfies commuta-

tive, monotonicity, associative and one act as identity element. And the same is for a *t-conorm* $\mathcal{S} : [0,1] \times [0,1] \rightarrow [0,1]$ by replacing the last constraint with zero identity constraint). Figure 9 shows some of well known *t-norms* and *t-conorms*. Choosing a pair of them to use for $\wedge_L$ and $\vee_L$ on the lattice L, we can define *meet* $\wedge$ and *join* $\wedge$ for partial order $\leq_t$, and *meet* $\otimes$ and *join* $\oplus$ for partial order $\leq_k$ on the bilattice $\mathcal{L}^2$ by the according to Equation 3 shown above. Therefore, considering the semantics of the Equation 1 (Definition 14), we can directly apply the same inference scheme to bilattice based fuzzy Belnap logic $\mathcal{L}^2$.

Similarly to square bilattice for fuzzy Belnap logic, triangle for IVFSs can be defined as follows.

Definition 22 ($\mathcal{I}(\mathcal{L})$ Triangle bilattice for IVFSs): *Let* $\mathcal{L} = (L, \leq_L)$ be a complete lattice, and $I(L) = \{[x_1, x_2] \mid (x_1, x_2) \in L^2, x_1 \leq_L x_2\}$. A (bilattice-based) triangle is a structure $\mathcal{I}(\mathcal{L}) = (I(L), \leq_t, \leq_k)$, where

a. $[x_1, x_2] \leq_t [y_1, y_2] \Leftrightarrow x_1 \leq_L y_1 \text{ and } x_2 \leq_L y_2 ;$

b. $[x_1, x_2] \leq_k [y_1, y_2] \Leftrightarrow x_1 \leq_L y_1 \text{ and } x_2 \geq_L y_2 .$

Though the definitions of triangle bilattice for IFSs are not explicitly defined in their work, we can easily introduce the triangle structure for IFSs following the Definition 22.

Definition 23 ($\mathcal{I}^*(\mathcal{L})$ Triangle bilattice for IFSs): *Let* $\mathcal{L} = (L, \leq_L)$ be a complete lattice, and $I(L) = \{[x_1, x_2] \mid (x_1, x_2) \in L^2, x_1 + x_2 \leq 1_L\}$. A (bilattice-based) triangle is a structure $\mathcal{I}^*(\mathcal{L}) = (I^*(L), \leq_t, \leq_k, \neg)$, where $\neg(x_1, x_2) = (x_2, x_1)$, and

Figure 9. Some of t-norms and t-conorms

	t-norms for $\wedge_L$	t-conorms for $\vee_L$
Min/Max	$\mathcal{T}_{\min}(a,b) = \min\{a,b\},$	$\mathcal{S}_{\max}(a,b) = \max\{a,b\}$
Product/Sum	$\mathcal{T}_{\mathrm{prod}}(a,b) = a \cdot b$	$\mathcal{S}_{\mathrm{sum}}(a,b) = a + b - a \cdot b$
Łukasewicz	$\mathcal{T}_{\mathrm{Luk}}(a,b) = \max\{0, a+b-1\}.$	$\mathcal{S}_{\mathrm{Luk}}(a,b) = \min\{a+b,1\}$
Drastic	$\mathcal{T}_{\mathrm{D}}(a,b) = \begin{cases} b & \text{if } a=1 \\ a & \text{if } b=1 \\ 0 & \text{otherwise.} \end{cases}$	$\mathcal{S}_{\mathrm{D}}(a,b) = \begin{cases} b & \text{if } a=0 \\ a & \text{if } b=0 \\ 1 & \text{otherwise,} \end{cases}$
Nilpotent min/max	$\mathcal{T}_{\mathrm{nM}}(a,b) = \begin{cases} \min(a,b) & \text{if } a+b>1 \\ 0 & \text{otherwise} \end{cases}$	$\mathcal{S}_{\mathrm{nM}}(a,b) = \begin{cases} \max(a,b) & \text{if } a+b<1 \\ 1 & \text{otherwise.} \end{cases}$
Hamacher Prod/Einstein	$\mathcal{T}_{\mathrm{H_0}}(a,b) = \begin{cases} 0 & \text{if } a=b=0 \\ \frac{ab}{a+b-ab} & \text{otherwise} \end{cases}$	$\mathcal{S}_{\mathrm{H_2}}(a,b) = \frac{a+b}{1+ab}$

a. $[x_1, x_2] \leq_t [y_1, y_2] \Leftrightarrow x_1 \leq_L y_1$ and $x_2 \geq_L y_2$;

b. $[x_1, x_2] \leq_k [y_1, y_2] \Leftrightarrow x_1 \leq_L y_1$ and $x_2 \leq_L y_2$.

As in the case of square bilattice, by setting $L = [0,1]$, the structure correspond to $\mathcal{L}^I$ and $\mathcal{L}^*$. However, Arieli et al. (2005) also showed that $\mathcal{I}(\mathcal{L})$ is in fact not a (pre-) bilattice, since the substructure $(I(L), \leq_k)$ is not a lattice because the *lub* (*least upper bound, join* $\wedge_k$) of any two elements does not always exist. This corresponds to the interesting aspect that, the triangles do not allow explicit representation of the epistemic state '*contradictory*' in terms of degree of information (note that opinion triangle of subjective logic has the same aspect). Therefore, for example, the full truth and full falsity in triangle are not comparable in terms of degree of information. But still, $(I(L), \leq_k)$ is a partially ordered set, therefore the triangle is very much in the same spirit as bilattices. This property is also same in the case of $\mathcal{I}^*(\mathcal{L})$. They have also proved that *t-norms* and *t-conorms* for the $\leq_k$ − order can't be properly defined by introducing some theorems such as *t-representability* theorem, etc. However, they

showed that any *t-norms* or *t-conorms* definable in classical fuzzy set theory have extensions to IVFSs along the partial order $\leq_t$ in a compositional manner. Due to this aspect, it seems that bilattices are not always the key to model the adequate properties of IVFL and IFL but is quite much adequate for modeling fuzzy Belnap logic. Therefore, in the context of bilattice, the default inference scheme, Equation (3) can not be set up on IVFL or IFL. While the *meet* $\otimes$ and *join* $\oplus$ operators can not be defined on $\mathcal{I}(\mathcal{L})$ and $\mathcal{I}^*(\mathcal{L})$, however, there is an useful mapping between *square* $\mathcal{L}_\square$ and *triangle* $\mathcal{L}^*$. Attanasov (2002), the founder of intuitionistic fuzzy logic, further studied on the relationship between the '*triangle*' and the '*square*', and defined following two bijective transformations F and G from $\mathcal{L}_\square$ to $\mathcal{L}^*$, defined for $(x_1, x_2) \in [0,1]^2$ such that,

$$F(x_1, x_2) = \begin{cases} (0,0) & \text{if } x_1 = x_2 = 0 \\ \left(\dfrac{x_1^2}{x_1 + x_2}, \dfrac{x_1 x_2}{x_1 + x_2} \right) & \text{if } x_1 \geq x_2 \\ \left(\dfrac{x_1 x_2}{x_1 + x_2}, \dfrac{x_2^2}{x_1 + x_2} \right) & \text{if } x_1 < x_2 \end{cases}$$

(4)

$$G(x_1, x_2) = \begin{cases} \left(x_1 - \dfrac{x_2}{2}, \dfrac{x_2}{2} \right) & \text{if } x_1 \geq x_2 \\[2ex] \left(\dfrac{x_1}{2}, x_2 - \dfrac{x_1}{2} \right) & \text{if } x_1 < x_2 \end{cases} \qquad (5)$$

Then later, Cornelis et al. (2004) showed that the bijective mapping does not preserve the order, therefore not lattice isomorphism. However, as for the *triangle* perspective interpretation of values in *square*, it is still useful. Therefore, rather than directly model default reasoning scheme for IFSs and IFSs, we do reasoning on *square* bilattice for fuzzy Belnap logic, then transform the derived result using above Equations 4 and 5. Definition 12, 13, and 14 hold on *square* $\mathcal{L}^2$, and we will again distinguish the inference on *square*, by denoting subscript $cl_{\mathcal{L}^2}$ to the closure operation and by denoting superscript on the *t-(co)norm* as $cl^{prod/sum}$ i.e. $cl_{\mathcal{L}^2_{di}}^{prod/sum}(\phi)(q)$. For $\mathcal{I}(\mathcal{L})$ and $\mathcal{I}^*(\mathcal{L})$, we define following projection function relying on the above two possible mappings.

Definition 24 ($cl_{\mathcal{I}^*(\mathcal{L})}^{F}$ F-Interpretation): *Given a reasoning result $cl_{\mathcal{L}^2_{di}}(\phi)(q)$ on square $\mathcal{L}^2$, the F-Interpretation is the function such that $cl_{\mathcal{I}^*(\mathcal{L})}^{F} = F(cl_{\mathcal{L}^2_{di}}(\phi)(q))$, where the function F corresponds to Equation (4).*

Definition 25 ($cl_{\mathcal{I}^*(\mathcal{L})}^{G}$ G-Interpretation): *Given a reasoning result $cl_{\mathcal{L}^2_{di}}(\phi)(q)$ on square $\mathcal{L}^2$, the G-Interpretation is the function such that $cl_{\mathcal{I}^*(\mathcal{L})}^{G} = G(cl_{\mathcal{L}^2_{di}}(\phi)(q))$, where the function G corresponds to Equation (5).*

Reminding that the IVFSs and IFSs are isomorphic (Cornelis, Deschrijver, & Kerrer, 2004), in this article, we will show default reasoning on $\mathcal{L}^2$ and its F and G interpretations to IFSs. The interpretations can give us a shedding insight on

comparing the reasoning result of the presented subjective logic based approach with IFL and fuzzy Belnap logic, because the uncertainty representation using μ and ν in IFL is pretty much similar to the one of subjective logic.

DEFAULT REASONING EXAMPLES IN VISUAL SURVEILLANCE

This section deals with illustrative default reasoning examples for visual surveillance scenarios. To verify our approach and also to contrast with *L*-fuzzy logic based approaches, we will reuse two examples demonstrated by Shet et al. (2006a, 2006b) and one scenario in typical airport scene that is also inspired by Shet et al. (2005). Then we compare the proposed default inference approach of Equation 2 to the one of bilattice based default reasoning and its extension to $\mathcal{L}^2$. The reasoning on $\mathcal{L}^2$ will be also interpreted in the view of $\mathcal{L}^*$ (i.e. $\mathcal{I}^*(\mathcal{L})$ psuedo-bilattice of $\mathcal{L}^*$) with the interpretations $cl_{\mathcal{I}^*(\mathcal{L})}^{F}$ and $cl_{\mathcal{I}^*(\mathcal{L})}^{G}$. In this section, we will not directly concern about IVFL due to the isomorphism between IVFSs and IFSs. We set truth values as follows:

$$T \simeq (1,0,0)_{sl} \simeq (1,0)_{\mathcal{L}^*} \simeq (1,0)_{\mathcal{L}^2},$$
$$F \simeq (0,1,0)_{sl} \simeq (0,1)_{\mathcal{L}^*} \simeq (0,1)_{\mathcal{L}^2},$$
$$DT \simeq (0.5,0,0.5)_{sl} \simeq (0.5,0)_{\mathcal{L}^*} \simeq (0.5,0)_{\mathcal{L}^2},$$
$$DF \simeq (0,0.5,0.5)_{sl} \simeq (0,0.5)_{\mathcal{L}^*} \simeq (0,0.5)_{\mathcal{L}^2}$$
$$U \simeq (0,0,1)_{sl} \simeq (0,0)_{\mathcal{L}^*} \simeq (0,0)_{\mathcal{L}^2},$$
$$* \simeq (x,x,1-2x)_{sl} \simeq (x,x)_{\mathcal{L}^*} \simeq (x,x)_{\mathcal{L}^2}$$

(i.e. undecided or contradiction with some amount of uncertainty (degree of information) on opinion triangle (on *L*-fuzzy sets)), and $\perp \simeq (0.5,0.5,0)_{sl} \simeq (0.5,0.5)_{\mathcal{L}^*} \simeq (1,1)_{\mathcal{L}^2}$ (i.e. the full contradiction). These mappings are reasonable in the sense that the uncertainty representation of opinion triangle and IFL $\mathcal{I}^*(\mathcal{L})$ are similar except the atomicity value a of opinion triangle. For the simplicity we assume that all the propositional knowledge we consider are balanced, therefore we set the atomicity of opinion triangle as default, $a = 0.5$ and we will not explicitly denote a. For the rest of truth values we will use opinion triple representation (b, d, i). For values of opinion triangle, $\mathcal{I}^*(\mathcal{L})$ and $\mathcal{L}^2$, that are slightly different to above symbols but still can be interpreted as one of them, we will denote it with superscript $'$ (e.g. $* \simeq *'$, $DT \simeq DT'$, etc.).

Example 2 (Identity Inference) (Shet, 2006a, 2006b): Assume the following truth assignment and set of rules about determining whether two individuals observed in an image should be considered as being one and the same.

$$\phi[\neg equal(P_1, P_2) \leftarrow distinct(P_1, P_2)] = DT$$
$$\phi[equal(P_1, P_2) \leftarrow appear\_similar(P_1, P_2)] = DT$$
$$\phi[appear\_similar(a, b)] = T$$
$$\phi[distinct(a, b)] = T$$

Given two default true rules and facts that can be seen as definite true, the inference for default logic shown in (Shet, 2006a) with bilattice and the default inference with subjective logic are as follows.

$$cl_{bl_{di}}(\phi)(equal(a, b))$$
$$= [U \vee (T \wedge DT)] \oplus \neg [U \vee (T \wedge DT)]$$
$$= [U \vee DT] \oplus \neg [U \vee DT]$$
$$= DT \oplus DF = *$$

$$cl_{sl_{di}}(\phi)(equal(a, b))$$
$$= [U \sqcup (T \bullet DT)] \oplus \neg [U \sqcup (T \bullet DT)]$$
$$= [U \sqcup (0.67, 0, 0.33)] \oplus \neg [U \sqcup (0.67, 0, 0.33)]$$
$$= (0.67, 0, 0.33) \oplus \neg(0.67, 0, 0.33)$$
$$= (0.67, 0, 0.33) \oplus (0, 0.67, 0.33)$$
$$= (0.4, 0.4, 0.2) = *'$$

And as shown in Figure 9, choosing one of *t-norm* and *t-conorm* pair, and applying Equation 3 in Definition 21, we get following inference result derived on $\mathcal{L}^2$, and its interpretations $cl^F_{\mathcal{I}^*(\mathcal{L})}$ and $cl^G_{\mathcal{I}^*(\mathcal{L})}$ on $\mathcal{I}^*(\mathcal{L})$. The reasoning results are as follows.

$$cl^{min/max}_{\mathcal{L}^2_{di}}(\phi)(equal(a, b))$$
$$= [U \vee (T \wedge DT)] \oplus \neg [U \vee (T \wedge DT)]$$
$$= [(0,0) \vee \{(1,0) \wedge (0.5, 0)\}] \oplus \neg$$
$$[(0,0) \vee \{(1,0) \wedge (0.5, 0)\}]$$
$$= [(0,0) \vee (min(1, 0.5), max(0, 0))] \oplus \neg$$
$$[(0,0) \vee (min(1, 0.5), max(0, 0))]$$
$$= [(0,0) \vee (0.5, 0)] \oplus \neg[(0,0) \vee (0.5, 0)]$$
$$= [max(0, 0.5), min(0, 0)] \oplus \neg$$
$$[max(0, 0.5), min(0, 0)]$$
$$= (0.5, 0) \oplus \neg(0.5, 0)$$
$$= (0.5, 0) \oplus (0, 0.5)$$
$$= (max(0.5, 0), max(0, 0.5))$$
$$= (0.5, 0.5) = *'$$

$$cl^F_{\mathcal{I}^*(\mathcal{L})}(cl^{min/max}_{\mathcal{L}^2_{di}}(\phi)(equal(a, b)))$$
$$= cl^F_{\mathcal{I}^*(\mathcal{L})}((0.5, 0.5))$$
$$= (\frac{0.5^2}{0.5 + 0.5}, \frac{0.5 \bullet 0.5}{0.5 + 0.5})$$
$$= (0.25, 0.25) = *'$$

$$cl^G_{\mathcal{I}^*(\mathcal{L})}(cl^{min/max}_{\mathcal{L}^2_{di}}(\phi)(equal(a, b)))$$
$$= cl^G_{\mathcal{I}^*(\mathcal{L})}((0.5, 0.5))$$
$$= (0.5 - \frac{0.5}{2}, \frac{0.5}{2})$$
$$= (0.25, 0.25) = *'$$

$$cl_{\mathcal{L}^2_{di}}^{prod/sum}(\phi)(equal(a,b))$$
$$= [U \vee (T \wedge DT)] \oplus \neg [U \vee (T \wedge DT)]$$
$$= [(0,0) \vee \{(1,0) \wedge (0.5,0)\}] \oplus \neg$$
$$[(0,0) \vee \{(1,0) \wedge (0.5,0)\}]$$
$$= [(0,0) \vee (1 \bullet 0.5, 0 + 0 - 0 \bullet 0)] \oplus \neg$$
$$[(1 \bullet 0.5, 0 + 0 - 0 \bullet 0)]$$
$$= [(0,0) \vee (0.5,0)] \oplus \neg [(0,0) \vee (0.5,0)]$$
$$= [0 + 0.5 - 0 \bullet 0.5, 0 \bullet 0] \oplus \neg$$
$$[0 + 0.5 - 0 \bullet 0.5, 0 \bullet 0]$$
$$= (0.5,0) \oplus \neg (0.5,0)$$
$$= (0.5,0) \oplus (0,0.5)$$
$$= (0.5 + 0 - 0.5 \bullet 0, 0.5 + 0 - 0.5 \bullet 0)$$
$$= (0.5,0.5) = *'$$

$$cl_{\mathcal{L}^2_{di}}^{drastic}(\phi)(equal(a,b))$$
$$= [U \vee (T \wedge DT)] \oplus \neg [U \vee (T \wedge DT)]$$
$$= [(0,0) \vee \{(1,0) \wedge (0.5,0)\}] \oplus \neg$$
$$[(0,0) \vee \{(1,0) \wedge (0.5,0)\}]$$
$$= [(0,0) \vee (\mathcal{T}_D(1,0.5), \mathcal{S}_D(0,0))] \oplus \neg$$
$$[(0,0) \vee (\mathcal{T}_D(1,0.5), \mathcal{S}_D(0,0))]$$
$$= [(0,0) \vee (0.5,0)] \oplus \neg [(0,0) \vee (0.5,0)]$$
$$= [\mathcal{S}_D(0,0.5), \mathcal{T}_D(0,0)] \oplus \neg$$
$$[\mathcal{S}_D(0,0.5), \mathcal{T}_D(0,0)]$$
$$= (0.5,0) \oplus \neg (0.5,0)$$
$$= (0.5,0) \oplus (0,0.5)$$
$$= (\mathcal{S}_D(0.5,0), \mathcal{S}_D(0,0.5))$$
$$= (0.5,0.5) = *'$$

$$cl_{\mathcal{I}^*(\mathcal{L})}^{F}(cl_{\mathcal{L}^2_{di}}^{prod/sum}(\phi)(equal(a,b)))$$
$$- cl_{\mathcal{I}^*(\mathcal{L})}^{F}((0.5,0.5)) - (0.25,0.25) = *'$$
$$cl_{\mathcal{I}^*(\mathcal{L})}^{G}(cl_{\mathcal{L}^2_{di}}^{prod/sum}(\phi)(equal(a,b)))$$
$$= cl_{\mathcal{I}^*(\mathcal{L})}^{G}((0.5,0.5)) = (0.25,0.25) = *'$$

$$cl_{\mathcal{I}^*(\mathcal{L})}^{F}(cl_{\mathcal{L}^2_{di}}^{drastic}(\phi)(equal(a,b)))$$
$$= cl_{\mathcal{I}^*(\mathcal{L})}^{F}((0.5,0.5)) = (0.25,0.25) = *'$$
$$cl_{\mathcal{I}^*(\mathcal{L})}^{G}(cl_{\mathcal{L}^2_{di}}^{drastic}(\phi)(equal(a,b)))$$
$$= cl_{\mathcal{I}^*(\mathcal{L})}^{G}((0.5,0.5)) = (0.25,0.25) = *'$$

$$cl_{\mathcal{L}^2_{di}}^{Luk}(\phi)(equal(a,b))$$
$$= [U \vee (T \wedge DT)] \oplus \neg [U \vee (T \wedge DT)]$$
$$= [(0,0) \vee \{(1,0) \wedge (0.5,0)\}] \oplus \neg$$
$$[(0,0) \vee \{(1,0) \wedge (0.5,0)\}]$$
$$= [(0,0) \vee (\max(0, 1 + 0.5 - 1), \min(0 + 0, 1))] \oplus \neg$$
$$[(0,0) \vee (\max(0, 1 + 0.5 - 1), \min(0 + 0, 1))]$$
$$= [(0,0) \vee (0.5,0)] \oplus \neg [(0,0) \vee (0.5,0)]$$
$$= [\min(0 + 0.5, 1), \max(0, 0 + 0 - 1)] \oplus \neg$$
$$[\min(0 + 0.5, 1), \max(0, 0 + 0 - 1)]$$
$$= (0.5,0) \oplus \neg (0.5,0)$$
$$= (0.5,0) \oplus (0,0.5)$$
$$= (\min(0.5 + 0, 1), \min(0 + 0.5, 1))$$
$$= (0.5,0.5) = *'$$

$$cl_{\mathcal{L}^2_{di}}^{Nilpotent}(\phi)(equal(a,b))$$
$$= [U \vee (T \wedge DT)] \oplus \neg [U \vee (T \wedge DT)]$$
$$= [(0,0) \vee \{(1,0) \wedge (0.5,0)\}] \oplus \neg$$
$$[(0,0) \vee \{(1,0) \wedge (0.5,0)\}]$$
$$= [(0,0) \vee (\mathcal{T}_{nM}(1,0.5), \mathcal{S}_{nM}(0,0))] \oplus \neg$$
$$[(0,0) \vee (\mathcal{T}_{nM}(1,0.5), \mathcal{S}_{nM}(0,0))]$$
$$= [(0,0) \vee (0.5,0)] \oplus \neg [(0,0) \vee (0.5,0)]$$
$$= [\mathcal{S}_{nM}(0,0.5), \mathcal{T}_{nM}(0,0)] \oplus \neg$$
$$[\mathcal{S}_{nM}(0,0.5), \mathcal{T}_{nM}(0,0)]$$
$$= (0.5,0) \oplus \neg (0.5,0)$$
$$= (0.5,0) \oplus (0,0.5)$$
$$= (\mathcal{S}_{nM}(0.5,0), \mathcal{S}_{nM}(0,0.5))$$
$$= (0.5,0.5) = *'$$

$$cl_{\mathcal{I}^*(\mathcal{L})}^{Luk}(cl_{\mathcal{L}^2_{di}}^{Luk}(\phi)(equal(a,b)))$$
$$= cl_{\mathcal{I}^*(\mathcal{L})}^{F}((0.5,0.5)) = (0.25,0.25) = *'$$
$$cl_{\mathcal{I}^*(\mathcal{L})}^{Luk}(cl_{\mathcal{L}^2_{di}}^{Luk}(\phi)(equal(a,b)))$$
$$= cl_{\mathcal{I}^*(\mathcal{L})}^{G}((0.5,0.5)) = (0.25,0.25) = *'$$

$$cl^F_{\mathcal{I}^*(\mathcal{L})}(cl^{Nilpotent}_{\mathcal{L}^2_{di}}(\phi)(equal(a,b)))$$
$$= cl^F_{\mathcal{I}^*(\mathcal{L})}((0.5,0.5)) = (0.25,0.25) = *'$$
$$cl^G_{\mathcal{I}^*(\mathcal{L})}(cl^{Nilpotent}_{\mathcal{L}^2_{di}}(\phi)(equal(a,b)))$$
$$= cl^G_{\mathcal{I}^*(\mathcal{L})}((0.5,0.5)) = (0.25,0.25) = *'$$

$$cl^{Hamacher}_{\mathcal{L}^2_{di}}(\phi)(equal(a,b))$$
$$= [U \vee (T \wedge DT)] \oplus \neg[U \vee (T \wedge DT)]$$
$$= [(0,0) \vee \{(1,0) \wedge (0.5,0)\}] \oplus \neg$$
$$[(0,0) \vee \{(1,0) \wedge (0.5,0)\}]$$
$$= [(0,0) \vee (\mathcal{T}_{H0}(1,0.5), \mathcal{S}_{H2}(0,0))] \oplus \neg$$
$$[(0,0) \vee (\mathcal{T}_{H0}(1,0.5), \mathcal{S}_{H2}(0,0))]$$
$$= [(0,0) \vee (0.5,0)] \oplus \neg[(0,0) \vee (0.5,0)]$$
$$= [\mathcal{S}_{H2}(0,0.5), \mathcal{T}_{H0}(0,0)] \oplus \neg$$
$$[\mathcal{S}_{H2}(0,0.5), \mathcal{T}_{H0}(0,0)]$$
$$= (0.5,0) \oplus \neg(0.5,0)$$
$$= (0.5,0) \oplus (0,0.5)$$
$$= (\mathcal{S}_{H2}(0.5,0), \mathcal{S}_{H2}(0,0.5))$$
$$= (0.5,0.5) = *'$$

$$cl^F_{\mathcal{I}^*(\mathcal{L})}(cl^{Hamacher}_{\mathcal{L}^2_{di}}(\phi)(equal(a,b)))$$
$$= cl^F_{\mathcal{I}^*(\mathcal{L})}((0.5,0.5)) = (0.25,0.25) = *'$$
$$cl^G_{\mathcal{I}^*(\mathcal{L})}(cl^{Hamacher}_{\mathcal{L}^2_{di}}(\phi)(equal(a,b)))$$
$$= cl^G_{\mathcal{I}^*(\mathcal{L})}((0.5,0.5)) = (0.25,0.25) = *'$$

Figure 10 shows the graphical representation of above reasoning results. The resulting opinion $(0.4, 0.4, 0.2)$ represents same amount of degree of truth and false with uncertainty. This can also be represented as undecided state $*'$. All reasoning results on $\mathcal{L}^2$ also yielded similar result $(0.5, 0.5)$ and its F/G interpretations $(0.25, 0.25)$. Thus, the semantics of results from the discrete bilattice for multivalued default logic, bilattice based L-fuzzy logics and subjective logic are the same. While the uncertainty representation semantics of subjective logic is similar to IFL, when the reasoning result on fuzzy Belnap logic is interpreted, the distance between subjective opinion and the value of IFL was bigger than the one to fuzzy Belnap.

Example 3 (Identity Inference with contextual cues) (Shet, 2006a, 2006b): Assume that a person enters an office room that we believe to be empty and closed (no other exit). Suppose that after a while, another person appears from the room who seems dissimilar from the first person. In this case, inferring equality based on appearance matching is a weaker default than inferring equality based on the fact that person entered and exited an empty closed world. This aspect can be represented as following truth assignment and set of rules.

Figure 10. Reasoning results of example 2 in opinion space, $\mathcal{L}^2$ and $\mathcal{I}^*(\mathcal{L})$

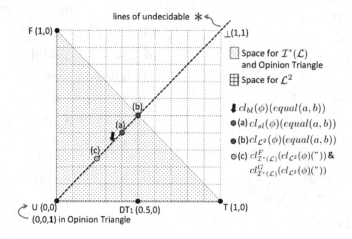

$\phi[\neg equal(P_1, P_2) \leftarrow \neg appear\_similar(P_1, P_2)] = DT_1$

$\phi[equal(P_1, P_2) \leftarrow enter\_closed\_world(P_1, X, T_1),$
$exit\_closed\_world(P_2, X, T_2), T_2 > T_1,$
$empty\_before(X, T_1), empty\_after(X, T_2),$
$not(enter\_or\_exit\_between(P_3, T_1, T_2)).] = DT_2$

$\phi[\neg appear\_similar(a, b)] = T$

$\phi[enter\_closed\_world(a, office, 400)] = T$

$\phi[exit\_closed\_world(b, office, 523)] = T$

$where, \; DT_1 \simeq (0.5, 0, 0.5)_{sl} \simeq (0.5, 0)_{\mathcal{L}^*} \simeq (0.5, 0)_{\mathcal{L}^2}$

$and \; DT_2 \simeq (0.8, 0, 0.2) \simeq (0.8, 0)_{\mathcal{L}^*} \simeq (0.8, 0)_{\mathcal{L}^2}$

The Inference in this setup is multivalued default reasoning and the bilattice based inference result shown in (Shet, 2006a) and the result of subjective logic based inference are as follows.

$cl_{bl_{di}}(\phi)(equal(a, b))$
$= [U \vee (T \wedge T \wedge T \wedge T \wedge T \wedge DT_2)]$
$\quad \oplus \neg[U \vee (T \wedge DT_1)]$
$= [U \wedge DT_2] \oplus \neg[U \wedge DT_1]$
$= DT_2 \oplus DF_1 = DT_2$

$cl_{sl_{di}}(\phi)(equal(a, b))$
$= [U \sqcup (T \bullet T \bullet T \bullet T \bullet T \bullet DT_2)]$
$\quad \oplus \neg[U \sqcup (T \bullet DT_1)]$
$= [U \sqcup (0.9, 0, 0.1)] \oplus \neg[U \sqcup (0.67, 0, 0.33)]$
$= (0.9, 0, 0.1) \oplus \neg(0.67, 0, 0.33)$
$= (0.9, 0, 0.1) \oplus (0, 0.67, 0.33)$
$= (0.75, 0.17, 0.08) = DT_2'$

Choosing a pair of *t-norm* and *t-conorm* inference result derived on $\mathcal{L}^2$, and its interpretations $cl^F_{\mathcal{I}^*(\mathcal{L})}$ and $cl^G_{\mathcal{I}^*(\mathcal{L})}$ on $\mathcal{I}^*(\mathcal{L})$ are as follows.

$cl^{\min/\max}_{\mathcal{L}^2_{di}}(\phi)(equal(a, b))$
$= [U \vee (T \wedge T \wedge T \wedge T \wedge T \wedge DT_2)]$
$\quad \oplus \neg[U \vee (T \wedge DT_1)]$
$= [U \vee (T \wedge DT_2)] \oplus \neg[U \vee (T \wedge DT_1)]$
$= [(0,0) \vee ((1,0) \wedge (0.8, 0))] \oplus \neg$
$\quad [(0,0) \vee ((1,0) \wedge (0.5, 0))]$
$= [(0,0) \vee (\min(1, 0.8), \max(0,0))] \oplus \neg$
$\quad [(0,0) \vee (\min(1, 0.5), \max(0,0))]$
$= [(0,0) \vee (0.8, 0)] \oplus \neg[(0,0) \vee (0.5, 0)]$
$= (\max(0, 0.8), \min(0,0)) \oplus \neg$
$\quad (\max(0, 0.5), \min(0,0))$
$= (0.8, 0) \oplus \neg(0.5, 0)$
$= (0.8, 0) \oplus (0, 0.5)$
$= (\max(0.8, 0), \max(0, 0.5))$
$= (0.8, 0.5) = DT_2'$

$cl^F_{\mathcal{I}^*(\mathcal{L})}(cl^{\min/\max}_{\mathcal{L}^2_{di}}(\phi)(equal(a, b)))$
$= cl^F_{\mathcal{I}^*(\mathcal{L})}((0.8, 0.5))$
$= (\dfrac{0.8^2}{0.8 + 0.5}, \dfrac{0.8 \bullet 0.5}{0.8 + 0.5})$
$= (0.49, 0.3) = DT_2'$

$cl^G_{\mathcal{I}^*(\mathcal{L})}(cl^{\min/\max}_{\mathcal{L}^2_{di}}(\phi)(equal(a, b)))$
$= cl^G_{\mathcal{I}^*(\mathcal{L})}((0.8, 0.5))$
$= (0.8 - \dfrac{0.5}{2}, \dfrac{0.5}{2})$
$= (0.55, 0.25) = DT_2'$

$$cl_{\mathcal{L}_{di}^{\ell}}^{prod/sum}(\phi)(equal(a,b))$$
$$= [U \vee (T \wedge T \wedge T \wedge T \wedge T \wedge DT_2)]$$
$$\quad \oplus \neg[U \vee (T \wedge DT_1)]$$
$$= [U \vee (T \wedge DT_2)] \oplus \neg[U \vee (T \wedge DT_1)]$$
$$= [(0,0) \vee ((1,0) \wedge (0.8,0))] \oplus \neg$$
$$\quad [(0,0) \vee ((1,0) \wedge (0.5,0))]$$
$$= [(0,0) \vee (1 \bullet 0.8, 0 + 0 - 0 \bullet 0)] \oplus \neg$$
$$\quad [(0,0) \vee (1 \bullet 0.5, 0 + 0 - 0 \bullet 0)]$$
$$= [(0,0) \vee (0.8,0)] \oplus \neg$$
$$\quad [(0,0) \vee (0.5,0)]$$
$$= (0 + 0.8 - 0 \bullet 0.8, 0 \bullet 0)) \oplus \neg$$
$$\quad (0 + 0.5 - 0 \bullet 0.5, 0 \bullet 0)$$
$$= (0.8,0) \oplus \neg(0.5,0)$$
$$= (0.8,0) \oplus (0,0.5)$$
$$= (0.8 + 0 - 0.8 \bullet 0, 0 + 0.5 - 0 \bullet 0.5)$$
$$= (0.8, 0.5) = DT_2'$$

$$cl_{\mathcal{I}^*(\mathcal{L})}^{F}(cl_{\mathcal{L}_{di}^{\ell}}^{prod/sum}(\phi)(equal(a,b)))$$
$$= cl_{\mathcal{I}^*(\mathcal{L})}^{F}((0.8,0.5)) = (0.49,0.3) = DT_2'$$
$$cl_{\mathcal{I}^*(\mathcal{L})}^{G}(cl_{\mathcal{L}_{di}^{\ell}}^{prod/sum}(\phi)(equal(a,b)))$$
$$= cl_{\mathcal{I}^*(\mathcal{L})}^{G}((0.8,0.5)) = (0.55,0.25) = DT_2'$$

$$cl_{\mathcal{L}_{di}^{\ell}}^{Luk}(\phi)(equal(a,b))$$
$$= [U \vee (T \wedge T \wedge T \wedge T \wedge T \wedge DT_2)]$$
$$\quad \oplus \neg[U \vee (T \wedge DT_1)]$$
$$= [U \vee (T \wedge DT_2)] \oplus \neg[U \vee (T \wedge DT_1)]$$
$$= [(0,0) \vee ((1,0) \wedge (0.8,0))] \oplus \neg$$
$$[(0,0) \vee ((1,0) \wedge (0.5,0))]$$
$$= [(0,0) \vee (\max(0, 1 + 0.8 - 1), \min(0 + 0, 1))]$$
$$\quad \oplus \neg[(0,0) \vee (\max(0, 1 + 0.5 - 1), \min(0 + 0, 1))]$$
$$= [(0,0) \vee (0.8,0)] \oplus \neg[(0,0) \vee (0.5,0)]$$
$$= (\min(0 + 0.8, 1), \max(0, 0 + 0))$$
$$\quad \oplus \neg(\min(0 + 0.5, 1), \max(0, 0 + 0))$$
$$= (0.8,0) \oplus \neg(0.5,0)$$
$$= (0.8,0) \oplus (0,0.5)$$
$$= (\min(0.8 + 0, 1), \min(0 + 0.5, 1))$$
$$= (0.8, 0.5) = DT_2'$$

$$cl_{\mathcal{I}^*(\mathcal{L})}^{F}(cl_{\mathcal{L}_{di}^{\ell}}^{Luk}(\phi)(equal(a,b)))$$
$$= cl_{\mathcal{I}^*(\mathcal{L})}^{F}((0.8,0.5)) = (0.49,0.3) = DT_2'$$
$$cl_{\mathcal{I}^*(\mathcal{L})}^{G}(cl_{\mathcal{L}_{di}^{\ell}}^{Luk}(\phi)(equal(a,b)))$$
$$= cl_{\mathcal{I}^*(\mathcal{L})}^{G}((0.8,0.5)) = (0.55,0.25) = DT_2'$$

$$cl_{\mathcal{L}_{di}^{\ell}}^{drastic}(\phi)(equal(a,b))$$
$$= [U \vee (T \wedge T \wedge T \wedge T \wedge T \wedge DT_2)]$$
$$\quad \oplus \neg[U \vee (T \wedge DT_1)]$$
$$= [U \vee (T \wedge DT_2)] \oplus \neg[U \vee (T \wedge DT_1)]$$
$$= [(0,0) \vee ((1,0) \wedge (0.8,0))] \oplus \neg$$
$$[(0,0) \vee ((1,0) \wedge (0.5,0))]$$
$$= [(0,0) \vee (\mathcal{T}_D(1,0.8), \mathcal{S}_D(0,0))]$$
$$\quad \oplus \neg[(0,0) \vee (\mathcal{T}_D(1,0.5), \mathcal{S}_D(0,0))]$$
$$= [(0,0) \vee (0.8,0)] \oplus \neg[(0,0) \vee (0.5,0)]$$
$$= (\mathcal{S}_D(0,0.8), \mathcal{T}_D(0,0))$$
$$\quad \oplus \neg(\mathcal{S}_D(0,0.5), \mathcal{T}_D(0,0))$$
$$= (0.8,0) \oplus \neg(0.5,0)$$
$$= (0.8,0) \oplus (0,0.5)$$
$$= (\mathcal{S}_D(0.8,0), \mathcal{S}_D(0,0.5))$$
$$= (0.8, 0.5) = DT_2'$$

$$cl_{\mathcal{I}^*(\mathcal{L})}^{F}(cl_{\mathcal{L}_{di}^{\ell}}^{drastic}(\phi)(equal(a,b)))$$
$$= cl_{\mathcal{I}^*(\mathcal{L})}^{F}((0.8,0.5)) = (0.49,0.3) = DT_2'$$
$$cl_{\mathcal{I}^*(\mathcal{L})}^{G}(cl_{\mathcal{L}_{di}^{\ell}}^{drastic}(\phi)(equal(a,b)))$$
$$= cl_{\mathcal{I}^*(\mathcal{L})}^{G}((0.8,0.5)) = (0.55,0.25) = DT_2'$$

$$cl^{Nilpotent}_{\mathcal{L}^2_{di}}(\phi)(equal(a,b))$$
$$= [U \vee (T \wedge T \wedge T \wedge T \wedge T \wedge DT_2)]$$
$$\quad \oplus \neg[U \vee (T \wedge DT_1)]$$
$$= [U \vee (T \wedge DT_2)] \oplus \neg[U \vee (T \wedge DT_1)]$$
$$= [(0,0) \vee ((1,0) \wedge (0.8,0))] \oplus \neg$$
$$[(0,0) \vee ((1,0) \wedge (0.5,0))]$$
$$= [(0,0) \vee (\mathcal{T}_{nM}(1,0.8), \mathcal{S}_{nM}(0,0))]$$
$$\quad \oplus \neg[(0,0) \vee (\mathcal{T}_{nM}(1,0.5), \mathcal{S}_{nM}(0,0))]$$
$$= [(0,0) \vee (0.8,0)] \oplus \neg[(0,0) \vee (0.5,0)]$$
$$= (\mathcal{S}_{nM}(0,0.8), \mathcal{T}_{nM}(0,0))$$
$$\quad \oplus \neg(\mathcal{S}_{nM}(0,0.5), \mathcal{T}_{nM}(0,0))$$
$$= (0.8,0) \oplus \neg(0.5,0)$$
$$= (0.8,0) \oplus (0,0.5)$$
$$= (\mathcal{S}_{nM}(0.8,0), \mathcal{S}_{nM}(0,0.5))$$
$$= (0.8,0.5) = DT'_2$$

$$cl^{F}_{\mathcal{I}^*(\mathcal{L})}(cl^{Nilpotent}_{\mathcal{L}^2_{di}}(\phi)(equal(a,b)))$$
$$= cl^{F}_{\mathcal{I}^*(\mathcal{L})}((0.8,0.5)) = (0.49,0.3) = DT'_2$$
$$cl^{G}_{\mathcal{I}^*(\mathcal{L})}(cl^{Nilpotent}_{\mathcal{L}^2_{di}}(\phi)(equal(a,b)))$$
$$= cl^{G}_{\mathcal{I}^*(\mathcal{L})}((0.8,0.5)) = (0.55,0.25) = DT'_2$$

$$cl^{Hamacher}_{\mathcal{L}^2_{di}}(\phi)(equal(a,b))$$
$$= [U \vee (T \wedge T \wedge T \wedge T \wedge T \wedge DT_2)]$$
$$\quad \oplus \neg[U \vee (T \wedge DT_1)]$$
$$= [U \vee (T \wedge DT_2)] \oplus \neg[U \vee (T \wedge DT_1)]$$
$$= [(0,0) \vee ((1,0) \wedge (0.8,0))] \oplus \neg$$
$$[(0,0) \vee ((1,0) \wedge (0.5,0))]$$
$$= [(0,0) \vee (\mathcal{T}_{H0}(1,0.8), \mathcal{S}_{H2}(0,0))]$$
$$\quad \oplus \neg[(0,0) \vee (\mathcal{T}_{H0}(1,0.5), \mathcal{S}_{H2}(0,0))]$$
$$= [(0,0) \vee (0.8,0)] \oplus \neg[(0,0) \vee (0.5,0)]$$
$$= (\mathcal{S}_{H2}(0,0.8), \mathcal{T}_{H0}(0,0))$$
$$\quad \oplus \neg(\mathcal{S}_{H2}(0,0.5), \mathcal{T}_{H0}(0,0))$$
$$= (0.8,0) \oplus \neg(0.5,0)$$
$$= (0.8,0) \oplus (0,0.5)$$
$$= (\mathcal{S}_{H2}(0.8,0), \mathcal{S}_{nM}(0,0.5))$$
$$= (0.8,0.5) = DT'_2$$

$$cl^{F}_{\mathcal{I}^*(\mathcal{L})}(cl^{Hamacher}_{\mathcal{L}^2_{di}}(\phi)(equal(a,b)))$$
$$= cl^{F}_{\mathcal{I}^*(\mathcal{L})}((0.8,0.5)) = (0.49,0.3) = DT'_2$$
$$cl^{G}_{\mathcal{I}^*(\mathcal{L})}(cl^{Hamacher}_{\mathcal{L}^2_{di}}(\phi)(equal(a,b)))$$
$$= cl^{G}_{\mathcal{I}^*(\mathcal{L})}((0.8,0.5)) = (0.55,0.25) = DT'_2$$

Figure 11 shows above reasoning results. The opinion DT'_2 $(0.75,0.17,0.08)$ in opinion triangle is the most closest one to DT_2 compared to L-fuzzy logic based results but a bit biased to center than original DT_2. In the sense of truth value, this is the same to the cases of yielded values on $\mathcal{L}^2$. However, in these cases, the amount of falsity is also relatively high therefore the point is located in the area of overflowed information $(\mu + \nu > 1)$. The F and G interpretations are also a bit different but very close to each other. Nonetheless, in the sense that all reasoning results are pointed on the right-hand side of the line of undecidable *, semantically, this can be interpreted as the meaning of week truth like DT_2. Thus, the semantics of results from the discrete bilattice for multivalued default logic, the bilattice based L-fuzzy logics and subjective logic are the same.

Example 4 (Theft Inference with contextual cues): The scenario and rules for 'theft' have been inspired by Shet et al. (2005). Assume a typical airport surveillance as depicted in Figure 12 with two cameras. Suppose that a human P_1 carrying an object (Baggage) B is observed and stayed around telephone booth in $Cam1$. After a while he disappears from the view of $Cam1$ without taking his baggage B. Subsequently, P_2 enters the scene, picks up the baggage and leaves. In parallel, according to $Cam2$, it seems that P_1 and P_2 belong to a same group of people so the two people are considered as friends. In this scenario, based on the possession relation between an object and person, we could build a default rule to infer whether a person is a thief or not. Similarly, based on

Figure 11. Reasoning results of example 3 in opinion space, $\mathcal{L}^2$ and $\mathcal{I}^*(\mathcal{L})$

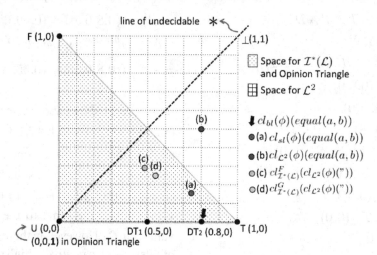

the friend relation we can also build a bit stronger default rule saying possessing object of friend is not thief. This aspect is depicted as following truth assignment and set of rules.

$\phi[\neg theft(P,B,T) \leftarrow human(P), package(B),$
$possess(P,B,T), \neg(belongs(B,P,T))] = DT_1$
$\phi[\neg theft(P,B,T) \leftarrow human(P), package(B),$
$possess(P,B,T), belongs(B,P,T)] = DT_1$
$\phi[\neg theft(P,B,T) \leftarrow human(P), package(B),$
$possess(P,B,T), \neg(belongs(B,P,T)),$
$friend(P,P'), belongs(B,P',T)] = DT_2$
$\phi[human(P)] = T$
$\phi[package(B)] = T$
$\phi[possess(P,B,T)] = T$
$\phi[\neg(belongs(B,P,T))] = T$
$\phi[friend(P,P')]_{cam2} = T$
$\phi[belongs(B,P',T)]_{cam2} = T$

where, $DT_1 \simeq (0.5, 0, 0.5)$ *and* $DT_2 \simeq (0.8, 0, 0.2)$

Given above rules and facts (gathered till P_2 is picking up the baggage B), inferring whether the person is a thief or not is shown as follows.

Case 1: (Inference relying only on Cam1).

$cl_{bl_{di}}(\phi)(theft(P,B,T))$
$= [U \vee (T \wedge T \wedge T \wedge T \wedge DT_1)]$
$= [U \vee DT_1] = DT_1$

$cl_{sl_{di}}(\phi)(theft(P,B,T))$
$= [U \sqcup (T \bullet T \bullet T \bullet T \bullet DT_1)]$
$= [U \sqcup (0.74, 0, 0.26)]$
$= (0.74, 0, 0.26)$
$= DT_2'$

Choosing a pair of *t-norm* and *t-conorm* inference result derived on $\mathcal{L}^2$, and its interpretations $cl^F_{\mathcal{I}^*(\mathcal{L})}$ and $cl^G_{\mathcal{I}^*(\mathcal{L})}$ on $\mathcal{I}^*(\mathcal{L})$ are as follows.

Figure 12. Illustrative scenario setup of example 4

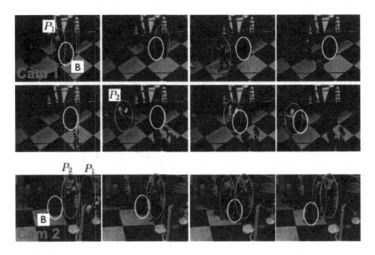

$$cl^{\min/\max}_{\mathcal{L}^2_{di}}(\phi)(theft(P,B,T))$$
$$= [U \vee (T \wedge T \wedge T \wedge T \wedge DT_1)]$$
$$= [U \vee (T \wedge DT_1)]$$
$$= [(0,0) \vee ((1,0) \wedge (0.5,0))]$$
$$= [(0,0) \vee (\min(1,0.5),\max(0,0))]$$
$$= [(0,0) \vee (0.5,0)]$$
$$= (\max(0,0.5),\min(0,0))$$
$$= (0.5,0) = DT_1$$

$$cl^{prod/sum}_{\mathcal{L}^2_{di}}(\phi)(theft(P,B,T))$$
$$= [U \vee (T \wedge T \wedge T \wedge T \wedge DT_1)]$$
$$= [U \vee (T \wedge DT_1)]$$
$$= [(0,0) \vee ((1,0) \wedge (0.5,0))]$$
$$= [(0,0) \vee (1\bullet 0.5, 0 + 0 - 0\bullet 0)]$$
$$= [(0,0) \vee (0.5,0)]$$
$$= (0 + 0.5 - 0\bullet 0.5), 0\bullet 0)$$
$$= (0.5,0) = DT_1$$

$$cl^F_{\mathcal{I}^*(\mathcal{L})}(cl^{\min/\max}_{\mathcal{L}^2_{di}}(\phi)(theft(P,B,T)))$$
$$= cl^F_{\mathcal{I}^*(\mathcal{L})}((0.5,0))$$
$$= (\frac{0.5^2}{0.5}, \frac{0.5\bullet 0}{0.5+0})$$
$$= (0.5,0) = DT_1$$
$$cl^G_{\mathcal{I}^*(\mathcal{L})}(cl^{\min/\max}_{\mathcal{L}^2_{di}}(\phi)(theft(P,B,T)))$$
$$= cl^G_{\mathcal{I}^*(\mathcal{L})}((0.5,0))$$
$$= (0.5 - \frac{0}{2}, \frac{0}{2})$$
$$= (0.5,0) = DT_1$$

$$cl^F_{\mathcal{I}^*(\mathcal{L})}(cl^{prod/sum}_{\mathcal{L}^2_{di}}(\phi)(theft(P,B,T)))$$
$$= cl^F_{\mathcal{I}^*(\mathcal{L})}((0.5,0)) = (0.5,0) = DT_1$$
$$cl^G_{\mathcal{I}^*(\mathcal{L})}(cl^{prod/sum}_{\mathcal{L}^2_{di}}(\phi)(theft(P,B,T)))$$
$$= cl^G_{\mathcal{I}^*(\mathcal{L})}((0.5,0)) = (0.5,0) = DT_1$$

$$cl^{Luk}_{\mathcal{L}^2_{di}}(\phi)(theft(P,B,T))[U \vee (T \wedge T \wedge T \wedge T \wedge DT_1)]$$
$$= [U \vee (T \wedge DT_1)]$$
$$= [(0,0) \vee ((1,0) \wedge (0.5,0))]$$
$$= [(0,0) \vee (\max(0,1+0.5-1),\min(0+0,1))]$$
$$= [(0,0) \vee (0.5,0)]$$
$$= (\min(0+0.5,1),\max(0,0+0-1))$$
$$= (0.5,0) = DT_1$$

$$cl^F_{\mathcal{I}^*(\mathcal{L})}(cl^{Luk}_{\mathcal{L}^2_{di}}(\phi)(theft(P,B,T)))$$
$$= cl^F_{\mathcal{I}^*(\mathcal{L})}((0.5,0)) = (0.5,0) = DT_1$$
$$cl^G_{\mathcal{I}^*(\mathcal{L})}(cl^{Luk}_{\mathcal{L}^2_{di}}(\phi)(theft(P,B,T)))$$
$$= cl^G_{\mathcal{I}^*(\mathcal{L})}((0.5,0)) = (0.5,0) = DT_1$$

$$cl^{drastic}_{\mathcal{L}^2_{di}}(\phi)(theft(P,B,T))$$
$$= [U \vee (T \wedge T \wedge T \wedge T \wedge DT_1)]$$
$$= [U \vee (T \wedge DT_1)]$$
$$= [(0,0) \vee ((1,0) \wedge (0.5,0))]$$
$$= [(0,0) \vee (\mathcal{T}_D(1,0.5), \mathcal{S}_D(0.5,0))]$$
$$= [(0,0) \vee (0.5,0)]$$
$$= (\mathcal{S}_D(0,0.5), \mathcal{T}_D(0,0))$$
$$= (0.5,0) = DT_1$$

$$cl^F_{\mathcal{I}^*(\mathcal{L})}(cl^{drastic}_{\mathcal{L}^2_{di}}(\phi)(theft(P,B,T)))$$
$$= cl^F_{\mathcal{I}^*(\mathcal{L})}((0.5,0)) = (0.5,0) = DT_1$$
$$cl^G_{\mathcal{I}^*(\mathcal{L})}(cl^{drastic}_{\mathcal{L}^2_{di}}(\phi)(theft(P,B,T)))$$
$$= cl^G_{\mathcal{I}^*(\mathcal{L})}((0.5,0)) = (0.5,0) = DT_1$$

$$cl^{Nilpotent}_{\mathcal{L}^2_{di}}(\phi)(theft(P,B,T))$$
$$= [U \vee (T \wedge T \wedge T \wedge T \wedge DT_1)]$$
$$= [U \vee (T \wedge DT_1)]$$
$$= [(0,0) \vee ((1,0) \wedge (0.5,0))]$$
$$= [(0,0) \vee (\mathcal{T}_{nM}(1,0.5), \mathcal{S}_{nM}(0.5,0))]$$
$$= [(0,0) \vee (0.5,0)]$$
$$= (\mathcal{S}_{nM}(0,0.5), \mathcal{T}_{nM}(0,0))$$
$$= (0.5,0) = DT_1$$

$$cl^F_{\mathcal{I}^*(\mathcal{L})}(cl^{Nilpotent}_{\mathcal{L}^2_{di}}(\phi)(theft(P,B,T)))$$
$$= cl^F_{\mathcal{I}^*(\mathcal{L})}((0.5,0)) = (0.5,0) = DT_1$$
$$cl^G_{\mathcal{I}^*(\mathcal{L})}(cl^{Nilpotent}_{\mathcal{L}^2_{di}}(\phi)(theft(P,B,T)))$$
$$= cl^G_{\mathcal{I}^*(\mathcal{L})}((0.5,0)) = (0.5,0) = DT_1$$

$$cl^{Hamacher}_{\mathcal{L}^2_{di}}(\phi)(theft(P,B,T))$$
$$= [U \vee (T \wedge T \wedge T \wedge T \wedge DT_1)]$$
$$= [U \vee (T \wedge DT_1)]$$
$$= [(0,0) \vee ((1,0) \wedge (0.5,0))]$$
$$= [(0,0) \vee (\mathcal{T}_{H0}(1,0.5), \mathcal{S}_{H2}(0.5,0))]$$
$$= [(0,0) \vee (0.5,0)]$$
$$= (\mathcal{S}_{H2}(0,0.5), \mathcal{T}_{H0}(0,0))$$
$$= (0.5,0) = DT_1$$

$$cl^F_{\mathcal{I}^*(\mathcal{L})}(cl^{Nilpotent}_{\mathcal{L}^2_{di}}(\phi)(theft(P,B,T)))$$
$$= cl^F_{\mathcal{I}^*(\mathcal{L})}((0.5,0)) = (0.5,0) = DT_1$$
$$cl^G_{\mathcal{I}^*(\mathcal{L})}(cl^{Nilpotent}_{\mathcal{L}^2_{di}}(\phi)(theft(P,B,T)))$$
$$= cl^G_{\mathcal{I}^*(\mathcal{L})}((0.5,0)) = (0.5,0) = DT_1$$

Relying only the facts generated by *Cam*1 (those are not explicitly subscripted with camera id), all of above inference concluded $cl(\phi)(theft(P_2,B,T)) = DT_1$ except subjective logic based approach that derived DT'_2. However, the semantic interpretation of the results are all the same. Namely. theft has taken place with low confidence.

Case 2: (Inference relying only on Cam1 and Cam2).

$$cl_{bl_{di}}(\phi)(theft(P,B,T))$$
$$= [U \vee (T \wedge T \wedge T \wedge T \wedge DT_1)]$$
$$\quad \oplus \neg [U \vee (T \wedge T \wedge T \wedge T \wedge T \wedge DT_2)]$$
$$= [U \vee DT_1] \oplus \neg [U \vee DT_2]$$
$$= DT_1 \oplus \neg DT_2$$
$$= DT_1 \oplus DF_2$$
$$= DF_2$$

$$cl_{sl_{di}}(\phi)(theft(P,B,T))$$
$$= [U \sqcup (T \bullet T \bullet T \bullet T \bullet DT_1)]$$
$$\oplus \neg [U \sqcup (T \bullet T \bullet T \bullet T \bullet T \bullet T \bullet DT_2)]$$
$$= [U \sqcup (0.74, 0, 0.26)] \oplus \neg [U \sqcup (0.9, 0, 0.1)]$$
$$= (0.74, 0, 0.26) \oplus \neg (0.9, 0, 0.1)$$
$$= (0.74, 0, 0.26) \oplus (0, 0.9, 0.1)$$
$$= (0.22, 0.7, 0.08)$$
$$= DF_2'$$

Choosing a pair of *t-norm* and *t-conorm* inference result derived on $\mathcal{L}^2$, and its interpretations $cl_{\mathcal{I}^*(\mathcal{L})}^F$ and $cl_{\mathcal{I}^*(\mathcal{L})}^G$ on $\mathcal{I}^*(\mathcal{L})$ are as follows.

$$cl_{\mathcal{L}^2_{di}}^{\min/\max}(\phi)(theft(P,B,T))$$
$$= [U \vee (T \wedge T \wedge T \wedge T \wedge DT_1)]$$
$$\oplus \neg [U \vee (T \wedge T \wedge T \wedge T \wedge T \wedge T \wedge DT_2)]$$
$$= [U \vee (T \wedge DT_1')] \oplus \neg [U \vee (T \wedge DT_2')]$$
$$= [(0,0) \vee ((1,0) \wedge (0.5,0))] \oplus \neg$$
$$[(0,0) \vee ((1,0) \wedge (0.8,0))]$$
$$= [(0,0) \vee (\min(1,0.5), \max(0,0))] \oplus \neg$$
$$[(0,0) \vee (\min(1,0.8), \max(0,0))]$$
$$= [(0,0) \vee (0.5,0)] \oplus \neg [(0,0) \vee (0.8,0)]$$
$$= (\max(0,0.5), \min(0,0)) \oplus \neg$$
$$(\max(0,0.8), \min(0,0))$$
$$= (0.5,0) \oplus \neg (0.8,0)$$
$$= (0.5,0) \oplus (0,0.8)$$
$$= (\max(0.5,0), \max(0,0.8))$$
$$= (0.5,0.8) = DF_2'$$

$$cl_{\mathcal{I}^*(\mathcal{L})}^F(cl_{\mathcal{L}^2_{di}}^{\min/\max}(\phi)(theft(P,B,T)))$$
$$= cl_{\mathcal{I}^*(\mathcal{L})}^F((0.5,0.8))$$
$$= (\frac{0.5 \bullet 0.8}{0.5+0.8}, \frac{0.8^2}{0.5+0.8}) = (0.3, 0.49) = DF_1'$$
$$cl_{\mathcal{I}^*(\mathcal{L})}^G(cl_{\mathcal{L}^2_{di}}^{\min/\max}(\phi)(theft(P,B,T)))$$
$$= cl_{\mathcal{I}^*(\mathcal{L})}^G((0.5,0.8))$$
$$= (\frac{0.5}{2}, 0.8 - \frac{0.5}{2}) = (0.25, 0.55) = DF_1'$$

$$cl_{\mathcal{L}^2_{di}}^{prod/sum}(\phi)(theft(P,B,T))$$
$$= [U \vee (T \wedge T \wedge T \wedge T \wedge DT_1)]$$
$$\oplus \neg [U \vee (T \wedge T \wedge T \wedge T \wedge T \wedge T \wedge DT_2)]$$
$$= [U \vee (T \wedge DT_1)] \oplus \neg [U \vee (T \wedge DT_2)]$$
$$= [(0,0) \vee ((1,0) \wedge (0.5,0))] \oplus \neg$$
$$[(0,0) \vee ((1,0) \wedge (0.8,0))]$$
$$= [(0,0) \vee (1 \bullet 0.5, 0 + 0 - 0 \bullet 0)] \oplus$$
$$[(0,0) \vee (1 \bullet 0.8, 0 + 0 - 0 \bullet 0)]$$
$$= [(0,0) \vee (0.5,0)] \oplus \neg [(0,0) \vee (0.8,0)]$$
$$= (0 + 0.5 - 0 \bullet 0.5, 0 \bullet 0) \oplus \neg (0 + 0.8 - 0 \bullet 0.8, 0 \bullet 0)$$
$$= (0.5, 0) \oplus \neg (0.8, 0)$$
$$= (0.5, 0) \oplus (0, 0.8)$$
$$= (0.5 + 0 - 0.5 \bullet 0, 0 + 0.8 - 0 \bullet 0.8)$$
$$= (0.5, 0.8) = DF_2'$$

$$cl_{\mathcal{I}^*(\mathcal{L})}^F(cl_{\mathcal{L}^2_{di}}^{prod/sum}(\phi)(theft(P,B,T)))$$
$$= cl_{\mathcal{I}^*(\mathcal{L})}^F((0.5,0.8)) = (0.3, 0.49) = DF_1'$$
$$cl_{\mathcal{I}^*(\mathcal{L})}^G(cl_{\mathcal{L}^2_{di}}^{prod/sum}(\phi)(theft(P,B,T)))$$
$$= cl_{\mathcal{I}^*(\mathcal{L})}^G((0.5,0.8)) = (0.25, 0.55) = DF_1'$$

$$cl_{\mathcal{L}^2_{di}}^{Luk}(\phi)(theft(P,B,T))$$
$$= [U \vee (T \wedge T \wedge T \wedge T \wedge DT_1)]$$
$$\oplus \neg[U \vee (T \wedge T \wedge T \wedge T \wedge T \wedge DT_2)]$$
$$= [U \vee (T \wedge DT_1)] \oplus \neg[U \vee (T \wedge DT_2)]$$
$$= [(0,0) \vee ((1,0) \wedge (0.5,0))] \oplus \neg$$
$$[(0,0) \vee ((1,0) \wedge (0.8,0))]$$
$$= [(0,0) \vee (\max(0,1+0.5-1), \min(0+0,1)]$$
$$\oplus \neg[(0,0) \vee (\max(0,1+0.8-1), \min(0+0,1)]$$
$$= [(0,0) \vee (0.5,0)] \oplus \neg[(0,0) \vee (0.8,0)]$$
$$= (\min(0+0.5,1), \max(0,0+0-1)) \oplus \neg$$
$$(\min(0+0.8,1), \max(0,0+0-1))$$
$$= (0.5,0) \oplus \neg(0.8,0)$$
$$= (0.5,0) \oplus (0,0.8)$$
$$= (\min(0+0.5,1), \min(0+0.8,1))$$
$$= (0.5,0.8) = DF_2'$$

$$cl_{\mathcal{I}^*(\mathcal{L})}^F(cl_{\mathcal{L}^2_{di}}^{Luk}(\phi)(theft(P,B,T)))$$
$$= cl_{\mathcal{I}^*(\mathcal{L})}^F((0.5,0.8)) = (0.3,0.49) = DF_1'$$
$$cl_{\mathcal{I}^*(\mathcal{L})}^G(cl_{\mathcal{L}^2_{di}}^{Luk}(\phi)(theft(P,B,T)))$$
$$= cl_{\mathcal{I}^*(\mathcal{L})}^G((0.5,0.8)) = (0.25,0.55) = DF_1'$$

$$cl_{\mathcal{L}^2_{di}}^{drastic}(\phi)(theft(P,B,T))$$
$$= [U \vee (T \wedge T \wedge T \wedge T \wedge DT_1)]$$
$$\oplus \neg[U \vee (T \wedge T \wedge T \wedge T \wedge T \wedge DT_2)]$$
$$= [U \vee (T \wedge DT_1)] \oplus \neg[U \vee (T \wedge DT_2)]$$
$$= [(0,0) \vee ((1,0) \wedge (0.5,0))] \oplus \neg$$
$$[(0,0) \vee ((1,0) \wedge (0.8,0))]$$
$$= [(0,0) \vee (\mathcal{T}_D(1,0.5), \mathcal{S}_D(0,0)] \oplus \neg$$
$$[(0,0) \vee (\mathcal{T}_D(1,0.8), \mathcal{S}_D(0,0)]$$
$$= [(0,0) \vee (0.5,0)] \oplus \neg[(0,0) \vee (0.8,0)]$$
$$= (\mathcal{S}_D(0,0.5), \mathcal{T}_D(0,0)) \oplus \neg(\mathcal{S}_D(0,0.8), \mathcal{T}_D(0,0))$$
$$= (0.5,0) \oplus \neg(0.8,0)$$
$$= (0.5,0) \oplus (0,0.8)$$
$$= (\mathcal{S}_D(0,0.5), \mathcal{S}_D(0,0.8))$$
$$= (0.5,0.8) = DF_2'$$

$$cl_{\mathcal{I}^*(\mathcal{L})}^F(cl_{\mathcal{L}^2_{di}}^{drastic}(\phi)(theft(P,B,T)))$$
$$= cl_{\mathcal{I}^*(\mathcal{L})}^F((0.5,0.8)) = (0.3,0.49) = DF_1'$$
$$cl_{\mathcal{I}^*(\mathcal{L})}^G(cl_{\mathcal{L}^2_{di}}^{drastic}(\phi)(theft(P,B,T)))$$
$$= cl_{\mathcal{I}^*(\mathcal{L})}^G((0.5,0.8)) = (0.25,0.55) = DF_1'$$

$$cl_{\mathcal{L}^2_{di}}^{Nilpotent}(\phi)(theft(P,B,T))$$
$$= [U \vee (T \wedge T \wedge T \wedge T \wedge DT_1)]$$
$$\oplus \neg[U \vee (T \wedge T \wedge T \wedge T \wedge T \wedge DT_2)]$$
$$= [U \vee (T \wedge DT_1)] \oplus \neg[U \vee (T \wedge DT_2)]$$
$$= [(0,0) \vee ((1,0) \wedge (0.5,0))] \oplus \neg$$
$$[(0,0) \vee ((1,0) \wedge (0.8,0))]$$
$$= [(0,0) \vee (\mathcal{T}_{nM}(1,0.5), \mathcal{S}_{nM}(0,0)] \oplus \neg$$
$$[(0,0) \vee (\mathcal{T}_{nM}(1,0.8), \mathcal{S}_{nM}(0,0)]$$
$$= [(0,0) \vee (0.5,0)] \oplus \neg[(0,0) \vee (0.8,0)]$$
$$= (\mathcal{S}_{nM}(0,0.5), \mathcal{T}_{nM}(0,0)) \oplus \neg$$
$$(\mathcal{S}_{nM}(0,0.8), \mathcal{T}_{nM}(0,0))$$
$$= (0.5,0) \oplus \neg(0.8,0)$$
$$= (0.5,0) \oplus (0,0.8)$$
$$= (\mathcal{S}_{nM}(0,0.5), \mathcal{S}_{nM}(0,0.8))$$
$$= (0.5,0.8) = DF_2'$$

$$cl_{\mathcal{I}^*(\mathcal{L})}^F(cl_{\mathcal{L}^2_{di}}^{Nilpotent}(\phi)(theft(P,B,T)))$$
$$= cl_{\mathcal{I}^*(\mathcal{L})}^F((0.5,0.8)) = (0.3,0.49) = DF_1'$$
$$cl_{\mathcal{I}^*(\mathcal{L})}^G(cl_{\mathcal{L}^2_{di}}^{Nilpotent}(\phi)(theft(P,B,T)))$$
$$= cl_{\mathcal{I}^*(\mathcal{L})}^G((0.5,0.8)) = (0.25,0.55) = DF_1'$$

$cl_{\mathcal{L}^2_{di}}^{Hamacher}(\phi)(theft(P,B,T))$

$= [U \vee (T \wedge T \wedge T \wedge T \wedge DT_1)]$

$\quad \oplus \neg [U \vee (T \wedge T \wedge T \wedge T \wedge T \wedge DT_2)]$

$= [U \vee (T \wedge DT_1)] \oplus \neg [U \vee (T \wedge DT_2)]$

$= [(0,0) \vee ((1,0) \wedge (0.5,0))] \oplus \neg$

$\quad [(0,0) \vee ((1,0) \wedge (0.8,0))]$

$= [(0,0) \vee (\mathcal{T}_{H0}(1,0.5), \mathcal{S}_{H2}(0,0)] \oplus \neg$

$\quad [(0,0) \vee (\mathcal{T}_{H0}(1,0.8), \mathcal{S}_{H2}(0,0)]$

$= [(0,0) \vee (0.5,0)] \oplus \neg [(0,0) \vee (0.8,0)]$

$= (\mathcal{S}_{H2}(0,0.5), \mathcal{T}_{H0}(0,0)) \oplus \neg$

$\quad (\mathcal{S}_{H2}(0,0.8), \mathcal{T}_{H0}(0,0))$

$= (0.5,0) \oplus \neg (0.8,0)$

$= (0.5,0) \oplus (0,0.8)$

$= (\mathcal{S}_{H2}(0,0.5), \mathcal{S}_{H2}(0,0.8))$

$= (0.5,0.8) = DF'_2$

$cl_{\mathcal{I}^*(\mathcal{L})}^{F}(cl_{\mathcal{L}^2_{di}}^{Hamacher}(\phi)(theft(P,B,T)))$

$= cl_{\mathcal{I}^*(\mathcal{L})}^{F}((0.5,0.8)) = (0.3,0.49) = DF'_1$

$cl_{\mathcal{I}^*(\mathcal{L})}^{G}(cl_{\mathcal{L}^2_{di}}^{Hamacher}(\phi)(theft(P,B,T)))$

$= cl_{\mathcal{I}^*(\mathcal{L})}^{G}((0.5,0.8)) = (0.25,0.55) = DF'_1$

Figure 13 shows above reasoning results. In case of Case1, subjective logic yielded a rather strong opinion $(0.74, 0, 0.26)$ that is rather close to DT_2 than DT_1 that other approaches yielded. Contrary to Case 1, when we take more information also from $Cam2$, both of above inference concluded $cl(\phi)(theft(P_2, B, T)) = DF_2$ and DF'_2. Namely, no theft has taken place with rather high confidence. The opinion DF'_2 $(0.22, 0.7, 0.08)$ in opinion triangle is the most closest one to DF_2 compared to L-fuzzy logic based results. In the sense of truth value, this is the same to the cases of yielded values on $\mathcal{L}^2$. However, in this case, the amount of falsity is also relatively high therefore the point is located in the area of overflowed information $(\mu + \nu > 1)$. The F and G interpretations are both close to each other however the interpretation is rather closer to DF_1. Nonetheless, in the sense that all reasoning results are pointed on the left-hand side of the line of undecidable *, semantically, this can be interpreted as the meaning of week false like DF_2. Thus, the semantics of results from the discrete bilattice for multivalued default logic, the bilattice based L-fuzzy logics and subjective logic are the same.

Figure 13. Reasoning results of example 4 in opinion space, $\mathcal{L}^2$ and $\mathcal{I}^*(\mathcal{L})$

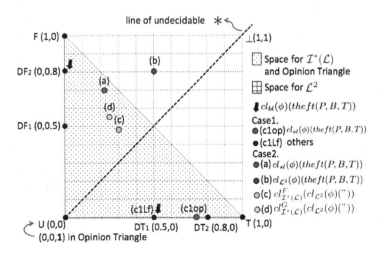

As shown with above illustrative visual surveillance inference scenarios, the proposed default reasoning mechanism Equation 2 semantically well models default reasoning and that is so in the case of *L*-fuzzy logics.

DISCUSSIONS

As shown in the previous section with examples of default reasoning in visual surveillance, both subjective logic and *L*-fuzzy logics (especially, IFL and fuzzy Belnap logic) seem relevant for the use of approximate default reasoning. What makes IFSs attractive compared to other fuzzy set extensions is that it makes geometrical interpretations possible, thereby, the combination of membership and non-membership functions can be calculated in the Euclidean plane with a Cartesian coordinate system (Atanassov, 2003). This aspect is also the same in Subjective logic because subjective logic also makes the geometrical interpretations of Beta probability distributions possible in the Euclidean plane. However, there are still some properties worth to discuss to contrast these approaches. In this section, we give a comparison on the property of both approaches in the view of logical soundness and feasibility in visual surveillance.

Which Way to Go? Subjective Logic vs. L-Fuzzy Logics

As we noted in the previous default reasoning section, the initial idea of discrete bilattice assumed an epistemic state called '*unknown*' and '*contradiction*' following Belnap's four-valued logic. In the sense of discrete valued logic such as multivalued default logic, the only way of reaching to the overflowed information state is through the handling of definite true and definite false, and '*contradiction*' $\perp$ is the only epistemic state that is defined in the overflowed information area. However, as shown in the previous examples,

this is not true on $\mathcal{L}^2$, because we can encounter values in the area of $(\mu + \nu > 1)$. Regarding the meaning of the area, and more specifically the epistemic state *contradiction,* there have been many discussions on the significance of the epistemic state in the view of logic. A critical review can be found in (Urquhart, 1986). There has been also some report on the possible problems that could be introduced for the formal specification of software systems such as non-termination error (Hähnle, 2005). Dubois (2008) formally showed the problems that can arise in Belnap logic, in the sense of logical soundness. In the following, we briefly review the discussions introduced by (Dubois, 2008).

Discussion 1 (Paradoxes in the truth table of multivalued logics): Figure 6 shows the truth table of the Belnap's four-valued logic and the default logic. In both logics, the conjunction and disjunction are problematic when applied to the two extreme epistemic states '*Unkown*' U and '*Contradiction*' $\perp$. For instance in Belnap logic, we have $U \wedge U = U$ and $U \vee U = U$. Assume that we attached U to a proposition p and consider $p \wedge \neg p$ and $p \vee \neg p$. In Belnap logic, the former and latter both are U because $U \wedge \neg U = U \wedge U = U$ and $U \vee \neg U = U \vee U = U$. However, in classical logic sense, the former should be false and the latter should be true. The same anomaly is also introduced in the case of $\perp$. According to the truth table, it claims $\perp \wedge \perp = \perp$ and $\perp \vee \perp = \perp$. For $p \wedge \neg p$ and $p \vee \neg p$, again, we get $\perp$ for both. It breaks the tautology in classical logic sense (Dubois, 2008). Similar anomaly can be found in the case of $U \wedge \perp = F$ and $U \vee \perp = T$. From a common sense, the results are counterintuitive and this was even to Belnap because he stated that this is an unavoidable consequence of his formal setting (Dubois, 2008).

This aspect can be problematic in the following scenario. Consider a proposition p and q, and agent A_1 and A_2 saying the p is T and F respectively and this is why p is $\bot$. Because A_1 and A_2 say nothing about q we assume q is U. Now, $p \wedge q = \bot \wedge U = F$ that is again counter intuitive (Dubois, 2008). This aspect also leads to debatable epistemic value assignments. Suppose two atomic propositions p and q with epistemic state assignment $\phi(p) = \bot$ and $\phi(q) = U$. Then $\phi(p \wedge q) = F$ as noted above. But since Belnap negation is such that $\phi(\neg p) = \bot$ and $\phi(\neg q) = U$, we also get
$$\phi(\neg p \wedge q) = \phi(p \wedge \neg q)$$
$$= \phi(\neg p \wedge \neg q) = F.$$
Hence,
$$\phi((p \wedge q) \wedge (\neg p \wedge q) \wedge (p \wedge \neg q) \wedge (\neg p \wedge \neg q)) =$$
$$\phi(p \wedge q) \wedge \phi(\neg p \wedge q) \wedge \phi(p \wedge \neg q) \wedge \phi(\neg p \wedge \neg q) = F,$$
however, according to the truth table,
$$(p \wedge q) \wedge (\neg p \wedge q) \wedge (p \wedge \neg q) \wedge (\neg p \wedge \neg q)$$
$$= F \wedge F \wedge T \wedge T = \bot .$$
This means $\phi(\bot) = F$, therefore hardly acceptable again. (Dubois, 2008). This aspect shows that, for any logical connectives $*$, $\phi(p) * \phi(q) \neq \phi(p * q)$ in Belnap logic. In other words, an epistemic value on each proposition can not characterize a single epistemic value for the combination of the propositions. This aspect also hold in the fuzzy Belnap logic as well, because regardless what *t-norms* and *t-conorms* we choose, the truth table values corresponding to definite true, definite false, unknown and contradictory values will have the same truth functional values as of discrete Belnap logic.

Unlike fuzzy Belnap logic, in subjective logic we can avoid this problem by the use of atomicity value a, therefore subjective logic better captures the spirit of classical logic. Consider the same case of $U \wedge U$ and $U \vee U$. As shown in Figure 14 (a), for a subjective logic opinion

$\omega = (0, 0, 1, 0.5)$ which corresponds to U, subjective logic conjunction also draws full ignorance but with different atomicity, namely
$$(0, 0, 1, 0.5) \wedge \neg(0, 0, 1, 0.5)$$
$$= (0, 0, 1, 0.25).$$
The semantics is clear. Namely, for a proposition that is known to be binary event that an agent has a full ignorance on the truth of it, the conjunction also draws full uncertainty but, following the spirit of probabilistic conjunction, it comes with the atomicity that is the product of both atomicity (i.e. $0.5 \bullet 0.5$ in this case). Therefore, even if we get full ignorance, when it is interpreted in terms of Beta distribution, the overall expectation should be biased to falsity as traditional logic yields F. This is the same in the case of $U \vee U$ that yields a full ignorance opinion but its atomicity is biased to T. The similar aspect holds in the case of $\bot \wedge \bot = \bot$ and $\bot \vee \bot = \bot$. For $p \wedge \neg p$ and $p \vee \neg p$, classical logic should draw T and F. As shown in Figure 14 (b), considering the epistemic state of contradiction as $\omega = (0.5, 0.5, 0, 0.5)$, we get
$$(0.5, 0.5, 0, 0.5) \wedge \neg(0.5, 0.5, 0, 0.5)$$
$$= (0.25, 0.75, 0, 0.25)$$
that is biased to disbelief. Note that, both in Figure 14 (a) and (b) we have the same probability expectation values. However, when represented as Beta distribution, while (b) is almost certain because we have rather pick distribution (b) is almost uncertain. This aspect is directly captured in the opinion triangle by the value of ignorance. Now, for the counter intuitive cases of $U \wedge \bot = F$ and $U \vee \bot = T$ in Belnap logic, subjective logic draws a bit different epistemic states. Figure 15 (a) depicts two cases of $U \wedge \bot$ one more biased to F and the other more biased to $\bot$. The basic idea is that we take more atomicity in the case of unknown opinion. The same aspect is captured in the case of $U \vee \bot$ as shown in Figure 15 (b). Figure 15 (a) more intuitively explains the above mentioned agent scenario with two propositions p and q. Again, consider the truth value on proposition p to be $\bot$ because agent A_1 and A_2 saying the p

Figure 14. (a) $U \wedge U$ *and* $U \vee U$ *(b)* $\bot \wedge \bot$ *and* $\bot \vee \bot$

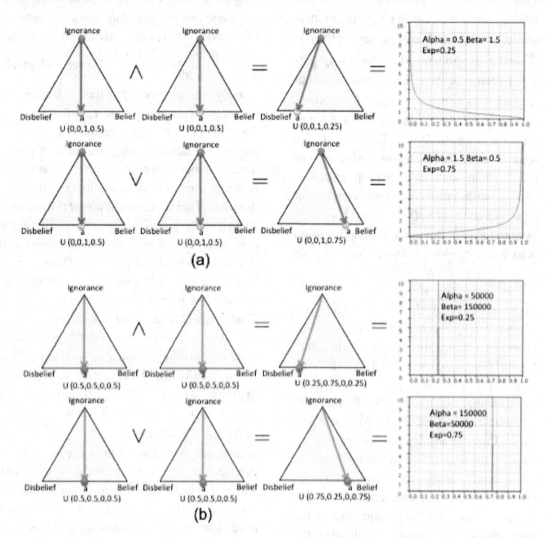

is T and F. For the proposition q, we assign U because agent A_1 and A_2 say nothing about q. Now, $p \wedge q$ can be determined differently as shown in Figure 15 (a). Finally, the last aspect on whether commutative computation is possible or not in Belnap logic, has no problem in subjective logic. Suppose two atomic propositions p and q with epistemic state assignment

$\phi(p) = \bot = (0.5, 0.5, 0, 0.5)$ and $\phi(q) = U$ $= (0, 0, 1, 0.5)$.

Then, $\phi(p \wedge q) = (0.17, 0.5, 0.33, 0.25)$. The negation in this case is $\phi(\neg p) = \bot = (0.5, 0.5, 0, 0.5)$ and $\phi(\neg q) = U = (0, 0, 1, 0.5)$, we also get $\phi(\neg p \wedge q) = \phi(p \wedge \neg q)$ $= \phi(\neg \wedge \neg q)$ Hence, $= (0.17, 0.5, 0.33, 0.25)$.

Figure 15. (a) Two examples of $U \wedge \bot$ (b) two examples of $U \vee \bot$ in subjective logic

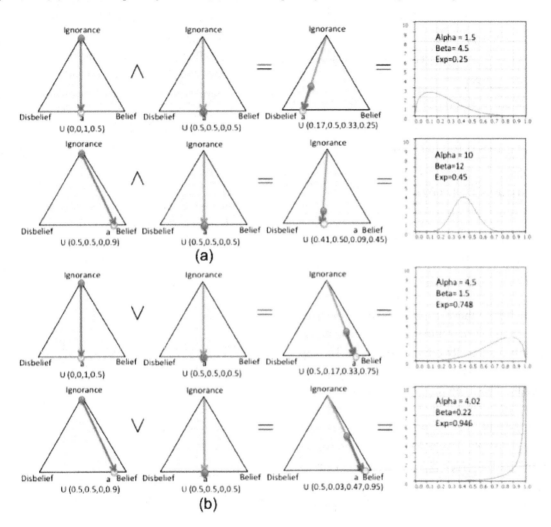

(a)

(b)

$\phi((p \wedge q) \wedge (\neg p \wedge q) \wedge (p \wedge \neg q) \wedge (\neg p \wedge \neg q))$

$= \phi(p \wedge q) \wedge \phi(\neg p \wedge q) \wedge \phi(p \wedge \neg q) \wedge \phi(\neg p \wedge \neg q)$

$= (0.17, 0.5, 0.33, 0.25) \wedge (0.17, 0.5, 0.33, 0.25) \wedge$

$(0.17, 0.5, 0.33, 0.25) \wedge (0.17, 0.5, 0.33, 0.25)$

$= (0.07, 0.75, 0.18, 0.07) \wedge (0.17, 0.5, 0.33, 0.25)$

$\wedge (0.17, 0.5, 0.33, 0.25)$

$= (0.03, 0.88, 0.1, 0.02) \wedge (0.17, 0.5, 0.33, 0.25)$

$= (0.01, 0.94, 0.05, 0.01)$

In subjective logic, regardless of the order how we calculate opinions, we get the same result as follows.

$\phi((p \wedge q) \wedge (\neg p \wedge q) \wedge (p \wedge \neg q) \wedge (\neg p \wedge \neg q))$

$= \phi((0.17, 0.5, 0.33, 0.25) \wedge (0.5, 0.5, 0, 0.5) \wedge$

$q \wedge p \wedge \neg q \wedge \neg p \wedge \neg q)$

$= \phi((0.11, 0.75, 0.14, 0.13) \wedge (0, 0, 1, 0.5) \wedge$

$p \wedge \neg q \wedge \neg p \wedge \neg q)$

$= \phi((0.05, 0.75, 0.2, 0.07) \wedge (0.5, 0.5, 0, 0.5) \wedge$

$\neg q \wedge \neg p \wedge \neg q)$

$= \phi((0.03, 0.88, 0.10, 0.04) \wedge (0, 0, 1, 0.5) \wedge$

$\neg p \wedge \neg q)$

$= \phi((0.01, 0.88, 0.11, 0.02) \wedge$

$(0.5, 0.5, 0, 0.5) \wedge \neg q)$

$= \phi((0.01, 0.94, 0.05, 0.01) \wedge (0, 0, 1, 0.5))$

$= \phi(0, 01, 0.94, 0.05, 0.01)$

$= (0, 01, 0.94, 0.05, 0.01)$

We believe, above aspect makes subjective logic more solid and sound logic formalism under uncertainty. Especially, compared to fuzzy Belnap logic, the operational order does not affect on the final result. This is an important aspect, because in fuzzy-Belnap logic, once we reach at the contradictory point, there is no easy way to escape from the state unless we use the meet operator $\otimes$ along the partial order $\leq_k$. Therefore, in fuzzy Belnap logic, the sequence of information arrival is important, however, so is not in subjective logic.

Discussion 2 (Feasibility in visual surveillance):

In the previous section for the examples, we assigned definite true T and definite false F for the logical facts. In practice, however, such symbolic logical facts are generated from the vision analytics. Because the vision analytics tend to rely on machine learning and pattern recognition techniques, in general, the values will be also noisy. Indeed, in practice, it would be more realistic to attach arbitrary amount of beliefs even to the logical rules rather than values such as DT, DF, DT_1, DF_1, etc. In the previous examples, the L-fuzzy logic based approaches generated the same result regardless how we choose *t-norms* and *t-conorms*. Therefore, in this discussion we will examine how the uncertainty introduced on facts and rules, and how the choices on *t-norms* and *t-conorms* could affect the reasoning result.

Consider Example 2 in the previous section with slightly different settings as follows.

$$\phi[\neg equal(P_1, P_2) \leftarrow distinct(P_1, P_2)] = (0.5, 0.1)_{\mathcal{L}^2}$$
$$= (0.5, 0.1, 0.4)_{sl} = r_1$$

$$\phi[equal(P_1, P_2) \leftarrow appear\_similar(P_1, P_2)]$$
$$= (0.5, 0.1)_{\mathcal{L}^2} = (0.5, 0.1, 0.4)_{sl} = r_2$$

$$\phi[appear\_similar(a, b)] = (0.6, 0.3)_{\mathcal{L}^2}$$
$$= (0.6, 0.3, 0.1)_{sl} = f_1$$

$$\phi[distinct(a, b)] = (0.3, 0.4)_{\mathcal{L}^2} = (0.3, 0.4, 0.3)_{sl} = f_2$$

In above setting, given two rules that are considered with the same amount of significance, we attach more strong belief to f_1. Therefore, the expected result is that the two persons maybe the same one but not quite certainly. Applying the same inference mechanism Equation 1 for *L*-fuzzy logics and (2) for subjective logic, the inference results are as follows. (note that, above setting is not applicable to the case of discrete bilattice species for multivalued default logic.).

$cl_{sl_{di}}(\phi)(equal(a,b))$

$= [U \sqcup (f_1 \bullet r_2)] \oplus \neg[U \sqcup (f_2 \bullet r_1)]$

$= [U \sqcup (0.6, 0.3, 0.1) \bullet (0.5, 0.1, 0.4)]$
$\quad \oplus \neg[U \sqcup (0.3, 0.4, 0.3) \bullet (0.5, 0.1, 0.4)]$

$= [(0, 0, 1) \sqcup (0.4, 0.37, 0.23)]$
$\quad \oplus \neg[(0, 0, 1) \sqcup (0.24, 0.46, 0.3)]$

$= (0.4, 0.07, 0.53)$
$\quad \oplus \neg(0.24, 0.09, 0.67)$

$= (0.4, 0.07, 0.53) \oplus (0.09, 0.24, 0.67)$

$= (0.37, 0.21, 0.42)$

As shown in Figure 9, choosing one of *t-norm* and *t-conorm* pair and applying Equation 3 in Definition 21, we get following inference results derived on $\mathcal{L}^2$, and its interpretations $cl^F_{\mathcal{I}^*(\mathcal{L})}$ and $cl^G_{\mathcal{I}^*(\mathcal{L})}$ on $\mathcal{I}^*(\mathcal{L})$.

$cl^{\min/\max}_{\mathcal{L}^2_{di}}(\phi)(equal(a,b))$

$= [U \vee (f_1 \wedge r_2)] \oplus \neg[U \vee (f_2 \wedge r_1)]$

$= [U \vee (0.6, 0.3) \wedge (0.5, 0.1)]$
$\quad \oplus \neg[U \vee (0.3, 0.4) \wedge (0.5, 0.1)]$

$= [U \vee (\min(0.6, 0.5), \max(0.3, 0.1))]$
$\quad \oplus \neg[U \vee (\min(0.3, 0.5), \max(0.4, 0.1))]$

$= [(0, 0) \vee (0.5, 0.3)]$
$\quad \oplus \neg[(0, 0) \vee (0.3, 0.4)]$

$= (\max(0, 0.5), \min(0, 0.3))$
$\quad \oplus \neg(\max(0, 0.3), \min(0, 0.4))$

$= (0.5, 0) \oplus \neg(0.3, 0)$

$= (0.5, 0) \oplus (0, 0.3)$

$= (\max(0.5, 0), \max(0, 0.3))$

$= (0.5, 0.3)$

$cl^F_{\mathcal{I}^*(\mathcal{L})}(cl^{\min/\max}_{\mathcal{L}^2_{di}}(\phi)(equal(a,b)))$

$= cl^F_{\mathcal{I}^*(\mathcal{L})}((0.5, 0.3))$

$= (\dfrac{0.5^2}{0.5 + 0.3}, \dfrac{0.5 \bullet 0.3}{0.5 + 0.3})$

$= (0.31, 0.19)$

$cl^G_{\mathcal{I}^*(\mathcal{L})}(cl^{\min/\max}_{\mathcal{L}^2_{di}}(\phi)(equal(a,b)))$

$= cl^G_{\mathcal{I}^*(\mathcal{L})}((0.5, 0.3))$

$= (0.5 - \dfrac{0.3}{2}, \dfrac{0.3}{2})$

$= (0.35, 0.15) = DF'_2$

$cl^{prod/sum}_{\mathcal{L}^2_{di}}(\phi)(equal(a,b))$

$= [U \vee (f_1 \wedge r_2)] \oplus \neg[U \vee (f_2 \wedge r_1)]$

$= [U \vee (0.6, 0.3) \wedge (0.5, 0.1)]$
$\quad \oplus \neg[U \vee (0.3, 0.4) \wedge (0.5, 0.1)]$

$= [U \vee (0.6 \bullet 0.5, 0.3 + 0.1 - 0.3 \bullet 0.1)]$
$\quad \oplus \neg[U \vee (0.3 \bullet 0.5, 0.4 + 0.1 - 0.4 \bullet 0.1)]$

$= [(0, 0) \vee (0.3, 0.37)]$
$\quad \oplus \neg[(0, 0) \vee (0.15, 0.46)]$

$= (0 + 0.3 - 0 \bullet 0.3, 0 \bullet 0.37)$
$\quad \oplus \neg(0 + 0.15 - 0 \bullet 0.15, 0 \bullet 0.15)$

$= (0.3, 0) \oplus \neg(0.15, 0)$

$= (0.3, 0) \oplus (0, 0.15)$

$= (0.3 + 0 - 0.3 \bullet 0, 0 + 0.15 - 0 \bullet 0.15)$

$= (0.3, 0.15)$

$$cl^F_{\mathcal{I}^*(\mathcal{L})}(cl^{prod/sum}_{\mathcal{L}^\mathcal{Q}_{di}}(\phi)(equal(a,b)))$$
$$= cl^F_{\mathcal{I}^*(\mathcal{L})}((0.3, 0.15))$$
$$= (\frac{0.3^2}{0.3 + 0.15}, \frac{0.3 \bullet 0.15}{0.3 + 0.15})$$
$$= (0.2, 0.1)$$
$$cl^G_{\mathcal{I}^*(\mathcal{L})}(cl^{prod/\overset{\ast}{sum}}_{\mathcal{L}^\mathcal{Q}_{di}}(\phi)(equal(a,b)))$$
$$= cl^G_{\mathcal{I}^*(\mathcal{L})}((0.3, 0.15))$$
$$= (0.3 - \frac{0.15}{2}, \frac{0.15}{2})$$
$$= (0.225, 0.075)$$

$$cl^{Luk}_{\mathcal{L}^\mathcal{Q}_{di}}(\phi)(equal(a,b))$$
$$= [U \vee (f_1 \wedge r_2)] \oplus \neg[U \vee (f_2 \wedge r_1)]$$
$$= [U \vee (0.6, 0.3) \wedge (0.5, 0.1)]$$
$$\quad \oplus \neg[U \vee (0.3, 0.4) \wedge (0.5, 0.1)]$$
$$= [U \vee (\max(0, 0.6 + 0.5 - 1), \min(0.3 + 0.1, 1)]$$
$$\quad \oplus \neg[U \vee (\max(0, 0.3 + 0.5 - 1), \min(0.4 + 0.1, 1)]$$
$$= [(0, 0) \vee (0.1, 0.4)]$$
$$\quad \oplus \neg[(0, 0) \vee (0, 0.5)]$$
$$= (\min(0 + 0.1, 1), \max(0, 0 + 0.4 - 1))$$
$$\quad \oplus \neg(\min(0 + 0, 1), \max(0, 0 + 0.5 - 1))$$
$$= (0.1, 0) \oplus \neg(0, 0)$$
$$= (0.3, 0) \oplus (0.0)$$
$$= (\min(0.3 + 0, 1), \min(0 + 0, 1))$$
$$= (0.3, 0)$$

$$cl^F_{\mathcal{I}^*(\mathcal{L})}(cl^{Luk}_{\mathcal{L}^\mathcal{Q}_{di}}(\phi)(equal(a,b))) = cl^F_{\mathcal{I}^*(\mathcal{L})}((0.3, 0))$$
$$= (\frac{0.3^2}{0.3 + 0}, \frac{0.3 \bullet 0}{0.3 + 0})$$
$$= (0.3, 0)$$
$$cl^G_{\mathcal{I}^*(\mathcal{L})}(cl^{Luk}_{\mathcal{L}^\mathcal{Q}_{di}}(\phi)(equal(a,b))) = cl^G_{\mathcal{I}^*(\mathcal{L})}((0.3, 0))$$
$$= (0.3 - \frac{0}{2}, \frac{0}{2})$$
$$= (0.3, 0)$$

$$cl^{drastic}_{\mathcal{L}^\mathcal{Q}_{di}}(\phi)(equal(a,b))$$
$$= [U \vee (f_1 \wedge r_2)] \oplus \neg[U \vee (f_2 \wedge r_1)]$$
$$= [U \vee (0.6, 0.3) \wedge (0.5, 0.1)]$$
$$\quad \oplus \neg[U \vee (0.3, 0.4) \wedge (0.5, 0.1)]$$
$$= [U \vee (\mathcal{T}_D(0.6, 0.5), \mathcal{S}_D(0.3, 0.1)]$$
$$\quad \oplus \neg[U \vee (\mathcal{T}_D(0.3, 0.5), \mathcal{S}_D(0.4, 0.1)]$$
$$= [(0, 0) \vee (0, 1)]$$
$$\quad \oplus \neg[(0, 0) \vee (0, 1)]$$
$$= (\mathcal{S}_D(0, 0), \mathcal{T}_D(0, 1))$$
$$\quad \oplus \neg(\mathcal{S}_D(0, 0), \mathcal{T}_D(0, 1))$$
$$= (0, 0) \oplus \neg(0, 0)$$
$$= (0, 0) \oplus (0, 0)$$
$$= (\mathcal{S}_D(0, 0), \mathcal{S}_D(0, 0))$$
$$= (0, 0)$$

$$cl^F_{\mathcal{I}^*(\mathcal{L})}(cl^{drastic}_{\mathcal{L}^\mathcal{Q}_{di}}(\phi)(equal(a,b)))$$
$$= cl^F_{\mathcal{I}^*(\mathcal{L})}((0, 0)) = (0, 0)$$
$$cl^G_{\mathcal{I}^*(\mathcal{L})}(cl^{drastic}_{\mathcal{L}^\mathcal{Q}_{di}}(\phi)(equal(a,b)))$$
$$= cl^G_{\mathcal{I}^*(\mathcal{L})}((0.3, 0)) = (0, 0)$$

$$cl^{Nilpotent}_{\mathcal{L}^\mathcal{Q}_{di}}(\phi)(equal(a,b))$$
$$= [U \vee (f_1 \wedge r_2)] \oplus \neg[U \vee (f_2 \wedge r_1)]$$
$$= [U \vee (0.6, 0.3) \wedge (0.5, 0.1)]$$
$$\quad \oplus \neg[U \vee (0.3, 0.4) \wedge (0.5, 0.1)]$$
$$= [U \vee (\mathcal{T}_{nM}(0.6, 0.5), \mathcal{S}_{nM}(0.3, 0.1)]$$
$$\quad \oplus \neg[U \vee (\mathcal{T}_{nM}(0.3, 0.5), \mathcal{S}_{nM}(0.4, 0.1)]$$
$$= [(0, 0) \vee (0.5, 0.3)]$$
$$\quad \oplus \neg[(0, 0) \vee (0, 0.4)]$$
$$= (\mathcal{S}_{nM}(0, 0.5), \mathcal{T}_{nM}(0, 0.3))$$
$$\quad \oplus \neg(\mathcal{S}_{nM}(0, 0), \mathcal{T}_{nM}(0, 0.4))$$
$$= (0.5, 0) \oplus \neg(0, 0)$$
$$= (0.5, 0) \oplus (0, 0)$$
$$= (\mathcal{S}_{nM}(0.5, 0), \mathcal{S}_{nM}(0, 0))$$
$$= (0.5, 0)$$

$$cl^F_{\mathcal{I}^*(\mathcal{L})}(cl^{Nilpotent}_{\mathcal{L}^2_{di}}(\phi)(equal(a,b))) = cl^F_{\mathcal{I}^*(\mathcal{L})}((0.5,0))$$

$$= (\frac{0.5^2}{0.5+0}, \frac{0.5 \cdot 0}{0.5+0})$$

$$= (0.5, 0)$$

$$cl^G_{\mathcal{I}^*(\mathcal{L})}(cl^{Nilpotent}_{\mathcal{L}^2_{di}}(\phi)(equal(a,b))) = cl^G_{\mathcal{I}^*(\mathcal{L})}((0.5,0))$$

$$= (0.5 - \frac{0}{2}, \frac{0}{2})$$

$$= (0.5, 0)$$

$$cl^{Hamacher}_{\mathcal{L}^2_{di}}(\phi)(equal(a,b))$$

$$= [U \vee (f_1 \wedge r_2)] \oplus \neg[U \vee (f_2 \wedge r_1)]$$

$$= [U \vee (0.6,0.3) \wedge (0.5,0.1)]$$

$$\oplus \neg[U \vee (0.3,0.4) \wedge (0.5,0.1)]$$

$$= [U \vee (\mathcal{T}_{H0}(0.6,0.5), \mathcal{S}_{H2}(0.3,0.1)]$$

$$\oplus \neg[U \vee (\mathcal{T}_{H0}(0.3,0.5), \mathcal{S}_{H2}(0.4,0.1)]$$

$$- [(0,0) \vee (0.375,0.39)]$$

$$\oplus \neg[(0,0) \vee (0.23,0.48)]$$

$$= (\mathcal{S}_{H2}(0,0.375), \mathcal{T}_{H0}(0,0.39))$$

$$\oplus \neg(\mathcal{S}_{H2}(0,0.23), \mathcal{T}_{H0}(0,0.48))$$

$$= (0.375,0) \oplus \neg(0.23,0)$$

$$= (0.375,0) \oplus (0,0.23)$$

$$= (\mathcal{S}_{H2}(0.375,0), \mathcal{S}_{H2}(0,0.23))$$

$$= (0.375,0.23)$$

$$cl^F_{\mathcal{I}^*(\mathcal{L})}(cl^{Hamacher}_{\mathcal{L}^2_{di}}(\phi)(equal(a,b)))$$

$$= cl^F_{\mathcal{I}^*(\mathcal{L})}((0.375,0.23))$$

$$= (\frac{0.375^2}{0.375+0.23}, \frac{0.375 \cdot 0.23}{0.375+0.23})$$

$$= (0.23,0.14)$$

$$cl^G_{\mathcal{I}^*(\mathcal{L})}(cl^{Hamacher}_{\mathcal{L}^2_{di}}(\phi)(equal(a,b)))$$

$$= cl^G_{\mathcal{I}^*(\mathcal{L})}((0.375,0.23))$$

$$= (0.375 - \frac{0.23}{2}, \frac{0.23}{2})$$

$$= (0.26,0.12)$$

Figure 16 shows above results in opinion space, $\mathcal{I}^*(\mathcal{L})$ and $\mathcal{L}^2$. Unlike the case of using values lying on the boundary of the spaces such as T, F, DT_1, DF_1, when internal values in spaces are used, the reasoning results are quite dependent on the choice of *t-norms* and *t-conorms*. However, what pair of *t-norms* and *t-conorms* to use is not easy to answer. This is a problem common to all fuzzy set based applications. Typically, connectives are categorized by the properties they satisfy. Lukasewicz connectives are in some sense the most interesting one because they satisfy the most properties of binary connectives, but it does not mean that they are best suited for each application. This aspect is sometimes also attacked by statisticians who prefer Bayesian theory. However, Product / Sum connectives are interesting in Bayesian sense, because Product *t-norm* and Sum *t conorm* resemble probabilistic conjunction and disjunction. For instance, following Equation 3, fuzzy Belnap connectives on $\mathcal{L}^2$ that are compositionally defined upon Product *t-norm* and Sum *t-conorm* pair are as follows:

$$(b_x,d_x) \wedge_{bl} (b_y,d_y) = (b_x b_y, d_x + d_y - d_x d_y)$$
$$(b_x,d_x) \vee_{bl} (b_y,d_y) = (b_x + b_y - b_x b_y, d_x d_y)$$
$$(b_x,d_x) \otimes_{bl} (b_y,d_y) = (b_x b_y, d_x d_y)$$
$$(b_x,d_x) \oplus_{bl} (b_y,d_y) = (b_x + b_y - b_x b_y, d_x + d_y - d_x d_y)$$

As mentioned throughout this article, subjective logic has solid mathematical basis in Bayesian perspective on dealing binary (crisp) event (see preliminaries and definitions operators). Therefore, it is worth to compare above Product / Sum connec- tives with the ones in subjective logic in the definition level. For example, given two opinions $\omega_x = (b_x, d_x, i_x, a_x)$ and $\omega_y = (b_y, d_y, i_y, a_y)$, the conjunction operator of subjective logic generates following elements (see Definition 15):

Figure 16. Reasoning results of extended example 2 in opinion space, $\mathcal{L}^2$ and $\mathcal{I}^*(\mathcal{L})$

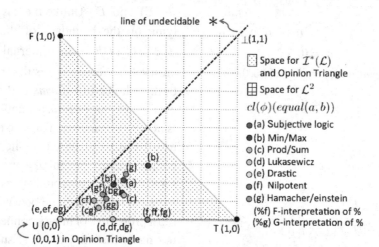

$$b_{x \wedge_{sl} y} = b_x b_y + \frac{(1-a_x)a_y b_x i_y + a_x(1-a_y)i_x b_y}{1-a_x a_y}$$

$$d_{x \wedge_{sl} y} = d_x + d_y - d_x d_y$$

$$i_{x \wedge_{sl} y} = i_x i_y + \frac{(1-a_y)b_x i_y + (1-a_x)i_x b_y}{1-a_x a_y}$$

$$a_{x \wedge_{sl} y} = a_x a_y$$

and the disjunction of the two opinions are defined as follows (see Definition 16):

$$b_{x \vee_{sl} y} = b_x + b_y - b_x b_y$$

$$d_{x \vee_{sl} y} = d_x d_y + \frac{a_x(1-a_y)d_x i_y + (1-a_x)a_y i_x d_y}{a_x + a_y - a_x a_y}$$

$$i_{x \vee_{sl} y} = i_x i_y + \frac{a_y d_x i_y + a_x i_x d_y}{a_x + a_y - a_x a_y}$$

$$a_{x \vee_{sl} y} = a_x + a_y - a_x a_y$$

Although conjunctions (disjunctions) of fuzzy Belnap on Product/Sum and of subjective logic look similar, they are not exactly the same. The reason is because the definition in subjective logic is defined so that it can model a beta distri-

bution that approximates the resulting function by multiplying (comultiplying) the two of corresponding beta distributions of the given two opinions ω_x and ω_y (Jøsang, 2004) (note that, the result of multiplication and comultiplication of two beta functions are not always beta function, Jøsang, 2004). Similarly, while the join operator $\oplus_{bl}$ on Product / Sum just sum both the belief and disbelief, subjective logic calculation is designed so that it can model the beta distribution derived by merging each pair of parameters of the beta distributions correspond to the given two opinions ω_x and ω_y (Jøsang, 2006). Due to this aspect, even compared with Product / Sum fuzzy Belnap connectives, subjective logic stays closer to the Bayesian aspect.

When it comes to visual surveillance, a number of vision analytics are based on the pattern recognition and machine learning techniques that are also (in many cases) based on Bayesian statistics rather than fuzzy theory. Noting this aspect, we advocate subjective logic could be better suited for visual surveillance applications especially when we want to stay closer to the way that usual vision analytics generate uncertain symbolic facts.

CONCLUSION

In this article, we proposed subjective logic based inference framework for default reasoning, and demonstrated its use for high level semantic analysis of visual surveillance scenes. Default reasoning is an important aspect of human like non-monotonic reasoning under incomplete and imprecise knowledge, that can play an important role for deriving plausible conclusions for many applications. Especially, in the forensic sense of visual surveillance that needs to reason about a propositional hypothesis to be investigated after an incident or a report, it is natural to examine all positive and negative contextual evidences that are related to the given hypothesis and fuse them to derive plausible conclusion based on default reasoning. The keys to enable default reasoning are 1) representing incompleteness of knowledge and 2) providing appropriate inference mechanism to draw plausible semantic conclusions by aggregating that knowledge. We adopted subjective logic due to its property of representing belief with ignorance and its rich set of operators for handling uncertain beliefs. To contrast the properties and advantage of the proposed approach, we also applied the inference scheme on L-fuzzy set based logics. The case study results show that the proposed approach and L-fuzzy set based approaches can be an alternative tool to model default reasoning. Among the L-fuzzy logics, intuitionistic fuzzy logic is very similar to the uncertainty representation scheme of subjective logic. While the generalized intuitionistic fuzzy logic (that is fuzzy Belnap logic) can be defined on a bilattice structure with operators regarding degree of information, intuitionistic fuzzy logic could not be fully defined on a bilattice structure because the *join* operator along the axis of degree of information cannot be defined. Contrary to intuitionistic fuzzy logic, even though it also has triangle structure, subjective logic provides an operator called *consensus* that has very similar behaviour as the *join* operator on degree of in-

formation in bilattice. This is because when two opinions are fused by the *consensus* operator, it always decreases ignorance in the derived opinion except in the case of fusing definite true (full belief) and definite false (full disbelief). Due to this aspect, the comparison of subjective logic based default reasoning with intuitionistic fuzzy logic was done via a mapping between the fuzzy Belnap logic and the intuitionistic fuzzy logic. The reasoning result of both the subjective logic and fuzzy Belnap logic seem reasonable. However, as noted in the discussion section, fuzzy Belnap logic has some problems. 1) the truth table has some problematic aspects, thereby logically not sound. 2) due to 1) the sequence of getting information is critical. 3) due to 1) once the epistemic state is reached to the *contradictory* state, it is not easy to escape that state. 4) the basic four logical operators in L-fuzzy logics can be determined in many ways, therefore, the semantics of the operators are not sound and clear in Bayesian sense. Due to these aspects, we advocate subjective logic has advantages as a tool for artificial reasoning in visual surveillance. Because, in visual surveillance, due to the flexibility, and instability of the vision analytics, we cannot guarantee the sequence of getting information, therefore, the reasoning system should be robust against the information acquisition sequence. Indeed, most of the vision analytics are based on probabilistic theory; therefore, the values from those analytic modules could be well interpreted in subjective logic. Beside these aspects, there is yet another advantage of the proposed approach, that is the ability of default reasoning can be fulfilled within a single subjective logic based reasoning framework that can also offer additional potential usage such as bidirectional conditional modeling (Han, Koo, Hutter, Shet, & Stechele, 2010a), reputation based belief decaying, etc. (Han, Koo, Hutter, & Stechele, 2010b). Therefore, enabling default reasoning to subjective logic could offer better expressive power for modeling and reflecting real world situation.

There are, however, still open issues such as comparing the introduced inference scheme to more complicated situational reasoning. Therefore, our future research will cover such comparisons and applying the shown approach to more complicated scenarios using automatically generated large scale data.

ACKNOWLEDGMENT

The work presented here was partially funded by the German Federal Ministry of Economy and Technology (BMWi) under the THESEUS project. The work presented here was partially funded by Siemens AG Corporate Technology and by the German Federal Ministry of economy and Technology (BMWi) under the THESEUS project. The authors would like thank Vinay D. Shet and Andreas Hutter for helpful discussions and valuable comments.

REFERENCES

Akdemir, U., Turaga, P., & Chellappa, R. (2008). An Ontology based approach for activity recognition from video. In *Proceedings of the ACM Conference on Multimedia* (pp. 709-712).

Anderson, D., Luke, R. H., Keller, J. M., Skubic, M., Rantz, M. J., & Aud, M. A. (2007). Modeling human activity from voxel person using fuzzy logic. *IEEE Transactions on Fuzzy Systems, 17*(1), 39–49. doi:10.1109/TFUZZ.2008.2004498

Arieli, O., Cornelis, C., Deschrijver, G., & Kerre, E. E. (2004). Relating intuitionistic fuzzy sets and interval-valued fuzzy sets through bilattices. In D. Ruan, P. D'hondt, M. De Cock, M. Nachtegael, & E. E. Kerre (Eds.), *Applied Computational Intelligence: Proceedings of the 6th International FLINS Conference,* Blankenberge, Belgium (pp. 57-64). Singapore: World Scientific.

Arieli, O., Cornelis, C., Deschrijver, G., & Kerre, E. E. (2005). Bilattice-Based Squares and Triangles. In *Symbolic and Quantitative Approaches to Reasoning with Uncertainty* (LNCS 3571, pp. 563-574).

Atanassov, K. T. (1986). Intuitionistic fuzzy sets. *Fuzzy Sets and Systems, 20,* 87–96. doi:10.1016/S0165-0114(86)80034-3

Atanassov, K. T. (1994). New operations defined over the intuitionistic fuzzy sets. *Journal of Fuzzy Sets and Systems, 61*(2), 137–142. doi:10.1016/0165-0114(94)90229-1

Atanassov, K. T. (2002). Remark on a property of the intuitionistic fuzzy interpretation triangles. *Notes on Intuitionistic Fuzzy Sets, 8,* 34–36.

Atanassov, K. T. (2003). Intuitionistic fuzzy sets: Past, present and future. In *Proceedings of the 3rd Conference of the European Society for Fuzzy Logic and Technology* (pp. 12-19).

Cornelis, C., Atanassov, K. T., & Kerre, E. E. (2003a). Intuitionistic fuzzy sets and interval-valued fuzzy sets: A critical comparison. In *Proceedings of the 3rd International Conference on Fuzzy Logic and Technology* (pp. 159-163).

Cornelis, C., Deschrijver, G., & Kerre, E. E. (2003b). Square and triangle: Reflections on two prominent mathematical structures for the representation of imprecision. *Notes on Intuitionistic Fuzzy Sets, 9*(3), 11–21.

Cornelis, C., Deschrijver, G., & Kerrer, E. E. (2004). Implication in intuitionistic and interval valued fuzzy set theory. *Journal of Approximate Reasoning, 35*(1), 55–95. doi:10.1016/S0888-613X(03)00072-0

Dubois, D. (2008). On ignorance and contradiction considered as truth-values. *Journal of the Interest Group of Pure and Applied Logic, 16*(2), 195–216.

Fitting, M. (1990). Bilattices in logic programming. In *Proceedings of the 20th International Symposium on Multiple-Valued Logic* (pp. 238-246).

Fitting, M. (1994). Kleenes three-valued logics and their children. *Fundamental Informaticae, 20*, 113–131.

Gehrke, M., Walker, C., & Walker, E. (1996). Some comments on interval-valued fuzzy sets. *International Journal of Intelligent Systems, 11*(10), 751–759. doi:10.1002/(SICI)1098-111X(199610)11:10<751::AID-INT3>3.3.CO;2-N

Ginsberg, M. L. (1988). Multivalued logics: A uniform approach to inference in artificial intelligence. *Computational Intelligence, 4*(3), 256–316. doi:10.1111/j.1467-8640.1988.tb00280.x

Goguen, J. A. (1967). L-fuzzy sets. *Journal of Mathematical Analysis and Applications, 8*(1), 145–174. doi:10.1016/0022-247X(67)90189-8

Hähnle, R. (2005). Many-valued logic, partiality, and abstraction in formal specification languages. *Journal of the Interest Group of Pure and Applied Logic, 13*(4), 415–433.

Han, S. H., Koo, B. J., Hutter, A., Shet, V., & Stechele, W. (2010a). Subjective logic based hybrid approach to conditional evidence fusion for forensic visual surveillance. In *Proceedings of the IEEE Conference on Advanced Video and Signal based Surveillance* (pp. 337-344).

Han, S. H., Koo, B. J., Hutter, A., & Stechele, W. (2010b). Forensic reasoning upon pre-obtained surveillance metadata using uncertain spatio-temporal rules and subjective logic. In *Proceedings of the International Workshop on Image Analysis for Multimedia Interactive Services* (pp. 1-4).

Jianbing, M., Weiru, L., Paul, M., & Weiqi, Y. (2009). Event composition with imperfect information for bus surveillance. In *Proceedings of the IEEE Conference of Advanced Video and Signal based Surveillance* (pp. 382-387).

Jøsang, A. (1997). Artificial reasoning with subjective logic. In *Proceedings of the 2nd Australian Workshop on Commonsense Reasoning*, Perth, Australia.

Jøsang, A. (2001). A logic for uncertain probabilities. *International Journal of Uncertainty. Fuzziness and Knowledge-Based Systems, 9*(3), 279–311. doi:10.1142/S0218488501000831

Jøsang, A. (2006). The consensus operator for combining beliefs. *Artificial Intelligence Journal, 38*(1), 157–170.

Jøsang, A., & Daniel, M. (2004) Multiplication and comultiplication of beliefs. *International Journal of Approximate Reasoning, 142*(1-2), 19–51.

Jøsang, A., Daniel, M., & Vannoorenberghe, P. (2003). Strategies for combining conflicting dogmatic beliefs. In *Proceedings of the 6th International Conference on Information Fusion* (pp. 1133-1140).

Pearl, J. (1988). *Probabilistic reasoning in intelligent systems: Networks of plausible inference.* San Mateo, CA: Morgan Kaufmann.

Reiter, R. (1980). A logic for default reasoning. *Artificial Intelligence, 13*, 81–132. doi:10.1016/0004-3702(80)90014-4

Shafer, G. (1976). *A mathematical theory of evidence.* Princeton, NJ: Princeton University Press.

Shet, V., Harwood, D., & Davis, L. (2005). Vidmap: Video monitoring of activity with prolog. In *Proceedings of the IEEE Conference of Advanced Video and Signal based Surveillance* (pp. 224-229).

Shet, V., Harwood, D., & Davis, L. (2006a). Multivalued default logic for identity maintenance in visual surveillance. In *Proceedings of the European Conference on Computer Vision* (pp. 119-132).

Shet, V., Harwood, D., & Davis, L. (2006b). Top-down, bottom-up multivalued default reasoning for identity maintenance. In *Proceedings of the ACM International Workshop on Video Surveillance & Sensor Networks* (pp. 79-86).

Shet, V., Neumann, J., Ramesh, V., & Davis, L. (2007). Bilattice-based logical reasoning for human detection. In *Proceedings of the IEEE Conference on Computer Vision and Pattern Recognition* (pp. 1-8).

Urquhart, A. (1986). Many-valued logics. In D. M. Gabbay & F. Guenthner (Eds.), *Handbook of Philosophical Logic: Volume III, Alternatives to Classical Logic* (pp. 71-116). Dordrecht, The Netherlands: Reidel.

Zadeh, L. A. (1965). Fuzzy sets. *Information and Control*, *8*, 338–353. doi:10.1016/S0019-9958(65)90241-X

Zadeh, L. A. (1973). Outline of a new approach to the analysis of complex systems and decision processes. *IEEE Transactions on Systems, Man, and Cybernetics*, *3*(1), 28–44. doi:10.1109/TSMC.1973.5408575

Zadeh, L. A. (2008). Is there a need for fuzzy logic? *Information Sciences*, *178*(13), 2751–2779. doi:10.1016/j.ins.2008.02.012

Section 2
Multimedia Content Management

Chapter 5
Navigating through Video Stories Using Clustering Sets

Sheila M. Pinto-Cáceres
University of Campinas, Brazil

M. Cecília C. Baranauskas
University of Campinas, Brazil

Jurandy Almeida
University of Campinas, Brazil

Neucimar J. Leite
University of Campinas, Brazil

Vânia P. A. Neris
Federal University of Sao Carlos, Brazil

Ricardo da S. Torres
University of Campinas, Brazil

ABSTRACT

The fast evolution of technology has led to a growing demand for video data, increasing the amount of research into efficient systems to manage those materials. Making efficient use of video information requires that data be accessed in a user-friendly way. Ideally, one would like to perform video search using an intuitive tool. Most of existing browsers for the interactive search of video sequences, however, have employed a too rigid layout to arrange the results, restricting users to explore the results using list- or grid-based layouts. This paper presents a novel approach for the interactive search that displays the result set in a flexible manner. The proposed method is based on a simple and fast algorithm to build video stories and on an effective visual structure to arrange the storyboards, called Clustering Set. It is able to group together videos with similar content and to organize the result set in a well-defined tree. Results from a rigorous empirical comparison with a subjective evaluation show that such a strategy makes the navigation more coherent and engaging to users.

INTRODUCTION

Recent advances in technology have facilitated the creation, storage, and distribution of digital videos. It led to an increase in the amount of video data deployed and used in many applications, such as search engines and digital libraries.

This scenario has created a strong requirement for systems that are able to efficiently manage video material (Chang et al., 1998; Hampapur et al., 1997; Snoek et al., 2007).

Making efficient use of video information requires that data to be accessed in a user-friendly way. For this, it is important to provide users

DOI: 10.4018/978-1-4666-2940-0.ch005

with a browsing tool to interactively search for (or query) a video in large collections, without having to look through many possible results at the same time, so that a user can easily find the video in which he/she is interested.

A lot of research has been done in browsing techniques for the interactive search of video sequences (De Rooij et al., 2008; De Rooij & Worring, 2010; Zavesky & Chang, 2008; Zavesky et al., 2008). However, many of those research works have considered a rigid layout to arrange the result set in some default order, typically according to the relevance to the query.

In this paper, we present a novel approach for the interactive search that displays the result set in a more flexible and intuitive way. It relies on two key strategies: (1) storyboard generation and (2) visualization of stories. The former is a simple and fast algorithm to convert videos into storyboards. The speed up of the computation makes our technique suitable for browsing video content in online tasks. The latter is an effective visual structure to organize the video stories in a well-defined tree, called Clustering Set. This innovative framework is significantly different from traditional paradigms, which often limit users to explore the results using list- or grid-based layouts.

Experiments were conducted both for evaluating the layout employed by the proposed method and for comparing it with several visualization techniques. Results from a subjective evaluation with 38 subjects show a clear preference by the display strategy of our approach.

The remainder of this paper is organized as follows. First, we introduce the background of interactive search problems. Next, we present our approach and show how to apply it for browsing a large video collection. After that, we report the results of our experiments and compare our technique with other methods. Finally, we offer our conclusions and directions for future work.

BACKGROUND

The exploration of large collections of video data is non-trivial. When a user requests a search, the query formulation (search criterion) can be quite difficult.

Most of search systems are based on textual metadata, which leads to several problems when searching for visual content. Generally, the user lacks information about which keywords best represent the content in which he/she is interested. In fact, different users tend to use different words to describe a same visual content. The lack of systematization in choosing query words can significantly affect the search results (De Rooij et al., 2008).

Modern systems have addressed those shortcomings by automatically detecting visual concepts derived from visual properties, such as color, texture, and shape. However, a minimum knowledge about the concept vocabulary is needed for performing a query, which is not appropriate for non-expert users (Zavesky & Chang, 2008).

Fully automated approaches have combined descriptors of multiple modalities (textual metadata, visual properties, and visual concepts). In spite of all the advances, the formulation of a query using such features is a difficult task for a human interested in a specific video (De Rooij & Worring, 2010).

Once the search results are returned, we can explore many different directions based on query type and user intention. Several visualization techniques have been proposed to assist users in the exploration of result sets (De Rooij et al., 2008; De Rooij & Worring, 2010; Zavesky & Chang, 2008; Zavesky et al., 2008).

Those methods often employ dimensionality reduction algorithms to map the high-dimensional feature space of visual properties into a fixed display. Afterwards, a display strategy is applied for producing user-browsable content (Zavesky et al., 2008).

There are two basic kinds of navigation (De Rooij et al., 2008): targeted search and exploratory search. The former performs a fast browsing in a single list of results. The latter allows the user to control the browsing procedure in several ways.

The major challenge of designing an interactive display is to minimize the fatigue and frustration that a user might experience. In general, users can spend a limited time to identify relevant videos for a query, thus they are hard-pressed to quickly inspect a large set of results.

The layout of videos is another concern for an interactive system. An effective tool for browsing in large collections should be suited for users without any expertise, providing an easy way to use the interface.

Most of existing approaches use list- or grid-based layouts, where the videos are disposed in a linear or grid manner according to their relevance to the query pattern (Flickner et al., 1995; Hampapur et al., 1997). Several techniques display the result set in a circular or elliptical form. These radial methods try to centralize the user vision by setting the query at the center of the available space and then place similar videos around it, allowing easy access and exploration of the result set (Guerin-Dugue et al., 2003; Moghaddam et al., 2002, 2004). Other methods exploit clustering algorithms in order to analyze the similarities between all the search results and, hence, display similar videos of the result set close to each other (Chen et al., 2000; Moghaddam et al., 2004; Nguyen & Worring, 2008).

On one hand, grid- and radial-based structures offer a good navigability and exploration of the result set in an organized way. However, they generally do not respect the intrinsic relationship among the results, displaying different similarity degrees at the same physical distance to the query pattern. On the other hand, cluster-based techniques provide a better understanding of the universe of available results. This approach usually

focuses on a large amount of information without, in many cases, taking care of an adequate design to distribute the clusters, which entails confusion for the users.

Different from all previous works, our approach combines the advantages of those strategies into a single structure, called Clustering Set. This strategy allows users to explore the result set in a more flexible and intuitive way.

OUR APPROACH

Save time in browsing, intuitively comprehend the results, and allow an exploratory search: those are the basic principles of our approach. In the following subsections, different design choices to achieve such goals are discussed in more details.

Features and Similarity

Humans judge more quickly the relevance of interrelated items. However, discovering the ideal relationship for such a judgment is non-trivial. The simplest approach is to group together video frames with similar content, so that a relevant judgment for one video frame could be applied to all near-duplicated ones and, hence, maximize the diversity.

In our approach, stories are the meaningful and manageable units for presenting the result set to the user. They consist of multiple shots and are represented by a collection of frames, as illustrated in Figure 1. This strategy provides an easy way for the user to visually judge whether a story is worth exploring.

We adopt a simple and fast algorithm to build storyboards described in Almeida et al. (2010b). This technique was designed to be simple and efficient in order to produce video stories in a reasonable time and with an acceptable quality, so as to allow online usage. It consists of three main steps: (1) feature extraction; (2) content

Figure 1. An example of storyboard produced for the video senses and sensitivity, introduction to lecture 3 presenter

selection; and (3) noise filtering. A flowchart of this approach is shown in Figure 2.

For each frame of an input sequence, visual features are extracted from the video stream for describing its visual content. After that, a simple and fast algorithm is used to detect groups of video frames with a similar content and for selecting a representative frame per each group. Finally, the selected frames are filtered in order to avoid possible redundant or meaningless frames in the storyboard. For a detailed discussion of this procedure, refer to Almeida et al. (2010b).

Numerous forms of raw features can be used to determine the similarity between video frames of different storyboards. Each type of feature spans a multidimensional feature space. The distance function determines the dissimilarity between features within this space. Thus, we coordinate the display positions of each story using its dissimilarity space.

Our technique was designed to be flexible and robust and, therefore, the feature input is not limited to a specific type. Instead, all possible data types can be used. The only requirement is that the dissimilarity between features must be numerically represented by an appropriate distance metric.

Intuitive Display

A problem regarding the interactive search of video sequences is the human understanding of what the system was trying to judge as relevant.

The most common approach for designing an interactive display is to use dimensionality reduction algorithms to map the multidimensional feature space into a fixed display and to apply a display strategy for producing user-browsable content.

The key advantage of our technique is to merge the positive aspects of different visualization strategies into a single structure, as illustrated in Figure 3. Such a visualization design is an original contribution of this work, called Clustering Set. It groups video stories into clusters, which are displayed in a radial manner. In this way, we take

Figure 2. Flowchart of the method used to build storyboards (adapted from Almeida et al., 2010b)

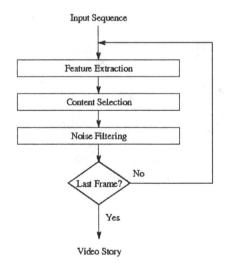

the advantages of a radial distribution while preserving the relationships between similar videos. This strategy allows the user to view the relationship between several clusters at once, providing a comfortable exploration and a better navigability.

In this figure, we display the stories for a sample of 50 videos randomly selected from the Open Video Project. All videos are in MPEG-1 format (at 352 × 240 resolution and 29.97 frames per second), in color and with sound. The se-

lected videos are distributed among several genres (e.g., documentary, educational, ephemeral, historical, lecture) and their duration varies from 1 to 4 minutes. Those videos are the same used in Almeida et al. (2010b) and their storyboards can be seen at http://www.liv.ic.unicamp.br/~jurandy/summaries/.

We converted each frame of those storyboards to a 64-dimensional feature vector by computing a Color Histogram (Swain & Ballard, 1991). The

Figure 3. An example of the visualization of our approach

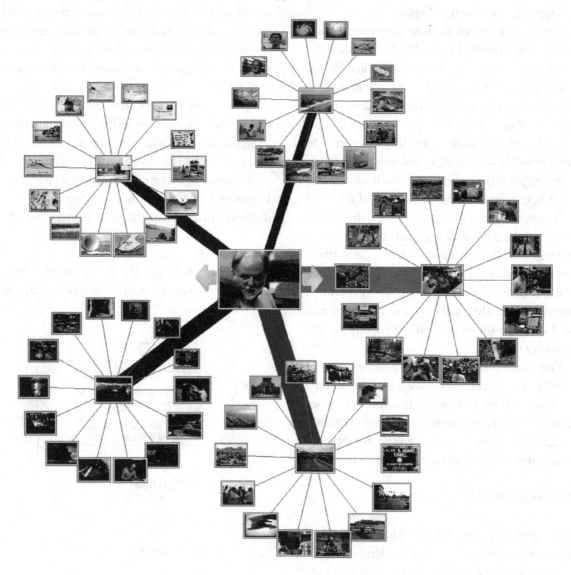

color histograms were extracted as follows: the RGB space is divided into 64 subspaces (colors), using four ranges in each color channel. The value for each dimension of a feature vector is the density of each color in the entire frame. The distance function used to compare the feature vectors is the Manhattan (L1) distance.

Our approach uses a clustering algorithm to group together video stories with similar content. In order to maintain the flexibility, we do not restrict the proposed scheme to use a specific algorithm and, hence, one can use the clustering method more appropriated for a specific domain or preference.

Then, the query pattern is placed in the center of the visualization display. Thus, we force the user to focus his/her attention on the center of the screen. The clusters are circularly distributed around the query in a clockwise order of similarity, which is represented by the width of the connecting line between them and by the size of the cluster being connected.

This strategy is also applied to each of the clusters. In this way, the user has a more intuitive understanding of the display. At the center, we place the most representative element of a cluster, which can be its centroid or medoid. The remaining results are sorted in a circular manner according to a clockwise order of similarity with respect to the center element, which is clearly denoted by their size and border color (in a color gamma from yellow to dark green).

Consider a polar coordinate system defined by an angle θ and a radius r. Initially, we put the center element at the origin. The remaining elements are placed at a constant radius R. For that, we set the first element at zero and include subsequent elements in a clockwise direction by considering an angle increment of $2\pi/M$, where M is the number of visible elements of a cluster. Thus, each element is equidistant to each other.

Each subsequent element is smaller than the previous one by a reduction factor f. In order to guarantee visibility and clarity of all elements in the structure, we compute this factor as a function of M. Denote s as the size of the first element of a cluster. We always adjust the last element to have a size equals to $s/2$. Therefore, the reduction factor must be set to $f = s/(2M)$.

Our technique provides the customization of some visualization parameters, such as the number of clusters and the number of elements inside them. For instance, let K be the number of clusters generated by the clustering algorithm and denote as k its respective parameter specified by the user. Thus, only a limited number $k \leq K$ of the most relevant clusters for the query will be displayed. If k is greater than $K,$ then all the clusters are exhibited. The same logic is used for the number of elements inside those clusters. It is important to note that the visual structure is automatically rearranged every time those parameters are changed, so to maintain a circular distribution around the center.

In order to minimize overlapping, we also consider an upper limit for those parameters, which guarantees a coherent and intuitive layout. In this way, we avoid the visual distortion of an overcrowded structure, whose elements usually do overlap. Moreover, it is useless to have many elements on a same display if they cannot be seen. Thus, we only show the most relevant ones according to the query pattern. Nevertheless, the navigation capabilities of our approach fulfill the needs of browsing the missing elements, as described in the following subsection.

In this way, we provide a coherent distribution of the query-related video universe by setting the results over a well-organized structure. This distribution, in most cases, avoids overlapping, which has been a challenge in the visualization area. Therefore, it represents a valuable advantage over other cluster-based visualization techniques (Chen et al., 2000; Moghaddam et al., 2004; Nguyen & Worring, 2008).

In our implementation, we used the well-known PAM (Partitioning Around Medoids) algorithm to divide the result set into groups. The parameters employed to display the visual structure were: the number of clusters equals to 5 and the number of elements inside them set to 15.

Engaged and Guided Browsing

The fully utilization of a user's inspection ability requires an engaging display which is guided by user preferences. Our approach fulfills such a principle by dynamically rearranging the result set. Figure 4 presents the navigation options of the propose method. Those options indicate all the possible browsing directions of a user.

Using a mouse click or a key press, the user can give an indication of which story is the most relevant. Then, we place the user at a new set of results which is most related to the last story

Figure 4. Overview of the navigation options of our approach

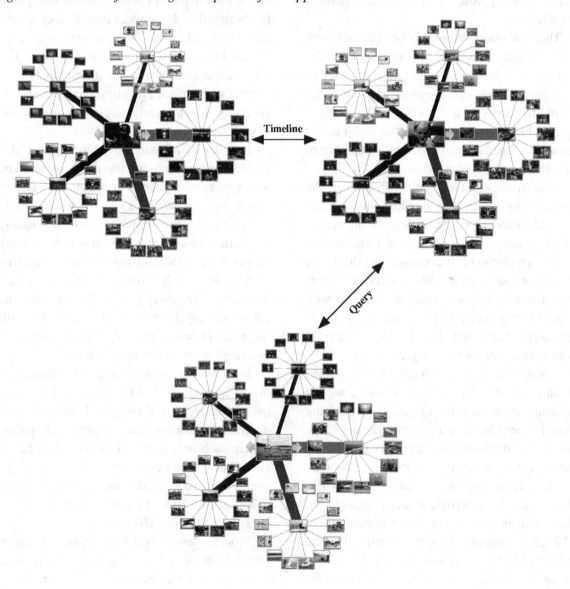

marked as relevant, as illustrated in the right column of Figure 4.

By clicking on the forward and backward arrows, users can navigate laterally in the timeline of the video. Thus, the result set is updated whenever they decide to focus on another story of a video. The top line of Figure 4 illustrates such a transition. In this way, the user can combine both targeted search and temporal browsing, which often yields more relevant results.

Additionally, we integrate different functionalities in the interface. By right-clicking on the stories, the user is presented with the operations that can be performed to them. This opens a pop-up window on the screen, as illustrated in Figure 5. On the top, we make available a video player. We display a click-able sequence of story collages and the selected story is highlighted in the video timeline. The frames from the shots in the selected story are expanded on the bottom.

Anytime users can also change the video-of-interest by choosing any of the stories visible in the screen. Thus, they can interleave between targeted search and exploratory search. Using

different searching and browsing methods into a single environment enhance the user's inspection ability. In this way, the user is in complete control and can change the current view at any time.

EXPERIMENTAL EVALUATION

In this section, we evaluate and compare the layout employed by the proposed method with previous work in visualization strategies.

Visual Structures

This section presents some visualization techniques widely used in the literature. In the following subsections, we compare these approaches to the proposed method.

- **Grid:** The most common approach employed to organize a set of results are the grid-based layouts (Flickner et al., 1995; Hampapur et al., 1997). This method disposes the result set in a matricial form. The

Figure 5. The pop-up window where a specific story is handled

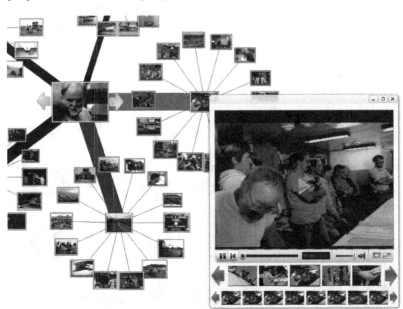

query is placed on top left and successive positions are sorted from left-to-right and top-to-down according to their relevance, as illustrated in Figure 6.

- **Concentric Rings:** Torres et al. (2003) introduced a visual structure that arranges the result set in a series of concentric rings. In this way, the most relevant results for the query (centroid) are located over a nearer ring, as showed in Figure 7.

- **Spiral:** Torres et al. (2003) proposed to organize the result set over a spiral structure. Thus, the query is placed at the origin of the spiral and successive results are distributed over the spiral line in increase order of relevance, as presented in Figure 8.

Experimental Protocol

Unlike other research areas, evaluating a display strategy is not a straightforward task due to the lack of an objective ground-truth. A consistent evaluation framework is seriously missing for visualization research. Presently, every work has its own evaluation methodology, often presented without any performance analysis.

In this work, we choose to incorporate the judgment of the user in evaluating the quality of visualization structures. For that reason, we adopted an evaluation framework known as *DECIDE* (Preece et al., 2002), which has been widely used, for nearly 10 years, by the HCI (Human-Computer Interaction) community for performing experiments involving users. Moreover, several areas in Computer Science have also been benefiting from the guidance provided by *DECIDE*, such as Information Retrieval and Digital Libraries (Blandford et al., 2008), Music Systems (Hsu & Sosnick, 2009) and Education (Anacleto et al., 2009).

DECIDE provides a comprehensive view over several important factors that need to be taken into account when designing a subjective evaluation, such as the selection of the target users and the identification of ethical and practical issues. It guides the experimental evaluation through six well-defined steps: Determine the goals, Explore the questions, Choose the evaluation paradigm and techniques, Identify the practical issues, Decide how to deal with the ethical issues, Evaluate, interpret, and present the data.

In the following subsections, each of those steps is explained in more detail.

- **Determine the goals:** The goal of the experiment is to validate the visual structure named Clustering Set. We are convinced that such a visualization technique will be

Figure 6. An example of a grid-based layout

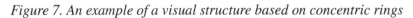

Figure 7. An example of a visual structure based on concentric rings

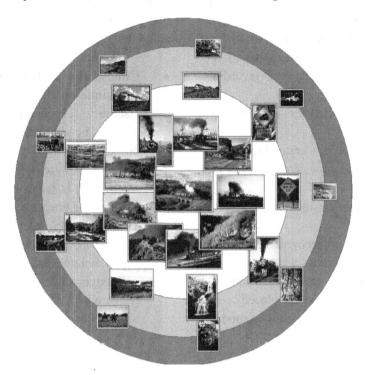

Figure 8. An example of a spiral-based layout

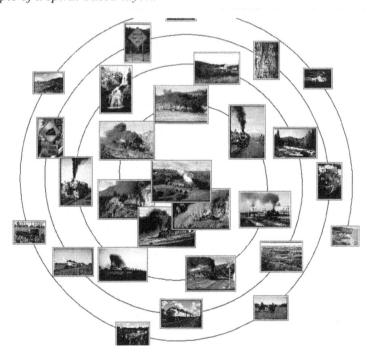

a valuable contribution for future video browsing and retrieval systems.

- **Explore the questions:** In order to achieve our goals, we defined some questions for assessing the user preferences regarding the introduced technique:
  - Is the user satisfied with the presented layout?
  - Is it possible to understand the visual structure and how it distributes the result set?
  - Is it possible to identify the query pattern?
  - Is it possible to recognize where the most relevant results are placed?
  - Is it possible to recognize where the least relevant results are placed?
  - What is the most suitable method to visualize the query results?

For obtaining unaware information, we also consider open questions for general comments about the evaluated approaches.

- **Choose the evaluation paradigms and techniques:** In this step, we adopted the Usability Test method (the standard ISO 9241). The evaluation instrument used in our experiments was a questionnaire. In this way, we are able to analyze a bigger sample in a faster manner.
- Identify the practical issues.
  - **Users:** In order to obtain significant results, we looked for a set of collaborators with background knowledge on interface design. Then, we invited a set of undergraduate and graduate students from three different courses related to interface design and human-computer interaction from the Institute of Computing at the University of Campinas, totalizing 38

Figure 9. An example of a Tukey-style boxplot

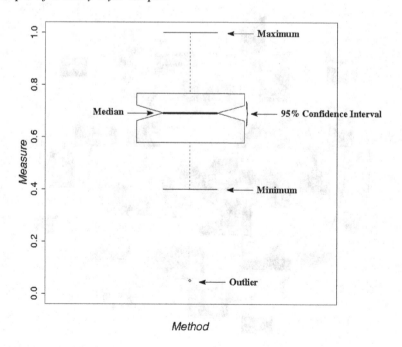

Figure 10. Satisfaction with the disposition of the results (SA)

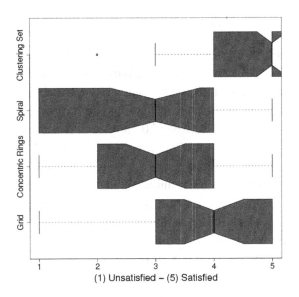

(1) Unsatisfied – (5) Satisfied

volunteers. It is important to point out that nobody had previous knowledge of the proposed method and, hence, they had never seen our strategy before the experiment.

- Equipment: Each experiment was carried out in several laboratories of the Institute of Computing at University of Campinas. Each participant had access to one computer and was free to use the operating system he/she prefers.
- Material: Each participant received a set of documents before evaluation starts. This set included:
  - **User Instructions:** It details what the user needs to know as experiment steps, available time, ethical issues, etc.
  - **Free and Clear Consent Terms:** It is a mandatory certificate in every investigation involving users. This document was signed by each user as a term of conformity with the experiments conditions.
  - **User Profile Form:** It allows registering relevant data of a user, such as his/her familiarity with the system and frequency of using the computer.
  - **Evaluation Form:** This is the main document of the experiment where the user opinion is captured. Basically, by using this form, users answer the aforementioned questions.

- **Decide how to deal with the ethical issues:** Ethical questions were clearly explained to the user verbally and in the user instructions. It was also specified in the Free and Clear Consent Terms, which was signed by the user as an acceptance condition.

- **Evaluate, interpret, and present the data:** The experiments were conducted at a laboratory of the university on a predefined hour. All users were invited to participate in the experiment. Users who accepted

Figure 11. Understanding degree (UD)

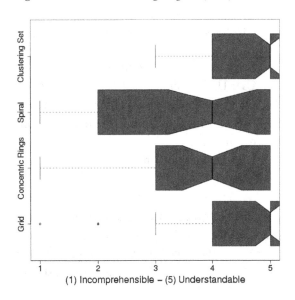

(1) Incomprehensible – (5) Understandable

Figure 12. Easiness of finding the query pattern (QP)

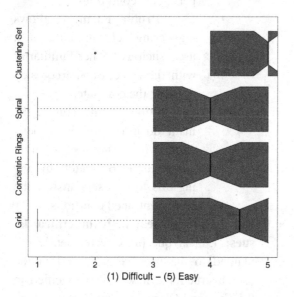

Experimental Results

We can compare different visual structures by exploiting the data collected from the *DECIDE* steps. Using the profile form we obtained information about age, studies, familiarity and frequency of using computers and search systems. Users were divided in two age groups: most of people (76.3%) were between 20 and 25 years old and the remainder (23.7%) were between 26 and 35 years old. At the moment of the experiment, 68.4% of them were in an undergraduate program and 31.6% were in a graduate program. They had a high level of familiarity and frequency with the use of computers and most of them had a lot of experience on search systems.

By collecting the data from the evaluation form, we can analyze the judgments of the users and compare different visual structures, as shown in Figures 10 through 14. Those graphs present an overall analysis of each criterion using boxplots. Figure 9 gives an explanation of the conventions used in the Tukey-style boxplots. The results indicate that the Clustering Set performs better than

the invitation were free to choose a computer and an operational system. Initially, we gave the users a set of aforesaid documents. Then, users read and signed the Free and Clear Consent Terms. After that, they filled the user profile form. Finally, they downloaded the structure prototypes and evaluate the visual structures by answering an evaluation form.

We analyzed five criteria:

1. **SA:** Satisfaction with the layout,
2. **UD:** Understanding degree,
3. **QP:** Easiness of finding the query pattern,
4. **MR:** Easiness of finding the most relevant results,
5. **LR:** Easiness of finding the least relevant results.

Each one of the 38 participants evaluated each of those criteria by allocating a number from 1 to 5 according to their opinion, where 1 represents the worst qualification and 5 represents the best one.

Figure 13. Easiness of finding the most relevant results (MR)

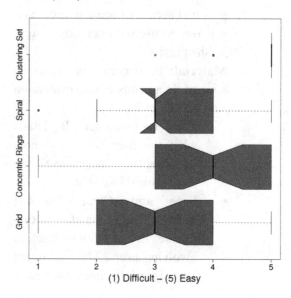

Figure 14. Easiness of finding the least relevant results (LR)

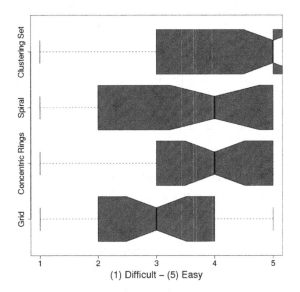

all the compared methods. Notice that it obtained the best punctuation on all the criteria. In addition, our approach presents the lowest dispersion of data, especially for the *MR* (easiness of finding the most relevant results) criterion. It means that, in general, the users agree on the score of the Clustering Set, as can be confirmed by the compact boxplot (thin line at level 5) in Figure 13.

In order to verify the statistical significance of those results, the confidence intervals for the differences between paired medians were computed to compare every pair of methods. If the confidence interval includes zero, the difference is not significant at that confidence level. If the confidence interval does not include zero, then the sign of the median difference indicates which alternative is better (Jain, 1991).

Table 1 presents the confidence intervals (with a confidence of 95%) for the differences between our technique and previous work. The analysis of the experiment shows that there is no significant difference between the Clustering Set and the Grid method with respect to the *UD* (understanding degree) and *QP* (easiness of finding the query

pattern) criteria, as shown in Figures 11 and 12, respectively.

Since the confidence intervals do not include zero for the other criteria (except *LR*), the results confirm that the Clustering Set outperforms all other methods regarding the satisfaction of the users with the layout (*SA*) and the easiness of finding the most relevant results (*MR*), as can be seen in Figures 10 and 13, respectively. Notice that the Clustering Set clearly overcomes the Grid method in those criteria. This is a remarkable fact once the latter is well-known and widely used in several contexts and, hence, it is certainly familiar to the participants.

Our approach also shared the best qualification with several other methods in relation to the *LR* (easiness of finding the least relevant results) criterion, as shown in Figure 14. Considering those observations, it is possible to conclude that the Clustering Set is a worth-full contribution for the result set presentation, visualization and exploration of a retrieval system.

Users were also asked to rank the analyzed structures according to their suitability for vi-

Figure 15. Distribution of ranks attributed by users for different approaches

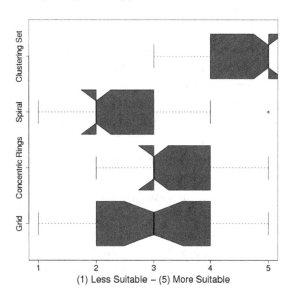

Table 1. Differences between our technique and previous work at a confidence of 95%

Criterion	Clustering Set – Grid		Clustering Set – Rings		Clustering Set - Spiral	
	min.	*max.*	*min.*	*max.*	*min.*	*max.*
SA	0.231	1.769	1.231	2.769	0.975	3.025
UD	-0.513	0.513	0.231	1.769	-0.025	2.025
QP	-0.269	1.269	0.231	1.769	0.231	1.769
MR	1.487	2.513	0.487	1.513	1.744	2.256
LR	0.975	3.025	-0.025	2.025	-0.282	2282

sualizing query results. Figure 15 compares the distribution of ranks attributed by the participants for different approaches. The comparison of the average rank of those methods in Table 2 shows that the majority of the participants indicated the Clustering Set as the best method, followed by the Concentric Rings, Grid, and Spiral methods, respectively.

The non-parametric Friedman test (Friedman, 1937) was performed to verify the statistical significance of those results. It checks whether the measured average ranks are significantly different from the mean rank. The analysis of the experiment shows that, with a confidence of 95%, there is statistical difference between those methods ($p < 0.001$).

According to a post-doc test of Nemenyi (1963), the critical distance for pairwise comparisons between different approaches at $p = 0.05$ is 0.761. Since our technique always differ by a value greater than the critical distance regarding the other methods, it clearly confirms the preference of users for the Clustering Set.

Open questions helped us to identify user opinions and aspects to take into account in future works. In general, the users' comments were favorable for the proposed method. Most of the comments were suggestions to extend or to add features to the Clustering Set, which demonstrates the interest of the users in our approach. One common suggestion was the possible combination with other techniques, creating a hybrid strategy.

Visual features are also relevant issues to take into account. For instance, the background color used by the Concentric Rings has assisted the users to understand the distribution of the results. For that reason, some participants suggested to use the same characteristic in the Spiral method. Eventually, this feature can be also included into the Clustering Set.

CONCLUSION

In this paper, we have presented a novel approach for the interactive search that displays the result set in a more flexible and intuitive way. Our technique relies both on a simple and fast algorithm to build storyboards and on a hierarchical structure named Clustering Set, where visually or semantically alike video stories are placed together. Such a strategy offers a guided browsing more coherent and engaging to users. These benefits were carefully demonstrated in our showcases.

Table 2. Average rank achieved by our technique and previous work

Method	Average Rank
Grid	3.026
Concentric Rings	3.395
Spiral	2.500
Clustering Set	4.658

We have performed a rigorous experimental design both for evaluating the layout employed by the proposed method and for comparing it with several visualization techniques. Results from a subjective evaluation with 38 subjects have shown that our approach clearly outperforms the most of the compared methods regarding the most of the evaluated criteria.

Future work includes a subjective evaluation of the whole approach. In addition, we plan to augment the proposed method for considering local features (Almeida et al., 2008) and/or motion analysis (Almeida et al., 2009, 2010a). We also want to augment the Clustering Set by including different types of visualization, creating a hybrid structure, as suggested by the users. Moreover, we intend to evaluate other visual features and similarity metrics. Finally, we plan to investigate the effects of integrating our technique into a complete system for search-and-retrieval of video sequences.

ACKNOWLEDGMENT

We would like to thank to all the participants of the experiments for their valuable contributions. This research was supported by Brazilian agencies FAPESP (Grant 07/52015-0, 08/50837-6, 09/04732-0, and 09/18438-7), CNPq (Grant 311309/2006-2, 472402/2007-2, 135526/2008-6, and 306587/2009-2), and CAPES (Grant 01P-05866/2007).

REFERENCES

Almeida, J., Minetto, R., Almeida, T. A., Torres, R. S., & Leite, N. J. (2009). Robust estimation of camera motion using optical flow models. In G. Bebis, R. D. Boyle, B. Parvin, D. Koracin, Y. Kuno, J. Wang et al. (Eds.), *Proceedings of the International Conference on Advances in Visual Computing* (LNCS 585, pp. 435-446).

Almeida, J., Minetto, R., Almeida, T. A., Torres, R. S., & Leite, N. J. (2010a). Estimation of camera parameters in video sequences with a large amount of scene motion. In *Proceedings of the IEEE International Conference on Systems, Signals and Image Processing* (pp. 348-351). Washington, DC: IEEE Computer Society.

Almeida, J., Rocha, A., Torres, R. S., & Goldenstein, S. (2008). Making colors worth more than a thousand words. In *Proceedings of the ACM International Symposium on Applied Computing* (pp. 1180-1186). New York, NY: ACM Press.

Almeida, J., Torres, R. S., & Leite, N. J. (2010b). Rapid video summarization on compressed video. In *Proceedings of the IEEE International Symposium on Multimedia* (pp. 113-120). Washington, DC: IEEE Computer Society.

Anacleto, J. C., Talarico Neto, A., & Neris, V. P. A. (2009). Cog-learn: An e-learning pattern language for web-based learning design. *eLearn Magazine, 2009*(8), 1-4.

Blandford, A., Adams, A., Attfield, S., Buchanan, G., Gow, J., & Makri, S. (2008). The PRET A Rapporter framework: Evaluating digital libraries from the perspective of information work. *Information Processing & Management, 44*(1), 4–21. doi:10.1016/j.ipm.2007.01.021

Chang, S.-F., Chen, W., Meng, H. J., Sundaram, H., & Zhong, D. (1998). A fully automated content-based video search engine supporting spatio-temporal queries. *IEEE Transactions on Circuits and Systems for Video Technology, 8*(5), 602–615. doi:10.1109/76.718507

Chen, C., Gagaudakis, G., & Rosin, P. (2000). Content-based image visualization. In *Proceedings of the International Conference on Information Visualization* (pp. 13-18). Washington, DC: IEEE Computer Society.

De Rooij, O., Snoek, C. G. M., & Worring, M. (2008). Balancing thread based navigation for targeted video search. In *Proceedings of the ACM International Conference on Image and Video Retrieval* (pp. 485-494). New York, NY: ACM Press.

De Rooij, O., & Worring, M. (2010). Browsing video along multiple threads. *IEEE Transactions on Multimedia, 12*(2), 121–130. doi:10.1109/TMM.2009.2037388

Flickner, M., Sawhney, H. S., Ashley, J., Huang, Q., Dom, B., & Gorkani, M. (1995). Query by image and video content: The QBIC system. *IEEE Computer, 28*(9), 23–32.

Friedman, M. (1937). The use of ranks to avoid the assumption of normality implicit in the analysis of variance. *Journal of the American Statistical Association, 32*, 675–701. doi:10.2307/2279372

Guerin-Dugue, A., Ayache, S., & Berrut, C. (2003). Image retrieval: A first step for a human centered approach. In *Proceedings of the International Conference on Information, Communications and Signal Processing* (pp. 21-25). Washington, DC: IEEE Computer Society.

Hampapur, A., Gupta, A., Horowitz, B., Shu, C.-F., Fuller, C., Bach, J. R., et al. (1997). Virage video engine. In *Proceedings of the SPIE International Conference on Storage and Retrieval for Image and Video Databases* (pp. 188-198).

Hsu, W., & Sosnick, M. (2009). Evaluating interactive music systems: An HCI approach. In *Proceedings of the International Conference on New Interfaces for Musical Expression* (pp. 25-28).

Jain, R. (1991). *The art of computer systems performance analysis: Techniques for experimental design, measurement, simulation, and modeling.* New York, NY: John Wiley & Sons.

Moghaddam, B., Tian, Q., Lesh, N., Shen, C., & Huang, T. (2002). PDH: A human-centric interface for image libraries. In *Proceedings of the IEEE International Conference on Multimedia and Expo* (pp. 901-904). Washington, DC: IEEE Computer Society.

Moghaddam, B., Tian, Q., Lesh, N., Shen, C., & Huang, T. S. (2004). Visualization and user-modeling for browsing personal photo libraries. *International Journal of Computer Vision, 56*(1-2), 109–130. doi:10.1023/B:VISI.0000004834.62090.74

Nemenyi, P. B. (1963). *Distribution-free multiple comparison.* Unpublished doctoral dissertation, Princeton University, Princeton, NJ.

Nguyen, G. P., & Worring, M. (2008). Interactive access to large image collections using similarity-based visualization. *Journal of Visual Languages and Computing, 19*(2), 203–224. doi:10.1016/j.jvlc.2006.09.002

Preece, J., Rogers, Y., & Sharp, H. (2002). *Interaction design.* New York, NY: John Wiley & Sons.

Snoek, C. G. M., Worring, M., Koelma, D., & Smeulders, A. W. M. (2007). A learned lexicon-driven paradigm for interactive video retrieval. *IEEE Transactions on Multimedia, 9*(2), 280–292. doi:10.1109/TMM.2006.886275

Swain, M. J., & Ballard, B. H. (1991). Color indexing. *International Journal of Computer Vision, 7*(1), 11–32. doi:10.1007/BF00130487

Torres, R. S., Silva, C. G., Medeiros, C. B., & Rocha, H. V. (2003). Visual structures for image browsing. In *Proceedings of the ACM International Conference on Information and Knowledge Management* (pp. 49-55). New York, NY: ACM Press.

Zavesky, E., & Chang, S.-F. (2008). CuZero: Embracing the frontier of interactive visual search for informed users. In *Proceedings of the ACM International Workshop on Multimedia Information Retrieval* (pp. 237-244). New York, NY: ACM Press.

Zavesky, E., Chang, S.-F., & Yang, C.-C. (2008). Visual islands: Intuitive browsing of visual search results. In *Proceedings of the ACM International Conference on Image and Video Retrieval* (pp. 617-626). New York, NY: ACM Press.

This work was previously published in the International Journal of Multimedia Data Engineering and Management, Volume 2, Issue 3, edited by Shu-Ching Chen, pp. 1-20, copyright 2011 by IGI Publishing (an imprint of IGI Global).

Chapter 6
Utilizing Context Information to Enhance Content-Based Image Classification

Qiusha Zhu
University of Miami, USA

Mei-Ling Shyu
University of Miami, USA

Lin Lin
University of Miami, USA

Dianting Liu
University of Miami, USA

ABSTRACT

Traditional image classification relies on text information such as tags, which requires a lot of human effort to annotate them. Therefore, recent work focuses more on training the classifiers directly on visual features extracted from image content. The performance of content-based classification is improving steadily, but it is still far below users' expectation. Moreover, in a web environment, HTML surrounding texts associated with images naturally serve as context information and are complementary to content information. This paper proposes a novel two-stage image classification framework that aims to improve the performance of content-based image classification by utilizing context information of web-based images. A new TF*IDF weighting scheme is proposed to extract discriminant textual features from HTML surrounding texts. Both content-based and context-based classifiers are built by applying multiple correspondence analysis (MCA). Experiments on web-based images from Microsoft Research Asia (MSRA-MM) dataset show that the proposed framework achieves promising results.

1. INTRODUCTION

With the proliferation of digital photo-capture devices like cameras, cell phones, and camcorders, and the exponential growth of web 2.0, people especially the youths are accustomed to utilize photographs to record their daily lives and to share images on social network websites (Flickr, Twitter, Facebook, etc.) to demonstrate their seeing and feeling. The new trend of lifestyle raises an issue to multimedia data management area, namely how to effectively organize these image data. Gener-

DOI: 10.4018/978-1-4666-2940-0.ch006

ally speaking, image classification experiences two developing phases: text-based and content-based. Traditional text-based approaches, which could be traced back to 1970s, usually rely on manual annotation (such as tagging and labeling) to perform image classification. The construction of an index (or a thesaurus) is mostly carried out by documentalists who manually assign a limited number of keywords describing the image content. However, the processing speed cannot meet the requirements of fast and automatic organization and search of images nowadays. In order to automatically organize the great amount of increasing online images, learning focused on image content analysis has gained popularity over traditional text-based analysis (Liu, Zhang, Lu, & Ma, 2007).

Content-based image classification approaches have been introduced in the early 1990s to classify and index images on the basis of low-level and mid-level visual features derived from color, texture or shape information (Lew, Sebe, Djeraba, & Jain, 2006). Although significant improvements have been achieved by using low-level visual features, the content-based approaches still face many challenges such as semantic gap and varied image qualities. Semantic gap characterizes the difference between the semantic meaning of an image and the extracted low-level visual features. A lot of effort has been put into bridging this gap, but it is still difficult to conquer (Naphade et al., 2006). On the other hand, context information for images can be utilized to be complementary to content information. Compared to low-level visual features, context information may better capture the semantics of images under the assumption that the textual terms are actually related to the images. An example of such context information is the HTML surrounding texts associated with images in a web environment. Therefore, a better image classification performance can be achieved by utilizing the context information to enhance the content-based image classification. To classify texts, or perform text categorization (TC) which

is defined as the task of labeling texts with thematic categories from a predefined set (Sebastiani, 2002), many techniques have been borrowed from information retrieval (IR) field. TF*IDF (term frequency-inverse document frequency) weighting scheme (Jones, 2004) is the most famous one and has achieved a great success.

In this paper, a novel two-stage image classification framework is proposed, which integrates content-based and context-based classification. A new TF*IDF weighting scheme is also introduced to calculate term weights for textual feature extraction. A classifier based on multiple correspondence analysis (MCA) transaction weights in (Lin, Shyu, & Chen, 2009) is trained by the visual features at the first stage. Then both predicted positive and negative results are refined by the classifiers trained by the textual features at the second stage. Fifteen concepts from MSRA-MM dataset (Li, Wang, & Hua, 2009) are used for evaluation, ranging from highly imbalanced datasets to balanced datasets. Experiments contain the evaluation of the proposed new TF*IDF weighting scheme and the whole framework. The proposed TF*IDF variant is compared with the conventional TF*IDF and two supervised term weighting methods. The evaluation of the framework is done by first comparing the separate content-based and context-based MCA classifiers with other seven existing well-known classifiers, and then comparing to these results, promising improvements are achieved by using our proposed framework. Furthermore, comparisons are made with two existing approaches that fuse visual and textual features (Kalva, Enembreck, & Koerich, 2007; Rafkind, Lee, Chang, & Yu, 2006) to be introduced in the Related Work Section. The experimental results demonstrate that our framework, via effective utilizing context-based information, can enhance content-based image classification performance.

This paper is organized as follows. Related work is introduced in Section 2. Our proposed framework is presented in Section 3, followed by experimental analyses in Section 4. We conclude this paper and discuss the future work in the last section.

2. RELATED WORK

A. Term Weighting Methods

To utilize context information, it is important to understand and choose the proper methods to extract and select useful textual features/terms. Among various term weighting methods, the most famous one is TF*IDF (term frequency-inverse document frequency) weighting method (Jones, 2004; Robertson, 2004), which is widely used in information retrieval and text mining, and many variants have been developed based on it. TF*IDF, as a common statistical measure, is employed to evaluate how important a word is to a document in a collection or corpus of documents. In conventional TF*IDF, the importance of a term increases proportionally to the number of times it appears in the document but is offset by the frequency of the term in the whole collection. Equation (1a) and Equation (1b) give the mathematic definitions of the *tf* and *idf* values, where n_{ij} is the number of term t_i appearing in document d_j, N is the total number of documents in the collection, and n_i out of it contain term t_i.

$$tf_i = \sum_{d_j \in N} \frac{n_{ij}}{\sum_{t_i \in d_j} n_{ij}}. \tag{1a}$$

$$idf_i = \log_2 \frac{N}{n_i}. \tag{1b}$$

Due to the success of TF*IDF, many variants have been consequently developed, aiming to improve the text categorization performance (Wang, Zhang, Wu, & Lin, 2010). Lan et al. used relevance frequency (*rf*) to substitute *idf* and proposed a novel supervised term weighting, i.e., *tf*rf*, aiming to improve the terms' discriminating power (Lan, Tan, Su, & Lu, 2009). Another study (Liu, Loh, & Sun, 2009) proposed a probability based supervised term weighting scheme (denoted as *prob-based*) to solve the imbalanced text classification problem and could better distinguish documents in minor categories. The scheme utilized two critical information ratios, i.e., relevance indicators, which were supported by probability estimates that might embody the category membership. The above two term weighting schemes have a similar term weighting function, except that the latter considers one factor more than the former.

B. Utilization of Context Information

One preceding work has studied computational models and techniques to combine textual and content features for the classification of images on the Internet (Gevers, Aldershoff, & Smeulders, 1999). The authors made use of weighted document terms and color invariant image features to obtain a high-dimensional similarity descriptor to be used as an index. Based on supervised learning, the k-nearest neighbor classifier was used to classify the Internet images into semantically meaningful concepts. The experiments were conducted on a large set of images downloaded from the Internet and showed good results by integrating textual and visual features. A similar idea was introduced (Cascia, Sethi, & Sclaroff, 1998) which built an image system that combined textual and visual statistics in a single index vector for content-based search of a WWW image database. Textual statistics were captured in the vector form using latent semantic indexing (LSI) (Deerwester, Dumais, Furnas, Landauer, & Harshman, 1990) based on texts in the containing HTML documents. Visual statistics were captured in the vector form using color and orientation histograms. The content of the documents (latent semantic content) and the content of the images (visual statistics) were integrated by using an early fusion approach. The combined approach gave an improved performance in conducting content-based classification. The study (Tollari, Glotin, & Maitre, 2003) combined textual and visual statistics in a single stochastic fusion process for content-based image classification. Textual statistics were captured in the vector form and first used in an ascendant hierarchical classification (AHC) approach for several semantic classes. Visual statistics were then drawn inside these classes, based on color and orientation histograms. Finally, a late fusion approach took advantages of coupling between visual and textual classification by assigning different weights.

The approach (Feng, Shi, & Chua, 2004) aimed to bootstrap the learning process by adopting a co-training approach involving classifiers based on two orthogonal sets of features - visual and text. The idea of co-training was to start from a small set of labeled training samples, and successively classify a larger set of unlabeled samples using the two orthogonal classifiers while updating them. They also exploited the evidences from both the HTML text and visual features of images and trained two independent probabilistic support vector machine (pSVM) classifiers. Several thresholds needed to be tuned in the co-training framework. The experimental results demonstrated that their co-training approach could achieve a level of performance comparable to that of the supervised learning, but it required a much smaller set of labeled training samples (less than 23% in their test).

Kalva et al. (2006) designed independent classifiers to deal with images and texts based on the hypothesis that contextual information related to an image can contribute in the image classification process. In their paper, image color, shape, and texture features were extracted and a neural network (NN) classifier was used to carry out image classification; while contextual information

was processed and used in a Naïve Bayes (NB) classifier. Since both classifiers could produce the posteriori probability of a data instance for each class, the fusion mechanism relied on such probabilities to decide on the class. Twelve heuristic rules obtained on the validation set through experimentation were used to combine the probability of each class produced by both classifiers. Their experimental results showed a meaningful improvement in the correct image classification rate relative to the results provided by the NN classifier alone.

Rafkind, Lee, Chang, and Yu (2006) explored supervised machine learning systems using support vector machines (SVM) to automatically classify biomedical images into six representative categories based on text, image, and the fusion of both. First, two SVM classifiers were trained by using the visual and textual features alone. Then a vector for each data point was constructed by extracting margins from the data point to the boundary in the feature space. For a five-class classifier, each data point would have five associated margins, each corresponding to the distance from the data point to the hyperplane that separated one class from the rest. Two five-dimensional vectors for each data point, generated from image-based and text-based classifiers, were normalized and concatenated to form a ten-dimensional fusion vector which was used to train a fusion SVM classifier. In their experiment, 554 images were downloaded; a half was used for training, a quarter for fusion, and a quarter for testing. The results showed a significant improvement in the average F1-score of the fusion classifier as compared to the image-based classifier or the text-based classifier.

To integrate content and context information, most existing approaches of late fusion use various ways to combine the results getting from two parallel classifiers trained by visual and textual features, respectively. In this paper, a novel image classification framework is proposed with two stages of classification. Instead of combining the results from two parallel classifiers, a MCA classifier is trained by the visual features at the first stage of our framework. Then both initial predicted positive (target concept) and negative (non-target concept) classes are refined by two additional MCA classifiers trained by the textual features at the second stage. In addition, a new TF*IDF weighting scheme is developed to calculate the term weights, so that those terms with high discriminant capabilities can be identified to be used as the textual features.

3. THE PROPOSED FRAMEWORK

A novel framework for image classification is proposed which contains the training model and testing phase, as shown in Figure 1 and Figure 2, respectively.

The training model consists of two stages which are enclosed in the dashed rectangular boxes, as shown in Figure 1. First, visual features are ex-

tracted from raw training images, and z-score normalization is performed on visual features to convert their scales and ensure that they are suitable for general data analysis. Table 1 shows the extracted visual features which belong to three main categories: color, edge, and texture. Considering the fact that extracted features usually include redundant or noisy features which would slow down the training process or diminish classification performance, feature selection is performed as a pre-processing step to reduce the feature space. A correlation and reliability based feature selection algorithm (Zhu, Lin, Shyu, & Chen, 2010) developed in our previous work is adopted to select a subset of features from the extracted visual features. Discretization is also required since the extracted features are numeric (for example, the value of the "color dominant" feature for an image may be 0.241), and multiple correspondence analysis (MCA) can only be applied to nominal feature data (for example, "sunny", "overcast", and "rainy" are values for

Figure 1. Training model of the proposed image classification framework

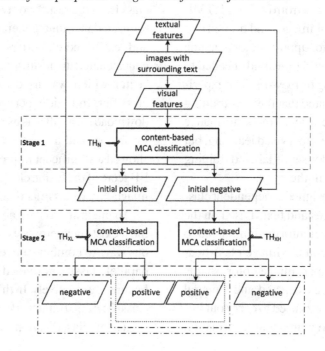

Figure 2. Testing phase of the proposed image classification framework

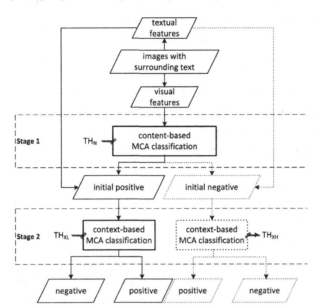

Table 1. Visual features

Category	Subcategory	Feature dimension
color	color dominant color histogram color moment	16 51 108
edge	edge histogram face detection	47 8
texture	texture cooccurrence texture wavelet texture tamura texture gabor local binary patterns	36 219 3 24 1

the "outlook" feature). For discretization, based on our knowledge and experimental results, so far no particular discretization method is clearly superior to the others for our dataset. Thus, a modified version of the minimum description length (MDL) method (Fayyad & Irani, 1993; Kononenko, 1995) available in WEKA (Witten & Frank, 2005) is used to discretize the features. For example, after discretization, there are two intervals for the dominant blue feature: [0, 0.234] and (0.235, 0.577]. Then the content-based MCA classifier is trained by the selected discretized visual features, which involves setting a threshold

TH_N to the content-based MCA classifier. A brief review of MCA classifier will be introduced in Subsection B.

After the first stage, an initial class label is assigned to each data instance, but there are some misclassified instances in both classes. Therefore, at the second stage, the context-based MCA classifiers are applied to refine the initial classification results. The textual features are extracted from the original training set, and those belonging to the initial positive set are used to train context-based MCA classifiers on the left hand side and the right hand side context-based MCA classifier are trained by the textual features belonging to the initial negative set. In the process of textual feature extraction, gaps between every two term weights in a sorted term list are calculated and the largest gap is used as the threshold to select textual features. The detailed textual feature extraction method will be introduced in Subsection A. The reason why training two classifiers in this stage is to eliminate as many false positive data instances as possible in the initial positive class on the left hand side, while getting as many false negative data instances as possible from the initial negative class on the right hand side. That is, a context-based MCA classifier is trained on the left hand side and a threshold (TH_{XL}) is set to eliminate as many false positive data instances as possible in the initial positive class so that those fuzzy positive data instances which probably contain true negative ones will be classified as the negative class in this stage. Thus the predicted positive set will eliminate those true negative data instances that have been misclassified in the first stage. Similarly, on the right hand side, another context-based MCA classifier is trained and a threshold (TH_{XH}) is set to get as many false negative data instances as possible from the initial negative class to improve the data instances in the predicted negative class. Lastly, the refined positive data instances from these two classifiers form the final positive set, enclosed by the dotted box, and the final negative set is enclosed by the chain dotted box, which are used to evaluate the training model.

The testing phase also consists of two stages as shown in Figure 2. When a testing image with its associated text comes, the same visual and textual features used in the training model are extracted from it, and the same pre-processing steps before classification as discussed in the training model are applied to the features. An initial label is assigned to it after the first stage, and then there are two possible routes, indicated in the solid line and the dotted line, depending on the initial label. If the initial label is positive, its textual features go to the left hand side context-based MCA classifier to get further classified. If the initial label is negative, the right hand side classifier is used instead.

A. A New TF*IDF Weighting Scheme

Based on the conventional TF*IDF and inspired by the relevance weight model (Robertson, 2004), a new TF*IDF variant is developed to weigh the terms in the associated texts. Terms with larger weights are supposed to have better discriminant capabilities and can better capture the semantics of the images, and thus are selected to serve as textual features for classification.

Figure 3 shows a collection of surrounding texts containing positive data instances and negative data instances, where each data instance refers to the context information of a corresponding image. For a certain concept, R denotes the number of relevant (positive) surrounding texts in a collection of total N texts. Thus, $N - R$ is the number of irrelevant (negative) surrounding texts. As shown in Figure 3, the left hand side part of the rectangle separated by the bold line is the positive set R and the right hand side part is the negative set $N - R$. The ellipse inside the rectangle refers to the total number of surrounding texts containing term t_i, which is n_i. r_i is the number of surrounding texts in the positive set that contain term t_i, and $n_i - r_i$ would be the number of surrounding texts in the negative set that have t_i in them.

$$tf_{ip} = \sum_{d_j \in N} \log_2 \left(\frac{n_{ij}}{\sum_{t_i \in d_j} n_{ij}} + 1 \right). \qquad (2a)$$

$$tf_{in} = \sum_{d_j \in N-R} \log_2 \left(\frac{n_{ij}}{\sum_{t_i \in d_j} n_{ij}} + 1 \right). \qquad (2b)$$

$$tf_i = \frac{tf_{ip}}{tf_{ip} + tf_{in}}. \qquad (2c)$$

$$idf_i = \log_2 \left(\frac{r_i \times \left(N - R - \left(n_i - r_i\right)\right)}{\left(R - r_i\right) \times \left(n_i - r_i\right)} + 1 \right). \qquad (3)$$

In order to find the terms that have the most capability to differentiate the positive set from the negative set, the *tf* value for each set or class needs to be considered. The *tf* value of the positive set for term t_i can be calculated from Equation (2a), and the corresponding *tf* value of the negative set can be calculated from Equation (2b), where n_{ij} is the number of term t_i appears in document d_j. Compared to the conventional definition of *tf* in Equation (1a), we take logarithm considering in most cases that the first appearance of a term gives the most evidence but successive appearances give successively less importance. Adding 1 to it before taking the logarithm is to ensure the *tf* value is larger than 0. The final *tf* value is given in Equation (2c), which calculates the ratio of *tf* value for term t_i in the positive document set versus it in the whole collection, in order to make the *tf* value lies between 0 to 1. Please note that the terms that do not appear in the positive set will have a *tf* value being 0.

The *idf* value can be calculated using Equation (3) which is similar to the one in (Robertson & Jones, 1976) but is added 1 to prevent the *idf*

Figure 3. Surrounding text collection

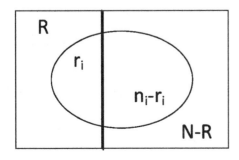

value from going below 0, since they are term weights and will not make sense if they are negative. In rare cases, $R - r_i$ could be 0, which means the term t_i appears in all the positive set. At the same time, $n_i - r_i$ is a small amount of surrounding texts, and then this term is supposed to be a good feature. However, if $n_i - r_i$ is a large proportion in the negative set, which means this term is common in both classes, like stop words, this term should not be considered as a good one. The same rule applies to $n_i - r_i$ when it is 0, which means t_i does not appear in any of the negative surrounding texts. In pseudo code for calculating *idf* the proportion is set to be 0.5 for the general purpose, but can be adjusted based on different datasets.

Pseudo code for calculating *idf*:

1.   If $R - r_i \equiv 0$ then

2.   If $\dfrac{n_i - r_i}{N - R} \geq 0.5$ then

3. $R - r_i \leftarrow 1$

4.   Else

5. $idf_i \leftarrow 0$

6.   End if

7.   Else if $n_i - r_i \equiv 0$ then

8.   If $\dfrac{r_i}{R} \geq 0.5$ then

9. $n_i - r_i \leftarrow 1$

10.   Else

11. $idf_i \leftarrow 0$

12.   End if

13.   Else

14. $idf_i \leftarrow \log_2 \left(\dfrac{r_i \times \left(N - R - \left(n_i - r_i\right)\right)}{\left(R - r_i\right) \times \left(n_i - r_i\right)} + 1 \right)$

15.   End if

Now, the weight of a term can be calculated by TF*IDF scheme using Equation (4). Terms with large weights indicate a better capability to differentiate the positive class from the negative class, and thus they should be selected as the textual features to train the context-based MCA classifier.

$$w_i = tf_i \times idf_i. \tag{4}$$

In addition, we looked into the textual features extracted by our developed TF*IDF variant algorithm. Take concept "Christmas" as an example. Terms like "Christmas", "holiday", "Christian", "shopping", and "winter" all have large TF*IDF weights, and these terms are intuitively related to the concept itself. Take another concept "Airplane" for example, terms like "airframe", "helicopter", and "emitter" also have large weights and can well imply the concept. Therefore, an effective text analysis can often well and directly capture the semantics of the images, which are usually hard to achieve by using low-level visual features alone.

B. MCA Classifier

Multiple correspondence analysis (MCA) has been applied in content-based video concept detection (Lin, Ravitz, Shyu, & Chen, 2008; Lin, Shyu, & Chen, 2009). Since the basic theory can also be used for image classification, MCA is adopted in both content-based and context-based classifiers in this paper. In other words, the content-based MCA classifier is trained by using the low-level visual features, while the context-based MCA classifier is trained by using the textual features. MCA can be considered as an extension of the standard correspondence analysis (CA) to more than two variables (Greenacre & Blasius, 2006). It is used to analyze a set of observations described by a set of nominal (categorical) variables. Thus, in order to apply MCA, each feature needs to be discretized into several intervals or nominal values (called feature-value pairs in our study). In this work, both content and textual features require discretization because they are represented by feature values and frequency counts, respectively, which are numerical values. Taking the textual features for example, the training dataset for concept "cloud" after discretization is shown in Table 2. Each of the T features is discretized into several feature-value pairs, for example, the first feature of the first instance is feature-value pair F_1^3.

Next, all features are combined with the class labels to form an indicator matrix with instances (images) as rows and categories of variables (feature-value pairs and classes) as columns. Assuming the i-th feature has j_i feature-value pairs and the number of classes is m, then the indicator matrix is denoted by Z with size $n \times \left(j_i + m \right)$, where n is the number of instances. Instead of performing on the indicator matrix, MCA analyzes the inner product of this indicator matrix, i.e., $Z^T Z$, called the Burt Table which is symmetric with size $\left(j_i + m \right) \times \left(j_i + m \right)$. Singular Value Decomposition (SVD) is then applied to the correspondence matrix which is transformed from the Burt Matrix by centering and standardizing. Now the feature-value pairs and classes can be projected into a two-dimensional space constructed by the first and second principal compo-

Table 2. Context-based training dataset

Feature 1	Feature 2	...	Feature T
F_1^3	F_2^1	...	F_T^2
F_1^1	F_2^1	...	F_T^1
...	...	...	...

nents due to the fact that over 95% of the total variance can be captured by the first two principal coordinates (Greenacre & Blasius, 2006).

Figure 4 shows an example of MCA geometrical representation, which is also called the symmetric map, for the textual feature "concourse" for concept "cloud". As can be seen from Figure 4, this "concourse" feature is discretized into four feature-value pairs, which correspond to four points in the map, namely, F_1^1, F_1^2, F_1^3, and F_1^4, respectively. The positive and negative classes are represented by two points lying in the x-axis, where C^1 is the positive class and C^2 is the negative class. Take F_1^1 as an example. The angle between F_1^1 and C^1 is a_1^1. Similar to the standard CA, the meaning of a_1^1 in MCA can be interpreted as the correlation between F_1^1 and C^1.

Since our goal is to identify the target concept (i.e., positive class), the angle between a feature-value pair and the positive class is analyzed. The cosine value of the angle represents the percentage of the variance that F_1^1 is explained by the positive class. A larger cosine value which is equal to a smaller angle indicates a strong correlation. F_1^4, on the other side, would have a negative cosine value regards to C^1, which means it has a stronger correlation with the negative class than it is with the positive class. The cosine value of the angle between the feature-value pair and the positive class can act as the weight for that feature-value pair regarding to its discriminant capability. For the j-th feature-value pair of the i-th feature, its weight W_i^j is indicated by Equation (5).

$$W_i^j = \cos\left(a_i^j\right). \tag{5}$$

$$TW_k = \sum_{i=1}^{T} W_i^j. \tag{6}$$

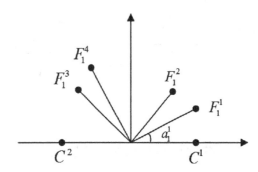

Figure 4. Geometrical representation of MCA

A transaction weight for each data instance in the original context-based training dataset in Table 2 can be calculated by summing the weights of the feature-value pairs along all the features. As shown in Table 3, the transaction weight for the k-th data instance, TW_k, can be calculated by Equation (6). Positive data instances are supposed to have larger transaction weights compared to the negative data instances since a feature-value pair with a large weight indicates a strong correlation with the positive class in comparison to a small weight. Thus, the threshold values can be set based on the training dataset to classify the testing data instances, as TH_N, TH_{XL}, and TH_{XH} in Figure 1 mentioned earlier. In this study, these thresholds are chosen from the mean transaction weight of the positive training data instances minus a constant multiplying its variance. The pseudo code seen is used to classify n testing data instances. Here, 1 denotes the positive label and 0 denotes the negative label.

Pseudo code used to classify n testing data instances:

1. For $k = 1$ to n do
2.   If $TW_k \geq mean_{pos} - const \times std_{pos}$ then
3. $Instance_k \leftarrow 1$
4.   Else
5. $Instance_k \leftarrow 0$
6.   End if
7. End for

Table 3. Context-based training dataset

Feature 1	Feature 2	...	Feature T	Weight
-0.71	0.57	...	-0.23	6.21
0.88	0.57	...	-0.23	4.93
...	...	...	...	...

4. EXPERIMENTS AND RESULTS

The dataset used in our experiments is the web image dataset from MSRA-MM (Li, Wang, & Hua, 2009) which contains 50000 images with ground truth. The download URLs of the images and term frequencies in their surrounding HTML are provided. The way they captured the context information of an image is to first segment the web pages into semantic blocks using VIPS algorithm (Cai, He, Ma, Wen, & Zhang, 2004), and then extract the texts in the block that surrounds the image URL. Texts are then split into words. Only those texts that appear in the WordNet are kept and their frequencies are recorded. We successfully downloaded and extracted visual features and surrounding texts from 8560 images with a landscape shape. Fifteen concepts are used with the positive to negative ratio (P/N ratio) scattered from slightly imbalanced (0.29) to extremely imbalanced (0.002), shown in Table 4. Three-fold cross-validation approach is adopted to evaluate our framework so that every image is tested. Precision (pre), recall (rec), and F1-score (F1) which are the harmonic mean of precision and recall, are adopted as our evaluation metrics for classification.

A. Evaluation of the New TF*IDF Weighting Scheme

Our proposed TF*IDF weighting scheme is compared with conventional TF*IDF (Robertson & Jones, 1976) and two other similar supervised weighting methods: *tf*rf* (Lan, Tan, Su, & Lu,

2009) and *prob-based* (Liu, Loh, & Sun, 2009). *tf*rf* only considers r_i and $n_i - r_i$ as shown in Figure 3, while *prob-based* takes $R - r_i$ into account but does not consider $(N - R) - (n_i - r_i)$. The MCA classifier is used to evaluate the classification result based on the textual features extracted from these four different weighting methods. Figure 5 shows the F1-scores of the fifteen concepts in Table 4, where the conventional TF*IDF is denoted as *tf*idf* and the new proposed variant is denoted as *tf*idfv*. As can be seen from Figure 5, *tf*idf* results in the worst performance in text classification, *tf*idfv* achieves the best on all fifteen concepts, and *tf*rf* achieves the second best F1-scores for eleven concepts.

B. Evaluation of the Framework

To fully evaluate our framework, we first evaluate the performance of the MCA classifier since it is an important component in the whole process. Next, the comparison is made among the results of mining pure content information, mining pure

Table 4. Concepts to be evaluated

No	Concept name	P/N ratio
1	Airplane	0.004
2	Baby	0.016
3	Building	0.066
4	Car	0.070
5	Christmas	0.005
6	Clothing	0.290
7	Cloud	0.273
8	Computer	0.022
9	Dog	0.026
10	Food	0.034
11	Logo	0.043
12	Panda	0.002
13	Sea	0.033
14	Sky	0.191
15	Woman	0.164

Figure 5. Evaluation of the proposed TD*IDF weighting scheme

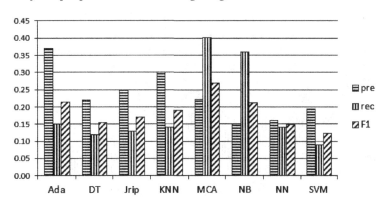

context information, and mining both content and context information. Finally, we compare our framework against two existing frameworks introduced in Section 2 using the same extracted visual and textual features.

The first part of the experiments is done by comparing the MCA classifiers with seven popular classifiers. WEKA provides an implementation of these seven classifiers, namely Adaptive Boosting (Ada), Decision Tree (DT), Rule based Jrip (Jrip), K Nearest Neighbor (KNN) where k=3, Native Bayes (NB), Neural Network (Multilayer-Perceptron) (NN), and Support Vector Machine (Sequential Minimal Optimization) (SVM). Here, the visual and textual features are used to train two sets of classifiers. In order to be fair to the other classifiers, the original non-discretized numeric features and default parameter setting

in WEKA are used to build them. Figure 6 and Figure 7 show the average precision, recall and F1-score of fifteen concepts for each classifier by using pure visual features and pure textual features, respectively. It can be seen that in both situations, MCA outperforms all the other classifiers in the F1-score values, which are the most important metric considering both precision and recall values.

The second part of the experiments aims to evaluate the improvement of the proposed framework based on mining both content and context information. As can be seen in Table 5, the MCA classifier trained by pure textual features usually performs better than the one trained by pure visual features, which is probably due to the reason that texts can better capture the semantics of the images than the low-level visual features. How-

Figure 6. Comparison with common classifiers using visual features

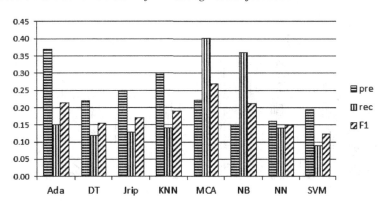

Figure 7. Comparison with common classifiers using textual features

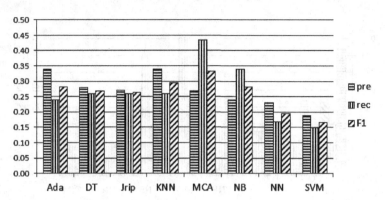

ever, since the surrounding texts are not always directly related to the images in the Internet, mining both information and integrating them in an effective way can achieve better and more reliable results. Table 5 shows that by effectively utilizing the context information, our framework achieves an average increase of 12.8% in the F1-scores compared to the F1-scores of the content-based classifier and an increase of 7.6% in the F1-scores compared to the F1-scores of the context-based classifier.

Finally, our framework (denoted as Combined MCA) is evaluated in comparison with the two state-of-the-art representative methods introduced in Section 2 (Kalva, Enembreck, & Koerich, 2007; Rafkind, Lee, Chang, & Yu, 2006). These two methods used late fusion to combine the results

getting from the classifiers individually trained by the visual and textual features. One is developed by Kalva et al. (2007) that used twelve rules to fuse the results from NB (trained by the visual features) and NN classifiers (trained by the textual features). The other one is developed by Rafkind et al. (2006) that constructed two margin vectors for each data instance, one generated by a SVM trained by the visual features, and the other one by a SVM trained by the textual features. Then a fusion SVM classifier is built by a vector that concatenates from the two margin vectors. Parameters and thresholds are set according to the descriptions of the two papers.

Figure 8 and Figure 9 show the precision and recall values of fifteen concepts for each method, where the numbers on the x-axis are the concept

Figure 8. Comparison of precision

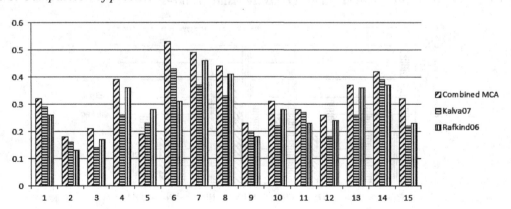

Figure 9. Comparison of recall

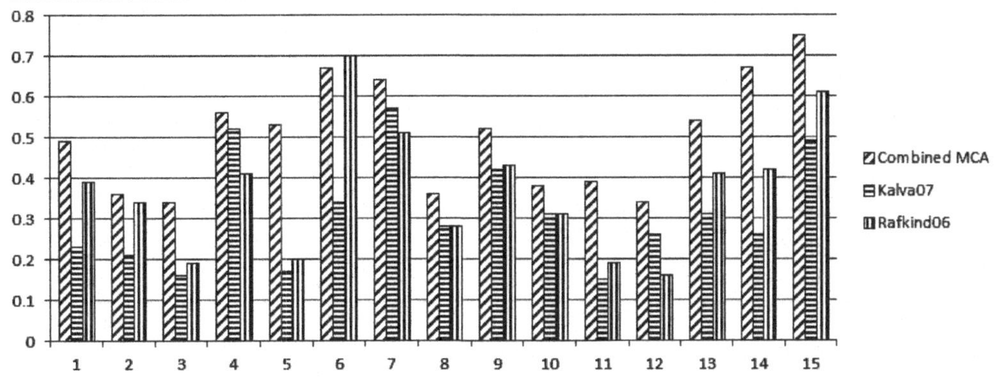

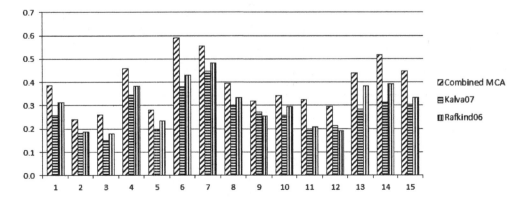

numbers. As can be seen from Figure 8, the precision values of our Combined MCA framework are higher than those of Rafkind (2006) and Kalva (2007), except for Concept 5 which is a little lower. Furthermore, by averaging the precision values of all fifteen concepts, our Combined MCA framework is 6.6% higher than that of Rafkind (2006)and 4.4% higher of Kalva et al. (2007). As for recall, our Combined MCA framework outperforms the other two by a considerable margin, in the averages of 19.1% and 13.3%, respectively. Moreover, our performance of F1-scores shown in Figure 10 is better than those of the other two methods in all fifteen concepts, with an average increase of 11.2% compared to Rafkind (2006) and 7.6% compared to Kalva et al. (2007).

CONCLUSION AND FUTURE WORK

In this paper, a two-staged image classification framework is proposed which utilizes context information to enhance content-based image classification. It first applies content analysis to extract visual features and classifies the images into an initial positive set and an initial negative set in the first stage. Then text analysis is conducted to extract textual features and further refine the classification results generated from the first stage. A new TF*IDF weighting scheme has been developed to weigh the terms in the surrounding texts of the images. This scheme aims to extract textual features that best discriminate the positive class from the negative class. MCA technique has been applied to perform classification and the MCA

Figure 10. Comparison of F1-score

Table 5. Classification via mining visual and textual features

Concept	Metric	Pure content	Pure context	Combined MCA
1. Airplane	pre	0.17	0.27	0.32
	rec	0.44	0.47	0.49
	F1	0.25	0.34	0.39
2. Baby	pre	0.07	0.16	0.18
	rec	0.23	0.25	0.36
	F1	0.11	0.20	0.24
3. Building	pre	0.11	0.12	0.21
	rec	0.23	0.41	0.34
	F1	0.15	0.19	0.26
4. Car	pre	0.28	0.34	0.39
	rec	0.43	0.46	0.56
	F1	0.34	0.39	0.46
5. Christmas	pre	0.10	0.14	0.19
	rec	0.45	0.42	0.53
	F1	0.16	0.21	0.28
6. Clothing	pre	0.45	0.48	0.53
	rec	0.52	0.58	0.67
	F1	0.48	0.53	0.59
7. Cloud	pre	0.39	0.46	0.49
	rec	0.58	0.52	0.64
	F1	0.47	0.49	0.56
8. Computer	pre	0.37	0.35	0.44
	rec	0.20	0.31	0.36
	F1	0.26	0.33	0.40
9. Dog	pre	0.09	0.14	0.23
	rec	0.46	0.49	0.52
	F1	0.15	0.22	0.32
10. Food	pre	0.22	0.26	0.31
	rec	0.27	0.29	0.38
	F1	0.24	0.27	0.34
12. Logo	pre	0.14	0.21	0.28
	rec	0.37	0.32	0.39
	F1	0.20	0.25	0.33
12. Panda	pre	0.13	0.16	0.26
	rec	0.24	0.28	0.34
	F1	0.17	0.20	0.29
13. Sea	pre	0.20	0.27	0.37
	rec	0.41	0.51	0.54
	F1	0.27	0.35	0.44
14. Sky	pre	0.38	0.36	0.42
	rec	0.58	0.57	0.67
	F1	0.46	0.44	0.52
15. Woman	pre	0.24	0.31	0.32
	rec	0.61	0.64	0.75
	F1	0.34	0.42	0.45

classifiers are trained by the visual and textual features, respectively. Experimental results show that the new developed TF*IDF outperforms the conventional TF*IDF and two other supervised weighting schemes in the task of context-based classification. Evaluation of the proposed framework using MSRA-MM web image dataset shows promising results as compared to two existing approaches that also utilize context information.

In the next steps, more concepts will be tested, and public image datasets from different sources such as Flickr and Picasa will be used to improve our framework. We will also keep exploring new approaches to better utilize and integrate context information with the content information. Moreover, MCA can be extended to handle multi-class classification instead of binary classification, which could avoid scalability issue when the number of concepts increases.

REFERENCES

Cai, D., He, X., Ma, W.-Y., Wen, J., & Zhang, H. (2004). Organizing www images based on the analysis of page layout and web link structure. In *Proceedings of the IEEE International Conference on Multimedia and Expo* (pp. 27-30).

Cascia, M. L., Sethi, S., & Sclaroff, S. (1998). Combining textual and visual cues for content-based image retrieval on the World Wide Web. In *Proceedings of the IEEE Workshop on Content-Based Access of Image and Video Libraries* (pp. 24-28).

Deerwester, S., Dumais, S. T., Furnas, G. W., Landauer, T. K., & Harshman, R. (1990). Indexing by latent semantic analysis. *Journal of the American Society for Information Science American Society for Information Science*, *41*(6), 391–407. doi:10.1002/(SICI)1097-4571(199009)41:6<391::AID-ASI1>3.0.CO;2-9

Fayyad, U. M., & Irani, K. B. (1993). Multi-interval discretization of continuous-valued attributes for classification learning. In *Proceedings of the International Joint Conference on Artificial Intelligence* (pp. 1022-1027).

Feng, H., Shi, R., & Chua, T.-S. (2004). A bootstrapping framework for annotating and retrieving www images. In *Proceedings of the ACM International Conference on Multimedia* (pp. 960-967).

Gevers, T., Aldershoff, F., & Smeulders, A. W. (1999). Classification of images on the internet by visual and textual information. In *Proceedings of the Society of Photo-Optical Instrumentation Engineers Conference Series* (pp. 16-27).

Greenacre, M. J., & Blasius, J. (2006). *Multiple correspondence analysis and related methods*. Boca Raton, FL: CRC Press.

Jones, K. S. (2004). A statistical interpretation of term specificity and its application in retrieval. *The Journal of Documentation*, *60*(5), 493–502. doi:10.1108/00220410410560573

Kalva, P., Enembreck, F., & Koerich, A. (2007). Web image classification based on the fusion of image and text classifiers. In *Proceedings of the International Conference on Document Analysis and Recognition* (pp. 561-568).

Kononenko, I. (1995). On biases in estimating multi-valued attributes. In *Proceedings of the International Joint Conference on Artificial Intelligence* (pp. 1034-1040).

Lan, M., Tan, C. L., Su, J., & Lu, Y. (2009). Supervised and traditional term weighting methods for automatic text categorization. *IEEE Transactions on Pattern Analysis and Machine Intelligence*, *31*(4), 721–735. doi:10.1109/TPAMI.2008.110

Lew, M. S., Sebe, N., Djeraba, C., & Jain, R. (2006). Content-based multimedia information retrieval: State of the art and challenges. *ACM Transactions on Multimedia Computing, Communications, and Applications, 2*(1), 1–19. doi:10.1145/1126004.1126005

Li, H., Wang, M., & Hua, X.-S. (2009). Msra-mm 2.0: A large-scale web multimedia dataset. In *Proceedings of the IEEE International Conference on Data Mining Workshops* (pp. 164-169).

Lin, L., Ravitz, G., Shyu, M.-L., & Chen, S.-C. (2008). Correlation-based video semantic concept detection using multiple correspondence analysis. In *Proceedings of the IEEE International Symposium on Multimedia* (pp. 316-321).

Lin, L., Shyu, M.-L., & Chen, S.-C. (2009). Enhancing concept detection by pruning data with mca-based transaction weights. In *Proceedings of the IEEE International Symposium on Multimedia* (pp. 304-311).

Liu, Y., Loh, H. T., & Sun, A. (2009). Imbalanced text classification: A term weighting approach. *Expert Systems with Applications, 36*(1), 690–701. doi:10.1016/j.eswa.2007.10.042

Liu, Y., Zhang, D. S., Lu, G., & Ma, W.-Y. (2007). A survey of content-based image retrieval with high-level semantics. *Pattern Recognition, 40*(1), 262–282. doi:10.1016/j.patcog.2006.04.045

Miller, G. A. (1995). WordNet: A lexical database for English. *Communications of the ACM, 38*(11), 39–41. doi:10.1145/219717.219748

Naphade, M., Smith, J. R., Tesic, J., Chang, S.-F., Hsu, W., & Kennedy, L. (2006). Large-scale concept ontology for multimedia. *IEEE Multimedia Magazine, 13*(3), 86–91. doi:10.1109/MMUL.2006.63

Rafkind, B., Lee, M., Chang, S.-F., & Yu, H. (2006). Exploring text and image features to classify images in bioscience literature. In *Proceedings of the Workshop on Linking Natural Language Processing and Biology: Towards Deeper Biological Literature Analysis* (pp. 73-80).

Robertson, S. E. (2004). Understanding inverse document frequency: On theoretical arguments for idf. *The Journal of Documentation, 60*(5), 503–520. doi:10.1108/00220410410560582

Robertson, S. E., & Jones, K. S. (1976). Relevance weighting of search terms. *Journal of the American Society for Information Science American Society for Information Science, 27*(3), 129–146. doi:10.1002/asi.4630270302

Sebastiani, F. (2002). Machine learning in automated text categorization. *ACM Computing Surveys, 34*(1), 1–47. doi:10.1145/505282.505283

Tollari, S., Glotin, H., & Maitre, J. L. (2003). Enhancement of textual images classification using their global and local visual contents. In *Proceedings of the International Workshop on Metadata and Adaptability in Web-Based Information Systems* (pp. 1-13).

Wang, D., Zhang, H., Wu, W. & Lin, M. (2010). Inverse category frequency based supervised term weighting scheme for text categorization. *ArXiv e-Prints*, 1-12.

Witten, I. H., & Frank, E. (2005). *Data mining: Practical machine learning tools and techniques* (2nd ed.). San Francisco, CA: Morgan Kaufmann.

Zhu, Q., Lin, L., Shyu, M.-L., & Chen, S.-C. (2010). Feature selection using correlation and reliability based scoring metric for video semantic detection. In *Proceedings of the IEEE International Conference on Semantic Computing* (pp. 462-469).

This work was previously published in the International Journal of Multimedia Data Engineering and Management, Volume 2, Issue 3, edited by Shu-Ching Chen, pp. 34-51, copyright 2011 by IGI Publishing (an imprint of IGI Global).

Chapter 7
Hybrid Query Refinement:
A Strategy for a Distance Based Index Structure to Refine Multimedia Queries

Kasturi Chatterjee
Florida International University, USA

Shu-Ching Chen
Florida International University, USA

ABSTRACT

This paper proposes a hybrid query refinement model for distance-based index structures supporting content-based image retrievals. The framework refines a query by considering both the low-level feature space as well as the high-level semantic interpretations separately. Thus, it successfully handles queries where the gap between the feature components and the semantics is large. It refines the low-level feature space, indexed by the distance based index structure, in multiple iterations by introducing the concept of multipoint query in a metric space. It refines the high-level semantic space by dynamically adjusting the constructs of a framework, called the Markov Model Mediator (MMM), utilized to introduce the semantic relationships in the index structure. A k-nearest neighbor (k-NN) algorithm is designed to handle similarity searches that refine a query in multiple iterations utilizing the proposed hybrid query refinement model. Extensive experiments are performed demonstrating an increased relevance of query results in subsequent iterations while incurring a low computational overhead. Further, an evaluation metric, called the Model_Score, is proposed to compare the performance of different retrieval frameworks in terms of both computation overhead and query result relevance. This metric enables the users to choose the retrieval framework appropriate for their requirements.

DOI: 10.4018/978-1-4666-2940-0.ch007

1. INTRODUCTION

An index structure is one of the major components of a database management system as it assists in efficiently organizing the data and enables quick and accurate retrieval. There are multidimensional index structures such as Berchtold and Keim (1996), Chatterjee and Chen (2006), Ciaccia, Patella, and Zezula (1997), and Guttman (1984), which can accommodate the atypical multidimensional representation of multimedia data. But enabling them to efficiently support the popular retrieval strategies, such as content-based image and video retrievals, is still a challenge due to the semantic information carried by them. The semantic interpretation of a multimedia data is subjective and varies from user to user or even from iteration to iteration for an individual user. This makes the similarity queries issued for multimedia data imprecise in nature. A single iteration or a fixed query representation is not enough to capture the user requirements during the retrieval process. Thus, attempts to capture the users' interest pattern are made with a strategy called *query refinement* having two major components namely *query modification* and *query re-weighting* (Porkaew, Chakrabarti, & Mehrotra, 1999). In query modification, the query representation is modified in each iteration to reach the region in the feature space which best describes the feature components of the users' requirement. In query re-weighting, the semantic component of a query is modified in subsequent iterations to better capture the users' perception. As a query is refined, the similarity search and the distance functions utilized to determine the similarity need to be modified as well. Automatically, it becomes necessary that the index structures, supporting the similarity searches, also accommodate the modified distance functions developed for the refined queries.

Multidimensional index structures can be broadly divided into two categories viz. feature-based and distance-based. A feature based indexing technique projects an image as a feature vector into a multidimensional space and index it. Some feature based index structures are KDB-tree (Robinson, 1981), R-tree (Guttman, 1984), etc. On the other hand distance based indexing structures are built based on the distances or similarities between two data objects. Some famous distance based index structures are M-Tree (Ciaccia, Patella, & Zezula, 1997) and vp-tree (Yianilos, 1993). Both categories are useful depending on the dataset in hand and the application that need to be supported. Though query refinement strategies have been designed for feature-based index structures as in Porkaew, Ortega, and Mehrotra (1999), Chakrabarti and Mehrotra (1999), and Chakrabarti, Porkaew, Ortega, and Mehrotra (2004) but to the best of our knowledge there has been no such attempt for distance-based index structures. Another major drawback is that if the semantic information of a multimedia object cannot be interpreted completely in terms of the inter and intra feature weights (when the semantic gap is large), refinement strategies (Porkaew, Chakrabarti, & Mehrotra, 1999) fail to produce satisfactory results. The *semantic gap* is a very common problem for multimedia data and is illustrated in Figure 1 for an image database where the feature-level similarity failed to capture users' high-level semantic perception. Figure 1(a) represents the inverse of the Euclidean Distance (similarity) between the feature vectors of an image with other images of a database. Figure 1(b) represents the high-level semantic relationship between the same image with other images in the database. It's seen that the image, with which the image under consideration shares a low similarity in terms of feature space, has a very high semantic relationship with it.

In this paper, we propose a hybrid query refinement model for distance based index structures, which organizes and manages mainly images. However, the refinement model used here can be utilized for indexing other multimedia objects such as videos as long as the distance based index structure can organize the particular data type. The proposed query refinement strategy is called *hybrid* because it refines and adjusts

Figure 1. Graphs depicting that feature-level similarity fail to capture users' high-level perception

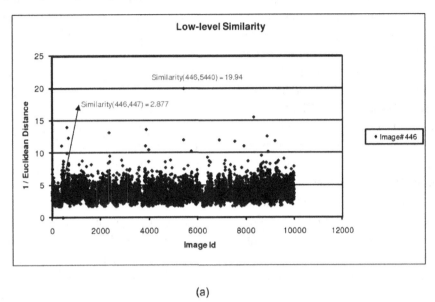

(a)

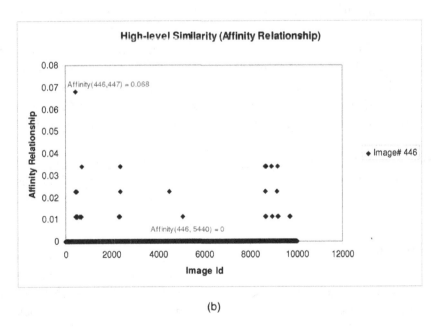

(b)

both the low-level feature space as well as high-level semantic interpretations individually during refining the queries in each iteration. It adopts a query expansion approach to refine the feature space. To refine the semantic interpretation of a query, it dynamically adjusts the parameter of a stochastic construct called Markov Model Mediator (MMM) (Shyu, Chen, Chen, Zhang, & Shu, 2003). We introduce the hybrid query refinement

ensemble in a distance-based index structure and enable the similarity search algorithms to implement it to improve query results progressively in subsequent iterations. We also propose a new evaluation score called the *Model_Score* that can compare the overall performance of the different multimedia retrieval frameworks in terms of both computation time and F1 Score (relevance). Both the response time and the relevance of a query result is important in case of similarity queries for multimedia data. Thus, while evaluating and comparing the performance of index structures for multimedia data, one should be able to view the combined effect of both these criteria on the retrieval process and how each affects the other. We chose Affinity Hybrid Tree (Chatterjee & Chen, 2006, 2007) (AH-Tree) as the distance-based index structure to introduce the hybrid query refinement model. The main motivation behind choosing Affinity Hybrid Tree, as the distance based index prototype, is that it has the capability to support the high-level semantic relationships between images without attempting to translate them into feature level equivalence.

The rest of the paper is organized as follows. Section 2 discusses the background and related works on query refinement strategies. Section 3 gives a brief overview of the AH-Tree and Section 4 discusses the MMM framework concisely. Section 5 and 6 discusses the query refinement approach in AH-Tree in details when introduced into the similarity search algorithms. It is followed by Section 7, which demonstrates the experiment results and data analysis along with the proposed evaluation metrics. And lastly, we have a conclusion and a brief outline of future work in the last section.

2. RELATED WORK

The concept of query refinement is found to be useful in areas such as web-search (Reynolds, Dickinson, & Grosvenor, 2009) and xml queries (Lu, Bao, Ling, & Meng, 2009) wherever there is a fuzzy component attached to the users' requirements. But, particularly it has been identified that the success of multimedia retrieval systems largely depends on how effectively the fuzzy/imprecise component of the query is handled with the help of different query refinement approaches. Content-Based Image Retrieval (CBIR) is one of the most popular retrieval strategies for multimedia data objects. Unlike traditional database queries, performance of multimedia data retrieval, such as Content-Based Image Retrieval (CBIR), depends largely on the efficiency with which the users' similarity concept is interpreted. Rui, Huang, Ortega, and Mehrotra (1998) pointed out two distinct characteristics of CBIR viz. (1) the gap between high-level concept and low level features and (2) subjectivity of human perception of visual content. Thus the queries issued during CBIR are imprecise in nature, i.e., the users' concept of subjectivity cannot be captured precisely in a single attempt. This results in CBIR requiring a frequently refined query (refined by information gathered from the user feedback) to increase the query precision in multiple iterations. Porkaew, Chakrabarti, and Mehrotra (1999) pointed out two steps to refine a query viz. (1) query modification and (2) query re-weighting. Query modification refines query representation to better suit the users' information need. Query re-weighting learns the users' notion of similarity by adjusting the weight of the features in the form of Relevance Feedback (RF).

In Porkaew, Chakrabarti, and Mehrotra (1999), two query modification techniques were proposed viz. (1) Query Point Movement and (2) Query Expansion. Query Point Movement (QPM) allows only a single query object per feature space. When, in multiple iteration of the refinement process, the user marks several objects as relevant, the weighted centroid of the relevant image objects is used as the new query. The weights are associated depending upon the relevance level as attached by the user.

The weighted centroid C is defined as:

$$c[j] = \frac{\sum_{i=1}^{n} w_i E_{ij}}{\sum_{i=1}^{n} w_i} \tag{1}$$

where, E_{ij} is the feature vector of image i along the jth dimension and w_i is the weight associated with the image i.

The similarity distance functions are modified with the new query point, represented as the centroid of multiple relevant image points. The above QPM technique is utilized in Ishikawa, Subramanya and Faloutsos (1998) and Ortega, Rui, Chakrabarti, Porkaew, Mehrotra, and Huang (1998). Its goal is to choose a single query point and re-weigh its feature dimensions such that the sum of its distances from the relevant points become minimum (Ishikawa, Subramanya, & Faloutsos, 1998). But, the QPM method results in some information loss as the characteristics of each relevant image is lost and their collective representation is treated as the refined query. Another technique was proposed in Porkaew, Chakrabarti, and Mehrotra (1999), the query expansion approach, where multiple objects marked relevant in a particular iteration are all considered as a new query. Such queries are also called Multipoint Queries. In this method, clustering of the relevant points are done and the centroid of the cluster is used as the representative. The representative points are used to form the new query. The weights get added to the multipoint query with the corresponding representative. The distance function of the multipoint query is the summation of the weighted distances of each representative query from an image object in the feature space. Porkaew, Ortega, and Mehrotra (1999) performed extensive experiments over large image collections and concluded that Query Expansion approach outperforms Query Point Movement approach in retrieval results based on precision and recall measures. Another important advantage of the query point expansion technique pointed out in Porkaew, Chakrabarti, and Mehrotra (1999) its enhanced general applicability as compared to the query point movement approach. Query expansion is usable even when the feature space is not defined but the metric space corresponding to

the particular feature space is known. Later, Liu, Hua, and Yu (2006) pointed out that the Query Point Movement technique has some additional limitation like having local maximum traps, which results in poor improvement of query results for refinement iterations. Thus, Liu, Hua, and Yu (2006) proposed four target search techniques viz. Naive Random Scan, Local Neighboring Movement, Neighboring Divide and Conquer Method and Global Divide and Conquer Methods to improve it.

To introduce a query refinement model into a multimedia data management framework, equipped with an appropriate index structure, the similarity search algorithms of those index structures should be revised as well. In Porkaew, Chakrabarti, and Mehrotra (1999), a feature-based multidimensional index structure, called Feature Index or F-Index, was used as a prototype multidimensional index structure to demonstrate the technique by which multipoint refined queries were supported during retrievals. The similarity queries were executed using a k-nearest neighbor algorithm that accesses nodes in a decreasing order of their distances (similarity measurement) from the query. A priority queue is implemented for the ordered traversal over the index structure. There are two approaches proposed by Chakrabarti, Porkaew, Ortega, and Mehrotra (2004) and Porkaew, Chakrabarti, and Mehrotra (1999) to implement similarity searches with the refined queries. One approach of evaluating the refined queries M (called multipoint query as multiple query points are gathered from the feedback of the users in the previous iteration to form them) is to retrieve nearest neighbors of a single point C and still guarantee that the set of answers S returned are the k-nearest neighbors of M i.e., $D(M, S_i) \leq D(M, T)$ for any $S_i \in S, T \notin S$. This is the criterion while using *query point movement*. An alternative approach is to retrieve results based on the distance from all the points in the multipoint query instead of the centroid only i.e., use *query expansion*. The distance between any intermediate node (N) and the multipoint refined query (M) using query expansion is defined as:

$$MINDIST(M,N) = \sum_{i=1}^{n} w_i D(P_i, NP(P_i, N))$$

(2)

where,

$$NP(P_i, N)[j] = \begin{cases} l_j, & \text{if } P_i[j] < l_j \\ h_j, & \text{if } P_i[j] > h_j \\ P_j[j], & \text{otherwise} \end{cases}$$

NP[j] denotes the position of *NP* along j^{th} dimension of the feature space R_F and P_i is the ith point of the multipoint query, and *D* is the distance function.

The distance between a leaf node and the multipoint query can be defined as:

$$D(M,N) = \sum_{i=1}^{n} w_i D_F(P_i, N)$$

(3)

To achieve query re-weighting, one needs to capture features that best describes the users' concept of high-level similarity and attach/modify weights to these features to get refined query results close to user perception. Extensive research was performed in this field to better capture users' perception and translate the high-level semantic interpretation of multimedia data to a feature-level model. In Huang and Rui (1997) and Rui, Huang, and Mehrotra (1997), an interactive mechanism was devised to include a human in the retrieval loop; in Daneels et al. (1993), an interactive region segmentation was employed etc. Later, Rui, Huang, Ortega, and Mehrotra (1998) proposed another technique called Relevance Feedback (RF) in which humans and computers interact to refine high-level queries to low-level representations. To introduce the query re-weighting component into the similarity search, the distance functions calculate the similarity as:

$$Sim_{xy} = \sum_{s=1}^{q} w_s Sim_s$$

(4)

where, $\sum_{s=1}^{q} w_s = 1$, Sim_{xy} is the similarity between the multimedia objects x and y, Sim_s is the similarity between the sth feature attribute of the multimedia objects x and y, q is the dimension of the feature space and w_s is the weight of the feature component s.

The weight w_s is modified at each iteration during query re-weighting while implementing query refinement.

Though, Chakrabarti, Porkaew, Ortega, and Mehrotra (2004) and Porkaew, Chakrabarti, and Mehrotra (1999) made the first attempt to enable a multidimensional index structure to support query refinement quite successfully, they have some limitations and disadvantages, such as:

- The query refinement technique proposed by Chakrabarti, Porkaew, Ortega, and Mehrotra (2004) and Porkaew, Chakrabarti, and Mehrotra (1999) can be used only in a feature-based index structure because distance-based index structures cannot handle arbitrary intra-feature weights. Varying the intra-feature weights (which makes it arbitrary) is the key step of the query re-weighting strategy as explained in Rui, Huang, Ortega, and Mehrotra (1998) and Rui, Huang, and Mehrotra (1997) Content based image retrieval with relevance feedback in mars and is utilized in the distance/similarity. computation following Equation 4.

- The query refinement methodology proposed in Chakrabarti, Porkaew, Ortega, and Mehrotra (2004) and Porkaew, Ortega, and Mehrotra (1999) is strongly based on the fact that high-level semantic relationship between image objects is closely related with their low-level similarity (calculated by the distance functions). But practical observations lead to the fact that many-a-time feature-level similarity fails to capture the users' similarity perception (an example is provided in Figure 1 for an image from our database). Under such circumstances, the query model laid down in Chakrabarti, Porkaew, Ortega, and Mehrotra (2004) and Porkaew, Chakrabarti, and Mehrotra (1999) and their approach to embed it into an index structure will not generate satisfactory results.

3. AFFINITY HYBRID TREE

Affinity Hybrid Tree (AH-Tree) is a novel multimedia indexing and access framework (Chatterjee & Chen, 2006, 2007) which devises a technique to embed feature-level similarity (low-level) and semantic closeness (high-level) of multimedia objects (at present images) in the retrieval mechanism efficiently. AH-Tree combines feature based and distance based indexing techniques seamlessly to produce semantically related query results with low computational overhead. It is a flexible index structure and is capable of supporting any feature space with a fairly high dimension and any representation of high-level multimedia object relationship.

At present we find that the AH-Tree built with the matrices (Feature Matrix, Affinity Matrix) derived from our proposed MMM model (Shyu, Chen, Chen, Zhang, & Shu, 2003) for image retrieval mechanism produces very promising results. However, it should be noted that with the advancement of research in fields like selecting appropriate features or determining high-level object similarity, the index structure will be able to leverage such improvements with little or no additional computational overheads. Thus, to the best of our knowledge, AH-Tree is the first attempt to introduce high-level semantic relationship into the similarity search routines of a distance-based index structure without deducing correlations among the feature components and the semantics.

The data/leaf nodes of the space-based (feature-based) index structure store pointers to the roots of the distance-based (similarity-based) index structures instead of pointers to the data objects. The space-based index structure acts as a filter and reduces the number of distance computation during building and querying, thus decreasing the computational overhead manifold. AH-Tree embeds the high-level image relationship in the metric space during the retrieval methods viz. the k-NN search and range search.

4. MARKOV MODEL MEDIATOR

Markov Model Mediator (MMM) (Shyu, Chen, Chen, Zhang, & Shu, 2003) is a stochastic approach that allows capturing the high-level image relationship called the affinity relationship, among image objects and uses it during searching the image database and providing query results. It is an effort to bridge the gap between low-level features and high-level concepts (the semantic gap). The MMM framework is represented as a 5-tuple $\lambda = (S, F, A, B, \Pi)$, where S is the set of images, A is the state transition probability distribution, B is the feature vector and Π is the initial state probability distribution. From this tuple, our point of interest is the state transition matrix denoted by A, where each entry (i, j) corresponds to the relationship between image i and j captured by off-line training processes. We use it during similarity search routines of the AH-Tree along with the distance measurement to produce semantically close results. It is also our point of interest for the query refinement model. The pair of user access pattern and user access frequency provides the capability to capture the user concepts in the training process {mmm}. The main idea is "the more frequent two images are accessed together, the more related they are".

The relative affinity measurement $aff_{m, n}$ between two images m and n is defined as follows:

$$aff_{m,n} = \sum_{k=1}^{q} use_{m,k} \times use_{n,k} \times access_k \qquad (5)$$

where, $use_{m,k}$ denotes the usage pattern of image m with respect to query q_k per time period, and $access_k$ denotes the access frequency of query q_k per time period.

The state transition probability matrix is built by having $a_{m,n}$ as the element in the $(m, n)^{th}$ position of A. The $a_{m,n}$ value is defined as:

$$a_{m,n} = \frac{aff_{m,n}}{\sum_{n \varepsilon d} aff_{m,n}} \qquad (6)$$

From the experimental results and analysis provided in {mmm}, it can be concluded that MMM mechanism can assist in retrieving very accurate results.

5. QUERY REFINEMENT IN AH-TREE

This is achieved by dynamically manipulating the $aff_{m,n}$ value (as explained in Equation 7) for each iteration. In each iteration, when a number of images from the result set for a query k are marked relevant by an user, the access frequency $access_k$ is increased by 1 while $use_{m,k}$ and $use_{n,k}$ are set to 1 for a pair of images m and n in the result set which are marked relevant. Thus, if the access frequency between two images at $(t-1)^{th}$ iteration be $access_{t-1}$, the affinity value at t^{th} iteration is refined as:

$$aff_{m,n_t} = 1 \times 1 \times (access_{t-1} + 1) \qquad (7)$$

Also, if the query image itself belongs to the database, the row of the affinity matrix corresponding to it is selected and all the entries in that row are refined according to Equation 7, where m is set as k and $n \ \varepsilon \ p_1, p_2, ..., p_x$, where p_x is the image id marked relevant by the user and $x \ \varepsilon$ ids of relevant images in each iteration. A normalization of each row, affected in the feedback process, of the affinity matrix is performed after each iteration as Equation 6 and the modified affinity relationship score is utilized during the similarity search in the next iteration. The original affinity value before normalization is stored to get the actual access value for refinement in subsequent iterations. With Equation 7, the affinity relationship scores between the relevant images are refined (increased) dynamically whereas the scores between all other pairs remain the same. Hence, those relevant images will have a greater probability of retrieval than the rest of the images during subsequent retrieval iterations and also for similar query types issued by different users later. Thus, the query is refined independently in terms of the high-level semantic relationship by manipulating the probabilistic measure of access frequencies without relying on the relationship between the semantics and the feature space.

The refinements or modifications of the affinity values that occur in a particular row of the affinity matrix for a particular feedback from the user, is distributed throughout the affinity matrix. The distribution takes place to pairs of affinity relationships that are directly or indirectly related to the modified/refined pairs of the affected row. For example, let, the $(i, j)^{th}$ pair of the affinity matrix be refined in iteration n. To distribute and reflect the update in the similarity perception throughout the affinity matrix, the affinity relationships for those elements in row i and j are refined with Equation 7, which have been marked relevant in the feedback in iteration n. The process is repeated for each pair marked relevant in a particular iteration. Thus with a single user feedback, quite a few number of semantic relationships are refined in a single go.

In addition, a separate data structure known as *profile_affinity_relationship*$_x$ is maintained, which copies the original Affinity Relationship matrix into a local profile specific to the xth user and updates it according to the users' perception and preference. Normalization is done for each updated row after each iteration. Such *profile_affinity_relationship* structures for different users are evaluated after a certain interval and the universal affinity relationship matrix is updated accordingly. In this way, high-level similarity is not biased by any one user's preference and each user need not take the heavy burden of correctness of his/her response. Since the universal affinity relationship matrix update takes place off-line, after a considerable amount of data is accumulated in the *profile_affinity_relationship* all the rows and every image pair that are affected by the feedback can be updated without causing considerable delays in query processing.

6. REFINEMENT MODEL FOR THE FEATURE SPACE

The hybrid query refinement model, for refining the feature space, uses a multiple point query representation as it has been pointed out in the literature (Porkaew, Chakrabarti, & Mehrotra, 1999) that multiple point query representations (query expansions) better capture users' perception than aggregated single point query representation (query point movement). Such a query is represented by the following tuple: $Q = (n, P, W)$, where n represents the number of image points present in the refined query, P stands for set of the feature vectors for each points and W the weights attached by the user with each refined query point to rank them in order of their relevance with the original submitted query. Thus, with each submitted feedback, the query representation is modified. The above method of representing the refined query modifies the requirement of the user

in terms of the target feature space. For example, for traditional queries when a k-NN query is submitted with a single image object, it meant "search the database and give me k images which are nearest to the query in terms of features". With the refined query, the requirement changes to "search the database and give me k images which are nearest to all the query images in terms of features". Thus, the above query representation expands the feature search space and adjusts it with each iteration.

To utilize the above representation of a refined query in a distance-based index structure to answer similarity searches, the distance function need to be modified. The distance function aids to calculate the (dis)similarity of an indexed object in the database with the query point. Since traditional metric distance functions, such as Euclidean Distance, were proposed with a single query point in mind, hence they need to be modified and the correctness need to be proved for multi-point queries. A distance function is correctly defined if after searching the metric space (containing the indexed data objects), based on the similarity score produced by the distance function, the top k results are indeed the k most nearest objects to the query point in the entire database. There are two basic search paradigms implemented by any index structures viz. range search and k-NN search. For the imprecise nature of multimedia query, k-NN search is preferred over range search since determining the range of an imprecise query is rather error-prone while simulating CBIR in the search routines for an index structure indexing multimedia data.

The k-NN search of AH-Tree follows the classical branch and bound technique (Roussopoulos, Kelley, & Vincent, 1995) and needs to determine (1) the distance between the query object and the image object in the leaf nodes and (2) the distance between the query object and the intermediate index nodes. Since the metric space of our index structure is Euclidean, hence each intermediate node which serves as a bounding region for the child nodes is represented by a sphere with a centroid C (an image object with a routing role) and a radius r (covering radius). Each data node (at the leaf level) is represented by a centroid with covering radius equal to zero. The distance function, DIST, is used to calculate the (dis)similarity between the query object and the index tree nodes (both intermediate and leaf nodes). Generalizing the definition of MINDIST in [?], the $DIST(O, P)$ in AH-Tree of an object O from query object P is defined as:

$$DIST(O, P) = |\, C - P\,|^2 - r. \qquad (8)$$

If, the object is a leaf node, the covering radius is zero and Equation 8 is reduced to:

$$DIST(O, P) = |\, C - P\,|^2 \qquad (9)$$

The above technique can be extended to query expansion for metric space with a multiple point refined query as follows: The DISTMULTI between an intermediate object O and an expanded query Q is defined as:

$$DISTMULTI(Q, O) = \sum_{i=1}^{n} W_i \,|\, C - F_i\,|^2 - r, \qquad (10)$$

where F is a feature vector consisting of features of each image object the user has marked to be a potential query object or relevant to a submitted query, n denotes the number of marked query objects and W corresponds to a set of weights attached to each returned additional query point.

As mentioned above, the correctness of the modified distance function or DISTMULTI with the multiple query points should be proved. It is correct if indeed it provides the k closest results in response to a similarity query, in each iteration. Thus, to ensure that there will be no false dis-

missal, it should be proved that $DISTMULTI(O, Q)$ lower bounds $D(T, Q)$, where T is any node of the subtree of O.

Lemma 1: *DISTMULTI for a multi-point query is correct iff $DISTMULTI(O, Q) \leq D(T, Q)$ for any node T in the subtree of O.*

Proof 2: *Let,* O be an intermediate node of the metric tree. Since, T is any object under O, it belongs to the subtree/covering tree of O. Since all nodes of the covering tree are within its bounding radius, we have:

$$D(P_i, T) - r(O_T) \geq D(P_i, O) - r(O_o) \qquad (11)$$

where P_i is the ith query point and $r(O_T)$ and $r(O_o)$ are the covering radii of the subtree T and O respectively. Which implies,

$$D(P_i, O) - r(O_o) \leq D(P_i, T) - r(O_T) \qquad (12)$$

Which implies,

$$\sum_{i=1}^{n} W_i D(P_i, O) - r(O_o) \leq \sum_{i=1}^{n} W_i D(P_i, T) - r(O_T) \qquad (13)$$

Thus,

$$DISTMULTI(O, Q) \leq D(T, Q) \qquad (14)$$

The summation of the distances over n refined query points ensures that the pruning is performed based upon the collective impact of each of the refined query points. The effect of each of the refined queries on the collective MINDIST function is determined by the weights assigned by the relevance attached by the user in each iteration.

7. SIMILARITY SEARCH WITH HYBRID QUERY REFINEMENT MODEL

The above discussed technique of hybrid query refinement is embedded in the metric space (distance-based index structure) of AH-Tree during similarity search as discussed in Refined_k-NN-Search algorithm in Table 1. The Refined_k-NN-Search explores the image database with a refined query Q, consisting of multiple image points marked as relevant by the user, and a refined affinity matrix to return k image points most similar in both feature-level similarity (computed by DISTMULTI) and high-level relationship (computed from the promoted affinity values). A priority queue of the sub-trees (for which at least one qualifying object has been found) is maintained and elements (intermediate nodes which are the roots of the subtrees) are popped from its top and checked for similarity criteria (both in terms of low-level features and high-level semantic relationship) until the priority queue consists of leaf nodes which are the k nearest neighbors of the multi-point query Q. During a k-NN search of the metric space, for each non-leaf node, the DISTMULTI is calculated between the node and each of the query points using Equation 10. If the DISTMULTI of the node is greater than the distance of the current k^{th} neighbor and does not have an affinity with any of the query point greater than or equal to the required affinity, the node is pruned. Otherwise the examined node is added to the priority queue and the entire queue is sorted based on the DISTMULTI function. Similarly, for each leaf-node, DISTMULTI is calculated using Equation 10 with r set to 0 since for leaf nodes there is no bounding region and the covering radius is 0 (Chatterjee & Chen, 2006). Here, the affinity condition is an *AND* (Equation 15) rather than an *OR* (Equation 16) as used in the intermediate node evaluation.

$$((aff(O_{leaf}, Q_1) \geq aff) \, \& \, \&(aff(O_{leaf}, Q_2) \geq aff) \, \& \, \& \ldots \& \, \&(aff(O_{leaf}, Q_n) \geq aff))$$

(15)

$$((aff(O_{router}, Q_1) \geq aff)PP(aff(O_{router}, Q_2) \geq aff) \, PP \ldots PP(aff(O_{router}, Q_n) \geq aff))$$

(16)

where $aff(O_{leaf}, Q_n)$ and $aff(O_{router}, Q_n)$ are the affinity between the leaf node and the intermediate node with the nth query point respectively. Q is the multi-point query and aff is the required affinity value.

This condition is utilized to push all the intermediate nodes into the priority queue with even a slight possibility to match the high-level similarity with at least a part of the multi-point query (at least with one of them). Thus, an optimistic guess is done to avoid any false dismissal. But for the leaf nodes, the final result set is determined based on the distance and the affinity criteria. Hence, the conditions are made more stringent and only those image points from the database are chosen which have the required high-level closeness with every query point. If there are not k image points satisfying the criteria, the refined query is re-executed with a more flexible *OR* condition for the leaf nodes and the intermediate nodes. Furthermore, it should be noted that based on the weights attached to each query point by the user, DISTMULTI is actually a weighted summation of the corresponding distances (bounding region or point). These weights (in the range of 0-3 as discussed in Section 7 are attached to each query point during the user feedback process.

The high level semantic relationships among the images in the form of affinity values cannot be embedded in the metric space as it makes the distance functions arbitrary (Chatterjee & Chen, 2006). Instead the affinity relationship is introduced in the metric structure prior to issuing a query, through a novel affinity promotion

Table 1. Refined_k-NN search algorithm

```
Refined_k-NN-Search(Q, N_child, r(Q), aff) { //Metric Search.
    Affinity_Promotion_RefinedQueries( ); //promotion of affinity value.
    if (((aff(O_r, Q_1) ≠ 0)|||| ((aff(O_r, Q_2) ≠ 0)|||| ... |||| ((aff(O_r, Q_n) ≠ 0)))
    { //affinity value available for at least one of the query points.
        if (O_r is a routing object){
            ∀ O_r in N_child do: {
                if ((∑_{i=1}^{n} W_i|C - F_i|^2 - r) ≤ r(Q)+r(O_r)) && ...
                    ((aff(O_r, Q_1) ≥ aff)|||| (aff(O_r, Q_2) ≥ aff)||||
                    |||| (aff(O_r, Q_n) ≥ aff))) {
                    //update and reshuffle the k least distance values by inserting
                    //(∑_{i=1}^{n} W_i|C - F_i|^2 - r) in the correct position.
                    aff = max_{i=1}^{n} (aff(O_r, Q_i));
                    Refined_k-NN-Search(ptr(T(O_r)), Q, aff);
                    //T(O_r): pointer to the subtree.
                }
            }//end of search for O_r
            //satisfying metric condition.
        }//end of search for all O_r in N_child.
    }//end of internal node search of the
    //metric tree.
    elseif (O_r is a leaf object){
        if ((∑_{i=1}^{n} W_i|C - F_i|^2) ≤ r(Q)+r(O_r)) &&
            ((aff(O_r, Q_1) ≥ aff)&&(aff(O_r, Q_2) ≥ aff)&& ... &&(aff(O_r, Q_n) ≥ aff))) {
            //add to the result set.
            //update and re-shuffle the k least distance values by inserting
            //(∑_{i=1}^{n} W_i|C - F_i|^2) in the correct position.
            aff = max_{i=1}^{n} (aff(O_r, Q_i));
        }
    } //end of search for query object with affinity.
    else {
        Refined_k-NN-Search with the absence of the affinity
        comparison;
    } //end of search for query object without affinity.
} //end of Metric Search Subroutine.
```

technique. In the affinity promotion routine, the affinity values are promoted from the leaf level to the intermediate nodes up to the root and thus distribute it throughout the tree structure so that each node has an affinity value with respect to the query. Since the query representation is modified, the affinity promotion technique should also be changed from to support multiple points in a query.

For a query space consisting of n query points $q_{i=1}^{n}$, the affinity relationship of an intermediate node p with child nodes a and b is set as:

$$max_{i=1}^{n} \begin{pmatrix} (\max(affinity_{a,q_i}, affinity_{b,q_i}), \\ \max(affinity_{a,q_{i-1}}, affinity_{b,q_{i-1}})), \end{pmatrix}$$

where $affinity_{a,q_i}$ represents the affinity value of child node a with the query point q_i. The above representation sets up a routine whereby the maximum of the affinity values among the values between all the child nodes with all the query points is promoted as the affinity value of the parent node p with respect to the multi-point query q. It is done by an iterative process whereby in the ith iteration the maximum of the affinity between all the children with the ith query point is compared with the maximum of the affinity between all the children with the $(i-1)^{th}$ query point. The maximum of these two values is set as the affinity value at the ith iteration and the process continues. Also, it should be mentioned here that for simplicity of representation, the above formula is presented for an intermediate node with only two children. But for implementation purposes, it could be extended for n number of child nodes without any loss of generality. This formula ensures that if there is any candidate node in the subtree which has an affinity value with each of the query points greater than or equal to the required affinity, the parent node is traversed and there is no false dismissal. It also ensures that if none of the child nodes has the required affinity, the parent node can be pruned altogether without any further investigation. The method executes bottom-up i.e., in the AH-Tree, first, for each leaf node, the affinity value between it and each of the query points are calculated and the maximum among them is determined. This maximum affinity value is assigned to each leaf node and then the index tree is traversed one level up to promote these affinity values to the intermediate nodes till the root is reached, using the above formula. The algorithm employed for the multi-point query promotion technique is presented in Table 2.

8. EMPIRICAL STUDY AND EVALUATION METRIC

In the experiments, the image database used consists of 10,000 color images from Corel dataset belonging to 72 semantic categories. The system allows the user to rank query results as 0 (Not Relevant), 1 (Very Close), 2 (Perfect), and 3 (Set as new query). These weights are utilized in formation of the refined queries. Extensive experiments are performed with 3 rounds of iteration for 10 query images randomly picked from the database. Four systems viz. AH-Tree Refinement Model, Feature-Based Refinement Model, AH-Tree Without Refinement Model and a Sequential Search Model(one which doesn't have any index structure but searches through the entire image database in terms of both low-level feature-wise similarity and high-level affinity relationships), are compared with one another. The comparison is performed in terms of 4 criteria viz. Accuracy, Computation Time, F1 Score and Number of Distance Computations (required to determine the feature-level similarity). The accuracy is measured as the percentage of retrieved results that were marked relevant by the user, computation time is the time taken to execute the query, F1 Score can be considered as the weighted average of the precision and recall and is expressed in Equation 17 and number of distance computation measures the computation overhead contributed by each model during the similarity calculation using distance functions (like Euclidean Distance Function).

$$F1 \quad Score = \frac{2 \times p \times r}{p + r} \qquad (17)$$

where, p is the precision and r is the recall.

The experimental results for 3 iterations averaged over 10 random queries are summarized in Table 3 and their graphical representations are presented in Figure 2, Figure 3, and Figure 4.

It can be seen from the results that the Naive system, having no index structure at all, performs the best in terms of Accuracy and F1 Score (since it searches through the entire database to provide the result) and thus obviously performs worst in terms of computation time and number of distance computations. On the other hand the feature-based index structure using a RF-based refinement model produces the best results in terms of computation time but the worst in terms of F1 Score (the feature-level weights failing to capture the users' similarity concept in this case where it has been seen that the query images are rather hard to distinguish in terms of low-level features alone). AH-Tree Refinement Model has a computation time far less than the Naive Model but the computation time is greater that the Feature-Based Index Structures Refinement Model (since an

Table 2. Affinity promotion for refined queries

Affinity_Promotion_RefinedQueries( );
Start from the leaf nodes of the distance-based index structure of the AH-Tree.
For each leaf node O_l:{
   Set aff(O_l, Q) = $max_{i=1}^n$ (aff(O_l, P_i));
   // Where, aff(O_l, Q) is the affinity of the leaf node with respect
   // to the multi-point query Q and aff(O_l, P_i) is the affinity of
   // the leaf node with respect to each query point P_i in Q.
}
Traverse the tree bottom-up.
For each intermediate node O_r:{
   aff(O_r, Q) = $max_{i=1}^n$(max(*aff(t_a, q_i), aff(t_b, q_i), ..., aff(tz, q_i),*
           max(*aff(t_a, q_{i-1}), aff(t_b, q_{i-1}), ..., aff(t_z, q_{i-1})*)) ;
   // Where, aff(O_r, Q) is the affinity of the intermediate node
   // with respect to the multi-point query Q consisting of q_i, aff(t_a, q_i)
   // is the affinity of each children t_a with each query point q_i and
   // z is the number of children of O_r.
}

Table 3. Experimental results

	Iterations	Accuracy (in %)	Computation Time (in sec)	F1 Score	# of Distance Computations	Model Score	Average Model Score
AH-Tree Refine	1st	70	0.086	0.215	3311	0.529	
	2nd	88	0.064	0.25	6361	0.584	0.564
	3rd	95	0.068	0.253	8966	0.580	
Feature Tree Refine	1st	30	0.011	0.092	1440	0.548	
	2nd	44	0.017	0.125	3475	0.565	0.552
	3rd	50	0.035	0.127	6769	0.543	
AH-Tree No Refine	1st	70	0.086	0.215	3311	0.529	
	2nd	70	0.086	0.215	3311	0.529	0.529
	3rd	70	0.086	0.215	3311	0.529	
Naive	1st	80	0.13	0.5	10000	0.617	
	2nd	90	0.26	0.6	10000	0.392	0.377
	3rd	99	0.39	0.7	10000	0.122	

additional similarity factor, the affinity relationship need to be considered). The AH-Tree without any refinement model obviously has a fixed value for each of the criteria for all the three iterations due to the lack of any refinement model.

From all the different criteria, it becomes rather difficult and confusing to determine which is the best model. Hence, an aggregate model score is proposed in terms of computation time (the main reason to introduce an index structure) and the F1 Score (the main reason for the requirement of an efficient refinement model). The main purpose behind proposing an efficient multidimensional index structure supporting multimedia retrieval strategies is twofold. First, to reduce the com-

putation overhead and second, to produce query results as close to human perception as possible.

Thus to compare different retrieval models (with and without index structures and refinement strategies) and justifying the need of an efficient index structure as well as a good refinement model, a metric should be formulated that will compare the models in terms of both the specified factors and thus help the users choose the appropriate method depending upon his/her need. A cost metric is proposed, called the Model_Score (expressed in Equation 18 in terms of computation time and F1 Score), to be utilized in comparing the different systems as discussed in the next subsection.

Figure 2. (a) Accuracy compared over three iterations, (b) computation time compared over three iterations

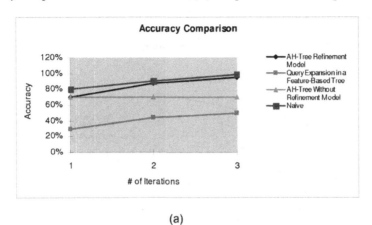

(a)

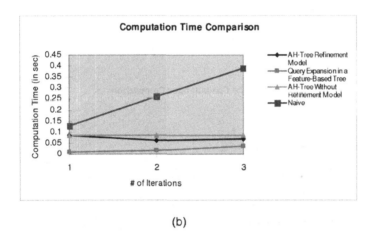

(b)

Evaluation Metric

This metric is determined with the consideration that the best model will be the one with minimum computation time and maximum F1 Score. Thus, the model score of a particular system is devised as the product of the inverse of its deviation from the maximum F1 Score (among all the models) and minimum computation time (among all the models). Thus, $\dfrac{T - T_{min}}{3 \times \sqrt{\left(\sum_{i=1}^{n}(T_i - T_{min})^2\right) / n}}$ determines the deviation of the computation time of a model from the best computation time (minimum) and produces a normalized error

value. The greater the error value, the farther is the computation time from the best possible computation time and lesser should be the computation time score. Thus, the value is subtracted from 1 and inversion is achieved. The same approach follows for determining the second part of the product, $\dfrac{F - F_{max}}{3 \times \sqrt{\left(\sum_{i=1}^{n}(F_i - F_{max})^2\right) / n}}$, with the only difference being the fact that now the best possible F1 Score is the maximum of all the available F1 Scores. Hence, the normalized error of the F1 Score with the best possible value for a particular model is determined and is subtracted from 1 to get the actual score. The value 3 is used

Figure 3. (a) F1 score compared over three iterations, (b) number of distance computations compared over three iterations

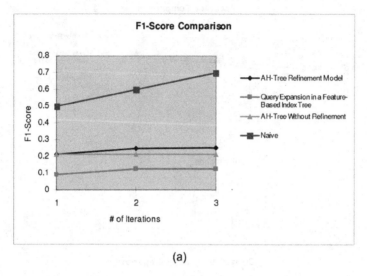

(a)

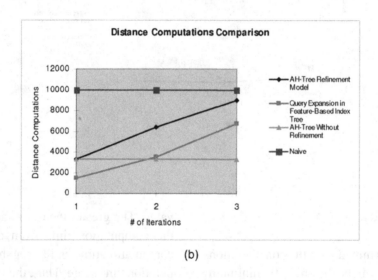

(b)

as a factor during determining the normalized error following Gaussian Normalization method, where using a factor of 3 increases the percentage of the probability of a value to lie in the range -1 and 1. Thus, the greater the model score, the better is its usefulness as multimedia retrieval framework. The current score is developed giving equal weights to the computation time and the F1 Score. But, depending upon users' prerogative, weights can be adjusted between them to modify the score.

$$
Model\_Score = (1 - \frac{T - T_{min}}{3 \times \sqrt{(\sum_{i=1}^{n}(T_i - T_{min})^2) / n}}) \times
$$

$$
(1 - |\frac{F - F_{max}}{3 \times \sqrt{(\sum_{i=1}^{n}(F_i - F_{max})^2) / n}}|)
$$

(18)

where, T is the computation time of the particular model, T_{min} is the minimum computation time

Figure 4. (a) Computation time score compared over three iterations, (b) similarity score compared over three iterations, (c) average model score

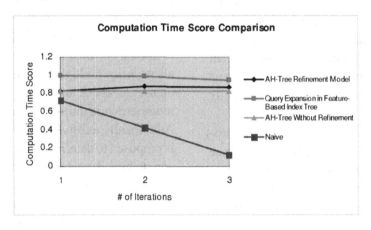

(a)

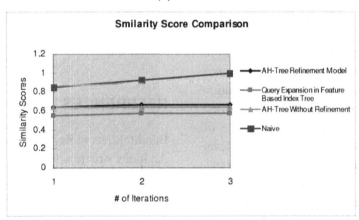

(b)

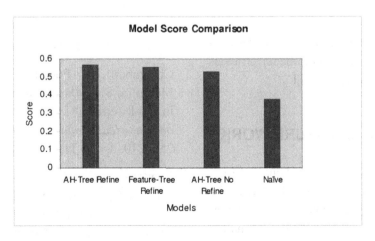

(c)

among all the models considered, F is the F1 Score of the particular model, F_{max} is the maximum F1 Score among all the models considered, and n is the total number of models.

The Model Score is computed for four different frameworks as presented in the last two columns of the table presented in Figure 4 and graphically in Figure 3(c).

From them, it can be concluded that the proposed query refinement approach on a distance based index structure has distinctively better performance than a framework without any refinement method and the sequential search framework. It has comparable and slightly better performance than the framework with query refinement approach on a feature based index structure. Thus, the proposed approach successfully achieved the two important goals of this research viz. (1) to develop a query refinement model for distance based index structure comparable in computation cost to the existing approaches for feature based index structures (2) improve the relevance of query results for scenarios where the low-level feature similarity do not follow the same pattern as the high-level semantic similarity (this is demonstrated by the higher F1 score for our proposed approach as compared to the query refinement approaches like Chakrabarti, Ortega, Porkaew, and Mehrotra (2001). It can be concluded from the experimental data analysis that the proposed method has potential of future extension and can be utilized in other genres of multimedia retrievals like content-based video retrieval.

CONCLUSION AND FUTURE WORK

In this paper, a technique to embed query refinement methodology into the metric space of a multidimensional distance based index structure is proposed. The refinement technique is mainly developed to enable a distance based index structure support CBIR with user feedback efficiently and improve query results at each iteration. The refinement model utilizes the query expansion approach and proposes ways to introduce multi-point queries into a metric space. It proposes techniques to not only refine the low-level feature space but also to refine the high-level image similarity based on user feedback and use them seamlessly in the index structure during similarity search routines. Additionally, a cost metric called the Model Score, is proposed to determine the overall performance of a multimedia data retrieval framework in terms of computation time and F1 Score. As future work, it is planned to introduce this query refinement model to the generalized index structure, GeM-Tree (Chatterjee & Chen, 2008) to refine queries and support content based information retrievals with relevance feedback for both images as well as videos.

REFERENCES

Berchtold, S., & Keim, D. A. (1996). The X-tree: An index structure for high-dimensional data. In *Proceedings of the 22th International Conference on Very Large Data Bases* (pp. 28-39).

Chakrabarti, K., Ortega, M., Porkaew, K., & Mehrotra, S. (2001). Query refinement in similarity retrieval systems. *A Quarterly Bulletin of the Computer Society of the IEEE Technical Committee on Data Engineering*, *24*(3), 3–13.

Chakrabarti, K., Porkaew, K., Ortega, M., & Mehrotra, S. (2004). Evaluating refined queries in top-k retrieval systems. *IEEE Transactions on Knowledge and Data Engineering*, *16*(2), 256–270. doi:10.1109/TKDE.2004.1269602

Chatterjee, K., & Chen, S.-C. (2006). Affinity hybrid tree: An indexing technique for content-based image retrieval in multimedia databases. In *Proceedings of the IEEE International Symposium on Multimedia*, San Diego, CA (pp. 47-54).

Chatterjee, K., & Chen, S.-C. (2007). A novel indexing and access mechanism using affinity hybrid tree for content-based image retrieval in multimedia databases. *International Journal of Semantic Computing, 1*(2), 147–170. doi:10.1142/S1793351X07000093

Chatterjee, K., & Chen, S.-C. (2008). GeM-tree: Towards a generalized multidimensional index structure supporting image and video retrieval. In *Proceedings of the Fourth IEEE International Workshop on Multimedia Information Processing and Retrieval in conjunction with the IEEE International Symposium on Multimedia* (pp. 631-636).

Ciaccia, P., Patella, M., & Zezula, P. (1997). M-tree: An efficient access method for similarity search in metric spaces. In *Proceedings of the 23rd Very Large Data Bases International Conference* (pp. 426-435).

Daneels, D., Campenhout, D., Niblack, W., Equitz, W., Barber, R., Bellon, E., et al. (1993). Interactive outlining: An improved approach using contours. In *Proceedings of the Storage and Retrieval for Image and Video Databases* (pp. 226-233).

Guttman, A. (1984). R-trees: A dynamic index structure for spatial searching. In *Proceedings of the ACM SIGMOD International Conference on Management of Data* (pp. 47-57).

Huang, T., & Rui, Y. (1997). Image retrieval: Past, present, and future. In *Proceedings of the International Symposium on Multimedia Information Processing.*

Ishikawa, Y., Subramanya, R., & Faloutsos, C. (1998). MindReader: Querying databases through multiple examples. In *Proceedings of the 24th International Conference of Very Large Data Bases* (pp. 218-227).

Liu, D., Hua, K., & Yu, N. (2006). Fast query point movement techniques with relevance feedback for content-based image retrieval. In *Proceedings of the International Conference on Extending Data Base Technology* (pp. 700-717).

Lu, J., Bao, Z., Ling, T. W., & Meng, X. (2009). XML keyword query refinement. In *Proceedings of the First International Workshop on Keyword Search on Structured Data* (pp. 41-42).

Ortega, M., Rui, Y., Chakrabarti, K., Porkaew, K., Mehrotra, S., & Huang, T. S. (1998). Supporting ranked Boolean similarity queries in MARS. *IEEE Transactions on Knowledge and Data Engineering, 10*(6), 905–925. doi:10.1109/69.738357

Porkaew, K., Chakrabarti, K., & Mehrotra, S. (1999). Query refinement for multimedia similarity retrieval in MARS. In *Proceedings of the ACM Multimedia Conference* (pp. 235-238).

Porkaew, K., Ortega, M., & Mehrotra, S. (1999). Query reformulation for content based multimedia retrieval in MARS. In *Proceedings of the IEEE International Conference on Multimedia Computing and Systems* (pp. 741-751).

Reynolds, D., Dickinson, I., & Grosvenor, D. (2009). *A query refinement model for exploratory semantic search* (Tech. Rep. No. HPL-2009-167). Palo Alto, CA: HP Laboratories.

Robinson, J. T. (1981). The K-D-B-tree: A search structure for large multidimensional dynamic indexes. In *Proceedings of the ACM SIGMOD International Conference on Management of Data* (pp. 10-18).

Roussopoulos, N., Kelley, S., & Vincent, F. (1995). Nearest neighbor queries. In *Proceedings of the ACM SIGMOD International Conference on Management of Data* (pp. 71-79).

Rui, Y., Huang, T., & Mehrotra, S. (1997). Content based image retrieval with relevance feedback in mars. In *Proceedings of the International Conference on Image Processing* (pp. 815-818).

Rui, Y., Huang, T., Ortega, M., & Mehrotra, S. (1998). Elevance feedback: A power tool for interactive content-based image retrieval. *IEEE Transactions on Circuits and Systems for Video Technology, 8*(5), 644–655. doi:10.1109/76.718510

Shyu, M.-L., Chen, S.-C., Chen, M., Zhang, C., & Shu, C.-M. (2003). MMM: A stochastic mechanism for image database queries. In *Proceedings of the IEEE Fifth International Symposium on Multimedia Software Engineering*, Taichung, Taiwan (pp. 188-195).

Yianilos, P. N. (1993). Data structures and algorithms for nearest neighbor search in general metric spaces. In *Proceedings of the 3rd Annual ACM-SIAM Symposium on Discrete Algorithms* (pp. 311-321).

This work was previously published in the International Journal of Multimedia Data Engineering and Management, Volume 2, Issue 3, edited by Shu-Ching Chen, pp. 52-71, copyright 2011 by IGI Publishing (an imprint of IGI Global).

Chapter 8
3D Model–Based Semantic Categorization of Still Image 2D Objects

Raluca-Diana Petre
TELECOM SudParis and Alcatel-Lucent Bell Labs, France

Titus Zaharia
TELECOM SudParis and UMR CNRS 8145 MAP5, France

ABSTRACT

Automatic classification and interpretation of objects present in 2D images is a key issue for various computer vision applications. In particular, when considering image/video, indexing, and retrieval applications, automatically labeling in a semantically pertinent manner/huge multimedia databases still remains a challenge. This paper examines the issue of still image object categorization. The objective is to associate semantic labels to the 2D objects present in natural images. The principle of the proposed approach consists of exploiting categorized 3D model repositories to identify unknown 2D objects, based on 2D/3D matching techniques. The authors use 2D/3D shape indexing methods, where 3D models are described through a set of 2D views. Experimental results, carried out on both MPEG-7 and Princeton 3D models databases, show recognition rates of up to 89.2%.

INTRODUCTION

The amount of multimedia content (still image, video, 2D/3D graphics, etc.) available today for the general public is continuously increasing due to the spectacular evolution in digital technologies. Within this context, disposing of powerful search and retrieval methods becomes a key issue for efficient indexing and intelligent access to audio-video material. When large databases are involved, user access to specific material of interest is not possible without efficient search engines and tools. Until recently, retrieval tools were exclusively based on keywords. However, the linguistic barriers represent an important drawback of such approaches. Also, a prior manual anno-

DOI: 10.4018/978-1-4666-2940-0.ch008

tation is required, which is a tedious and highly subjective process.

Within this context, the need of automatic object categorization tools appears as a crucial challenge. The objective is to determine automatically the semantic meaning of an object present in an image or video. A large number of existing methods use prior knowledge in order to accomplish such an objective. Such approaches, so-called machine learning (ML) techniques (Mitchel, 1997; Xue *et al.,* 2009), automatically learn to recognize complex structures based on examples. ML techniques involve two main stages. First, some characteristic features are extracted starting from a set of examples involved in a given training dataset. Then, these features are used in order to recognize new cases. Such methods should be able to generalize the features of a given class while ensuring the accuracy of the recognition process.

However, when a large number of categories involved, the number of recognition criteria (and implicitly the number of exploited features) increases and thus the computational complexity may become intractable (Li, 2006). In addition, in order to allow generalization, a large variety of models should be used in the training set. Notably, we have to take into account that even a given object may present very different appearances due to pose variation. Thus, the training set should include not only a variety of examples but also different instances of the same object, corresponding to different poses.

In this paper we present a new recognition method able to deal with a large variety of objects. Instead of using machine learning techniques, exploit categorized 3D models from existing 3D repositories in the classification process.

The paper is structured as follows. The following chapter presents the 2D/3D shape-based indexing approaches, with basic principle and related work. The proposed 2D/3D indexing methodology, with viewing angle selection strategies and adopted 2D shape descriptors, is then detailed.

After introducing the recognition framework, we present and discuss the experimental results obtained. Finally, we conclude the paper and open some perspectives of future work.

SHAPE-BASED 2D/3D INDEXING

Let us first present the general principle of 2D/3D indexing methods.

Basic Principle

The principle of 2D/3D indexing approach is to represent a 3D model, denoted by M as a set of 2D views obtained according to different projection angles. The main hypothesis is that if the models are similar, then they should present similar views. On the contrary, if the two 3D models are different, then there is no correspondence between the sets of views.

A main advantage of the 2D/3D indexing methodology is that it allows different types of comparison. Thus, a 3D model can be compared with other 3D models based on their respective projections. In the same time, a 3D model can be compared in this framework with a 2D object extracted from a 2D image.

The set of views is generated using a set of viewing angles (i.e., positions of the camera in the 3D space). Before generating the set of views, the model is normalized in size and position in order to obtain a canonical representation. First, the object is centered in the origin of the Cartesian system and resized such that it fits the unit sphere. Next, a Principal Component Analysis (PCA) (Schwengerdt *et al.,* 1997) is performed in order to compute the axes of inertia of the 3D model. Finally, the rotation invariance is obtained by rotating the 3D model such that its principal axes coincide with those of the coordinate system (Figure 1).

Figure 1. 3D model alignement. Left: 3D model presenting an arbitrary position: the object's axes of inertia (in red) are not aligned with respect to the coordinate system (in black). Right: 3D model aligned with respect to the coordinate system: here, the object's axes of inertia coincide with the coordinate system.

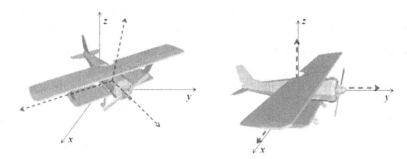

The model is projected and rendered in 2D from N_P different viewing angles, resulting in a set of N_P projections, denoted by $P_i(M)$, with $i = 1..N_P$.

The projection may represent a binary image (the silhouette of the object) or a gray level image representing the depth map. In our case, we have exclusively used binary images corresponding to the projected silhouettes (Figure 2), since our goal is to match 2D objects, which do not have any depth information, with a set of 3D models.

Finally, each projection $P_i(M)$ is described by a 2D shape descriptor $d_i(M)$. The set of all de-scriptors $\{d_i(M)\}$ yields the 2D/3D representation of the considered 3D object (Figure 2).

In order to fully implement a 2D/3D indexing approach, several issues have to be specified. The first one is the set of viewing directions $\{n_i\}$ used to perform the projections. Let us note that the number of considered projection images is a parameter that has to be carefully considered, since a large number of silhouettes provides a more complete description but also increases the computational cost of the subsequent matching algorithms.

Figure 2. Projecting a 3D model. Left: the projection of the 3D model M using the Ox axis as viewing direction. Right: sample of 2D projections $P_i(M)$.

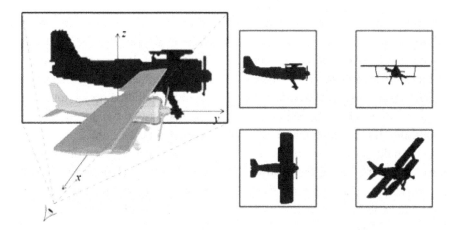

The second important issue involved concerns the 2D shape descriptors used for characterizing the projections: in order to ensure a discriminant description, a fundamental aspect is the choice of appropriate 2D shape descriptors.

Before describing the indexing approaches considered in our work, let us briefly present the state of the art in the field of 2D/3D indexing methods.

Related Work

Among the existing approaches, let us first mention those proposed by the MPEG-7 standard (International Organization for Standardization, 2002). Here, the *Multiview description scheme* (*DS*) makes it possible to obtain 2D/3D object representations. Concerning the shape description, the following two descriptors are supported: the *Angular Radial Transform* (ART) (Kim *et al.*, 1999) and the *Contour Scale Space* (CSS) (Mokhtarian *et al.*, 1992). The first descriptor is obtained by decomposing the support region function in the 2D-ART basis functions while the second one aims at describing the contour behavior at different scales. The viewing angle selection strategy is based on PCA, with either three or seven views.

Another multi-scale contour-based representation was proposed in Napoleon *et al.* (2007). Here, the sampled contour of the 2D shape is described by analyzing the variation in position of each sample when convoluting the contour with a set of Gaussian filters.

One of the most effective 2D/3D indexing method is the Light Field Descriptor (LFD) (Chen *et al.*, 2003) which uses a set of 100 views, derived from the vertices of a dodecahedron, and evenly distributed around the 3D model. Each view is represented with the help of two descriptors: one for the contour of the shape (using the contour-based Fourier coefficients) (Zhang *et al.*, 2002) and another descriptor exploiting the region (using the Zernike Moments) (Mukundan *et al.*, 1998).

In Daras *et al.* (2009) the same descriptors (i.e., the Zernike Moments and the Fourier co-efficients) are combined with the Krawtchouk moments (Yap *et al.*, 2003) in order to describe the 18 views composing the Compact MultiView Descriptor (CMVD). These views are obtained by evenly distributing 18 cameras around the model.

As the viewing angle selection is a key issue to be considered, the work presented in Cyr *et al.* (2001) and Yamauchi *et al.* (2006) exclusively addresses this issue. The principle here consists of selecting the most representative views among a large number of projections evenly distributed around the 3D model.

The research work described here-above tackles exclusively the issue of 3D-to-3D indexing, which supposes that a query 3D model is available. In our case, the objective is to perform 2D-to-3D matching. In this case, the query is represented as a 2D object.

However, the idea of using categorized 3D models for 2D image recognition purposes has been recently exploited in Toshev *et al.* (2009) and Liebelt *et al.* (2008).

Thus, in Liebelt *et al.* (2008) authors use textured 3D models in the recognition process. For each class to be recognized, a visual codebook is constructed by extracting appearance features from the views of the textured 3D models.

In Toshev *et al.* (2009) authors use non-textured 3D models in order to classify 2D objects segmented from videos. Thus, in order to recognize an object, several of its instances are supposed to be available. For 2D/3D indexing purposes, authors exploit a set of 20 views per model which are determined by k-means clustering of 500 evenly distributed projections. The main limitation concerns the reduced number of categories supported (only 2 or 3).

In this paper, we propose a new recognition framework which, as the algorithms proposed in Toshev *et al.* (2009) and Liebelt *et al.* (2008), exploits 3D model information in order to recognize 2D objects. However, in our work, we do not use neither textured 3D models nor video objects, but solely binary and static 2D regions. Our choice is motivated by the fact that the amount of textured models available today is not sufficient for recognition purposes. Also, in contrast with the previous work we are able to deal with a larger number of object categories (up to 161 possible categories).

In order to achieve this goal, we consider different sets of viewing angles as well as combinations of various shape descriptors, as described in the following section.

THE PROPOSED 2D/3D INDEXING METHODOLOGY

Let us first present the adopted viewing angle selection strategies.

Viewing Angle Selection

Several strategies for selecting a set of viewing angles can be considered.

Let us first mention the MPEG-7 approach (Zaharia *et al.*, 2004), which uses a PCA-based strategy. The underlying assumption is that the views corresponding to the projections on the principal planes are the three most discriminant views (Figure 3). From now on, this strategy will

be referred to as PCA3. Furthermore, for a better description, four secondary views may be additionally considered, resulting in a total of seven views (so-called PCA7 strategy). The secondary views are obtained by considering the bisectors of the eight octants defined by the principal planes.

A second strategy exploits an even distribution of the cameras around the 3D model. A simple manner to construct such a distribution is to consider the set of vertices of a regular dodecahedron. The viewing angles are determined as the lines relying the set of vertices with the coordinate system's origin.

Two sub-cases may be further considered: in a first case the 3D model has an arbitrary orientation in the 3D space (Figure 4, left). In the second case, the model is first aligned with the help of PCA (Figure 4, right). Because the dodecahedron-based positioning of the cameras was introduced in Chen *et al.* (2003) when computing the Light Field Descriptor (LFD), the two strategies will be referred to as LFD (in the case where the 3D model has an arbitrary position) and LFDPCA (in the case where the 3D model is first aligned by using the PCA).

Finally, a third projection strategy exploits the vertices of a regular octahedron (Petre *et al.*, 2010). In order to obtain additional views, the faces of the octahedron are successively subdivided and

Figure 3. PCA-based positioning of the camera. Left: using the three axes of inertia as viewing angle directions. Center: the PCA3 projections. Right: the four additional views of the PCA7.

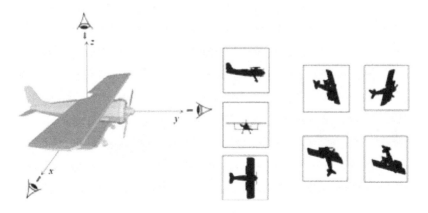

Figure 4. Dodecahedron-based positioning of the camera: the cameras are placed on the vertices of the dodecahedron and oriented toward the 3D model (placed in the center of the coordinate system). Left: random orientation of the 3D model (the LFD strategy). Right: 3D model aligned with respect to the coordinate system (the LFDPCA strategy).

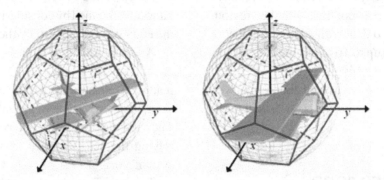

thus the number of views increases from three to nine and thirty three (Figure 5). From now on, the octahedron-based strategies will be referred to as OCTA3, OCTA9 and OCTA33, depending on the number of views obtained.

For each viewing angle, a projection binary image, representing the object's silhouette, is obtained and further characterized with the help of 2D shape descriptors. The next section presents the 2D shape descriptors considered in our work.

2D Shape Descriptors

As the views are binary images representing only the object's silhouette (without internal contours, shadows, textures, etc.), the only features that can be exploited are the external contour and the corresponding region of support. In our work, we have retained two contour-based and two region-based descriptors, briefly recalled here below.

Figure 5. Octahedron-based camera positioning: the cameras are placed on the vertices of the octahedron and oriented toward the 3D model. Left: the OCTA3 strategy. Center: the OCTA9 strategy. Right: the OCTA33 strategy.

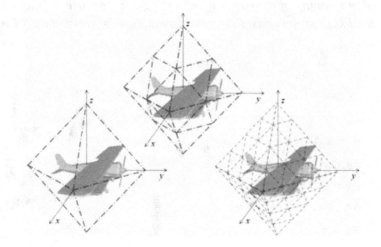

Let us start with the Contour Shape (*CS*) descriptor (Mokhtarian *et al.*, 1992) proposed by the MPEG-7 standard (Bober *et al.*, 2002; Manjunath *et al.*, 2001; International Organization for Standardization, 2002). In order to obtain the CS descriptor, the first step is to extract the contour of the 2D shape. This contour is successively filtered with a Gaussian kernel. Thus, a set of several contours in a Gaussian scale space is obtained. For each of them, the curvilinear positions of the inflexion points are computed. Finally, for each curve, the inflexion points are represented in the (σ, u) space (the Contour Scale Space - CSS), where σ represents the standard deviation used to generate the curve and u represents the curvilinear position of the considered inflexion point. Once the CSS representation is obtained, the curvature peaks are determined. For each peak, the corresponding curvature value and position (expressed in curvilinear abscise) are retained as the CS descriptor. The associated similarity measure between two CSS representations is based on a matching procedure which takes into account the cost of fitted and unfitted curvatures peaks (International Organization for Standardization, 2002).

The second approach adopted is the MPEG-7 Region Shape (*RS*) descriptor, based on the 2D Angular Radial Transform (ART) (Kim *et al.*, 1999). In this case, the object's support function is represented as a weighted sum of 34 ART basis functions ($f_{m,n}$) defined in equation 1.

$$\forall m \in \{0,1,2\}, \ \forall n \in \{0,\ldots,11\},$$
$$f_{m,n}(\rho,\theta) = \frac{1}{A}\cos(An\acute{A})e^{jm.}$$

where,

($f_{m,n}$) = the ART basis function of order *m*, *n*;

ρ, θ = the polar coordinates, of a point in the image.

The decomposition coefficients constitute the descriptor. The distance between two shapes is simply defined as the L_1 distance between the absolute values of the ART coefficients.

Another region-based descriptor adopted is based on the 2D Hough Transform (HT) (Hart, 2009). Each point *p* corresponding to the silhouette of the object is represented in the (s, θ) space. Let us assume a given coordinate system (xOy). If we consider a line *l* passing through a point $p(x,y)$, then let us denote by θ the angle between the line *l* and the *Ox* axis, and by *s* the distance from the coordinate system origin to the line.

In order to represent a point of the support region of the object with the help of the HT, we generate a family of lines passing through the point, and represent each of these lines in the (s, θ) space. The HT descriptor is obtained by transforming each object pixel in the (s, θ) cumulative space. The associated similarity measure between two HT representations is the L_1 distance between the (s, θ) coefficients.

Finally, we propose a new contour-based descriptor, so-called *Angle Histogram* (AH). The shape contour is first sub-sampled in a number of successive 2D points (Figures 6a and 6b). The angular histogram is created by computing the angles defined by each three consecutive samples and accumulating them into a histogram. When the three considered samples are closed to each another (green and orange angles in Figure 6d), they encode the local features of the curve; on the contrary, when the distance between the considered samples increases (see red or purple angles in Figure 6d), the resulting histogram describes the global behavior of the shape. Since local and global features capture different characteristics of the shape, we compute five angular histograms, each one obtained with a different distance between each three samples. The 2D AH descriptor is obtained by concatenating the five angular histograms. A simple L_1 distance between histograms is used as similarity measure.

Let us now describe the 2D shape recognition framework proposed.

2D Shape Recognition Framework

Figure 7 briefly illustrates the 2D shape recognition process. In order to classify an unknown 2D object, the system needs to dispose of a categorized 3D model repository. In the 2D/3D indexing stage, a set of 2D views is generated for each model, using one of the presented projection strategies (i.e., PCA3, PCA7, LFD, LFDPCA, OCTA9, OCTA33) and the 2D shape descriptor of each view is extracted. This stage is performed offline and the resulting descriptors are stored and used for object recognition.

The input for the system is an unknown binary object that we want to identify. The binary image may be obtained with the help of some semi-automatic segmentation methods (Sapna Varshney *et al.*, 2010). Furthermore, the same 2D shape descriptor as the one used in the 2D/3D indexing stage is extracted for the current unknown image.

In the 2D-3D shape matching stage the distance $d(O,M)$ between the unknown 2D object O and the 3D model M is computed. This distance is defined as the minimum distance between the 2D object and all the projections $P_i(M)$ $(i=1..N_P)$.

$$d\left(O,\ M\right) = \min_i d\left(O, P_i\left(M\right)\right).$$

Thus, the current image is compared with all N_M 3D models from the 3D model database and the corresponding distance is computed.

Finally, the results analyzer module examines which are the most probable categories that might fit the unknown image. First, the 3D models are sorted by decreasing order of similarity and only the N top retrieved models are retained. Next, for each category we count the number of occurrences among the N top retrieved 3D models. Finally, the N_C most represented categories are presented to the user as proposed categories.

In the next section, we provide an experimental evaluation of this 2D/3D recognition framework as well as a comparison of all the 2D shape descriptors and viewing angle selection strategies previously presented.

EXPERIMENTAL EVALUATION

Experiments have been carried out on different 3D model and query databases, described in the following section.

3D Model and Query Databases

Concerning the 3D categorized respositories, we have considered two different 3D model databases

Figure 6. Computing the angular histograms: a) the 2D contour; b) sampling the contour; c) the sampled contour (in red the current sample for which we compute the angles); d) the angles considered for the current sample. Each color corresponds to a different sampling level; the five angles (green, orange, blue, red and purple) are added in five different angular histograms. The AH descriptor is obtained by concatenating the five angular histograms (characterized by different sampling levels).

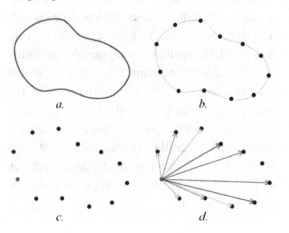

First, we retained the MPEG-7 dataset (Zaharia *et al.*, 2004), which is composed of N_M=362 mesh models divided into 23 semantic classes. Categories include humanoids, airplanes, helicopters, cars, race cars, trees (with and without leafs), rifles, missiles, pistols, etc. These models present intra-class variability as well as inter-class similarity.

The second 3D database considered is the Princeton Shape Benchmark (PSB) (Shilane *et al.*, 2004), which includes N_M=1814 models semantically categorized in 161 classes. Compared to the MPEG-7 database, the Princeton classification is more precise and presents a hierarchical tree structure which supports sub-classes, For example, a distinction between commercial airplanes, biplanes, fighter jet, glider airplane... is done for the "airplane" category. The PSB database includes various models representing aircrafts, animals, furniture, plants, sea vessels, musical instruments, tools, vehicles, etc.

Some sample models from both MPEG-7 and PSB databases are illustrated in Figure 8.

We also considered two different 2D object databases in order to obtain a ground truth collection of queries, adapted to an objective evaluation.

The first query database has been created with the help of synthetic images. Thus, we have selected 3 MPEG-7 models for each of the 13 categories which are common for both MPEG-7 and PSB 3D model databases. For each selected model, we have considered 10 views, obtained with the LFD projection strategy. Thus, we have obtained 390 synthetic query objects derived from the MPEG-7 database and attempted to recognize them by using, as categorized repository, the PSB database.

In order to test the performances of the proposed approach in real-life conditions, we have also created a 2D object database consisting of 115 real images. A number of 5 different users (without any knowledge of the MPEG-7 and PSB 3D model databases) have been asked to retrieve from the web images corresponding to each of the 23 MPEG-7 categories with the help of commercial search engines. In this way, we have gathered 5 images for each MPEG-7 category (Figure 9). The images have been then manually segmented in order to extract the support region of the objects

Figure 7. The 2D shape recognition framework

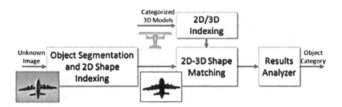

Figure 8. Sample 3D meshes from the MPEG-7 and PSB 3D models databases

of interest. Let us note that when using the PSB, only 65 objects can be used (corresponding to the 13 categories that are common for the MPEG-7 and the PSB databases).

In the second stage, we have defined the objective performance measures needed to evaluate the methods.

Performance Measures

The performance measure adopted is the recognition rate (RR), defined as the percentage of cases where the correct category is assigned to the input image.

For each 2D object O to be recognized, the N_C most probable categories ($C_1...C_{Nc}$) are determined. If one of the retrieved categories coincides with the category of the object $C(O)$ then the recognition is considered as successful. A binary recognition label per object, denoted by $R(O, N_C)$, is defined as follows:

$$R\left(O, N_C\right) = \begin{cases} 1; & if\, C(O) \in \left\{ C_1 \dots \; C_{Nc} \right\} \\ 0; & otherwise \end{cases}.$$

$$(3)$$

The recognition rate, denoted by $RR(N_C)$, is defined as described by the following equation:

$$RR\left(N_C\right) = \frac{\sum_{i=0}^{N_O} R\left(O_i, N_C\right)}{N_O}.$$

$$(4)$$

where N_O is the number of 2D objects. The recognition rate $RR(N_C)$ represents the percentage of successfully recognized objects.

In order to illustrate the recognition process, let us consider the example presented in Figure 10. Here, the 2D object to be recognized represent a humanoid ($C(O)$=humanoid). Let us examine the first N=8 top retrieved 3D models. The first $Nc = 3$ most represented categories are the following: C_1=cars; C_2=humanoids and C_3=pistols. Therefore, in this case the corresponding recognition rates are: RR(1)=0, RR(2)=1, and RR(3)=1.

In our experiments, the parameter N representing the number of 3D models taken into account for the analysis of results has been set to 20, which represents the average category size. The recognition rate was computed by taking into account one, two or three most probable categories (Nc =

Figure 9. Sample images from the test 2D object dataset

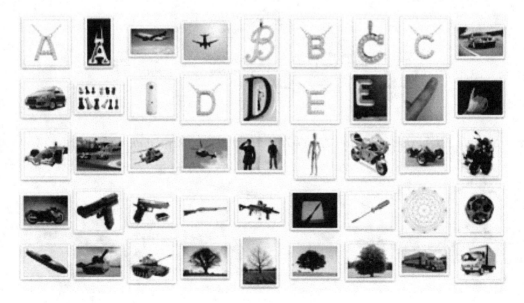

Figure 10. Example of 3D models retrieval. Top: the 2D object and its silhouette. Bottom: the eight images representing a view of the eight most similar 3D models. They represent four cars, three humanoids and one pistol.

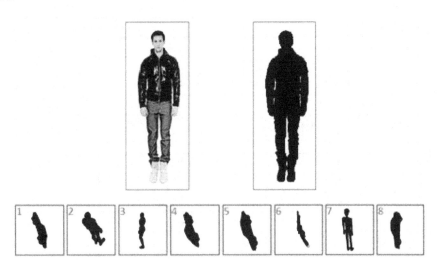

1,2,3). However, for the case of Princeton database we have also considered the score $RR(N_C=10)$ because of the higher number of available categories (161 classes).

Recognition Results

We have first tested the performances of the proposed recognition method on the synthetic query dataset of 390 objects. The obtained results are presented in Table 1. More precisely, Table 1a, b, c, and d summarize the results obtained for each retained descriptor (Contour Shape – CS, Region Shape – RS, Angular Histogram – AH and Hough Transform –H, respectively).

We can observe that in this case, the highest performances are obtained by the CS and AH descriptors, with recognition rates RR(3) of 71,3% and 66,9%, respectively. This shows that these two contour-based shape description approaches outperform the region-based techniques.

Concerning the viewing angle selection strategy, the best performances are provided by the OCTA33 and LFD approaches, with the advantage, in the case of the LFD strategy of a less

important number of views (10, with respect to 33 when OCTA33 is considered).

We have also proposed a strategy of combining the two descriptors with the highest performances (i.e., CS and AH). The idea here is to attempt to exploit the potential complementarities between the two descriptors. Thus, instead of computing the scores based on the N most similar models given by the CS, we have also considered the N most similar models retrieved when using the AH descriptor. The analysis of the numbers of most representative categories has been thus performed based on the (2N) top retrieved models obtained with both CS and AH descriptors. The results, presented in Table 1e, show a slight enhancement of results with RR(3) and RR(10) of 74,4% and 88,5%, respectively. Here again the OCTA33 viewing angle selection strategy provides the best results.

In a similar manner, we have also tested a combination of viewing angles strategies. Since LFD provides high results with a limited number of views, we have added the LFD results to each of the other considered projection methods. The results are presented in Table 1f (in the case of

Table 1. Recognition rate for synthetic images using the PSB

a						
CS	**PCA3**	**PCA7**	**LFD**	**LFDPCA**	**OCTA9**	**OCTA33**
RR(1)	29,5	42,8	47,7	45,1	45,4	50,0
RR(2)	42,3	55,6	62,1	57,4	57,9	65,4
RR(3)	49,7	61,0	66,9	65,4	63,6	71,3
RR(10)	65,9	76,7	79,5	79,0	78,7	83,1
b						
RS	**PCA3**	**PCA7**	**LFD**	**LFDPCA**	**OCTA9**	**OCTA33**
RR(1)	28,2	27,9	40,8	34,1	33,6	45,4
RR(2)	36,7	42,1	54,6	48,7	49,5	59,7
RR(3)	40,0	50,5	57,9	55,4	54,6	64,6
RR(10)	51,8	65,4	75,6	70,0	67,7	77,9
c						
AH	**PCA3**	**PCA7**	**LFD**	**LFDPCA**	**OCTA9**	**OCTA33**
RR(1)	25,6	35,4	39,2	39,7	36,2	40,8
RR(2)	34,9	49,0	54,6	53,3	48,7	56,9
RR(3)	40,0	55,1	60,3	61,3	54,9	66,9
RR(10)	59,7	72,6	77,4	75,9	72,1	82,3
d						
H	**PCA3**	**PCA7**	**LFD**	**LFDPCA**	**OCTA9**	**OCTA33**
RR(1)	15,4	23,1	35,1	24,6	29,2	36,7
RR(2)	23,1	31,8	44,1	34,4	40,8	50,3
RR(3)	27,4	37,9	49,2	37,9	45,9	55,9
RR(10)	41,8	53,3	69,5	57,4	61,3	73,6
e						
CS + AH	**PCA3**	**PCA7**	**LFD**	**LFDPCA**	**OCTA9**	**OCTA33**
RR(1)	35,1	46,4	48,7	51,3	48,7	54,6
RR(2)	45,4	59,7	64,6	64,1	59,0	69,7
RR(3)	51,3	66,4	70,8	71,0	66,4	74,4
RR(10)	67,7	80,8	83,1	81,5	80,0	88,5
f						
CS + AHLFD	**PCA3**	**PCA7**	**LFD**	**LFDPCA**	**OCTA9**	**OCTA33**
RR(1)	44,4	48,5	48,7	51,8	51,5	52,3
RR(2)	61,3	63,6	64,6	66,9	64,1	69,2
RR(3)	67,9	71,0	70,8	74,1	72,3	75,1
RR(10)	83,6	86,2	83,1	85,4	85,9	88,5

Table 2. Recognition rate using the MPEG-7 database

a						
S	**PCA3**	**PCA7**	**LFD**	**LFDPCA**	**OCTA9**	**OCTA33**
RR(1)	33.9	34.8	37.4	33.9	37.4	37.4
RR(2)	41.7	53.9	52.2	50.4	51.3	51.3
RR(3)	53.9	61.7	59.1	60.0	56.5	60.0
b						
RS	**PCA3**	**PCA7**	**LFD**	**LFDPCA**	**OCTA9**	**OCTA33**
RR(1)	24.3	22.6	28.7	27.0	26.1	30.4
RR(2)	36.5	37.4	40.9	37.4	42.6	46.1
RR(3)	40.9	45.2	46.1	45.2	50.4	54.8
c						
AH	**PCA3**	**PCA7**	**LFD**	**LFDPCA**	**OCTA9**	**OCTA33**
RR(1)	30.4	35.7	44.3	42.6	32.2	38.3
RR(2)	47.8	55.7	60.9	56.5	48.7	60.0
RR(3)	56.5	61.7	67.0	62.6	60.0	70.4
d						
H	**PCA3**	**PCA7**	**LFD**	**LFDPCA**	**OCTA9**	**OCTA33**
RR(1)	18.3	20.9	27.0	24.3	28.7	34.8
RR(2)	27.0	29.6	35.7	30.4	36.5	41.7
RR(3)	37.4	37.4	46.1	35.7	43.5	49.6
e						
CS + AH	**PCA3**	**PCA7**	**LFD**	**LFDPCA**	**OCTA9**	**OCTA33**
RR(1)	37.4	40.0	41.7	41.7	38.3	39.1
RR(2)	47.0	53.0	60.0	55.7	53.9	60.0
RR(3)	58.3	62.6	71.3	67.8	61.7	70.4
f						
CS + AH LFD	**PCA3**	**PCA7**	**LFD**	**LFDPCA**	**OCTA9**	**OCTA33**
RR(1)	41.7	40.9	41.7	41.7	40.9	39.1
RR(2)	55.7	54.8	60.0	56.5	58.3	57.4
RR(3)	66.1	68.7	71.3	68.7	65.2	68.7

CS+AH combined approach). Here again, we observe a slight, but global enhancement of the recognition rates.

Concerning the results obtained on the real images query set, Tables 2 and 3 respectively present the scores obtained using the MPEG-7 and Princeton Shape Benchmark databases.

Globally, when considering real query images, we can observe that the overall recognition rates are slightly decreasing. This result is without surprise, because of the complexity/diversity of objects encountered in real life and because of segmentation issues. However, even in this case, the obtained recognition rates, which reach more than 70% for RR(3) score and almost 90% for the RR(10) score, still offer interesting perspectives.

Here again, and for both databases, we observe the same global behavior with respect to the

Table 3. Recognition rate using the PSB database

a						
CS	**PCA3**	**PCA7**	**LFD**	**LFDPCA**	**OCTA9**	**OCTA33**
RR(1)	32.3	41.5	40.0	41.5	41.5	44.6
RR(2)	43.1	53.8	53.8	50.8	49.2	58.5
RR(3)	49.2	58.5	58.5	55.4	56.9	64.6
RR(10)	63.0	76.9	72.3	69.2	69.2	72.3
b						
RS	**PCA3**	**PCA7**	**LFD**	**LFDPCA**	**OCTA9**	**OCTA33**
RR(1)	26.2	20.0	23.1	24.6	29.2	32.3
RR(2)	30.8	27.7	32.3	41.5	43.1	40.0
RR(3)	38.5	35.4	38.5	41.5	46.2	46.2
RR(10)	55.4	49.2	55.4	55.4	63.1	60.0
c						
AH	**PCA3**	**PCA7**	**LFD**	**LFDPCA**	**OCTA9**	**OCTA33**
RR(1)	27.7	40.0	40.0	36.9	35.4	44.6
RR(2)	40.0	50.8	49.2	53.8	50.8	52.3
RR(3)	49.2	55.4	52.3	58.5	60.0	53.8
RR(10)	66.2	70.8	72.3	73.8	73.8	76.9
d						
H	**PCA3**	**PCA7**	**LFD**	**LFDPCA**	**OCTA9**	**OCTA33**
RR(1)	10.8	12.3	21.5	18.5	26.2	26.2
RR(2)	12.3	15.4	32.3	23.1	32.3	33.8
RR(3)	15.4	20.0	36.9	24.6	35.4	40.0
RR(10)	30.8	35.4	41.5	29.2	49.2	52.3
e						
CS + AH	**PCA3**	**PCA7**	**LFD**	**LFDPCA**	**OCTA9**	**OCTA33**
RR(1)	36.9	49.2	46.2	46.2	43.1	44.6
RR(2)	47.7	60.0	56.9	60.0	49.2	61.5
RR(3)	53.8	66.2	61.5	63.1	56.9	67.7
RR(10)	67.7	81.5	81.5	83.1	80.0	84.6
f						
CS + AHLFD	**PCA3**	**PCA7**	**LFD**	**LFDPCA**	**OCTA9**	**OCTA33**
RR(1)	44.6	50.8	46.2	50.8	47.7	44.6
RR(2)	56.9	60.0	56.9	56.9	53.8	60.0
RR(3)	64.6	66.2	61.5	63.1	61.5	66.2
RR(10)	83.1	83.1	81.5	89.2	84.6	86.2

viewing angle selection, with LFD and OCTA33 strategies offering the highest recognition rates, whatever the considered descriptor. More precisely, we achieve 60% of RR(3) recognition rate for the CS descriptor and 70.4% for AH when employing the MPEG-7 database. In the case of PSB database, the same global behaviors were observed. CS and AH are the descriptors providing

Figure 11. 2D/3D retrieval and categorization with the proposed system, with a query representing a car

the highest recognition rates, with *RR(3)* scores of 64.6% and respectively 60%. When considering the *RR(10)* scores, the recognition rates increase up to 76.9% for both CS and AH descriptors.

The combination of the CS and AH descriptors (Tables 2e and 3e) significantly increases the performances. Thus, the *RR(3)* scores have increased up to 71.3% when using the MPEG-7 database and up to 67.7% in the case of the PSB dataset. Also, the recognition rate of the combined descriptors has improved to 84.6% when analyzing the *RR(10)*.

Finally, the introduction into the process of the additional LFD strategy (Tables 2f and 3f) makes it possible, here again, to further improve the results. Thus, the RR(10) score obtained on the PSB database is here of 89,2%, when LFD is combined with LFDPCA.

The experimental results obtained demonstrate the interest of integrating some *a priori* knowledge (driven from existing 3D models) in the recognition process. Even if the system outputs several candidate categories ($N_C \neq 1$), such a multiple response process can be helpful as a preliminary analysis stage within the framework of a more complete recognition system. Let us note that the proposed descriptors are very compact and the associated similarity measures are fast to compute. This first recognition method can be completed with a second analysis phase, which can be based for example on machine learning techniques. This second phase can be allowed to present higher computational complexity, since the number of candidate categories has been significantly reduced after the first stage. Such a hybrid system would also allow achieving superior recognition rates while speeding-up the process.

Finally, an important aspect in 2D/3D object retrieval and recognition is to dispose of appropriate user interfaces. Thus, we have developed an

Figure 12. 2D/3D retrieval and categorization with the proposed system, with a query representing a motorcycle

interface designed to compare and evaluate the 2D/3D indexing methods previously presented. The proposed system is illustrated in Figures 11, 12, and 13. First, the user has the possibility to select the 3D model database (i.e., MPEG-7 or PSB database) to be used in the recognition process. Several 2D/3D indexing methods (projection strategies and 2D shape descriptors) and 2D query objects are also available. Finally, the system returns as response three proposed categories and also sorts all the 3D models by decreasing order of similarity to the query object (with respect to a given indexing method). Several examples are illustrated in Figures 11, 12, and 13. It can be observed that the category of the given query image (symbolically represented with some icons) is always retrieved within the first three returned positions.

The 2D/3D retrieval and categorization system has been developed with the help of web technologies/services and thus can be remotely accessed by multiple users.

CONCLUSIONS AND FUTURE WORK

In this paper, we have addressed the issue of 2D object recognition from a single binary view. The novel recognition framework proposed allows semantic labeling of 2D objects by integrating, in the recognition process, some *a priori* knowledge, driven from existing 3D models and exploited with the help of 2D/3D indexing techniques. The projection strategy and the 2D shape descriptor represent key issues that are discussed in details. A comparative experimental evaluation is performed

Figure 13. 2D/3D retrieval and categorization with the proposed system, with a query representing a chess piece

in order to analyze the performances of different approaches. Concerning the viewing angle selection methods, experimental results have shown that in most cases LFD and OCTA33 strategies provide the best recognition rates. Four different descriptors, including contour-based and region-based approaches, have been retained. Results obtained have shown that the highest recognition rates are obtained by the two contour-based CS and AH descriptors. In order to further increase the recognition performances, we have also tested a combined descriptor, based on the two best performing descriptors. Similarly, we have combined all the projection strategies with the LFD strategy. As a result, the recognition scores were further improved (up to 89.2%).

In our future work, we intend to exploit the information included in the internal edges of the shape in order to obtain more discriminant representations.

A second axis of future research concerns the extension of the purposed method to video objects. In this case, the system will dispose of several instances of the query object. This additional information could greatly help the recognition process.

ACKNOWLEDGMENT

This work has been performed within the framework of the UBIMEDIA Research Lab, between Institut TELECOM and Alcatel-Lucent Bell-Labs. We also wish to thank Princeton University for supplying their 3D shape database.

REFERENCES

Bober, M. (2002). MPEG-7 visual shape descriptors. *IEEE Transactions on Circuits and Systems for Video Technology*, *11*(6), 716–719. doi:10.1109/76.927426

Chen, D.-Y., Tian, X.-P., Shen, Y.-T., & Ouhyoung, M. (2003). On visual similarity based 3D model retrieval. *Computer Graphics Forum*, *22*(3), 223–232. doi:10.1111/1467-8659.00669

Cyr, C. M., & Kimia, B. (2001). 3D object recognition using shape similarity-based aspect graph. In *Proceedings of the 8th IEEE International Conference on Computer Vision*, Vancouver, BC, Canada (Vol. 1, pp. 254-261).

Daras, P., & Axenopoulos, A. (2009). A compact multi-view descriptor for 3D object retrieval. In *Proceedings of the International Workshop on Content-Based Multimedia Indexing* (pp. 115-119).

Hart, P. E. (2009). How the Hough transform was invented. *IEEE Signal Processing Magazine*, *26*(6), 18–22. doi:10.1109/MSP.2009.934181

International Organization for Standardization. (2002). *ISO/IEC 15938-3: MPEG-7-Visual, Information Technology – Multimedia content description interface – Part 3: Visual*. Geneva, Switzerland: ISO/IEC.

Kim, W.-Y., & Kim, Y.-S. (1999). *ISO/IEC MPEG99/M5472: New Region-Based Shape Descriptor*. Geneva, Switzerland: ISO/IEC.

Li, L. (2006). Data complexity in machine learning and novel classification algorithms (Unpublished doctoral dissertation). California Institute of Technology, Pasadena, CA.

Liebelt, J., Schmid, C., & Schertler, K. (2008). Viewpoint-independent object class detection using 3D Feature Maps. In *Proceedings of the IEEE Conference on Computer Vision and Pattern Recognition* (pp. 1-8).

Manjunath, B. S., Salembier, P., & Sikora, T. (2002). *Introduction to MPEG-7: Multimedia content description interface*. New York, NY: John Wiley & Sons.

Mitchell, T. M. (1997). *Machine learning*. New York, NY: McGraw-Hill.

Mokhtarian, F., & Mackworth, A. K. (1992). A theory of multiscale, curvature-based shape representation for planar curves. *IEEE Transactions on Pattern Analysis and Machine Intelligence*, 789–805. doi:10.1109/34.149591

Mukundan, R., & Ramakrishnan, K. R. (1998). *Moment functions in image analysis: Theory and applications*. Singapore: World Scientific. doi:10.1142/9789812816092

Napoléon, T., Adamek, T., Schmitt, F., & O'Connor, N. E. (2007). Multi-view 3D retrieval using silhouette intersection and multi-scale contour representation. In *Proceedings of the Shape Retrieval Contest*, Lyon, France.

Petre, R., Zaharia, T., & Preteux, F. (2010). An overview of view-based 2D/3D indexing methods. In *Proceedings of the 12th SPIE Conference on Mathematics of Data/Image Coding, Compression, and Encryption with Applications* (Vol. 7799, p. 779904).

Sapna Varshey, S., & Rajpal, R. (2010). Comparative study of image segmentation techniques and object matching using segmentation. In *Proceedings of the International Conference on Methods and Models in Computer Science* (pp. 1-6).

Schwengerdt, R. A. (1997). *Remote Sensing: Models and methods for image processing* (2nd ed.). New York, NY: Academic Press.

Shilane, P., Min, P., Kazhdan, M., & Funkhouser, T. (2004). The Princeton Shape Benchmark. In *Proceedings of the Shape Modeling International Conference*, Genoa, Italy.

Toshev, A., Makadia, A., & Daniilidis, K. (2009). Shape-based object recognition in videos using 3D synthetic object models. In *Proceedings of the IEEE Conference on Computer Vision and Pattern Recognition*, Miami, FL (pp. 288-295).

Xue, M., & Zhu, C. (2009). A study and application on machine learning of artificial intelligence. In *Proceedings of the International Joint Conference on Artificial Intelligence* (p. 272).

Yamauchi, H., Saleem, W., Yoshizawa, S., Karni, Z., Belyaev, A., & Seidel, H.-P. (2006). Towards stable and salient multi-view representation of 3D shapes. In *Proceedings of the IEEE International Conference on Shape Modeling and Applications* (p. 40).

Yap, P. T., Paramesran, R., & Ong, S. H. (2003). Image Analysis by Krawtchouk Moments. *IEEE Transactions on Image Processing*, *12*(11), 1367–1377. doi:10.1109/TIP.2003.818019

Zaharia, T., & Prêteux, F. (2004). 3D versus 2D/3D Shape Descriptors: A comparative study. In *Proceedings of the SPIE Conference on Image Processing: Algorithms and Systems*, Toulouse, France.

Zhang, S., & Lu, G. (2002). An integrated approach to shape based image retrieval. In *Proceedings of the 5th Asian Conference on Computer Vision* (pp. 652-657).

This work was previously published in the International Journal of Multimedia Data Engineering and Management, Volume 2, Issue 4, edited by Shu-Ching Chen, pp. 19-37, copyright 2011 by IGI Publishing (an imprint of IGI Global).

Section 3
Multimodal Content Retrieval

Chapter 9
Building Multi–Modal Relational Graphs for Multimedia Retrieval

Jyh-Ren Shieh
National Taiwan University, Taiwan

Shun-Xuan Wang
National Taiwan University, Taiwan

Ching-Yung Lin
IBM T. J. Watson Research Center, USA

Ja-Ling Wu
National Taiwan University, Taiwan

ABSTRACT

The abundance of Web 2.0 social media in various media formats calls for integration that takes into account tags associated with these resources. The authors present a new approach to multi-modal media search, based on novel related-tag graphs, in which a query is a resource in one modality, such as an image, and the results are semantically similar resources in various modalities, for instance text and video. Thus the use of resource tagging enables the use of multi-modal results and multi-modal queries, a marked departure from the traditional text-based search paradigm. Tag relation graphs are built based on multi-partite networks of existing Web 2.0 social media such as Flickr and Wikipedia. These multi-partite linkage networks (contributor-tag, tag-category, and tag-tag) are extracted from Wikipedia to construct relational tag graphs. In fusing these networks, the authors propose incorporating contributor-category networks to model contributor's specialization; it is shown that this step significantly enhances the accuracy of the inferred relatedness of the term-semantic graphs. Experiments based on 200 TREC-5 ad-hoc topics show that the algorithms outperform existing approaches. In addition, user studies demonstrate the superiority of this visualization system and its usefulness in the real world.

INTRODUCTION

The last few years we have witnessed the phenomenal success of Web 2.0, which has enabled users to create and exchange self-organized resources on the web, resulting in a huge amount of resources in "folksonomy" systems such as Flickr, YouTube, and De.li.ci.ous. As of October 2009, Flickr for example hosted more than four billion images with manual, user-annotated tags. Tagging functions are widely available in Web 2.0 applications. A tag is a non-hierarchical keyword or term assigned to

DOI: 10.4018/978-1-4666-2940-0.ch009

a piece of information such as an Internet bookmark, an image, or a video. This kind of metadata helps describing an item and allows it to be found again by browsing or searching. Tags are typically created by the media creator or by the viewers in a more or less discretionary manner, but are assumed to be semantically related to their target resources. Image tags in Flickr, for example, help users to understand the background, location, and people in each specific image. Intuitively, if two multimedia resources are tagged with similar tags, a semantic relatedness between them can be established with higher confidence, regardless of their media types. As such, an accurate measure of semantic relatedness among tags will go a long way to realizing the holy grail of semantically relevant multimedia search.

Content-based image retrieval (CBIR) techniques involve understanding the image content directly and automatically annotating these images with keyword terms. However, due to the semantic gap between low-level features and high-level concepts, visually similar images are likely to be judged as semantically unrelated, further associating unrelated concepts with the images. Moreover, errors introduced in annotation mapping or in central topic-cohesive tag detection may result in false concepts being assigned to the resources, which leads to mistaken query results.

In addition to finding an effective way to retrieve semantic related multimedia, we also discovered that the query itself need not be limited to a single modality. Tagging is widely used in Web 2.0 systems, and where a resource is represented in the uniform resource model by its semantically-rich tags, the modality it belongs to is ignored. Therefore, the resources relevant to specific query terms can be determined using tags. Moreover, users can use a single keyword to search for resources from different modalities. Significantly, the queries themselves may also be in various forms, such as text, images, and video. Suppose, for instance, that a user comes across an image on Flickr and is eager to find more information on the subject, such as relevant documents on De.li.ci.ous or videos on Youtube. Unfortunately, such a search is not trivial, as most current systems do not support cross references to related materials and media. In pursuit of this goal, our approach is to create ways to support the discovery of relevant connections across various media as shown in Figure 1. However, establishing connections between related media using naive tag similarity matching can result in either inappropriate relationships or poor search performance. These problems have made finding semantically related tags one of the most challenging issues in Web 2.0 search.

The conventional approach for finding related tags involves the extraction of co-occurring key terms from retrieved documents that are highly ranked. Such approaches are referred to as document-based approaches. To extract high-ranking terms, i.e., tags for media, these approaches must ensure that the extracted terms are representative and that word boundaries are correctly identified (Vectomova et al., 2006). Another problem is that the resultant documents might not all be relevant to the queries. In addition, document-based approaches cannot identify key terms that are highly semantically related, but do not frequently co-occur in documents (Xu, 1996). A variation of the document-based approach is to consider the hyperlink graphs of terms (Gracia et al., 2008).

The second approach is log-based term suggestion, where stored logs of previous users' queries are investigated. Beeferman and Berger (2000) proposed a query clustering method based on "click-through" data, each record of which consists of a user's query to the search engine and the URLs within the list provided by the search engine that the user actually visited. One can cluster queries with similar clicked URLs by treating click-through data set as a bipartite graph and identifying the mapping between queries and clicked URLs (Ma et al., 2008). The main problem

Figure 1. Multi-modal query system that combines information from different input modalities, which may include video, audio, image, and text

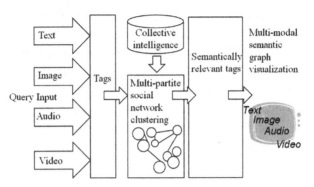

with log-based approaches is that a user normally browses only the most highly-ranked search results, regardless of how long the result list might be. As a result, most queries are associated with only a few URLs that are already limited to the top list of the search engine, and many URLs are not associated with any queries. Additionally, although we could use the click history of a given user to improve his or her current search results, this clicked set of documents is likely to be different from the documents relevant to the current query. Some differences also arise because we are aggregating clicks across users, who may simply disagree about which documents are relevant. Clearly, log-based approaches deserve further investigation.

The third approach for term suggestion is to rely on ontologies inferred from lexical reference systems such as WordNet (Fellbaum, 1998; Budanitsky et al., 2006). However, WordNet is a manually constructed system based on individual words; hence, using it to compute semantic relatedness on the basis of bi-gram or multi-gram words is of only limited benefit. Additionally, its manual nature renders it difficult to update.

Given these difficulties, search term suggestions for most web search engines are generated primarily based on word completion rather than semantically relevant keywords. That is, given the user query tag "3D television", it could be valu-

able to be able to show additional search results like the in-depth related word "anaglyph image," which is a more informed suggestion than only those phrases that start with "3D".

In this paper, we propose enhancing the quality of search term suggestions by utilizing the "collective intelligence" that is embedded in user-intensive social media such as Wikipedia (Watts, 1999; Jin et al., 2001). We propose modeling contributor specialization and fusing it with multi-partite graphs of four different types of pairs – contributor-tag, contributor-category, tag-category, and tag-tag. The hidden networks which link Wikipedia's contributors (i.e., article editors) to tags on Wikipedia pages can help us estimating the semantic distance between any two tags (Jin et al., 2001). We not only calculate the relatedness of two terms using hyperlinks on a Wiki page or the related links section on each Wikipedia page (Gracia et al., 2008), but also rely on contributor specialization inference and the implicit linkage of terms that can be uncovered through the overall knowledge of contributors. We find that modeling contributor specialization is crucial to construct good tag-relation graphs.

We present an implementation of the proposed algorithms, a prototype system which shows a weighted suggested tag-relation graph to users for a given tagged multimedia document (i.e., a text document, an image, a video, or an audio segment), allowing users to easily visualize the semantic relationships between those tags. These graphs can be used for search, regardless of the modality. For multimedia visualization, we can also change the center tag of a graph. This allows users to observe the semantic distances between the new center tag and the other tags. Moreover, we can use this system to conduct multi-modal tag queries and induce the most common tag; i.e., given the input "small world", "cliques", and "power law", we can infer the main concept "social network".

The rest of this paper is organized as follows. We review related work in Section 2, and Section 3 presents the framework of our multi-modal relational graph for multimedia retrieval. We provide details about how to construct the system in Section 4. In Section 5, we report on the promising evaluation results of the proposed system based on a common dataset from TREC and on user studies, and in Section 6, we conclude and suggest directions for future work.

2. RELATED WORK

2.1. Multi-Modal Data Retrieval

Josgim et al. (2006) developed an approach for image search, in which they first extract semantic keywords from a paragraph describing the image and then perform the search on a database of annotated images. Most research works on image search depend essentially on content-based image retrieval techniques (Datta, 2008) in which the similarity between images is computed from an image's low level features. Such techniques can be seen as the foundation of searching similar images using images as input query. The widespread use of mobile camera-equipped devices has increased the demand of text search using image queries. The search for keywords using images is commonly referred to as automatic image annotation; as a result a set of related words is

generated for the image. Furthermore, in Yeh et al. (2004), they proposed techniques for recognizing locations by Web searching. Users can optionally provide texts to aid the search. In addition, was also developed a photo-based question answering system to help people finding useful information given an image. In summary, although the above research is to some extent related to multi-modal search, most of which is limited either to certain input query types or in the returned result type. In contrast, in our work, a general framework to support different kinds of search by integrating resources across various modalities is proposed. In addition, we also provide a semantically-relevant method to support the various requirements of multi-modal search.

2.2. Knowledge Repository

The major challenge for suggesting effective tags is how to ferret out the meaningful semantic relationships among tags (Salton & Buckley, 1998). Repository-based query expansion, which is highly dependent on the quality and relevance of the thesaurus, has been attempted using lexical reference systems such as WordNet (Fellbaum, 1998), as stated in the introduction. However, WordNet-yielded term suggestion results are of limited value since WordNet is a manually-constructed system that focuses primarily on single words; its limitation lies in its inability to easily compute or update the semantic relatedness of bi-gram or multi-gram words. That is, a general-purpose repository is not specific enough to offer synonyms for words used in the corresponding document collection. Researchers have therefore attempted to use Wikipedia to replace WordNet as a more effective ontology. However, this generally works out to using Wikipedia merely as an online dictionary and utilizing it only as a structured knowledge database. That is, researchers have exploited the Wikipedia structure using text processing techniques (Gabrilovich & Markovitch, 2005, 2006), or its associated hyperlinks (Milne et al., 2007; Wang & Domeniconi, 2008) all the while neglecting the important role that Wikipedia has played in the rise of Web 2.0 applications to promote information sharing, interoperability, and Web collaboration, This exploitation, however, has underpinning the role of Wikipedia played in Web-based communities, such as the collection of contributor specialization embedded in Wikipedia social networks (Shieh et al., 2009). Recently, there has been work (Brandes et al., 2009) that analyzes and visualizes the networks that represent the collaborative social process of Wikipedia editing. However, this work focused on identifying the characteristics inherent to the structure and community of Wikipedia, instead of using these properties to benefit data retrieval, i.e., how to design a powerful algorithm that uses social network-derived weighting approaches to incorporate each contributor's expertise in constructing the output relational graphs. Notably, in the approaches presented here, we have attempted to leverage this role that other systems have not exploited.

2.3. Expertise-Mining

A number of automatic expert-finding prototypes reported in the literature have been proposed to solve the expert-mining problem using traditional information retrieval techniques. In their approaches, expertise is described in terms of a vector and does not include any relational information. NASA's Expert Finder (Becerra-Fernandez, 2001; Staab, 2001) uses name-entity extraction to process resumes and documents published by her employees as well as corporate newsletters, so as to identify keywords for creating expertise profiles. I-Help (Bull et al., 2001) models a user's characteristics so that it can assist the user in identifying a peer who is of help. To select the most appropriate peer for a particular request, it uses a matchmaking agent that communicates with the personal agents of other users, by accessing various kinds of vector-based user information.

Link analysis has long been studied as a way to capture relationships between entities (Wasserman & Faust, 1995), for instance, both Google search engine (Page et al., 1998) and Kleinberg's HITS algorithm (1998) use link analysis on the web to find "hubs" and "authorities". The success of these approaches has led to a flurry of research including link analysis into the traditional information retrieval area (Henzinger, 2001). Other researchers have proposed approaches for expert finding in a social network which taken into account not only the information about which topic a person has edited but also the interpersonal relationships (Lappas et al., 2009; Dmitriev et al., 2010). However, information about a single topic is inadequate, as it does not include editing behavior for terms related to the key term. Moreover, although based on the propagation theory it may make use of interpersonal relationships to improve the accuracy of "important contributor" finding, it still is unable to identify a person's "expertise". In this paper, we leverage the structure of Wikipedia to assess the expertise of contributors based on multi-modal link analysis to mine the expertise of each of the contributors.

3. SYSTEM FRAMEWORK

The proposed framework includes ten components, as illustrated in Figure 2. Given the search media, we parse its related documents or tags to find the meaningful (i.e., non-spam) tags. Then, we use Wikipedia as an interpreter to deal with tags that have more than one meaning by adopting the top meaning from the corresponding Wikipedia disambiguation page.

Data sampling starts from the query keyword tag. First, the system collects all the terms that exist as concept links within the page of the query keyword. We then identify the contributors for these terms to construct the previously-defined social network; given these contributors, we continue to identify even more terms. We repeat this

Figure 2. Block diagram of the proposed framework

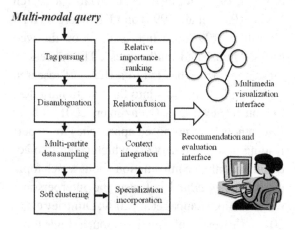

process iteratively to glean a large set of related tags and contributors. After data sampling, we construct a multi-partite network composed of layers of contributors and terms, as shown in Figure 3. We also go on to construct multi-partite networks, that describe tagging term-category relationship, and single partite networks that illustrate term-term hyperlinks.

Then, we apply a soft clustering technique to fold these networks into a term relationship graph called the related-tag graph. In this graph, tags are expressed as nodes and the degree of semantic relatedness are represented as edge weights. The folded related-term graph is viewed as having another layer of graph consists of the contributors who link to the nodes of this related-tag graph.

Furthermore, we crawl the contributor histories in Wikipedia to construct the contributor-category networks based on their editing histories to infer the expertise of individual contributors. These expertise distributions help us set the edge weights in the related-tag graph.

Cosine similarity is effective for divergence measurements in several scenarios (Zhang et al., 2002). Using the cosine similarity measure, we analyze the Wikipedia-derived term-category relationships to calculate the specialization level

of each contributor to each term – the degree to which a given contributor is focused solely on a given term – and then proceed. We also construct another semantic graph where the nodes of the network are distinct tags and the edges are their Wikipedia co-occurrences, that is, the number of times they appear together on the same Wikipedia page. Using ensemble fusion we can capture the relationship between different modalities in Wikipedia to adjust edge weights in the semantic relatedness graph. These finer edge weights are used to determine a form of semantic similarity between any two terms, which can be further used to calculate the relative importance and resultant rank of a term with respect to another given term, in a similar fashion to PageRank with Priors.

The user is then given the related-term graph visualization as suggested search terms to facilitate further searches. Note that a limitation of the proposed system is that related-term graphs can only be generated if the term already exists in Wikipedia. It may help to combine these graphs with other document-based and log-based approaches to ensure that all terms have related graphs; however, that is beyond the scope of this

Figure 3. The construction procedure of the term-contributor graph. Given a term, we can find the term's contributors; in turn, we can find the terms associated with these contributors. The procedure repeats itself layer by layer.

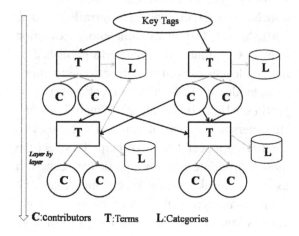

paper. We also want to point out that a thorough real-time use of this system would require periodic large-scale crawling of Wikipedia to construct graphs beforehand. However, that would require significant computing resources which are typically not available in academics. Hence for our prototype experiments we limited the use of terms and generated the related-term graphs off-line. Throughout the paper, we use the 200 query terms derived from the TREC-5 ad-hoc topics (TREC-5, 1996) in our experiments.

4. SYSTEM CONSTRUCTION

4.1. Tag Parsing

We parse the content related to the input media to find the most meaningful tags associated with it. The parsing code is developed in C# and makes use of regular expressions.

4.2. Disambiguation

Using the tags as a query, we perform a search in Wikipedia, the resultant article titles of which we adopt as the concepts of the resource for use in constructing the different semantic tag graphs. The hierarchical structure of Wikipedia guarantees that each concept is unique, and hence that unambiguous tags and phrases will be used as the initial terms (below referred to as set T_{tag}^0) for data sampling.

4.3. Multi-Partite Data Sampling

Our data sampling method differs from intuitive approaches which simply use Wikipedia's hyperlinks to connect each term with the next term. We believe that such methods capture only the simplest relationships among terms. In contrast, we note that information from Wikipedia contains not only hyperlinks among terms, but also contributors; that is, editors (or authors) who have created or modified the Wikipedia pages for these terms. This information, taken together, can be used to induce a social relationship network among contributors; thus, we are able not only to identify the contributors for query terms but also those who have contributed to related terms. We describe the associated mathematical models below. Let $\mathbb{T}_{tag}$ be the set of terms which constitutes the topics of Wikipedia, and let $\mathbb{U}_{ctb}$ be the set of contributors to Wikipedia. Note that, in this notation, we treat as equivalent the contributors of the final and previous versions of a given Wikipedia page. We define the sets

$$\mathcal{TC} = \left\{ \begin{matrix} \left(t_{tag}, u_{ctb} \right) \in \mathbb{T}_{tag} \times \mathbb{U}_{ctb} \mid \\ \text{where } u_{ctb} \text{ contributes to } t_{tag} \end{matrix} \right\}$$

and

$$\mathcal{TL} = \left\{ \begin{matrix} \left(t_{tag}, l_{cat} \right) \in \mathbb{T}_{tag} \times \mathbb{L}_{cat} \mid \\ \text{where } t_{tag} \text{ belongs to } l_{cat} \end{matrix} \right\}$$

as associations between tag t_{tag} and contributor u_{ctb} and the categories that tag t_{tag} belongs to. We then define the set

$$T_{tag}^0 = \left[t_{tag}^0 \right] = \left\{ \begin{matrix} t_{tag} \in \mathbb{T}_{tag} \mid \\ t_{tag} \text{ appears in page } t_{tag}^0 \end{matrix} \right\}$$

as the topics that appear within Wikipedia's top tag page t_{tag}^0 with respect to the initial search tag t_{tag}^{query}. For every $t_{tag}^0 \in \mathbb{T}_{tag}$, there exists an $u_{ctb} \in \mathbb{U}_{ctb}$ such that $\left(t_{tag}, u_{ctb} \right) \in \mathcal{TC}$.

By definition, every contributor has edited at least one tag; that is, for every $u_{ctb} \in \mathbb{U}_{ctb}$, there exists a $t_{tag} \in \mathbb{T}_{tag}$ such that $\left(t_{tag}, u_{ctb} \right) \in \mathcal{TC}$. Thus from the initial search term t_{tag}^{query} we can find the internal term links in the article of the query term which we can follow to find other contributors who have edited these terms.

For a given $t_{tag}^0 \in \mathbb{T}_{tag}$, we have,

$$\mathbb{U}_{ctb}^1 = \left\{ \begin{array}{l} u_{ctb} \in \mathbb{U}_{ctb} \mid \left(t_{tag}, u_{ctb} \right) \in \\ \mathcal{TC}, \text{for every } t_{tag} \in \mathbb{T}_{tag}^0 \end{array} \right\}$$

and thus we can have

$$\mathbb{T}_{tag}^1 = \left\{ \begin{array}{l} t_{tag} \in \mathbb{T}_{tag} \mid \left(t_{tag}, u_{ctb} \right) \in \\ \mathcal{TC}, \text{ for every } u_{ctb} \in \mathbb{U}_{ctb}^1 \end{array} \right\}.$$

and

$$\mathbb{L}_{cat}^1 = \left\{ \begin{array}{l} l_{cat} \in \mathbb{L}_{cat} \mid \left(t_{tag}, l_{cat} \right) \in \\ \mathcal{TL}, \text{ for every } t_{tag} \in \mathbb{T}_{tag}^1 \end{array} \right\}.$$

In this fashion, given a term we can find its contributors, and given a contributor we can find the terms associated with the contributor, layer by layer. Thus, in the kth layer, we have

$$\mathbb{U}_{ctb}^k = \left\{ \begin{array}{l} u_{ctb} \in \mathbb{U}_{ctb} \mid \left(t_{tag}, u_{ctb} \right) \in \\ \mathcal{TC} \text{ for any } t_{tag} \in \mathbb{T}_{tag}^k \end{array} \right\},$$

$$\mathbb{T}_{tag}^k = \left\{ \begin{array}{l} t_{tag} \in \mathbb{T}_{tag} \mid \left(t_{tag}, u_{ctb} \right) \in \\ \mathcal{TL} \text{ for any } u_{ctb} \in \mathbb{U}_{ctb}^k \end{array} \right\}$$

and

$$\mathbb{L}_{cat}^k = \left\{ \begin{array}{l} l_{cat} \in \mathbb{T}_{tag} \mid \left(t_{tag}, l_{cat} \right) \in \\ \mathcal{TL} \text{ for any } t_{tag} \in \mathbb{T}_{tag}^k \end{array} \right\}.$$

Figure 3 illustrates this multi-partite network.

In graph theory, the clustering coefficient is used to measure the degree to which nodes in a graph are clustered together (i.e., the probability that two nodes are linked, given that they are both linked to a third node). Evidence suggests that in social networks, nodes tend to create tightly knit groups characterized by a relatively high density clustering coefficient. At each layer k of the crawling process, we calculate the cluster coefficient of the current graph to identify the level k^* at which the coefficient saturates. It is at layer k^* that we conduct soft clustering to generate the idealist relational graph for the network, or what is called the related-tag graph in the following.

From the resulting networks, we observed that Wikipedia is strongly characterized by the "small world" property. As illustrated in Figure 4, two-hundred-term experiments reveal that by the fourth layer, both the cluster coefficient and number of discovered terms have become saturated. Thus, we empirically select $k = 4$ as the ideal number of layers. Notably, this is in notable contrast to most social networks which saturate at $k = 6$.

4.4. Soft Clustering

After sampling, we generate a related-tag graph from the contributors and their associated terms. That is, we construct a bipartite graph by dividing all of the contributors $\mathbb{U}_{ctb}$ and terms $\mathbb{T}_{tag}$ into two separate parts. Given this graph, we apply a soft clustering technique to calculate the semantic relatedness of every tag pair. Here, we first define the bipartite graph and its corresponding probability descriptions, and then conducting the soft clustering based on (Yu et al., 2002).

Let $\mathbb{B}(\mathbb{U}_{ctb}, \mathbb{T}_{tag}, \mathbb{E}_{ct})$ be a bipartite graph, where

$$\mathbb{T}_{tag} = \left\{ t_{tag}^i \right\}_{i=1}^n$$

and $\mathbb{U}_{ctb} = \left\{ u_{ctb}^k \right\}_{k=1}^m$ are the two disjoint vertex sets and $\mathbb{E}_{CT}$ denotes all of the edges that connect $\mathbb{U}_{ctb}$ and $\mathbb{T}_{tag}$. Let $R_{UT} = \left\{ r_{UT}^{ik} \right\}$ denote

Figure 4. (a) The average clustering coefficient increases with the level of coverage and plateaus at k=4. (b) The number of discovered terms also increases with the level of coverage. (c) The delta of (b) peaks at k=3; therefore, the ideal coverage is set to k=4.

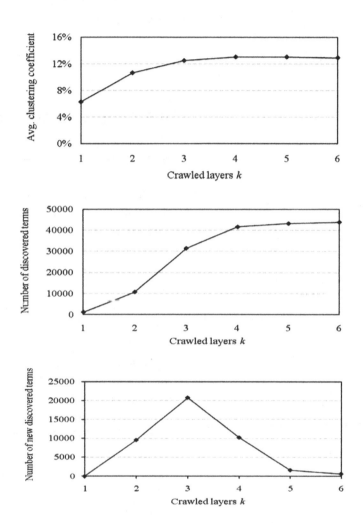

the $n \times m$ adjacency matrix with $r_{UT}^{ik} \geq 0$ being the weight of the edge between u_{ctb}^{k} and t_{tag}^{i}. Graph $\mathbb{B}$ induces a similarity between t_{tag}^{i} and t_{tag}^{j}, that is,

$$\text{SIM}\left(t_{tag}^{i}, t_{tag}^{j}\right) = \sum_{k=1}^{m} \frac{r_{UT}^{ik} r_{UT}^{jk}}{\aleph_k} = \left(R_{UT} \Lambda^{-1} R_{UT}^{\ T}\right)_{ij},$$

$$(1)$$

where $\aleph = \text{diag}\left(\aleph_1, \cdots, \aleph_m\right)$ and $\aleph_k = \sum_{i=1}^{m} r_{UT}^{ik}$ denotes the degree of the vertex $u_{ctb}^{k} \in \mathbb{U}_{ctb}$. Equation (1) can be interpreted from the perspective of Markov random walks on graphs. $\text{SIM}\left(t_{tag}^{i}, t_{tag}^{j}\right)$ is essentially proportional to the stationary probability of a direct transition between t_{tag}^{i} and t_{tag}^{j}, denoted by $p_r\left(t_{tag}^{i}, t_{tag}^{j}\right)$.

Without loss of generality, we normalize the similarity to ensure $\sum_{ij} \mathrm{SIM}(t_{tag}^i, t_{tag}^j) = 1$. For graph $\mathbb{B}(\mathbb{U}_{ctb}, \mathbb{T}_{tag}, \mathbb{E}_{ct})$, there are no direct links between vertices in $\mathbb{T}_{tag}$, and all paths from t_{tag}^i to t_{tag}^j must go through vertices in $\mathbb{U}_{ctb}$. Thus

$$p_r\left(t_{tag}^i, \ t_{tag}^j\right) = p_r\left(t_{tag}^i\right) p_r\left(t_{tag}^j | t_{tag}^i\right), \qquad (2)$$

where $p_r\left(t_{tag}^j | t_{tag}^i\right)$ is the conditional transition probability from t_{tag}^i to t_{tag}^i, $\deg_i = p_r\left(t_{tag}^i\right)$ is the degree (i.e., the marginal probability) of t_{tag}^i, and $\gg_k = p_r\left(u_{ctb}^k\right)$ is similarly the degree of $u_{ctb}^k \in \mathbb{U}_{ctb}$. This leads directly to Equation (1) with $r_{UT}^{ik} = p_r\left(u_{ctb}^k, \ t_{tag}^i\right)$. For graph $\mathbb{B}$, the relation $p_r\left(t_{tag}^j \ | t_{tag}^i\right) = \dfrac{r_{UT}^{ik} r_{UT}^{jk}}{\deg_i}$ is the conditional probability of the transition from t_{tag}^i to u_{ctb}^k. If the size of $\mathbb{U}_{ctb}$ is smaller than that of $\mathbb{T}_{tag}$, namely $m < n$, then $p_r\left(u_{ctb}^k | t_{tag}^i\right)$ indicates the likelihood that contributor c_{ctb}^k contributes to term t_{tag}^i is contributed by contributor. T; this suggests that one can construct graph $\mathbb{B}(\mathbb{U}_{ctb}, \mathbb{T}_{tag}, \mathbb{E}_{ct})$ to approximate a given semantic graph $\mathbb{S}_{softcluster}\left(\mathbb{T}_{tag}, \mathbb{R}_{tag}\right)$, in which each node $t_{term}^i \in \mathbb{T}_{term}$ represents an individual and each edge $r_{tag}^{ij} \in \mathbb{R}_{tag}$ denotes the presence of interactions between t_{tag}^i and t_{tag}^j. Since graph $\mathbb{B}$ is constructed via soft clustering, the corresponding graph $\mathbb{S}_{softcluster}$ represents the affinity of the clusters.

In the following, we use a small example to describe how to model semantic relatedness weighting from on the Wikipedia community structure and how to compute the semantic relatedness between terms. We asume there are m contributors at time t, We further assume and that the interaction (similarity) $\mathrm{SIM}(t_{tag}^i, t_{tag}^j)$ is a combined effect due to all contributors. We approximate $\mathrm{SIM}(t_{tag}^i, t_{tag}^j)$ using with a simple model, that is

$$\mathrm{SIM}^k\left(t_{tag}^i, t_{tag}^j\right) \approx \ p_{r_{ctb}}^k \cdot p_r\left(t_{tag}^i | u_{ctb}^k\right) \cdot p_r\left(t_{tag}^j | u_{ctb}^k\right). \qquad (3)$$

4.5. Contributor Specialization

a. Estimate Specialization

So far, we have proposed using soft clustering to calculate the semantic relatedness of every tag pair based on unsupervised models. However, so doing fails to take into account an important factor in Wikipedia, that is, the specialization – or expertise – of each contributor. To incorporate contributor specialization may greatly refine the final semantic relatedness. In the Wikipedia social network, taking into account a contributor's specialization greatly helps to improve recommendation quality, as there are some contributors who are able to expertly formulate related terms, while other contributors are not experts in certain fields. While experts may not appear frequently, many of their opinions and suggestion terms have a profound influence on the development of semantic relatedness due to their high level of academic specialization. For instance, in many universities there are seminars offered outside of the regular academic curriculum. These seminars are comprised of lectures on specialized themes; thus, although they do not require much school time, these seminars often still uncover many unforeseen solutions and profound relationships due to their level of academic specialization. For instance, when we consider the example of "homographic encryption", the general suggestive tags are "*RSA*", *ElGamal*"; and "*paillier*"; however, since some experts believe that the "secure voting systems", may result in further development of the cloud computing market.

Hence, we refine our semantic relatedness model by incorporating information about contributor's specialization. In other words, the prescribed tag-tag relatedness model

$$\text{SIM}\left(t^i_{tag}, t^j_{tag}\right) \approx \sum_{k=1}^{m} \left(p^k_{rctb}\right) \cdot p_r\left(t^i_{tag}|u^k_{ctb}\right) \cdot p_r\left(t^j_{tag}|u^k_{ctb}\right),$$
(4)

does not take into account a contributor's specialization, but considers only the prior probability of a contributor editing Wikipedia as well as trip-respective editing probabilities for the terms t^i_{tag} and t^j_{tag}. In order to incorporate contributor expertise, we consider the contributor specialization factor $Spec\left(u^k_{ctb}, t^j_{tag}\right)$ as the degree to which contributor u^k_{ctb} specializes in term t^j_{tag}. To incorporate contributor specialization with respect to a given term, we find the categories that the contributor is familiar with and then estimate the specialization factors between those categories and the categories related to each of the tags which the contributor has edited. We thus restate the tag-tag relatedness model as

$$\text{SIM}_{opt}\left(t^i_{tag}, t^j_{tag}\right) =$$
$$\sum_{k=1}^{m} Spec\left(u^k_{ctb}, t^j_{tag}\right) \cdot Spec\left(u^k_{ctb}, t^j_{tag}\right) \cdot$$
(5)
$$\left(p^k_{rctb}\right) \cdot p_r\left(t^i_{tag}|u^k_{ctb}\right) \cdot p_r\left(t^j_{tag}|u^k_{ctb}\right),$$

which takes the contributor's specialization in t^i_{tag}, $Spec\left(u^k_{ctb}, t^i_{tag}\right)$, and t^j_{tag}, $Spec\left(u^k_{ctb}, t^j_{tag}\right)$, into account. Clearly, $\text{SIM}_{opt}\left(t^i_{tag}, t^j_{tag}\right)$ thus provides a better estimate of the semantic relatedness between t^i_{tag} and t^j_{tag} than $\text{SIM}\left(t^i_{tag}, t^j_{tag}\right)$ does. The remaining question is how to calculate $Spec\left(u^k_{ctb}, t^j_{tag}\right)$, the specialization capacity of contributor u^k_{ctb} for tag t^i_{tag} .

As stated above, contributor specialization will lead to a refined estimate of semantic relatedness. The corresponding specialization factor of contributors can be calculated from the list of changes in specific fields that the contributor has made, which can be found in the history section of each Wikipedia topic or term pages. We first list the tags that the contributor has edited and the categories related to those terms (for example, the term "Lattice-based cryptography" falls into the categories "Cryptography", "Post-quantum cryptography", etc.). A contributor's specialization is related to the categories he or she typically edits; thus the specialization for a given tag can be calculated as the similarity between the related categories for that tag and the various categories for the tags that the contributor has edited (a similar idea was addressed in (Schonhofen, 2006). For instance, if the contributor u^k_{ctb} edits many cryptography related pages, he or she would be considered highly specialized in "NTRUcrypt". Note that because specialization is calculated according to related categories, u^k_{ctb}'s specialization in "Lattice-based cryptography" would also be high, because "Lattice-based cryptography" and "NTRUcrypt" same share the category "Post-quantum cryptography". In addition, according to the structure of Wikipedia, the page for a given term (here called the original term) generally contains references to other terms in the form of internal Wikipedia links; therefore, following these links to other terms yields even more terms. From a reference link network point of view, a contributor's editorial works for these referenced terms also represents contributions to the original term. The impact factor for terms relative to the original term can, therefore, be quantified. In this way, once contributor specialization has been taken into account, a user query of "NTRUcrypt" can yield valuable but not immediately obvious search results, such as the educational videos "Lattice-based cryptography" and "Post-quantum cryptography" can be retrieved.

b. Category Similarity-Based Weighting

The algorithm for calculating contributor's specialization is as follows. First, we use cosine distance to determine the similarity between the categories a contributor is familiar with and the categories that the original term belongs to. As demonstrated in Zhang et al. (2002), cosine similarity is effective for information detection and has been shown to outperform KL divergence in several scenarios. Likewise, we adopt cosine distance as our similarity measure. We calculate contributor specialization by first deleting contributors who have contributed little. For Wikipedia, this amounts to ignoring edits that have been marked "minor". We perform latent Dirichlet allocation (LDA) (Blei et al., 2003) to reduce data dimensionality.

Given the two attribute vectors v_{tag}^i and v_{ctb}^k, their cosine similarity $f_0\left(v_{tag}^i, v_{ctb}^k\right)$, is represented as the normalized inner product

$$f_0\left(v_{tag}^i, v_{ctb}^k\right) = \frac{v_{tag}^i \cdot v_{ctb}^k}{\left|v_{tag}^i\right|\left|v_{ctb}^k\right|}, \tag{6}$$

where $v_{tag}^i = v\left(t_{tag}^i\right)$ is the category vector to which the term t_{tag}^i belongs, and $v_{ctb}^k = v\left(u_{ctb}^k\right)$ is the vector representing the categories that contributor u_{ctb}^k is familiar with, and $|\mathcal{V}|$ denotes the length of the vector $\mathcal{V}$. Secondly, the link structure can provide related terms or phrases for the original term which elaborate on the original term's concept. By proceeding layer-by-layer, we connect these internal links as cross references. Therefore, if contributors have edited such internal linked reference terms, they are said to also contribute in part to the original term, and are thus seen to be more specialized in this area.

c. Weighting Based on Category Concept Network

Most generally, domain knowledge is the knowledge in an area of endeavor or in a specialized discipline which should contribute to contributor's specialization. In order to model domain knowledge, we find tags that are related to the original tag one layer at a time by leveraging the links in every Wikipedia page to include relevant information in a specific field. The following formulation clarifies this property:

$$I\left(t_{tag}, r\right) = \left\{ \begin{matrix} t_{tag}' \in \mathbb{T}_{tag} \mid x \text{ links to } t_{tag}' \\ \text{for every } x \in I\left(t_{tag}, r-1\right) \end{matrix} \right\}, \tag{7}$$

where r is the distance in links between the original term and x, where x is one of the tagging terms linked to the original term. Thus, $I\left(t_{tag}^i, 0\right) = \left\{t_{tag}^i\right\}$ is the original term t_{tag}^i and $I\left(t_{tag}^i, 1\right)$ is all of the terms linked directly from the original term page. Likewise, the specialization level of a contributor can be measured using the following two factors: one is the cosine distance between the category vectors of the contributor u_{ctb}^k and the linked concept term t_{tag}', while the other is the importance of the concept term with respect to the original term. That is, the specialization can be computed as

$$\begin{aligned} f_n\left(v_{tag}', v_{ctb}^k\right) &= \sum_{t_{tag}' \in I\left(t_{tag},n\right)\setminus I(tag, n-1)} W_{t_{tag}'} f_{n-1}\left(v_{tag}', v_{ctb}^k\right) \\ &= \sum_{t_{tag}' \in I\left(t_{tag},n\right)\setminus I\left(t_{tag}, n-1\right)} W_{t_{tag}'} \frac{v_{tag}' \cdot v_{ctb}^k}{\left|v_{tag}'\right|\left|v_{ctb}^k\right|}, \end{aligned} \tag{8}$$

where $v_{tag}' = v\left(t_{tag}'\right)$ is the category vector for t_{tag}', $v_{ctb}^k = v\left(u_{ctb}^k\right)$ is the category vector for contributor u_{ctb}^k, and $W_{t_{tag}'}$ is the importance factor of t'_{term} with respect to the original term t_{tag} while $I\left(t_{tag}, n\right) \setminus I\left(t_{tag}, n-1\right)$ denotes the difference between the sets $I\left(t_{tag}, n\right)$ and $I\left(t_{tag}, n-1\right)$ which is included to avoid duplicated tags. In practice, due to the presence of dangling nodes (nodes that do not have any outlinks) and cyclic paths in the network, $W_{t'_{tag}}$ can be reformulated as

$$\overline{W}_{t'_{tag}} = \pm\left(W_{t'_{tag}} + \frac{1}{u}\left(\overline{e}\,\overline{a}^{T}\right)\right) + \frac{1}{u}\left(1-\alpha\right)\left(\overline{e}\,\overline{e}^{T}\right).$$
(9)

As in PageRank (Page et al., 1998), we apply the remedy of "random jumps", where $\pm$ is the probability that the random walk follows a link, $\left(1-\pm\right)$ is the probability of a "random jump", and $1/n$ is the probability that a particular random node is chosen to make this random jump. In Equation (9), $\overline{e}$ is an $u-length$ vector of all ones and $\overline{a}$ is an $u-length$ vector with components $a_i = 1$ if the ith row of $W_{t'_{tag}}$ corresponds to a dangling node, and $a_i = 0$ otherwise. Thus, each $u-length$ vector represents the connections between nodes. Moreover, we set

$$f_1\left(v'_{tag}, v^k_{ctb}\right) = \sum_{t'_{tag} \in I\left(t_{tag},1\right)\setminus 1\left(t_{tag},0\right)} W_{t'_{tag}} f_0\left(v'_{tag}, v^k_{ctb}\right)$$
$$= \sum_{t'_{tag} \in I\left(t_{tag},1\right)\setminus 1\left(t_{tag},0\right)} W_{t'_{tag}} \frac{v'_{tag} \cdot v^k_{ctb}}{\left|v'_{tag}\right|\left|v^k_{ctb}\right|}$$
(10)

on the basis of the reference link networks. Contributor specialization is defined to be the composition of functions f_0 and f_1, that is

$$Spec\left(u^k_{ctb}, t^i_{tag}\right) = \beta f_0 + \left(1-\beta\right)f_1,$$
(11)

where $\hat{a}$ is the weighting factor between the key tagging term and the related concept terms. $Spec\left(u^k_{ctb}, t^j_{tag}\right)$ can be calculated similarly. After we incorporating contributor specialization, the optimized graph $S_{softcluster}\left(\mathbb{T}_{tag}, \mathbb{R}_{opt}\right)$ can be constructed, where each node $t^i_{tag} \in \mathbb{T}_{tag}$ represents an individual tag and each refined edge $r^{ij}_{opt} \in \mathbb{R}_{opt}$ represents the optimized semantic tag relatedness.

4.6. Co-Occurrence Network

In addition to calculating semantic tag relatedness using multi-partite hyperlink social networks, tag similarity can also be derived from the Wikipedia document context, that is, the text surrounding the tags can be useful to find semantic relatedness for tags. We first extract the key term from each Wikipedia document using *tf* (term frequency) multiplied by *idf* (inverse document frequency). *tf* * *idf* is a method widely used in many keyword extraction systems to score individual words within text documents in order to select concepts that accurately represent the content of the document. The *tf* * *idf* score of a word t^i_{cont} can be calculated by multiplying the number of times the word appeared in a document by the inverse of the logarithm of the total number of documents (corpora) the word appears in. *idf* is defined as

$$idf = \log\left(DOCn \, / \, DOCfq\left(t^i_{ctxt}\right)\right) + 1,$$
(12)

where $DOCn$ is the number of pages sampled from Wikipedia and $DOCfq\left(t^i_{ctxt}\right)$ is the number of pages in which word t^i_{ctxt} occurs. We construct the co-occurrence network, in which the nodes are distinct words and each edge is the number of co-occurrences for the two words, that is, the number of times they appear together on the same Wikipedia page. We observe that this network demonstrates the social network property, which has been described as a relatively small diameter and short average path length compared to its size. On the other hand, this network has a relatively large clustering coefficient compared with the clustering coefficient of a random network of the same size and average degree. Graph $\mathbb{S}_{context}(\mathbb{T}_{ctxt}, \mathbb{R}_{ctxt})$ is created based on word co-occurrence information, each node $t^i_{ctxt} \in \mathbb{T}_{ctxt}$ represents an individual tag and each edge $r^{ij}_{ctxt} \in \mathbb{R}_{ctxt}$ represents another type of semantic tag relatedness derived from Wikipedia context. Clearly, this approach can also facilitate the content-based extraction of relevant tags and thus contribute to media retrieval.

4.7. Semantic Graph Ensemble Fusion

We then use ensemble fusion to integrate the semantic relationship tag graph generated using soft tag clustering, $\mathbb{S}_{softcluster}(\mathbb{T}_{tag}, \mathbb{R}_{opt})$, with that

generated using word co-occurrences, $\mathbb{S}_{context}(\mathbb{T}_{ctxt}, \mathbb{R}_{ctxt})$, both of which are derived from the collective intelligence embedded in Wikipedia. Therefore, all semantically-related tags can be merged as $\mathbb{T}_{fusion\,tag} = \mathbb{T}_{tag} \bigcup \mathbb{T}_{ctxt}$. Weights between tags can be composed as $\mathbb{R}_{fusion\,tag} = \mathbb{R}_{opt} + \mathbb{R}_{ctxt}$, and the fused semantic relationship tag graphs, as illustrated in Figure 5, can be expressed as $\mathbb{S}_{semantic}(\mathbb{T}_{fusion\,tag}, \mathbb{R}_{fusion\,tag}) = \mathbb{S}_{softcluster}(\mathbb{T}_{tag}, \mathbb{R}_{opt}) \bigcup \mathbb{S}_{context}(\mathbb{T}_{ctxt}, \mathbb{R}_{ctxt})$. Note that for tensor analysis approaches (Lebedev, 2003; Harvey, 2010), the ability to measure semantic relatedness is both limited by the dimension of the relational vector and is more difficult to implement; our graph-based approach leverages knowledge bases that are much richer and much more comprehensive.

Figure 5. The semantic graph with its center node as the search keyword "web search engine." The distance of a tag from the center represents its semantic divergence from the search topic, and the thickness of an edge represents semantic relatedness. For instance, while "Google" and "Page Rank" are widely divergent tags, semantically speaking, they are highly related media.

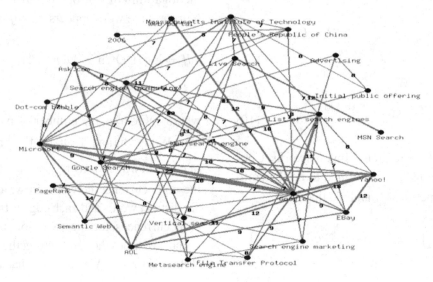

5. RELATED-TAG GRAPH APPLICATIONS

5.1. User-Driven Tag Suggestions

In the proposed system, we incorporate a user-driven tag suggestion function. In order to learn more about a given topic, or to get an answer to an open-ended question, users can select a group of media with specific tags by clicking on or circling the desired cluster media. After the selection has been made, a query is then submitted based on the selected tags and the user is presented with a number of text, image, and video results provided by the search engine. This user-driven tag suggestion function helps users searching for media in a more focused and efficient fashion.

5.2. Estimation of Relative Importance of All Tags in the Graph

In fact, users are not really interested in suggestion terms per se; they are really only interested in one term – the one they are looking for but can't seem to think of. So they are very interested in a more precise nature of the connections between the query and suggestion terms, as evidenced by the importance rankings in the semantic graph, illustrated in Figure 5. Thus, a user may also click on any term in the graph to display a completely new semantic graph which shows that term's relative importance with respect to the other terms. In this way – by a process of guided discovery consisting of traversing the proposed semantic graph – a user may find the query term he or she is looking for. Below, we describe a procedure to measure the relative importance of suggested terms, in which a PageRank with Priors (White & Smyth, 2003) mechanism is used to make semantic relatedness recommendations. We define the target tag as the root set RT, and a vector of prior probabilities $P_{RT} = \{ P_1, ..., P_{|v_{st}|}\}$ such

that the probabilities sum to 1. $P_{v_{st}}$ denotes the relative importance (or "prior bias") attached to node v_{st}. In general, we have $P_{v_{st}} = \dfrac{1}{|RT|}$ for $v_{st} \in RT$; otherwise, $P_v = 0$. Thus, all nodes in the root set have an equal prior probability. In addition to P_{RT}, we also define a "back probability" [3], with $0 \leq {}^3 \leq 1$, which determines how often we can jump back to the set of root nodes in RT. Integrating these two extensions into the original PageRank formula yields the following probability equation:

$$\grave{A}\left(v_{st}\right)^{(i+1)} = \left(1 - {}^3\right)\left(\sum_{u=1}^{d_{in}\left(v_{st}\right)} p\left(v_{st}|u_{st}\right)\grave{A}\left(u_{st}\right)^i\right) + {}^3 p_v,$$

(13)

where $\grave{A}\left(u_{st}\right)^i$ defines the probability of a net surfer staying at node u_{st} in the ith iteration, $p\left(v_{st}|u_{st}\right)$ defines the transition probability from node u_{st} to node v_{st}, and $d_{in}\left(v_{st}\right)$ defines the set of nodes that link to node v_{st}. The transition probabilities $p\left(v_{st}|u_{st}\right)$ are obtained by normalizing the weights of the outgoing edges of node u_{st}. That is,

$$p\left(v_{st}|u_{st}\right) = \frac{w\left(v_{st}, u_{st}\right)}{\sum_{a=1}^{d_{out}\left(u_{st}\right)} w\left(a, u_{st}\right)}, \quad v_{st} \in d_{out}\left(u_{st}\right),$$

(14)

where $w(v_{st}, u_{st})$ defines the weight on the edge $\left(v_{st}, u_{st}\right)$ and $d_{out}\left(u_{st}\right)$ defines the set of nodes that link to node u_{st}. After convergence, the ranking result, which is biased toward the prior set R is reported and serves as the new relative importance ranking. Equation (13) represents the Markov chain of a random surfer who transits "back" to the root set R with probability ^{3} at each time step. Under this assumption, we evaluate the probability of landing on a node in a modified Markov chain, where the random surfer starts at any element in set R (associated with appropriate prior probabilities) and executes a random walk that ends stochastically with probabilities ^{3} (at which point the process restarts). This process defines an infinite set of walks of variable lengths starting at the root set. In fact, they will follow a geometric distribution with mean $1/^3$. The ranking equation, given in Equation (13), estimates the relative probability of landing on any particular node during this set of walks.

5.3. Expert Finding

Using the expert mining algorithm presented in Section 2.3, we are able to add an expert finding function into our system: when a user clicks on any tag shown in the suggestion tag graph, the system displays a window showing the ranking list of the mined experts based on this tag. From that the user can not only determine the semantic relatedness between any two tags by calculating the relative importance with respect to one another, but can also find related experts for in-depth information.

6. EVALUATION

The evaluation of the proposed system includes two major parts, one of which concerns usability and the other concerns the quality of the semantic relatedness measure obtained. We evaluate usability with user studies. For semantic relatedness, evaluation is difficult in particular for user-generated content, as there are no standard linguistic resources available. We conducted our performance evaluation by choosing 200 query tags according to the TREC-5 ad-hoc topics. Such tag-based approaches for calculating precision and recall for multimedia retrieval have been adopted by others as well, for example, Sigurbjörnsson, (2008) and Harvey (2010). Following the approaches of related work on tag suggestion, we calculate precision based on the ODP database (2002) and recall based on normalized Google distance (NGD) (Gligorov et al., 2007). In order to ensure fair human evaluations, we performed multiple searches with the same set of terms using different search engines to achieve a variety of tagging term suggestions to examine the performance of our approaches. The superior performance, as judged by randomized human subject test shows that our work offers very constructive suggestion tags to users.

6.1. Usability

User interaction with such a system plays a crucial role; therefore, the usability of the system must be evaluated. We conducted our experiments using Internet Explorer 6, Windows XP PC with 19-inch monitors set at 1280 by 1024 pixels in 24-bit color. 103 participants were invited to experiment on their own with term-based suggestions for the TREC-5 ad-hoc topics using commercial search tools for three weeks, after which they were asked to use our system to conduct searches on the same topics, and then answer questions regarding novelty, flexibility, and usability.

User studies showed that 82% of the participants prefer the proposed semantic relatedness results to those provided by a traditional search interface, 86% felt that the obtained relatedness helped them to learn more about the collection, 71% found our system to be more flexible, and 82% found it easier to use. These results indicate that the proposed multi-modal relational semantic graph-based approach is a promising method for users for everyday search tasks.

6.2. Precision

We used the ODP database to automatically evaluate search precision. ODP, also known as DMOZ, is the largest and the most comprehensive human-edited directory on the Web. We adopt the same method used in (Baeza-Yates & Tiberi, 2007) to evaluate the quality of the suggested terms. Queries submitted to ODP yield not only site matches but also categories, in the form of paths between directories; moreover, the categories are ordered by relevance. Hence, to measure the strength of the relation between two suggestion tags, we compare the corresponding categories (as provided by ODP). In particular, we measure the similarity between the two categories $\mathcal{D}_c$ and $\mathcal{D}'_c$ as the length of their longest common prefix $O\left(\mathcal{D}_0, \mathcal{D}'_0\right)$, divided by the length of the longest path of $\mathcal{D}_c$ or $\mathcal{D}'_c$. More precisely, we denote the length of a path as $\left|\mathcal{D}_c\right|$, and define the similarity as

$$\mathrm{ODP}sim\left(\mathcal{D}_c, \mathcal{D}'_c\right) = \left|O\left(\mathcal{D}_c, \mathcal{D}'_c\right)\right| / \mathrm{MAX}\left\{\left|\mathcal{D}_c\right|, \left|\mathcal{D}'_c\right|\right\}. \quad (15)$$

We evaluate the similarity between two suggestion tags by measuring the similarity between the most similar categories for the two suggestion tags from the top five ODP results. As shown in Figure 6, the proposed algorithm yielded an average suggestion precision of 73.9%, as compared to 69.3% and 50.2% for WordNet and Bag-of-Words (Xu, 1996; Lewis, 1998) approaches, respectively. We also evaluated the system performance when the related-term graphs do not incorporate contributor specialization and the resultant precision becomes 67.2%, which is significantly lower than that of the proposed approach.

6.3. Recall

Recall is the probability that a relevant document was retrieved in a search. It is defined as

$$\mathrm{Recall} = \frac{\left|\begin{array}{c}\left\{\text{relevant document}\right\} \cap \\ \left\{\text{retrieved document}\right\}\end{array}\right|}{\left|\left\{\text{relevant document}\right\}\right|}. \quad (16)$$

Because the dataset used to evaluate our tag suggestion system is derived from commercial search engines, we do not know how many documents in the system are relevant to the query. To approximate recall, we have adopted normalized Google distance (NGD) as a kind of semantic relatedness measure of concepts (Gligorov et al., 2007). The normalized Google distance between two search terms x and y is defined as

Figure 6. We automatically evaluate the precision using the ODP database, which divides the results into ten categories. These results show that in terms of precision, the proposed system performs very well. In particular, for specialized terms or jargons, we are able to provide useful term suggestions, as compared with WordNet and Bag-of-Words (Xu, 1996; Lewis, 1998) approaches.

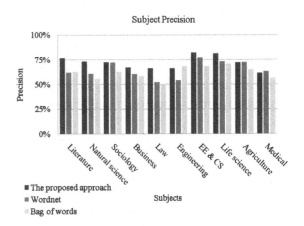

$$NGD(x,y) = \frac{MAX\begin{bmatrix} \log g(x), \\ \log g(y) \end{bmatrix} - \log g(x,y)}{\log M - MIN\{\log g(x), \log g(y)\}},$$

(17)

where M is the total number of web pages searched by Google, $g(x)$ a and $g(y)$ are the numbers of hits for search terms x and y, respectively, and $g(x,y)$ is the number of web pages on which both x and y co-occurred. If the two search terms x and y never co-occur on the same web page, but do occur separately, the normalized Google distance between them is infinite. If both terms always occur together, their NGD is zero. To approximate the recall, in our system, we denote x_{qry} as a query tag and y_{sugg} as a suggestion tag. Let $g(x_{qry})$ be the number of hits returned by the Google search engine for x_{qry}, $g(y_{sugg})$ be that for y_{sugg} and $g(x_{qry}, y_{sugg})$ be the number of web pages on which both x_{qry} and y_{sugg} co-occur. Then, our NGD-based measure of recall, for query tag x_{qry} and suggested tag y_{sugg}, can be written as

$$Recall_{NGD}(x_{qry}, y_{sugg}) = \frac{\log g(x_{qry}, y_{sugg})}{MAX\{\log g(x_{qry}), \log g(y_{sugg})\}}.$$

(18)

We calculate recall based on different suggestion terms and average the results by the number of suggestion terms to obtain the overall recall, that is

$$Suggestion\ Term\ Recall_{NGD}(x_{qry}) = \frac{\sum_{y_{sugg} \in Y_{sugg\ x_{qry}}} Recall_{NGD}(x_{qry}, y_{sugg})}{|Y_{sugg\ x_{qry}}|},$$

(19)

where $y_{sugg\ x_{qry}}$ denotes the suggested tag for query tag x_{qry}, as returned by Google search engine. As shown in Figure 7, when evaluating using NGD with 200 ad-hoc terms, the average suggestion recall of our approaches is 77.4%.

This indicates that the proposed term suggestion algorithm is very effective in querying specialized topics. Similarly, if contributor expertise is not taken into account, the average recall is only 72.3%.

6.4. Comparison with Other Tag Suggestion Algorithms

We first compare our method with SimRank (Jeh & Widom, 2002) and latent semantic query suggestion (LSQS) algorithms (Ma et al., 2008), respectively. In terms of recall and precision, the semantic similarity in SimRank is based on the intuition that two terms are very similar if they link too many similar items. That is, SimRank is a hyperlink-based approach that takes no human factors into account. In LSQS, on the other hand, the suggestion quality is improved from SimRank using the relationship between users and queries; however, it does not incorporate contributor's spe-

Figure 7. We calculate the recall using NGD and divide the terms into ten categories

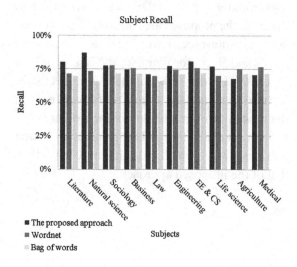

Figure 8. The results of our user study. Users feel that our system's term suggestions outperform those of the other search engines.

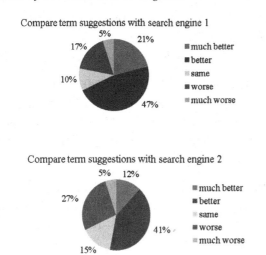

cialization, therefore, in contrast to our approaches, these two methods do not take into account the human factors which are hidden in the Wikipedia social network, nor do they leverage contributor's specialization. Thus, as shown in Table 1, the proposed approach outperformed these methods under the same testing conditions, yielding the highest precision (73.9%) and the highest recall (77.4%), followed by LSQS, and then SimRank.

6.5. Comparison with Other Tag Suggestion Algorithms

In order to ensure a fair human evaluation, we performed randomized experiments to compare the proposed approach with commercial search engines. We first conducted searches using each of the 200 terms using commercial search engines 1 and 2 and then selected the top eight suggestion terms provided by these two engines. For further comparison, similar search keywords were submitted to our system, from which we also selected the top eight suggestion terms. We then randomly combined the 24 suggestion terms selected from the output of the three systems into a single list

of suggestion terms and displayed the results on a web page. We asked for 103 volunteers in two computer science courses (one undergraduate and one graduate-level) to conduct user studies. Each subject was asked to examine ten randomly selected search terms, for each of those terms, the subject was asked to choose the eight most appropriate suggestion terms by a secret vote, in which the subject is not informed which terms are generated by which systems. In the end, our system garnered 47% of the votes, and search engines 1 and 2 garnered 31% and 22% of the votes respectively. In addition, we used our system and the other search engines to generate three different sets of search results. We then asked the subjects to complete an evaluation form in which they estimated the degree of semantic relatedness between the suggestion terms and the search query: scoring 5 if our system's suggestion terms are much more related to the search query than the suggestion terms from other search engines, and 1 if they are much less relevant than those from the other systems. Figure 8 shows the experimental results for these three systems, including pie chart analyses for comparison.

CONCLUSION

We proposed a new multi-modal tag suggestion graph for multimedia retrieval. Our framework is highly extensible and flexible in its processing of multi-modal search and relevant media retrieval. We make explicit use of Wikipedia's multi-partite networks and contributor specialization to com-

Table 1. Performance comparison in term of precision and recall

Algorithms	Precision	Recall
Proposed approach	**73.9%**	**77.4%**
LSQS	68.2%	73.1%
SimRank	57.9%	63.9%

pute the semantic relatedness between tags and use the resultant semantic graphs to suggest related tags. Our experiments have shown promising results for effective tag suggestions. We see a potential advantage in using such semantic graphs for various search tasks in people's daily search activities. Compared with WordNet, as information retrieval ontology, our approach leverages knowledge bases that are orders of magnitude larger and more comprehensive, and therefore, provides much better performance. Compared with commercial search engines, our system results in better semantically-related tag suggestions. Moreover, our system does not require a pre-defined vocabulary (because the Wikipedia vocabulary is maintained by a large number of contributors) and does not require extensive storage space for query logs (because richer relationships are embedded in the editorial history of Wikipedia); therefore, our system is able to perform term suggestions more simply, efficiently, and semantically. Our future work will focus on enhancing our system's search capabilities by adding personalization factors into the design. Moreover, we will try to further understand the latent relationships in the related semantic terms. For example, why are certain synonyms or antonyms are closely connected? A better understanding of this might help us to extend the query expansions and suggestions of the system one step further.

REFERENCES

Baeza-Yates, R., & Tiberi, A. (2007). Extracting semantic relations from query logs. In *Proceedings of the 13th ACM SIGKDD International Conference on Knowledge Discovery and Data Mining* (pp.76-85).

Becerra-Fernandez, I. (2001). Searching for experts with expertise-locator knowledge management systems. In *Proceedings of the 39th Annual Meeting of the Association for Computational Linguistics Workshop Human Language Technology and Knowledge Management* (pp. 9-16).

Beeferman, D., & Berger, A. (2000). Agglomerative clustering of a search engine query log. In *Proceedings of the 6th ACM SIGKDD International Conference on Knowledge Discovery and Data Mining* (pp. 407-416).

Blei, D. M., Ng, A. Y., & Jordan, M. I. (2003). Latent Dirichlet allocation. *Journal of Machine Learning Research, 3*(5), 993–1022. doi:10.1162/jmlr.2003.3.4-5.993

Budanitsky, A., & Hirst, G. (2006). Evaluating WordNet-based measures of lexical semantic relatedness. *Computational Linguistics, 32,* 13–47. doi:10.1162/coli.2006.32.1.13

Bull, S., Greer, J., Mccalla, G., Lori, K., & Bowes, J. (2001). User modeling in I-Help: What, why, when and how. In *Proceedings of the 8th International Conference on User Modeling*, Sonthofen, Germany (pp. 117-126).

Datta, R., Joshi, D., Li, J., & Wang, J. Z. (2008). Image retrieval: Ideas, influences, and trends of the new age. *ACM Computing Surveys, 40*(2), 1–60. doi:10.1145/1348246.1348248

Dmitriev, P., Serdyukov, P., & Chernov, S. (2010). Enterprise and desktop search. In *Proceedings of the 19th International World Wide Web Conference* (pp. 1345-1346).

Fellbaum, C. (Ed.). (1998). *WordNet: An electronic lexical database*. Cambridge, MA: MIT Press.

Gabrilovich, E., & Markovitch, S. (2005). Feature generation for text categorization using world knowledge. In *Proceedings of the International Joint Conference on Artificial Intelligence* (pp. 1048-1053).

Gabrilovich, E., & Markovitch, S. (2006). Overcoming the brittleness bottleneck using Wikipedia: Enhancing text categorization with encyclopedic knowledge. In *Proceedings of the 21st American Association for Artificial Intelligence* (pp.1301-1306).

Gligorov, R., Aleksovski, Z., Kate, W., & Harmelen, F. (2007). Using Google distance to weight approximate ontology matches. In *Proceedings of the 16th International Conference on World Wide Web* (pp. 767-776).

Gracia, J., & Mena, E. (2008). Web-based measure of semantic relatedness. In *Proceedings of the 9th International Conference on Web Information Systems Engineering* (pp. 136-150).

Harvey, M., Baillie, M., Ruthven, I., & Carman, M. (2010). Tripartite hidden topic models for personalized tag suggestion. In *Proceedings of the 32nd European Conference on Advances in Information Retrieval Research* (pp. 432-443).

Henzinger, M. (2001). Hyperlink analysis for the Web. *IEEE Internet Computing*, *5*(1), 45–50. doi:10.1109/4236.895141

Jin, E., Girvan, M., & Newman, M. (2001). The structure of growing social networks. *Physical Review E: Statistical, Nonlinear, and Soft Matter Physics*, *64*(4), 046132. doi:10.1103/PhysRevE.64.046132

Josgim, D., Wang, J. Z., & Li, J. (2006). The story picturing engine-a system for automatic text illustration. *ACM Transactions on Multimedia Computing, Communications, and Applications*, *2*(1), 68–89. doi:10.1145/1126004.1126008

Kleinberg, J. (1998). Authoritative sources in a hyperlinked environment. In *Proceedings of the 9th ACM SIAM Symposium on Discrete Algorithms* (pp. 668-677).

Lappas, T., Liu, K., & Terzi, E. (2009). Finding a team of experts in social networks. In *Proceedings of the 15th ACM SIGKDD International Conference on Knowledge Discovery and Data Mining* (pp. 467-476).

Lebedev, L. P., & Cloud, M. J. (2003). *Tensor analysis*. Singapore: World Scientific. doi:10.1142/9789812564467

Lewis, D. D. (1998). Naive (Bayes) at forty: The independence assumption in information retrieval. In *Proceedings of the 10th European Conference on Machine Learning* (pp. 4-15).

Ma, H., Yang, H., King, I., & Lyu, M. (2008). Learning latent semantic relations from click through data for query suggestion. In *Proceedings of the 17th ACM Conference on Information and Knowledge Management* (pp. 709-718).

Milne, D., Witten, I., & Nichols, D. (2007). A knowledge-based search engine powered by Wikipedia. In *Proceedings of the 16th ACM Conference on Information and Knowledge Management* (pp. 445-454).

Page, L., Brin, S., Motwani, R., & Winograd, T. (1999). *The PageRank citation ranking: Bringing order to the Web* (Tech. Rep. No. SIDL-WP-1999-0120). Stanford, CA: Stanford University.

Salton, G., & Buckley, C. (1988). Term-weighting approaches in automatic text retrieval. *International Journal of Information Processing and Management*, *24*(5), 513–523. doi:10.1016/0306-4573(88)90021-0

Sarwar, B., Karypis, G., Konstan, J., & Riedl, J. (2001). Item-based collaborative filtering recommendation algorithms. In *Proceedings of the 10th International World Wide Web Conference* (pp. 285-295).

Schonhofen, P. (2006). Identify document topics using the Wikipedia category network. In *Proceedings of the International Conference on Web Intelligence* (pp. 456-462).

Shieh, J. R., Hsieh, Y. H., Yeh, Y. T., Su, T. C., Lin, C. Y., & Wu, J. L. (2009). Building term suggestion relational graphs from collective intelligence. In *Proceedings of the 18th International World Wide Web Conference* (pp. 713-721).

Sigurbjörnsson, F., & Zwol, R. (2008). Flickr tag recommendation based on collective knowledge. In *Proceedings of the 17th International Conference on World Wide Web* (pp. 327-336).

Silverstein, C., Henzinger, M., Marais, H., & Moricz, M. (1998). *Analysis of a very large AltaVista query log* (Tech. Rep. No. 1998014). Palo Alto, CA: Digital Systems Research Center.

Staab, S. (2001). Human language technologies for knowledge management. *IEEE Intelligent Systems, 16*(6), 84–94. doi:10.1109/5254.972104

Vectomova, O., & Wang, Y. (2006). A study of the effect of term proximity on query expansion. *Journal of Information Science, 32*(4), 324–333. doi:10.1177/0165551506065787

Waatts, D. (1999). *Small worlds: The dynamics of networks between order and randomness.* Princeton, NJ: Princeton University Press.

Wang, P., & Domeniconi, C. (2008). Building semantic kernels for text classification using Wikipedia. In *Proceedings of the 14th ACM SIGKDD International Conference on Knowledge Discovery and Data Mining* (pp. 713-721).

Wasserman, S., & Faust, K. (1995). *Social network analysis: Theory and methods.* Cambridge, UK: Cambridge University Press.

White, S., & Smyth, P. (2003). Algorithms for estimating relative importance in networks. In *Proceedings of the 9th ACM SIGKDD International Conference on Knowledge Discovery and Data Mining* (pp. 266-275).

Woodruff, A., Faulring, A., Rosenholtz, R., Morrison, J., & Pirolli, P. (2001). Using thumbnails to search the Web. In *Proceedings of the SIGCHI Conference on Human Factors in Computing Systems*, Seattle, WA (pp. 198-205).

Xu, J. (1996). Query expansion using local and global document analysis. In *Proceedings of the 19th Annual International ACM SIGIR Conference on Research and Development in Information Retrieval* (pp. 4-11).

Yeh, T., Lee, J. J., & Darrell, T. (2008). Photo-based question answering. In *Proceedings of the 16th ACM International Conference on Multimedia* (pp. 389-398).

Yeh, T., Tollmar, K., & Darrell, T. (2004). Searching the web with mobile images for location recognition. In *Proceedings of the Conference on Computer Vision and Pattern Recognition* (pp. 76-81).

Yu, K., Yu, S., & Tresp, V. (2005). Soft clustering on graphs. In *Advances in neural information processing systems.* Cambridge, MA: MIT Press.

Zhang, Y., Callan, J., & Minka, T. (2002). Novelty and redundancy detection in adaptive filtering. In *Proceedings of the 25th Annual International ACM SIGIR Conference on Research and Development in Information Retrieval* (pp. 81-88).

This work was previously published in the International Journal of Multimedia Data Engineering and Management, Volume 2, Issue 2, edited by Shu-Ching Chen, pp. 19-41, copyright 2011 by IGI Publishing (an imprint of IGI Global).

Chapter 10
Client–Side Relevance Feedback Approach for Image Retrieval in Mobile Environment

Ning Yu
University of Central Florida, USA

Kien A. Hua
University of Central Florida, USA

Danzhou Liu
Symantec Corporation, USA

ABSTRACT

During the last decade, high quality (i.e. over 1 megapixel) built-in cameras have become standard features of handheld devices. Users can take high-resolution pictures and share with friends via the internet. At the same time, the demand of multimedia information retrieval using those pictures on mobile devices has become an urgent problem to solve, and therefore attracts attention. A relevance feedback information retrieval process includes several rounds of query refinement, which incurs exchange of images between the mobile device and the server. With limited wireless bandwidth, this process can incur substantial delay, making the system unfriendly to use. This issue is addressed by considering a Client-side Relevance Feedback (CRF) technique. In the CRF system, Relevance Feedback (RF) is done on client side along. Mobile devices' battery power is saved from exchanging images between server and client and system response is instantaneous, which significantly enhances system usability. Furthermore, because the server is not involved in RF processing, it is able to support more users simultaneously. The experiment indicates that the system outperforms the traditional server-client relevance feedback systems on the aspects of system response time, mobile battery power saving, and retrieval result.

DOI: 10.4018/978-1-4666-2940-0.ch010

1. INTRODUCTION

Mobile devices with high resolution built-in camera are becoming ubiquitous. It is desirable to support multimedia information retrieval using the images taken from the camera. As examples, a student can use pictures of a plant to search for information of similar species in a remote digital library. Providing this capability calls for efficient techniques to facilitate *Content-Based Image Retrieval* (CBIR) in mobile environment. In a CBIR system, images are characterized by their low level features such as color, texture, and shape. Since it is difficult to "describe" a query through those features, RF is widely used and plays an important role (Binderberger & Mehrotra, 2004; Chen et al., 2009; Fu et al., 2008; Goh et al., 2004; Gevers & Smeulders, 2004; Hoi et al., 2006, Kim & Chung, 2003). It helps the system to understand the user's intention. In such a system, the user interacts with the system as follows: In each round, he helps by identifying the relevant images within the returned set; the system then utilizes this feedback to modify the query and thus to improve its retrieval results in the next round. This process can be repeated until the user is satisfied with the results.

Lots of information retrieval systems in mobile environment have been introduced in recent years (Bezerra et al., 2005; Jia et al., 2006; Kim et al., 2006; Lee & Jayant, 2006; Shyu et al., 2006; Sonobe et al., 2004; Sarvas et al., 2004; Tollmar et al., 2004). In Bezerra et al. (2005), the query is composed by keywords and visual sub-queries. The keyword part is submitted to an existing search engine and the resulting images are passed to a query refinement agent that processes the visual part of the query in the client side. In Jia et al. (2006) and Kim et al. (2006), visual features are used to search in a large database and the result is returned to the user for relevance feedback. In summary, in those systems, the user needs to interact with the server for result. The mobile device

works as an interface. However, this computation model is not suitable for RF because the wireless bandwidth is limited for exchanging images in each round of user RF. The long delay in feedback would affect the usability of the mobile system. Moreover, communication is generally hundreds of times more demanding on mobile power than computation is (Pottie & Kaiser, 2000; Stemm & Katz, 1997). Constantly sending and receiving queries and results can quickly exhaust mobile device's battery power. In practice, power required by CPU is minimal compared to sending data over the wireless radio. For example, the energy cost of transmitting 1Kb message over a distance of 100 meters is approximately 3 joules. By contrast, a general-purpose processor with 100 MIPS/W power could efficiently execute 3 million instructions for the same amount of energy (Pottie & Kaiser, 2000). Also the storage power for mobile devices is always some hundred mW (Zheng et al., 2003), which is 20-30% of the communication power consumption. Therefore, saving the communication power will be more urgent in mobile RF system.

Another issue in the existing image retrieval techniques is the semantic gap between the high level semantic concept and the low level visual features. In most of the current systems (Ishikawa et al., 1998; Kim & Chung, 2003), the searching range is always confined in a single neighborhood. This is not consistent with the reality: a semantic concept can have very different representation (for example, side view of a sedan and front view of a sedan can be very different). Trying to bridge the gap, some mobile information management systems use tags generated at the point of picture was taken: In Davis et al. (2004), Liu et al. (2005), and Lahti et al. (2005), location, temporal, and sometimes social contextual metadata are used as image features instead of the visual features. However, a picture is worth a thousand words. It is hard and tedious to fully describe an image using concise verbal terms. The most convenient and common way for a mobile user to express himself is to use the picture he took as the query (Bentley et al., 2006).

To address the aforementioned issues, we investigate a *Client-side Relevance Feedback* (CRF) technique in this paper. In this model, all RF except the last round is processed in the mobile device to avoid the communication cost. To achieve this, we adapt the *Relevance Feedback Support* (RFS) structure (Hua et al., 2006; Yu et al., 2007) to address the storage and computation limitation of mobile devices. In the CRF system, the initial user query might be decomposed to cover more semantically relevant images, thus to bridge the semantic gap. We list the contributions as below:

1. The CRF technique is detailed described and investigated.
2. We take the interface design into consideration. We develop different interfaces for different mobile users.
3. We conduct extensive experimental studies on the CRF system to examine the mobile device power saving and the accuracy of the system.

The remainder of this paper is organized as follows. The CRF technique is introduced in Section 2. In Section 3, we discuss the interface design. We then analyze our experiment results in Section 4. Finally, we conclude this study in the last section.

2. CLIENT-SIDE RELEVANCE FEEDBACK TECHNIQUE

To support client side RF, we adapt *Query Decomposition* technique (QD) (Hua et al., 2006), and use the RFS structure to facilitate the query processing: The system provides RF retrieval result to the user based on the RFS structure; Also, to cover more semantically similar image

clusters, user's query is decomposed based on the RFS structure. In this section, we describe RFS structure and discuss the CRF retrieval technique in details.

2.1. RFS Structure

Since low-level visual features are not sufficient to capture the semantics of general images, semantically identical images may exhibit very different visual characteristics and thus may be projected to data points lying far apart in the multi-dimensional feature space. Standard retrieval techniques which are trying to find the cluster with the more relevant images cannot achieve good recall (Hua et al., 2006). QD approach addresses this problem by finding all semantically-related clusters. To cover those clusters, the system decomposes the user's query based on the relevance feedback and the RFS structure.

The RFS structure is constructed in two stages: *Data Clustering* and *Representative Images Selection*. In the Data Clustering stage, a hierarchical clustering technique is used to organize the entire image database into a tree structure. Then in the Representative Images Selection stage, a bottom-up representative image selection procedure is performed as follows. At the bottom level of the RFS structure, unsupervised k-mean clustering algorithm is applied to the images in each leaf node. For each of the resulted subclusters, one or more images nearest to its center are selected as the *representative images*. For each cluster in the upper level of the hierarchy, the representative images from its child clusters are aggregated and clustered again. Then representative images are selected for the current node. The number of representative images for each cluster is chosen proportional to the number of images in that cluster (i.e. 5% of the images). Finally, the list of the representative images and their corresponding subcluster identifications (i.e. to which they belong to) are stored in the RFS structure in the corresponding tree node. Thus, all of the information needed to support relevance feedback is self-contained in the RFS structure.

2.2. Query Processing with RFS Structure

To help the user formulate the initial query, the system displays some randomly selected representative images from the root node of the RFS structure. From these images, the user identifies the most relevant ones. If necessary, this process can be repeated. To process the initial query, the system determines the relevant subclusters to which the selected representative images are from. If this process results in more than one relevant subcluster, the initial query is "split" into separate localized subqueries for RF, one for each relevant subcluster. We claim that because real-world objects can have very different appearances when represented in 2-dimensional images, multiple independent subqueries are better suited for their retrieval.

We illustrate the query decomposition process with an example in Figure 1 (only tree nodes and images relevant to the discussion are presented in this figure). In this example, the RFS structure has three levels, with *Node 1* representing the root cluster, which is the entire image database. Suppose the user wants to find images of cars. In the first feedback iteration, he found two relevant images in *Node 1* - a steamed car and a modern

car. Based on the RFS structure, the system determines that these two images came from *Node 2* and *Node 3* in *Level 2*, respectively; then the initial query is split into two subqueries as follows. At the beginning of the second iteration, random representative images from *Node 2* and *Node 3* are presented to the user for RF. The user can now find more relevant images according to his interest, say, a steamed car and an antique car in *Node 2*, plus two modern cars with different colors in *Node 3*. With these new relevant images, the system recognizes the corresponding relevant subclusters to be *Nodes 4, 5, 6, and 7* in *Level 3*. Finally, the user identifies the relevant images in these subclusters as illustrated in Figure 1. These images are then used as the final localized *k-NN* subqueries to search the corresponding subclusters independently; and their results are merged to form the overall result of car.

2.3. Procedures of Client-Side Relevance Feedback

Given a RFS structure stored on the mobile device, we can use this structure to process the user's relevance feedback without any support from the remote server. The client-side relevance feedback is performed starting at the root node as follows:

1. A user has two ways to formulate the initial query: (1) By identifying initial relevant images (i.e. query images) from the set of

Figure 1. A 3-level RFS structure

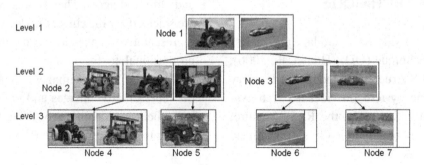

images randomly selected from the representative images corresponding to the root node in the RFS structure. (This step can be repeated until the user is satisfied with the initial query.) (2) A set of pictures, taken by the user, can be submitted as the initial query. In response to this initial query, the mobile device presents the top k similar images from the representative images in the root node; and the user marks the relevant images.

2. The images marked for the current query identify the relevant clusters in the next (lower) level of the RFS structure. A cluster in the next level is relevant if one or more of its representative images is selected as query images. With the help of RFS structure, it only takes $O(1)$ time to determine which subcluster to explore next.

3. Localized relevance feedback is processed independently for each relevant subcluster. The user chooses query images from the set of images, randomly selected from the representative images from each relevant subcluster.

4. Recursively repeat Steps 2 and 3 until the RF process reaches a relevant cluster at the leaf level (i.e., a semantically relevant cluster) of the RFS structure. Then the query is sent to the server for final image retrieval. We note that the user has the option to submit the final query before the search reaches the leaf level.

We note that the CRF approach requires storing the RFS structure on the mobile device. Although the capacity of flash memory continues to quadruple each year, it is desirable to keep the size of this RFS structure small. Typically, the RFS structure contains less than 5% of the database images. Since it is sufficient to use low-resolution image icons for feedback purposes, this RFS structure is generally very small. For instance, if each image icon requires 10 KB of storage space, a mobile device with 100MB of available flash memory can hold an RFS structure that can support an image database with 200,000 images. Considering 1 GB flash memory in a cell phone becomes a standard, the proposed approach is feasible.

2.4. Final Query Processing on Server

When the final query is sent to the server, localized k-NN queries are performed on the corresponding leaf cluster to retrieve the semantically relevant images. This time, the server searches all the images in the relevant cluster, not just the representative images. Finally, the candidates from different relevant clusters are merged and ranked to form the final result. A distinct benefit of CRF is that the RFS scheme only needs to do k-NN computation over the much smaller data subspaces, represented by the relevant leaf nodes in the RFS structure, in the final round of retrieval. Existing RF techniques must perform the k-NN computation over the entire database for each round of RF.

2.5. Active Learning in RF

According to the basic idea of QD technique, the relevance feedback procedure refines the initial query by decompose it into subqueries. However, the user might not satisfy with the images in the chosen subclusters. This might happen when the image's semantic meaning is different from the rest of the cluster, but similar on the features; or the selected relevant image is at the boundary of a cluster, the real relevant images should be in the nearby cluster. This situation is caused by the semantic gap. The user may not always be able to choose the "right" images. In the QD system (Hua et al., 2006), the system provides a "back" function to allow user to go back to the previous step to recover his "wrong" operation. However, we do not want to leave all these responsibility on users. Also, it is more difficult to use a mobile interface than a PC interface. Therefore, in order to save the mobile user's time and improve the system's usability, we adapt the QD technique to learn the user's activity and use this short term learning knowledge to adjust the relevance feedback procedure. In detail, if the user does not select any images from the returned subclusters, then the system considers that the user does not interested in any image contained within. Therefore, the system brings representatives to the user from other clusters that are not explored.

In Figure 2, we have a multi-level RFS structure. Under the root level, there are n clusters, which are $C_1, ..., Cn$. Each of those clusters contains some subclusters. To simplify the graph, we did not draw all the clusters and subclusters. In the image retrieval procedure, user picks images from the representatives as examples. For instance, the user selects some images from C_1 and C_2. After a relevance feedback retrieval procedure on the RFS structure, the searching space is refined to the subclusters contains the selected relevant images. Say, S_{1i} $(1 \leq i \leq p)$, S_{21}, and S_{2q} are the identified subclusters. In the new round, the user does not further select any representative from S_{1i}. There are two schemes to handle the situation.

Scheme 1: Due to the semantic gap, some unrelated images might be clustered together based on the similarity in the low-level features. Therefore, the selected subcluster, S_{1i}, does not contain the images that the user interested in. In this case, the system suggests representative image from the upper level clusters, which are siblings of S_{1i}'s parent cluster.

Scheme 2: when the selected representative image is near the boundary of S_{1i}, the images that the user interested in might be in the sibling of S_{1i}. In this case, the system needs to show images from the nearby subcluster of S_{1i}. The nearby subcluster is determined by calculating the distance from the selected representative to the centers of the subclusters.

Figure 2. A multi-level RFS structure

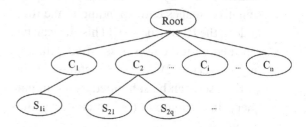

Considering these two cases, the system's RF result for the next round includes images from the subclusters containing the selected images and those from the clusters of the nearest sibling and upper level. After all, the relevance feedback procedure in CRF system can be summarized as in Algorithm 1.

3. INTERFACE DESIGN

To better help the user and present more information as possible, we take the interface design into consideration. There have been studies to investigate the design rules (Brewster, 2002; Mohomed et al., 2006). With small screen space, mobile devices can only present limited amount of information at one time. So thumbnails are used for browsing. As smart phone and cell phone has different screen sizes, we want to maximize the screen usage on each device. Therefore we designed different interfaces as shown in Figure 3

Figure 3. CRF mobile user interface for smart phone device

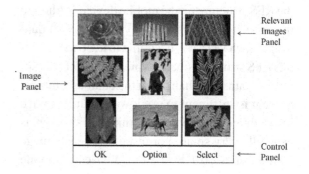

Algorithm 1. Relevance feedback procedure

1) **CandidateCluster** = {RFS Root}
2) Do{
3) Randomly present images **CandidateCluster**;
4) User selects relevant images $I = \{I_1, I_2, ..., I_l\}$;
5) For each query image, the system identifies the corresponding RFS subcluster $S_i, 0 \leq i \leq l$;
6) **NewCandidateCluster** = $S_i, 0 \leq i \leq l$
7) IF($S_q, (I_j S_q); 1 \leq q \leq l, 1 \leq j \leq t$)
8) THEN **NewCandidateCluster** = **NewCandidate-Cluster** - S_q + *sibling(parent(S_q))* + *sibling(S_q)*)
9) **CandidateCluster** = **NewCandidateCluster**
10) } WHILE USER IS NOT SATISFIED

(for smart phone) and 4 (for cell phone user). The thumbnails shown in the *Result Panel* are the retrieval result from last round's relevance feedback, and are sorted according to the similarity to the query images. When the user is interested in one of the images, he can click "Select" to choose it as relevant images, then the image is added to the *Relevant Image Panel*. When the user finds enough relevant images, he can click "Option" from the *Control Panel* to choose whether to "submit" a query or "exit" the system.

4. EXPERIMENTAL RESULT

To evaluate our CRF system's performance, we compared the CRF technique to the existing client-server technique. The experiment systems' interface is sized to fit smart phone and cell phones as shown in Figures 3 and 4. Our test images are from the Corel image database, which are classified into distinct categories by domain professionals. There are 100 images under each category and the category information is used as the ground truth. We constructed a 19,200 image database with about 15,000 Corel images and new images we took. 37 features were extracted: 9 color moment features, 10 Wavelet-based Texture features, and 18 edge-based structural features. There were 100 queries for each experiment from which the average results were calculated.

4.1. Evaluation Criteria

The performance metrics selected for this study are as follows:

1. **Mobile Energy Consumption:** For a mobile device, power saving is very important. By reducing the messages transmitted between server and client, our system can save a lot of energy compared to traditional client-server systems.

2. **Precision, Recall, and GTIR:** To measure retrieval accuracy. GTIR (Ground Truth Inclusion Ratio) is defined as:

$$GTIR = \frac{Num\ of\ retrievad\ subconcept(s)}{Num\ of\ Total\ subconcepts\ in\ groud\ truth},$$

(1)

Figure 4. CRF mobile user interface for cell phone

4.2. Mobile Power Consumption Measurement

In our CRF system, the mobile device does not interact with the server in the query refining stage, hence there is no message been sent or received. For conventional client-server techniques, the mobile communication cost includes sending and receiving messages. We can see that the more information been exchanged, the more battery power consumed, and the longer the mobile user need to wait.

4.2.1. Communication Cost

In this study, we first report the message size sent and received by the mobile device when the numbers of query images and returned image various in one RF round. Suppose the number of messages exchanged between server and client is between 11 and 60 in the conventional system (1 to 10 query images; and 10 to 50 returned image). Duplicate images are omitted from transferring. The result is shown in Figure 5. We can see that there is no communication between server and mobile in CRF system in the query refinement stage, therefore, no communication cost associated. For the traditional systems, the RF process includes sending, waiting, and receiving message from the server. We conclude that the CRF system saves considerable amount of power and time on refining query.

Second, in Figure 6, we show the message exchanged when the number of RF rounds changes in the whole RF process. Suppose in each RF round, 2 new relevant images were selected as query. 20 images were returned. The last round is for final result retrieval. Apparently, our CRF system can severely save the communication cost by process the RF on the mobile device alone.

Figure 5. Size of images exchanged between server and client in CRF and traditional system in one round when number of query and result images changes

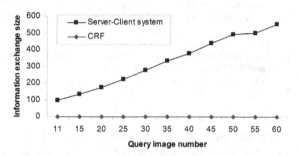

Figure 6. Size of images exchanged between server and client in CRF and Traditional system in the whole process when number of RF round changes

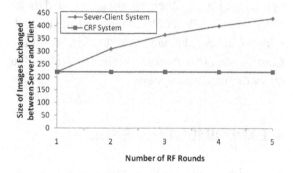

4.2.2. User's Waiting Time

To give a general idea of our system's advantage, we listed the waiting time for users with different bandwidth settings in Table 1. Usually users in our system need 3 rounds to find the desired images, so we use this transferred image size, averagely 3184kb, to calculate the waiting times. From the result, we can see that, in the traditional system, the user with 56kbps bandwidth needs to wait about 1 minute to refine a query before the final round. In fact, the delay in traditional system can be significantly longer since the server needs to

Table 1. Waiting time comparison of client-server systems

Total RF Info. Trans (kb)	Total waiting time (s)			
	5 kbps	56 kbps	114 kbps	384 kbps
3184	636.8	56.9	27.9	8.3

multiplex among a large number of concurrent users to support their RF. At the same time, there is no waiting time for the user in CRF system. The only time needed for CRF is to identify the next searching subclusters, which takes $O(1)$ time.

4.3. Accuracy of CRF

As we described previously, the CRF system is able to bridge the semantic gap hence improve the accuracy of relevance feedback. In this section, we evaluate the system's accuracy in the context of bridging the semantic gap, precision and recall.

4.3.1. Performance on Bridging the Semantic Gap

To test the CRF system's accuracy, we compared our system with one of the state-of-the-art

techniques, namely Multiple Viewpoint (MV) (French & Jin, 2004). The reason we compare our technique with the MV technique is that the MV technique is similar to our idea: it is trying to search for relevant images using multiple queries. However, each of the MV query changes only a subset of the visual features, therefore the retrieved images are still in one neighborhood. When the objects' appearances are very different (no common features), the MV technique can never cover all the relevant images. In this study, we used 10 representative queries. Some of the test queries allow us to compare the two techniques when the subject is different in a subset of visual features (e.g., red rose and yellow rose). We compared the precision (P_{MV} and P_{CRF}) and GTIR (G_{MV} and G_{CRF}) of MV and our CRF system as shown in Figure 7. To illustrate the GTIR, we consider the query "a person." In this case, the MV only captures 1 out of 3 ground truth subcategories, thus resulting in GTIR=1/3; while CRF can capture all three subcategories achieving a GTIR of 1. The result shows the merit of using separate queries in the CRF system. We notice that for most of the cases, the CRF approach can capture all the semantic subclusters therefore achieves better precision and GTIR than MV.

Figure 7. Precision and GTIR comparison for CRF and MV. Queries: 1. a person (hair-model, fitness, Kongfu); 2. airplane (single, multiple); 3. bird (eagle, owl, sparrow); 4. car (modern, antique, steamed car); 5. horse (polo, wild horse, race); 6. rose (yellow, red); 7. water sports (surfing, sailing); 8. computer (server, desktop, laptop); 9. personal computer (desktop, laptop); and 10. laptop (clear background, complicated background)

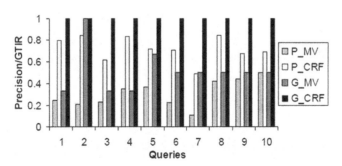

4.3.2. Effects of Different RFS Settings

From the design of RFS technique, we notice that choosing a different leaf size results in a new RFS structure with different representative images due to its construction property. To investigate the performance impact of this change, we changed the leaf cluster size to be 30, 50, 70, 100, 150, and 200, respectively. 2 new images were selected as relevant images in each round. We plot the precision-recall performance in Figure 8. The result shows that the performance is the best when the cluster size is 100. This cluster size matches the characteristic of the databases: there are about 100 images in each category.

CONCLUSION

In this paper, we described a Client-side Relevance Feedback system for mobile device image retrieval. The RFS structure is stored in the client side for RF processing. Only in the final round for the result, the query is sent back to the server. In traditional client-server systems, each round of the RF and the final query are sent to the server. With the limited wireless bandwidth, the user suffers the long delay of transferring the query and result images. The significance of the proposed CRF technique is trifold. First, since processing of RF incurs no communication delay, CRF enhances system usability. Second, it leverages distributed mobile computing to significantly reduce server load and therefore improve system throughput. Third, our experimental studies indicate that substantial improvement in retrieval precision and recall can be achieved.

Figure 8. Precision-recall for different cluster size in 19000 database

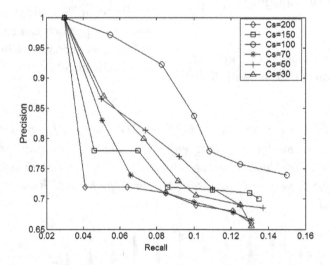

REFERENCES

Bentley, F., Metcalf, C., & Harboe, G. (2006). Personal vs. commercial content: The similarities between consumer use of photos and music. In *Proceedings of the International Conference on Human Factors in Computing Systems* (pp. 667-676).

Bezerra, F. N., Werbet, E., & Silva, W. B. (2005). Client-side content-based refinement for image search in the web. In *Proceedings of the Brazilian Symposium on Multimedia and the Web* (pp. 1-3).

Binderberger, M. O., & Mehrotra, S. (2004). Relevance feedback techniques in the MARS image retrieval system. *Multimedia Systems*, 9(6), 535–547. doi:10.1007/s00530-003-0126-z

Brewster, S. (2002). Overcoming the lack of screen space on mobile computers. *Personal and Ubiquitous Computing*, 6(3), 188–205. doi:10.1007/s007790200019

Chen, X., Zhang, C., Chen, S.-C., & Rubin, S. H. (2009). A human-centered multiple instance learning framework for semantic video retrieval. *IEEE Transactions on Systems, Man, and Cybernetics. Part C*, 39(2), 228–233.

Davis, M., King, S., Good, N., & Sarvas, R. (2004). From context to content: Leveraging context to infer media metadata. In *Proceedings of the ACM Multimedia Conference* (pp. 188-195).

French, J., & Jin, X. Y. (2004). An empirical investigation of the scalability of a multiple viewpoint CBIR system. In *Proceedings of the International Conference on Image and Video Retrieval* (pp. 252-260).

Fu, Y., Li, Z., Huang, T. S., & Katsaggelos, A. K. (2008). Locally adaptive subspace and similarity metric learning for visual clustering and retrieval. *Computer Vision and Image Understanding*, 111(3), 390–402. doi:10.1016/j.cviu.2007.09.017

Gevers, T., & Smeulders, A. (2004). Content-based image retrieval: An overview. In Medioni, G., & Kang, S. B. (Eds.), *Emerging topics in computer vision*. Upper Saddle River, NJ: Prentice Hall.

Goh, K., Chang, E., & Lai, W.-C. (2004). Concept-dependent multimodal active learning for image retrieval. In *Proceedings of the ACM Multimedia Conference* (pp.564-571).

Hoi, S. C. H., Lyu, M. R., & Jin, R. (2006). A unified log-based relevance feedback scheme for image retrieval. *IEEE Transactions on Knowledge and Data Engineering*, 18(4), 509–524. doi:10.1109/TKDE.2006.1599389

Hua, K. A., Yu, N., & Liu, D.-Z. (2006). Query decomposition: A multiple neighborhood approach to relevance feedback processing in content-based image retrieval. In *Proceedings of the International Conference on Data Engineering* (pp. 84-93).

Ishikawa, Y., Subramanya, R., & Faloutsos, C. (1998). MindReader: Querying databases through multiple examples. In *Proceedings of the Very Large Database Conference* (pp. 218-227).

Jia, M., Fan, X., Xie, X., Li, M. J., & Ma, W. Y. (2006). Photo-to-search: Using camera phones to inquire of the surrounding world. In *Proceedings of the Conference on Mobile Data Management* (pp. 46-48).

Kim, D. H., & Chung, C. W. (2003). Qcluster: Relevance feedback using adaptive clustering for content-based image retrieval. In *Proceedings of SIGMOD International Conference on Management of Data* (pp. 599-610).

Kim, S., Tak, Y., Nam, Y., & Hwang, E. (2006). mCLOVER: Mobile content-based leaf image retrieval system. In *Proceedings of the ACM Multimedia Conference* (pp.215-216).

Lahti, J., Westermann, U., Palola, M., Peltola, J., & Vildjiounaite, E. (2005). MobiCon: Integrated capture, annotation, and sharing of video clips with mobile phones. In *Proceedings of the ACM Multimedia Conference* (pp. 798-799).

Lee, J., & Jayant, N. (2006). Mixed-initiative multimedia for mobile devices: A voting-based user interface for news videos. In *Proceedings of the ACM Multimedia Conference* (pp. 611-614).

Liu, X., Corner, M., & Shenoy, P. (2005). SEVA: Sensor-enhanced video annotation. In *Proceedings of the ACM Multimedia Conference* (pp. 618-627).

Mohomed, I., Cai, J. C., Chavoshi, S., & Lara, E. (2006). Context-aware interactive content adaptation. In *Proceedings of the International Conference on Mobile Systems, Applications, and Services* (pp. 42-55).

Pottie, G., & Kaiser, W. (2000). Wireless integrated network sensors. *Communications of the ACM*, *43*(5), 51–58. doi:10.1145/332833.332838

Sarvas, R., Viikari, M., Pesonen, J., & Nevanlinna, H. (2004). MobShare: Controlled and immediate sharing of mobile images. In *Proceedings of the International Conference on ACM Multimedia* (pp. 724-731).

Shyu, M.-L., Chen, S.-C., Chen, M., Zhang, C., & Shu, C.-M. (2006). Probabilistic semantic network-based image retrieval using MMM and relevance feedback. *Multimedia Tools and Applications*, *30*(2), 131–147. doi:10.1007/s11042-006-0023-5

Sonobe, H., Takagi, S., & Yoshimoto, F. (2004). Image retrieval system of fishes using a mobile device. In *Proceedings of the International Workshop on Advanced Image Technology* (pp. 33-37).

Stemm, M., & Katz, R. H. (1997). Measuring and reducing energy consumption of network interfaces in hand-held devices. *IEICE Transactions on Communication*, *80*(8), 1125–1131.

Tollmar, K., Yeh, T., & Darrell, T. (2004). IDeixis - searching the Web with mobile images for location-based information. In *Proceedings of the International Symposium on Mobile Human-Computer Interaction* (pp. 288-299).

Yu, N., Hua, K. A., & Liu, D.-Z. (2007). Client-side relevance feedback approach for image retrieval in mobile environment. In *Proceedings of the International Conference on Multimedia & Expo* (pp. 552-555).

Zheng, F., Garg, N., Sobti, S., Zhang, C., & Joseph, R. E. (2003). Considering the energy consumption of mobile storage alternatives. In *Proceedings of the International Symposium on Modeling, Analysis and Simulation of Computer Telecommunications Systems* (pp. 36-45).

This work was previously published in the International Journal of Multimedia Data Engineering and Management, Volume 2, Issue 2, edited by Shu-Ching Chen, pp. 42-53, copyright 2011 by IGI Publishing (an imprint of IGI Global).

Chapter 11
Video Segmentation and Structuring for Indexing Applications

Ruxandra Tapu
TELECOM SudParis, France

Titus Zaharia
TELECOM SudParis, France

ABSTRACT

This paper introduces a complete framework for temporal video segmentation. First, a computationally efficient shot extraction method is introduced, which adopts the normalized graph partition approach, enriched with a non-linear, multiresolution filtering of the similarity vectors involved. The shot boundary detection technique proposed yields high precision (90%) and recall (95%) rates, for all types of transitions, both abrupt and gradual. Next, for each detected shot, the authors construct a static storyboard by introducing a leap keyframe extraction method. The video abstraction algorithm is 23% faster than existing techniques for similar performances. Finally, the authors propose a shot grouping strategy that iteratively clusters visually similar shots under a set of temporal constraints. Two different types of visual features are exploited: HSV color histograms and interest points. In both cases, the precision and recall rates present average performances of 86%.

INTRODUCTION

Recent advances in the field of image/video acquisition and storing devices have determined a spectacular increase of the amount of audio-visual content transmitted, exchanged and shared over the Internet. In the past years, the only method of searching information in multimedia databases was based on textual annotation, which consists of associating a set of keywords to each individual item. Such a procedure requires a huge amount of human interaction and is intractable in the case of large multimedia databases. Today, existing video repositories (e.g., Youtube, Google Videos, DailyMotion, etc.) include millions of items. Thus, attempting to manually annotate

DOI: 10.4018/978-1-4666-2940-0.ch011

such huge databases is a daunting job, not only in terms of money and time, but also with respect to the quality of annotation.

When specifically considering the issue of video indexing and retrieval applications, because of the large amount of information typically included in a video document, a first phase that needs to be performed is to structure the video into its constitutive elements: chapters, scenes, shots and keyframes This paper specifically tackles the issue of video structuring and proposes a complete and automatic segmentation methodology.

Figure 1 presents the proposed analysis framework. The main contributions proposed in this paper concern: an enhanced shot boundary detection method, a fast static storyboard technique and a new scene/chapter detection approach.

The rest of this paper is organized as follows. After a brief recall of some basic theoretical aspects regarding the graph partition model exploited, we introduce the proposed shot detection algorithm. Then, we describe the keyframe selection procedure. The following section introduces a novel scene/chapter extraction algorithm based on temporal distances and merging strategies. The experimental results obtained are then presented and discussed in details. Finally, we conclude the paper and open some perspectives of future work.

SHOT BOUNDARY DETECTION

Related Work

The first methods introduced in the literature were based on pixels color variation between successive frames (Zhang *et al.*, 1993; Lienhart *et al.*, 1997). Such algorithms offer the advantage of simplicity but present serious limitations. Thus, in the presence of large moving objects or in the case of camera motion, a significant number of pixels change their intensity values, leading to false alarms. In addition, such methods are highly

sensitive to noise that may be introduced during the acquisition process.

Among the simplest, most effective and common used methods, the color histogram comparison and its numerous variations assume that frames from the same shot have similar histograms (Yuan *et al.*, 2007; Gargi *et al.*, 2000). Histogram-based methods are more robust to noise and motion than pixel-based approaches due to the spatial invariance properties. However, they also present some strong limitations. First of all, let us mention the sensitivity to abrupt changes in light intensity: two images taken in the same place but with different lightening conditions will be described by distinct histograms. Furthermore, a color histogram does not take into account the spatial information of an image, so two identical histograms could actually correspond to two visual completely different images, but with similar colors and appearance probability (Matsumoto *et al.*, 2006).

Let us also cite the methods based on edges/contours (Zabih *et al.*, 1995). Such methods are useful in removing false alarms caused by abrupt illumination change, since they are less sensitive to light intensity variation then color histogram

Figure 1. The proposed framework for high level video segmentation

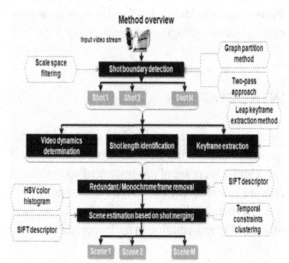

(Yuan *et al.*, 2007). However, their related detection performances are inferior to the histogram-based approaches.

Algorithms using motion features (Porter *et al.*, 2000) or developed in the compressed domain (Fernando *et al.*, 2001) propose an interesting alternative solution to pixel and histogram-based methods. Notably, such approaches are fairly robust with respect to camera and object motion. In addition, in this case, the detection is performed only on a partial decoded video stream therefore the computation time is reduced. However, such methods lead to inferior precision rates when compared to other methods because of incoherencies in the motion vector field. The compromise solution consists in decompressing the data up to a certain level of detail (Truong *et al.*, 2007).

In the following section, we propose an improved shot boundary detection algorithm, based on the graph partition (GP) model firstly introduced in Yuan *et al.* (2007) and considered as state of the art technique for both types of transitions: abrupt (cuts) and gradual (e.g., fades and wipes).

Graph Partition Model

The graph partition model was firstly introduced in Hendrickson *et al.* (2000). The technique can be applied for video temporal segmentation by considering the input image sequence as an undirected weighted graph. In this context, we denote with G a set (V, E) where V represents the set of vertices, $V = \{v_1, v_2, ..., v_n\}$, and $E \subset V \times V$ denote a set of pair-wise relationships, called edges. An edge $e_{i,j} = \{v_i, v_j\}$ is established between two adjacent nodes.

A shot boundary detection process relaying on a graph partition system represents each video frame as a node in the hierarchical structure, connected with the other vertexes by edges (e_{ij}). The weight (w_{ij}) of an edge (e_{ij}), expresses the similarity between the corresponding nodes (v_i and v_j). In our work, we have adopted, as visual similarity

measure the chi-square distance between color histograms in the HSV color space (Equation 1):

$$w_{i,j} = \sum_k \frac{\left(H_k^i - H_k^j\right)^2}{H_k^i + H_k^j} \times e^{|i-j|} \quad , \qquad (1)$$

where H^i denotes the HSV color histogram associate to frame *i*. The exponential term in Equation (1) takes into account the temporal distance between frames: if two frames are located at an important temporal distance it is highly improbable to belong to the same shot.

The video is segmented using a sliding window that selects a constant number of N frames, centered on the current frame *n*. The window size should be large enough to capture usual transitions. In practice, such transitions are most often greater than 10–15 frames. Thus in our work, we have considered a value of $N = 25$ frames.

For each position of the sliding window, the system computes a sub-graph G_n and its associated similarity matrix that stores all the chi-square distances between the frames considered for analysis at the current moment. Let $V_n = \{v_n^1, v_n^2, ..., v_n^N\}$ denote the vertices of graph G_n at frame *n*. For each integer $k \in \{1, ..., N-1\}$, a partition of the graph G_n into two sets $(A_n^k = v_n^1, ..., v_n^k)$, $(B_n^k = v_n^{k+1}, ..., v_n^N)$ is defined.

To each partition, the following objective function is associated with:

$$Mcut\left(A_n^k, B_n^k\right) = \frac{cut\left(A_n^k, B_n^k\right)}{assoc(A_n^k)} + \frac{cut\left(A_n^k, B_n^k\right)}{assoc\left(B_n^k\right)},$$
$$(2)$$

where *cut* and *assoc* respectively denote the measures of cut (i.e., dissimilarity between the two elements of the partition) and association (i.e., homogeneity of each element of the partition) and are defined as described in (3) and (4):

$$assoc\left(A_n^k\right) = \sum_{i,j \in A_n^k} w_{i,j} ; assoc\left(B_n^k\right) = \sum_{i,j \in B_n^k} w_{i,j},$$

$$(3)$$

$$cut\left(A_n^k, B_n^k\right) = \sum_{i \in A_n^k, j \in B_n^k} w_{i,j} , \qquad (4)$$

The objective is to determine an optimal value for the k parameter that maximizes the $Mcut\left(A_n^k, B_n^k\right)$ function defined in Equation (2). This optimization requires to maximize the *cut* function, while simultaneously minimizing both *association* values involved in Equation 2. The optimal value, determined for each image n of the video flow, is stored in a *dissimilarity vector* $v = (v(n))$ constructed as follows:

$$v\left(n\right) = \max_{k \in \{1,...,N-1\}} \left\{Mcut\left(A_n^k, B_n^k\right)\right\} , \qquad (5)$$

Figure 2 illustrates the *dissimilarity vector* obtained for different values N of the temporal analysis window.

A straightforward manner to identify a shot boundary is determine the peaks of the dissimilarity vector v that are higher than a considered threshold T_{shot}.

However, in practice the selection of the threshold parameter T_{shot} is highly difficult due mostly to various visual content variation caused by camera and large object movement, or by changes in the lightening conditions. An inadequate threshold may thus lead to both false alarms and missed detections. For these reasons, in contrast with Yuan

Figure 2. Local minimum vector variation with different window sizes (a. 10 frames, b. 15 frame, c. 25 frames, and d. 35 frames)

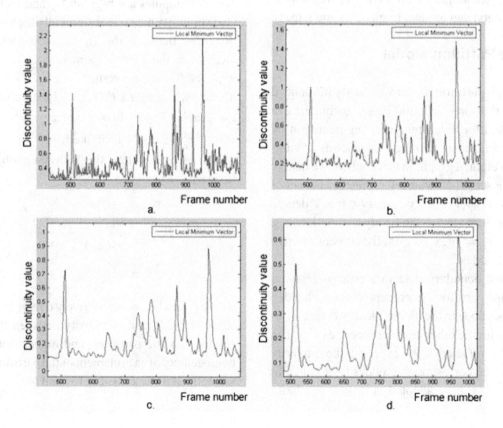

et al. (2007) and Hendrickson *et al.* (2000), we propose to perform the analysis within the scale space of the derivatives of the local minimum vector *v*, as described in the next section.

Scale Space Filtering

The discrete derivative *v'(n)* of the dissimilarity vector *v(n)*, can be defined in the discrete space based on the first order finite difference as:

$$v'(n) = v(n) - v(n-1), \tag{6}$$

Based on this simple relation we can construct a set of cumulative sums $\left\{ v'_k(n) \right\}_{k=1}^{N}$ on the derivative signal up the sliding window size (*N*) based on the following equation:

$$v'_k \left(n \right) = \sum_{p=0}^{k} v'(n-p), \tag{7}$$

The resulted signals *v'$_k$(n)* represent low-pass filtered versions of the derivative signal *v'(n)*, with increasingly larger kernels, and constitute

our scale space analysis. After summing all the above equations, within a window of analysis, *v'$_k$(n)* can be simply expressed as:

$$v'_k \left(n \right) = v \left(n \right) - v \left(n-k \right); \tag{8}$$

Figure 3 presents the dissimilarity signal obtained at different scales. As it can be observed, smoother and smoother versions of the original signal are produced, which can be useful to remove undesired variations caused by camera/large object motions.

The peaks which are persistent at multiple resolutions correspond to large variations in the feature vector and are used to detect the shot transitions.

The selection of the identified peaks is performed based on a different non-linear filtering operation that is applied at each scale of analysis, defined as described by the following equation.

$$d \left(n \right) = \max_{k} \left\{ \left| v'_k(n) \right| \cdot h(k) \right\} = \max_{k} \left\{ \left| v \left(n \right) - v(n-k) \right| \cdot h(k) \right\}, \tag{9}$$

Figure 3. The set of scale space derivatives obtained

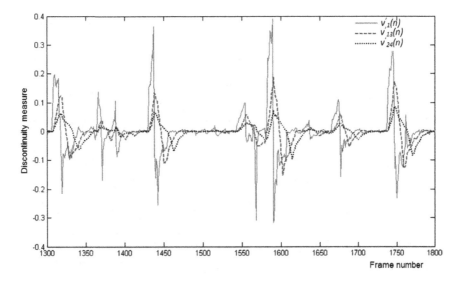

where the weights $h(k)$ are defined as:

$$h(k) = \begin{cases} e^{-k}, & k \in \left[0, \dfrac{N-1}{2}\right] \\ e^{N-1-k}, & k \in \left[\dfrac{N+1}{2}, N\right] \end{cases}, \quad (10)$$

The shot boundaries detection process is applied directly on the $d(n)$ signal. The weighting mechanism adopted, given by the $h(n)$ function, privileges derivative signals located at the extremities of the scale space analysis (Figure 4). In this way, solely peaks that are persistent through all scales are retained and considered as transitions.

The second step of the proposed shot boundary detection system is focused on reducing the computational complexity of the proposed shot detector. In this context, a two pass analysis technique is introduced.

Two Pass Analysis Approach

The principle consists of successively applying two different analysis stages.

In a first stage, the objective is to determine video segments that can be reliable classified as belonging to the same shot. In order to identify such segments, a simple and fast chi-square comparison on HSV color histogram between each two successive frames is performed. In this step we can identify also abrupt transition that characterized by large discontinuity values (Figure 5).

Concerning the detection process we have considered two thresholds. The first one, denoted by T_{g1} has to be selected high enough to avoid the false positives. The second threshold T_{g2} is used in order to determine uncertain time intervals. If the dissimilarity values are above the second threshold ($D(I_t, I_{t-1}) > T_{g2}$), and also inferior to T_{g1} a more detailed analysis is required and the method passes to the second step. All frames presenting lower similarity values (i.e., smaller than T_{g2}) are classified as belonging to the same shot.

In a second stage, for the remaining uncertain intervals (for which a reliable classification could not be made only by performing a simple chi-square distance analysis), we apply the graph partition method with scale space filtering previously described.

In this manner, the total number of images that require a detailed analysis is considerably reduced. The second phase helps us differentiate between actual gradual transition and local variations in the feature vector caused by object or camera motion.

Figure 4. False alarms due to flash lights, large object/camera motion are avoided when using the scale-space filtering approach

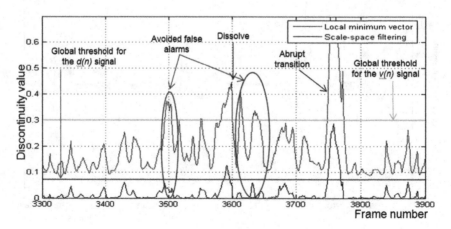

Figure 5. Classification of video in certain/uncertain segments

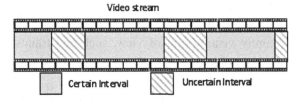

For each detected shot, we aim at determining a set of keyframes that can represent in a significant manner the associated content.

KEYFRAME EXTRACTION

Related Work

One of the first attempts to automate the keyframe extraction process was to consisted in selecting as a keyframe the first, the middle or the last frame (or even a random one) of each detected shot (Hanjalic *et al.*, 1999). However, while being sufficient for stationary shots, a single frame does not provide an acceptable representation of the visual content in the case of dynamic sequences that exhibit large camera/object motion. Therefore, it is necessary to consider more sophisticated approaches (Fu *et al.*, 2009).

The challenge in automatic keyframe extraction is given by the necessity of adapting the selected keyframes to the underlying content, while maintaining, as much as possible, the original message and removing all the redundant information. In Zhang *et al.* (1999), the first keyframe is set as the first frame in a shot appearing after a shot boundary. A set of additional keyframes is determined based on the variation in color/motion appearance with respect to this first frame. However, the approach does not take into account of the case of gradual transitions, where the first keyframe is not an optimal choice and might negatively influence the whole keyframe selection process.

A clustering algorithm (Girgensohn *et al.*, 1999) is the natural solution to solve the problems described above. The limitations here are related to the threshold parameters that need to be specified and which have a strong impact on both the cluster density and on the related computational cost.

A mosaic-based approach can generate, in an intuitive manner, a panoramic image of all informational content existed in a video stream. The summarization procedure in this case is based on the assumption that there is only one dominant motion among all the others various object motions found in the sequence (Aner *et al.*, 2002). Mosaic-based representations of shot / scene include more information and are visually richer than regular keyframe approaches. However, creating mosaics is possible solely for videos with specific camera motion, such as pan, zoom or tilling.

In the case of movies with complex camera effects such as a succession of background/foreground changes, mosaic-based representations return less satisfactory results due to physical location inconsistency. Furthermore, mosaics can blur certain foreground objects and thus present a degraded image quality.

In our case, we have developed a keyframe representation system that extracts a variable number of images from each detected shot, adaptively with the visual content variation.

Leap-Extraction Method

For each detected shot, a first keyframe is defined as the frame located N frames away after the detected transition (i.e., the beginning of the shot). Let us recall that N denotes the window size used for the shot boundary detection method. In this way, we make sure that the first selected keyframe does not belong to a gradual effect.

In the second phase, we developed a *leap-extraction method* that analyzes only the frames spaced by multiple integers of window size N and not the entire set of frames as in the case of the reference techniques introduced in Zhang *et al.* (1999) and Rasheed *et al.* (2005). Then, in order to select a new keyframe the current image is compared (i.e., chi-square distance of HSV color histograms) with all the keyframes already extracted. If the visual dissimilarity is above a pre-established threshold the new image is marked as representative and is added to the set of keyframes (Figure 6).

The leap keyframe extraction method takes advantage of the shot boundary detection system that computes the graph partition within a sliding window of analysis. In this way, the proposed method ensures that all the relevant information will be taken into account. As it can be observed, the number of keyframes necessary to describe the informational content of a shot is not *a priori* fixed, but automatically adapted to the dynamics of the content.

An additional post-processing step is introduced. The goal is to eliminate, from the selected set of keyframes, all the blank images that might appear (Chasanis *et al.*, 2008). Such images can appear due to gradual transitions developed over a large number of frames or to false alarms. They are often encountered in real life videos and it is necerssaryto remove them in order to ensure the quality of the detected summary (Li *et al.*, 2010). . The adopted technique exploits a contour-based approach. Here, the total number of edges detected in a keyframe is analyzed in order to determine such blank images.

A final contribution concerns the shot clustering within scenes.

SCENE SEGMENTATION

A scene is defined in the Webster's dictionary as follows: "a subdivision of an act or a play in which the setting is fixed, the time is continuous and the action is developed in one place".

Such a definition involves some purely semantic elements, related to the unity of time, place and action that are difficult to determine automatically when performing solely vision-based analysis. This makes the scene detection process a highly difficult issue.

In addition, in some circumstances and from a purely visual point of view, such constraints may not hold, as in the case of scenes with large camera/object motion.

For all these reasons, elaborating methods for pertinent and automatic scene identification is still an open issue of research. Let us first analyze how these aspects are treated in the rich literature dedicated to this subject.

Related Work

In Rasheed *et al.* (2005), authors transform the detection problem into a graph partition task. Each shot is represented as a node being connected with the others through edges based on the visual similarity and the temporal proximity between the shots. A new measure, so-called *shot goodness* (SG), is here introduced. The SG measure quantifies the degree of representativeness of each shot, based on its temporal length, visual activity and action content.

In Hanjalic *et al.* (1999), the detection process relays on the concept of logical story units (LSU) and inter-shot dissimilarity measure. The LSU

Figure 6. Keyframe selection based on leap-extraction technique

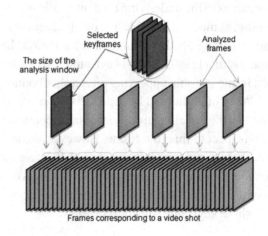

definition is based on the temporal consistency of the visual content assuming that similar elements (e.g., people, faces, locations, etc.) appear and some of them even repeat. So, a LSU gathers a set of successive shots, connected by overlapping links. The shots regrouped in a same LSU present similarity values superior to an adaptive threshold set by the user.

Different approaches (Ariki *et al.*, 2003) propose to use both audio features and low level visual descriptors in order to detect scenes separately based on both characteristics. In this case, two types of boundaries are detected and used to make a final decision. A scene is defined based on audio sequences as a succession of shots in which a similar audio pattern occurs (e.g., dialog between two characters, cheering crowd, etc.) (Truong *et al.*, 2007). The audio segments are divided in: background and foreground. Only the foreground segments are analyzed in order to make a decision because the background soundtrack is assumed not to carry any information that may be relevant to the film story.

In Ngo *et al.* (2002), color and motion information are integrated in order to take a decision. The motion analysis is based on the tensor determination in order to establish the slices (set of 2D images in a *x*, *y* *t* space) with horizontal and vertical positions.

A mosaic-based approach is introduced in Aner *et al.* (2002). The value of each pixel in the mosaic is defined as the median value of pixels corresponding to all the frames mapped in the mosaic image. The scene boundaries are determined after segmenting the mosaic in small regions and analyzing the similarities between such adjacent regions.

More recent techniques (Chasanis *et al.*, 2009; Zhu *et al.*, 2009) introduce in the analysis process useful concepts such as temporal constraints and visual similarity.

However, the existing approaches show strong limitations and present limited precision and recall rates (77% to 82%).

In order to deal with the complexity of the scene detection task this paper proposes a novel approach, based on a hierarchical clustering algorithm with and temporal constraints.

Scene Detection Method

The algorithm takes as input the set of keyframes detected for the whole set of video shots as described in the previously. A clustering process is then applied. The principle consists of iteratively grouping shots encountered in a temporal sliding analysis window that satisfy simultaneously a set of similarity constraints.

The size of the sliding window (denoted by *dist*) is adaptively determined, based on the input video stream dynamics and is proportional to the average number of frames per shot. The parameter *dist* can be computed as:

$$dist = \alpha \cdot \frac{Total\,number\,of\,frames}{Total\,number\,of\,shots}, \qquad (11)$$

where α denotes a user-defined parameter. We consider further that a scene is completely described by its constituent shots:

$$S_l : s\left(S_l\right) = \left\{s_{l,p}\right\}_{p=1}^{N_l} \rightarrow \left\{\left\{f_{l,p,i}\right\}_{i=1}^{n_{l,p}}\right\}_{p=1}^{N_l}, \qquad (12)$$

$S_1 = \{S_1\} = \left\{\{k_i^{s_1}\}_i^{n_i}\right\}$ where S_l denotes the lth video scene, N_l the number of shots included in scene S_l, $s_{l,p}$ the pth shot in scene S_l, and $f_{l,p,i}$ the ith keyframe of shot $s_{l,p}$ containing $n_{l,p}$ keyframes.

The proposed scene change detection algorithm based on shot clustering consists of the following steps:

Step 1: Initialization – The technique starts by assigning the first shot of the input video stream to the first scene S_l. Scene counter l is set to 1.

Step 2: Shot to scene comparison – The next shot being analyzed (i.e., a shot that is not assigned to any already created scene) is considered as the current shot and denoted by s_{crt}: the technique determines The subset Ω of all anterior scenes located at a temporal distance inferior to the parameter *dist* with respect to the current shot s_{crt} is then determined. The visual similarity between each scene S_k in Ω and the shot s_{crt} is computed as described by the following relation:

$$\forall S_k \in \copyright, SceneShotSim\left(s_{crt}, S_k\right) =$$

$$\frac{n_{matched}}{n_{k,p} \cdot N_k \cdot n_{crt}} \quad , \quad (13)$$

where n_{crt} is the number of keyframes of the considered shot and $n_{matched}$ represents the number of *matched* keyframes of the scene S_k. A keyframe from scene S_k is considered to be matched with a keyframe from shot s_{crt} if a given *visual similarity measure* between the two keyframes is superior to a threshold T_{group}. Let us note that a keyframe from the scene S_k can be matched with multiple frames from the current shot.

Two different types of visual similarity measures have been considered:

1. The total number of common interest points established based on a SIFT descriptor

(Lowe, 2004) and matched with the help of a KD-tree technique (Vedaldi *et al.*, 2010), and (2) the chi-square distance between HSV color histograms.

2. The current shot s_{crt} is identified to be similar to a scene S_k if the following condition is satisfied:

$$SceneShotSim\left(S_k, s_{crt}\right) \geq 0.5, (14)$$

The relation 13 expresses that at least half of the keyframes belonging to the current shot s_{crt} need to be similar with the scene's S_k keyframes.

In this case, the current shot s_{crt} is clustered in the scene S_k. In the same time, all the shots between the current shot and the scene S_k will also be attached to scene S_k and marked as *neutralized*. Then all scenes containing neutralized shots are automatically removed, in the sense that they are attached to the scene S_k. The list of detected scenes is consequently updated.

The neutralization process allows us to identify the most representative shots for a current scene (Figure 7), which are the remaining non-neutralized shots. In this way, the influence of outlier shots which might correspond to some punctual digressions from the main action in the considered scene is minimized.

If the condition described in Equation (13) is not satisfied, go to step 3.

Figure 7. Neutralizing shots (marked with red) based on visual similarity

Step 3: Shot by shot comparison – Here, we determine the set of *highly similar* shots (i.e., with a similarity value at least two times bigger than the grouping threshold T_{group}). Here, for the current shot (s_{crt}) we compute its visual similarity with respect to all shots of all scenes included in the sub-set Ω determined at step 2. If the shot s_{crt} is found as being highly similar with a scene in Ω, then it is merged with the corresponding scene, together with all the intermediate shots. If s_{crt} is found highly similar to multiple scenes, than the scene which is the most far away from the considered shot is retained.

Both the current shot and all its highly similar matches are unmarked and for the following clustering process will contribute as normal, non-neutralized shots (Figure 8).

This step ensures that shots that are highly similar with other shots in a previous scene are be grouped into this scene. In this way, the number of false alarms (i.e., false scene transitions) is considerably reduced.

Step 4: Creation of a new scene – If none of the conditions introduced in steps 2 and 3 are satisfied, then a new scene, containing the current shot (s_{crt}), is created.
Step 5: Refinement –The scenes containing only one shot are automatically deleted and their

shot is attached to the adjacent scenes based on the highest similarity value. In the case of the first scene, the corresponding shot will be grouped to the following one by default.

The grouping threshold T_{group} is established adaptively with respect to the input video stream visual content variation, for each visual similarity measure considered (i.e., HSV color histogram or interest points). Thus, T_{group} is defined as as the average chi-square distance / number of interest points between the current keyframe and all anterior keyframes located at a temporal distance smaller then *dist*.

EXPERIMENTAL RESULTS

Shot Boundary Detection

In order to evaluate our shot boundary detection algorithm, we have considered a sub-set of videos from the "TRECVID 2001 and 2002 campaigns", which are available on Internet (www.archive.org and www.open-video.org). The videos are mostly documentaries that vary in style and date of production, while including multiple types of both camera/object motion (Table 1).

As evaluation metrics, we have considered the traditional Recall (R) and Precision (P) measures, defined as follows:

Figure 8. Unmarking shots based on high similarity values (red – neutralized shots; green – non-neutralized shots)

Table 1. Movie database features

Video Title	Number of Frames	Number of Transition	Abrupt Transition	Gradual Transition			File Name
				Fade In / Out	Dissolve	Other Type	
NAD 55	26104	185	107	21	57	-	NASA Anniversary
NAD 57	10006	73	45	6	22	-	NASA Anniversary
NAD 58	13678	85	40	7	38	-	NASA Anniversary
UGS09	23918	213	44	25	144	-	Wrestling with Uncertainty
UGS01	32072	180	86	6	88	-	Exotic Terrane
23585a	14797	153	80	2	71	-	Adelante Cubanos
10558a	19981	141	79	20	42	1	Desert Venture
06011	23918	153	81	26	46	-	The Egg and US
TOTAL	**164474**	**1183**	**562**	**113**	**508**	**1**	

$$R = \frac{D}{D + MD}; P = \frac{D}{D + FA}; F1 = \frac{2 \cdot P \cdot R}{R + P}. \quad (15)$$

Here, D is the number of the detected shot boundaries, MD is the number of missed detections, and FA the number of false alarms. Ideally, both recall and precision should be equal to 100%, which correspond to the case where all existing shot boundaries are correctly detected, without any false alarm.

Table 2 presents the precision, recall and F1 rates obtained for the reference graph partition shot boundary detection method proposed by Yuan *et*

al. (2007), while Table 3 summarizes the detection performances of our proposed scale-space filtering approach.

The results presented clearly demonstrate the superiority of our approach, for both types of abrupt (Figure 9) and gradual transitions (Figure 10). The global gains in recall and precision rates are of 9.8% and 7.4%, respectively (Figure 11).

Moreover, when considering the case of gradual transitions, the improvements are even more significant. In this case, the recall and precision rates are respectively of 94,1% and 88,3% (with respect to R = 81.5% and P = 79% for the

Table 2. Precision, recall and F1 rates obtained for the Yuan et al. algorithms

Video Title	Abrupt Transitions			Gradual Transitions			All Transitions		
	R	P	F1	R	P	F1	R	P	F1
NAD 55	0.9626	0.824	0.8879	0.8717	0.7391	0.7999	0.9243	0.788	0.8507
NAD 57	0.8666	0.8666	0.8666	0.7857	0.8148	0.7999	0.8472	0.8472	0.8472
NAD 58	0.95	0.8444	0.8940	0.7777	0.6603	0.7142	0.8588	0.7448	0.7977
UGS09	0.9727	0.8431	0.9032	0.8106	0.7740	0.7918	0.8866	0.7894	0.8351
UGS01	0.9069	0.8472	0.8760	0.8404	0.7523	0.7939	0.8722	0.8579	0.8649
23585a	0.75	0.923	0.8275	0.7945	0.9666	0.8721	0.7712	0.944	0.8488
10558a	0.8607	0.8717	0.8661	0.7741	0.923	0.8420	0.8226	0.8923	0.8560
06011	0.9135	0.9024	0.9079	0.8333	0.7228	0.7741	0.8756	0.8121	0.8426
TOTAL	**0.8950**	**0.8627**	**0.8785**	**0.8164**	**0.7812**	**0.7984**	**0.8610**	**0.8198**	**0.8398**
P – Precision ; R – Recall ; F1 – F1 norm									

Table 3. Precision, recall and F1 rates obtained for the scale-space filtering algorithm

Video Title	Abrupt Transitions			Gradual Transitions			All Transitions		
	R	P	F1	R	P	F1	R	P	F1
NAD 55	1	0.922	0.9594	0.935	0.802	0.8634	0.972	0.869	0.9176
NAD 57	0.955	0.955	0.955	0.857	0.888	0.8722	0.917	0.931	0.9239
NAD 58	0.95	0.904	0.9264	0.955	0.811	0.8771	0.952	0.852	0.8992
UGS09	1	0.916	0.9561	0.941	0.919	0.9298	0.953	0.918	0.9351
UGS01	0.976	0.884	0.9277	0.989	0.861	0.9205	0.983	0.871	0.9236
23585a	0.937	0.949	0.9429	0.917	0.985	0.9497	0.928	0.965	0.9461
10558a	0.962	0.894	0.9267	0.967	0.857	0.9086	0.964	0.877	0.9184
06011	0.938	0.926	0.9319	0.944	0.871	0.9060	0.941	0.904	0.9221
TOTAL	**0.9661**	**0.917**	**0.9409**	**0.945**	**0.877**	**0.9097**	**0.955**	**0.896**	**0.9245**
P – Precision ; R – Recall ; F1 – F1 norm									

Figure 9. Recall (a.) precision (b.) and F1 norm (c.) rates when detecting abrupt transitions for: a. Yuan et al. algorithm (blue), b. the novel scale space derivative technique (red)

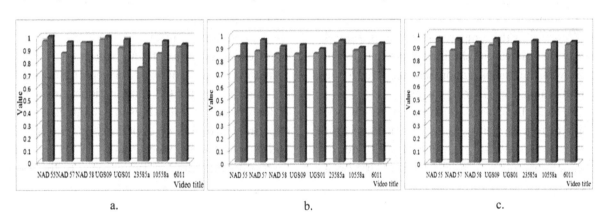

a.   b.   c.

Figure 10. Recall (a.) precision (b.) and F1 norm (c.) rates when detecting gradual transitions for: a. Yuan et al. algorithm (blue), b. the novel scale space derivative technique (red)

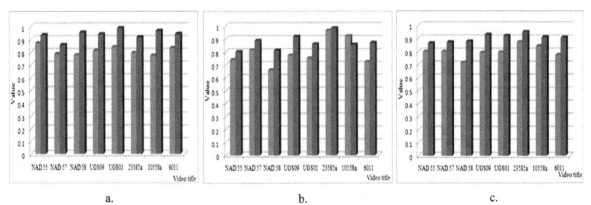

a.   b.   c.

Figure 11. Recall (a.) precision (b.) and F1 norm (c.) rates when detecting all types of transitions for: a. Yuan et al. algorithm (blue), b. the proposed technique (red)

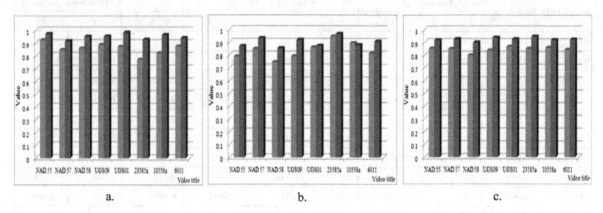

a.   b.   c.

reference method) (Yuan *et al.*, 2007). This shows that the scale space filtering approach makes it possible to eliminate the errors caused by camera/object motion.

Concerning the computational aspects, Table 4 synthesizes the results obtained, in computational time, with the two-pass approach compared to the initial scale-space filtering method.

Here, for the chi-square, frame-to-frame HSV color histogram comparison we considered for the first threshold (T_{g1}) a value of 0.9 to detect abrupt transition, while the second (T_{g2}) has been set to 0.35.

Such values ensure the same overall performance of the shot boundary detection as the multi-resolution graph partition method applied on the entire video stream. A smaller value for the T_{g1} will determine an increase in the number of false alarms while a higher values for T_{g2} will increase the number of missed detected transitions.

Table 5 presents the computational times for different values for the threshold parameter. The experimental results were obtained for T_{g1} constant and T_{g2} variable and vice-versa.

Results presented in Table 5 lead to the following conclusion. With the increase of the

Table 4. Computation time for GP and two-pass approach

Video Title	Video Duration Time (s)	Two-Pass Approach Time (s)	Graph Partition Method Time (s)	Gain (%)
NAD55	871	153	221	**30.7**
NAD57	417	72	107	**32.7**
NAD58	455	102	141	**27.5**
UGS09	1768	355	457	**22.3**
UGS01	1337	292	399	**26.8**
23585a	615	125	155	**19.3**
10558a	833	169	225	**25.3**
06011	997	168	215	**21.8**
TOTAL	**7293**	**1436**	**1920**	**25.2**

Table 5. Computation time for different values of the threshold parameters

Threshold	Value	NAD55 Time (s)	NAD57 Time (s)	NAD58 Time (s)	UGS09 Time (s)	UGS01 Time (s)	23585a Time (s)	10558a Time (s)	06011 Time (s)
T_{g1}	0.05	214	101	135	450	391	151	223	208
	0.1	207	93	131	439	376	148	215	203
	0.15	197	89	127	426	361	144	201	193
	0.2	188	85	119	411	342	138	188	185
	0.25	173	81	111	399	319	134	175	178
	0.3	161	75	105	373	305	129	172	171
	0.35	153	72	102	355	292	125	169	168
T_{g2}	0.9	153	72	102	355	292	125	169	168
	0.95	162	79	107	367	306	128	177	172
	1	166	83	114	378	315	133	184	182
	1.05	174	88	118	389	332	137	193	189
	1.1	183	95	123	404	345	141	202	194
	1.15	192	101	132	421	368	146	211	199
	1.2	218	103	138	448	389	149	221	211

threshold T_{g1} and respectively with the reduction of the T_{g2} the computational time is decreasing. Let us also mention that the values parameter T_{g1} should be inferior to 0,35 and the value of T_{g2} greater than 0.9 in order to maintain the same performances in terms of detection efficiency.

Leap Keyframe Extraction

For each detected shot we applied the leap extraction method described. Figure 12 presents a set of keyframes detected from of a complex shot which exhibits important visual content variation (because of very large camera motion). In this case,

the proposed algorithm automatically determines a set of 6 keyframes.

Table 6 presents the computational time[1] necessary to extract keyframes for two methods: (1) the proposed leap-extraction strategy, and (2) the state-of-the-art method (Zhang *et al.*, 1999; Rasheed *et al.*, 2005) based on direct comparison of all adjacent frames inside a shot. Let us note that the obtained key-frames are quite equivalent in both cases.

The results presented in Table 6 demonstrate that the proposed approach makes it possible to significantly reduce the computational complexity for the keyframe detection algorithms, for

Figure 12. Shot boundary detection and keyframe extraction

Table 6. Computation time for LEM and CE approach

Video Title	Video Duration Time (s)	LEM Time (s)	CE Time (s)	Gain (%)
Seinfeld	1313	297	434	31.56
Two and a half men	1200	384	509	24.55
Prison Break	2512	990	1260	21.42
Ally McBeal	2607	1269	1642	22.71
Sex and the city	1801	854	1067	19.96
Friends	1506	309	371	16.71
TOTAL	**10936**	**4103**	**5283**	**22.33**
LEM- Leap Extraction Method, CE – Classical Extraction				

equivalent performances. Thus, the leap keyframe extraction method leads to a gain of 22% in computational time when compared to the state of the art method.

Scene/DVD Chapter Extraction

The validation of our scene extraction method has been performed on a corpus of 6 sitcoms and 6 Hollywood movies (Tables 6 and 7) also used for evaluation purposes in the state of the art algorithms presented in Rasheed *et al.* (2005), Chasanis *et al.* (2009), and Zhu *et al.* (2009).

Figure 13 illustrates some examples of scene boundary detection, obtained with the HSV-based approach.

We can observe that in this case the two scenes of the movie have been correctly identified.

In order to establish an objective evaluation, for the considered database, a ground truth has been established by human observers. Table 7 summarizes the scene detection results obtained with both visual similarity measures adopted (i.e., SIFT descriptors and HSV color histograms).

As it can be observed, the detection efficiency is comparable in both cases. The α parameter has been set here to a value of 7.

The average precision and recall rates are the following:

- R=88% and P=78%, for the SIFT-based approach, and

Figure 13. Detected scenes

Table 7. Evaluation of the scene extraction: precision, recall and F1 rates

Video Name	Ground Truth Scenes	SIFT Descriptor						HSV Color Histogram					
		D	FA	MD	R (%)	P (%)	F1 (%)	D	FA	MD	R (%)	P (%)	F1 (%)
Sienfeld	24	19	1	5	95.00	79.16	86.36	20	0	4	100	83.33	90.88
Two and a half men	21	18	0	3	100	81.81	90.00	17	2	4	89.47	80.95	85.01
Prison Break	39	31	3	8	91.17	79.48	84.93	33	0	6	100	84.61	91.66
Ally McBeal	32	28	11	4	71.79	87.50	78.87	24	4	8	84.00	75.00	79.24
Sex and the city	20	17	0	3	100	85.00	91.89	15	1	5.	93.75	75.00	83.33
Friends	17	17	7	0	70.83	100	82.92	17	7	0	70.83	100	82.92
5th Element	63	55	24	8	69.62	87.30	77.46	54	10	9	83.05	84.48	83.76
Ace -Ventura	36	34	11	2	75.55	94.44	83.95	29	2	7	92.85	78.78	85.24
Lethal Weapon 4	67	63	39	4	61.76	94.02	74.55	64	25	3	71.97	95.52	82.05
Terminator 2	66	61	11	5	84.72	92.42	88.41	60	7	6	89.55	90.90	90.22
The Mask	44	40	5	4	88.88	90.91	89.88	38	7	6	84.44	86.36	85.39
Home Alone 2	68	56	6	12	90.32	82.35	86.15	57	5	11	90.90	81.96	86.20
TOTAL	**497**	**439**	**118**	**58**	**88.32**	**78.81**	**83.29**	**428**	**70**	**69**	**86.11**	**85.94**	**86.02**

D – Detected ; FA – False Alarms ; MD – Missed Detected; P – Precision ; R – Recall ; F1 – F1 norm

- R=86% and P=85%, for the HSV histogram approach.

These results demonstrate the superiority of the proposed scene detection method with respect to existing state of the art techniques (Rasheed *et al.*, 2005; Chasanis *et al.*, 2009; Zhu *et al.*, 2009), which provide precision/recall rates between 82% and 77%.

We also analyzed the impact of the different temporal constraints lengths on the scene detection performances. Thus, Figure 14 presents the precision, recall and F1 scores obtained for various values of the α parameter.

As it can be noticed, a value between 5 and 10 returns quite similar results in terms of the overall efficiency.

Let us also observe that increasing the α parameter lead to lower recall rates. That means that for higher values of the α parameter, different scenes are grouped within a same one. In the same time, the number of false alarms (i.e., false scene breaks) is reduced.

This observation led us to investigate the utility of our approach for a slightly different application, related to DVD chapter detection. For the considered Hollywood videos, the DVD chapters were identified by movie producers and correspond to access points in the considered video. The DVD chapters are highly semantic video units with low level of detail containing a scene ore multiple scenes that are grouped together based on a purely semantic meaning.

The value of the α parameter has been here set to 10.

The average recall (R) and precision (P) rates obtained in this case (Figure 15) are the following:

- R=93% and P=62%, for the SIFT-based approach, and
- R=68% and P=87%, for the HSV histogram approach.

Figure 14. Precision, recall and F1 scores obtained for different α values

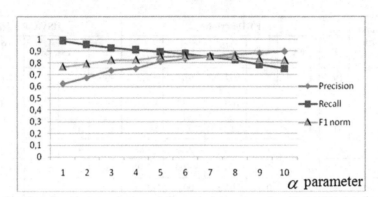

Figure 15. Recall, precision and F1 norm rates when extracting DVD chapter using: a. HSV color histogram, b. interest points extracted based on SIFT descriptor

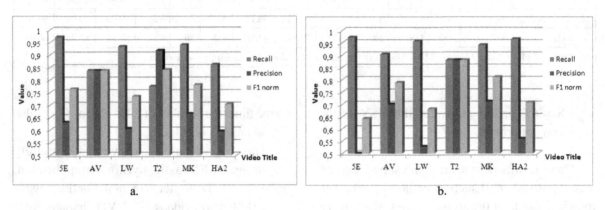

Table 8. Evaluation of the DVD chapter extraction: precision, recall and F1 rates

Video Name	Ground Truth Scenes	SIFT Descriptor						HSV Color Histogram					
		D	FA	MD	R (%)	P (%)	F1 (%)	D	FA	MD	R (%)	P (%)	F1 (%)
5th Element	37	36	39	1	97.29	48.00	64.28	35	25	2	58.33	94.59	72.16
Ace -Ventura	31	28	12	3	90.32	70.00	78.87	25	5	6	83.87	80.64	82.23
Lethal Weapon 4	46	44	41	2	95.65	52.87	68.09	43	28	3	60.56	93.47	73.5
Terminator 2	58	51	7	7	87.93	87.93	87.93	45	4	13	91.83	77.58	84.11
The Mask	34	32	12	2	94.11	71.11	81.01	32	16	2	66.66	94.11	78.04
Home Alone 2	29	28	22	1	96.55	56.00	70.88	25	17	4	59.52	86.21	70.41
TOTAL	**235**	**219**	**133**	**16**	**93.19**	**62.42**	**74.76**	**205**	**95**	**30**	**68.33**	**87.23**	**76.66**
D – Detected ; FA – False Alarms ; MD – Missed Detected; P – Precision ; R – Recall ; F1 – F1 norm													

Such a result is quite competitive with the state of the art techniques introduced in Rasheed *et al.* (2005), Chasanis *et al.* (2009), and Zhu *et al.* (2009) which yield precision/recall rates varying between 65% and 72%.

The obtained chapter detection results, with precision, recall and F1 rates are further detailed in Table 8.

The analysis of the obtained results leads to the following conclusions.

The keyframe similarity based on HSV color histogram is much faster than the SIFT extraction process. In addition, it can be successfully used when feature detection and matching becomes difficult due to the complete change of the background, important variation of the point of view, or complex development in the scene's action.

The matching technique based on interest points is better suited for scenes that have undergone some great changes but where some persistent, perennial features (such as objects of interest) are available for extraction and matching. In addition, the technique is robust to abrupt changes in the intensity values introduced by noise or changes in the illumination condition.

It would be interesting, in our future work, to investigate how the two methods can be efficiently combined in order to increase the detection performances.

CONCLUSION AND PERSPECTIVES

In this paper, we have proposed a novel methodological framework for temporal video structuring and segmentation, which includes shot boundary detection, keyframe extraction and scene identification methods.

The main contributions proposed involve: (1) an enhanced shot boundary detection method based on multi-resolution non-linear filtering and with low computational complexity; (2) a leap keyframe extraction strategy that generates adaptively static storyboards; and (3) a novel shot clustering technique that creates semantically relevant scenes, by exploiting a set of temporal constraints, a new concept of neutralized/ non-neutralized shots as well as an adaptive thresholding mechanism.

The shot boundary detection methods is highly efficient in terms of precision and recall rates (with gains up to 9.8% and 7.4%, respectively in the case all transitions with respect to the reference state of the art method), while reducing with 25% the associated computational time.

Concerning the shot grouping into scenes, we have validated our technique by using two different types of visual features: HSV color histograms and interest points with SIFT descriptors. In both cases, the experimental evaluation performed validates the proposed approach, with a F1 performance measure of about 86%.

Finally, we have shown that for larger temporal analysis windows, the proposed algorithm can also be used to detect DVD chapters. The experimental results demonstrate the robustness of our approach, which provides an average F1 score of 76%, regardless the movie's type or gender.

Our perspectives of future work will concern the integration of our method within a more general framework of video indexing and retrieval applications, including object detection and recognition methodologies. Finally, we intend to integrate within our approach motion cues that can be useful for both reliable shot/scene/keyframe detection and event identification.

REFERENCES

Aner, A., & Kender, J. R. (2002). Video summaries through mosaic-based shot and scene clustering. In *Proceedings of the European Conference on Computer Vision* (pp. 388-402).

Ariki, Y., Kumano, M., & Tsukada, K. (2003). Highlight scene extraction in real time from baseball live video. In *Proceedings of the ACM International Workshop on Multimedia Information Retrieval* (pp. 209-214).

Chasanis, V., Kalogeratos, A., & Likas, A. (2009). Movie segmentation into scenes and chapters using locally weighted bag of visual words. In *Proceeding of the ACM International Conference on Image and Video Retrieval.*

Chasanis, V., Likas, A., & Galatsanos, N. P. (2008). Video rushes summarization using spectral clustering and sequence alignment. In *Proceedings of the ACM International Conference on Multimedia and the TRECVID BBC Rushes Summarization Workshop* (pp. 75-79).

Fernando, W. A. C, Canagarajah, C. N., & Bull, D. R. (2001). Scene change detection algorithms for content-based video indexing and retrieval. *IEEE Electronics and Communication Engineering Journal,* 117-126.

Fu, X., & Zeng, J. (2009). An improved histogram based image sequence retrieval method. In *Proceedings of the International Symposium on Intelligent Information Systems and Applications* (pp. 15-18).

Furini, M., & Ghini, V. (2006). An audio–video summarization scheme based on audio and video analysis. In *Proceedings of the IEEE Consumer Communications and Networking Conference* (Vol. 2, pp. 1209-1213).

Gargi, U., Kasturi, R., & Strayer, S. (2000). Performance characterization of video shot-change detection methods. *IEEE Transactions on Circuits and Systems for Video Technology, 10*(1), 1–13. doi:10.1109/76.825852

Girgensohn, A., & Boreczky, J. (1999). Time-constrained keyframe selection technique. In *Proceedings of the IEEE International Conference on Multimedia Systems* (Vol. 1, pp. 756-761).

Hanjalic, A., Lagendijk, R. L., & Biemond, J. (1999). Automated high-level movie segmentation for advanced video-retrieval systems. *IEEE Transactions on Circuits and Systems for Video Technology, 9,* 580–588. doi:10.1109/76.767124

Hanjalic, A., & Zhang, H. J. (1999). An integrated scheme for automated video abstraction based on unsupervised cluster-validity analysis. *IEEE Transactions on Circuits and Systems for Video Technology, 9*(8). doi:10.1109/76.809162

Hendrickson, B., & Kolda, T. G. (2000). Graph partitioning models for parallel computing. *Parallel Computing Journal, 26,* 1519–1534. doi:10.1016/S0167-8191(00)00048-X

Li, Y., & Merialdo, B. (2010). VERT: a method for automatic evaluation of video summaries. In *Proceedings of the ACM Conference on Multimedia* (pp. 851-854).

Lienhart, R., Pfeiffer, S., & Effelsberg, W. (1997). Video abstracting. *Communications of the ACM,* 1–12.

Lowe, D. (2004). Distinctive image features from scale-invariant keypoints. *International Journal of Computer Vision,* 1–28.

Matsumoto, K., Naito, M., Hoashi, K., & Sugaya, F. (2006). SVM-based shot boundary detection with a novel feature. In *Proceedings of the IEEE International Conference Multimedia and Expo* (pp. 1837-1840).

Ngo, C. W., & Zhang, H. J. (2002). Motion-based video representation for scene change detection. *International Journal of Computer Vision, 50*(2), 127–142. doi:10.1023/A:1020341931699

Porter, S. V., Mirmehdi, M., & Thomas, B. T. (2000). Video cut detection using frequency domain correlation. In *Proceedings of the 15th International Conference on Pattern Recognition* (pp. 413-416).

Rasheed, Z., Sheikh, Y., & Shah, M. (2005). On the use of computable features for film classification. *IEEE Transactions on Circuits and Systems for Video Technology*, *15*(1), 52–64. doi:10.1109/TCSVT.2004.839993

Truong, B., & Venkatesh, S. (2007). Video abstraction: A systematic review and classification. *ACM Transactions on Multimedia Computing, Communications, and Applications*, *3*(1), 3. doi:10.1145/1198302.1198305

Vedaldi, A., & Fulkerson, B. (2010). *VLFeat: An open and portable library of computer vision algorithm*. Retrieved from http://www.vlfeat.org

Yuan, J., Wang, H., Xiao, L., Zheng, W., Li, J., Lin, F., & Zhang, B. (2007). A formal study of shot boundary detection. *IEEE Transactions on Circuits and Systems for Video Technology*, *17*, 168–186. doi:10.1109/TCSVT.2006.888023

Zabih, R., Miller, J., & Mai, K. (1995). A feature-based algorithm for detecting and classifying scene breaks. In *Proceedings of the Third ACM International Conference on Multimedia* (pp. 189-200).

Zhang, H., Wu, J., Zhong, D., & Smoliar, S. W. (1999). An integrated system for content-based video retrieval and browsing. *Pattern Recognition*, *30*(4), 643–658. doi:10.1016/S0031-3203(96)00109-4

Zhang, H. J., Kankanhalli, A., & Smoliar, S. W. (1993). Automatic partitioning of full-motion video. *Multimedia Systems*, *1*, 10–28. doi:10.1007/BF01210504

Zhu, S., & Liu, Y. (2009). Video scene segmentation and semantic representation using a novel scheme. *Multimedia Tools and Applications*, *42*(2), 183–205. doi:10.1007/s11042-008-0233-0

ENDNOTES

[1]   The algorithms have been tested on a Pentium IV machine with 3.4 GHz and 2 Go RAM, under a Windows XP SP3 platform.

This work was previously published in the International Journal of Multimedia Data Engineering and Management, Volume 2, Issue 4, edited by Shu-Ching Chen, pp. 38-58, copyright 2011 by IGI Publishing (an imprint of IGI Global).

Chapter 12

Constructing and Utilizing Video Ontology for Accurate and Fast Retrieval

Kimiaki Shirahama
Kobe University, Japan

Kuniaki Uehara
Kobe University, Japan

ABSTRACT

This paper examines video retrieval based on Query-By-Example (QBE) approach, where shots relevant to a query are retrieved from large-scale video data based on their similarity to example shots. This involves two crucial problems: The first is that similarity in features does not necessarily imply similarity in semantic content. The second problem is an expensive computational cost to compute the similarity of a huge number of shots to example shots. The authors have developed a method that can filter a large number of shots irrelevant to a query, based on a video ontology that is knowledge base about concepts displayed in a shot. The method utilizes various concept relationships (e.g., generalization/ specialization, sibling, part-of, and co-occurrence) defined in the video ontology. In addition, although the video ontology assumes that shots are accurately annotated with concepts, accurate annotation is difficult due to the diversity of forms and appearances of the concepts. Dempster-Shafer theory is used to account the uncertainty in determining the relevance of a shot based on inaccurate annotation of this shot. Experimental results on TRECVID 2009 video data validate the effectiveness of the method.

There is significant demand for a video retrieval method that is capable of retrieving shots of interest from a large number of videos efficiently. Based on how to represent a query, existing methods can be classified as *Query-By-Keyword* (QBK) or *Query-By-Example* (QBE). In the QBK approach, the user provides keywords that represent the query. The system then retrieves shots that are annotated with the same or related keywords. Under the QBE approach, the user provides ex-

DOI: 10.4018/978-1-4666-2940-0.ch012

ample shots to represent the query. The system then retrieves shots that are similar to example shots in terms of features like color, edge, motion, etc. QBE has two advantages over QBK. The first advantage is that through features in example shots, the query is represented with no subjectivity. In QBK, representing semantic content with keywords is affected by user subjectivity and lexical ambiguity, as different users may perceive the same content differently (Rui, Huang, & Chang, 1999). The second advantage is that QBE requires no shot annotation as features can be automatically extracted from shots. In contrast, QBK requires shot annotation, but it is impractical to annotate a huge number of shots with keywords for all possible queries. Therefore, the video retrieval method we developed is based on the QBE approach.

However, applying QBE to large-scale video data involves two crucial problems: The first one is that similarity in features does not necessarily imply similarity in semantic content. In other words, QBE retrieves several irrelevant shots that contain similar features to example shots, but show different semantic content. One main reason is *overfitting*, resulting from the insufficiency of example shots, compared to the high-dimensionality of features. A user can only provide a small number of example shots for a query. However, each shot is represented using high-dimensional features, for example, a *bag-of-visual-words* representation having over 1,000 dimensions. Due to the small number of example shots available, obtaining reliable statistical information about feature dimen-

sions is difficult. Consequently, retrieved shots are similar to example shots in terms of feature dimensions that are very specific to the example shots, but are not useful for characterizing the query. For example, in Figure 1, when *Ex. 1, 2, and 3* are provided as example shots for the query "tall buildings are shown", *Shot 1, 2, and 3* are incorrectly retrieved. This is because *Shot 1, 2, and 3* are similar to *Ex. 1, 2, and 3* in terms of feature dimensions that characterize few edges in sky regions. The second problem is an expensive computational cost to calculate the similarity of a huge number of shots to example shots. The computational cost of QBE linearly increases depending on the number of shots.

To overcome the above problems, as preprocessing of QBE, we develop a method that filters a large number of irrelevant shots to a query based on concept detection results. Figure 1 shows detection results for three concepts: *Building*, *Cityspace*, and *Person*. Each shot is represented as a vector of detection scores, each of which represents the presence of a concept in the shot. A higher detection score for a concept indicates that this concept is more likely to appear in a shot. In Figure 1, *Building* and *Cityspace* are likely to appear in *Ex. 1, 2, and 3*, although unlikely to appear in *Shot 1, 2, and 3*. Several researchers have used concept detection results in video retrieval recently (Ngo et al., 2009; Snoek et al., 2009). Unlike a small number of example shots in QBE, the detector for each concept is built using a large number of shots (more than 10,000 shots), that are annotated to represent the

Figure 1. Example of an overfit retrieval result

Query: Tall buildings are shown				Retrieved by overfitting		
	Ex. 1	Ex. 2	Ex. 3	Shot 1	Shot 2	Shot 3
Building:	0.9	0.85	0.7	0.1	0.02	0.05
Cityspace:	0.7	0.95	0.8	0.03	0.0	0.01
Person:	0.0	0.1	0.05	0.8	0.02	0.0

presence or absence of the concept. Hence, the concept can be detected robustly irrespective of their size, position and direction on the screen. This kind of concept detection results alleviate overfitting.

It is crucial how to use concept detection results for accurately filtering irrelevant shots to a query. For example, if one knows that *Building* and *Cityspace* are related to the query "tall buildings are shown", *Shot 1*, *2*, and *3* can be filtered because of their low detection scores for *Building* and *Cityspace*. To implement this idea, we construct a *video ontology* that is knowledge based about concepts present in a shot, where concept properties and relationships are defined in a formal and explicit way. This video ontology is used to select concepts related to a query. Shots are then filtered by referring to detection scores for selected concepts. In addition, to further filter shots, we use rules that are derived from concept properties and relationships defined in the video ontology.

The main contributions of this paper are three-fold:

1. **Construction of the video ontology:** Most of existing methods try to automatically extract concept relationships using a set of annotated shots and external resources like WordNet (Koskela, Smeaton, & Laaksonen, 2007; Wei & Ngo, 2008; Weng & Chuang, 2009; Yan, Chen, & Hauptmann 2006). However, in these methods, relationships among concepts are simply defined as the degrees of their relatedness. In comparison, we manually construct a detailed video ontology, where various concept relationships (e.g., generalization/specialization, sibling, part-of, co-occurrence, etc.) are defined based on the design patterns of general ontologies. As described in the next contribution, using these relationships provides us with several effective inferences for deciding the relevance of a shot to a query.

2. **Use of concept relationships:** Only using the degree of relatedness among concepts limits the kinds of inferences. A linear combination of concept detection scores is typically used (Natsev, Haubold, Tesic, Xie, & Yan 2007; Ngo 2009; Snoek et al., 2007, 2009; Wei & Ngo, 2008). Compared to this, we demonstrate that several rules for filtering irrelevant shots can be derived from concept relationships and properties, defined in the video ontology. Suppose that *Hand* is defined as a part of *Person* in the video ontology. This leads to the rule: "If *Hand* is detected in a shot, *Person* should also be detected."

3. **Uncertainty of inference:** Traditional ontology formalisms do not account for uncertainty. In other words, an ontology itself is not uncertain, by its very nature; it is a presentation of a priori knowledge that has been accepted to be true. However, concept detection results generally contain several errors. If the above kind of inference is directly applied to concept detection results, many relevant shots will be filtered incorrectly due to concept detection errors. To overcome this, we use *Dempster-Shafer* Thery (DST) (Shafer, 1976), that is a generalization of the Bayesian theory to deal with the uncertainty of hypotheses. In addition to the probability of a hypothesis, DST considers the probability of a set of hypotheses. The latter probability represents the uncertainty in which of hypotheses in the set is true. We use DST to represent the uncertainty resulting from error-prone concept detection results for determining if a shot is relevant to a query.

Related Works

A popular current ontology for video retrieval is Large-Scale Concept Ontology for Multimedia (LSCOM) (Naphade et al., 2006). LSCOM defines a standardized set of 1,000 concepts, such as *Person*, *Car*, and *Building*. Concepts are selected based on their utility for classifying content in videos, their coverage in being responding to a variety of user queries, their feasibility for automatic detection, and the availability (observability) of large annotated data sets. As was exemplified in the high-level feature extraction (concept detection) in TRECVID (Smeaton, Over, & Kraaij, 2006), a lot of research effort has been spent on developing a method to accurately detect LSCOM concepts in shots. However, a crucial problem with LSCOM is that it just provides a list of concepts. For LSCOM concepts to be utilized in video retrieval, they need to be organized into a meaningful structure. Then, it will become possible to select concepts related to a given query based on the structure. In what follows, we describe the contributions of this paper in the areas of concept structuring (concept relationship extraction) and the selection of concepts related to the query.

A number of researchers have studied the extraction of relationships among LSCOM concepts. Koskela et al. (2007) proposed a method that computes the degree of concept relationships by analyzing the result of clustering shots based on features. Two concepts are considered to be related if shots annotated with those concepts are distributed on the same clusters. Yan et al. (2006) proposed a method for extracting dependences among concepts using a probabilistic graphical model. Wei and Ngo (2008) developed a method that extracts relationships among concepts using WordNet. It is a large lexical database where synonym sets (synsets) of nouns, verbs, adjectives, and adverbs are interlinked based on their meanings (Fellbaum, 1998). In addition, the method in Wei and Ngo (2008) extracted the co-occurrence relationships among concepts using annotated shots. Weng and Chuang (2008) developed a method that extracts co-occurrence relationships among concepts and inter-shot relationships by conducting the chi-square test on annotated shots.

As these examples demonstrate, most existing methods adopt an *inductive* approach to automatically extracts relations among concepts using annotated shots and external resources (e.g., WordNet). However, the concept relationships extracted by this inductive approach are very coarse as they only indicate the degree of interrelatedness between concepts. For example, *Car* has a high correlation with *Road*, whereas *Kitchen* has a very low correlation with *Outdoor*. In the field of ontology engineering, ontologies are constructed using several other types of concept relationships, such as generalization/specialization, part-of, attribute-of, and self-defined relationships. It is difficult to extract such relationships automatically. We therefore adopt a *deductive* approach whereby concept relationships and properties are defined manually, based on the design patterns of general ontologies. This allows us to define various concept relationships and draw effective inferences. For example, suppose the concept *Hand* is defined as a part of *Person*. If *Hand* is detected in a shot, we can infer that *Person* too appears in the shot. Zha, Mei, Wang, and Hua (2007) used an inductive approach to define generalization/ specialization (hierarchical) relationships among concepts. However, they extracted concept properties and co-occurrence relationships based on an inductive approach, which meant they did not consider part-of, attribute-of, or other types of relationships.

Several methods exist for selecting concepts that are related to a given query. These can be classified into the following four types: the *Ontology-based*, *Text-based*, *Corpus-based*, and *Visual-based* approaches. Ontology-based methods select concepts that are related to words in the text description of the query using an external knowledge base (typically WordNet). The relatedness between a concept and a word is measured using a lexical similarity measure, such as Resnik's measure (Snoek et al., 2007) and Lesk semantic relatedness score (Natsev et al., 2007). Text-based methods work by selecting concepts based on the extent to which their text descriptions match the text description of a query. This typically involves using a document retrieval approach, such as vector space model (Snoek et al., 2007). Corpus-based methods select concepts that significantly co-occur with words in the text description of a query. The use of annotated video collections (Wei & Ngo, 2008) and external resources like Flickr (Ngo et al., 2009) facilitates the extraction of co-occurrence patterns in advance. Visual-based methods select concepts that have high detection scores in example shots (Natsev et al., 2007; Snoek et al., 2007, 2009).

In contrast to existing concept selection methods, we select concepts related to a query using our own video ontology. The advantage is that it enables us to use concept relationships defined in our video ontology for filtering irrelevant shots. For example, our video ontology defines *Tower* as a subconcept of *Building*. Thus, if *Tower* is detected in a shot, and *Building* is not, we can infer that *Tower* has been incorrectly detected in this shot. In contrast to this use of concept relationships, many existing methods opt to use a linear combination of detection scores for selected concepts (Natsev et al., 2007; Ngo et al., 2009; Snoek et al., 2007, 2009; Wei & Ngo, 2008). To the best of our knowledge, no existing methods deal with the uncertainty in determining the relevance of a shot to a query based on error-prone concept detection results. We present a first study on this issue using DST.

SHOT FILTERING USING VIDEO ONTOLOGY

Construction of the Video Ontology

We assume that all shots have already been assigned concept detection scores, and use the concept detection scores provided by the City University of Hong Kong (Jiang, Yang, Ngo, & Hauptmann, 2010). Detection scores for 374 LSCOM concepts are assigned to all shots in TRECVID 2009 video data (Smeaton et al., 2006). Researchers have prepared a large amount of training data (61,901 shots), in which shots are annotated manually to indicate the presence or absence of 374 LSCOM concepts. Three Support Vector Machines (SVMs) (Vapnik, 1998) are constructed for each concept, based on local edge (i.e., Scale-Invariant Feature Transform (SIFT)), color moment, and wavelet texture features. For a shot, each SVM provides a probabilistic output that represents the probability of the concept's presence, based on the distance between the shot and the decision boundary of the SVM (Liu, Lin, & Weng, 2007). The detection score of the concept is then computed as the average of probabilistic outputs of the above SVMs. That is, this score ranges from 0 to 1. The final representation of a shot is a 374-dimensional vector, where each dimension represents the detection score of a concept. Please refer to Jiang et al. (2010) for more detail. The discussion that follows, explains how to organize 374 LSCOM concepts into a video ontology.

Figure 2 shows a part of our video ontology, with LSCOM concepts represented as upper case followed by lower case. As LSCOM concepts alone are incapable of constructing a meaningful structure, a series of new concepts are defined; they are represented using only upper case. In addition, the properties of concepts are represented by names that begin in lower case.

As shown in Figure 2(a), a shot is represented by eight attributes; each attribute represents a concept present in the shot. This representation satisfies the disjoint partition requirement, which is a well-known ontology design pattern that makes an ontology easily interpretable by both humans and machines (Horridge, Knublauch, Rector, Stevens, & Wroe, 2004). To meet the disjoint partition requirement, a concept C_l should be

Figure 2. Part of the video ontology: a) shot representation using eight attributes, and b) concept hierarchies and properties for PERSON, OBJECT, and ROLE

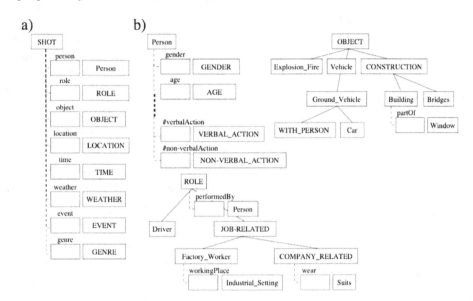

separable into disjoint subconcepts, C_2, C_3, and so on. That is, for $i, j \geq 2$ and $i \neq j$, $C_i \cap C_j = \varphi$. Thus, an instance of C_1 cannot be an instance of more than one subconcept, C_2, C_3, and so on. For example, *Vehicle* and *Car* should not be placed at the same level of the concept hierarchy, because an instance of *Car* is also an instance of *Vehicle*. Consider the above eight attributes of a shot: If we organize all concepts into a single hierarchy, it is clearly impossible to satisfy the disjoint partition requirement. Instead, we define the eight attributes as categories of semantic content that may appear in a shot, and organize concepts to satisfy the disjoint partition requirement in each category.

As shown in Figure 2(b), *Person*-related concepts (e.g., *Male_Person*, *Female_Person*, *Child*) are not defined as subconcepts of *Person*. Instead, they are defined as attributes of *Person* in order to satisfy the disjoint partition requirement. For example, if *Person* is first divided into *Male_Person* and *Female_Person*, it is impossible to define *Child*, because shots can show both male and female children (i.e., the disjoint partition re-

quirement is violated). We do not define concepts related to *Person* that are context dependent. For example, an instance of *Person* can also be an instance of *Driver* in one shot, or an instance of *Factory_Worker* in another shot. To ensure the identity of the instance, we define such context dependent concepts as *roles* (Masolo et al., 2004).

We also consider visual characteristics in when defining the concept hierarchy. For example, in Figure 2(b) we define *WITH_PERSON* as a subconcept of *Ground_Vehicle*, because *Person* is likely to coexist with subconcepts of *WITH_PERSON*, such as *Bicycle* and *Motorcycle*. In Figure 2, some concept properties are preceded by #. This *# operator* represents a concept property that is used only when it is specified in the description of a query. This aims to overcome the problem of the insufficiency of concepts that are applicable to the concept property. For example, for *#nonverbalAction* property, LSCOM only defines nine concepts, such as *Sitting*, *Walking_Running*, and *Dancing*. Consider a query related to a person that does not specify the person's action (e.g., "a person is indoors"). If the nine LSCOM concepts for

231

#non-verbalAction property are selected, we may miss many shots where a person performs other non-verbal actions, such as jumping, sleeping, and squatting and so on. Therefore, we use concepts for *#non-verbalAction* property, if a non-verbal action is specified in the query, for example, "a person is dancing indoors".

Concept Selection and Shot Filtering Based on Video Ontology

Using the video ontology defined in the previous section, we can now select concepts related to a query and filter shots that are clearly irrelevant. First, we select concepts that match words in the text description of the query. Next, we select subconcepts of each selected concept. At the above processes, we also select concepts that are specified as properties of selected concepts. In addition, we select concepts whose properties match words in the text description of the query, and select their subconcepts. Figure 3 shows this concept selection process for the query "buildings are shown". First, *Building* and all its subconcepts (e.g., *Office_Building*, *Tower*, and *Factory*) are selected. *Window* is selected from *hasPartOf* property of *Building*. Finally, as *Building* is *appearWith* property of *Artificial_Site*, we select all subconcepts of *Artificial_Site* (e.g., *Cityspace*, *Urban*, and *Suburban*).

As this process of concept selection selects all concepts that could possibly be related to the query, it inevitably selects many unrelated concepts as well. For example, for the query "buildings are shown", 80 concepts, including *White_House*, *Military_Base*, and *Ruins*, are selected. However, only some of them are actually related to the query. Hence, we validate selected concepts using example shots. All shots are associated with detection scores for LSCOM concepts, as shown in the example of *Building* in Figure 3. We compute the average detection score among example shots for each shot and list concepts in the descending order of their scores. Using this ranking, we select concepts that are chosen by the video ontology, and are ranked in the top T positions (here we use $T=20$). In this way, selected concepts are validated from both semantic and statistical perspectives.

These select concepts are used to filter shots without relevance to a query. The objective at this stage is to retain as many relevant shots as possible. Thus, we filter shots in which none of the selected concepts are detected. Our preliminary experiment showed that the distribution of detection scores varies significantly with the concepts. The result of checking concept detection scores in 97,150 shots in TRECVID 2009 test videos indicated that, most shots where *Person* appears have detections scores from 0.7 to 1, most shots

Figure 3. Part of the concept hierarchies and properties for LOCATION and OBJECT

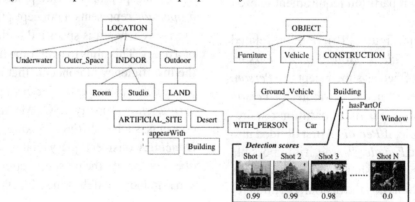

where *Building* is present have scores from 0.3 to 0.9, most shots where *Airplane* is present have scores from 0.1 to 0.5, and so forth. This implies that the distribution of shots where a concept is present significantly varies depending on concepts. Hence, for each concept, we manually assign a threshold detection score for the presence of that concept in a shot. It should be noted that even if concept detection scores are normalized to have zero mean and unit standard deviation, manual threshold assignment is required. This is because the number of shots where one concept is present is significantly different from the one where another concept is present.

However, as concept detection is very error prone, in many shots the concept is detected incorrectly (i.e., false positive). Therefore, we further filter shots using the following two functions that examine the inconsistencies of concept detection, based on concept relationships defined in the video ontology. The first function examines the inconsistencies in concept detection in a shot based on the generalization/specialization relations among concepts. We define the following rule to refine concept results: "If a concept is detected in a shot, its superconcept should also be detected". For example, if *Office_Building* is detected in a shot, *Building* should also have been detected in the shot. If this condition does not hold, we assume that *Office_Building* was detected incorrectly. In this manner, we reduce the number of incorrect concept detections and irrelevant shots can safely be filtered. Highly specific concepts are increasingly difficult to detect with accuracy. Hence, the above rule is applied to general concepts like *Building* and *Person* (in the case of *Person*, we restate the above rule as: "If a concept that is specified as a property of *Person* is detected in a shot, and *Person* is not detected, this property was detected incorrectly").

The second function looks for inconsistencies in concept detection based on the disjoint partition requirement, which prevents that an instance of a concept become an instance of a 'sibling'

concept. A sibling *S* of a selected concept *C* is another subconcept of *C*'s superconcept (Horridge et al., 2004). Thus, we filter shots based on the following the rule: "A shot is filtered if a sibling of a selected concept is detected in the shot". For example, in Figure 3, *Underwater*, *Outer_Space* and *INDOOR* are siblings of *Outdoor*. So, if the concept *Outdoor* is selected, shots where its siblings (i.e., *INDOOR*, *Outer_Space* and *Underwater*) are detected are considered irrelevant to the query. It is important to note that this rule is applicable only for concepts that are global visual characteristics of a shot. Such concepts are defined for five attributes at the bottom of Figure 2, *LOCATION*, *TIME*, *WEATHER*, *EVENT*, and *GENRE*; these affect the global color and edge features of a video frame, whereas concepts for the attributes *Person*, *ROLE* and *OBJECT* appear in a specific region of the video frame. Thus, for concepts that are global visual characteristics of a shot, their siblings should not be detected.

Managing Uncertainty Using Dempster-Shafer Theory

The two shot filtering functions described in the previous section fail to work as designed because concept detection results are prone to have several errors. For example, when the query is related to the concept *Outdoor*, several relevant shots are incorrectly filtered due to the failed detection of *Outdoor* in these shots. This is because traditional ontology formalisms lack support for uncertainty (Bellenger & Gatepaille, 2011). In other words, an ontology is not uncertain by its very nature; it is a specification of a priori knowledge that is considered to be true. In the ideal case, inferences can be performed based on the following assumptions (Russell & Norvig, 2003):

1. **Locality:** If we have $A \Rightarrow B$, then we can conclude B is true given A, without worrying about any other rules.

2. **Detachment:** Once a logical proof is found for a proposition, we can use it regardless of how it was derived.

3. **Truth functionality:** The truth of complex sentences can be computed from the truth of their components.

However, if uncertainty is involved, the assumptions are invalid. In our case, based on the first and second assumptions, we cannot conclude that if a concept A is detected in a shot, the shot is relevant to a query B. Instead, we need to estimate the detection accuracy of A. In addition, it is not desirable to use the following combination rule based on the third assumption: For a shot to be relevant to B, each selected concept needs to be detected. It is better to assess the relevance of a shot based on the overall detection result of selected concepts. Therefore, a shot may be relevant to a query even if only a small number of selected concepts are detected in it.

Due to these factors, we use DST (Shafer, 1976) which is a generalization of Bayesian theory that defines the probability of a hypothesis based on the degree of belief (i.e., how certain the hypothesis is). DST provides two functionalities that are effective in handling violations of the above assumptions. If the first and second assumptions are violated, DST can represent the degree of ignorance in deciding if a shot is relevant to a query based on error-prone concept detection results. If the third assumption is violated, DST provides an effective combination rule for integrating multiple decisions which are based on detection results of different concepts.

Multiple shot filtering results are required to use the DST combination rule. In addition to filtering shots based on the video ontology, we also filter shots based on a visual approach that selects concepts having high detection scores in example shots. Furthermore, in order to represent the degree of belief, we require both kinds of shot filtering results, those relevant and those irrelevant to the query. Thus, we conduct two types of shot filtering based on the video ontology. The first type of filtering, called *ontology positive* filtering (*onto_pos* for short), filters shots using concepts selected by the video ontology, with the aim of retaining shots relevant to the query. The second type of filtering, called *ontology negative* filtering (*onto_neg* for short), aims to filter irrelevant shots using concepts, that were not selected by the video ontology. Similarly, two kinds of filtering are performed based on the visual approach, namely *vis_pos* (*visual positive* filtering) using selected concepts, and *vis_neg* (*visual negative* filtering) using not-selected concepts. We apply DST to the above four types of shot filtering results.

In DST, we first define a *Basic Belief Assignment* (BBA), which is a function m that estimates the degree of belief of shot filtering results, signifying the relevance or irrelevance of a shot to a query. For shot filtering results by *onto_pos* and *onto_neg* (or *vis_pos* and *vis_neg*), BBA is defined as shown in Table 1, where + represents a positive conclusion with high certainty. For *onto_pos* or *vis_pos*, + denotes that a shot is considered relevant to a query with high certainty, whereas for *onto_neg* or *vis_neg*, + implies that the shot is considered irrelevant with high certainty. In contrast, - represents a negative conclusion with high certainty. For *onto_pos* or *vis_pos*, - implies that a shot is considered irrelevant to a query with high certainty, whereas for *onto_neg* or *vis_neg*, - implies that it is considered relevant to a query with high certainty. Furthermore, the symbol 0 implies that the conclusion is not certain, that is, the filtering method could not determine if the shot is relevant or not. Each element in Table 1 shows *belief masses* (probabilities) obtained by combining conclusions from *onto_pos* and *onto_neg* (or *vis_pos* and *vis_neg*). For example, the element that combines positive conclusions by *onto_pos* and *onto_neg* shows that the belief mass of a shot being relevant is $0.7 (=m(\{rel\}))$. Furthermore, the belief mass that denotes if the shot is irrelevant is $0.2 (=m(\{irr\}))$, whereas the belief mass denoting uncertainty in deciding relevance is $0.1 (=m(\{rel,$

irr}). Through *m({rel, irr})*, DST represents uncertainty as a disjunction of hypotheses. In addition, because our preliminary experiment showed that *onto_neg* (or *vis_neg*) is not very accurate, we define *m* to favor the conclusion reached by *onto_pos* (or *vis_pos*).

Using belief masses of a shot obtained by the pairs *onto_pos* and *onto_neg*, and *vis_pos* and *vis_neg*, we calculate the *joint mass*, which is the final evaluation value of shot's relevance to a query, by the following combination rule:

$$jm(\{rel\}) = \frac{\sum_{A_{onto,i} \cap A_{vis,j} \neq \varphi} m_{onto}(A_{onto,i}) \bullet m_{vis}(A_{vis,j})}{1 - \sum_{A_{onto,i} \cap A_{vis,j} = \varphi} m_{onto,i}(A_{onto,i}) \bullet m_{vis,j}(A_{vis,j})}$$

(1)

where *jm({rel})* is the joint mass, m_{onto} and m_{vis} represent the belief masses from the pairs *onto_pos* and *onto_neg*, and *vis_pos* and *vis_neg*, respectively. $A_{onto,i}$ and $A_{vis,j}$ represent sets of hypotheses associated with m_{onto} and m_{vis}, respectively. Equation (1) implies that *jm({rel})* becomes large if belief masses from *onto_pos* and *onto_neg* agree with those from *vis_pos* and *vis_neg*. It is desirable that these belief masses are associated with the same sets of hypotheses. Finally, we retain shots which have joint masses larger than a threshold (*T=0.5*).

Video Retrieval Using Rough Set Theory

To obtain a final retrieval result, we perform QBE on shots that remain after shot filtering in the previous section. One of the major problems associated with QBE is the large variation in shots that are relevant to a query. There are significant differences in the features of such shots due to variation in camera techniques and settings. We apply *Rough Set Theory* (RST) to overcome this issue; RST is a set-theoretic classification method for extracting *rough* descriptions of a class from imprecise or noisy data (Komorowski, Ohrn, & Skowron, 2002). The term rough here indicates that RST does not extract a single classification rule to characterize the entire set of examples belonging to the class. Rather it extracts multiple rules that characterize different subsets of examples. The class is represented as a union of rules. We use RST to extract multiple rules, each of which characterizes a subset of example shots. By accumulating shots retrieved using such rules, it becomes possible to retrieve a variety of shots that are relevant to the query.

RST extracts classification rules that make it possible to discriminate between relevant and irrelevant shots to a query. Thus, we require both example shots representing relevant shots and *counter-example shots* representing irrelevant

Table 1. Basic Belief Assigment (BBA) in our DST

		onto_pos (or vis_pos)		
		-	0	+
onto_neg (or vis_neg)	-	m({rel}) = 0.1 m({irr}) = 0.8 m({rel, irr}) = 0.1	m({rel}) = 0.3 m({irr}) = 0.7	m({rel}) = 0.9 m({irr}) = 0.1
	0	m({rel}) = 0.2 m({irr}) = 0.8	m({rel}) = 0.2 m({irr}) = 0.6 m({rel, irr}) = 0.2	m({rel}) = 0.8 m({irr}) = 0.2
	+	m({rel}) = 0.1 m({irr}) = 0.9	m({rel}) = 0.2 m({irr}) = 0.5 m({rel, irr}) = 0.3	m({rel}) = 0.7 m({irr}) = 0.2 m({rel, irr}) = 0.1

shots. However, counter-example shots are not provided in QBE. We developed a method that collects counter-example shots based on example shots. This method selects counter-example shots that are similar to example shots, but irrelevant to the query. These counter-example shots are useful for characterizing the boundary between relevant and irrelevant shots. Space limitations prevent us from describing the method in full. Please refer to Shirahama, Matsuoka, and Uehara (in press-b) for more details. In the following discussion, it is assumed that counter-example shots have already been selected.

To extract rules that cover a variety of relevant shots, RST requires *diverse* features, each of which characterizes a different set of shots. Using the software developed by Sande, Gevers, and Snoek (2010), from the middle video frame (i.e., key-frame) of each shot, we extract six local image features, *SIFT*, *Dense SIFT*, *Opponent SIFT*, *RGB SIFT*, *Hue SIFT*, and *RGB Histogram*. The diversity of these features has been validated in Sande et al. (2010) and Zhang, Marszalek, Lazebnik, and Schmid (2007), as they represent different color and edge properties in local image regions. Each of the above features is represented using a 1,000 dimensional bag-of-visual-words representation.

In addition, RST requires features that classify example and counter-example shots imperfectly. It is not appropriate to apply RST directly to the above features. The reason is the high-dimensionality of the bag-of-visual-words representation having 1,000 dimensions. It is likely that example and counter-example shots can be perfectly classified by a hyperplane in the high-dimensional feature space. Consequently, RST only extracts a small number of rules that characterize the entire set of example shots. Such rules are only useful for retrieving shots that are very similar to example shots; they are not useful for retrieving a variety of relevant shots. Therefore, we construct a classifier on each feature, and use its classification result as a feature in RST. In order to retain the possibility

of incorrectly classifying example and counter-example shots, the classifier is constructed using only a subset of example and counter-example shots. Hence, the classifier may incorrectly classify example and counter-example shots that were excluded during classifier construction. In this way, we construct many classifiers using different subsets of randomly selected example and counter-example shots. Also, we use a *Support Vector Machine* (SVM), which is generally acknowledged as being one of the most effective classifiers for high-dimensional features (Vapnik, 1998). In the experiment, we construct 18 SVMs, where three SVMs are built on each of six features using different sets of randomly selected example and counter-example shots.

Although the above SVMs characterize different sets of shots, they are not very accurate. A simple combination of these SVMs like majority voting can result in the potential retrieval of many irrelevant shots. To overcome this, we utilize RST to analyze SVM classification results and extract rules as combinations of SVMs. Each rule can correctly discriminate a subset of example shots from the whole set of counter-example shots. This enables us to cover a range of relevant shots by alleviating the retrieval of irrelevant shots. In what follows, we summarize the rule extraction procedure of RST. Please refer to Shirahama, Matsuoka, and Uehara (in press-a) for more detail.

For each pair of an example shot ex_i and a counter-example shot c_ex_j, we first determine $SVM_{i,j}$ that is a set of SVMs useful for discriminating ex_i from c_ex_j. If an SVM can correctly classify ex_i and c_ex_j as relevant and irrelevant respectively, it is included in $SVM_{i,j}$. In other words, ex_i can be discriminated from c_ex_j when at least one SVM in $SVM_{i,j}$ is utilized. Next, we compute the *discernibility function* df_i, that represents sets of SVMs, required to discriminate ex_i from all counter-example shots. This is achieved by using at least one SVM in $SVM_{i,j}$ for all counter-example shots. That is, df_i is computed by taking the disjunction of SVMs in $SVM_{i,j}$, and then taking the conjunction of such disjunctions for all counter-example shots. Afterwards, df_i is simplified into the minimal disjunctive normal form, where each conjunctive term, called *reduct*, represents a minimal set of SVMs required to discriminate ex_i from all counter-example shots. Such a reduct forms a rule: A shot is regarded as relevant to a query, if all SVMs in the reduct classify it as such (i.e., it matches the rule). Shots that match many shots comprise the retrieval result.

Experimental Results

We examined the effectiveness of our shot filtering method using TRECVID 2009 video data (Smeaton et al., 2006). This data set consists of 219 development and 619 test videos, comprising 36,106 and 97,150 shots, respectively. In addition, the detection scores for all these shots, based on 374 LSCOM concepts were provided by the City University of Hong Kong (Jiang et al., 2010). We test the following three queries:

- **Query 1:** A view of one or more tall buildings and the top story visible,
- **Query 2:** One or more people, each at a table or desk with a computer visible,
- **Query 3:** One or more people, each sitting in a chair, talking.

We manually collect example shots from development videos for each query, and retrieve relevant shots in test videos. In other words, our shot filtering method examines whether shots in test videos are clearly irrelevant to the query based on our video ontology.

Evaluation of Shot Filtering

To evaluate the effectiveness of our video ontology, we first compare the following three shot filtering methods:

1. **Onto:** This method selects concepts that are related to a query using our video ontology.
2. **WordNet:** This method selects concepts related to a query using WordNet (Fellbaum, 1998). Based on Snoek (2007), we perform pre-processing, where WordNet synsets are manually associated with some LSCOM concepts. We first select synsets based on words in the text description of the query, using hypernymy, hyponymy and meronym relationships among synsets. We then select LSCOM concepts which are associated with the above synsets.
3. **Visual:** This method selects concepts having the highest detection scores in example shots.

In order to evaluate the usefulness of the selected concepts, it should be noted that all three filter shots based on the same criterion: Shots in which none of selected concepts are detected are filtered.

We evaluate the shot filtering result based on the following evaluation measures:

1. **F-score:** A shot filtering result should contain as few irrelevant shots as possible. This is evaluated by a *precision*, representing the probability that a remaining shot is relevant. In addition, the shot filtering result should retain as many relevant shots as possible, which is evaluated by a *recall* representing the probability that a relevant shot is successfully retained. To simultaneously consider the precision and recall, we use the F-score that is defined as their harmonic mean: $F-score = \dfrac{2 \bullet precision \bullet recall}{(precision + recall)}$ (Han & Kamber, 2006).
2. **Filter recall:** For shot filtering, it is important what fraction of irrelevant shots are filtered. Hence, we use a *filter recall* to represent the probability that an irrelevant shot is successfully filtered.

Figure 4 shows the shot filtering performances of *Onto*, *WordNet*, and *Visual*. The performances of all methods are comparable. We cannot conclusively say that any method is significantly better than other methods. This similar performance is observed because concepts selected by each method are relatively similar. In other words, simply selecting concepts related to a query does not significantly change the shot filtering performance. However, unlike *WordNet* and *Visual*, our video ontology defines various relationships among LSCOM concepts. In the following discussion, we use the performance of *Onto* as a baseline to evaluate the effectiveness of concept relations in shot filtering.

In Figure 5, we show the performance of *Onto* (the left bar for each query) alongside the following two shot filtering methods:

1. **No-DST:** This method uses the same set of concepts to *Onto*, but filters shots by examining the consistency of concept detection using the generalization/specialization and disjoint partition relationships among concepts (as described in the section *Concept Selection and Shot Filtering Using Video Ontology*). In Figure 5, this method is represented by the middle bar for each query.

2. **DST:** In addition to the generalization/specialization and disjoint partition relations in *No-DST*, this method uses DST to account the uncertainty in determining the relevance of a shot based on error-prone concept detection results. In Figure 5, this method is represented by the right bar for each query.

As clear from the performance of *No-DST* in Figure 5(a) and (b), using concept relations sig-

Figure 4. Shot filtering performance comparison between Onto, WordNet, and Visual

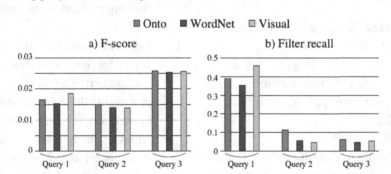

Figure 5. Shot filtering performance comparison between Onto, No-DST, and DST

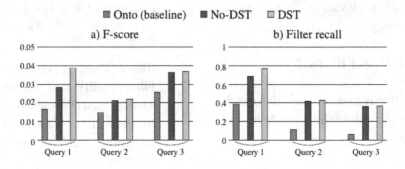

nificantly improves the F-score and filter recall. Specifically, in *Onto*, the majority of irrelevant shots are erroneously retained, leading to its low filter recalls in Figure 5(b), especially for *Query 2* and *Query 3*. In comparison, *No-DST* successfully filters significantly more irrelevant shots using concept relationships. Accordingly, the F-score is also improved as shown in Figure 5(a). From now, we closely compare *No-DST* to *DST* using Figure 6 that represents their precisions and recalls. As *No-DST* ignores incorrect concept detection results, it wrongly filters several relevant shots. Figure 6(b) shows that this problem is alleviated in *DST*, where the recall of *DST* is higher than that of *No-DST*. In addition, as shown in Figure 6(a), the precision of *DST* is also higher than that of *No-DST*. The above results validate the effectiveness of using concept relationships and accounting for the uncertainty of shot filtering resulting from error-prone concept detection.

Evaluation of Shot Filtering from the Retrieval Perspective

In this section, we examine whether our shot filtering method is effective in both improving retrieval performance and reducing retrieval time. We compare two retrieval methods, *No-ontology* and *Ontology*. *No-ontology* is basically our QBE method that is used on all shots in test videos. For *Ontology*, our QBE method is applied to shots

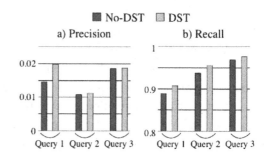

Figure 6. Performance comparison between No-DST and DST in terms of precision (a) and recall (b)

that remain after the shot filtering performed using *DST* in the previous section. This experiment was conducted on the following hardware setting: *No-ontology* and *Ontology* were run on the same PC with Intel Core i7 X990 CPU (3.47GHz) and 24 GB memory. Both methods were executed on a single core, although the CPU has multiple cores. Also, the difference between *No-ontology* and *Ontology* is just the number of shots examined by our QBE method. To concentrate on the effect caused by this difference, the following data were prepared before the retrieval for each query: Counter-example shots were collected based on 10 example shots using the method in Shirahama et al. (in press-b). *No-ontology* and *Ontology* used the same set of example and counter-example shots. Concept detection scores and six features described in the section *Video Retrieval Using*

Figure 7. Comparison of Ontology and No-ontology in terms of retrieval performance (a) and retrieval time (b)

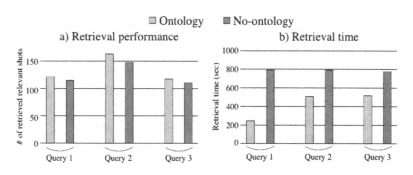

Rough Set Theory were extracted for each shot. The retrieval time of *No-ontology* or *Ontology* was computed as the time that was spent to obtain a retrieval result using the above data.

Figure 7(a) compares the retrieval performance of *Ontology* and *No-ontology*. We quantify the retrieval performance of each method as the number of relevant shots found for 1,000 retrieved shots. Figure 7(b) compares the retrieval times of *Ontology* and *No-ontology*. In Figure 7(a) and (b), for each query, the left and right bars indicate the performances of *Ontology* and *No-ontology*, respectively. From Figure 7(a), for all queries, *Ontology* is superior to *No-ontology* in terms of performance. This validates the effectiveness of filtering irrelevant shots using our method. In addition, Figure 7(b) shows that the retrieval time of *Ontology* is much less than that of *No-ontology*. This is because, for each query, *DST* can successfully filter approximately 40% to 70% of irrelevant shots, as per Figure 5(b). Therefore, our shot filtering method is not only effective in improving retrieval performance, but also in significantly reducing retrieval time.

CONCLUSION AND FUTURE WORK

In order to improve the retrieval performance of QBE and reduce its retrieval time, we proposed a method that can filter a large number of irrelevant shots to a query based on a video ontology. We constructed a detailed video ontology based on the design patterns of general ontologies. We filtered shots by referring to detection results of concepts that are selected based on the hierarchical structure and concept properties of the video ontology. The inconsistencies of concept detection results were also examined based on concept properties and relationships. Furthermore, we used DST to account for the uncertainty in shot filtering based on error-prone concept detection results. The experimental results based on TRECVID 2009 video data validate the effectiveness of our shot filtering method.

We plan to explore the following two issues in future studies: First, our current method does not use detection scores for concepts, which we define to construct a meaningful concept structure (see concepts denoted by capital letters in Figure 2 and Figure 3). We plan to compute detection scores for these concepts, and incorporate them into our shot filtering method. Second, DST requires a BBA function consisting of many parameters, as shown in Table 1. At present, we manually define this BBA function. There is no guarantee that these manually defined parameters (i.e., belief masses) are optimal. Thus, we plan to estimate an optimal BBA function based on the method proposed by Zribi and Benjelloun (2003).

ACKNOWLEDGMENT

This research is supported in part by Strategic Information and Communications R&D Promotion Programme (SCOPE) by the Ministry of Internal Affairs and Communications, Japan.

REFERENCES

Bellenger, A., & Gatepaille, S. (2011). *Uncertainty in ontologies: Dempster-Shafer theory for data fusion applications.* Retrieved October 10, 2011, from http://arxiv.org/abs/1106.3876

Fellbaum, C. (Ed.). (1998). *WordNet: An electronic lexical database.* Cambridge, MA: MIT Press.

Han, J., & Kamber, M. (2006). *Data Mining: Concepts and techniques* (2nd ed.). Waltham, MA: Morgan Kaufmann.

Horridege, M., Knublauch, H., Rector, A., Stevens, R., & Wroe, C. (2004). *A practical guide to building OWL ontologies using the Protege-OWL plugin and CO-ODE tools edition 1.0.* Retrieved September 14, 2011, from http://owl.cs.manchester.ac.uk/tutorials/protegeowltutorial/

Jiang, Y., Yang, J., Ngo, C., & Hauptmann, A. (2010). Representations of keypoint-based semantic concept detection: A comprehensive study. *IEEE Transactions on Multimedia, 12*(1), 42–53. doi:10.1109/TMM.2009.2036235

Komorowski, J., Ohrn, A., & Skowron, A. (2002). The ROSETTA rough set software system. In W. Klosgen & J. Zytkow (Eds.), *Handbook of data mining and knowledge discovery* (Ch. D.2.3). Oxford, UK: Oxford University Press.

Koskela, M., Smeaton, A., & Laaksonen, J. (2007). Measuring concept similarities in multimedia ontologies; Analysis and evaluations. *IEEE Transactions on Multimedia, 9*(5), 912–922. doi:10.1109/TMM.2007.900137

Liu, H., Lin, C., & Weng, R. (2007). A note on platt's probabilistic outputs for support vector machines. *Machine Learning, 68*(3), 267–276. doi:10.1007/s10994-007-5018-6

Masolo, C., Vieu, L., Bottazzi, E., Catenacci, C., Ferrario, R., Gangemi, A., & Guarino, N. (2004). Social roles and their descriptions. In *Proceedings of the 9th International Conference on the Principles of Knowledge Representation and Reasoning* (pp. 267-277).

Naphade, M., Smith, J., Tesic, J., Chang, S., Hsu, W., & Kennedy, L. (2006). Large-scale concept ontology for multimedia. *IEEE MultiMedia, 13*(3), 86–91. doi:10.1109/MMUL.2006.63

Natsev, A., Haubold, A., Tesic, J., Xie, L., & Yan, R. (2007). Semantic concept-based query expansion and re-ranking for multimedia retrieval. In *Proceedings of the 15th International Conference on Multimedia* (pp. 991-1000).

Ngo, C., Jiang, Y., Wei, X., Zhao, W., Liu, Y., Wang, J., et al. (2009). VIREO/DVM at TRECVID 2009: High-level feature extraction, automatic video search and content-based copy detection. In *Proceedings of the TREC Video Retrieval Evaluation Conference* (pp. 415-432).

Rui, Y., Huang, T., & Chang, S. (1999). Image retrieval: Current techniques, promising directions and operations. *Journal of Visual Communication and Image Representation, 10*(1), 39–62. doi:10.1006/jvci.1999.0413

Russell, S., & Norvig, P. (2003). *Artificial Intelligence: A modern approach.* Upper Saddle River, NJ: Prentice Hall.

Sande, K., Gevers, T., & Snoek, C. (2010). Evaluating color descriptors for object and scene recognition. *IEEE Transactions on Pattern Analysis and Machine Intelligence, 32*(9), 1582–1596. doi:10.1109/TPAMI.2009.154

Shafer, G. (1976). *A mathematical theory of evidence.* Princeton, NJ: Princeton University Press.

Shirahama, K., Matsuoka, Y., & Uehara, K. (in press). -a). Event retrieval in video archives using rough set theory and partially supervised learning. *Multimedia Tools and Applications.*

Shirahama, K., Matsuoka, Y., & Uehara, K. (in press). -b). Hybrid negative example selection using visual and conceptual features. *Multimedia Tools and Applications.*

Smeaton, A., Over, P., & Kraaij, W. (2006). Evaluation campaigns and TRECVid. In *Proceedings of the 8th International Workshop on Multimedia Information Retrieval* (pp. 321-330).

Snoek, C., et al. (2009). The MediaMill TRECVID 2009 semantic video search engine. In *Proceedings of TREC Video Retrieval Evaluation* (pp. 226-238).

Snoek, C., Huurnink, B., Hllink, L., Rijke, M., Schreiber, G., & Worring, M. (2007). Adding semantics to detectors for video retrieval. *IEEE Transactions on Multimedia, 9*(5), 975–986. doi:10.1109/TMM.2007.900156

Vapnik, V. (1998). *Statistical learning theory.* Hoboken, NJ: Wiley-Interscience.

Wei, X., & Ngo, C. (2008). Fusing semantics, observability, reliablity and diversity of concept detectors for video search. In *Proceedings of the 16th International Conference on Multimedia* (pp. 81-90).

Weng, M., & Chuang, Y. (2008). Multi-cue fusion for semantic video indexing. In *Proceedings of the 16th International Conference on Multimedia* (pp. 71-80).

Yan, R., Chen, M., & Hauptmann, A. (2006). Mining relationship between video concepts using probabilistic graphical models. In *Proceedings of the IEEE International Conference on Multimedia and Expo* (pp. 3010-304).

Zha, Z., Mei, T., Wang, Z., & Hua, X. (2007). Building a comprehensive ontology to refine video concept detection. In *Proceedings of the 9th International Workshop on Multimedia Information Retrieval* (pp. 227-236).

Zhang, J., Marszalek, M., Lazebnik, S., & Schmid, C. (2007). Local features and kernels for classification of texture and object categories: A comprehensive study. *International Journal of Computer Vision, 73*(2), 213–238. doi:10.1007/s11263-006-9794-4

Zribi, M., & Benjelloun, M. (2003). Parametric estimation of Dempster-Shafer belief functions. In *Proceedings of the 6th International Conference on Information Fusion* (pp. 485-491).

This work was previously published in the International Journal of Multimedia Data Engineering and Management, Volume 2, Issue 4, edited by Shu-Ching Chen, pp. 59-75, copyright 2011 by IGI Publishing (an imprint of IGI Global).

Section 4
Multimedia Delivery and Applications

Chapter 13

A Real–Time 3D Visualization Framework for Multimedia Data Management, Simulation, and Prediction:
Case Study in Geospatial–Temporal Biomedical Disease Surveillance Networks

Nathaniel Rossol
University of Alberta, Canada

Iqbal Jamal
AQL Management Consulting Inc., Canada

Irene Cheng
University of Alberta, Canada

John Berezowski
*Food Safety and Animal Health Division,
Government of Alberta, Canada*

Anup Basu
University of Alberta, Canada

ABSTRACT

Geographic Information Systems (GISs), which map spatiotemporal event data on geographical maps, have proven to be useful in many applications. Time-based Geographic Information Systems (GISs) allow practitioners to visualize collected data in an intuitive way. However, while current GIS systems have proven to be useful in post hoc analysis and provide simple two-dimensional geographic visualizations, their design typically lacks the features necessary for highly targeted real-time surveillance with the goal of spread prevention. This paper outlines the design, implementation, and usage of a 3D framework for real-time geospatial temporal visualization. In this case study, using livestock movements, the authors show that the framework is capable of tracking and simulating the spread of epidemic diseases. Although the application discussed in this paper relates to livestock disease, the proposed framework can be used to manage and visualize other types of high-dimensional multimedia data as well.

DOI: 10.4018/978-1-4666-2940-0.ch013

INTRODUCTION

Multimedia data streams used in real world applications have been growing at an astonishing rate. Often, cross data streams are collected from different sources without obvious correlations. Integration typically generates data of high dimensionality, which needs further processing to be useful. Although computer systems and artificial intelligence techniques can assist data processing and, to a certain extent, replace human intensive procedural tasks, incomplete data records and insufficient input from domain experts still pose challenges and make it impossible to implement a fully automatic simulation and prediction system. The goal of our visualization framework is to present cross data streams collected from multiple sources in an interactive and intuitive format, so that domain experts can navigate within the visualization space and identify trends that would not have been discovered using traditional analysis techniques. As a result, data record irregularities can be rectified and important expert input can be built in as system parameters, so that sophisticated machine learning and data mining algorithms can be applied.

In addition to simulating, tracking, and predicting diseases, our framework can be applied to analyze financial data, e.g., currency and interest rate movements, which have important impacts on economies. In this case, the visualization network parameters include the flows of import and export, national and domestic consumer indices. The duration of political instability, natural and seasonal disasters, e.g., hurricanes and other storms can be additional factors affecting the network flows. Another example would be tracking the source-destination and responsiveness of message exchanges in social webs. The visualization framework can also be used to improve traffic movements, and thus city planning. Traffic patterns, which can be denoted by the number of vehicles passing a certain bottleneck, can be plotted

along a time scale. The time of the day and day of the week, as well as holiday seasons, can be used as filtering parameters to visualize selected data sets. Residential dispersion can be used to refine the analysis further. Consumer preferences and purchasing patterns are important analytic criteria in grocery chains. Identifying associations between product sale quantities and other factors, such as weather, holiday seasons, pay days, etc., helps stocking and pricing. In general, the proposed framework is useful in modeling flows over geographical areas, communication networks, business networks and human disease spread. Note that one common characteristic among these applications is that data or information flows can be modeled using *nodes* and *edges*, and a value can be assigned to each edge to reflect the probability of occurrence.

Although we use geospatial-temporal biomedical disease surveillance in our case study, the visualization framework can be applied in many applications. Visualization helps the understanding of data by making use of our human visual system's highly tuned ability and visual encoding, e.g., position, size, shape and color; to recognize patterns, identify trends, and discriminate exceptions, as well as making data more appealing to engage a larger audience in exploration and analysis (Heer, Bostock, & Ogievetsky, 2010). Observation and simulation of flows and trends are keys for proving scientific theories and discovering facts that the human brain would otherwise never imagine (Ailamaki, Kantere, & Dash, 2010). In response to these application demands, constant improvements of observational instruments and simulation mechanisms such as our visualization framework are launched in scientific research.

The rest of the paper is structured as follows: the Related Works Section reviews visualization and network analysis techniques; the Background Section introduces our case study and disease surveillance; the Design Section and the Implementation Section describe the challenges and technical details, as well as feedback from a case study. The final sections include the conclusion and describe future work.

RELATED WORKS

Visualization tools have become attractive to users because of their graphical presentations which often have higher expressive powers than simple text, images and videos alone. Properly structured graphics can convey the underlying associations between otherwise seemingly independent elements, and can perceptually attract more attention from the viewers (Compieta, Di-Martino, Bertolotto, Ferrucci, & Kechadi, 2007). The idea is to highlight possible associations between the displayed data and alert the viewers, if necessary, for more in-depth examinations, possibly through data mining or clustering (Bailey-Kellogg, Ramakrishnan, & Marathe, 2006). Due to the wide variations in design, implementation and even original purpose of the most closely related systems, there is no well defined state-of-the-art system by which to make a comprehensive comparison with our framework. Instead, this section describes various approaches similar to our framework, and then compares the unique features among them.

GeoTime (Proulx et al., 2007) is one such commercial analytics tool designed for processing temporal geospatial information. This tool takes in sequential event data and displays it over a map, with the vertical dimension indicating progression of time. GeoTime imports data using Excel, has a high degree of customizability, and facilitates detection of interesting events.

Another approach to deal with highly dimensional data is to arrange it into a hierarchical structure. Systems such as n-Vision (Beshers & Feiner, 1990) split the highly dimensional data space into a group of simpler, lower-dimensional subspaces. These subspaces are then arranged in a hierarchy to facilitate comprehension, although the ease of understanding in such visualizations naturally depends quite closely on the nature of the data and the partitioning used to generate the subspace hierarchy.

Not all visualization techniques are focused on just visualizing the raw data of interest. Some visualizations deal with high dimensional data by first processing it before visualization (Ferreira de Oliveira & Levkowitz, 2003). For example, some systems perform clustering or some other data mining task, and then visualize the corresponding processed data instead of the actual raw data itself (Gross, Sprenger, & Finger, 1995). While this approach aids in comprehension by breaking down large raw datasets into a more meaningful and structured form, the issue remains that the data pre-processing step might have removed or obfuscated patterns that were in the raw data that would have otherwise been of great interest or importance to the domain experts using the system.

Visual analytics (Lawton, 2009) has generated growing interest in the research community and in industry. An important contribution to the field of visual analytics was made by the National Visualization and Analytics Center in the United States (Thomas & Cook, 2005). Their approach focuses on information visualization relevant to homeland security and their research includes the state-of-the-art in the field, as it details the needs and expectations of stakeholders in order to map out a vision of future development. Visual analytics has four target areas: analytical reasoning techniques, visual representation and interaction techniques, data representation and transformation, and finally, production and presentation (Thomas & Cook, 2005). Such analytical reasoning techniques maximize the human capacity to perceive, understand, and reason. Significant research was done on the analysis of data that can be represented in terms of networks, investigation techniques such as graph partitioning, reorder-able matrix representations, and flow maps (Guo, 2007).

Other related work includes the development of EpiScanGIS which is a GIS-based research prototype designed to detect and visualize epidemics in order to aid decision-makers enact control measures (Reinhardt et al., 2008). It is similar to our proposed framework and implementation in that it is designed to visualize multiple layers of data in the same geographic visualization space, and can animate these visualizations within an adjustable time window in order to observe how they interact or change over time. In contrast to our proposed framework, EpiScanGS is currently designed primarily with human health in mind, and thus does not use network analysis or network visualization due to the inherent logistical realities of attempting to obtain a complete and accurate social network graph for a large human population. The system also does not provide a mechanism for simulating disease spread or explicitly tracing epidemics back to their possible source(s).

Burns et al. (2006) in collaboration with the University of Michigan used ArcObjects (available online at: http://edndoc.esri.com/arcobjects/8.3/) to implement a GIS for epidemic disease surveillance in human populations. Although their system is similar to this paper's proposed framework in that it is designed to be capable of modeling network connections (in this case road networks) to visualize and even simulate disease spread over time, unlike this paper's proposed framework, the ArcObject's-based GIS does not allow for multiple visualization layers to be rendered and animated in the same space, and still does not provide any explicit mechanism for tracing disease propagation backwards through networks in order to identify potential sources. Also, much like EpiScanGIS, the ArcObjects GIS employs visually limited 2-dimensional visualizations, and is designed primarily with human epidemiology in mind.

In order to study the complex interactions that led to disease spread in the 1878 Yellow Fever epidemic of New Orleans, a 3-Dimensional GIS was implemented that was capable of geospatially mapping recorded mortalities over the Urban geography of New Orleans (Curtis, 2008). The system is capable of filtering datasets based on cultural groups and as a result patterns of disease spread through cultural clusters became quite apparent. The system is similar to this paper's proposed framework in that it uses a 3D GIS visualization approach to visually enhance understanding beyond what is normally possible with only a standard 2D GIS visualization. The system also considers factors beyond simple proximity in determining disease spread, although it does not use any explicit network-based approach in either disease modeling or visualization, and simulation through such networks is therefore not part of the design, rather, the system is designed specifically for post hoc analysis and not real-time use by practitioners.

Related work was also recently achieved by Bigras-Poulin et al. (2006) who used networks to analyze the Danish cattle industry in order to examine the risk for disease spread. The approach was similar to the framework proposed in this paper as cattle operation premises were represented as nodes or vertices on the graph, and cattle movements or trade between premises served as connections or edges for the graph in their model. Although the authors were able to perform useful analysis with this approach, they stopped short of proposing or implementing a software framework suggesting how such data may be gathered and visualized in real-time to aid in epidemic disease management.

Data representation and transformation for more effective analysis is also an active area of research. For instance, Heath, Vernon, and Webb (2008) investigated the temporal structure of UK cattle movement data using a network model in which nodes represent movements instead of locations, and links between nodes indicate sequences of movements. Their subsequent analysis demonstrated that this approach was especially effective in analyzing the effect of transmission rates on disease spread. However, once again, the authors stop short of proposing any multimedia software framework for visualizing or managing the data.

Datasets involved in disease surveillance are often quite large, and can typically involve data that are highly dimensional. Expressing large volumes of these data in a way that is understandable, meaningful, and from which useful knowledge can be extracted can often be a challenge (Reinhardt et al., 2008). As a result, GIS-based methods have become an increasingly popular choice for analysis because they offer a highly intuitive means by which to examine and visualize disease surveillance data (Boulos, 2004; Burns et al., 2006; Curtis, 2008; Janies et al., 2007; Jerrett et al., 2003; Reinhardt et al., 2008; Zeng et al., 2004).

BACKGROUND OF DISEASE SURVEILLANCE

Geographic Information Systems (GISs)

A biomedical GIS visualization typically displays a variety of health surveillance data over a geographical overview of the area of interest. The data rendered on top of the geographical map can be as simple as two-dimensional shapes representing various important disease events or clusters (Reinhardt et al., 2008) or as complex as three-dimensional height-maps representing disease mortality rates within an urban environment (Curtis, 2008). Regardless of the specific visuals used to display the data, the key is that the visuals are spatially aligned with the underlying geography of the region in some meaningful way. This approach allows for non-obvious complex interactions, such as the manner by which environmental, climatic, or other spatial factors affect epidemic behaviours, to be more easily viewed and understood (Jerrett et al., 2003).

Network-Based Approach to Modelling Disease Spread

Although traditionally epidemics in human populations were largely modeled via spatial and/or proximity measures, recent research has shown great promise in applying a network-based modeling approach through creating and analyzing a Disease Transmission Network (Luke & Harris, 2007). Network-based models have proven to be particularly effective in modeling the spread of human sexually transmitted diseases such as Syphilis and Human Immunodeficiency Virus (HIV) through social networks given that such diseases have more to do with contacts in one's social network rather than simple proximity (Rothenberg et al., 1998). Further research has concluded that even in the case of highly contagious diseases, social and cultural networks still play a large role in determining the risk of exposure (Curtis, 2008; Dunham, 2005).

Similarly, research in the field of veterinary medicine has highlighted the merits of a network-based visualization approach to modeling disease spread. For example, research into the United Kingdom foot-and-mouth disease epidemic of 2001 revealed that the social business network between farms may be more important than simple proximity in determining disease spread, and that a lack of understanding of the livestock movement network at the time was a factor in the difficulties encountered whilst attempting to halt the spread of disease (Lawson & Zhou, 2005; Shirley & Rushton, 2005). Since then, networks and graph theory when applied to livestock movement data, have proven to be useful in the analysis and understanding of disease transmission in real-world animal movement networks (Bigras-Poulin, Thompson, Chriel, Mortensen, & Greiner, 2006; Shirley & Rushton, 2005; Staubach, Schmid, Knorr-Held, & Ziller, 2002).

Challenges and Motivations

Similar to other surveillance systems, the challenges of interpreting disease data are mainly due to the high data dimensionality and many hidden patterns. Technical knowledge combined with professional experience is necessary in order to understand and analyze the associations between data streams and predict future trends.

The current process for active livestock disease surveillance and epidemic prevention is tedious and often involves experts searching through archived records, many of which may not exist in consistently formatted digital databases. Furthermore, any suspected livestock disease outbreaks are typically only communicated to affected farms directly via telephone. However, this highly-manual procedure is not feasible when mega- to terabyte sized data management is involved. Moreover, the data formats range from manual records to video recordings and even satellite imagery. This significantly increases the complexity in data analysis. Association rules need to be applied before transforming the diversified data into meaningful information comprehensible to the users. An effective data visualization framework for domain experts thus plays an important role in evaluating multiple cross-correlated data streams, and reporting possible "suspicious events" for further investigation.

Many government agencies already actively update and maintain large disease surveillance and livestock movement databases (Zeng et al., 2004) so therefore, the potential exists to leverage online multimedia systems to aid in disease tracking and management. Naturally, these databases by themselves simply provide vast repositories of information and are not inherently useful without some form of analysis framework. Knowledge is typically gathered in a post hoc fashion by most current GIS applications as the system is used to find geospatial and/or temporal patterns and correlations well after the date on which the data were gathered (Curtis, 2008; Janies et al., 2007; Shirley & Rushton, 2005). Thus, the desire remains for a GIS framework that allows for disease surveillance practitioners to visualize, simulate, and predict the spread of disease through livestock movement networks in real-time. Real-time software tools to track diseases backwards to their potential source(s) are of particular interest.

SYSTEM DESIGN

In collaboration with a publically funded veterinarian disease surveillance network organization, a framework was designed and a GIS-based system was implemented. The framework offers a uniquely targeted combination of features that distinguishes it from existing GIS systems in many key areas. Major contributions of the system include:

- A flexible graphical GIS interface that allows for 3D display to multiple platforms including web-based and stereoscopic displays.
- The ability to visualize and animate an arbitrarily-sized time window of movements between operations over time.
- The ability to select any time-continuous sub-network of the overall graph.
- The ability to simulate the forward spread over time.
- The ability to trace backwards through time in order to determine event sources and the ability to use different propagation or network prediction models via a flexible plug-in style interface.
- The framework is designed to maximize the ability of domain experts to understand and control network spread in a real-time visualization space.

The proposed framework was implemented and tested using real data provided by the disease surveillance organization. The results were well received by our industrial partners as a model for future GIS-based online livestock disease surveillance systems.

Design Overview

The proposed framework contains several components (Figure 1). The main visualization user interface component is designed to accept input from databases, as well as to dispatch visual information created by users to the databases.

There are two different plug-in style interfaces designed to maximize system flexibility and utility. The Disease Model Interface, allows for any compatible external disease modeller (i.e., a software module built that implements the interface specifications) to be used with the disease simulation features of the system. Likewise, in order to predict and visualize the livestock movement network data beyond what is available, the Network Prediction Interface allows for any compatible external prediction model to be used with the system. For testing purposes, a basic "worst case" disease modeller and a simple prediction model were implemented. The prediction model assumes fixed and repeating annual patterns. Under normal circumstances, only a percentage of contacted livestock are infected. The worst case model assumes 100% infection once in contact. The percentage parameter can be adjusted depending on the choice of modeler.

Since our framework is not designed for one specific application, a flexible plug-in interface allowing different prediction models and adjustable parameter values is important. As mentioned in the Challenges and Motivations subsection, high dimensionality and hidden patterns are two major issues to address. In the following, we will explain how our proposed framework is designed to handle dimensionality reduction and knowledge exploration using our geospatial-temporal visualization schema, and thus can support effective simulation and prediction in a real-time environment.

Database Schema for Geospatial-Temporal Visualization

Data to be displayed by the network visualization component is classified into two tables just prior to data loading: one table for network vertices and the second for edges. The Vertices Table allows an arbitrarily large number of data columns (i.e., dimensions) but the framework requires at least one column which contains a unique identifier (primary key) for the vertex, and two more columns for its X and Y position in the visualization space. Similarly, the Edges Table can support an arbitrarily large number of data dimensions, with a minimum of three for a valid edge: the sender, receiver, and time of transaction. The sender and receiver are identified by their unique identifiers

Figure 1. Conceptual overview of the proposed framework

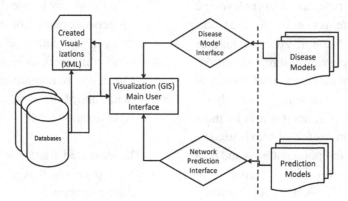

in the Vertices Table governed by the foreign key constraint. The sender, receiver, and time of transaction uniquely identify every row and thus collectively form a primary key for the Edges Table. A fourth, optional data dimension that is specific to the network visualization Edges Table is a column for transaction volume. If left empty, the framework will simply assume the transaction is of unit size (i.e., a size of 1).

Geospatial-temporal attributes play an important role in movement visualization. Our Vertices and Edges Tables design specification precisely captures the characteristics of network-based data visualization.

Reduction of High Dimensional Data

In the proposed framework, the management of high dimensional data occurs in two separate phases: preprocessing prior to visualization and during visualization. Due to the complex nature of integrating the visualization framework with an incomplete existing database, a flexible approach was chosen for the initial data population. Specifically, prior to being loaded by the network visualization component, the data must be preprocessed to create a data view in the simple two-table database schema specification described in the previous section. This specification approach allows for integration into any existing database setup as long as a basic conversion script is implemented to organize the data according to the defined format. A second major benefit of this preprocessing step is that it allows for integration of any other existing data dimensionality reduction solutions, e.g., KNIME (available at: http://www.knime.org), to be used prior to visualization. When implemented in a web-based solution, any preprocessing steps can be configured alongside the visualization interface, and have the new data loaded into the framework on the fly.

The second level of data dimensionality management occurs after the preprocessed data have been loaded. So long as the data loaded adhere

to the format specifications, several tools are offered to the user to manipulate the data presentation both temporally and spatially. Reducing the data into manageable views is largely achieved by adjusting the size and position of a sliding window to only visualize data in the time-domain of interest. Similarly, if the focus is instead on a small spatial region over a large time interval, the framework allows for selections of spatial regions over any time window. In addition to the temporal and spatial mechanisms of manipulating the data presentation, the framework also includes or excludes data based on the results of the network prediction model plug-ins, which make use of the other data dimensions available. The framework is composed of multiple layers. These multimedia visualization layers (e.g., weather data, incident reports, etc.) can be manipulated by similar spatial and temporal tools so as to keep all layers fully aligned and consistent in both space and time.

Knowledge Exploration via Network Visualization

The main GIS visualization user interface is designed to allow users to navigate and explore the movement network data space over time in a geographical context. It is designed to support various visual display options including standard desktop computers, the World Wide Web, and specialized stereoscopic 3D projectors.

In our case study, cattle operations (which include farms, feedlots, slaughterhouses, etc.) are represented as vertices on the movement network (Figure 2), and cattle trade movements between operations are represented as directed edges (i.e., node connections or arrows). The network is rendered in three dimensions to provide different viewing perspectives, as many regions often have several cattle operations clustered closely together. In this framework, such clusters of cattle operations are arranged vertically in the third dimension so that complex transactions between large numbers of operations can be rendered simultaneously in the same visualization space with minimized edge intersections. At any point in time, even during animation of the network, the user may freely adjust their viewing position, angle, and zoom with mouse gestures.

The visualization also includes an adjustable "time window" feature allowing the user to change the interval of time for viewing. By default, the cattle movement network for a single day is rendered as this is the finest level of granularity available in the dataset used, but the user may expand the time dimension to include weeks, months, an entire year, or any size in-between. As shown in Figure 3, the weekly view shows clearly the general trend that cattle tend to flow from north to south in Alberta from northern farms and feedlots to slaughterhouses and other businesses which tend to be located predominately in the southern part of the province. Animating this time window over the course of a year reveals other macro-scale patterns such as the seasonal increase of transaction volume during the spring and fall, and the relative lull in transactions (seen as a reduction in network density) during the summer months.

Besides adjusting the time window, the user may also view any desired "sub-network" of the movement network. Hence, selecting a single vertex, and setting the desired time window to one year, essentially allows the user to view exclusively the entire movement sub-network for a single cattle operation for a year. Selecting two vertices will likewise visualize all livestock movements involving the two selected operations for the chosen time window. The selection tool also includes additive and subtractive modes which allow for any vertices to be added or deleted from the selection sub-network at any time. This essentially allows for any arbitrary combination of vertices to form a sub-network of the overall network.

Propagation Simulation

One of the key features offered by the proposed framework is its ability to visualize a simulation of event spread, and also the ability to automatically track "backwards" in order to identify potential sources. Once the users enter the framework's Forward Disease Simulation Mode, they may

Figure 2. User interface of the implemented framework with Alberta cattle movements shown in the visualization pane. The user may click on any cattle operation or transaction to bring up a large list of detailed information about it.

Figure 3. A zoomed-out top-down view of part of the cattle movement network across Alberta for one week in mid-January. Note that arrow heads are rendered in green and tails are rendered in orange, thus cattle movements flow from orange to green.

select any livestock operations in the region (i.e., vertices on the graph) to mark them as the starting point for an infection. Using the disease model currently plugged into the framework (i.e., different diseases would likely necessitate different models) the framework will calculate how the disease will propagate over time. The infected or potentially exposed livestock operations and transactions will then be highlighted in a separate, visually distinguishing colour. A special visualization mode also exists that exclusively renders only the sub-network of vertices representing those operations marked as potentially exposed to disease by the disease model (Figure 4).

The test prototype aims to assist practitioners in understanding the manner in which livestock diseases may behave or spread throughout the region. For example, if a practitioner were to

receive information that a serious disease was detected at a certain operation three days ago, using the framework will allow the user to view, in real-time, cattle movements that may have exposed other nearby or even remote operations to the disease. The practitioner may also use previous statistics to model where the disease is likely to spread in the near future. Ideally, this will reduce the risk of herd-to-herd disease transmission by isolating the sub-network of potentially exposed livestock operations (i.e., via quarantine or other measures) from the rest of the livestock movement network.

The Reverse Disease Tracking Mode was specifically identified as being a high priority by the epidemiologist practitioners involved in the research project. When the users enter this mode, they may select any livestock operation in the movement network to mark them as locations where a specific disease has been detected. From these starting points, the system will then run the plugged-in disease modeller "backwards" through time in order to mark all the livestock operations that may be a possible source of infection. For example, in Figure 5, the user has identified the cattle operation in the top-left corner of the visualization as being infected, and has chosen to identify all possible sources of infection within the past week. The system has identified three such locations, which are visually marked close to the bottom of the visualization viewport. Even though no cattle were moved explicitly from the two cattle operations in the bottom left-hand corner to the infected operation near the top, both sent cattle to an operation to the east which then later sent cattle to the infected operation in the north. Thus, all three operations are identified as a potential source of the infection. The practitioner may then click on any of the operations to bring up further details, including contact information, and likewise clicking on a transaction brings up all the relevant details available about the infected shipment. By identifying multiple infected locations,

Figure 4. An example of the Disease Propagation system in use. The node in the centre-left has been identified as infected, and the system has simulated its probable spread through the network over the given time period according to the disease propagation model currently plugged-in. The option to disable rendering of the geography layers was also selected for visual clarity in this case. Information about the affected nodes can be revealed by clicking on them (personal information was removed from figure for privacy reasons).

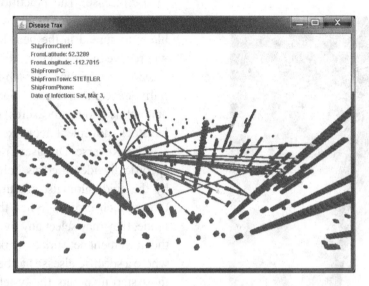

Figure 5. An example of the Reverse Disease Tracking Mode feature in use. The yellow vertex in the top left corner of the viewport was marked as a confirmed infected operation, and the three yellow vertices along the bottom are identified as being potential infection sources.

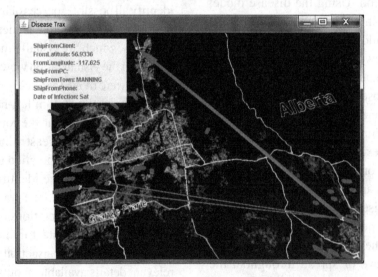

and looking for overlaps in the locations identified as sources, a user can help narrow down or rank the likely candidates for an infection source.

Network Prediction and Disease Model Interface Design

Both the network prediction and disease model interfaces are implemented by constructing a software module that adheres to the simple input-output specifications of the interfaces.

In the case of the Disease Model interface, the module is supplied three data arrays as input. The first two arrays contain all of the vertices and edges, respectively for the network including any and all extra data dimensions associated with each element. The third array is a list of all vertex-time index pairs that indicate which vertices are affected, and at what time. From these data, the spread models are expected to return the vertex and transactions list with new data columns appended onto them. In the case of the vertex list, each vertex now contains an element indicating what time the vertex was first exposed to the disease in question, or null if it was never exposed. Likewise, each transaction contains an additional data column specifying whether or not the transaction was potentially spreading exposed units. The framework is flexible in the sense that models are optionally allowed to output additional details such as the level of infection of a vertex, the stage of infection, etc., if the disease model computes such details. The disease modeller can be chosen by the user at runtime, and different modellers can be used for different types of diseases to account for differences in epidemic behaviours.

As mentioned previously, for the purposes of the case study, a basic worst-case model was implemented. Given a single starting point or a set of starting points, this model simply computes all the vertices in the graph that can possibly have received transactions either directly or indirectly from one of the starting points. The model iterates over each time step, in ascending chronological order and marks a vertex as exposed if it is a receiver of a transaction where the sender of said transaction has already been exposed. The pseudo-code for the algorithm is outlined below:

Assume V is the set of all vertices in the graph, E is the set of all edges, and T is the set of all time indices in ascending order, and $E(v_1, v_2, t_1)$ represents a directed edge from vertex v_1 to vertex v_2 at time index t_1.

In reality, a contacted entity may not be infected. The worst case scenario assumes an infection rate of 100% once contacted. The percentage parameter can be adjusted depending on the model chosen. Disease modeller modules may load any additional model configuration parameters as desired from a configuration file.

The network prediction module interface is almost identical in design to the disease model interface except that in place of the list of vertex/time pairs, it instead takes as input a time value indicating up to what time index the modeller should stop creating the predicted network. The model then returns a list of predicted transactions between vertices up to the time limit specified.

IMPLEMENTATION AND CASE STUDY VALIDATION

The implementation of the framework presented in this paper was written as a Java application using JOGL: the Java Open Graphics Library (available online at https://jogl.dev.java.net/) for 3D visualization. Java was chosen as the programming language due to its cross-platform compatibly, the ease of deployment on the web, and strong flexible interfaces and dynamic library loading ideal for loading external components such as the disease or network prediction models during runtime. JOGL was chosen due to its built-in graphics hardware acceleration available on most major platforms, and its wide, flexible feature-set.

Box 1.

```
for t=0, t < size(T), t++
foreach v1 in V
if isExposed(v1)
 then
 foreach v2 in V
 if exists(E(v1,v2,T(t)))
 then
 setExposed(v2, true)
 end if
 end foreach loop
end if
end foreach loop
end for loop
```

Real-Time Challenges and a Hybrid Caching Solution

Several design challenges needed to be overcome in implementing a visualization framework that could remain sufficiently responsive for real-time interactivity in spite of the large volumes of highly dimensional data present. In particular, the computational costs involved with rendering and animating a large number of transactions concurrently with different time windows was of particular concern, because although the number of vertices is known and constant, the number of transactions can be comparatively much larger. Assuming that there are n vertices in the network graph, and that there are t discrete time-steps, we can see that for each individual time-step there are a total of n^2 possible transactions. Therefore, given a time window of size 1, we have $n^2 \times t$ possible transactions for the entire dataset.

To keep the system performing in real-time, it becomes apparent that for large numbers of transactions, attempting to compute the position, scale, and direction of all 3D transaction meshes every frame, or after every parameter change, will quickly become too costly. Thus, a caching option for the 3D meshes in the visualization scene is required to keep the system responsive. One such caching approach that might be considered would be to pre-cache every scene for every possible time window configuration. However, in terms of the actual number of unique data views that can be created by the user, we can see that the total is actually significantly larger than just the value of t. Given that the upper bound of the sliding time window "u" can be of any value between 0 and t and likewise, the lower bound of the sliding time window "l" can be of any value between 0 and t as long as $l \leq u$, we can see that there are approximately up to $t^2/2$ possible unique views that can be created by the user just by using the time window feature alone. For large timescales involving several years of data, the value of t will be quite large and the space requirements for pre-caching a 3D scene mesh for every possible time view will quickly become unmanageable. This is complicated even further by all the possible unique spatial restrictions the user may configure let alone the additional possible views introduced by the disease or network prediction modellers.

Thus, to solve the dilemma, a hybrid caching solution was chosen whereby the three-dimensional positions, scales, and orientations of every transaction mesh were pre-cached only on a per-transaction basis. Each transaction mesh then contains a single Boolean flag indicating whether or not it should draw itself at the current time index, and these flags are toggled only on affected transactions during a change of a relevant visualization parameter. With this approach, the transaction caching step is linear in the number of transactions, as are the parameter updates, even in the rare worst case where all transactions must have their flags updated all at once.

Case Study and Results

The dataset used in the case study was tested on a standard 2.20GHz dual core personal computer with a 475 MHz graphics processor and 256MB of video RAM. The dataset contained 1,418 vertices with 6 dimensions per vertex, and 218,391 transactions with 14 dimensions per transaction, spread over 365 time-steps whereby each time-step corresponded to a single day of the year. Initial data loading and one-time pre-caching of the entire dataset took approximately 3 seconds to complete, with the majority of the time taken due to the unavoidable hard-disc read time rather than the pre-caching step. During normal operation with daily, weekly, or monthly time-windows (i.e., viewing up to 50,000 transactions at once), the visualization was able to maintain a frame-rate of between 30 to 40 frames per second regardless of other configuration parameters or animation settings. Visualization view updates due to new data or parameter configuration changes were all completed in less than 1 second.

Although the framework proposed in this paper can be used for multimedia data management and visualization in a wide range of applications, we chose disease surveillance of livestock production systems and the detection of possible outbreaks in our case study by examining historic trends and using disease spread models. The complex and high-dimensional multiple cross data streams collected over time and throughout the entire production continuum used in our case study was provided by a publicly funded animal disease surveillance network organization.

Although the surveillance network's databases contain ample data, there were few means by which to understand the data or draw conclusions from them. Previous efforts were made by the surveillance network organization to use statistical models and data mining in order to help detect alarming events, but these approaches are not useful for understanding and predicting long-term trends and behaviors. The proposed visualization framework was therefore developed and implemented with input and feedback from the organization's veterinarian epidemiologist practitioners for using multimedia data visualization and animation in order to practically and effectively perceive meaningful long-term patterns and trends. A similar computer-based real-time

visualization framework is simply non-existent, as advised by the epidemiologist professionals.

The visualization framework was presented to several groups of scientists and middle managers in the government food safety and animal health divisions. The senior scientists were interested in using the framework to simulate their assumptions about relationships in the data. From another perspective, the managers could see value for them to better understand these assumptions/relationships and then be able to communicate them to fellow managers and improve their deliberations about impacts of policy decisions. In general, the team of domain experts found the network-based visualization approach of live-stock production system data very helpful in the discovery of underlying patterns and interesting events, which may lead to the understanding of historic trends and the prediction of future disease outbreaks. The forward prediction and backward tracking both proved helpful in providing information for controlling disease spread.

Using the implemented visualization framework, the veterinarian epidemiologist practitioners were already able to make several preliminary discoveries and new knowledge gains:

- A large number of long-standing assumptions regarding the most at-risk regions for infection were validated and confirmed by the visualization framework, and several new smaller high-risk hotspots were shown as well.

- The visualization framework also clearly demonstrated that the overall risk of herd-to-herd secondary infections were surprisingly small as the vast majority of cattle operations appear only to buy or sell cattle, but not do both. Of the operations that did frequently both buy and sell cattle, they typically did not do both types of transactions inside small time windows or sell to a large number of clients all at once. However, whether this is a result of cattle operations failing to report certain trans-actions remains unknown until new larger and more robust datasets become available.

- In addition to the preliminary discoveries made by the intended use of the framework, a number of additional unexpected benefits of the system also manifested during the case study. Practitioners were quickly able to notice anomalies in the visualization where certain cattle operations appeared to sell large numbers of cattle without show-ing any source of obtaining them. Further investigation revealed that the operations involved, perhaps due to misunderstanding of proper procedures, had not submitted the proper paperwork for their cattle pur-chases. In fact, this issue turned out to be quite common amongst several operations across the province. Given the relative ease with which such operations could be iden-tified by the visualization, remedial action could be undertaken immediately.

Overall, the users described the visualization interface as straightforward and easy to under-stand. As the system continues to be used by the practitioners over time, and as user familiar-ity increases, additional discoveries and further knowledge gains are expected.

FUTURE WORK

Future works include plans to implement and incorporate additional models into the system, including models for other applications that use geospatial-temporal data for simulation and predi-cation. In addition, there are plans to incorporate additional visualization layers to examine any possible relationship with geography and envi-ronmental properties. Lastly, we will enhance the visualization further by distinguishing the various states. For example, "susceptible", "exposed", "infected", "immune", etc., which in our case study, a herd at a livestock operation might exist in.

CONCLUSION

This paper proposes the design of a multimedia data management and visualization framework for a 3D, online, real-time network-based GIS, and presents a case study where the framework proved effective in aiding veterinarian epidemiologists in understanding herd-to-herd disease spread through livestock movement networks with the ultimate goal of assisting in the management and prevention of such diseases. Through its network based visualization approach, the framework of-fers unique tools and approaches to movement visualization and simulation including the ability to model where current events will possibly spread in the near future, and predict where a known event may have come from in the recent past. The software implementation of the system was created with an interdisciplinary research team involv-ing computing science researchers, veterinarian epidemiologist practitioners, and an industrial partner. The unique features of the framework are, to the best of the authors' knowledge and the knowledge of the participating veterinarian epidemiologist practitioners, a novel and useful approach to multimedia utilization in the field of biomedical multimedia computing and multime-dia forensics, particularly in the field of disease surveillance. Although the proposed framework was tested with the management, simulation and predication of events and visualization of high-dimensional multimedia biomedical data, it can be readily applied to other similar forms of complex multimedia data as well.

REFERENCES

Ailamaki, A., Kantere, V., & Dash, D. (2010). Managing scientific data. *Communications of the ACM, 53*(8), 88–78.

Bailey-Kellogg, C., Ramakrishnan, N., & Marathe, M. V. (2006). Mining and visualizing spatial interaction patterns for pandemic response. *ACM SIGKDD Explorations Newsletter*, 80-82.

Beshers, C. G., & Feiner, S. K. (1990). Visualizing n-dimensional virtual worlds within n-Vision. *Computer Graphics, 24*(2), 37–38. doi:10.1145/91394.91412

Bigras-Poulin, M., Thompson, R. A., Chriel, M., Mortensen, S., & Greiner, M. (2006). Network analysis of Danish cattle industry trade patterns as an evaluation of risk potential for disease spread. *Preventive Veterinary Medicine, 76*(1-2), 11–39. doi:10.1016/j.prevetmed.2006.04.004

Boulos, M. (2004). Descriptive review of geographic mapping of severe acute respiratory syndrome (SARS) on the Internet. *International Journal of Health Geographics, 3*(1), 2. doi:10.1186/1476-072X-3-2

Burns, J., Hatt, C., Brooks, C., Keefauver, E., Wells, E. V., Shuchman, R., & Wilson, M. L. (2006). Visualization and simulation of disease outbreaks: Spatially-explicit applications using disease surveillance data. In *Proceedings of the ESRI Users conference*.

Compieta, P., Di-Martino, S., Bertolotto, M., Ferrucci, F., & Kechadi, T. (2007). Exploratory spatio-temporal data mining and visualization. *Journal of Visual Languages and Computing, 18*(3), 255–279. doi:10.1016/j.jvlc.2007.02.006

Curtis, A. (2008). Three-dimensional visualization of cultural clusters in the 1878 yellow fever epidemic of New Orleans. *International Journal of Health Geographics, 7*(1), 47. doi:10.1186/1476-072X-7-47

Dunham, J. B. (2005). An agent-based spatially explicit epidemiological model in MASON. *Journal of Artificial Societies and Social Simulation, 9*(1), 3.

Ferreira de Oliveira, M. C., & Levkowitz, H. (2003). From visual data exploration to visual data mining: A survey. *IEEE Transactions on Visualization and Computer Graphics, 9*(3), 378–394. doi:10.1109/TVCG.2003.1207445

Gross, M. H., Sprenger, T. C., & Finger, J. (1995). Visualizing information on a sphere. In *Proceedings of the IEEE Symposium on Information Visualization* (pp. 11-16).

Guo, D. (2007). Visual analytics of spatial interaction patterns for pandemic decision support. *International Journal of Geographical Information Science, 21*(8), 859–877. doi:10.1080/13658810701349037

Heath, F. M., Vernon, M. C., & Webb, C. R. (2008). Construction of networks with intrinsic temporal structure from UK cattle movement data. *BMC Veterinary Research, 4*(1), 11. doi:10.1186/1746-6148-4-11

Heer, J., Bostock, M., & Ogievetsky, V. (2010). A tour through the visualization zoo. *Communications of the ACM, 53*(8), 59–67. doi:10.1145/1743546.1743567

Janies, D., Hill, A. W., Guralnick, R., Habib, F., Waltari, E., & Wheeler, W. C. (2007). Genomic analysis and geographic visualization of the spread of avian influenza (H5N1). *Systematic Biology, 56*, 321–329. doi:10.1080/10635150701266848

Jerrett, M., Burnett, R., Goldberg, M., Sears, M., Krewski, D., & Catalan, R. (2003). Spatial analysis for environmental health research: Concepts, methods, and examples. *Journal of Toxicology and Environmental Health. Part A: Current Issues, 66*(19), 1783–1810. doi:10.1080/15287390306446

Lawson, A. B., & Zhou, H. (2005). Spatial statistical modeling of disease outbreaks with particular reference to the UK foot and mouth disease (FMD) epidemic of 2001. *Preventive Veterinary Medicine*, *71*(3-4), 141–156. doi:10.1016/j.prevetmed.2005.07.002

Lawton, G. (2009). Users take a close look at visual analytics. *IEEE Computer Magazine*, *42*(2), 19–22.

Luke, D. A., & Harris, J. K. (2007). Network analysis in public health: History, methods, and applications. *Annual Review of Public Health*, *28*, 16.1-16.25.

Proulx, P., Chien, L., Harper, R., Schroh, D., Kapler, D., & Jonker, D. (2007). nSpace and GeoTime: A VAST 2006 case study. *IEEE Computer Graphics and Applications*, *27*(5), 46–56. doi:10.1109/MCG.2007.131

Reinhardt, M., Elias, J., Albert, J., Frosch, M., Harmsen, D., & Vogel, U. (2008). EpiScanGIS: An online geographic surveillance system for meningococcal disease. *International Journal of Health Geographics*, *7*(1), 33. doi:10.1186/1476-072X-7-33

Rothenberg, R. B., Potterat, J. J., Woodhouse, D. E., Muth, S. Q., Darrow, W. W., & Klovdahl, A. S. (1998). Social network dynamics and HIV transmission. *AIDS (London, England)*, *12*(12), 1529–1536. doi:10.1097/00002030-199812000-00016

Rothenberg, R. B., Sterk, C., Toomey, K. E., Potterat, J. J., Johnson, D., & Schrader, M. (1998). Using social network and ethnographic tools to evaluate syphilis transmission. *Sexually Transmitted Diseases*, *25*(3), 154–160. doi:10.1097/00007435-199803000-00009

Shirley, M. D. F., & Rushton, S. P. (2005). Where diseases and networks collide: Lessons to be learnt from a study of the 2001 foot-and-mouth disease epidemic. *Epidemiology and Infection*, *133*, 1023–1032. doi:10.1017/S095026880500453X

Staubach, C., Schmid, V., Knorr-Held, L., & Ziller, M. (2002). A Bayesian model for spatial wildlife disease prevalence data. *Preventive Veterinary Medicine*, *56*(1), 75–87. doi:10.1016/S0167-5877(02)00125-3

Thomas, J. J., & Cook, K. A. (2005). *Illuminating the path: The research and development agenda for visual analytics*. Berkeley, CA: National Visualization and Analytics Center.

Zeng, D., Chen, H., Tseng, C., Larson, C. A., Eidson, M., Gotham, I., et al. (2004). Towards a national infectious disease information infrastructure: A case study in West Nile virus and botulism. In *Proceedings of the Annual National Conference on Digital Government Research*, Seattle, WA (pp. 1-10).

This work was previously published in the International Journal of Multimedia Data Engineering and Management, Volume 2, Issue 2, edited by Shu-Ching Chen, pp. 1-18, copyright 2011 by IGI Publishing (an imprint of IGI Global).

Chapter 14
A Cross–Layer Design for Video Streaming Over 802.11e HCCA Wireless Network

Hongli Luo
Indiana University-Purdue University Fort Wayne, USA

ABSTRACT

Video transmission over wireless networks has quality of service (QoS) requirements and the time-varying characteristics of wireless channels make it a challenging task. IEEE 802.11 Wireless LAN has been widely used for the last mile connection for multimedia transmission. In this paper, a cross-layer design is presented for video streaming over IEEE 802.11e HCF Controlled Channel Access (HCCA) WLAN. The goal of the cross-layer design is to improve the quality of the video received in a wireless network under the constraint of network bandwidth. The approach is composed of two algorithms. First, an allocation of optimal TXOP is calculated which aims at maintaining a short queuing delay at the wireless station at the cost of a small TXOP allocation. Second, the transmission of the packets is scheduled according to the importance of the packets in order to maximize the visual quality of video. The approach is compared with the standard HCCA on NS2 simulation tools using H.264 video codec. The proposed cross-layer design outperforms the standard approach in terms of the PSNRs of the received video. This approach reduces the packet loss to allow the graceful video degradation, especially under heavy network traffic.

1. INTRODUCTION

Because of the increase of the multimedia data and wireless networks, there is an increasing demand for wireless multimedia transmission over the Internet. IEEE 802.11 Wireless LAN (WLAN) is widely used for the mobile and ubiquitous multimedia networking because of its low cost and ease of configurations. Video transmission has its quality of service (QoS) requirements, such as bandwidth, packet loss and delay. Because of the dynamics of the wireless channels, the quality of service (QoS) poses challenges to the design of the wireless networks.

Since IEEE 802.11 WLAN cannot provide QoS for multimedia applications, the IEEE 802.11

DOI: 10.4018/978-1-4666-2940-0.ch014

Working Group has proposed 802.11e (IEEE Computer Society, 2003) as a new enhancement with QoS features. It can provide differentiated services for real-time multimedia applications, such as video and audio. 802.11e standards specified two QoS medium access mechanism: Enhanced Distributed Channel Access (EDCA) and HCF (Hybrid Coordinator Function) Controlled Channel Access (HCCA). EDCA is a contention based channel access mechanism which provides differentiated services for different traffic categories. HCCA is a polling-based and contention free medium access. It uses a centralized scheduling scheme at the Access Point (AP) to allocate the transmission opportunities to the stations. However the current design of 802.11e still cannot guarantee the QoS for multimedia applications. There are lots of researches on the EDCA and HCCA of 802.11e MAC layer to improve the QoS. A major research issue for HCCA is the design of an efficient scheduling algorithm to provide QoS for different traffic.

Cross-layer design of wireless multimedia transmission (Van Der Schaar & Shankar, 2005) provides a promising direction to improve the overall performance of wireless networks since it takes into account the interactions among layers. In this paper, a cross-layer design for video streaming over 802.11e HCCA WLAN is proposed. Our approach involves interactions between the application layers and MAC layers to exchange information about the traffic. The actual queue length of wireless stations is provided as feedback information to the central controller. To maximize the quality of video, the proposed approach is designed to minimize the loss rate of the packets of high importance and provide a bounded delay for the packets. The length of transmission opportunity (TXOP) allocated to each wireless station provides an efficient bandwidth management, at the same time the scheduling of the packets maximizes the video quality under the allocated TXOP. In our previous work (Luo & Shyu, 2009; Luo, 2009), an optimized TXOP

allocation algorithm was proposed for 802.11e to achieve a small delay for video packets. This paper extends our previous work to optimize the end-to-end video quality over IEEE 802.11e HCCA wireless networks with the consideration of importance of video packets.

The rest of the paper is organized as follows. Section 2 gives a brief introduction of the IEEE 802.11e MAC layer mechanisms. Related research in the QoS support in the IEEE 802.11e is reviewed in Section 3. The cross-layer scheduling algorithm is proposed in Section 4. Section 5 presents the simulation results of the cross-layer design. Finally, the last section gives the conclusions.

2. IEEE 802.11E MAC

This section gives a brief introduction of IEEE 802.11e MAC layer, which is composed of HCCA and EDCA.

2.1. IEEE 802.11e HCCA

IEEE 802.11e HCCA provides a centralized polling scheme to allocate the access to the channel to traffic flows according to their QoS requirements. A beacon interval is divided into contention period (CP) and contention-free period (CFP). During the CP, the access to the medium is controlled by the EDCA. But the hybrid coordinator (HC) can initiate controlled access periods (CAPs) at any time. HCCA is in charge of the contention-free medium access and collocated at the access point. A transmission opportunity (TXOP) is an interval of time in which a wireless station (STA) or the HC can transmit a burst of data separated by a short interframe space (SIFS) interval. The major responsibility of the HC is to perform bandwidth allocation via assigning TXOPs to each STA.

A reference scheduler was proposed by the IEEE 802.11 working group to determine the TXOP for each traffic flow. Each traffic flow declares its QoS characteristics in traffic specification (TSPEC). The reference scheduler uses several TSPEC parameters for the calculation, such as the mean data rate, nominal MAC service data unit (MSDU) size, and maximum service interval (SI). N_i is the number of MSDUs that arrive at the mean data rate for each traffic stream during one SI for stream i, which is calculated as follows:

$$N_i = \left\lceil \frac{SI \ x \ \rho_i}{L_i} \right\rceil \tag{1}$$

where Li is the nominal MSDU size of stream i and ρi is the Mean Data Rate of stream i.

Then the transmission opportunity for stream i, $TXOP_i$ is obtained by

$$TXOP_i = \max(\frac{N_i x L_i}{R_i} + O, \frac{M}{R_i} + O) \tag{2}$$

where R_i is the minimum physical rate for stream i, and M is the maximum allowable size of MSDUs. o is the overhead in time units, including the PHY and MAC headers, interframe space, ACK and the polling overhead. As can be observed from the formula, the reference scheduler allocates fixed-length TXOPs for each station based on the declared TSPEC parameters. It works well for the constant bit rate (CBR) traffic; while not efficient for the variable bit rate (VBR) traffic with varying data rates. With constant TXOPs, there may be overflow at the queues of the station under VBR traffic, which results in packet loss.

2.2. IEEE 802.11e EDCA

IEEE 802.11e EDCA provides differentiated service in a distributed manner with the introduction of access categories (ACs). It assigns different access opportunities to each AC by differentiating channel access delay among ACs. Each AC defines a different set of channel access parameters to specify how a station should backoff its transmission if a busy channel is sensed. Some parameters to differentiate the services include:

contention window (CW), CW_{max}, CW_{min}, arbitrary interframe space (AIFS). A smaller CW_{max} or CW_{min} is assigned to traffic of higher priority, so higher priority traffic will have a better chance of accessing the wireless medium and being transmitted before low priority ones. EDCA defines 4 ACs: AC_VO for voice, AC_VI for video, AC_BE for best effort traffic, and AC_BK for background traffic.

3. RELATED WORK

3.1. QoS Scheduling at the 802.11e HCCA

Since the reference scheduler of 802.11e HCCA cannot efficiently utilize the bandwidth, many scheduling algorithms have been proposed to overcome the shortcomings of the reference scheduler. An efficient scheduler should be adaptive to the network traffic and application requirement. Since the queue length at the wireless station is an indicator of the network traffic, it is used as feedback information for several adaptive schedulers. The FHCF scheme proposed in Ansel, Ni, and Turletti (2006) adjusts the TXOP of each flow according to the estimation of the queue length. It considers the varying traffic and application requirements by using the queue length to calculate the current demands of flows. The TXOP will be increased if the current demand is higher than the reserved transmission time. In Giro, Macedo, and Nunes (2003), the scheduling of the queued packets follows a delay-earliest-due-date algorithm. The TXOPs are assigned based on earliest deadlines to reduce transmission delay and packet losses. In Boggia, Camarda, Grieco, and Mascolo (2007), two schedulers that utilize the discrete-time feedback control theory are proposed: feedback based dynamic scheduler and proportional-integral scheduler. Inan, Keceli, and Ayanoglu (2006) proposed a scheduler that adaptively adjusted service intervals, transmission opportunities, and polling order based on the instantaneous network conditions and traffic characteristics.

Reference scheduling schedules all streams with a common spacing. Zhao and Tsang (2008) proposed an equal-spacing-based (equal-SI) design, where spacing is defined as the interval between two successive scheduling of stream. In the equal-SI design, each stream is scheduled with equal spacing and different streams are scheduled with different spacings. In Skyrianoglou, Passas, and Salkintzis (2006), the available bandwidth is allocated based on the actual amount of data waiting at every STA. Cicconetti, Lenzini, Mingozzi, and Stea (2007) proposed a scheduler for IEEE 802.11e HCCA which provides traffic streams with a minimum reserved rate and accounts for CBR and VBR traffic simultaneously. Bheemarjuna, John, and Siva Ram Murthy (2007) aims at improving the ratio of packets that reach the destination within the deadline in 802.11e based multi-hop ad hoc wireless network. It dynamically changes the priorities of packets in the MAC queue and modifies the TXOP based on the packets in the queue. Adaptive TXOP allocation proposed in Arora, Yoon, Choi, & Bahk (2010) exploits the channel condition to increase system efficiency. Minimal length of TXOP is allocated to stations with bad channel condition, so more TXOP can be allocated to stations with a better channel condition.

3.2. Cross-Layer Design for 802.11e

Cross-layer design improves QoS of networking applications by jointly considering several network layers. There are lots of cross-layer approaches proposed for the QoS provision of 802.11e WLAN that can considerably improve the throughput and delay performance. Most approaches cover a variety of techniques at the application layer, MAC layer or physical (PHY) layer. Zhu, Zeng, and Li (2007) considers transport layer in their cross-layer approach, which consists of source rate control at the application layer, congestion control at the transport layer, and wireless loss ratio at MAC layer.

Cai, Gao, and Wu (2007) proposed a cross-layer approach for IEEE 802.11e HCCA WLAN, which includes admission control and resource allocation at the MAC layer and video adaptation at the application layer. Van Der Schaar, Andreopoulos, and Hu (2006) optimized the scalable video over IEEE 802.11 HCCA across application-MAC-PHY layer by maximizing the number of admitted stations. Hsu and Hefeeda (2011) jointly sets parameters at application layer, link layer, and physical layers to optimize the video quality of all streams considering different power levels and channel conditions of the wireless stations. Shankar and Van Der Schaar (2007) provides a cross-layer design that adapts both EDCA and HCCA parameters to optimize the quality of video at the receiver.

Ksentini, Naimi, and Gueroui (2006) proposed a method to improve the QoS over EDCA of 802.11e, which utilized the data partitioning technique at the application layer and QoS mapping technique at the EDCA-based MAC layer. Van Der Schaar and Turaga (2007) introduced an application-MAC layer design that jointly decides the optimal packet size at the application layer and retransmission limits at the MAC layer. The cross-layer design in Chilamkurti, Zeadally, Soni, and Giambene (2010) maps video packets at the application layer to the appropriate access categories of 802.11e EDCA at the MAC layer according to the significance of the video data.

4. THE PROPOSED CROSS-LAYER DESIGN

The proposed cross-layer scheduling algorithms are adaptive to the varying network traffic and the requirements of the real-time applications. To reflect the current network traffic and the requirements of the application, the information of the queue size at STA is used for the calculation of TXOP. There are two major mechanisms in the proposed approach. First, an optimized TXOP is calculated at access point with the objective of maintaining small queuing delay at each STA at the cost of a small TXOP. Then each STA schedules the transmission of the packets under the constraint of allocated TXOP with the goal of maximizing the video quality at the receiver.

4.1. Architecture of the Cross-Layer Design

The video transmitted over the Internet are compressed video using different standards, such as MPEG and H.264 (Joint Video Team of ISO/IEC MPEG and ITU-T VCEG, 2002). The video standards define three types of video frames, I frame, P frame and B frame. Since I frame has the highest importance to the quality of the video, I frame packet is considered as the highest priority.

At each STA, video stream is encoded using H.264 codec at the application layer. The video packets are generated at the application layer and passed to the lower layers. The information of the packet is also passed to the lower layers, such as the frame type of the packet and the size of the packet. Different from most of the existing methods which use the estimation of the queue length, the actual queue length is used here. Queue length reflects the network traffic, and size of packets represents the application requirements. Both the size of the packets and actual queue length will be transmitted back to the access point as feedback information.

Access point polls each STA and receives the information from STA. At access point, the MAC layer calculates TXOPs assigned to STAs based on the actual queue length and the application requirement, which determines the time duration each station can send out the packets. With the allocated TXOP, the priority scheduling algorithm

at the MAC layer of the STA sender determines which packets to transmit based on several factors, such as the importance and size of the packets.

4.2. Admission Control

The traffic flows of the wireless stations are admitted under the admission control policy. The admission control guarantees that the admission of a new flow will not affect the quality of service experienced by the existing flows.

Assume the number of existing flows is j, the service interval is SI, the beacon interval is T, and the time allocated for EDCA traffic is T_{cp}. The admission control policy decides a new stream $j+1$ is admitted if the following formula is satisfied.

$$\frac{TXOP_{j+1}}{SI} + \sum_{i=1}^{j} \frac{TXOP_i}{SI} \leq \frac{T - T_{CP}}{T} \tag{3}$$

The number of admitted flows is determined by SI, T, T_{cp} and TXOP. The calculation of TXOP is based on the data rates declared by each flow in TSPEC.

4.3. Optimized TXOP Allocation at the Access Point

The adaptive TXOP allocation in our approach is designed to improve the average QoS of all the stations under the heavy network traffic. A large TXOP allocated for a traffic stream will reduce the queue length and consequently reduce the delay, but an over allocation of TXOP is a waste of network bandwidth. At the other hand, a small TXOP allocated for a traffic stream will degrade the QoS with large end-to-end delay and packet loss. With a small TXOP, the packets need to be waiting in the queue too long to be transmitted, which results in a large end-to-end delay. There is packet loss at the STA if there are a large number of packets coming from the application layer and buffer overflow occurs. So an optimal TXOP is a TXOP that is small but at the same time it will not result in buffer flow at the queue and it can maintain an acceptable queue length and delay. Based on this analysis, an objective index for optimized TXOP allocation is introduced in Equation (5).

At the kth interval, $q[k]$ is the actual queue length of traffic flow at a STA at the beginning of kth interval, $p[k]$ is the size of the packets arriving at the queue during the kth interval, $d[k]$ is the size of the packets that are transmitted and depleted at the queue at the kth interval. The dynamics of the queue length at the kth interval can be described as

$$q[k] = q[k-1] + p[k-1] - d[k-1] \qquad (4)$$

The $d[k-1]$ is determined by the TXOP allocated to the STA during each time interval. $p[k-1]$ can be obtained from the sizes of the video packets. Since the goal of our approach is to maintain a small queue length at the cost of a small allocation of network bandwidth, the objective index J can be written as follows,

$$J = \frac{1}{2}\sum_{K=0}^{N-1}(h*(q[k]-q_r)^2 + c*(d[k]-d_r)^2) \qquad (5)$$

where q_r is the reference queue length or the ideal queue length that should be achieved at the beginning of each time interval. Q_r is set to 0 which means the ideal allocation of TXOP can deplete the queue and reduce the queuing delay. Minimizing the $q[k]-q_r$ means the queuing delay of packets should be as small as possible at the cost of the small transmission opportunities. d_r is the expected depletion rates assigned to the queue, which is set to 0. The objective is to minimize $d[k]$ and at the same time $q[k]$. h and c are the weight coefficients assigned for each traffic flow. For traffic flows that have higher real-time requirements, for example, small end-to-end delay, a shorter queue

length should be maintained, so a larger h value will be assigned.

The optimal TXOP is calculated according to the current queue length and the incoming packet size. Both the current queue length and the incoming packet size are transmitted to the HC as feedback information. An optimal $d[k]$ schedule minimizes the performance index J. So the optimized problem is to find a sequence of $d[k]$: $k= 0, 1, ..., N-1$ that minimizes J.

The first step to solve this optimization problem is to form the Hamilton equation as

$$H[k] = \frac{1}{2}h(q[k]-q_r)^2 + \frac{1}{2}c(d[k]-d_r)^2 + \lambda[k+1](q[k]+p[k]-d[k]) \qquad (6)$$

The optimal sequence of $d[k]$ can be solved from $\dfrac{\partial H(k)}{\partial d(k)} = 0$,

$$d[k] = d_r + \frac{\lambda[k+1]}{c} \qquad (7)$$

$\lambda[k]$ can be sequentially solved from the following Equation (8).

$$\lambda[k+1] = \lambda[k] - h(q[k]-q_r) \qquad (8)$$

After the $\lambda[k]$ and $\lambda[k+1]$ are obtained, $d[k]$ can be solved from Equation (7).

Inside the Equation (8), the initial value of $\lambda[k]$ is calculated as

$$\lambda[0] = \omega^{-1}\left(-[0 \ 1]A^N\begin{bmatrix}1\\0\end{bmatrix}q[0] - [0 \ 1]\sum_{k=0}^{N-1}A^{N-k-1}G[k]\right) \qquad (9)$$

where the variables ω, A and $G[k]$ are calculated as

$$A = \begin{bmatrix}1+\frac{h}{c} & -\frac{1}{c}\\ -h & 1\end{bmatrix} \qquad (10)$$

$$\omega = [0 \quad 1] A^N \begin{bmatrix} 0 \\ 1 \end{bmatrix} \tag{11}$$

and

$$G[k] = \begin{bmatrix} -\frac{h}{c} q_r - d_r + p[k] \\ h q_r \end{bmatrix} \tag{12}$$

The details of the solving of the optimization problem can be seen in our previous work (Luo & Shyu, 2009). Since depletion rate $d[k]$ is a non-negative value, the optimal depletion rate is determined as max$\{d[k], 0\}$. The performance index J obtained under the optimal schedule $d[k]$ is smaller than any other sequences of $d[k]$.

$d[k]$ is represented in the number of packets that should be depleted in the given time interval, which will be converted to TXOP. If the queue for ith traffic flow is depleted at rate $d[k]$, the TXOP allocated to the ith traffic flow during the time interval k is,

$$TXOP_i(k) = \max(\frac{t*d[k]}{R_i} + O, \frac{M}{R_i} + O) \tag{13}$$

where t is the time interval used for the calculation of $d[k]$. The allocated TXOP is rounded in order to guarantee a queuing delay smaller than or equal to the bounded queuing delay. O is the overhead assigned to ACK packets and interframe spaces.

4.4. Priority Scheduling at the Wireless Station

After the TXOP for each traffic stream is calculated at the access point, it will be sent to the STA. The priority scheduling algorithm at each STA decides which packets to transmit under the constraint of allocated TXOP. The purpose of the priority scheduling is to maximize the quality of the received video via minimizing the distortion resulted from packet loss.

The priority scheduling plays an important role in improving the quality of video especially when the network traffic is heavy and the TXOP is not large enough to deplete the packets waiting at the queue. Since packets have different contributions to the video quality, packets with higher importance should be transmitted with higher priority. Multiple virtual queues are created for the packets of different priorities. In a simplified case, 3 virtual queues are created for three frame

Algorithm 1. Priority scheduling

Wireless station receives the TXOP allocation $TXOP_{allocated}$ from the access point
Create L_{max} priority virtual queues
Map the frame type of the packet into priority value
Enqueue the packets to the corresponding priority virtual queue

for (i=L$_{max}$; i>0 and $\sum_{j=1}^{L\,max} txop_j(k) < TXOP_{Allocated}$; i--) do

fetch a packet in virtual priority queue i and calculate txop

if $\sum_{j=1}^{L\,max} txop_j(k) < TXOP_{Allocated}$

transmit the packet
else
skip the packet
end if
end for

Table 1. Parameters setting used in the simulation

Parameter	Value
Beacon Interval	0.5 s
SIFS	16 μs
DIFS	34 μs
Slot time	9 μs
ACK frame length	14 Bytes
MAC header length	38 Bytes
PLCP preamble	16 μs

types, Virtual priority queue I, Virtual priority queue P, and Virtual priority queue B. Each virtual queue is for packets belonging to the same frame type. Since packet arrives at the MAC layer with its frame type information, the frame type of each incoming packet is checked at the MAC layer and will be mapped into a specific priority value. Packets belonging to the same traffic stream will be categorized into different priority virtual queues according to their priorities.

The total queue length of the traffic stream $q[k]$ is the sum of the queue length of the multiple virtual queues at time interval k.

$$q[k] = \sum_{j=1}^{L_{max}} q_j[k] \qquad (14)$$

where $q_j[k]$ is the size of virtual queue j at the time interval k. L_{max} is the total number of virtual queues. The scheduling algorithm redistributes the allocated TXOP among the packets of different priorities. It first decides the number of packets that will be transmitted in each virtual queue. Then it calculates the time required to transmit each packet.

Assume S_i is the number of packets that will be transmitted in the virtual priority queue i, the total TXOP $txop_i$ it will consume is

$$txop_i = S_i * (\frac{M_i}{R} + 2 * SIFS + ACK) \qquad (15)$$

The priority scheduling algorithm implemented at each STA can be written as seen in Algorithm 1.

In the algorithm, L_{max} is the number of priority virtual queues created. L_{max} queue has the highest priority, which is assigned for I frame packets. L_1 queue has the lowest priority, which

Table 2. The average PSNR of the received video under different scenarios

Bandwidth	Cross-layer Approach	Standard HCCA
10 Mbps	36.80	36.02
6 Mbps	36.80	34.47
5 Mbps	36.79	33.78
4 Mbps	35.51	29.13
3 Mbps	33.18	26.56

Table 3. Comparison of number of packet loss

	Packet loss in Cross-layer Approach	Packet loss in Standard HCCA	Total number of packets transmitted
I frame packet	0	23	436
P frame packet	0	13	351
B frame packet	5	9	332

Figure 1. The PSNRs of the cross-layer approach

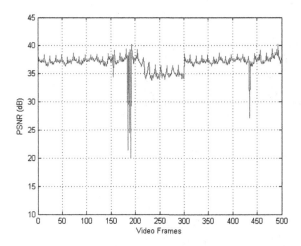

is assigned to B frame packets. The transmissions of packets are scheduled in a greedy manner from the highest priority queue to the lowest priority queue. Starting from the highest priority virtual queue, each time a packet is fetched from the virtual queue, the txop used to transmit this packet is calculated. This procedure will be repeated for each virtual queue, until the allocated TXOP for this traffic stream has been used up.

5. SIMULATION RESULTS

In this section, the performance of the proposed cross-layer scheduling is evaluated in ns-2 (NS2, 2011) environment. The proposed cross-layer design is compared to a baseline approach to demonstrate that the proposed scheme can improve the quality of video.

5.1. Simulation Setup

In the simulations, we consider that wireless stations operate in infrastructure mode, where the access point provides centralized control. The proposed cross-layer approach is implemented at the access point. Multiple wireless stations send out the H.264 video to the access point, and the access point polls each station and allocates the transmission time. Standard video sequence Foreman (Video Trace Library, n. d.) is used as the test video. The sequence is in CIF resolution (352 x 288 pixels) with the format of YUV 4:2:0. The video is encoded using the H.264 encoder in the group-of-pictures (GOP) sequence IPBBPBB-PBB. Besides the H.264 VBR traffic, there are two classes of background traffic with different QoS requirements, CBR traffic and Audio traffic. At the receiver side, the received packets are used to reconstruct the H.264 video stream, which is then decompressed into raw video. Peak Signal to Noise Ratio (PSNR) value (Ke, Shieh, Hwang & Ziviani, 2008) is calculated to measure the quality of received video.

The parameters of the 802.11e MAC are set as suggested by IEEE 802.11 WG (IEEE Computer Society, 2009). Table 1 shows the parameters used for the simulations. We need to study how the approaches perform under different network traffic load. There are several ways to generate different network traffic load in the simulations, for example, changing the number of traffic flows, the data requirements of the traffic flow, or the bandwidth of the channel. In this simulation we vary the PHY rates of the wireless channels to generate different traffic load, while keep the

Figure 2. The PSNRs of standard HCCA method

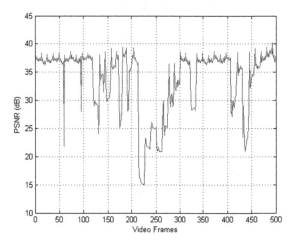

Figure 3. Decoded frames in cross-layer approach

Figure 4. Decoded frames in standard HCCA approach

number of traffic flow constant. The PHY rates of the wireless channel range from 3Mbps to 10 Mbps. The total number of the wireless stations is 9.

The computation complexity of the optimization algorithm depends on the value of the N and the duration of time interval t. The optimization period N is set to 10 to achieve a lower computation complexity. The duration of time interval t used for the calculation of optimized TXOP is 50ms, which is equivalent to one SI period. For each traffic flow the optimized TXOP is calculated for each SI period. Each optimization period starts at the beginning of the beacon interval.

5.2. Results and Analysis

To evaluate the performance of the proposed cross-layer approach, we choose the standard HCCA approach as the baseline for comparison. The standard HCCA approach uses the reference scheduler. It treats packets equally without differentiating their frame types. The simulations are run under different scenarios. Each run of the simulation lasts 30 seconds. The total number of packets sent out from each wireless station is 1119, among which 436 packets are I frames, 351 packets are P frames and 332 packets are B frames.

The bandwidth of the channel is varied in the simulation to study the performance of the two approaches under different network traffic load. Table 2 displays the comparison of the average PSNR of the received video frames under different scenarios. As can be seen from the table, both approaches can achieve good PSNR values under light network traffic when bandwidth is 10 Mbps. When the network traffic becomes congested, the PSNR of the standard approach degrades severely, while the PSNR of the cross-layer approach maintains at a higher level. The advantage of the cross-layer approach is more obvious under heavy traffic load when the bandwidth is 4 Mbps or 3 Mbps, because the cross-layer can more efficiently allocate the TXOP to the packets. It can also be observed from the table, when the link bandwidth decreased from 10 Mbps to 3 Mbps, the average PSNR of standard approach is reduced by 9.5 dB, while the average PSNR of the cross-layer approach is only reduced by 3.6 dB. The average PSNR of the cross-layer method outperforms the standard method, and the cross-layer approach provides a more graceful degradation of the video quality.

Figure 1 and Figure 2 display the PSNRs of the 500 received video frames under the cross-layer design and the standard method when the link bandwidth is 5 Mbps, respectively. The average PSNR of the cross-layer approach is 36.75 dB, and the average PSNR of the standard approach is 34.6 dB. Although the cross-layer approach only outperforms the standard approach by around 2 dB, the cross-layer approach maintains its PSNR values at a more stable level and experiences a small degradation of PSNRs among frames. In standard approach, the PSNRs range between 15 dB and 40 dB and suffer from frequent degradation. In the cross-layer approach, the PSNRs maintain at a stable level higher than 35 dB except for occasional drop of values. The cross-layer approach can effectively recover from the occasional drop of PSNRs and maintain the PSNR at higher values.

Table 3 displays the corresponding packet loss for the two traffic flows in the Figure 1 and Figure 2. The packet loss in standard approach is much higher than the cross-layer approach. Also the packets of different frames experience different loss rate under the two approaches. In the cross-layer approach, there is only packet loss for B frame, since the B frame packets have the lowest priority and are dropped with higher probability. The packet loss in the standard approach occurs at packets of all the types of frames with equal probability since all of the packets are treated equally.

Figure 3 and Figure 4 illustrate the decoded frames under cross-layer approach and standard approach, respectively. The frames of the standard approach have distortion because of the loss of the packets. The frames of the cross-layer approach maintain good quality without much distortion, since I frame packets are transmitted with higher probability. The visual effect of video is better because of the low loss rate of I frame packets which makes important contribution to the quality of received video.

CONCLUSION

IEEE 802.11 WLAN has been widely used to provide the wireless connection. QoS provision over the wireless networks is challenging because of the characteristics of wireless channels. IEEE 802.11e was proposed as QoS enhancement of 802.11. This paper presents a cross-layer design for the video streaming over 802.11e WLAN. The proposed approach is designed for 802.11e HCCA to optimize the quality of video streaming. The cross-layer design focuses on MAC layer scheduling which can improve quality of video under heavy traffic load. First the allocation of the TXOP is based on the current queue length of the wireless station and application requirements. Then the transmission of the packets is scheduled according to the priorities of the packets. The proposed scheme is implemented in ns-2 simulation tools and compared with the standard HCCA. The PSNRs of the received video sequence under the proposed cross-layer approach are much higher than the standard HCCA. The simulation results demonstrate the proposed cross-layer design can efficiently improve the quality of received video over 802.11e WLAN.

REFERENCES

Ansel, P., Ni, Q., & Turletti, T. (2006). FHCF: A simple and efficient scheduling scheme for IEEE 802.11e wireless LAN. *Mobile Networks and Applications*, *11*(3), 391–403. doi:10.1007/s11036-006-5191-z

Arora, A., Yoon, S., Choi, Y., & Bahk, S. (2010). Adaptive TXOP allocation based on channel conditions and traffic requirements in IEEE 802.11e networks. *IEEE Transactions on Vehicular Technology*, *58*(3), 1087–1099. doi:10.1109/TVT.2009.2031677

Bheemarjuna Reddy, T., John, J. P., & Siva Ram Murthy, C. (2007). Providing MAC QoS for multimedia traffic in 802.11e based multi-hop ad hoc wireless networks. *Computer Networks*, *51*(1), 153–176. doi:10.1016/j.comnet.2006.04.015

Boggia, G., Camarda, P., Grieco, L. A., & Mascolo, S. (2007). Feedback-based control for providing real-time services with the 802.11e MAC. *IEEE/ACM Transactions on Networking*, *15*(2), 323–333. doi:10.1109/TNET.2007.892881

Cai, J., Gao, D., & Wu, J. (2007). MAC-layer QoS management for streaming rate-adaptive VBR video over IEEE 802.11e HCCA WLANs. *Advances in Multimedia*, (1): 1–11. doi:10.1155/2007/94040

Chilamkurti, N., Zeadally, S., Soni, R., & Giambene, G. (2010). Wireless multimedia delivery over 802.11e with cross-layer optimization techniques. *Multimedia Tools and Applications*, *47*(1), 189–205. doi:10.1007/s11042-009-0413-6

Cicconetti, C., Lenzini, L., Mingozzi, E., & Stea, G. (2007). An efficient cross layer scheduler for multimedia traffic in wireless local area networks with IEEE 802.11e HCCA. *ACM Mobile Computing and Communications Review*, *11*(3), 31–46. doi:10.1145/1317425.1317428

Giro, A., Macedo, M., & Nunes, M. (2003). A scheduling algorithm for QoS support in IEEE802.11 networks. *IEEE Wireless Communications*, *10*(3), 36–43. doi:10.1109/MWC.2003.1209594

Hsu, C.-H., & Hefeeda, M. (2011). A framework for cross-layer optimization of video streaming in wireless networks. *ACM Transactions on Multimedia Computing, Communications, and Applications*, *7*(1), 1–28. doi:10.1145/1870121.1870126

IEEE. Computer Society. (2003). *IEEE 802.11 WG: IEEE 802.11e/D4.1: Wireless MAC and physical layer specifications: MAC enhancements for QoS*. Washington, DC: IEEE Computer Society.

IEEE. Computer Society. (2009). *IEEE 802.11 WG: IEEE standard for information technology – Telecommunications and information exchange between systems – LAN/MAN specific requirements, Part 11: Wireless LAN MAC and PHY specifications*. Washington, DC: IEEE Computer Society.

Inan, I., Keceli, F., & Ayanoglu, E. (2006). An adaptive multimedia QoS scheduler for 802.11e wireless LANs. In *Proceedings of the IEEE International Conference on Communications* (pp. 5263-5270).

Joint Video Team of ISO/IEC MPEG and ITU-T VCEG. (2002). *Joint model number 1, revision 1 (JM-1R1)*. Retrieved from http://ip.hhi.de/image-com_G1/assets/pdfs/JVT-A003r1.pdf

Ke, C. H., Shieh, C. K., Hwang, W. S., & Ziviani, A. (2008). An evaluation framework for more realistic simulations of MPEG video transmission. *Journal of Information Science and Engineering*, *24*(2), 425–440.

Ksentini, A., Naimi, M., & Gueroui, A. (2006). Toward an improvement of H.264 video transmission over IEEE 802.11e through a cross-layer architecture. *IEEE Communications Magazine*, *44*(1), 107–114. doi:10.1109/MCOM.2006.1580940

Luo, H. (2009). An optimized scheduling scheme for 802.11e MAC. *International Journal of Electronics and Computer Systems*, *11*(2), 1–8.

Luo, H., & Shyu, M.-L. (2009). An optimized scheduling scheme to provide quality of service in 802.11e wireless LAN. In *Proceedings of the Fifth IEEE International Workshop on Multimedia Information Processing and Retrieval* (pp. 651-656).

NS-2. (2011). *Network simulator*. Retrieved from http://www.isi.edu/nsnam/ns/

Shankar, N. S., & Van Der Schaar, M. (2007). Performance analysis of video transmission over IEEE 802.11a/e WLANs. *IEEE Transactions on Vehicular Technology*, *56*(4), 2346–2362. doi:10.1109/TVT.2007.897646

Skyrianoglou, D., Passas, N., & Salkintzis, A. K. (2006). ARROW: An efficient traffic scheduling algorithm for IEEE 802.11e HCCA. *IEEE Transactions on Wireless Communications*, *5*(12), 3558–3567. doi:10.1109/TWC.2006.256978

Van Der Schaar, M., Andreopoulos, Y., & Hu, Z. (2006). Optimized scalable video streaming over IEEE 802.11 a/e HCCA wireless networks under delay constraints. *IEEE Transactions on Mobile Computing*, *5*(6), 755–768. doi:10.1109/TMC.2006.81

Van Der Schaar, M., & Shankar, N. S. (2005). Cross-layer wireless multimedia transmission: Challenges, principles, and new paradigms. *IEEE Wireless Communications*, *12*(4), 50–58. doi:10.1109/MWC.2005.1497858

Van Der Schaar, M., & Turaga, D. (2007). Cross-layer packetization and retransmission strategies for delay-sensitive wireless multimedia transmission. *IEEE Transactions on Multimedia*, *9*(1), 185–197. doi:10.1109/TMM.2006.886384

Video Trace Library. (n. d.). *MPEG-4 and H.263 video traces for network performance evaluation.* Retrieved from http://trace.eas.asu.edu/TRACE/trace.html

Zhao, Q., & Tsang, D. H. K. (2008). An equal-spacing-based design for QoS guarantee in IEEE 802.11e HCCA wireless networks. *IEEE Transactions on Mobile Computing*, *7*(12), 1474–1490. doi:10.1109/TMC.2008.71

Zhu, P., Zeng, W., & Li, C. (2007). Cross-layer design of source rate control and congestion control for wireless video streaming. *Advances in Multimedia*, (1): 3–15.

This work was previously published in the International Journal of Multimedia Data Engineering and Management, Volume 2, Issue 3, edited by Shu-Ching Chen, pp. 21-33, copyright 2011 by IGI Publishing (an imprint of IGI Global).

Chapter 15
A Novel Strategy for Recommending Multimedia Objects and its Application in the Cultural Heritage Domain

Massimiliano Albanese
George Mason University, USA

Vincenzo Moscato
University of Naples, Italy

Antonio d'Acierno
ISA, National Research Council, Italy

Fabio Persia
University of Naples, Italy

Antonio Picariello
University of Naples, Italy

ABSTRACT

One of the most important challenges in the information access field, especially for multimedia reposi-tories, is information overload. To cope with this problem, in this paper, the authors present a strategy for a recommender system that computes customized recommendations for users' accessing multimedia collections, using semantic contents and low-level features of multimedia objects, past behaviour of individual users, and social behaviour of the users' community as a whole. The authors implement their strategy in a recommender prototype for browsing image digital libraries in the Cultural Heritage domain. They then investigate the effectiveness of the proposed approach, based on the users' satisfac-tion. The preliminary experimental results show that the approach is promising and encourages further research in this direction.

DOI: 10.4018/978-1-4666-2940-0.ch015

1. INTRODUCTION

Multimedia data allow fast and effective communication and sharing of information about people lives, their behaviors, work, interests, but they also are the digital testimony of facts, objects, and locations. The widespread availability of cheap media technologies (e.g., digital and video cameras, MP3 players, and smart phones) dramatically increased the availability of multimedia data. Images and videos are used, by media companies as well as the public at large, to record daily events, to report local, national, and international news, to enrich and emphasize web content, as well as to promote cultural heritage. Furthermore, through digitization of all types of data and records, multimedia data plays an increasingly critical role in government administration, from security and justice to the health system.

As a result, huge data collections, in the form of digital video and image libraries, digital documents, news archives, shopping catalogs, virtual museums, and so on, are widely available, determining the well-known problem of *information overload*. From such a massive amount of data, it is very difficult for a common user to obtain her/his preferred ones, and despite the great amount of research work done in the last decade, retrieving and suggesting information of interest from very large repositories still remains an open issue, especially in the case of multimedia collections.

To cope with this problem, a number of algorithms and tools – generally referred to as *Recommender Systems* – are being proposed to facilitate browsing of large data repositories, and thus to realize the transition from the "era of search" to the "era of discovery". Recommender systems help people in retrieving information that match their preferences by recommending products or services from large number of candidates and support people in making decision in various contexts: what items to buy (Zhang & Wang, 2005), which movie to watch (Qin et al., 2010) or even who they can invite to their social networks (Kazienko & Musial, 2006).

They are especially useful in the environments with a vast amount of information where it is difficult to express the semantics of a query since they allow an automatic selection of a small subset of items that appears to fit to the user needs (Adomavicius & Tuzhilin, 2005). The main problem for multimedia is that the *semantic gap* between users and contents is sometimes so large that very little previous work succeeds in building an effective multimedia recommender system.

In such a context, the main goal of this work is to present a novel approach to recommendation for multimedia objects, based on an "importance ranking" algorithm that strongly resembles the well known *PageRank* ranking strategy (Albanese et al., 2011). We propose a method that computes customized recommendations by originally combining intrinsic features of multimedia objects (low level and semantic similarities), past behavior of individual users and overall behavior of the entire community of users. Eventually, we have implemented the propose strategy in a software prototype for browsing digital libraries related to a famous on-line collection of paintings and measured its effectiveness with respect to a user-centric evaluation.

The paper is organized as follows. Section 2 presents some motivating examples that justify the utility our work in different contexts related to Cultural Heritage domain. Section 3 discusses the state of the art of recommender systems, including those applied in the multimedia realm. Section 4 shortly describes the proposed strategy for recommending multimedia objects. Section 4 illustrates the system architecture and provides some implementation details. Section 6 reports preliminary experimental results; finally, Section 7 gives some concluding remarks and discusses future work.

2. MOTIVATING EXAMPLES

In this section we report two typical scenarios in the Cultural Heritage domain that aim at showing how a recommendation system could desirably work during both a virtual -- but also a real -- visit of an art gallery.

First, let us consider an on-line art museum offering web-based access to a multimedia collection of digital reproductions of paintings. For instance, let us consider users visiting such a virtual museum and suppose that they request, at the beginning of their tour, some paintings depicting the "Bacchus" subject. While observing such paintings, they are attracted, for example by Caravaggio's painting entitled "Self-Portrait as Sick Bacchus" (Figure 1a). It would be helpful if the system could learn the preferences of the users, based on these first interactions and predict their future needs by suggesting other paintings representing the same or related subjects, depicted by the same or other related authors or items that have been requested by users with similar preferences, thus avoiding the use of a classical keyword-based search engine.

As an example, a user who is currently watching the Carvaggio's painting in Figure 1a might be recommended to see a the Feodor Bruni's painting entitled "Bacchante Giving Wine to Cupid" (Figure 1b), that is quite similar to the current picture in terms of color, shape and texture, and "Andrians or The Great Bacchanal with Woman Playing a Lute" by Nicolas Poussin (Fig-

ure 1c), that is not similar in terms of low level features but has the same subject and belongs to the same artistic movement.

As another example, let us consider the case of a real museum (i.e., Uffizi Gallery in Florence) offering by means of a WiFi connection, a web-based access to a multimedia collection containing: digital reproductions of paintings, educational videos, audio guides, textual and hypermedia documents with description of authors and paintings. In order to make the user's experience in the museum more interesting and stimulating, the access to information should be customized based on the specific profile of a visitor, which includes learning needs, level of expertise and personal preferences, on user effective location in the museum, and on the "paintings similarity".

In particular, let us consider a user visiting the room 20 of the museum containing some paintings depicting by Albrecht Dűrer's and suppose that she is attracted, for example, by the painting entitled "Madonna col Bambino" (Figure 2). Also in this case, it would be helpful if the system could learn the preferences of the user (e.g., interests in paintings depicting the Holy Mary subject), based on the user current behaviour and past interactions of other museum visitors, and predict her future needs, by suggesting other paintings (or any other multimedia objects) representing the same or related subjects, depicted by the same or other related authors, or items that have been requested by users with similar preferences.

Figure 1. Paintings depicting "Bacchus"

a   b   c

Similarly to the previous case, as an example, the user who is currently observing the Dûrer's painting in Figure 2 might be recommended to see in the room 27 a Jacopo Carucci's painting entitled "Madonna col Bambino e San Giovannino" (Figure 2), that is quite similar to the current picture in terms of color and texture, and in the room 3 "Madonna col Bambino" by Andrea Vanni (Figure 2), that is not very similar in terms of low level features but is more similar in terms of semantic content. Moreover, if in the past a lot of visitors after having seen the Dûrer's painting visited the room containing the special Pontormo and Rosso Fiorentino collection, the system could suggest visiting it and recommending some paintings within. If it is requested, the system could suggest by using museum maps and given the user location the way to reach each room from the current position.

During the visit, a user by her mobile device could read multimedia documents related to authors or paintings that she is viewing and listening to audio guides available for different languages.

Finally, the activities suggested to the user should be the following ones:

- "See the painting Madonna col Bambino by Dûrer in the room 20"

Figure 2. Paintings depicting the subject "Holy Mary"

- "See the painting Madonna col Bambino e San Giovannino by Carucci in the room 27"
- "See some paintings by Carrucci in the room 27"

In both cases, from the *user perspective* there is the advantage of having a guide suggesting paintings which the users might be interested in, whereas, from the *system perspective*, there is the undoubted advantage of using the suggestions for pre-fetching and caching the objects that are more likely to be requested.

3. RELATED WORK AND BASIC IDEA BEHIND THE PROPOSED APPROACH

In the most common formulation, the *recommendation problem* is the problem of estimating *ratings* - sometimes called also *utilities* - for the set of items that has not yet been seen by a given user.

In *Content Based recommender systems* (Pazzani & Billsus, 2007), the utility r^i_j of item o_j is estimated using the utilities $r(u_p, o_k)$ assigned by the user u_i to items o_k that are in some way "similar" to item o_j. For example, in a movie recommendation application, in order to recommend movies to user u, the content-based recommender system tries to understand the commonalities among the movies user u has rated highly in the past (specific actors, directors, genres, subject matter, etc.). Then, only the movies that have a high degree of similarity to the user's preferences would be recommended.

One of the main drawbacks of these techniques is that they do not benefit from the great amount of information that could be derived by analyzing the behavior of other users. Moreover, the content must either be in a form that can be automatically parsed or the features and if two different items are represented by the same set of features, they are indistinguishable. Eventually, a subtle problem is that the system can only recommend items that are similar to those already rated by the user itself (*overspecialization*).

Collaborative Filtering (Adomavicius & Tuzhilin, 2005) is, in the opposite, the process of filtering or evaluating items using the opinions of other people. Thus, unlike content-based recommendation methods, collaborative systems predict the utility of items r^i_j for a particular user u_i based on the utility $r(u_h, o_k)$ of items o_k previously rated by other users u_h "similar" to u_i. It takes its root from something human beings have been doing for centuries: sharing opinions with others. These opinions can be processed in real time to determine not only what a much larger community thinks of an item, but also develop a truly personalized view of that item using the opinions most appropriate for a given user or group of users (Resnick et al., 1994; Schafer et al., 2007; Kim et al., 2009).

The main problem behind collaborative filtering clearly is to associate each user to a set of other users having similar profiles. In order to make any recommendations, the system has to collect data mainly using two methods: the first one is to ask for explicit ratings from a user, while it is also possible to gather data implicitly logging actions performed by users. Once the data has been gathered, there are two basic ways of filtering through it to make predictions. The most basic method is *passive filtering*, which simply uses data aggregates to make predictions (such as the average rating for an item) and each user will be given the same predictions for a particular item (e.g., *digg.com*). In the opposite, *active filtering* uses patterns in user history to make predictions obtaining user-specific and context-aware recommendations (e.g., *Amazon*).

Collaborative systems have their own limitations that can be grouped under the name of the *cold start problem* that describes situations in which a recommender is unable to make meaningful recommendations due to an initial lack of ratings thus degrading the filtering performance. It can occur under three scenarios: *new user*, *new item,* and *new community*.

Content-based filtering and collaborative filtering may be manually combined by the end-user specifying particular features, essentially constraining recommendations to have certain content features. More often they are automatically combined in the so called *hybrid approach* (Basilico & Hofmann, 2004; Anand et al., 2007; Lam et al., 2008) that helps to avoid certain limitations of each method. Different ways to combine collaborative and content-based methods into a hybrid recommender system can be classified as follows: (i) implementing collaborative and content-based methods separately and combining their predictions; (ii) incorporating some content-based characteristics into a collaborative approach; (iii) incorporating some collaborative characteristics into a content-based approach; and (iv) constructing a general unifying model that incorporates both content-based and collaborative characteristics.

More recently, the discussed strategies have been extended to multimedia realm (e.g., multimedia repositories, digital libraries, multimedia sharing system, etc.) with the aim of considering in the more effective way multimedia content of recommended objects, both in terms of low-level and high-level characteristics (i.e., multimedia features and semantics), in the recommendation process together with user social behavior and preferences.

For what content-based techniques concerns, Maidel et al. (2008) proposes a method that exploits some ontologies for ranking items' relevancy in the electronic paper domain, while in Hijikata et al. (2006) a content based filtering has been applied to music data using decision trees. In the framework of multimedia sharing system, Musial et al. (2008) introduces a recommender system that use two ontologies (one for multimedia objects and one for users) in the context of a photo sharing system. To generate suggestions a new concept of "multirelational" social network was introduced, covering both direct as well as multimedia object-based relationships that reflect social and semantic links between users. Eventually, Manzato and Goularte (2009) propose a content-based recommender architecture which explores information that is available at the time users enhance content in order to capture a certain level of semantic information from the multimedia content and from user preferences that is at the base of their video recommender system.

Among collaborative-filtering proposals, authors in Baloian et al. (2004) propose a collaborative recommender system, which suggests multimedia learning material based on the learner's background and preferences. Kim et al. (2008) proposes a collaborative filtering-based multimedia contents recommender system in P2P architectures that rates multimedia objects of nearest peers with similar preference through peer-based local information only. Tseng et al. (2008) propose a system, which combines discovered relations between user preferences and conceptualized multimedia contents by annotation and association mining techniques, can provide a suitable recommendation list to assist users in making a decision among a massive amount of multimedia items (images, videos and music).

As hybrid solutions, the *uMender* system (Su & Ye, 2010) exploits context information, musical content and relevant user ratings to perform music recommendations on mobile devices. Knijnenburg et al. (2010) propose a user-centric approach to media recommendations that exploits subjective and objective measures of user experience, while users interact with multimedia data. A framework for recommendation of multimedia objects based on processing of individual ontologies is then proposed in Juszczyszyn et al. (2010): the recommendation process takes into account similarities calculated both between objects (metadata) and users' ontologies, which reflect the social and semantic features existing in the system. Another example of hybrid approach, implemented in *MoRe*, a movie recommendation system, has been described in Lekakos and Caravelas (2008). Finally, low and high level features have been used

to define the similarity among multimedia items in Albanese, Chianese et al. (2010); this measure is then used to compare patterns of past users in order to identify users with similar browsing behavior.

As we can note, the majority of approaches to recommendation in the multimedia realm exploits high level metadata - extracted in automatic or semi-automatic way from low level features - that are in different manners correlated and compared with user preferences, usually mapped in the shape of ontologies. These approaches suffer from some drawbacks:

- It is not always possible to extract in automatic and effective way useful high level information from multimedia features (automatic annotation algorithms have not always high performances);
- For some kinds of multimedia data there is not a precise correlation between high and low level information (e.g., in images the concept of "moon" is related to a region with a circular shape and white color with a given *uncertainty*);
- There are not always available explicit and useful information (knowledge) about user preferences (e.g., usually a user can retrieve information from a multimedia system without the necessity of a registration, as in youtube or flickr);
- In the recommendation process and for particular kinds of multimedia data sometimes it is useful to take into account features of the objects that user is currently observing as content information (e.g., the main colours of a painting are often an indication of the related artistic movement or school).

Our approach tries to avoid such drawbacks:

- Supposing the existence of a-priori knowledge about metadata values and their relationships (i.e., a taxonomy is used to define high-level concepts);

- Considering in a separate way low and high level information, i.e., both contribute to determine the utility of an object in the recommendation process;
- Exploiting system logs to implicitly determine information about a user and the related community and considering their browsing sessions as a sort of ratings;
- Considering as relevant content for the recommendation the features of the object that a user is currently watching.

Thus, we try to meet in a unique strategy some aspects of multimedia information retrieval with the basic theory of modern recommender systems.

4. THE RECOMMENDATION STRATEGY

An effective multimedia recommender system for supporting intelligent browsing of multimedia collections has the capability of reliably identify the objects that are most likely to satisfy the interests of a user at any given point of her exploration. In our case, we have to address four fundamental questions:

1. How can we select a set of objects from the collection that are good candidates for recommendation?
2. How can we rank the set of candidates?
3. How can we capture, represent and manage semantics related to multimedia objects to reduce the semantic gap between what the user is watching and what she is looking for?
4. How can we take into account such semantics in the recommendation process?

To give an answer to the first two questions, we have based our recommendation algorithm on an importance ranking method that strongly resembles the *PageRank* ranking system (Albanese, d'Acierno et al., 2010) and model recommendation

as a social choice problem, proposing a method that computes customized recommendations by originally combining several features of multimedia objects (low-level and semantics), past behavior of individual users and overall behavior of the entire community of users. Our basic idea is to assume that when an object o_i is chosen after an object o_j in the same browsing session, this event means that o_j "is voting" for o_i. Similarly, the fact that an object o_i is very similar to o_j can also be interpreted as o_j "recommending" o_i (and viceversa).

Thus, our idea is to model a browsing system for a set of object O as a labeled graph (G,l), where $G=(O,E)$ is a directed graph and $l: E \rightarrow \{pattern, sim\} \times R^+$ is a function that associates each edge in $E \subseteq O \times O$ with a pair (t,w), where t is the type of the edge which can assume two enumerative values (*pattern* and *similarity*) and w is the weight of the edge. According to this model, we can list two different cases:

- A *pattern label* for an edge (o_j, o_i) denotes the fact that an object o_i was accessed immediately after an object o_j and, in this case, the weight w^i_j is the number of times o_i was accessed immediately after o_j;
- The *similarity label* for an edge (o_j, o_i) denotes the fact that an object o_i is similar to o_j and, in this case, the weight w^i_j is the similarity between o_j and o_i.

Thus, a link from o_j to o_i indicates that part of the importance of o_j is transferred to o_i. Given a labeled graph (G,l), we can formulate the definition of recommendation grade of a multimedia object more formally as follows.

Definition 3.1: (Recommendation Grade ρ)

$$\forall o_i \in O \; \rho(o_i) = \sum_{o_j \in PG(oi)} w^i_j \, o_j \qquad (1)$$

where $P_G=\{o_j\in O|(o_j,o_i)\in E\}$ is the set of predecessors of o_i in G, and w^i_j is the normalized weight of the edge from o_j to o_i. For each $o_i\in O$, $\sum_{oi\in S_{G(oj)}} w^i_j=1$ must hold, where $S_G=\{o_i\in O|(o_j,o_i)\in E\}$ is the set of successors of o_j in G.

It is easy to see that the vector $R = [\rho(o_i)...\rho(o_n)]^T$ can be computed as the solution to the following equation:

$$R = C \cdot R \tag{2}$$

where $C=\{w^i_j\}$ is an ad-hoc matrix that defines how the importance of each object is transferred to other objects and can be seen as a linear combination of the following elements (Albanese et al., 2011):

- A *local browsing matrix* $A_l=\{a^l_{ij}\}$ for each user $u_l\in U$. Its generic element a^l_{ij} is defined as the ratio of the number of times object o_i has been accessed by user u_l immediately after o_j to the number of times any object in O has been accessed by u_l immediately after o_j.

- A *global browsing matrix* $A=\{a_{ij}\}$. Its generic element a_{ij} is defined as the ratio of the number of times object o_i has been accessed by any user immediately after o_j to the number of times any object in O has been accessed immediately after o_j.

- A *multimedia similarity matrix* $B=\{b_{ij}\}$ such that $b_{ij}=\sigma(o_i,o_j)/\Gamma$ if $\sigma(o_i,o_j)\geq\tau$ $\forall i\neq j$, 0 otherwise. σ is any similarity function defined over O which calculates for each couple of objects their multimedia relatedness in terms of low (features) and high level (semantics) descriptors; τ is a threshold and Γ is a normalization factors which guarantees that $\sum_i b_{ij}=1$.

The introduction of matrix B allows to address the two last questions that we introduced at the beginning of the section and thus to introduce a sort of content-based image retrieval with high-level semantics in the recommendation process. In particular, to compute B matrix, we have decided to adopt 5 sets of the most diffused multimedia features (Tamura descriptors, MPEG-7 color-based descriptors, MPEG-7 edge-based descriptors, MPEG-7 color layout- based descriptors and all MPEG7 descriptors (Lux & Chatzichristofis, 2008) and the related similarity metrics have been implemented by LIRE tool. In addition, we exploit specific image metadata (*artist*, *genre* and *subject*) and the semantic similarity has been computed used the most diffused metrics for semantic relatedness of concepts based on a vocabulary (Li-Bandar-McLean, Wu-Palmer, Rada, Leacock-Chodorow) (Budanitsky & Hirst, 2001). In particular the semantic similarity combines similarities among artists, genres and subjects obtained by using a fixed taxonomy produced by domain experts with image features.

In Albanese et al. (2011) the experimental protocol to determine the best combination of the proposed metrics is reported for images representing artistic paintings. In particular, the combination between high and low level descriptors is Sugeno fuzzy integral of Li and MPEG-7 color layout-based similarities in order to have more high values of precision, and Sugeno fuzzy integral of Wu-Palmer and MPEG-7 color based similarities in order to have more high level values of recall, thus we use this combination for matrix B computation.

So far we have a suitable manner to represent object features and to compare the related similarity also considering semantics in terms of object metadata; now, our main goal is to compute customized rankings for each individual user.

In this case, we can then rewrite Equation 2 considering the ranking for each user as follows:

$$R_l = C \cdot R_l \tag{3}$$

where $R_l=[\rho(o_i)...\rho(o_n)]^T$ is the vector of recommendation grades, customized for a user u_l.

We note that solving Equation 3 corresponds to find the stationary vector of C, i.e., the eigenvector with eigenvalue We demonstrated in Albanese, d'Acierno et al. (2010) - here all the details for computation of recommendation grades are also reported - that C, under certain assumptions and transformations, is a real square matrix having positive elements, with a unique largest real eigenvalue and the corresponding eigenvector has strictly positive components. In such conditions, Equation 3 can be solved used the *Power Method* algorithm.

The matrix C does not have to be computed for all database objects, but only for those objects that are good candidates to recommendation. Assuming that a user u_i is currently watching object o_j, we can generate the final set of candidate recommendations by considering:

$$C = \cup_{k=1...M} (\{o_i \in O | A^k{}_{ij} > 0\} \cup \{o_i \in O | B_{ij} > 0\})$$

$$(4)$$

The set of candidates includes the objects that have been accessed by at least one user within k steps from o_j, with k between 1 and M, and the objects that are most similar to o_j. Note that a positive element $a^k{}_{ij}$ of A^k indicates that o_i was accessed exactly k steps after o_j at least once.

In Figure 3 there is an easy example of how to compute the set of candidates in the case the collection has only ten paintings and the most similar images to the current image are only four. As we can see, after selecting the most similar images, from each of these the images accessed within 2 steps are selected.

5. THE SYSTEM

In this section, we describe a case study in the cultural heritage domain for a web recommendation system that provides browsing facilities for a multimedia collection of paintings. In particular, our recommender helps the users for finding paintings of interest from a large set of choices, proposing a set of suggestions for each observed object; the recommendations are computed combining the user's behaviour with low and high

level image descriptors, following the previous described approach.

We use a *memory-based* algorithm so that low and high level similarities are evaluated once; this reflect the unchanging nature of these measures while, clearly, if we add new paintings, similarity matrices have to be conveniently updated. Instead, to capture the dynamic nature of user's behaviour, we periodically re-compute connection matrices; specifically, each connection matrix is updated as soon the browsing session ends. To solve the cold start problem, when there is no information about user's behaviour, our system uses low or/ and high level similarities, in addition to the extracted behaviour of the whole community. For new items, of course, recommendation is based just on similarities.

Our data collection can consist of different digital reproductions of paintings (managed by *MySQL* DBMS) to which it is possible to associate artists and artistic genres. Each painting can be also linked to a pair of subjects, chosen among a list containing the available ones; such an information roughly represents what the painting represents. A user can interact with our system (Figure 4) using a web browser that communicates with the server by means of straight http requests or by means of an *Android* application. In the first case, the presentation logic is based on *JavaFX* technology that allows interaction with users using advanced graphical functionalities. The client requests are elaborated by *JAVA Servlets* and results are sent to the client in form of XML data (according to the *Service Oriented Architecture* paradigm). The core functionality of the system, the recommendation process, can be described as follow.

As soon as a user interacts with the system, the core process starts defining the set of candidates for the recommendation by considering the union of:

• The set of paintings which are the most similar to the current one, according the similarity matrices;

Figure 3. How to compute the set of candidates

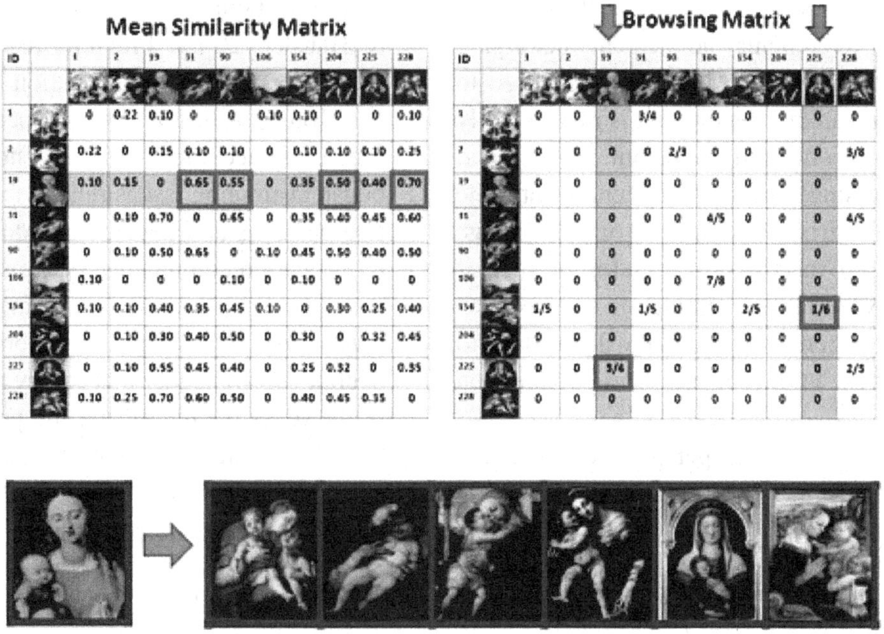

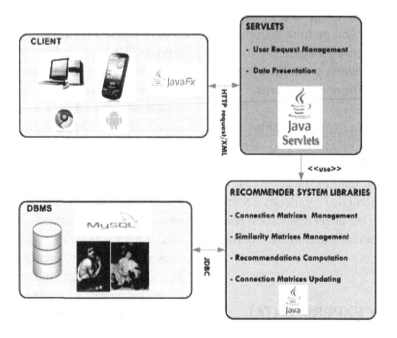

Figure 4. The system architecture

- The set of paintings which have been accessed by at least one user within a certain number of steps from the current one; to reach this goal, if the user is logged in and there exits the related user connection matrix, the past user's behaviour is considered; otherwise the global connection matrix is taken into account.

The set of candidates, of course, takes into account the user's context and, thus, the C matrix is built just referencing the elements belonging to such set; the Power Method is then used to compute the ranking vector, that is in eventually exploited to recommend new paintings. At the end of each browsing session, the system updates the connection matrix extracting a set of pairs (image to be accessed - accessed image); for instance, if once observed the j-th painting the user sees the i-th painting, then an occurrence will be added to the A_{ij} element in the corresponding connection matrix.

From the final users perspective, the client application has the following features:

- A set of forms to provide users log in or registration;
- A gallery to visualize images which are returned after a search by author, subject or artistic genre;
- Visualization of an image and of the related information and multimedia presentation of recommended images;
- Storing of user session with the information related to the browsing patterns.

The client side of our system can be adapted both for a mobile and PC device and customized for different applications, while the serve side can host different multimedia collection of images (e.g., *Uffizi* and *Olga's* galleries). Some screenshots related to the client application realized for browsing of a real museum are reported in Figure 5.

6. PRELIMINARY EXPERIMENTAL RESULTS

Recommender systems are complex applications that are based on a combination of several models, algorithms and heuristics. This complexity makes evaluation efforts very difficult and results are hardly generalizable, which is apparent in the literature about recommender evaluation (Schulz & Hahsler, 2002). Previous research work on recommender system evaluation has mainly focused on algorithm *accuracy*, especially objective prediction accuracy. More recently, researchers began examining issues related to users' subjective opinions and developing additional criteria to evaluate recommender systems. In particular, they suggest that user's satisfaction does not always (or, at least, not only) correlate with the overall recommender's accuracy and evaluation frameworks for measuring the perceived qualities of a recommender and for predicting user's behavioural intentions as a result of these qualities should be taken into account.

In Albanese et al. (2011) a user-centric evaluation is proposed and reported some preliminary experimental results about user satisfaction in using a recommendation strategy for browsing the *Uffizi Gallery* (containing only 474 paintings). The goal was to establish how helpful our system was to provide an exploration of digital reproductions of paintings. Moreover from these experiments we wanted to understand how helpful recommendations offered by our recommender system were to address users toward paintings which satisfied their interests. In particular, it has been demonstrated that the introduction of recommendation techniques can improve the system usability with respect to assigned browsing tasks and we evaluated such an improvement in terms of empirical measurements of access complexity and *TLX* factors (with regards to a system that does not exploit recommendation, i.e., Picasa) provided by different kinds of users.

In this paper we want to repeat the proposed experimental protocol, adding an evaluation on browsing effectiveness, using a more large multimedia collection, the paintings belonging to the *Olga's Gallery* on-line art museum; in particular, the collection includes about 10,000 paintings encompassing 28 genres (e.g., Cubism, Baroque, Early Renaissance), more than 200 authors (e.g.,

Figure 5. Screenshots of the client application

Caravaggio, Rubens), and about 100 subjects (e.g., Landscapes, Portraits).

In the training phase, we have chosen 20 users among students and graduate students that used for 5 days the system without recommendation facilities to capture their browsing sessions and build a consistent matrix A. As comparing system we consider the web site of Olga's Gallery (http://www.abcgallery.com) that provides a classical keywords-based search engine and some indexes (on artist and genre names) to facilitate retrieval of painting of interest. Finally we have set $k=3$ for computing the candidates set and used a (sliding) window of 50 recommended items.

Browsing Effectiveness

This first set of experiments aims at comparing the ranking provided by our system using the proposed recommendation degree with the ranking provided by a human observer. To this end, we have slightly modified a test proposed by Santini (2000), in order to evaluate the difference between the two rankings ("treatments") in terms of hypothesis verification on the entire dataset.

Consider a weighted displacement measure defined as follows.

Let q be a query (example painting) on a database of n images that produces k results (recommended items). There is one ordering (usually given by one or more human subjects) which is considered as the ground truth, represented as:

$$R_h = \{o_1, \ldots, o_k\} \tag{5}$$

Every image in the ordering has also associated a measure of relevance $0 \leq S(o, q) \leq 1$ such that (for the ground truth), $S(o_i, q) \geq S(o_{i+1}, Q), \forall i$. This is compared with an (experimental) ordering:

$$Rs = \{o_{\pi 1}, \ldots, o_{\pi k}\} \tag{6}$$

where $\{\pi 1, \ldots, \pi k\}$ is a permutation of $1, \ldots, n$. The displacement of o_i is defined as:

$$d_q(o_i) = |i - \pi i| \tag{7}$$

Table 1. Mean and variance of the weighted displacement for the three treatments (two human subjects and system)

	Human 1	**Human 2**	**System**
μ_i	0.0475	0.0412	0.0304
σ^2_i	8.266e⁻⁴	8.895e⁻⁴	8.951e⁻⁴

while, the relative weighted displacement of *Rs* is defined as:

$$W_q = \sum_i (S(o_i,q) \cdot d_q(o_i))/\Omega \qquad (8)$$

$\Omega = \lceil n^2/2 \rceil$ being a normalization factor.

Relevance *S* is obtained from the subjects asking them to divide the results in three groups: *very similar* ($S(o_i, q) = 1$), *quite similar* ($S(o_i,q) = 0.5$) and *dissimilar* ($S(o_i,q) = 0.05$).

In our experiments, on the basis of the ground truth provided by human subjects, treatments provided either by humans or by our system are compared. The goal is to determine whether the observed differences can indeed be ascribed to the different treatments or are caused by random variations. In terms of hypothesis verification, if μ_i is the average score obtained with the *i-th* treatment, a test is performed in order to accept or reject the null hypothesis H_0 that all the averages μ_i are the same (i.e., the differences are due only to random variations).

Clearly the alternate hypothesis H_1 is that the means are not equal, that is the experiment actually revealed a difference among treatments. The acceptance of the H_0 hypothesis can be checked with the *F* ratio. Let us assume that there are *M* treatments and *N* measurements (experiments) for each treatment. Let us define:

- t_{ij} the result of the *j*-th experiment performed with the *i*-th treatment in place;
- $\mu_i = (\sum_{j=1,N} t_{ij})/N$ the average for treatment t_{ij};

- $\mu = (\sum_{i=1,M} \mu_i)/M$ the total average;
- $\sigma^2_A = (\sum_{i=1,M} (\mu_i - \mu)^2)/(N/(M-1))$ the between treatments variance;
- $\sigma^2_W = ((\sum_{i=1,M} \sum_{j=1,N} (t_{ij} - \mu_i)^2)/(M/(N-1))$ the within treatments variance.

Then, the *F* ratio is:

$$F = \sigma^2_A / \sigma^2_W \qquad (9)$$

A high value of *F* means that the between treatments variance is preponderant with respect to the within treatment variance, that is, that the differences in the averages are likely to be due to the treatments.

In our experiments we employed 12 subjects, experts on art. Ten users, randomly chosen among the 12, were employed to determine the ground truth ranking and the other two served to provide the treatments to be compared with our system. 10 example images were selected, and for each of them we run the recommendation algorithm returning a result set of ten best candidates, for a total of 100 objects.

Result sets were randomly ordered to prevent bias and the two students were then asked to rank images in each set in terms their level of recommendation with respect to the query object. Each subject was also asked to divide the ranked objects in three groups: the first group consisted of images judged *very relevant* to the query, the second group consisted of images judged *quite relevant* to the query, and the third of *non relevant* images.

Table 2. The f ratio measured for pairs of distances (human vs. human and human vs. system)

F	**Human 1**	**Human 2**	**System**
System	0.484	0.713	0
Human 2	0.0899	0	
Human 1	0		

Table 3. Comparison between our system and Olga's gallery in terms of t_a and n_c

Task Class	System	t_a (sec.)	n_c
Q1	Olga	58.7	14.5
Q1	Our System	53.8	13.2
Q2	Olga	174.2	41.8
Q2	Our System	62.5	21.5
Q3	Olga	309.2	77.1
Q3	Our System	145.1	38.2
Q4	Olga	500.7	144.2
Q4	Our System	232.9	56.7

The mean and variance of the weighted displacement of the two subjects and of our system with respect to the ground truth are reported in Table 1. Then, the *F* ratio for each pair of distances was computed in order to establish which differences were significant. As can be noted from Table 2, the *F* ratio is always less than 1 and since the critical value F_0, regardless of the confidence degree (the probability of rejecting the right hypothesis), is greater than 1, the null hypothesis can be statistically accepted.

User Satisfaction

In order to evaluate the impact of the system on the users we have conducted the following experiments. We asked a different group of about 20 people (all medium experts in art) to browse a collection of images and complete several browsing tasks (20 tasks per user) of different complexity (five tasks for each complexity level), using the Olga's Gallery web site. After this test, we asked them to browse once again the same collection with the assistance of our recommender system and complete other 20 tasks of the same complexity.

We have subdivided browsing tasks in the following four broad categories:

- **Low Complexity tasks (Q1):** e.g., "explore at least 10 paintings of *Baroque* style

authored by *Caravaggio* and depicting a *religious* subject";
- **Medium Complexity tasks (Q2):** e.g., "explore at least 20 paintings of *Baroque* authors that have *nature* as their subject";
- **High Complexity tasks (Q3):** e.g., "explore at least 30 paintings of *Baroque* authors with subject *nature* and with a predominance of *red color*";
- **Very High Complexity tasks (Q4):** e.g., "explore at least 50 paintings of *Baroque* authors depicting a *religious* subject with a predominance of *red color*".

Note that the complexity of a task depends on several factors: the number of objects to explore, the type of desired features (either low or high-level), and the number of constraints (genre, author, subject). Two strategies were used to evaluate the results of this experiment: empirical measurements of access complexity in terms of *mouse clicks* and *time*, and *TLX* (*NASA Task Load Index* factors).

With respect to the first strategy, we measured the following parameters:

- **Access Time (t_a):** The average time spent by the users to request and access all the objects for a given class of tasks.
- **Number of Clicks (n_c):** The average number of clicks necessary to collect all the requested objects for a given class of tasks.

Table 4. Comparison between our system and Olga's gallery in terms of TLX factors

TLX Factor	Our System	Olga's Gallery
Effort	49.3	60.5
Mental Demand	53.2	58.3
Physical Demand	44.4	50.2
Temporal Demand	50.6	70.1
Frustration	58.3	72.8
Own Performance	39.5	44.2

Table 3 reports the average values of t_a and n_c, for both Picasa and our system, for each of the four task complexity levels defined earlier.

In the second experiment, we asked the users to express their opinion about the capability of Olga's gallery and our system respectively to provide an effective user experience in completing the assigned browsing tasks. To this end, we used the TLX evaluation form to assess the workload on operators of various human–machine systems. Specifically, TLX is a multi-dimensional rating procedure that provides an overall workload score based on a weighted average of ratings on six sub-scales: mental demand, physical demand, temporal demand, own performance, effort and frustration (lower TLX scores are better). In other words, this experiment was aimed at measuring how difficult is for a user to use either our system or Olga's gallery to complete a browsing task. We obtained the average result scores reported in Table 4, which show that our system outperforms Olga in every sub-scale.

It is evident that the two aspects where our system beats Olga by the largest margin are temporal demand and frustration. This result implies that our system completes browsing tasks faster and provides a better (less frustrating) user experience. In addition, the fact that browsing tasks can be completed faster using our system is an indication that recommendations are effective, as they allow a user to explore interesting and related objects one after another, without the interference of undesired items that would necessarily slow down the process.

CONCLUSION AND FUTURE WORK

In this paper we proposed a novel approach to recommendation for multimedia browsing systems, based on a method that computes customized recommendations by combing in an original way intrinsic features (semantic contents and low-level features) of the objects, past behaviour of individual users and behaviour of the users' community as a whole. In particular, we realized a recommender system which helps users to browse digital reproductions of Uffizi paintings, providing them suggestions computed by our novel method for recommendations. Then we investigated the effectiveness of the proposed approach in the considered scenario, based on the browsing effectiveness and user satisfaction. Experimental results showed that our approach is promising and encourages further research in this direction.

Future works will be devoted to: (i) introduce explicit user profiling mechanism based on the creation of users' categories, (ii) extend experimentation on a larger image data set, and (iii) compare our algorithm with respect to other recommendation strategies.

REFERENCES

Adomavicius, G., & Tuzhilin, A. (2005). Toward the next generation of recommender systems: A survey of the state-of-the-art and possible extensions. *IEEE Transactions on Knowledge and Data Engineering*, *17*(6), 734–749. doi:10.1109/TKDE.2005.99

Albanese, M., Chianese, A., d'Acierno, A., Moscato, V., & Picariello, A. (2010). A multimedia recommender integrating object features and user behavior. *Multimedia Tools and Applications*, *50*(3), 563–585. doi:10.1007/s11042-010-0480-8

Albanese, M., d'Acierno, A., Moscato, V., Persia, F., & Picariello, A. (2010). Modeling recommendation as a social choice problem. In *Proceedings of the 4th ACM Conference on Recommender Systems* (pp. 329-332).

Albanese, M., d'Acierno, A., Moscato, V., Persia, F., & Picariello, A. (2011). A multimedia semantic recommender system for cultural heritage applications. In *Proceedings of the 5th IEEE Conference on Semantic Computing – Semantic Multimedia Management Workshop*.

Anand, S. S., Kearney, P., & Shapcott, M. (2007). Generating semantically enriched user profiles for web personalization. *ACM Transactions on Internet Technology*, *7*(4). doi:10.1145/1278366.1278371

Baloian, N. A., Galdames, P., Collazos, C. A., & Guerrero, L. A. (2004). A model for a collaborative recommender system for multimedia learning material. In G.-J. de Vreede, L. A. Guerrero, & G. M. Raventos (Eds.), *Proceedings of the 10th International Workshop on Groupware: Design, Implementation, and Use* (LNCS 3198, pp. 281-288).

Basilico, J., & Hofmann, T. (2004). Unifying collaborative and content-based filtering. In *Proceedings of the 21st Conference on Machine Learning*.

Budanitsky, A., & Hirst, G. (2001). Semantic distance in Wordnet: An experimental, application oriented evaluation of five measures. In *Proceedings of the Workshop on WordNet and Other Lexical Resources*.

Herlocker, J. L., Konstan, J. A., Terveen, L. G., & Riedl, J. T. (2004). Evaluating collaborative filtering recommender systems. *ACM Transactions on Information Systems*, *22*(1), 5–53. doi:10.1145/963770.963772

Hijikata, Y., Iwahama, K., & Nishida, I. S. (2006). Content-based music filtering system with editable user profile. In *Proceedings of the ACM Symposium on Applied Computing* (pp. 1050-1057).

Juszczyszyn, K., Kazienko, P., & Musiał, K. (2010). Personalized ontology-based recommender systems for multimedia objects, agent and multi-agent technology for internet and enterprise systems. In Hakansson, A., Hartung, R., & Nguyen, N.-T. (Eds.), *Agent and multiagent technology for Internet and enterprise systems* (*Vol. 289*, pp. 275–292). Berlin, Germany: Springer-Verlag. doi:10.1007/978-3-642-13526-2_13

Kazienko, P., & Musial, K. (2006). Recommendation framework for online social networks. *Advances in Web Intelligence and Data Mining*, *23*, 111–120. doi:10.1007/3-540-33880-2_12

Kim, H. K., Kim, J. K., & Ryu, Y. U. (2009). Personalized recommendation over a customer network for ubiquitous shopping. *IEEE Transactions on Services Computing*, *2*(2), 140–151. doi:10.1109/TSC.2009.7

Kim, J. K., Kim, H. K., & Cho, Y. H. (2008). A user-oriented contents recommendation system in peer to peer architecture. *Expert Systems with Applications*, *34*(1), 300–312. doi:10.1016/j.eswa.2006.09.034

Knijnenburg, B., Meesters, L., Marrow, P., & Bouwhuis, D. (2010). User-centric evaluation framework for multimedia recommender systems. In P. Daras & O. M. Ibarra (Eds.), *Proceedings of the First International Conference on User Centric Media* (LNICST 40, pp. 366-369).

Lam, X. N., Vu, T., Le, T. D., & Duong, A. D. (2008). Addressing cold-start problem in recommendation systems. In *Proceedings of the 2nd International ACM Conference on Ubiquitous Information Management and Communication* (pp. 208-211).

Lekakos, G., & Caravelas, P. (2008). A hybrid approach for movie recommendation. *Multimedia Tools and Applications*, *36*(1-2), 55–70. doi:10.1007/s11042-006-0082-7

Lux, M., & Chatizichristofis, A. (2008). LIRE: Lucene Image REtrieval - an extensible java cbir library. In *Proceedings of the 16th ACM International Conference on Multimedia* (pp. 1085-1088).

Maidel, V., Shoval, P., Shapira, B., & Taieb-Maimon, M. (2008). Evaluation of an ontology-content based filtering method for a personalized newspaper. In *Proceedings of the ACM Conference on Recommender Systems* (pp. 91-98).

Manzato, M. G., & Goularte, R. (2009). Supporting multimedia recommender systems with peer-level annotations. In *Proceedings of the 15th Brazilian Symposium on Multimedia and the Web.*

Musiał, K., Kazienko, P., & Kajdanowicz, T. (2008). Social recommendations within the multimedia sharing systems. In M. D. Lytras, J. M. Carroll, E. Damiani, & R. D. Tennyson (Eds.), *Proceedings of the First World Summit on Emerging Technologies and Information Systems for the Knowledge Society* (LNCS 5288, pp. 364-372)

Pazzani, M., & Billsus, D. (2007). Content-based recommendation systems. In P. Brusilovsky, A. Kobsa, & W. Nejdl (Eds.), *Proceedings of the Methods and Strategies of Web Personalisation: The Adaptive Web* (LNCS 4321, pp. 325-341).

Qin, S., Menezes, R., & Silaghi, M. (2010). A recommender system for Youtube based on its network of reviewers. In *Proceedings of the IEEE Second International Conference on Social Computing* (pp. 323-328).

Resnick, P., Iacovou, N., Suchak, M., Bergstrom, P., & Riedl, J. (1994). GroupLens: an open architecture for collaborative filtering of netnews. In *Proceedings of the ACM Conference on Computer Supported Cooperative Work* (pp. 175-186).

Santini, S. (2000). Evaluation vademecum for visual information systems. In *Proceedings of the SPIE Conference on Storage and Retrieval for Image and Video Databases* (Vol. 3972, pp. 132-143).

Schafer, J. B., Frankowsky, D., Herlocker, J. L., & Sen, S. (2007). Collaborative filtering recommender systems. In P. Brusilovsky, A. Kobsa, & W. Nejdl (Eds.), *Proceedings of the Methods and Strategies of Web Personalisation: The Adaptive Web* (LNCS 4321, pp. 291-324).

Schulz, A. G., & Hahsler, M. (2002). Evaluation of recommender algorithms for an internet information broker based on simple association rules and on the repeat-buying theory. In *Proceedings of the Fourth WebKDD Workshop: Web Mining for Usage Patterns & User Profiles* (pp. 100-114).

Su, J. W., & Yeh, H. H. (2010). Music recommendation using content and context information mining. *IEEE Intelligent Systems, 25*(1), 16–26. doi:10.1109/MIS.2010.23

Tseng, V. S., Su, J.-H., Wang, B.-W., Hsiao, C.-Y., Huang, J., & Yeh, H.-H. (2008). Intelligent multimedia recommender by integrating annotation and association mining. In *Proceedings of the IEEE International Conference on Sensor Networks, Ubiquitous, and Trustworthy Computing* (pp. 492-499).

Zhang, X., & Wang, H. (2005). Study on recommender systems for business-to-business electronic commerce. *Communications of the IIMA, 5*(4), 53–61.

This work was previously published in the International Journal of Multimedia Data Engineering and Management, Volume 2, Issue 4, edited by Shu-Ching Chen, pp. 1-18, copyright 2011 by IGI Publishing (an imprint of IGI Global).

Compilation of References

Abdel-Mottaleb, M. (2000). Image retrieval based on edge representation. In *Proceedings of the 2000 International Conference on Image Processing,* Vancouver, BC, Canada (Vol. 3, pp. 734-737).

Adami, N., Benini, S., & Leonardi, R. (2006). An overview of video shot clustering and summarization techniques for mobile applications. In *Proceedings of the 2nd International Conference on Mobile Multimedia Communications,* Alghero, Italy. New York: ACM.

Adomavicius, G., & Tuzhilin, A. (2005). Toward the next generation of recommender systems: A survey of the state-of-the-art and possible extensions. *IEEE Transactions on Knowledge and Data Engineering, 17*(6), 734–749. doi:10.1109/TKDE.2005.99

Ailamaki, A., Kantere, V., & Dash, D. (2010). Managing scientific data. *Communications of the ACM, 53*(8), 88–78.

Akdemir, U., Turaga, P., & Chellappa, R. (2008). An Ontology based approach for activity recognition from video. In *Proceedings of the ACM Conference on Multimedia* (pp. 709-712).

Al-Asmari, A. K., & Al-Enizi, F. A. (2009). A pyramid-based watermarking technique for digital color images copyright protection. In *Proceedings of the International Conference on Computing, Engineering and Information,* Fullerton, CA (pp. 44-47).

Albanese, M., d'Acierno, A., Moscato, V., Persia, F., & Picariello, A. (2010). Modeling recommendation as a social choice problem. In *Proceedings of the 4th ACM Conference on Recommender Systems* (pp. 329-332).

Albanese, M., d'Acierno, A., Moscato, V., Persia, F., & Picariello, A. (2011). A multimedia semantic recommender system for cultural heritage applications. In *Proceedings of the 5th IEEE Conference on Semantic Computing – Semantic Multimedia Management Workshop.*

Albanese, M., Chianese, A., d'Acierno, A., Moscato, V., & Picariello, A. (2010). A multimedia recommender integrating object features and user behavior. *Multimedia Tools and Applications, 50*(3), 563–585. doi:10.1007/s11042-010-0480-8

Almeida, J., Minetto, R., Almeida, T. A., Torres, R. S., & Leite, N. J. (2009). Robust estimation of camera motion using optical flow models. In G. Bebis, R. D. Boyle, B. Parvin, D. Koracin, Y. Kuno, J. Wang et al. (Eds.), *Proceedings of the International Conference on Advances in Visual Computing* (LNCS 585, pp. 435-446).

Almeida, J., Minetto, R., Almeida, T. A., Torres, R. S., & Leite, N. J. (2010). Estimation of camera parameters in video sequences with a large amount of scene motion. In *Proceedings of the IEEE International Conference on Systems, Signals and Image Processing* (pp. 348-351). Washington, DC: IEEE Computer Society.

Almeida, J., Rocha, A., Torres, R. S., & Goldenstein, S. (2008). Making colors worth more than a thousand words. In *Proceedings of the ACM International Symposium on Applied Computing* (pp. 1180-1186). New York, NY: ACM Press.

Almeida, J., Torres, R. S., & Leite, N. J. (2010). Rapid video summarization on compressed video. In *Proceedings of the IEEE International Symposium on Multimedia* (pp. 113-120). Washington, DC: IEEE Computer Society.

Anacleto, J. C., Talarico Neto, A., & Neris, V. P. A. (2009). Cog-learn: An e-learning pattern language for web-based learning design. *eLearn Magazine, 2009*(8), 1-4.

Anand, S. S., Kearney, P., & Shapcott, M. (2007). Generating semantically enriched user profiles for web personalization. *ACM Transactions on Internet Technology, 7*(4). doi:10.1145/1278366.1278371

Anderson, D., Luke, R. H., Keller, J. M., Skubic, M., Rantz, M. J., & Aud, M. A. (2007). Modeling human activity from voxel person using fuzzy logic. *IEEE Transactions on Fuzzy Systems*, *17*(1), 39–49. doi:10.1109/TFUZZ.2008.2004498

Aner, A., & Kender, J. R. (2002). Video summaries through mosaic-based shot and scene clustering. In *Proceedings of the European Conference on Computer Vision* (pp. 388-402).

Ansel, P., Ni, Q., & Turletti, T. (2006). FHCF: A simple and efficient scheduling scheme for IEEE 802.11e wireless LAN. *Mobile Networks and Applications*, *11*(3), 391–403. doi:10.1007/s11036-006-5191-z

Arieli, O., Cornelis, C., Deschrijver, G., & Kerre, E. E. (2004). Relating intuitionistic fuzzy sets and interval-valued fuzzy sets through bilattices. In D. Ruan, P. D'hondt, M. De Cock, M. Nachtegael, & E. E. Kerre (Eds.), *Applied Computational Intelligence: Proceedings of the 6th International FLINS Conference,* Blankenberge, Belgium (pp. 57-64). Singapore: World Scientific.

Arieli, O., Cornelis, C., Deschrijver, G., & Kerre, E. E. (2005). Bilattice-Based Squares and Triangles. In *Symbolic and Quantitative Approaches to Reasoning with Uncertainty* (LNCS 3571, pp. 563-574).

Ariki, Y., Kumano, M., & Tsukada, K. (2003). Highlight scene extraction in real time from baseball live video. In *Proceedings of the ACM International Workshop on Multimedia Information Retrieval* (pp. 209-214).

Arora, A., Yoon, S., Choi, Y., & Bahk, S. (2010). Adaptive TXOP allocation based on channel conditions and traffic requirements in IEEE 802.11e networks. *IEEE Transactions on Vehicular Technology*, *58*(3), 1087–1099. doi:10.1109/TVT.2009.2031677

Atanassov, K. T. (2003). Intuitionistic fuzzy sets: Past, present and future. In *Proceedings of the 3rd Conference of the European Society for Fuzzy Logic and Technology* (pp. 12-19).

Atanassov, K. T. (1986). Intuitionistic fuzzy sets. *Fuzzy Sets and Systems*, *20*, 87–96. doi:10.1016/S0165-0114(86)80034-3

Atanassov, K. T. (1994). New operations defined over the intuitionistic fuzzy sets. *Journal of Fuzzy Sets and Systems*, *61*(2), 137–142. doi:10.1016/0165-0114(94)90229-1

Atanassov, K. T. (2002). Remark on a property of the intuitionistic fuzzy interpretation triangles. *Notes on Intuitionistic Fuzzy Sets*, *8*, 34–36.

Bae, M. H., Pan, R., Wu, T., & Badea, A. (2009). Automated segmentation of mouse brain images using extended MRF. *NeuroImage*, *46*(3), 717–725. doi:10.1016/j.neuroimage.2009.02.012

Baeza-Yates, R., & Tiberi, A. (2007). Extracting semantic relations from query logs. In *Proceedings of the 13th ACM SIGKDD International Conference on Knowledge Discovery and Data Mining* (pp.76-85).

Bailey-Kellogg, C., Ramakrishnan, N., & Marathe, M. V. (2006). Mining and visualizing spatial interaction patterns for pandemic response. *ACM SIGKDD Explorations Newsletter*, 80-82.

Baker, C. R. (1973). Joint measures and cross-covariance operators. *Transactions of the American Mathematical Society*, *2*, 273–289. doi:10.1090/S0002-9947-1973-0336795-3

Baloian, N. A., Galdames, P., Collazos, C. A., & Guerrero, L. A. (2004). A model for a collaborative recommender system for multimedia learning material. In G.-J. de Vreede, L. A. Guerrero, & G. M. Raventos (Eds.), *Proceedings of the 10th International Workshop on Groupware: Design, Implementation, and Use* (LNCS 3198, pp. 281-288).

Basilico, J., & Hofmann, T. (2004). Unifying collaborative and content-based filtering. In *Proceedings of the 21st Conference on Machine Learning*.

Becerra-Fernandez, I. (2001). Searching for experts with expertise-locator knowledge management systems. In *Proceedings of the 39th Annual Meeting of the Association for Computational Linguistics Workshop Human Language Technology and Knowledge Management* (pp. 9-16).

Beeferman, D., & Berger, A. (2000). Agglomerative clustering of a search engine query log. In *Proceedings of the 6th ACM SIGKDD International Conference on Knowledge Discovery and Data Mining* (pp. 407-416).

Bellenger, A., & Gatepaille, S. (2011). *Uncertainty in ontologies: Dempster-Shafer theory for data fusion applications.* Retrieved October 10, 2011, from http://arxiv.org/abs/1106.3876

Bentley, F., Metcalf, C., & Harboe, G. (2006). Personal vs. commercial content: The similarities between consumer use of photos and music. In *Proceedings of the International Conference on Human Factors in Computing Systems* (pp. 667-676).

Berchtold, S., & Keim, D. A. (1996). The X-tree: An index structure for high-dimensional data. In *Proceedings of the 22th International Conference on Very Large Data Bases* (pp. 28-39).

Beshers, C. G., & Feiner, S. K. (1990). Visualizing n-dimensional virtual worlds within n-Vision. *Computer Graphics*, *24*(2), 37–38. doi:10.1145/91394.91412

Bezerra, F. N., Werbet, E., & Silva, W. B. (2005). Client-side content-based refinement for image search in the web. In *Proceedings of the Brazilian Symposium on Multimedia and the Web* (pp. 1-3).

Bheemarjuna Reddy, T., John, J. P., & Siva Ram Murthy, C. (2007). Providing MAC QoS for multimedia traffic in 802.11e based multi-hop ad hoc wireless networks. *Computer Networks*, *51*(1), 153–176. doi:10.1016/j.comnet.2006.04.015

Bigras-Poulin, M., Thompson, R. A., Chriel, M., Mortensen, S., & Greiner, M. (2006). Network analysis of Danish cattle industry trade patterns as an evaluation of risk potential for disease spread. *Preventive Veterinary Medicine*, *76*(1-2), 11–39. doi:10.1016/j.prevetmed.2006.04.004

Binderberger, M. O., & Mehrotra, S. (2004). Relevance feedback techniques in the MARS image retrieval system. *Multimedia Systems*, *9*(6), 535–547. doi:10.1007/s00530-003-0126-z

Blandford, A., Adams, A., Attfield, S., Buchanan, G., Gow, J., & Makri, S. (2008). The PRET A Rapporter framework: Evaluating digital libraries from the perspective of information work. *Information Processing & Management*, *44*(1), 4–21. doi:10.1016/j.ipm.2007.01.021

Blei, D. M., Ng, A. Y., & Jordan, M. I. (2003). Latent Dirichlet allocation. *Journal of Machine Learning Research*, *3*(5), 993–1022. doi:10.1162/jmlr.2003.3.4-5.993

Bober, M. (2002). MPEG-7 visual shape descriptors. *IEEE Transactions on Circuits and Systems for Video Technology*, *11*(6), 716–719. doi:10.1109/76.927426

Boggia, G., Camarda, P., Grieco, L. A., & Mascolo, S. (2007). Feedback-based control for providing real-time services with the 802.11e MAC. *IEEE/ACM Transactions on Networking*, *15*(2), 323–333. doi:10.1109/TNET.2007.892881

Boulos, M. (2004). Descriptive review of geographic mapping of severe acute respiratory syndrome (SARS) on the Internet. *International Journal of Health Geographics*, *3*(1), 2. doi:10.1186/1476-072X-3-2

Brewster, S. (2002). Overcoming the lack of screen spaces on mobile computers. *Personal and Ubiquitous Computing*, *6*(3), 188–205. doi:10.1007/s007790200019

Browning, J. D., & Tanimoto, S. L. (1982). Segmentation of pictures into regions with a tile-by-tile method. *Pattern Recognition*, *15*(1), 1–10. doi:10.1016/0031-3203(82)90055-3

Budanitsky, A., & Hirst, G. (2001). Semantic distance in Wordnet: An experimental, application oriented evaluation of five measures. In *Proceedings of the Workshop on WordNet and Other Lexical Resources*.

Budanitsky, A., & Hirst, G. (2006). Evaluating Word-Net-based measures of lexical semantic relatedness. *Computational Linguistics*, *32*, 13–47. doi:10.1162/coli.2006.32.1.13

Bull, S., Greer, J., Mccalla, G., Lori, K., & Bowes, J. (2001). User modeling in I-Help: What, why, when and how. In *Proceedings of the 8th International Conference on User Modeling*, Sonthofen, Germany (pp. 117-126).

Burns, J., Hatt, C., Brooks, C., Keefauver, E., Wells, E. V., Shuchman, R., & Wilson, M. L. (2006). Visualization and simulation of disease outbreaks: Spatially-explicit applications using disease surveillance data. In *Proceedings of the ESRI Users conference*.

Cai, D., He, X., Ma, W.-Y., Wen, J., & Zhang, H. (2004). Organizing www images based on the analysis of page layout and web link structure. In *Proceedings of the IEEE International Conference on Multimedia and Expo* (pp. 27-30).

Caicedo, J. C., Cruz, A., & Gonzalez, F. A. (2009). Histopathology image classification using bag of features and kernel functions. *Artificial Intelligence in Medicine, 5651*, 126–135. doi:10.1007/978-3-642-02976-9_17

Cai, J., Gao, D., & Wu, J. (2007). MAC-layer QoS management for streaming rate-adaptive VBR video over IEEE 802.11e HCCA WLANs. *Advances in Multimedia*, (1): 1–11. doi:10.1155/2007/94040

Carpenter, A. E., Jones, T. R., Lamprecht, M. R., Clarke, C., Kang, I. H., & Friman, O. (2006). CellProfier: Image analysis software for identifying and quantifying cell phenotypes. *Genome Biology, 7*(10), 100. doi:10.1186/gb-2006-7-10-r100

Cascia, M. L., Sethi, S., & Sclaroff, S. (1998). Combining textual and visual cues for content-based image retrieval on the World Wide Web. In *Proceedings of the IEEE Workshop on Content - Based Access of Image and Video Libraries* (pp. 24-28).

Chakrabarti, K., Ortega, M., Porkaew, K., & Mehrotra, S. (2001). Query refinement in similarity retrieval systems. *A Quarterly Bulletin of the Computer Society of the IEEE Technical Committee on Data Engineering, 24*(3), 3–13.

Chakrabarti, K., Porkaew, K., Ortega, M., & Mehrotra, S. (2004). Evaluating refined queries in top-k retrieval systems. *IEEE Transactions on Knowledge and Data Engineering, 16*(2), 256–270. doi:10.1109/TKDE.2004.1269602

Chang, S.-F., Hsu, W., Kennedy, L., Xie, L., Yanagawa, A., Zavesky, E., et al. (2005). *Columbia university trecvid-2005 video search and high-level feature extraction*. Paper presented at the NIST TRECVID Workshop, Gaithersburg, MD.

Chang, S.-F., Chen, W., Meng, H. J., Sundaram, H., & Zhong, D. (1998). A fully automated content-based video search engine supporting spatio-temporal queries. *IEEE Transactions on Circuits and Systems for Video Technology, 8*(5), 602–615. doi:10.1109/76.718507

Chasanis, V., Kalogeratos, A., & Likas, A. (2009). Movie segmentation into scenes and chapters using locally weighted bag of visual words. In *Proceeding of the ACM International Conference on Image and Video Retrieval*.

Chasanis, V., Likas, A., & Galatsanos, N. P. (2008). Video rushes summarization using spectral clustering and sequence alignment. In *Proceedings of the ACM International Conference on Multimedia and the TRECVID BBC Rushes Summarization Workshop* (pp. 75-79).

Chatterjee, K., & Chen, S.-C. (2006). Affinity hybrid tree: An indexing technique for content-based image retrieval in multimedia databases. In *Proceedings of the IEEE International Symposium on Multimedia*, San Diego, CA (pp. 47-54).

Chatterjee, K., & Chen, S.-C. (2008). GeM-tree: Towards a generalized multidimensional index structure supporting image and video retrieval. In *Proceedings of the Fourth IEEE International Workshop on Multimedia Information Processing and Retrieval in conjunction with the IEEE International Symposium on Multimedia* (pp. 631-636).

Chatterjee, K., & Chen, S.-C. (2007). A novel indexing and access mechanism using affinity hybrid tree for content-based image retrieval in multimedia databases. *International Journal of Semantic Computing, 1*(2), 147–170. doi:10.1142/S1793351X07000093

Chen, C., Gagaudakis, G., & Rosin, P. (2000). Content-based image visualization. In *Proceedings of the International Conference on Information Visualization* (pp. 13-18). Washington, DC: IEEE Computer Society.

Chen, S.-C., Shyu, M.-L., & Chen, M. (2008). An effective multi-concept classifier for video streams. In *Proceedings of the IEEE International Conference on Semantic Computing* (pp. 80-87).

Chen, B. W., Wang, J. C., & Wang, J. F. (2009). A novel video summarization based on mining the story-structure and semantic relations among concept entities. *IEEE Transactions on Multimedia, 11*, 295–312. doi:10.1109/TMM.2008.2009703

Chen, D.-Y., Tian, X.-P., Shen, Y.-T., & Ouhyoung, M. (2003). On visual similarity based 3D model retrieval. *Computer Graphics Forum, 22*(3), 223–232. doi:10.1111/1467-8659.00669

Cheng, X., Hu, Y., & Chia, L.-T. (2008). Image near-duplicate retrieval using local dependencies in spatial-scale space. In *Proceedings of the ACM 2008 Conference on Multimedia,* Vancouver, BC, Canada (pp. 627-630).

Chen, S. C. (2010). Multimedia databases and data management: A survey. *International Journal of Multimedia Data Engineering and Management, 1*(1), 1–11. doi:10.4018/jmdem.2010111201

Chen, X., Zhang, C., Chen, S.-C., & Rubin, S. H. (2009). A human-centered multiple instance learning framework for semantic video retrieval. *IEEE Transactions on Systems, Man, and Cybernetics. Part C, 39*(2), 228–233.

Chilamkurti, N., Zeadally, S., Soni, R., & Giambene, G. (2010). Wireless multimedia delivery over 802.11e with cross-layer optimization techniques. *Multimedia Tools and Applications, 47*(1), 189–205. doi:10.1007/s11042-009-0413-6

Chum, O., Philbin, J., Isard, M., & Zisserman, A. (2007). Scalable near identical image and shot detection. In *Proceedings of the ACM Conference on International Video Retrieval,* Amsterdam, The Netherlands (pp. 549-556).

Ciaccia, P., Patella, M., & Zezula, P. (1997). M-tree: An efficient access method for similarity search in metric spaces. In *Proceedings of the 23rd Very Large Data Bases International Conference* (pp. 426-435).

Cicconetti, C., Lenzini, L., Mingozzi, E., & Stea, G. (2007). An efficient cross layer scheduler for multimedia traffic in wireless local area networks with IEEE 802.11e HCCA. *ACM Mobile Computing and Communications Review, 11*(3), 31–46. doi:10.1145/1317425.1317428

Compieta, P., Di-Martino, S., Bertolotto, M., Ferrucci, F., & Kechadi, T. (2007). Exploratory spatio-temporal data mining and visualization. *Journal of Visual Languages and Computing, 18*(3), 255–279. doi:10.1016/j.jvlc.2007.02.006

Cornelis, C., Atanassov, K. T., & Kerre, E. E. (2003). Intuitionistic fuzzy sets and interval-valued fuzzy sets: A critical comparison. In *Proceedings of the 3rd International Conference on Fuzzy Logic and Technology* (pp. 159-163).

Cornelis, C., Deschrijver, G., & Kerre, E. E. (2003). Square and triangle: Reflections on two prominent mathematical structures for the representation of imprecision. *Notes on Intuitionistic Fuzzy Sets, 9*(3), 11–21.

Cornelis, C., Deschrijver, G., & Kerrer, E. E. (2004). Implication in intuitionistic and interval valued fuzzy set theory. *Journal of Approximate Reasoning, 35*(1), 55–95. doi:10.1016/S0888-613X(03)00072-0

Curtis, A. (2008). Three-dimensional visualization of cultural clusters in the 1878 yellow fever epidemic of New Orleans. *International Journal of Health Geographics, 7*(1), 47. doi:10.1186/1476-072X-7-47

Cyr, C. M., & Kimia, B. (2001). 3D object recognition using shape similarity-based aspect graph. In *Proceedings of the 8th IEEE International Conference on Computer Vision,* Vancouver, BC, Canada (Vol. 1, pp. 254-261).

Damnjanovic, U., Piatrik, T., Djordjevic, D., & Izquierdo, E. (2007). Video summarisation for surveillance and news domain. In *Proceedings of the 2nd International Conference on Semantics and Digital Media Technologies,* Genoa, Italy.

Daneels, D., Campenhout, D., Niblack, W., Equitz, W., Barber, R., Bellon, E., et al. (1993). Interactive outlining: An improved approach using contours. In *Proceedings of the Storage and Retrieval for Image and Video Databases* (pp. 226-233).

Daras, P., & Axenopoulos, A. (2009). A compact multi-view descriptor for 3D object retrieval. In *Proceedings of the International Workshop on Content-Based Multimedia Indexing* (pp. 115-119).

Das, M., Farmer, J., Gallagher, A., & Loui, A. (2008). Event-based location matching for consumer image collections. In *Proceedings of the International Conference on Image and Video Retrieval* (pp. 339-348).

Datta, R., Joshi, D., Li, J., & Wang, J. Z. (2008). Image retrieval: Ideas, influences, and trends of the new age. *ACM Computing Surveys, 40*(2), 1–60. doi:10.1145/1348246.1348248

Davis, M., King, S., Good, N., & Sarvas, R. (2004). From context to content: Leveraging context to infer media metadata. In *Proceedings of the ACM Multimedia Conference* (pp. 188-195).

De Rooij, O., Snoek, C. G. M., & Worring, M. (2008). Balancing thread based navigation for targeted video search. In *Proceedings of the ACM International Conference on Image and Video Retrieval* (pp. 485-494). New York, NY: ACM Press.

De Rooij, O., & Worring, M. (2010). Browsing video along multiple threads. *IEEE Transactions on Multimedia*, *12*(2), 121–130. doi:10.1109/TMM.2009.2037388

Deerwester, S., Dumais, S. T., Furnas, G. W., Landauer, T. K., & Harshman, R. (1990). Indexing by latent semantic analysis. *Journal of the American Society for Information Science American Society for Information Science*, *41*(6), 391–407. doi:10.1002/(SICI)1097-4571(199009)41:6<391::AID-ASI1>3.0.CO;2-9

Dmitriev, P., Serdyukov, P., & Chernov, S. (2010). Enterprise and desktop search. In *Proceedings of the 19th International World Wide Web Conference* (pp. 1345-1346).

Doyle, S., Feldman, M., Tomaszewski, J., & Madabhushi, A. (2010). A boosted bayesian multi-resolution classifier for prostate cancer detection from digitized needle biopsies. *IEEE Transactions on Bio-Medical Engineering*, *99*, 1.

Dubois, D. (2008). On ignorance and contradiction considered as truth-values. *Journal of the Interest Group of Pure and Applied Logic*, *16*(2), 195–216.

Dunham, J. B. (2005). An agent-based spatially explicit epidemiological model in MASON. *Journal of Artificial Societies and Social Simulation*, *9*(1), 3.

Fayyad, U. M., & Irani, K. B. (1993). Multi-interval discretization of continuous-valued attributes for classification learning. In *Proceedings of the International Joint Conference on Artificial Intelligence* (pp. 1022-1027).

Fellbaum, C. (Ed.). (1998). *WordNet: An electronic lexical database*. Cambridge, MA: MIT Press.

Feng, H., Shi, R., & Chua, T.-S. (2004). A bootstrapping framework for annotating and retrieving www images. In *Proceedings of the ACM International Conference on Multimedia* (pp. 960-967).

Fernandes, L. A. F., & Oliveira, M. M. (2008). Real-time line detection through an improved hough transform voting scheme. *Pattern Recognition*, *41*(1), 299–314. doi:10.1016/j.patcog.2007.04.003

Fernando, W. A. C, Canagarajah, C. N., & Bull, D. R. (2001). Scene change detection algorithms for content-based video indexing and retrieval. *IEEE Electronics and Communication Engineering Journal*, 117-126.

Ferreira de Oliveira, M. C., & Levkowitz, H. (2003). From visual data exploration to visual data mining: A survey. *IEEE Transactions on Visualization and Computer Graphics*, *9*(3), 378–394. doi:10.1109/TVCG.2003.1207445

Fitting, M. (1990). Bilattices in logic programming. In *Proceedings of the 20th International Symposium on Multiple-Valued Logic* (pp. 238-246).

Fitting, M. (1994). Kleenes three-valued logics and their children. *Fundamental Informaticae*, *20*, 113–131.

Flickner, M., Sawhney, H. S., Ashley, J., Huang, Q., Dom, B., & Gorkani, M. (1995). Query by image and video content: The QBIC system. *IEEE Computer*, *28*(9), 23–32.

French, J., & Jin, X. Y. (2004). An empirical investigation of the scalability of a multiple viewpoint CBIR system. In *Proceedings of the International Conference on Image and Video Retrieval* (pp. 252-260).

Friedman, M. (1937). The use of ranks to avoid the assumption of normality implicit in the analysis of variance. *Journal of the American Statistical Association*, *32*, 675–701. doi:10.2307/2279372

Fu, X., & Zeng, J. (2009). An improved histogram based image sequence retrieval method. In *Proceedings of the International Symposium on Intelligent Information Systems and Applications* (pp. 15-18).

Furini, M., & Ghini, V. (2006). An audio–video summarization scheme based on audio and video analysis. In *Proceedings of the IEEE Consumer Communications and Networking Conference* (Vol. 2, pp. 1209-1213).

Fu, Y., Li, Z., Huang, T. S., & Katsaggelos, A. K. (2008). Locally adaptive subspace and similarity metric learning for visual clustering and retrieval. *Computer Vision and Image Understanding*, *111*(3), 390–402. doi:10.1016/j.cviu.2007.09.017

Gabrilovich, E., & Markovitch, S. (2005). Feature generation for text categorization using world knowledge. In *Proceedings of the International Joint Conference on Artificial Intelligence* (pp. 1048-1053).

Gabrilovich, E., & Markovitch, S. (2006). Overcoming the brittleness bottleneck using Wikipedia: Enhancing text categorization with encyclopedic knowledge. In *Proceedings of the 21st American Association for Artificial Intelligence* (pp.1301-1306).

Gao, Y., & Dai, Q. H. (2008). Shot-based similarity measure for content-based video summarization. In *Proceedings of the 15th IEEE International Conference on Image Processing,* San Diego, CA (pp. 2512-2515).

Gargi, U., Kasturi, R., & Strayer, S. (2000). Performance characterization of video shot-change detection methods. *IEEE Transactions on Circuits and Systems for Video Technology, 10*(1), 1–13. doi:10.1109/76.825852

Gatica-perez, D., Loui, A., & Sun, M.-T. (2003). Finding structure in home video by probabilistic hierarchical clustering. *Circuits and Systems for Video Technology, 13*(6), 539–548. doi:10.1109/TCSVT.2003.813428

Gehrke, M., Walker, C., & Walker, E. (1996). Some comments on interval-valued fuzzy sets. *International Journal of Intelligent Systems, 11*(10), 751–759. doi:10.1002/(SICI)1098-111X(199610)11:10<751::AID-INT3>3.3.CO;2-N

Gevers, T., Aldershoff, F., & Smeulders, A. W. (1999). Classification of images on the internet by visual and textual information. In *Proceedings of the Society of Photo-Optical Instrumentation Engineers Conference Series* (pp. 16-27).

Gevers, T., & Smeulders, A. (2004). Content-based image retrieval: An overview. In Medioni, G., & Kang, S. B. (Eds.), *Emerging topics in computer vision.* Upper Saddle River, NJ: Prentice Hall.

Ginsberg, M. L. (1988). Multivalued logics: A uniform approach to inference in artificial intelligence. *Computational Intelligence, 4*(3), 256–316. doi:10.1111/j.1467-8640.1988.tb00280.x

Girgensohn, A., & Boreczky, J. (1999). Time-constrained keyframe selection technique. In *Proceedings of the IEEE International Conference on Multimedia Systems* (Vol. 1, pp. 756-761).

Giro, A., Macedo, M., & Nunes, M. (2003). A scheduling algorithm for QoS support in IEEE802.11 networks. *IEEE Wireless Communications, 10*(3), 36–43. doi:10.1109/MWC.2003.1209594

Gligorov, R., Aleksovski, Z., Kate, W., & Harmelen, F. (2007). Using Google distance to weight approximate ontology matches. In *Proceedings of the 16th International Conference on World Wide Web* (pp. 767-776).

Goguen, J. A. (1967). L-fuzzy sets. *Journal of Mathematical Analysis and Applications, 8*(1), 145–174. doi:10.1016/0022-247X(67)90189-8

Goh, K., Chang, E., & Lai, W.-C. (2004). Concept-dependent multimodal active learning for image retrieval. In *Proceedings of the ACM Multimedia Conference* (pp.564-571).

Gracia, J., & Mena, E. (2008). Web-based measure of semantic relatedness. In *Proceedings of the 9th International Conference on Web Information Systems Engineering* (pp. 136-150).

Greenacre, M. J., & Blasius, J. (2006). *Multiple correspondence analysis and related methods.* Boca Raton, FL: CRC Press.

Gross, M. H., Sprenger, T. C., & Finger, J. (1995). Visualizing information on a sphere. In *Proceedings of the IEEE Symposium on Information Visualization* (pp. 11-16).

Guerin-Dugue, A., Ayache, S., & Berrut, C. (2003). Image retrieval: A first step for a human centered approach. In *Proceedings of the International Conference on Information, Communications and Signal Processing* (pp. 21-25). Washington, DC: IEEE Computer Society.

Guo, D. (2007). Visual analytics of spatial interaction patterns for pandemic decision support. *International Journal of Geographical Information Science, 21*(8), 859–877. doi:10.1080/13658810701349037

Guttman, A. (1984). R-trees: A dynamic index structure for spatial searching. In *Proceedings of the ACM SIGMOD International Conference on Management of Data* (pp. 47-57).

Hagen, L., & Kahng, A. (1992). New spectral methods for ratio cut partitioning and clustering. *Transactions on Computer-Aided Design, 11*(9), 1074–1085. doi:10.1109/43.159993

Hähnle, R. (2005). Many-valued logic, partiality, and abstraction in formal specification languages. *Journal of the Interest Group of Pure and Applied Logic, 13*(4), 415–433.

Hamilton, N., Pantelic, R., Hanson, K., Fink, J. L., Karunaratne, S., & Teasdale, R. D. (2006). Automated sub-cellular phenotype classification: An introduction and recent results. In *Proceedings of the Workshop on Intelligent Systems for Bioinformatics* (pp. 67-72).

Hampapur, A., Gupta, A., Horowitz, B., Shu, C.-F., Fuller, C., Bach, J. R., et al. (1997). Virage video engine. In *Proceedings of the SPIE International Conference on Storage and Retrieval for Image and Video Databases* (pp. 188-198).

Han, S. H., Koo, B. J., Hutter, A., & Stechele, W. (2010). Forensic reasoning upon pre-obtained surveillance metadata using uncertain spatio-temporal rules and subjective logic. In *Proceedings of the International Workshop on Image Analysis for Multimedia Interactive Services* (pp. 1-4).

Han, S. H., Koo, B. J., Hutter, A., Shet, V., & Stechele, W. (2010). Subjective logic based hybrid approach to conditional evidence fusion for forensic visual surveillance. In *Proceedings of the IEEE Conference on Advanced Video and Signal based Surveillance* (pp. 337-344).

Han, J., & Kamber, M. (2006). *Data Mining: Concepts and techniques* (2nd ed.). Waltham, MA: Morgan Kaufmann.

Hanjalic, A., Lagendijk, R. L., & Biemond, J. (1999). Automated high-level movie segmentation for advanced video-retrieval systems. *IEEE Transactions on Circuits and Systems for Video Technology*, *9*, 580–588. doi:10.1109/76.767124

Hanjalic, A., & Zhang, H. J. (1999). An integrated scheme for automated video abstraction based on unsupervised cluster-validity analysis. *IEEE Transactions on Circuits and Systems for Video Technology*, *9*(8). doi:10.1109/76.809162

Hart, P. E. (2009). How the Hough transform was invented. *IEEE Signal Processing Magazine*, *26*(6), 18–22. doi:10.1109/MSP.2009.934181

Harvey, M., Baillie, M., Ruthven, I., & Carman, M. (2010). Tripartite hidden topic models for personalized tag suggestion. In *Proceedings of the 32nd European Conference on Advances in Information Retrieval Research* (pp. 432-443).

Heath, F. M., Vernon, M. C., & Webb, C. R. (2008). Construction of networks with intrinsic temporal structure from UK cattle movement data. *BMC Veterinary Research*, *4*(1), 11. doi:10.1186/1746-6148-4-11

Heer, J., Bostock, M., & Ogievetsky, V. (2010). A tour through the visualization zoo. *Communications of the ACM*, *53*(8), 59–67. doi:10.1145/1743546.1743567

Hendrickson, B., & Kolda, T. G. (2000). Graph partitioning models for parallel computing. *Parallel Computing Journal*, *26*, 1519–1534. doi:10.1016/S0167-8191(00)00048-X

Henzinger, M. (2001). Hyperlink analysis for the Web. *IEEE Internet Computing*, *5*(1), 45–50. doi:10.1109/4236.895141

Herlocker, J. L., Konstan, J. A., Terveen, L. G., & Riedl, J. T. (2004). Evaluating collaborative filtering recommender systems. *ACM Transactions on Information Systems*, *22*(1), 5–53. doi:10.1145/963770.963772

Hijikata, Y., Iwahama, K., & Nishida, I. S. (2006). Content-based music filtering system with editable user profile. In *Proceedings of the ACM Symposium on Applied Computing* (pp. 1050-1057).

Hirose, S., Yoshimura, M., Hachimura, K., & Akama, R. (2008). Authorship identification of ukiyo by using rakkan image. In *Proceedings of the Eighth IAPR Workshop on Document Analysis Systems*, Nara, Japan (pp. 143-150).

Hoi, S. C. H., Lyu, M. R., & Jin, R. (2006). A unified log-based relevance feedback scheme for image retrieval. *IEEE Transactions on Knowledge and Data Engineering*, *18*(4), 509–524. doi:10.1109/TKDE.2006.1599389

Horridege, M., Knublauch, H., Rector, A., Stevens, R., & Wroe, C. (2004). *A practical guide to building OWL ontologies using the Protege-OWL plugin and CO-ODE tools edition 1.0*. Retrieved September 14, 2011, from http://owl.cs.manchester.ac.uk/tutorials/protegeowltutorial/

Hsu, W., & Sosnick, M. (2009). Evaluating interactive music systems: An HCI approach. In *Proceedings of the International Conference on New Interfaces for Musical Expression* (pp. 25-28).

Hsu, C.-H., & Hefeeda, M. (2011). A framework for cross-layer optimization of video streaming in wireless networks. *ACM Transactions on Multimedia Computing, Communications, and Applications*, 7(1), 1–28. doi:10.1145/1870121.1870126

Hua, K. A., Yu, N., & Liu, D.-Z. (2006). Query decomposition: A multiple neighborhood approach to relevance feedback processing in content-based image retrieval. In *Proceedings of the International Conference on Data Engineering* (pp. 84-93).

Huang, T., & Rui, Y. (1997). Image retrieval: Past, present, and future. In *Proceedings of the International Symposium on Multimedia Information Processing*.

Huang, C. H., & Wu, J. L. (2004). Attacking visible watermarking schemes. *IEEE Transactions on Multimedia*, 6(1), 16–30. doi:10.1109/TMM.2003.819579

Huang, Y., Sun, X., & Hu, G. (2009). An automatic integrated approach for stained neuron detection in studying neuron migration. *Microscopy Research and Technique*, 73(2), 109–118.

IEEE. Computer Society. (2003). *IEEE 802.11 WG: IEEE 802.11e/D4.1: Wireless MAC and physical layer specifications: MAC enhancements for QoS*. Washington, DC: IEEE Computer Society.

IEEE. Computer Society. (2009). *IEEE 802.11 WG: IEEE standard for information technology – Telecommunications and information exchange between systems – LAN/MAN specific requirements, Part 11: Wireless LAN MAC and PHY specifications*. Washington, DC: IEEE Computer Society.

Inan, I., Keceli, F., & Ayanoglu, E. (2006). An adaptive multimedia QoS scheduler for 802.11e wireless LANs. In *Proceedings of the IEEE International Conference on Communications* (pp. 5263-5270).

International Organization for Standardization. (2002). *ISO/IEC 15938-3: MPEG-7-Visual, Information Technology – Multimedia content description interface – Part 3: Visual*. Geneva, Switzerland: ISO/IEC.

Ishikawa, Y., Subramanya, R., & Faloutsos, C. (1998). MindReader: Querying databases through multiple examples. In *Proceedings of the Very Large Database Conference* (pp. 218-227).

Jahne, B., Scharr, H., & Korkel, S. (1999). Principles of filter design. In *Handbook of Computer Vision and Applications* (pp. 125–152). New York, NY: Academic Press.

Jain, R. (1991). *The art of computer systems performance analysis: Techniques for experimental design, measurement, simulation, and modeling*. New York, NY: John Wiley & Sons.

Janies, D., Hill, A. W., Guralnick, R., Habib, F., Waltari, E., & Wheeler, W. C. (2007). Genomic analysis and geographic visualization of the spread of avian influenza (H5N1). *Systematic Biology*, 56, 321–329. doi:10.1080/10635150701266848

Jerrett, M., Burnett, R., Goldberg, M., Sears, M., Krewski, D., & Catalan, R. (2003). Spatial analysis for environmental health research: Concepts, methods, and examples. *Journal of Toxicology and Environmental Health. Part A: Current Issues*, 66(19), 1783–1810. doi:10.1080/15287390306446

Jia, M., Fan, X., Xie, X., Li, M. J., & Ma, W. Y. (2006). Photo-to-search: Using camera phones to inquire of the surrounding world. In *Proceedings of the Conference on Mobile Data Management* (pp. 46-48).

Jianbing, M., Weiru, L., Paul, M., & Weiqi, Y. (2009). Event composition with imperfect information for bus surveillance. In *Proceedings of the IEEE Conference of Advanced Video and Signal based Surveillance* (pp. 382-387).

Jiang, Y., Yang, J., Ngo, C., & Hauptmann, A. (2010). Representations of keypoint-based semantic concept detection: A comprehensive study. *IEEE Transactions on Multimedia*, 12(1), 42–53. doi:10.1109/TMM.2009.2036235

Jin, E., Girvan, M., & Newman, M. (2001). The structure of growing social networks. *Physical Review E: Statistical, Nonlinear, and Soft Matter Physics*, 64(4), 046132. doi:10.1103/PhysRevE.64.046132

Joint Video Team of ISO/IEC MPEG and ITU-T VCEG. (2002). *Joint model number 1, revision 1 (JM-1R1)*. Retrieved from http://ip.hhi.de/imagecom_G1/assets/pdfs/JVT-A003r1.pdf

Jones, K. S. (2004). A statistical interpretation of term specificity and its application in retrieval. *The Journal of Documentation*, 60(5), 493–502. doi:10.1108/00220410410560573

Jøsang, A. (1997). Artificial reasoning with subjective logic. In *Proceedings of the 2nd Australian Workshop on Commonsense Reasoning,* Perth, Australia.

Jøsang, A., Daniel, M., & Vannoorenberghe, P. (2003). Strategies for combining conflicting dogmatic beliefs. In *Proceedings of the 6th International Conference on Information Fusion* (pp. 1133-1140).

Jøsang, A. (2001). A logic for uncertain probabilities. *International Journal of Uncertainty. Fuzziness and Knowledge-Based Systems, 9*(3), 279–311. doi:10.1142/S0218488501000831

Jøsang, A. (2006). The consensus operator for combining beliefs. *Artificial Intelligence Journal, 38*(1), 157–170.

Jøsang, A., & Daniel, M. (2004). Multiplication and comultiplication of beliefs. *International Journal of Approximate Reasoning, 142*(1-2), 19–51.

Josgim, D., Wang, J. Z., & Li, J. (2006). The story picturing engine-a system for automatic text illustration. *ACM Transactions on Multimedia Computing, Communications, and Applications, 2*(1), 68–89. doi:10.1145/1126004.1126008

Juszczyszyn, K., Kazienko, P., & Musiał, K. (2010). Personalized ontology-based recommender systems for multimedia objects, agent and multi-agent technology for internet and enterprise systems. In Hakansson, A., Hartung, R., & Nguyen, N.-T. (Eds.), *Agent and multiagent technology for Internet and enterprise systems* (*Vol. 289*, pp. 275–292). Berlin, Germany: Springer-Verlag. doi:10.1007/978-3-642-13526-2_13

Kalva, P., Enembreck, F., & Koerich, A. (2007). Web image classification based on the fusion of image and text classifiers. In *Proceedings of the International Conference on Document Analysis and Recognition* (pp. 561-568).

Kazienko, P., & Musial, K. (2006). Recommendation framework for online social networks. *Advances in Web Intelligence and Data Mining, 23,* 111–120. doi:10.1007/3-540-33880-2_12

Ke, Y., Suthankar, R., & Huston, L. (2004). An efficient parts-based near-duplicate and sub-image retrieval system. In *Proceedings of the ACM Multimedia Conference* (pp. 869–876).

Ke, C. H., Shieh, C. K., Hwang, W. S., & Ziviani, A. (2008). An evaluation framework for more realistic simulations of MPEG video transmission. *Journal of Information Science and Engineering, 24*(2), 425–440.

Kim, D. H., & Chung, C. W. (2003). Qcluster: Relevance feedback using adaptive clustering for content-based image retrieval. In *Proceedings of SIGMOD International Conference on Management of Data* (pp. 599-610).

Kim, S., Tak, Y., Nam, Y., & Hwang, E. (2006). mCLOVER: Mobile content-based leaf image retrieval system. In *Proceedings of the ACM Multimedia Conference* (pp.215-216).

Kim, H. K., Kim, J. K., & Ryu, Y. U. (2009). Personalized recommendation over a customer network for ubiquitous shopping. *IEEE Transactions on Services Computing, 2*(2), 140–151. doi:10.1109/TSC.2009.7

Kim, J. K., Kim, H. K., & Cho, Y. H. (2008). A user-oriented contents recommendation system in peer to peer architecture. *Expert Systems with Applications, 34*(1), 300–312. doi:10.1016/j.eswa.2006.09.034

Kim, W.-Y., & Kim, Y.-S. (1999). *ISO/IEC MPEG99/M5472: New Region-Based Shape Descriptor.* Geneva, Switzerland: ISO/IEC.

Kleinberg, J. (1998). Authoritative sources in a hyperlinked environment. In *Proceedings of the 9th ACM SIAM Symposium on Discrete Algorithms* (pp. 668-677).

Knijnenburg, B., Meesters, L., Marrow, P., & Bouwhuis, D. (2010). User-centric evaluation framework for multimedia recommender systems. In P. Daras & O. M. Ibarra (Eds.), *Proceedings of the First International Conference on User Centric Media* (LNICST 40, pp. 366-369).

Kohavi, R. (1995). A study of cross-validation and bootstrap for accuracy estimation and model selection. In *Proceedings of the Fourteenth International Joint Conference on Artificial Intelligence* (Vol. 2, pp. 1137-1143).

Komorowski, J., Ohrn, A., & Skowron, A. (2002). The ROSETTA rough set software system. In W. Klosgen & J. Zytkow (Eds.), *Handbook of data mining and knowledge discovery* (Ch. D.2.3). Oxford, UK: Oxford University Press.

Kononenko, I. (1995). On biases in estimating multi-valued attributes. In *Proceedings of the International Joint Conference on Artificial Intelligence* (pp. 1034-1040).

Koskela, M., Smeaton, A., & Laaksonen, J. (2007). Measuring concept similarities in multimedia ontologies; Analysis and evaluations. *IEEE Transactions on Multimedia*, *9*(5), 912–922. doi:10.1109/TMM.2007.900137

Ksentini, A., Naimi, M., & Gueroui, A. (2006). Toward an improvement of H.264 video transmission over IEEE 802.11e through a cross-layer architecture. *IEEE Communications Magazine*, *44*(1), 107–114. doi:10.1109/MCOM.2006.1580940

Kwitt, R., Uhl, A., Hafner, M., Gangl, A., Wrba, F., & Vecsei, A. (2010). Predicting the histology of colorectal lesions in a probabilistic framework. In *Proceedings of the IEEE Computer Society Conference on Computer Vision and Pattern Recognition Workshops* (pp.103-110).

Lahti, J., Westermann, U., Palola, M., Peltola, J., & Vildjiounaite, E. (2005). MobiCon: Integrated capture, annotation, and sharing of video clips with mobile phones. In *Proceedings of the ACM Multimedia Conference* (pp. 798-799).

Lam, X. N., Vu, T., Le, T. D., & Duong, A. D. (2008). Addressing cold-start problem in recommendation systems. In *Proceedings of the 2nd International ACM Conference on Ubiquitous Information Management and Communication* (pp. 208-211).

Lan, M., Tan, C. L., Su, J., & Lu, Y. (2009). Supervised and traditional term weighting methods for automatic text categorization. *IEEE Transactions on Pattern Analysis and Machine Intelligence*, *31*(4), 721–735. doi:10.1109/TPAMI.2008.110

Lappas, T., Liu, K., & Terzi, E. (2009). Finding a team of experts in social networks. In *Proceedings of the 15th ACM SIGKDD International Conference on Knowledge Discovery and Data Mining* (pp. 467-476).

Lawson, A. B., & Zhou, H. (2005). Spatial statistical modeling of disease outbreaks with particular reference to the UK foot and mouth disease (FMD) epidemic of 2001. *Preventive Veterinary Medicine*, *71*(3-4), 141–156. doi:10.1016/j.prevetmed.2005.07.002

Lawton, G. (2009). Users take a close look at visual analytics. *IEEE Computer Magazine*, *42*(2), 19–22.

Lazebnik, S., Schmid, C., & Ponce, J. (2006). Beyond bags of features: Spatial pyramid matching for recognizing natural scene categories. In *Proceedings of the IEEE Computer Society Conference on Computer Vision and Pattern Recognition* (pp. 2169-2178).

Lebedev, L. P., & Cloud, M. J. (2003). *Tensor analysis*. Singapore: World Scientific. doi:10.1142/9789812564467

Lee, C. F., & Lee, H. E. (2008). A blind associative watermark detection scheme using self-embedding technique. In *Proceedings of the International Conference on Intelligent Information Hiding and Multimedia Signal Processing* (pp.1122-1125).

Lee, J., & Jayant, N. (2006). Mixed-initiative multimedia for mobile devices: A voting-based user interface for news videos. In *Proceedings of the ACM Multimedia Conference* (pp. 611-614).

Lekakos, G., & Caravelas, P. (2008). A hybrid approach for movie recommendation. *Multimedia Tools and Applications*, *36*(1-2), 55–70. doi:10.1007/s11042-006-0082-7

Lewis, D. D. (1998). Naive (Bayes) at forty: The independence assumption in information retrieval. In *Proceedings of the 10th European Conference on Machine Learning* (pp. 4-15).

Lew, M. S., Sebe, N., Djeraba, C., & Jain, R. (2006). Content-based multimedia information retrieval: State of the art and challenges. *ACM Transactions on Multimedia Computing, Communications, and Applications*, *2*(1), 1–19. doi:10.1145/1126004.1126005

Li, H., Wang, M., & Hua, X.-S. (2009). Msra-mm 2.0: A large-scale web multimedia dataset. In *Proceedings of the IEEE International Conference on Data Mining Workshops* (pp. 164-169).

Li, L. (2006). Data complexity in machine learning and novel classification algorithms (Unpublished doctoral dissertation). California Institute of Technology, Pasadena, CA.

Li, Y., & Merialdo, B. (2010). VERT: a method for automatic evaluation of video summaries. In *Proceedings of the ACM Conference on Multimedia* (pp. 851-854).

Liebelt, J., Schmid, C., & Schertler, K. (2008). Viewpoint-independent object class detection using 3D Feature Maps. In *Proceedings of the IEEE Conference on Computer Vision and Pattern Recognition* (pp. 1-8).

Lienhart, R., Pfeiffer, S., & Effelsberg, W. (1997). Video abstracting. *Communications of the ACM*, 1–12.

Lin, L., Chen, C., Shyu, M.-L., Fleites, F., & Chen, S.-C. (2009). *Florida International University and University of Miami TRECVID 2009-high level feature extraction.* Retrieved from http://www-nlpir.nist.gov/projects/tvpubs/tv9.papers/fiu-um.pdf

Lin, L., Ravitz, G., Shyu, M.-L., & Chen, S.-C. (2008). Correlation-based video semantic concept detection using multiple correspondence analysis. In *Proceedings of the IEEE International Symposium on Multimedia* (pp. 316-321).

Lin, L., Shyu, M.-L., & Chen, S.-C. (2009). Enhancing concept detection by pruning data with mca-based transaction weights. In *Proceedings of the IEEE International Symposium on Multimedia* (pp. 304-311).

Lin, L., & Shyu, M.-L. (2010). Correlation-based ranking for large-scale video concept retrieval. *International Journal of Multimedia Data Engineering and Management*, *1*(4), 60–74. doi:10.4018/jmdem.2010100105

Liu, D., Hua, K., & Yu, N. (2006). Fast query point movement techniques with relevance feedback for content-based image retrieval. In *Proceedings of the International Conference on Extending Data Base Technology* (pp. 700-717).

Liu, X., Corner, M., & Shenoy, P. (2005). SEVA: Sensor-enhanced video annotation. In *Proceedings of the ACM Multimedia Conference* (pp. 618-627).

Liu, H., Lin, C., & Weng, R. (2007). A note on platt's probabilistic outputs for support vector machines. *Machine Learning*, *68*(3), 267–276. doi:10.1007/s10994-007-5018-6

Liu, Y., Loh, H. T., & Sun, A. (2009). Imbalanced text classification: A term weighting approach. *Expert Systems with Applications*, *36*(1), 690–701. doi:10.1016/j.eswa.2007.10.042

Liu, Y., Zhang, D. S., Lu, G., & Ma, W.-Y. (2007). A survey of content-based image retrieval with high-level semantics. *Pattern Recognition*, *40*(1), 262–282. doi:10.1016/j.patcog.2006.04.045

Long, X., Cleveland, W., & Yao, Y. (2010). Multiclass detection of cells in multicontrast composite images. *Computers in Biology and Medicine*, *40*(2), 168–178. doi:10.1016/j.compbiomed.2009.11.013

Love, H. (2002). *Attributing authorship: An introduction.* Cambridge, UK: Cambridge University Press. doi:10.1017/CBO9780511483165

Lowe, D. (2004). Distinctive image features from scale-invariant key points. *International Journal of Computer Vision*, *60*(2), 91–110. doi:10.1023/B:VISI.0000029664.99615.94

Lu, J., Bao, Z., Ling, T. W., & Meng, X. (2009). XML keyword query refinement. In *Proceedings of the First International Workshop on Keyword Search on Structured Data* (pp. 41-42).

Luke, D. A., & Harris, J. K. (2007). Network analysis in public health: History, methods, and applications. *Annual Review of Public Health*, *28*, 16.1-16.25.

Luo, H., & Shyu, M.-L. (2009). An optimized scheduling scheme to provide quality of service in 802.11e wireless LAN. In *Proceedings of the Fifth IEEE International Workshop on Multimedia Information Processing and Retrieval* (pp. 651-656).

Luo, H. (2009). An optimized scheduling scheme for 802.11e MAC. *International Journal of Electronics and Computer Systems*, *11*(2), 1–8.

Lux, M., & Chatizichristofis, A. (2008). LIRE: Lucene Image REtrieval - an extensible java cbir library. In *Proceedings of the 16th ACM International Conference on Multimedia* (pp. 1085-1088).

Luxburg, U. V. (2007). A tutorial on spectral clustering. *Statistics and Computing*, 17.

Ma, H., Yang, H., King, I., & Lyu, M. (2008). Learning latent semantic relations from click through data for query suggestion. In *Proceedings of the 17th ACM Conference on Information and Knowledge Management* (pp. 709-718).

Madhloom, H. T., Kareem, S. A., Ariffin, H., Zaidan, A. A., Alanazi, H. O., & Zaidan, B. B. (2010). An automated white blood cell nucleus localization and segmentation using image arithmetic and automatic threshold. *Journal of Applied Sciences*, *10*(11), 959–966. doi:10.3923/jas.2010.959.966

Maidel, V., Shoval, P., Shapira, B., & Taieb-Maimon, M. (2008). Evaluation of an ontology-content based filtering method for a personalized newspaper. In *Proceedings of the ACM Conference on Recommender Systems* (pp. 91-98).

Manjunath, B. S., Salembier, P., & Sikora, T. (2002). *Introduction to MPEG-7: Multimedia content description interface*. New York, NY: John Wiley & Sons.

Manning, C. D., Raghavan, P., & Schütze, H. (2008). Introduction to information retrieval. In *Evaluation of Clustering* (pp. 356–360). Cambridge, UK: Cambridge University Press.

Manzato, M. G., & Goularte, R. (2009). Supporting multimedia recommender systems with peer-level annotations. In *Proceedings of the 15ᵗʰ Brazilian Symposium on Multimedia and the Web*.

Masolo, C., Vieu, L., Bottazzi, E., Catenacci, C., Ferrario, R., Gangemi, A., & Guarino, N. (2004). Social roles and their descriptions. In *Proceedings of the 9th International Conference on the Principles of Knowledge Representation and Reasoning* (pp. 267-277).

Matsumoto, K., Naito, M., Hoashi, K., & Sugaya, F. (2006). SVM-based shot boundary detection with a novel feature. In *Proceedings of the IEEE International Conference Multimedia and Expo* (pp. 1837-1840).

Meng, T., Lin, L., Shyu, M.-L., & Chen, S.-C. (2010). Histology image classification using supervised classification and multimodal fusion. In *Proceedings of the IEEE International Symposium on Multimedia* (pp. 145-152).

Miller, G. A. (1995). WordNet: A lexical database for English. *Communications of the ACM*, *38*(11), 39–41. doi:10.1145/219717.219748

Milne, D., Witten, I., & Nichols, D. (2007). A knowledge-based search engine powered by Wikipedia. In *Proceedings of the 16th ACM Conference on Information and Knowledge Management* (pp. 445-454).

Minamikawa, R., Kabuyama, N., Gotoh, T., Kagei, S., Naruse, M., & Kisu, Y. (2003). High-throughput classification of images of cell transfected with cDNA clones. *Molecular Biology and Genetics*, *326*, 993–1001.

Misselwitz, B., Strittmatter, G., Periaswamy, B., Schlumberger, M. C., Rout, S., & Horvath, P. (2010). Enhanced cell classifier: A multi-class classification tool for Microscopy images. *BMC Bioinformatics*, *11*(30).

Mitchell, T. M. (1997). *Machine learning*. New York, NY: McGraw-Hill.

Moghaddam, B., Tian, Q., Lesh, N., Shen, C., & Huang, T. (2002). PDH: A human-centric interface for image libraries. In *Proceedings of the IEEE International Conference on Multimedia and Expo* (pp. 901-904). Washington, DC: IEEE Computer Society.

Moghaddam, B., Tian, Q., Lesh, N., Shen, C., & Huang, T. S. (2004). Visualization and user-modeling for browsing personal photo libraries. *International Journal of Computer Vision*, *56*(1-2), 109–130. doi:10.1023/B:VISI.0000004834.62090.74

Mohomed, I., Cai, J. C., Chavoshi, S., & Lara, E. (2006). Context-aware interactive content adaptation. In *Proceedings of the International Conference on Mobile Systems, Applications, and Services* (pp. 42-55).

Mokhtarian, F., & Mackworth, A. K. (1992). A theory of multiscale, curvature-based shape representation for planar curves. *IEEE Transactions on Pattern Analysis and Machine Intelligence*, 789–805. doi:10.1109/34.149591

Mukundan, R., & Ramakrishnan, K. R. (1998). *Moment functions in image analysis: Theory and applications*. Singapore: World Scientific. doi:10.1142/9789812816092

Musiał, K., Kazienko, P., & Kajdanowicz, T. (2008). Social recommendations within the multimedia sharing systems. In M. D. Lytras, J. M. Carroll, E. Damiani, & R. D. Tennyson (Eds.), *Proceedings of the First World Summit on Emerging Technologies and Information Systems for the Knowledge Society* (LNCS 5288, pp. 364-372)

Naphade, M., Smith, J., Tesic, J., Chang, S., Hsu, W., & Kennedy, L. (2006). Large-scale concept ontology for multimedia. *IEEE MultiMedia*, *13*(3), 86–91. doi:10.1109/MMUL.2006.63

Napoléon, T., Adamek, T., Schmitt, F., & O'Connor, N. E. (2007). Multi-view 3D retrieval using silhouette intersection and multi-scale contour representation. In *Proceedings of the Shape Retrieval Contest*, Lyon, France.

Natsev, A., Haubold, A., Tesic, J., Xie, L., & Yan, R. (2007). Semantic concept-based query expansion and re-ranking for multimedia retrieval. In *Proceedings of the 15th International Conference on Multimedia* (pp. 991-1000).

Nemenyi, P. B. (1963). *Distribution-free multiple comparison*. Unpublished doctoral dissertation, Princeton University, Princeton, NJ.

Ngo, C., Jiang, Y., Wei, X., Zhao, W., Liu, Y., Wang, J., et al. (2009). VIREO/DVM at TRECVID 2009: High-level feature extraction, automatic video search and content-based copy detection. In *Proceedings of the TREC Video Retrieval Evaluation Conference* (pp. 415-432).

Ngo, C. W., & Zhang, H. J. (2002). Motion-based video representation for scene change detection. *International Journal of Computer Vision*, *50*(2), 127–142. doi:10.1023/A:1020341931699

Nguyen, K., Jain, A. K., & Allen, R. L. (2010). Automated gland segmentation and classification for Gleason grading of prostate tissue images. In *Proceedings of the 20th International Conference on Pattern Recognition* (pp. 1497-1500).

Nguyen, G. P., & Worring, M. (2008). Interactive access to large image collections using similarity-based visualization. *Journal of Visual Languages and Computing*, *19*(2), 203–224. doi:10.1016/j.jvlc.2006.09.002

NS-2. (2011). *Network simulator*. Retrieved from http://www.isi.edu/nsnam/ns/

Odobez, J.-M., Gatica-Perez, D., & Guillemot, M. (2003). Spectral structuring of home videos. In *Proceedings of the ACM International Conference on Image and Video Retrieval. Urbana (Caracas, Venezuela)*, *IL*, 310–320.

Ortega, M., Rui, Y., Chakrabarti, K., Porkaew, K., Mehrotra, S., & Huang, T. S. (1998). Supporting ranked Boolean similarity queries in MARS. *IEEE Transactions on Knowledge and Data Engineering*, *10*(6), 905–925. doi:10.1109/69.738357

Page, L., Brin, S., Motwani, R., & Winograd, T. (1999). *The PageRank citation ranking: Bringing order to the Web* (Tech. Rep. No. SIDL-WP-1999-0120). Stanford, CA: Stanford University.

Pazzani, M., & Billsus, D. (2007). Content-based recommendation systems. In P. Brusilovsky, A. Kobsa, & W. Nejdl (Eds.), *Proceedings of the Methods and Strategies of Web Personalisation: The Adaptive Web* (LNCS 4321, pp. 325-341).

Pearl, J. (1988). *Probabilistic reasoning in intelligent systems: Networks of plausible inference*. San Mateo, CA: Morgan Kaufmann.

Pei, S. C., & Zeng, Y. C. (2006). A novel image recovery algorithm for visible watermarked images. *IEEE Transactions on Information Forensics and Security*, *1*(4), 543–550. doi:10.1109/TIFS.2006.885031

Peker, K. A., & Bashir, F. I. (2005). *Content-based video summarization using spectral clustering*. Paper presented at the International Workshop on Very Low-Bitrate Video, Sardinia, Italy.

Peng, H. (2008). Bioimage informatics: A new area of engineering biology. *Bioinformatics (Oxford, England)*, *24*(17), 1827–1836. doi:10.1093/bioinformatics/btn346

Petre, R., Zaharia, T., & Preteux, F. (2010). An overview of view-based 2D/3D indexing methods. In *Proceedings of the 12th SPIE Conference on Mathematics of Data/Image Coding, Compression, and Encryption with Applications* (Vol. 7799, p. 779904).

Porkaew, K., Chakrabarti, K., & Mehrotra, S. (1999). Query refinement for multimedia similarity retrieval in MARS. In *Proceedings of the ACM Multimedia Conference* (pp. 235-238).

Porter, S. V., Mirmehdi, M., & Thomas, B. T. (2000). Video cut detection using frequency domain correlation. In *Proceedings of the 15th International Conference on Pattern Recognition* (pp. 413-416).

Pottie, G., & Kaiser, W. (2000). Wireless integrated network sensors. *Communications of the ACM*, *43*(5), 51–58. doi:10.1145/332833.332838

Preece, J., Rogers, Y., & Sharp, H. (2002). *Interaction design*. New York, NY: John Wiley & Sons.

Proulx, P., Chien, L., Harper, R., Schroh, D., Kapler, D., & Jonker, D. (2007). nSpace and GeoTime: A VAST 2006 case study. *IEEE Computer Graphics and Applications*, *27*(5), 46–56. doi:10.1109/MCG.2007.131

Qamra, A., Meng, Y., & Cheng, E. Y. (2005). Enhanced perceptual distance functions and indexing for image replica recognition. *IEEE Transactions on Pattern Analysis and Machine Intelligence*, *27*, 379–391. doi:10.1109/TPAMI.2005.54

Qin, S., Menezes, R., & Silaghi, M. (2010). A recommender system for Youtube based on its network of reviewers. In *Proceedings of the IEEE Second International Conference on Social Computing* (pp. 323-328).

Quirino, T., Xie, Z., Shyu, M.-L., Chen, S.-C., & Chang, L. (2006). Collateral representative subspace projection modeling for supervised classification. In *Proceedings of the IEEE International Conference on Tools with Artificial Intelligence* (pp. 98-105).

Qureshi, H., Raipoot, N., Nattkemper, T., & Hans, V. (2009). A robust adaptive wavelet-based method for classification of Meningioma histology images. In *Proceedings of the MICCAI Workshop on Optical Tissue Image Analysis in Microscopy, Histology and Endoscopy.*

Rafailidis, D., Nanopoulos, A., & Manolopoulos, Y. (2010). Building tag-aware groups for music high-order ranking and topic discovery. *International Journal of Multimedia Data Engineering and Management, 1*(3), 1–18. doi:10.4018/jmdem.2010070101

Rafkind, B., Lee, M., Chang, S.-F., & Yu, H. (2006). Exploring text and image features to classify images in bioscience literature. In *Proceedings of the Workshop on Linking Natural Language Processing and Biology: Towards Deeper Biological Literature Analysis* (pp. 73-80).

Rasheed, Z., & Shah, M. (2005). Detection and Representation of scenes in videos. *IEEE Transactions on Multimedia, 7*(6), 1097–1105. doi:10.1109/TMM.2005.858392

Rasheed, Z., Sheikh, Y., & Shah, M. (2005). On the use of computable features for film classification. *IEEE Transactions on Circuits and Systems for Video Technology, 15*(1), 52–64. doi:10.1109/TCSVT.2004.839993

Reinhardt, M., Elias, J., Albert, J., Frosch, M., Harmsen, D., & Vogel, U. (2008). EpiScanGIS: An online geographic surveillance system for meningococcal disease. *International Journal of Health Geographics, 7*(1), 33. doi:10.1186/1476-072X-7-33

Reiter, R. (1980). A logic for default reasoning. *Artificial Intelligence, 13*, 81–132. doi:10.1016/0004-3702(80)90014-4

Resnick, P., Iacovou, N., Suchak, M., Bergstrom, P., & Riedl, J. (1994). GroupLens: an open architecture for collaborative filtering of netnews. In *Proceedings of the ACM Conference on Computer Supported Cooperative Work* (pp. 175-186).

Reynolds, D., Dickinson, I., & Grosvenor, D. (2009). *A query refinement model for exploratory semantic search* (Tech. Rep. No. HPL-2009-167). Palo Alto, CA: HP Laboratories.

Rice, J. A. (2007). *Mathematical statistic and data analysis* (3rd ed.). Belmont, CA: Duxbury.

Robertson, S. E. (2004). Understanding inverse document frequency: On theoretical arguments for idf. *The Journal of Documentation, 60*(5), 503–520. doi:10.1108/00220410410560582

Robertson, S. E., & Jones, K. S. (1976). Relevance weighting of search terms. *Journal of the American Society for Information Science American Society for Information Science, 27*(3), 129–146. doi:10.1002/asi.4630270302

Robine, M., Hanna, P., Ferraro, P., & Allali, J. (2007). Adaptation of string matching algorithms for identification of near-duplicate music documents. In *Proceedings of the International SIGIR Workshop on Plagiarism Analysis, Authorship Identification, and Near-Duplicate Detection (PAN),* Amsterdam, The Netherlands (pp. 37-43).

Robinson, J. T. (1981). The K-D-B-tree: A search structure for large multidimensional dynamic indexes. In *Proceedings of the ACM SIGMOD International Conference on Management of Data* (pp. 10-18).

Rosenberg, A., & Hirschberg, J. (2007). V-Measure: A conditional entropy-based external cluster evaluation measure. In *Proceedings of the 2007 Joint Conference on Empirical Methods in Natural Language Processing and Computational Natural Language Learning (EMNLP-CoNLL),* Prague, Czech Republic (pp. 410-420).

Rothenberg, R. B., Potterat, J. J., Woodhouse, D. E., Muth, S. Q., Darrow, W. W., & Klovdahl, A. S. (1998). Social network dynamics and HIV transmission. *AIDS (London, England), 12*(12), 1529–1536. doi:10.1097/00002030-199812000-00016

Rothenberg, R. B., Sterk, C., Toomey, K. E., Potterat, J. J., Johnson, D., & Schrader, M. (1998). Using social network and ethnographic tools to evaluate syphilis transmission. *Sexually Transmitted Diseases, 25*(3), 154–160. doi:10.1097/00007435-199803000-00009

Roussopoulos, N., Kelley, S., & Vincent, F. (1995). Nearest neighbor queries. In *Proceedings of the ACM SIGMOD International Conference on Management of Data* (pp. 71-79).

Rui, Y., Huang, T., & Mehrotra, S. (1997). Content based image retrieval with relevance feedback in mars. In *Proceedings of the International Conference on Image Processing* (pp. 815-818).

Rui, Y., & Huang, T. (2000). A unified framework for video browsing and retrieval. In *Image and Video Processing Handbook* (pp. 705–715). New York: Academic Press.

Rui, Y., Huang, T., & Chang, S. (1999). Image retrieval: Current techniques, promising directions and operations. *Journal of Visual Communication and Image Representation, 10*(1), 39–62. doi:10.1006/jvci.1999.0413

Rui, Y., Huang, T., Ortega, M., & Mehrotra, S. (1998). Elevance feedback: A power tool for interactive content-based image retrieval. *IEEE Transactions on Circuits and Systems for Video Technology, 8*(5), 644–655. doi:10.1109/76.718510

Russell, S., & Norvig, P. (2003). *Artificial Intelligence: A modern approach.* Upper Saddle River, NJ: Prentice Hall.

Sainani, V., & Shyu, M.-L. (2009). A hybrid layered multiagent architecture with low cost and low response time communication protocol for network intrusion detection system. In *Proceedings of the IEEE International Conference on Advanced Information Networking and Applications* (pp. 154-161).

Salton, G., & Buckley, C. (1988). Term-weighting approaches in automatic text retrieval. *International Journal of Information Processing and Management, 24*(5), 513–523. doi:10.1016/0306-4573(88)90021-0

Sande, K., Gevers, T., & Snoek, C. (2010). Evaluating color descriptors for object and scene recognition. *IEEE Transactions on Pattern Analysis and Machine Intelligence, 32*(9), 1582–1596. doi:10.1109/TPAMI.2009.154

Santini, S. (2000). Evaluation vademecum for visual information systems. In *Proceedings of the SPIE Conference on Storage and Retrieval for Image and Video Databases* (Vol. 3972, pp. 132-143).

Sapna Varshey, S., & Rajpal, R. (2010). Comparative study of image segmentation techniques and object matching using segmentation. In *Proceedings of the International Conference on Methods and Models in Computer Science* (pp. 1-6).

Sarvas, R., Viikari, M., Pesonen, J., & Nevanlinna, H. (2004). MobShare: Controlled and immediate sharing of mobile images. In *Proceedings of the International Conference on ACM Multimedia* (pp. 724-731).

Sarwar, B., Karypis, G., Konstan, J., & Riedl, J. (2001). Item-based collaborative filtering recommendation algorithms. In *Proceedings of the 10th International World Wide Web Conference* (pp. 285-295).

Schafer, J. B., Frankowsky, D., Herlocker, J. L., & Sen, S. (2007). Collaborative filtering recommender systems. In P. Brusilovsky, A. Kobsa, & W. Nejdl (Eds.), *Proceedings of the Methods and Strategies of Web Personalisation: The Adaptive Web* (LNCS 4321, pp. 291-324).

Schonhofen, P. (2006). Identify document topics using the Wikipedia category network. In *Proceedings of the International Conference on Web Intelligence* (pp. 456-462).

Schulz, A. G., & Hahsler, M. (2002). Evaluation of recommender algorithms for an internet information broker based on simple association rules and on the repeat-buying theory. In *Proceedings of the Fourth WebKDD Workshop: Web Mining for Usage Patterns & User Profiles* (pp. 100-114).

Schwengerdt, R. A. (1997). *Remote Sensing: Models and methods for image processing* (2nd ed.). New York, NY: Academic Press.

Sebastiani, F. (2002). Machine learning in automated text categorization. *ACM Computing Surveys, 34*(1), 1–47. doi:10.1145/505282.505283

Sertel, O. Catalyurek, Shimada, U. V., & Guican, M. N. (2009). Computer-aided prognosis of Neuroblastoma: Detection of Mitosis and Karyorrhexis cells in digitized histological images. In *Proceedings of the IEEE International Conference on Engineering in Medicine and Biology Society* (pp.1433-1436).

Shafer, G. (1976). *A mathematical theory of evidence.* Princeton, NJ: Princeton University Press.

Shamir, L. Eckley, D. M., & Goldberg, I. G. (2007). Image tiling vs. cell segmentation – a case study. In *Proceedings of the 47th American Society for Cell Biology Meeting* (p. 35).

Shamir, L., Orlov, N., Eckley, D. M., Macura, T., Johnston, J., & Goldberg, G. (2008). Wndchm - an open source utility for biological image analysis. *Source Code for Biology and Medicine, 3*(13), 943–947.

Shankar, N. S., & Van Der Schaar, M. (2007). Performance analysis of video transmission over IEEE 802.11a/e WLANs. *IEEE Transactions on Vehicular Technology*, *56*(4), 2346–2362. doi:10.1109/TVT.2007.897646

Shet, V., Harwood, D., & Davis, L. (2005). Vidmap: Video monitoring of activity with prolog. In *Proceedings of the IEEE Conference of Advanced Video and Signal based Surveillance* (pp. 224-229).

Shet, V., Harwood, D., & Davis, L. (2006). Multivalued default logic for identity maintenance in visual surveillance. In *Proceedings of the European Conference on Computer Vision* (pp. 119-132).

Shet, V., Harwood, D., & Davis, L. (2006). Top-down, bottom-up multivalued default reasoning for identity maintenance. In *Proceedings of the ACM International Workshop on Video Surveillance & Sensor Networks* (pp. 79-86).

Shet, V., Neumann, J., Ramesh, V., & Davis, L. (2007). Bilattice-based logical reasoning for human detection. In *Proceedings of the IEEE Conference on Computer Vision and Pattern Recognition* (pp. 1-8).

Shieh, J. R., Hsieh, Y. H., Yeh, Y. T., Su, T. C., Lin, C. Y., & Wu, J. L. (2009). Building term suggestion relational graphs from collective intelligence. In *Proceedings of the 18th International World Wide Web Conference* (pp. 713-721).

Shilane, P., Min, P., Kazhdan, M., & Funkhouser, T. (2004). The Princeton Shape Benchmark. In *Proceedings of the Shape Modeling International Conference,* Genoa, Italy.

Shirahama, K., Matsuoka, Y., & Uehara, K. (in press). Event retrieval in video archives using rough set theory and partially supervised learning. *Multimedia Tools and Applications*.

Shirahama, K., Matsuoka, Y., & Uehara, K. (in press). Hybrid negative example selection using visual and conceptual features. *Multimedia Tools and Applications*.

Shirley, M. D. F., & Rushton, S. P. (2005). Where diseases and networks collide: Lessons to be learnt from a study of the 2001 foot-and-mouth disease epidemic. *Epidemiology and Infection*, *133*, 1023–1032. doi:10.1017/S095026880500453X

Shyu, M.-L., Chen, S.-C., Chen, M., Zhang, C., & Shu, C.-M. (2003). MMM: A stochastic mechanism for image database queries. In *Proceedings of the IEEE Fifth International Symposium on Multimedia Software Engineering*, Taichung, Taiwan (pp. 188-195).

Shyu, M.-L., Chen, S.-C., Chen, M., Zhang, C., & Shu, C.-M. (2006). Probabilistic semantic network-based image retrieval using MMM and relevance feedback. *Multimedia Tools and Applications*, *30*(2), 131–147. doi:10.1007/s11042-006-0023-5

Shyu, M.-L., Quirino, T., Xie, Z., Chen, S.-C., & Chang, L. (2007). Network intrusion detection through adaptive sub-eigenspace modeling in multiagent systems. *ACM Transactions on Autonomous and Adaptive Systems*, *2*(3), 1–37. doi:10.1145/1278460.1278463

Shyu, M.-L., Xie, Z., Chen, M., & Chen, S.-C. (2008). Video semantic event/concept detection using a subspace-based multimedia data mining framework. *IEEE Transactions on Multimedia*, *10*(2), 252–259. doi:10.1109/TMM.2007.911830

Sigurbjörnsson, F., & Zwol, R. (2008). Flickr tag recommendation based on collective knowledge. In *Proceedings of the 17th International Conference on World Wide Web* (pp. 327-336).

Silverstein, C., Henzinger, M., Marais, H., & Moricz, M. (1998). *Analysis of a very large AltaVista query log* (Tech. Rep. No. 1998014). Palo Alto, CA: Digital Systems Research Center.

Skyrianoglou, D., Passas, N., & Salkintzis, A. K. (2006). ARROW: An efficient traffic scheduling algorithm for IEEE 802.11e HCCA. *IEEE Transactions on Wireless Communications*, *5*(12), 3558–3567. doi:10.1109/TWC.2006.256978

Smeaton, A., Over, P., & Kraaij, W. (2006). Evaluation campaigns and TRECVid. In *Proceedings of the 8th International Workshop on Multimedia Information Retrieval* (pp. 321-330).

Snoek, C., et al. (2009). The MediaMill TRECVID 2009 semantic video search engine. In *Proceedings of TREC Video Retrieval Evaluation* (pp. 226-238).

Snoek, C. G. M., Worring, M., Koelma, D., & Smeulders, A. W. M. (2007). A learned lexicon-driven paradigm for interactive video retrieval. *IEEE Transactions on Multimedia*, *9*(2), 280–292. doi:10.1109/TMM.2006.886275

Snoek, C., Huurnink, B., Hllink, L., Rijke, M., Schreiber, G., & Worring, M. (2007). Adding semantics to detectors for video retrieval. *IEEE Transactions on Multimedia*, *9*(5), 975–986. doi:10.1109/TMM.2007.900156

Sonobe, H., Takagi, S., & Yoshimoto, F. (2004). Image retrieval system of fishes using a mobile device. In *Proceedings of the International Workshop on Advanced Image Technology* (pp. 33-37).

Sprinthall, R. C. (2002). *Basic Statistical Analysis* (7th ed.). Boston, MA: Allyn and Bacon Publishers.

Staab, S. (2001). Human language technologies for knowledge management. *IEEE Intelligent Systems*, *16*(6), 84–94. doi:10.1109/5254.972104

Staubach, C., Schmid, V., Knorr-Held, L., & Ziller, M. (2002). A Bayesian model for spatial wildlife disease prevalence data. *Preventive Veterinary Medicine*, *56*(1), 75–87. doi:10.1016/S0167-5877(02)00125-3

Stemm, M., & Katz, R. H. (1997). Measuring and reducing energy consumption of network interfaces in hand-held devices. *IEICE Transactions on Communication*, *80*(8), 1125–1131.

Su, J. W., & Yeh, H. H. (2010). Music recommendation using content and context information mining. *IEEE Intelligent Systems*, *25*(1), 16–26. doi:10.1109/MIS.2010.23

Swain, M. J., & Ballard, B. H. (1991). Color indexing. *International Journal of Computer Vision*, *7*(1), 11–32. doi:10.1007/BF00130487

Thomas, J. J., & Cook, K. A. (2005). *Illuminating the path: The research and development agenda for visual analytics*. Berkeley, CA: National Visualization and Analytics Center.

Tollari, S., Glotin, H., & Maitre, J. L. (2003). Enhancement of textual images classification using their global and local visual contents. In *Proceedings of the International Workshop on Metadata and Adaptability in Web-Based Information Systems* (pp. 1-13).

Tollmar, K., Yeh, T., & Darrell, T. (2004). IDeixis - searching the Web with mobile images for location-based information. In *Proceedings of the International Symposium on Mobile Human-Computer Interaction* (pp. 288-299).

Torres, R. S., Silva, C. G., Medeiros, C. B., & Rocha, H. V. (2003). Visual structures for image browsing. In *Proceedings of the ACM International Conference on Information and Knowledge Management* (pp. 49-55). New York, NY: ACM Press.

Toshev, A., Makadia, A., & Daniilidis, K. (2009). Shape-based object recognition in videos using 3D synthetic object models. In *Proceedings of the IEEE Conference on Computer Vision and Pattern Recognition*, Miami, FL (pp. 288-295).

TRECVID. (2006). *Guidelines*. Retrieved January, 24, 2006, from http://www-nlpir.nist.gov/projects/tv2006/tv2006.html#3

Truong, B., & Venkatesh, S. (2007). Video abstraction: A systematic review and classification. *ACM Transactions on Multimedia Computing, Communications, and Applications*, *3*(1), 3. doi:10.1145/1198302.1198305

Tseng, V. S., Su, J.-H., Wang, B.-W., Hsiao, C.-Y., Huang, J., & Yeh, H.-H. (2008). Intelligent multimedia recommender by integrating annotation and association mining. In *Proceedings of the IEEE International Conference on Sensor Networks, Ubiquitous, and Trustworthy Computing* (pp. 492-499).

Urquhart, A. (1986). Many-valued logics. In D. M. Gabbay & F. Guenthner (Eds.), *Handbook of Philosophical Logic: Volume III, Alternatives to Classical Logic* (pp. 71-116). Dordrecht, The Netherlands: Reidel.

Van Der Schaar, M., Andreopoulos, Y., & Hu, Z. (2006). Optimized scalable video streaming over IEEE 802.11 a/e HCCA wireless networks under delay constraints. *IEEE Transactions on Mobile Computing*, *5*(6), 755–768. doi:10.1109/TMC.2006.81

Van Der Schaar, M., & Shankar, N. S. (2005). Cross-layer wireless multimedia transmission: Challenges, principles, and new paradigms. *IEEE Wireless Communications*, *12*(4), 50–58. doi:10.1109/MWC.2005.1497858

Van Der Schaar, M., & Turaga, D. (2007). Cross-layer packetization and retransmission strategies for delay-sensitive wireless multimedia transmission. *IEEE Transactions on Multimedia*, 9(1), 185–197. doi:10.1109/TMM.2006.886384

Vapnik, V. (1998). *Statistical learning theory*. Hoboken, NJ: Wiley-Interscience.

Vectomova, O., & Wang, Y. (2006). A study of the effect of term proximity on query expansion. *Journal of Information Science*, 32(4), 324–333. doi:10.1177/0165551506065787

Vedaldi, A., & Fulkerson, B. (2010). *VLFeat: An open and portable library of computer vision algorithm*. Retrieved from http://www.vlfeat.org

Video Trace Library. (n. d.). *MPEG-4 and H.263 video traces for network performance evaluation*. Retrieved from http://trace.eas.asu.edu/TRACE/trace.html

Waatts, D. (1999). *Small worlds: The dynamics of networks between order and randomness*. Princeton, NJ: Princeton University Press.

Wang, D., Zhang, H., Wu, W. & Lin, M. (2010). Inverse category frequency based supervised term weighting scheme for text categorization. *ArXiv e-Prints*, 1-12.

Wang, P., & Domeniconi, C. (2008). Building semantic kernels for text classification using Wikipedia. In *Proceedings of the 14th ACM SIGKDD International Conference on Knowledge Discovery and Data Mining* (pp. 713-721).

Wang, W., Ozolek, J. A., & Rohde, G. K. (2010). Detection and classification of Thyroid Follicular lesions based on nuclear structure from histopathology images. *Cytometry. Part A*, 77(5), 485–494.

Wasserman, S., & Faust, K. (1995). *Social network analysis: Theory and methods*. Cambridge, UK: Cambridge University Press.

Wei, X., & Ngo, C. (2008). Fusing semantics, observ-ability, reliablity and diversity of concept detectors for video search. In *Proceedings of the 16th International Conference on Multimedia* (pp. 81-90).

Weng, M., & Chuang, Y. (2008). Multi-cue fusion for semantic video indexing. In *Proceedings of the 16th International Conference on Multimedia* (pp. 71-80).

White, S., & Smyth, P. (2003). Algorithms for estimating relative importance in networks. In *Proceedings of the 9th ACM SIGKDD International Conference on Knowledge Discovery and Data Mining* (pp. 266-275).

Witten, I. H., & Frank, E. (2005). *Data mining: Practical machine learning tools and techniques* (2nd ed.). San Francisco, CA: Morgan Kaufmann.

Woodruff, A., Faulring, A., Rosenholtz, R., Morrison, J., & Pirolli, P. (2001). Using thumbnails to search the Web. In *Proceedings of the SIGCHI Conference on Human Factors in Computing Systems*, Seattle, WA (pp. 198-205).

Wu, X., Zhao, W. L., & Ngo, C. W. (2007). Near-duplicate keyframe retrieval with visual keywords and semantic context. In *Proceedings of the ACM Conference of International Video Retrieval*, Amsterdam, The Netherlands (pp. 162-169).

Xie, Z., Shyu, M.-L., & Chen, S.-C. (2008). Video event detection with combined distance-based and rule-based data mining techniques. In *Proceedings of the IEEE International Conference on Multimedia & Expo* (pp. 2026-2029).

Xu, D., Cham, T., Yan, S., & Chang, D.-F. (2008). Near duplicate image identification with spatially aligned pyramid matching. In *Proceedings of the IEEE Computer Vision and Pattern Recognition Conference*, Anchorage, AK (pp. 1-7).

Xu, J. (1996). Query expansion using local and global document analysis. In *Proceedings of the 19th Annual International ACM SIGIR Conference on Research and Development in Information Retrieval* (pp. 4-11).

Xue, M., & Zhu, C. (2009). A study and application on machine learning of artificial intelligence. In *Proceedings of the International Joint Conference on Artificial Intelligence* (p. 272).

Yamauchi, H., Saleem, W., Yoshizawa, S., Karni, Z., Belyaev, A., & Seidel, H.-P. (2006). Towards stable and salient multi-view representation of 3D shapes. In *Proceedings of the IEEE International Conference on Shape Modeling and Applications* (p. 40).

Yan, R., Chen, M., & Hauptmann, A. (2006). Mining relationship between video concepts using probabilistic graphical models. In *Proceedings of the IEEE International Conference on Multimedia and Expo* (pp. 3010-304).

Yap, P. T., Paramesran, R., & Ong, S. H. (2003). Image Analysis by Krawtchouk Moments. *IEEE Transactions on Image Processing*, *12*(11), 1367–1377. doi:10.1109/TIP.2003.818019

Yeh, T., Lee, J. J., & Darrell, T. (2008). Photo-based question answering. In *Proceedings of the 16th ACM International Conference* on *Multimedia* (pp. 389-398).

Yeh, T., Tollmar, K., & Darrell, T. (2004). Searching the web with mobile images for location recognition. In *Proceedings of the Conference on Computer Vision and Pattern Recognition* (pp. 76-81).

Yianilos, P. N. (1993). Data structures and algorithms for nearest neighbor search in general metric spaces. In *Proceedings of the 3rd Annual ACM-SIAM Symposium on Discrete Algorithms* (pp. 311-321).

Younessian, E., Rajan, D., & Chng, E. S. (2009). *Improved keypoint matching method for near-duplicate keyframe retrieval*. Paper presented at the International Symposium on Multimedia, San Diego, CA.

Yu, N., Hua, K. A., & Liu, D.-Z. (2007). Client-side relevance feedback approach for image retrieval in mobile environment. In *Proceedings of the International Conference on Multimedia & Expo* (pp. 552-555).

Yuan, J., Wang, H., Xiao, L., Zheng, W., Li, J., Lin, F., & Zhang, B. (2007). A formal study of shot boundary detection. *IEEE Transactions on Circuits and Systems for Video Technology*, *17*, 168–186. doi:10.1109/TCSVT.2006.888023

Yu, D., Sattar, F., & Ma, K. K. (2002). Watermark detection and extraction using independent component analysis method. *Journal on Applied Signal Processing*, *1*, 92–104. doi:10.1155/S111086570200046X

Yu, K., Yu, S., & Tresp, V. (2005). Soft clustering on graphs. In *Advances in neural information processing systems*. Cambridge, MA: MIT Press.

Zabih, R., Miller, J., & Mai, K. (1995). A feature-based algorithm for detecting and classifying scene breaks. In *Proceedings of the Third ACM International Conference on Multimedia* (pp. 189-200).

Zadeh, L. A. (1965). Fuzzy sets. *Information and Control*, *8*, 338–353. doi:10.1016/S0019-9958(65)90241-X

Zadeh, L. A. (1973). Outline of a new approach to the analysis of complex systems and decision processes. *IEEE Transactions on Systems, Man, and Cybernetics*, *3*(1), 28–44. doi:10.1109/TSMC.1973.5408575

Zadeh, L. A. (2008). Is there a need for fuzzy logic? *Information Sciences*, *178*(13), 2751–2779. doi:10.1016/j.ins.2008.02.012

Zaharia, T., & Prêteux, F. (2004). 3D versus 2D/3D Shape Descriptors: A comparative study. In *Proceedings of the SPIE Conference on Image Processing: Algorithms and Systems*, Toulouse, France.

Zavesky, E., & Chang, S.-F. (2008). CuZero: Embracing the frontier of interactive visual search for informed users. In *Proceedings of the ACM International Workshop on Multimedia Information Retrieval* (pp. 237-244). New York, NY: ACM Press.

Zavesky, E., Chang, S.-F., & Yang, C.-C. (2008). Visual islands: Intuitive browsing of visual search results. In *Proceedings of the ACM International Conference on Image and Video Retrieval* (pp. 617-626). New York, NY: ACM Press.

Zeng, D., Chen, H., Tseng, C., Larson, C. A., Eidson, M., Gotham, I., et al. (2004). Towards a national infectious disease information infrastructure: A case study in West Nile virus and botulism. In *Proceedings of the Annual National Conference on Digital Government Research*, Seattle, WA (pp. 1-10).

Zha, Z., Mei, T., Wang, Z., & Hua, X. (2007). Building a comprehensive ontology to refine video concept detection. In *Proceedings of the 9th International Workshop on Multimedia Information Retrieval* (pp. 227-236).

Zhang, D. Q., & Chang, S. F. (2004). Detecting image near-duplicate by stochastic attributed relational graph matching with learning. In *Proceedings of the ACM Multimedia Conference* (pp. 877-884).

Zhang, J., Sun, L., Yang, S., & Zhong, Y. (2005). Joint inter and intra shot modeling for spectral video shot clustering. In *Proceedings of the International Conference of Multimedia and Expo*, Amsterdam, The Netherlands (pp. 1362-1365).

Zhang, S., & Lu, G. (2002). An integrated approach to shape based image retrieval. In *Proceedings of the 5th Asian Conference on Computer Vision* (pp. 652-657).

Zhang, Y., Callan, J., & Minka, T. (2002). Novelty and redundancy detection in adaptive filtering. In *Proceedings of the 25th Annual International ACM SIGIR Conference on Research and Development in Information Retrieval* (pp. 81-88).

Zhang, H. J., Kankanhalli, A., & Smoliar, S. W. (1993). Automatic partitioning of full-motion video. *Multimedia Systems, 1*, 10–28. doi:10.1007/BF01210504

Zhang, H., Wu, J., Zhong, D., & Smoliar, S. W. (1999). An integrated system for content-based video retrieval and browsing. *Pattern Recognition, 30*(4), 643–658. doi:10.1016/S0031-3203(96)00109-4

Zhang, J., Marszalek, M., Lazebnik, S., & Schmid, C. (2007). Local features and kernels for classification of texture and object categories: A comprehensive study. *International Journal of Computer Vision, 73*(2), 213–238. doi:10.1007/s11263-006-9794-4

Zhang, X., & Wang, H. (2005). Study on recommender systems for business to-business electronic commerce. *Communications of the IIMA, 5*(4), 53–61.

Zhao, W.-L., & Ngo, C.-W. (2006). Fast tracking of near-duplicate keyframes in broadcast domain with transitivity propagation. In *Proceedings of the ACM Special Interest Group on Multimedia Conference,* Santa Barbara, CA (pp. 845-854).

Zhao, M., Bu, J. J., & Chen, C. (2002). Robust Background Subtraction in HSV Color Space. In. *Proceedings of SPIE: Multimedia Systems and Applications, 4861*, 325–332.

Zhao, Q., & Tsang, D. H. K. (2008). An equal-spacing-based design for QoS guarantee in IEEE 802.11e HCCA wireless networks. *IEEE Transactions on Mobile Computing, 7*(12), 1474–1490. doi:10.1109/TMC.2008.71

Zhao, W.-L., & Ngo, C.-W. (2007). Near-duplicate keyframe identification with interest point matching and pattern learning. *IEEE Transactions on Multimedia, 9*, 1037–1048. doi:10.1109/TMM.2007.898928

Zhao, Y., & Zobel, J. (2005). *Effective and scalable authorship attribution using function words*. Melbourne, Australia: RMIT University.

Zheng, F., Garg, N., Sobti, S., Zhang, C., & Joseph, R. E. (2003). Considering the energy consumption of mobile storage alternatives. In *Proceedings of the International Symposium on Modeling, Analysis and Simulation of Computer Telecommunications Systems* (pp. 36-45).

Zhu, J. Zou, H., Rosset, S., & Hastie, T. (2009). Multi-class AdaBoost. *Statics and its Interface, 2*(3), 349-360.

Zhu, J., Hoi, S. C. H., Lyu, M. R., & Yan, S. (2008). Near-duplicate keyframe retrieval by nonrigid image matching. In *Proceedings of the ACM Multimedia Conference,* Vancouver, BC, Canada (pp. 41-50).

Zhu, Q., Lin, L., Shyu, M.-L., & Chen, S.-C. (2010). Feature selection using correlation and reliability based scoring metric for video semantic detection. In *Proceedings of the IEEE International Conference on Semantic Computing* (pp. 462-469).

Zhu, P., Zeng, W., & Li, C. (2007). Cross-layer design of source rate control and congestion control for wireless video streaming. *Advances in Multimedia,* (1): 3–15.

Zhu, S., & Liu, Y. (2009). Video scene segmentation and semantic representation using a novel scheme. *Multimedia Tools and Applications, 42*(2), 183–205. doi:10.1007/s11042-008-0233-0

Zribi, M., & Benjelloun, M. (2003). Parametric estimation of Dempster-Shafer belief functions. In *Proceedings of the 6th International Conference on Information Fusion* (pp. 485-491).

About the Contributors

Shu-Ching Chen is a Full Professor at School of Computing and Information Sciences (SCIS), Florida International University (FIU), Miami since August 2009. Prior to that, he was an Assistant/Associate Professor in SCIS at FIU from 1999. He received Ph.D. degree in Electrical and Computer Engineering in 1998, and Master's degrees in Computer Science, Electrical Engineering, and Civil Engineering, all from Purdue University, West Lafayette, IN, USA. His main research interests include distributed multimedia database management systems and multimedia data mining. He is the Editor-in-Chief of *International Journal of Multimedia Data Engineering and Management*. He is a Fellow of SIRI.

Mei-Ling Shyu has been an Associate Professor at Department of Electrical and Computer Engineering (ECE), University of Miami (UM) since June 2005. Prior to that, she was an Assistant Professor in ECE at UM from 2000. She received her Ph.D. degree from Electrical and Computer Engineering in 1999, and her Master's degrees from Computer Science, Electrical Engineering, and Restaurant, Hotel, Institutional, and Tourism Management, all from Purdue University, West Lafayette, IN, USA. Her research interests include multimedia data mining, management & retrieval, and security. She received 2012 IEEE Computer Society Technical Achievement Award. She is a Fellow of SIRI.

* * *

Massimiliano Albanese received a Laurea degree in computer science and engineering from the University of Naples "Federico II" in 2002. In 2005, he received his PhD degree in Computer Science and Engineering from the same University, where he then served until 2006 as a research and teaching assistant with the Multimedia Information Systems Group. He e joined in 2006 the University of Maryland Institute for Advanced Computer Studies, College Park, as a post doctoral researcher and in 2011 the Center of Secure Info Systems of George Mason University as Assistant Professor. His primary areas of interest are in multimedia databases, information extraction, activity detection, knowledge representation and management.

Jurandy Almeida received a B.Sc. in Computer Science from Sao Paulo State University (UNESP, 2005), Brazil. He finished his Masters in Computer Science at University of Campinas (UNICAMP, 2007). Nowadays, he is a Ph.D. student at Institute of Computing, UNICAMP. His research interests include Pattern Analysis, Database Systems, and Content-Based Image/Video Retrieval.

M. Cecília C. Baranauskas is Professor at the Institute of Computing, UNICAMP, Brazil. She received a B.Sc. and M.Sc. in Computer Science and a Ph.D. in Electrical Engineering at UNICAMP, Brazil. She was Honorary Research Fellow at the Staffordshire University and Visiting Fellow at the University of Reading (2001-2002), and she received a Cátedra Ibero-Americana Unicamp-Santander Banespa to study accessibility issues in software engineering at the Universidad Politécnica de Madrid (2006-2007). In 2010, she received the ACM SIGDOC Rigo Award. Her research interests have focused on issues in Human-Computer Interaction, particularly investigating different formalisms (including Participatory Design and Semiotics) in the design and evaluation of user interfaces.

Anup Basu received the Ph.D. degree in computer science from the University of Maryland, College Park. He was a Visiting Professor at the University of California, Riverside, a Guest Professor at the Technical University of Austria, Graz, and the Director at the Hewlett-Packard Imaging Systems Instructional Laboratory, University of Alberta, Edmonton, Canada, where, since 1999, he has been a Professor at the Department of Computing Science, and is currently an Informatics Circle of Research Excellence-Natural Sciences and Engineering Research Council Industry Research Chair. He originated the use of foveation for image, video, stereo, and graphics communication in the early 1990s, an approach that is now widely used in industrial standards. He also developed the first robust (correspondence free) 3-D motion estimation algorithm, using multiple cameras, a robust (and the first correspondence free) active camera calibration method, a single camera panoramic stereo, and several new approaches merging foveation and stereo with application to 3-D TV visualization and better depth estimation. His current research interests include 3-D/4-D image processing and visualization especially for medical applications, multimedia in education and games, and wireless 3-D multimedia transmission.

John Berezowski graduated from the Western College of Veterinary Medicine in 1981 and spent 18 years in food animal practice in Western Canada. He completed his PhD in epidemiology in 2004 and has been pursuing his interests in surveillance epidemiology by designing, leading and participating in large and small surveillance projects for the Alberta Veterinary Surveillance Network of Alberta Agriculture and Rural Development. He has a strong interest in developing new surveillance methodologies and has published, presented and taught in the field. His current focus is method development to support knowledge generation from complex real-time surveillance, by combining data from many varied sources (human, livestock, wildlife, and environment) and across complete livestock based food supply chains. He represents Alberta on many provincial and national boards and committees including the board of directors for Prairie Diagnostic Services and the Surveillance and Epidemiology Support Committee for the Council of Canadian Chief Veterinary Officers.

Kasturi Chatterjee is a Software Engineer in Analytics at Hi5 Networks, a social gaming company. She received her Ph.D. is Computer Science from Florida International University in 2010. Her dissertation concentrates on designing a multimedia database management system to organize multimedia data accessed in a collaborative search environment. During her Ph.D. study, she received several awards from Florida International University as well from other organization such as IBM Research and NSF.

Shu-Ching Chen is a Full Professor in the School of Computing and Information Sciences (SCIS), Florida International University (FIU), Miami since August 2009. Prior to that, he was an Assistant/Associate Professor in SCIS at FIU from 1999. He received Master's degrees in Computer Science, Electrical Engineering, and Civil Engineering in 1992, 1995, and 1996, respectively, and the Ph.D. degree in Electrical and Computer Engineering in 1998, all from Purdue University, West Lafayette, IN, USA. His main research interests include distributed multimedia database management systems and multimedia data mining. Dr. Chen received the best paper award from the 2006 IEEE International Symposium on Multimedia. He was awarded the IEEE Systems, Man, and Cybernetics (SMC) Society's Outstanding Contribution Award in 2005 and was co-recipient of the IEEE Most Active SMC Technical Committee Award in 2006. He is the Editor-in-Chief of International Journal of Multimedia Data Engineering and Management.

Irene Cheng received the Ph.D. degree in computing science from the University of Alberta, Edmonton, Canada. She is currently the Scientific Director of the Information Circle of Research Excellence-Natural Sciences and Engineering Research Council Multimedia Research Center, Department of Computing Science, University of Alberta, where she is also an Adjunct Faculty. From 2006 to 2007, she was involved in design of a multimedia framework, incorporating innovative interactive 3-D item types for online multimedia education. She is the author or coauthor of two books and more than 90 papers published in international journals and peer-reviewed conferences. Her research interests include incorporating human perception—Just-Noticeable-Difference—following psychophysical methodology, to improve multimedia transmission techniques. She is also engaged in research on 3-D TV and perceptually motivated technologies in multimedia, high-dimensional visualization, and transmission. Dr. Cheng is the Chair of the IEEE Northern Canada Section Engineering in Medicine and Biology Society Chapter 2009–2011 and the Chair of the Multimedia Communications Technical Committee (TC) Interest Group on 3-D Rendering, Processing and Communication 2010–2012 in IEEE Communication Society. She is a Guest Editor for International Journal of Digital Multimedia Broadcasting special issue on Advances in 3-D TV. She serves as a Program Chair and as a TC Member in numerous conferences including the IEEE International Conference on Multimedia and Expo 2008–2010 and International Symposium on Visual Computing 2006–2009.

Antonio d'Acierno received the Laurea degree com laude in electronics engineering from the University of Naples Federico II . Since 1988 to 1999, he was actively integrated into the research group of IRSIP (Institute for Research on Parallel Informatics Systems) of the National Research Council of Italy (CNR). In 1999 he joined the Institute of Food Science (ISA) of CNR. He is currently a contract professor of Data Base Systems at the Faculty of Computer Science Engineering of the University of Salerno. His current research interests lie in the field of mobile transactions, information retrieval, semantic web, multimedia ontologies and applications, multimedia knowledge extraction and management, and bioinformatics.

Iqbal Jamal received an M.A.Sc. in engineering and an M.Sc. in operations research from the University of British Columbia. He spent 4 years in the resource engineering sector, followed by 11 years in municipal government with a focus on the development of analytical, performance and management frameworks to improve the efficiency and effectiveness of public sector programs. After a number of years with an information technology company, he became a principal in a management consulting practice with a focus on strategies, methods and tools to link business operations to organizational strategy and is a registered professional engineer and a Certified Management Consultant. Mr. Jamal has a keen interest in the development and use of analytical tools using disparate data sources to support operational improvement, program monitoring, and performance measurement through innovative data capture, analytics, visualization and knowledge management. He is currently involved in a number of research projects in support of new methodologies applied to complex real-time surveillance across varied sources (human, livestock, wildlife, and environment) and food supply chains.

Neucimar J. Leite received the B.Sc. and M.Sc. in Electrical Engineering from Federal University of Paraiba (UFPB), Brazil, in 1986 and 1988, respectively, and the Ph.D. degree in Computer Science from University Pierre et Marie Curie, Paris, France, in 1993. He is currently an Associate Professor with the Institute of Computing at the University of Campinas (UNICAMP), Brazil. His main research interests include Mathematical Morphology, Image Filtering and Segmentation, Multiscale Representation, and Content-Based Video/Image Retrieval.

Ching-Yung Lin is a Research Scientist in the Event and Streaming Systems Department, IBM T. J. Watson Research Center, New York. He is currently leading projects on Collective Intelligence and Network Science researches. He is also an affiliate faculty at the University of Washington since 2003 and Columbia University since 2005. He received his B.S. and M.S. from National Taiwan University, in 1991 and 1993, respectively, and Ph.D. from Columbia University in 2000, all in electrical engineering.

Lin Lin received her PhD degree Department of Electrical and Computer Engineering (ECE), University of Miami (UM), Coral Gables, Florida, USA in 2010, and her Master degree in Electrical and Systems Engineering from University of Pennsylvania, Philadelphia, Pennsylvania, USA in 2006. Her research interests include multimedia information retrieval, multimedia database, and data mining. She received the "Best Student Paper Award" from the Third IEEE International Conference on Semantic Computing (ICSC) in September 2009.

Dianting Liu currently is a PhD candidate at the Department of Electrical and Computer Engineering (ECE), University of Miami (UM). She received her PhD and BS degree at School of Mechanical Engineering from Dalian University of Technology, Dalian, China in Oct. 2009 and Jul. 2003, respectively. Her PhD research focused on face recognition of infrared and visible image fusion. During Jun. 2004 and May 2005, she worked as a software engineer at Dalian Hi-Think Computer (DHC) Technology Corp., Dalian, China. Her current research interests include multimedia data mining, video object detection and segmentation, key frame detection, pattern recognition, and image processing.

Hongli Luo is currently an assistant professor in the Department of Computer and Electrical Engineering Technology and Information Systems and Technology at Indiana University Purdue University Fort Wayne, Fort Wayne, IN, USA. She received her Ph.D degree from the Department of Electrical and Computer Engineering, University of Miami, Coral Gables, Florida, USA in 2006. Her research interests are multimedia networking, wireless networking, video streaming and quality of service. She was a program co-chair of the IEEE International Workshop on Semantic Computing and Multimedia Systems and program vice co-chair of the 2010 International Conference on Multimedia and Ubiquitous Engineering. She also serves on the editorial boards for Journal of Information Processing Systems and International Journal of Smart Home.

Vincenzo Moscato received the Laurea degree (cum laude) in computer science and engineering from the University of Naples "Federico II", Italy, in 2002. In 2005, he received the PhD degree in computer science and engineering at the same University. In 2009 he joined the Dipartimento di Informatica e Sistemistica of University of Napoli "Federico II", where he is currently an assistant professor of data base and computer engineering. He has been active in the field of computer vision, video and image indexing and multimedia data sources integration. His current research interests lie in the area of multimedia databases, video-surveillance applications and knowledge representation and management.

Vânia P. A. Neris is Associate Professor at the Computing Department at the Federal University of Sao Carlos (UFSCar), Brazil. She graduated in Computer Engineering and received a Master degree in Computer Science at UFSCar. She received a Ph.D. degree in Computer Science at the University of Campinas (UNICAMP) and was a visitor student at the Informatics Research Centre (IRC) at the University of Reading, UK. Her actual research focus on the design and evaluation of Interactive Systems, Universal Design and Semiotics.

Fabio Persia received in 2009 the Laurea degree in computer science and engineering from the University of Naples "Federico II", Italy, where he is currently a PhD student in computer science and engineering. His current research interests lie in the field of video surveillance applications, multimedia databases and knowledge representation and management.

Raluca-Diana Petre received her engineering degree in telecommunications at POLITEHNICA University of Bucharest and the Master's degree in High Tech Imaging at Télécom SudParis in 2009. During her master, she gained extensive experience in medical imagery within the R and D department of General Electric Healthcare. She is currently a PhD student at the ARTEMIS Department of Télécom SudParis, within the framework of the UBIMEDIA Research Lab between Institut Télécom and Alcatel-Lucent Bell Labs. Her research interests include 2D/3D indexing and recognition techniques, shape analysis and multimedia indexing systems.

Antonio Picariello received the laurea degree in electronics engineering and the PhD degree in computer science and engineering from the University of Naples "Federico II," Italy, in 1991 and 1998, respectively. In 1993, he joined the Istituto Ricerca sui Sistemi Informatici Paralleli, National Research Council, Naples, Italy. In 1999, he joined the Dipartimento di Informatica e Sistemistica, University of Naples "Federico II" and is currently an associate professor of databases and computer engineering. He has been active in the field of computer vision, medical image processing and pattern recognition, object-oriented models for image processing, multimedia databases, and information retrieval. His current research interests include knowledge extraction and management, multimedia integration, and image and video databases.

Sheila M. Pinto-Cáceres received her B.Sc. in Systems Engineering from the National University of San Agustin of Arequipa (UNSA), Peru, in 2006. She got her Master degree in Computer Science at the University of Campinas (UNICAMP), Brazil, in 2010. She is currently a researcher at Sofist company, Brazil. Her actual research focus on Visualization for Content-Based Image/Video Retrieval, Visual Data Mining, Image Analysis, and Test Automation.

Nathaniel Rossol received a B.Sc. and M.Sc. degree in software engineering and intelligent systems from the Department of Electrical and Computer Engineering at the University of Alberta, Edmonton, Canada. He is currently working toward a Ph.D. degree in computing science at the University of Alberta. He is the author or coauthor of several papers published in international conferences. His current research interests include multimodal data analysis, image processing, and data visualization. Mr. Rossol is a recipient of the Alberta Advanced Education and Queen Elizabeth II Graduate Scholarships.

Jyh-Ren Shieh received his M.S. and the professional degree at Columbia University, New York, USA, in 1997 and 2000, all in Electrical Engineering. He is Ph.D. candidate at National Taiwan University, Taipei, Taiwan.

Kimiaki Shirahama received his BE, ME and DE degrees in engineering from Kobe University, Japan in 2003, 2005 and 2011, respectively. Currently, he is an assistant professor in the Graduate School of Economics at Kobe University. His research interests include multimedia data processing, data mining and virtual reality. He has presented his research outcome in 1 book chapter, 4 journal papers and 25 papers of international conferences and workshops. He is a member of ACM SIGKDD, ACM SIGMM, the Institute of Image Information and Television Engineers in Japan (ITE), Information Processing Society of Japan (IPSJ) and the Institute of Electronics, Information and Communication Engineering in Japan (IEICE).

Mei-Ling Shyu has been an Associate Professor at the Department of Electrical and Computer Engineering (ECE), University of Miami (UM) since June 2005. Prior to that, she was an Assistant Professor in ECE at UM dating from January 2000. She received her Ph.D. degree from the School of Electrical and Computer Engineering, Purdue University, West Lafayette, Indiana, USA in 1999 and her three master degrees from Computer Science, Electrical Engineering, and Restaurant, Hotel, Institutional, and Tourism Management from Purdue University in 1992, 1995, and 1997. Her research interests include multimedia data mining and information systems. She has co-authored more than 190 technical papers published in prestigious journals, book chapters, and refereed conference proceedings. She received the "Best Student Paper Award" from the Third IEEE International Conference on Semantic Computing in September 2009 and the "Johnson A. Edosomwan Scholarly Productivity Award" from the College of Engineering at UM in 2007.

Ruxandra Tapu received as valedictorian the BS degree in electronics from the faculty of electronics, Telecommunications and Information Technology of Bucharest in 2008. She is currently working toward a PhD degree at the University "Politehnica" of Bucharest (Romania) and University "Pierre et Marie Currie" (France). She is part of the ARTEMIS department within IT/TELECOM SudParis having as major research interest content-based video retrieval, pattern recognition and machine learning techniques.

Ricardo da S. Torres received a B.Sc. in Computer Engineering from University of Campinas, Brazil, in 2000. He got his doctorate in Computer Science at the same university in 2004. He is an Associate Professor at Institute of Computing, University of Campinas. His research interests include Image Analysis, Content-Based Image Retrieval, Databases, Digital Libraries, and Geographic Information Systems.

Kuniaki Uehara received his BE, ME and DE degrees in Information and computer sciences from Osaka University, Japan in 1978, 1980 and 1984, respectively. He was an assistant professor in the Institute of Scientific and Industrial Research, Osaka University from 1984 to 1990, an associate professor in the Department of Computer Science and Systems Engineering, Kobe University from 1990 to 1997, a professor in the Research Center for Urban Safety and Security, Kobe University since 1997. Currently, he is a professor in the Graduate School of System Informatics, Kobe University. He has published a number of books, articles and conference papers in wide areas of artificial intelligence, especially in machine learning and natural language processing. He is a member of the Association for the Advancement of Artificial Intelligence (AAAI).

Shun-Xuan Wang received his B.S. degree in computer science and information engineering as major degree and electrical engineering as minor degree in 2010. He is now a graduate researcher in Graduate Institute of Networking and Multimedia, all in National Taiwan University, Taipei, Taiwan.

Ja-Ling Wu received the B.S. degree in electronic engineering from TamKang University, Tamshoei, Taiwan, in 1979, and the M.S. and Ph.D. degrees in electrical engineering from Tatung Institute of Technology, Taipei, Taiwan, in 1981 and 1986. Since 1987, he has been with the Department of Computer Science and Information Engineering, National Taiwan University, where he is a Lifetime Distinguished Professor. He has published more than 200 journal and conference papers. Prof. Wu was the recipient of the Excellent Research Award from NSC, Taiwan, in 1999, 2001 and 2004. He is the IEEE Fellow from 2008.

Titus Zaharia received an engineer degree in Electronics and Telecommunications, and a MS degree from University POLITEHNICA (Bucharest, Romania) in 1995 and 1996, respectively. In 2001, he obtained a PhD in mathematics and computer science from University Paris V – Rene Descartes (Paris, France). He joined the ARTEMIS department at Institut Télécom, Télécom Sudparis as an Associate Professor in 2002 and has become a full professor, in 2011. His research interests include visual content representation methods, with 2D/3D compression, reconstruction, recognition and indexing applications. Since 1998, Titus Zaharia actively contributes to the ISO/MPEG-4 and MPEG-7 standards.

Qiusha Zhu currently is a PhD candidate at the Department of Electrical and Computer Engineering (ECE), University of Miami (UM). She received her M.S. degree of Electronic Engineering from School of Electronic, Information and Electrical Engineering, Shanghai Jiao Tong University in Mar. 2009 and BS degree of Electronic Engineering from Shanghai University as an Outstanding Graduate in Jun. 2006, Shanghai, China. She worked as a database apprentice at DOW Chemical from Nov. 2007 to Jun. 2008, Shanghai. Her research interests include multimedia information retrieval and data mining, especially how to effectively retrieve online images and videos, how to fuse information available from different sources to boost this process.

Index